CU-A

Renaissance Venice

Contents

7

Contents

Note: Nos. 1, 8, 9, 11, 12 and 14 were translated by J. R. and Sheila Hale

Illustrations

PLATES

between pp. 256 and 257

9

Illustrations

Acknowledgements are made to the British Museum for plates A, 5 and 18 and to the Trustees, The National Gallery, London for plate 52.

Plate A illustrates 'Naval actions and fleet organization, 1499–1502' (Lane); the rest of the plates illustrate 'The relationship between German and Venetian painting in the late quattrocento and early cinquecento' (Pignatti).

MAP

Abbreviations

Albèri	Eugenio Albèri, *Relazioni degli ambasciatori veneti al Senato* (Florence, 1839–1863)
A.S.I.	*Archivio Storico Italiano*
A.S.V.	Archivio di Stato, Venice
A.V.	*Archivio Veneto*
B.I.S.	*Bollettino dell' Istituto di Storia della Società e dello Stato Veneziano*
B.M.V.	Biblioteca Marciana, Venice
M.C.V.	Museo Correr, Venice
N.A.V.	*Nuovo Archivio Veneto*
R.I.S.	Muratori, *Rerum italicarum scriptores*, orig. ed.
R.I.S.2	Ibid., revised ed.
Riv. Stor. Ital.	*Rivista Storica Italiana*
Romanin	Samuele Romanin, *Storia documentata di Venezia*, new ed., 10 vols (Venice, 1912–1921)
Sanuto	*I diarii di Marino Sanuto*, ed. Rinaldo Fulin and others, 58 vols (Venice, 1879–1903). References are to columns, not pages
S.M.	The Venetian archival series *Senato, Mar*
S.S.	The Venetian archival series *Senato, Secreta*
S.T.	The Venetian archival series *Senato, Terra*

Note: All dates are modernized

NOTES

1. *Crisis and Change in the Venetian Economy*, ed. Brian Pullan (London, 1968).

2. Sir John Smythe, *Instructions, observations and orders mylitarie* (London 1595, written 1591) 214-5, from a long passage which bears ample, if unsophisticated, witness to the potency of the 'myth' referred to in the last two essays.

3. But see, among the most recent publications dealing with Venice in this period, William J. Bouwsma, *Venice and the defense of republican liberty* (U. of California, 1968); D. S. Chambers, *The imperial age of Venice 1380–1580* (London, 1970) and Brian Pullan, *Rich and poor in Renaissance Venice: the social institutions of a catholic state to 1620* (Oxford, Blackwell, 1971).

4. *La nouvelle Cynée ou discours d'estat* (Paris, 1623).

5. *The reason of state*, tr. P. J. and D. P. Waley (London, 1956) 109.

I

ALBERTO TENENTI

The Sense of Space and Time in the Venetian World of the Fifteenth and Sixteenth Centuries

I

National consciousness, by having become since the Enlightenment part of almost every European's collective inheritance, has powerfully contributed to looking upon a political entity like that of the *Serenissima* as a hybrid, a sport of nature. Only one other polity which bore some resemblance to it remained in existence, the Papal State. But it hardly modified this opinion. It had never stretched over something like a thousand miles; it had remained huddled, as it were, like a patchwork cope about the shoulders of the pope. To those who are familiar with the unique character of the city of the lagoon today, it might seem banal to underline the singularity of the Venetian case. Still, it is perhaps worth recalling that the extent and duration of the Venetian empire were based neither on a coherent geographic configuration nor on ethnic, religious, or linguistic homogeneity. It is thus not totally out of place to bring to mind, at least briefly, the co-ordinates of a state so different from others. The assertion that Venice was a channel between Orient and Occident can no longer be seen in such simple terms. At the start, and for a long time thereafter, such a function was the making of its economic fortune; but the fact remains that this channel soon expanded into becoming a flexible but nevertheless potentially resistant zone which did not survive by mere force of inertia or by chance. Unquestionably, a lasting and favourable combination of circumstances accompanied this growth. The mediocre – and by no means continuous – power of the Balkan kings, the ever more precarious existence of the Byzantine empire, the sluggish assertion of Habsburg power and the political fragmentation of the Italian peninsula figured among the conditions which permitted the creation and the strengthening of a coherent Venetian empire. Venice found itself, that is, strengthening the centre of an international field of low political and military pressure, which came in time to constitute a virtual power-vacuum. It knew how to take advantage of this situation in order to establish and root itself there firmly enough to evolve effective and original functions of government and civilization.

As far as space is concerned, the hallmarks of Venetian control can still be recognized today, from such clearly Lombard centres as Bergamo or Brescia to the cities of Friuli, Istria and Dalmatia, to the islands of Corfu and Crete and as far as Cyprus. As for time, this was probably the last example in history of a cycle of human endeavour in which Rome and Byzantium are among the most striking examples. Its art and its legal system characterized it no less than a particular way of fortifying, defending and administering itself. Energy, organizing power, a native faculty for government – not, certainly, simply the benevolence of fate alone – secured for it a continuity which thrust it so far forward into history as to render it, finally, an anachronism.

The fifteenth and sixteenth centuries constitute without doubt the era in which this organism assumed its completest form in almost all respects. But that period of maturity was at the same time the one in which vital and contrasting tendencies were emerging within Venice itself and it was in that period, moreover, following the phase of initial growth and structuring, that the overall situation in which it found itself came to be radically modified. The Byzantine empire was succeeded by the altogether more threatening and invasive Turk; Venice's fundamental economic function was seriously disturbed and weakened by new factors, the Portuguese spice route among them; finally, political equilibrium on the Italian peninsula was destroyed by the invasion of the 'barbarians', first the French, then the Spanish. Furthermore, it was in this stormy atmosphere and under the impact of such outstanding events that there developed a complex awareness of the nature and the destiny of the world of St. Mark.

The voices to be heard in this present inquiry will be almost exclusively Venetian and patrician. But it would be unjustified to expect anything else. Venice was above all an occupying power. Practically none of the centres which made up its territory was inhabited predominantly by Venetians, none was governed by local representatives. For all that the rule of the *Signoria* was counted among the shrewdest, if not the most just, of its time, an insurmountable barrier existed everywhere (with the partial and far from comforting exception of Crete) between governors and governed. Venice was at once the soul, heart[1] and brain of the entire body, the other members being held in lesser account than the parts of a real organism would have been. Whether they were near or far, all possessions were regarded more or less as alike, and the Venetians, on the whole, aroused less sympathy and support than aversion or indifference. Venice probably did not treat its own subjects any worse than did the king of France, for example, or the king of Spain. But between its own ruling class and the other levels of the population beyond the lagoon there was neither the potential attachment nor the amount of collective solidarity which constituted a reserve and a potential source of strength for the monarchies of the West. The actual power at Venice's command was considerably greater than that of the princely states of Italy; but it was not enough to induce the *Signoria's* subjects to consider their lot as indissolubly linked with that of the *Serenissima*. And the situation was duplicated, *mutatis mutandis*, within the ruling city itself. About two thousand patricians, assisted by a fringe of citizens with no real political rights, governed the entire community as well as the whole state. The people were hardly more than a spineless multitude who felt bound to the fortunes of its rulers chiefly by the immediate advantages or disadvantages to be derived from them. A Venetian patriotism certainly existed, but from the *quattrocento* it is decreasingly in evidence. Even as it gained in strength, the state had become cut off from the masses, while a more and more restricted group was consolidating power within the patrician class itself.[2] The people were left with, above all, the satisfaction, touched with pride, of constituting the body of a powerful community, full of prestige, occupying a privileged site of natural no less than man-made beauty.[3]

Within the circle of this Venetian world, space and time had a particularly forceful, one could even say existential, significance, amounting to personal and meaningful projections from a unique centre of activity and power. Both the 'stato da mar' and that of the *terraferma* were created as functions of the lagoon city and its interests. Therefore one could hardly not mention their dimensions, the ties which Venice felt it had with them, the tensions to which the patrician community was subjected in the effort to conserve and defend them in order to safeguard itself.

II

The first characteristic of Venetian space, as has been noted, is that of not having had any natural geographic or geopolitical coherence. Insofar as there was cohesion, Venice had had to create it, and the level of coherence achieved by its empire was largely acquired thanks to the initiative of its merchants and *gentiluomini*. A second aspect, however, especially characterizes the period considered here. While by and large until the end of the fourteenth century the Venetian empire is almost exclusively maritime – and is therefore marked by a fairly homogeneous set of problems – from the beginning of the *quattrocento* the situation changes radically. To the modest possession of the Trevigiano the *Signoria* added in a short space of time that of Padua, Vicenza, Verona, and Friuli, not to mention Brescia and Bergamo with their respective territories. It is true that Venice had to go to war against the expansionism of the Visconti of Milan; but it quickly transformed this obligation into a valid territorial projection of its strength and statecraft. Until the beginning of the fifteenth century its patriciate was divided between the need to maintain and defend a maritime supremacy based on possessions in the Levant and the move to consolidate acquisitions on the *terraferma*. In fact, Venetian power came to move with more and more ease on the chess-board of Italy, where its adversaries were weaker and more divided, and with more and more difficulty in the East because of the continuous advance of the Turks.

That Francesco Foscari's dogeship, which was marked by a deep penetration of the Italian mainland, should have followed that of Tommaso Mocenigo has with good reason been considered emblematic. Before dying (1423) the latter is supposed to have reaffirmed in an eloquent political testament that the destiny of Venice lay primarily across the sea.[4] The great debate, which hardly emerged in publicly expressed antagonism owing to the restraints exercised by the leading political magistracies, troubled the patrician class for several generations. It was not simply an abstract question. The Venetians were profoundly convinced that the fundamental basis of their fortune and power had been and still was the sea, meaning, that is, the total position, economic, military, and political which they had secured from the Black Sea to the North Sea. They realized, however, that one of the conditions of their success was the absence of a formidable power (which could become an adversary) on Italian soil. The best way of perpetuating the division of the peninsula and therefore the weakness of its principalities was by settling a considerable portion of it in such a way as to be able to exert a direct influence, hopefully a determining one, on relations between the various states. The success of the *Signoria's* policy quickly aroused the rancour of its neighbours, beginning with the Milanese and Ferrarese, soon followed by the Florentines and the popes. When, after the peace of Lodi, the conclusion of the Italian League (1454) sanctioned the *status quo* in Italy, Venice appeared to be the predominant power and a real threat to the political equilibrium of the peninsula.[5]

However effectively the *Serenissima* tried to enlarge its possessions on the *terraferma*, however consistently it plotted against its neighbours, it did not really pursue a policy of conquest on a national scale. For the Venetians the acquisitions on the mainland were in the first place a security measure, then a basis for international prestige, and finally a kind of compensation or counterweight for damages and losses sustained in the Levant. On the other hand, for almost the whole of the *quattrocento*, the key positions in the East and the system of maritime trade showed little sign of being compromised. It was, in fact, that very period which saw the full and almost consistently successful functioning of the maritime organization which formed the keystone of Venetian prosperity: the voyages of the merchant galleys.[6] With a rhythm worthy of comparison with a superb piece of clock-work, these voyages timed the economic life of the West, to the very great advantage of the Venetians. Their sequence and interconnection constituted, indeed, a kind of masterpiece.[7] The appearance of Florentine, Ragusan or Marseillais competitors constituted no more serious a danger than had the old Genoese or Catalan rivals. The Turks were advancing, it is true, but on the sea they remained inferior, still preferring territorial objectives which did not seriously jeopardize the domains of the *Signoria*.

The fifteenth century represented, then, a phase of equilibrium, though it was in more than one respect an unstable one. The new body of land that was added to the maritime state did not yet seem to imperil the financial balance of the traditional economy. A maritime crisis was smouldering, but remained in part latent; it did not seem incautious to surrender to the investments and pleasures of the *terraferma*. The old ideal values and the new preferences co-existed, each turning a deaf ear to the other in a conflict that grew daily more intense. The whole glorious past, the whole structure of the maritime commune, the persistent commercial success – an irrefutable source of wealth – constituted a sum of factors which gave the partisans of the sea the sense of being the true interpreters of the city's destiny as well as of defending their own prevailing interests.[8] And yet the tranquil charms of landed possession and the costly delights of the country villa were converting an ever more conspicuous number not only of patricians, but also of *cittadini* and even simple *popolani*.[9] The *terraferma* was progressively seducing the Venetians, a people still without cultural myths in spite of the prestige of maritime tradition and the evidently greater profits to be derived from overseas trade.[10] At the end of the *quattro-cento*, when the Venetians had finally to acknowledge the massive and irresistible power of the Turks and the serious problems raised by the Italian possessions, the unstable equilibrium between the two zones which they controlled was in danger of breaking down.[11]

The long history of control and colonization, as well as the persistence of economic interests, operated in such a way that the 'stato da mar' enjoyed a set of conditions of which the *terraferma* did not have the advantage; however, it was the *terraferma* which was to gain in some measure the upper hand. The Venetians had entered on their course of territorial appropriation in the fifteenth century, still before the economic conditions in the Mediterranean and in the world were to reduce and seriously limit the advantages of the mediating role between East and West played by the Venetians, and still before they were to perceive clearly the crisis in their commerce. It was not, in fact, just a question of a measure of territorial security or of a skilful politico–military manoeuvre; nor was it simply done for the sake of a more tranquil and agree-able way of investing money. The often moralistic but at the same time frequently just observations of Girolamo Priuli[12] to this effect did not prevent his recognizing that, besides the by now impressive mass of economic interests which bound his fellow citizens to the *terraferma*,[13] there was an ulterior and probably decisive motive driving them forward and holding them there: politically and socially, it was a step up. In a manner not very dissimilar from that of other great Italian mercantile communities, most notably Florence, the *quattrocento* was for Venice the era in which rich patricians wanted to climb to a higher social level: that of the nobleman, for which landed property and a certain style of country life were the indispensable conditions and prerogatives. Here the Venetians found not only a way of enjoying their wealth but a promotion and prestige that satisfied them still more. No Venetian was count or marquis, nor even baron: but all the patricians were joint lords of vast domains and as such were almost the equals of territorial princes. Though an unshakeable supporter of maritime trade, Priuli lucidly observed: 'Before these forefathers of ours had the *terraferma* they devoted themselves to voyages and navigation to the great advantage and emolument of the city and they earned much money each year, and yet they were not renowned throughout the world and were regarded as fishermen. Whereas, having conquered the *stato* of the mainland, they have gained great reputation and name on that account and are much esteemed and appreciated and honoured by the *signori* of the world and respected by all.'[14]

III

Up to what point, however, did the landward space and the possessions on the *terraferma* successfully challenge the hold of maritime reality on the Venetian sensibility between the *quattrocento* and the *cinquecento*? To an impassioned witness like Priuli there seemed to be no doubt: Venice's fortune came, and could not but come, from the sea; navigation and commerce were the positive pole of the lagoon world, the *terraferma* the negative pole. The premise of the syllogism on which he based his own argument was to be found in the official minutes of the Senate debates[15] as well as in his *Diarii*: 'money . . . is the chief component of the Republic.'[16] As long as maritime trade prospered, money would never be lacking.[17] Trade, apart from representing 'the nutriment and profit of the city',[18] had made possible 'the wars and the acquisition of the state of the *terraferma*', which, on the contrary, yielded no more than the *Signoria* had to spend there.[19] If trade were to decline or failed to maintain its leading role, or if Venice were to lose its possessions in the Levant, 'it would also lose the *terraferma* in a very few years'.[20] In sum, 'if trade falls off and men live on income little progress will be possible.'[21] Instead of neglecting to keep the affairs of the *terraferma* to a budget, instead of being quite so eager to garrison all the little forts and castles there, however small,[22] the government would do better not to overlook, as it was doing, the defence of its maritime bases.[23]

Priuli was right, all too right, when his arguments were reiterated on the morrow of the disaster provoked by the League of Cambrai. These, however, related to a much broader problem and it is only when they are seen in this context that they take on their full meaning. Since it had become established on the seas, Venice had despatched there not only merchants and sailors but magistrates and citizen soldiers. Free as he may have been to ignore a duty that was in no way codified, until the fourteenth century the average Venetian had faced the risks of piracy and war as well as those of peaceful traffic. There had been striking losses from the end of the *quattrocento*. In the conquest of the *terraferma*, however, the *Signoria* sent mainly mercenary soldiers into the field. This was not because its ancient and hallowed laws prohibited its inhabitants from taking up arms to this purpose, nor simply because men accustomed to the sea would have been ill at ease on land. For centuries patriotism had been shaped by the city itself and its *alter ego* overseas. Though the capital counted for more than its maritime extension, the possessions in the Levant and the Adriatic amounted to an integral part of the collective patrimony, with a quite different status – more structured, more deeply rooted – from that of the *terraferma*.

The syllogism based on the determinant character of money on the life of the Republic was therefore embodied in a broader horizon. Besides this (and its circumstantial validity) was the fact that the Venetians were used to regarding the seaward zone as vital, even if they could no longer contemplate the loss of their mainland acquisitions and would have done anything possible to regain them. In the collective psyche of the inhabitants of the lagoon in the *quattrocento* the Levant and the *terraferma* were by no means on equal terms. To a large extent this was to remain true of the sixteenth century also. In the Italian territories (with the partial exception of Friuli, whose frontier was especially vulnerable to the Turks) the patricians behaved as sovereigns rather than administrators, taking little notice of local sensibilities. In the maritime localities they were primarily the protectors of the community and at the same time of their own interests. To the ties deriving from partnership in economic profit were added – between Venetians and Dalmatians or Greeks – those resulting from a common life on the sea involving both day to day navigation and moments of armed combat. Although, from the *quattrocento*, such relationships entered a long series of crises, Venice was to persist, in spite of everything, in considering them fundamental; it tried to plug every leak that sprang within its maritime structure, never admitting that the 'stato da mar' could be lost without diminishing and wounding Venice itself.

The zone conquered on the Italian hinterland was another matter altogether, involving sharply different circumstances. While in the Levant one crisis had followed another for more than three centuries – from the first Turkish attacks to the loss of Crete (1669) and beyond – the *terraferma*, during four centuries of occupation, saw only a few years of really serious danger. Thunderstruck as they were to find their enemies on the banks of the lagoon and to hear the thunder of their cannon, the Venetian senators resolved at the most dramatic moment, in June 1509, 'as the least of evils and in order to save the city of Venice, to abandon the whole of the *stato di terraferma*'.[24] The Treaty of Cambrai, in fact, had provided that it should be divided among Pope Julius II, Louis XII of France, the Emperor Maximilian and the king of Spain. The decision of the Senate – it was argued – would not only establish the ground for negotiations but would also safeguard Venice itself, especially as those sovereigns 'have not discussed what might become of the city of Venice in the aforementioned league'.[25] The significance of this line of reasoning was almost the opposite of what had been maintained in the face of the Turkish threat until 1470, – again in the Senate: 'Quante importantie sint nova que ex apparatibus Turchorum habentur omnes intelligunt; et non agitur in huiusmodi materia de honore vel utilitate sed de ipsa salute status et libertatis nostre.'[26] Obviously, at the first glimpse of hope that the loss could be recovered, the

Venetians employed every means of returning to their Italian possessions. On one occasion, even if the aim was mainly a demonstrative one, several members of the patrician class – including the doge's sons – took up arms to save Padua. The motives behind the struggle for the *terraferma* were nevertheless various: 'It was not possible that the city fathers and senators of Venice should wish to abandon the *stato di terraferma*; it seemed too fine a thing, nor did they think of anything except its recovery, and were so involved with the possessions, cattle, sheep and livestock that they desired nothing but to regain them and return, each one, to his farms and estates.'[27]

IV

At the beginning of the *quattrocento*[28] the 'stato da mar' made up a good part of Dalmatia, the island of Corfu, the coasts of the Morea and various islands in the Aegean (the most important of which was Negroponte) and Crete. At that time, as we have seen, the growing Turkish power troubled the Venetians very little, as their almost exclusive concern was with territorial objectives. It was one of these, indeed – the recently acquired Salonica – which first fell into the hands of the Ottomans (March, 1429); this was an important but peripheral position, and its loss could be considered largely compensated by the settlement of Corfu from 1386. The importance of this island continued to grow in the eyes of the Venetians, who were forced to turn it into the keystone of their maritime defence system. If the fall of Constantinople made an impression on and caused notable damage to their commerce, especially among the communities on the Black Sea, they suffered their first real defeat by the Ottomans at Negroponte. Yet, even in 1466, a merchant resident in Constantinople assured the Captain general of the Venetian fleet that the Turks thought they needed four or five of their warships to confront a single light galley of St. Mark.[29] In his letter Antonio Michiel guaranteed Vittore Capello that 'as long as you have 40 *galie sotil*, 20 *nave grosse* of 500 to 600 *botte*, with 100 men for each and 10 *galie grosse* you will be able to follow them up vigorously and have the victory, let the Turks strike where they will.'[30]

Such forecasts were destined to be rapidly modified. In the following year there was much anxiety that for the first time the *Serenissima* should have agreed to draw up a treaty with Mahomet II without the usual clause prohibiting the Turkish fleet from leaving the Straits.[31] In July, 1470, the Ottomans, at some cost to themselves, took Negroponte. One of the Venetian commanders, Girolamo Longo, captured the image of the enemy army and his own reaction to it in a metaphor: 'The sea is like a forest; to hear it seems an incredible thing: but to see it is stupendous'; no less significant was his comment 'the time is passed when one could say a fig for the Turkish fleet, for they have put their affairs in order'.[32] Against this background of bitter stupefaction, a change was taking place: the security of the *Signoria*'s space by sea was endangered irreversibly. Henceforth, and for a full century, the Venetian empire 'da mar' passed through a phase of drama, punctuated by threats and serious losses, underscored and pervaded by constant tension.

The drama stemmed mainly from the fact that for many decades Venice had confronted the enemy on the sea almost singlehanded.[33] The aid which the Knights of Rhodes or the papacy could have proffered was less than mediocre; there was none from Spain or France throughout the first half of the fifteenth century, and later, even when Spanish support proved powerful, it remained desultory and was always uncertain. Finally, the Genoese could hardly have been expected to lend a hand spontaneously to the Venetians. For all practical purposes no other military fleets existed. In the second place, that prolonged politico–military depression which had allowed the lagoon city to establish an autonomous area of its own between East and West began to lift. The appearance of the great Turkish war fleet was to coincide – after a considerable delay – with the creation of the joint forces of Spain and Genoa. The Mediterranean was to be transformed into a battlefield, and the sea space of the *Serenissima* in its midst was to be encroached upon by both contestants. Nevertheless, despite the crushing nature of the Turkish offensive and later periodic conflicts between the Ottomans and the Spanish, the empire 'da mar' not only continued to exist but – at the cost, of course, of certain losses, the Morea for example, and later Cyprus – retained its essential nature thanks to a prolonged and constantly renewed capacity for defence and combat. The structural bias towards maritime affairs within the lagoon community continued to show its worth and enabled the Venetians to emerge from their gravest crisis with the space which was really essential to them and which they had conquered previously, intact.

The initial phase – between the loss of Negroponte and of Modone (1500) – was undoubtedly the hardest. An increasingly unhealthy inferiority complex grew out of encounters with the Turks and was aggravated by a shipping crisis which was by no means unrelated to concern for the *terraferma*. An old symptom was the desertion by young patricians of the places (called *balestrarie*) reserved for them on the trading galleys.[34] More recent and more serious was the clear-cut subordination of economic interests to those of defence. Reaction to Ottoman naval power proved to be neither prompt nor courageous. The senators recognized it bitterly by 1471: 'in tanta agitatione status nostri, in tanto tamque periculoso Turcorum bello, nisi id quod maiores nostri fecere consueverunt qui sanguinem proprium exponebant pro conservatione status nostri facere volumus, saltem pecuniis nos adiuvare et statum nostrum conservare debemus.'[35] Restlessness[36] and malaise[37] went together with a desire to avoid danger, a feeling of abandon and of panic[38] as well as of rage.[39] Without effective defence, Crete felt itself in danger of occupation as early as 1475.[40] Breaking clear through the boundary of the 'stato da mar' nearest to Venice itself, the Turks had arrived on the Isonzo by 1472,[41] and again in the following years they repeatedly raided in Friuli. When therefore, after years of repeated but until then false alarms,[42] it came once again to a trial of arms, it seemed that the entire Venetian maritime zone must be engulfed. The naval encounter at Porto Longo (August 12, 1499) showed up the weaknesses of the *Serenissima's* fleet, in particular the selfish cowardice of the captains of the great merchant galleys[43]; the fall of Modone underlined the government's lack of foresight.[44] Consternation[45] was increased by the derision of Christians[46] and Turks. A pasha is said to have commented allusively to Alvise Manenti, an emissary of the *Signoria*: 'Until now, you have been married to the sea; for the future, that is for us, who are more powerful by sea than you.'[47] It was a turning point and Venice felt it suddenly. 'Faced by the Turkish threat,' Priuli wrote of his co-citizens in 1499, 'they are in a worse condition than slaves.'[48] Before the end of that year the Ottomans were at the gates of Treviso.[49]

Fear and alarm – justified, indeed, though not impeding eventual Venetian recovery – are the words which best describe the atmosphere of the lagoon at the beginning of the sixteenth century. So preoccupied was the governing class in September, 1499, that in their anguished wait for news from the Levant[50] even the public celebrations for the victory reported over Lodovico Sforza on the *terraferma* were suspended. They ordered instead that an announcement of this success be circulated at top speed through the maritime cities in the hope that the spectacle of Venetian rejoicing might check the Turkish advance.[51] But in vain. Venice was now facing the hardest test: knowing it was on the losing side,[52] to fight for Modone and the Levant as though for its very life.[53] 'This Turkish engagement', wrote Priuli again in the summer of 1501, 'meant everything; it was not a matter of losing a city or a fort, but of something much more serious';[54] in other words, the entire 'stato da mar'.[55] There was no alternative but to hold firm in the hope of an acceptable peace. As the sixteenth century dawned, convictions which had been growing in the minds of the patricians during the dramatic struggle as a whole crystallized under the impact of events. The rival empire was undeniably stronger: while the Venetians would never make a single conquest from it, the enemy would inevitably succeed in snatching something with every raid.[56] To avoid ruin it was necessary to obtain a truce allowing for the reconstruction of the Venetian forces: 'such a republic, recognizing its manifest ruin, must gain time, and then come what God wills.'[57] The consciousness of what it was, of its own greatness and valour, forced Venice to safeguard itself with every means: peace, now, 'meant life, liberty and wealth'.[58] Along with this 'ragion di stato' went a novel and clear-cut belief that the principal duty was now simply to endure, to continue to live in spite of the overpowering neighbour which was threatening its very existence.[59] And so, next to God, it was Time that appeared insistently to be the protecting deity.

It was an ancient idea, a physiological vision of existence which Machiavelli, for example, was to express.[60] But at this juncture it took on a particular prominence because, in the final analysis, the sea space of the *Serenissima* must henceforward satisfy above all the requirements of survival: 'Having to deal with so great and powerful a ruler . . . it was necessary to do what one could to gain time.'[61] In this way there took place within the collective Venetian sensibility a phenomenon analogous to the one recorded contemporaneously on an individual level by Erasmus in his *Carmen de senectutis incommodis*: a sudden loss of equilibrium in the assessment of its own energies with a consequent unsteadying of the subjective sense of time and space.[62]

V

The fifteenth century had witnessed the successful expansion of Venice in the West and there was no general movement of recoil in the East almost until its close – where, indeed, Cyprus had been acquired in 1479. Political malaise and socio-economic imbalance had been the mute companions of this otherwise prestigious phase in the life of the *Serenissima*. The dimensions of the *quattrocento* world were still, however, in harmony with the nature of the water-bound city state itself, extended equally across the seas and into the Italian peninsula. This harmony was no longer possible in the *cinquecento*.[63] Hitherto, the space which had been of value to Venice had been predominantly economic: settlement had almost always been made with a commercial end in view. The occupation of the *terraferma*, which involved, of course, a variety of economic motives, had altered this traditional pattern. But now, at the beginning of the sixteenth century, more critical factors intervened, requiring a new approach on the part of the *Serenissima* to its space as a whole. While the Ottoman empire was imposing its presence in the east, the king of France, then the king of Spain, and finally the Emperor Charles V asserted themselves no less effectively on the continental chess-board. It was now a matter of steadily transforming the mercantile republic into a true political organism. The game had changed. Each specific piece seemed to have taken on a distinctly new value, all the more so since the transoceanic voyages, particularly the Portuguese rounding of Africa, had led to new relationships within the main trading areas. Throughout the fifteenth century space and time in Venice had been co-ordinated in terms of commerce. Throughout the merchant class the sense of time had been unusually acute, especially so with regard to the complex planning required in the search for profit.[64] But it was involved with a space which – including the Middle East as well as the Atlantic countries of Europe, the Black Sea as well as North Africa – was anything but exclusively Venetian. With the advent of the sixteenth century the politico–military dimension became a priority, if not the predominant one, for the Venetian world: it was as if the sense of space and time still proceeded *pari passu* but in a fresh relationship, more straightforward on the one hand, more circumscribed on the other. Acquired mercantile experience, long tied to government management and practice, was bound to prove valuable in the new climate of the *cinquecento*; but the challenges were severe. The complementary inter-dependence between *terraferma* and Levant was accentuated; military needs – especially on the maritime side – became brutally clear; economic interests, although shrinking, became more diverse: industry and landed property coming to rival the position of trade.

One of the principal consequences, even if it were not yet fully apparent, was that Venice, instead of continuing in its profitable role as universal intermediary, was obliged to concentrate on itself and to make choices. The barbarians were overrunning the peninsula, wreaking havoc: before long they would bring fire and sword to the *terraferma* itself. On the other hand there was the Turk: and between the two barbarians Venice felt constrained to choose the Christian one – if not, perhaps, for purely religious motives. This is seen in the clearest way in 1509 when, to save itself from the fury of the allies of Cambrai, the Senate seriously considered inviting the Turks into Italy to aid the *Serenissima*.[65] They would willingly have seen the Ottoman army expel the threat from across the mountains and humiliate the fierce and dogged pope Julius II had shown himself to be. But who then would have induced the Turks to quit Italy or not to touch the Venetian empire in the Levant? In the dire necessity of the summer of 1509, many came to see falling back on Turkey as the only escape route;[66] but no sooner was there renewed hope of saving the city by themselves than it was agreed not to put the maritime possessions at risk. Just as their loss would have opened the gate of Italy to Islam, so a Turkish establishment on the peninsula would have put an end to the 'stato da mar' and to Venice itself.[67] The image of the *Serenissima* as Christianity's first line of defence, for so long mainly a convenient but empty publicity device for the use of western princes little inclined to support Venice's position in the East, was becoming a reality for Venice itself.[68] The *Signoria* was no more anxious to shield the faith with its own territorial body than were the faithful of the West to consider safeguarding that same shield. Circumstances forced the 'stato da mar' to take on the function of a protective wall;[69] with many variants[70] this leitmotif could be said to span the whole history of *cinquecento* Venice.[71] The Venetian ambassadors at the court of Philip II turned chiefly to this theme in order to explain their abandoning the Holy League and concluding a separate peace with the Turks.[72]

The radical change in the relative naval forces of the *Signoria* and the Ottomans and the breakthrough in ballistic power of the most recent artillery, which put the majority of the old fortifications out of date, did not cause the Venetians to lose heart. The capacity of the arsenal was vigorously strengthened[73] while, in spite of their immense cost, some almost impregnable fortresses – most notably that of Corfu – were built at Sebenico, at Zara, and elsewhere. It would be easy to make a long list of Venetian insufficiencies in all sectors of maritime defence from commanders and crews to supplies and tactics.[74] It is far more pertinent here to stress that the 'sea wall' role of the *Serenissima* was maintained in spite of the extremely serious economic and demographic crisis that affected the whole of the 'stato da mar' in the course of the sixteenth century.[75] Around 1550 raids, military operations and mere terror of the Turks had reduced the inhabitants of Venetian Dalmatia to 100,000;[76] Cefalonia and Corfu were depopulated on a no less impressive scale[77] while in Crete it was ever more difficult to produce an adequate naval defence.[78] To this one must add the installation of Turkish bases at the heart of the Venetian defence system, at Valona, at Santa Maura, at Lepanto, where the Ottoman authorities regularly recruited squadrons of Barbary pirates. It was only thanks to Venice's remarkable and continued diligence, to the many patricians who served in its fleet or administration, that the sea wall was strengthened and made capable of safeguarding navigation and the majority of the maritime possessions themselves. The old maritime institutions of the Republic furnished a further proof of their vitality as long as the *Signoria* still knew how to turn to account the geopolitical and economic elements on which it had founded its original fortune. The fleet was reorganized and transformed into a permanent instrument of intervention despite a grave shortage of men for its crews.[79] New and better integrated systems were created for the navy, various methods of enlistment and armament were tried and introduced.[80] On the other hand, not even the Turks could surmount the natural obstacle formed by the impervious and almost uninterrupted mountain barrier which protected Dalmatia from the hinterland they occupied. Sovereignty of the Adriatic waters remained substantially in Venetian hands. The *Serenissima* had always regarded that sea as 'its' gulf, in the most possessive sense of the term, that is, as an integral part of its jurisdiction. Not even the formation of the Spanish empire and the revived crusading spirit could lead to the establishment of bases for a non-Venetian army on the inhospitable shores of eastern Italy. Despite increasingly frequent and ill-omened pirate raids and the attacks of the Turkish fleet, the Adriatic remained the watery but well-garrisoned scarp of the sea wall which wound down from the lagoon to the Levant.

VI

Broadly speaking, Venice had undoubtedly declined from being a power of the first order to becoming a second-rate state. The world which at the end of the fifteenth century it could still call its own had been unexpectedly enlarged by the great oceanic discoveries. One in particular, the Portuguese discovery of a sea passage to India, came to diminish and, to some extent, nullify the mediating role of the lagoon city. Around 1455, after having reached the equator with some Portuguese vessels, the Venetian Alvise da Ca' da Mosto wrote, significantly: 'Truly, in comparison with our own [places], those that I saw and came to know could be called another world.'[81] Nevertheless, when – in mid-July, 1501 – the first news arrived at Venice of the caravels that had returned from India,[82] the reaction was one of deep depression.[83]

As men used to the most various and far-flung trade, as merchants in touch then as they had been for so long with Indian markets,[84] the Venetians were more impressed and stunned than surprised. The hardest blow was not, as it turned out, to their concept of geographic space, but to that of economic space, their most direct source of profit, their livelihood.[85] Because they did not want to adapt to the idea of having to give up their accustomed profitable earnings, the majority were seized with alarm and a minority took refuge for years in refusing to believe what was being confirmed again and again from all sides.[86] It was, then, the dimension of profit, psychological and not theoretical, that the Portuguese voyage had injured and disturbed: 'There were still many who would not believe, even when the aforesaid caravels had arrived, because they did not wish it to be.'[87] Perception of the damage at the level of commercial strategy was immediate and – apart from the excessive pessimism, no less understandable than the incredulity – far more lucid.[88] If the sea passage to the Indies was also held to be 'almost incredible' this was because it was a matter of 'things undiscovered for such a great and infinite time' and of a route that was 'new . . . and neither heard of nor seen in the days of the ancients or of our ancestors'.[89] The roots of this suspension of belief grew naturally enough, that is, from an attachment to a world of economic relationships as convenient as they were time-honoured. On the surface there was no sense of theoretical or practical impossibility, rather a revulsion against the breaking of an almost patrimonial tradition. The initial astonishment was quickly dispelled. They continued instead to cling to every hope while unanimously considering this 'the worst news the Venetian Republic could ever have had, excepting only the loss of our freedom'.[90] Nothing could have more serious results, neither war with the Turks[91] nor loss of the *terraferma*.[92] Hope was looked for in the excessive length of the journey, in the difficulty of finding men disposed to face such dangers, in the reaction of the other injured parties: the Sultan of Egypt and the 'Moor'. For these reasons – as well as their lack of faith in the real advantages of such a venture – the *Signoria* did not take up the king of Portugal's offer to make the port of Lisbon the centre of the Venetian distributive network.[93] German merchants, on the other hand, did not hesitate to run the risk.[94]

With verification not only of the accuracy of the first news but also of the increasing continuity and profit of the new maritime route, there were few left in Venice able to think that 'this voyage could have no effect' and to persist in this belief 'because for the good of the city they would not believe it'.[95] To the political and military forces working on their *quattrocento* world was added an even more irreparable prospect: the drying up of their most profitable trade with the east. The economic foresightedness which had served the Venetians, smiling on them so abundantly in the past, seemed to offer them no escape either in the short or in the long run: 'everyone knew that, with time, this would be the total ruin of the Venetian city'.[96] At first, hope had even been placed in good luck, a change of fortune dictated by the heavens.[97] But after a decade, how could one dare to hope? The horizon had changed and appeared closed; now merchants looked with renewed interest towards the *terraferma*.[98] There was nothing left but for men to take their own desires for reality[99] or to day-dream – on one of the dismal nights of June, 1509 – of a moral palingenesis. Had the League of Cambrai stripped Venice of its Italian domains? From that very evil, regeneration might come. Indeed, 'the *terraferma* being lost, the nobles, citizens and populace of Venice, I mean the younger ones among them, will concentrate on the sea and voyages of trade, and beyond the profit we will produce brave men, skilled in the use of the sea and in every other way, and perhaps this will be of more benefit to the Venetian Republic than the revenues of the *terraferma*'.[100]

VII

For the Venetian, from the economic, political and even psychological points of view, space was restructured by events between the end of the *quattrocento* and the beginning of the following century. At the same time, a critical perception of the community as something which must endure and the adoption of values which underlined this were becoming more instinctive, more existential.

After the alarm raised by the Turk, amid the sense of ruin spread by the Portuguese voyage, the *Serenissima* had experienced a moment's fear that all was over. In the eyes of its citizens, and also in those of the world, Venice's position at the beginning of the *cinquecento* appeared absolutely secure: its diminishment seemed out of the question. The loss of Modone was certainly no small thing for a republic more accustomed to growth than withdrawal: it could have led to doubts about the future.[101] But to lose all the *terraferma* in fifteen days, to gather that the enemy had reached the 'salt marges' of the lagoon[102] was unheard of. The Venetians had been so sure of themselves that they had fortified the outer border of their empire – Cremona, Bergamo, Brescia, etc. – but not the nearer cities like Verona, Vicenza and Padua.[103] Sebastiano Giustinian, *podestà* of Brescia, expressed his astonishment in these words: 'If an angel from heaven had said that the state of the *Signoria* would be lost in fifteen days, I would not have believed him.'[104] No one, inside or out of Venice, had so much as thought of such a thing: 'There was no human mind or intellect which would have considered it, nor any astrologer, nor philosopher, nor necromancer, nor expert practitioner in predicting the future who would have considered it nor prophesied it, seeming as it did to them, *ut ita dicam*, a thing impossible . . .'[105]

Immediately after Agnadello (14th May, 1509), the Venetians had to prepare themselves not only for a siege of the city but also, at least in part, for surrender. One must say 'at least in part' because the centuries-long belief in the city's security could not be cancelled point blank in the collective subconscious, even by the most open threat. Almost no one had even his personal arms left,[106] the last serious conflict dating back to the end of the fourteenth century: 'In the city of Venice men held themselves to be as far from hostile and warlike threats as they would have been in heaven.'[107] During the first days of con-

31

fusion the patricians did not (if they ever had) feel entirely safe from popular insurrection.[108] It was, perhaps, in order to close ranks that they gave currency to the fear that the enemy might not only enslave them but drive them from the city and force them to scatter 'throughout the whole world'.[109] Probably anachronistic, this was a fear which arose from long memory of the banishments and sentences of exile which had regularly characterized the struggles between the other medieval Italian cities.

Thrown back on themselves alone (and on the bands of countrymen on the *terraferma* who still declared themselves for St. Mark), together with the will to resist the most profound themes of survival emerged, ideological reference points of particular significance to the patrician class but not without meaning among the less exclusive layers of Venetian society. How could they not have great faith in themselves in the 'impregnable site and wonderful strength of the glorious city of Venice'?[110] Was it not impossible to take possession of Venice without a powerful fleet?[111] The enemy did not have one, and thus it could not come closer than three miles.[112] The encircling fortress of water was admired *pari passu* with the city itself.[113] Self-satisfaction apart, the inhabitants' attachment to their community was a not unimportant factor; it was an element, moreover, inherent in a by now long cultural tradition. In the *quattrocento* and *cinquecento*, as in previous centuries, the site of Venice was considered ideal, almost uniquely fortunate, and this was a by no means secondary aspect of the city's myth. This impregnability – 'virginea'[114] or 'virginale, never conquered by any ruler'[115] – was not based on the events of the moment: it stretched back through a long and luminous past, it reached forward into the future. Venice had arisen, as civic historiography had underlined, as a refuge, a place of escape from the invading barbarians.[116] There was no patrician who could be ignorant of this moment of his community's birth: and it, in its turn, was closely linked with the idea of its age. Bankers, sea captains, ambassadors[117] all knew, with equal readiness, how old Venice was. For this reason also, the city to whose history they so often referred their own was the one which – in addition to its glorious repute – reinforced this sense of era: Rome. It was easier for the nobility to disagree about the date of the acquisition of Padua or Vicenza, of which their grandfathers had been witnesses.[118]

The nature of the site, its extraordinary security, a political longevity almost unparalleled throughout the world: all helped to drive home the conviction that Venice was unique and therefore as profoundly different from other states as it was superior to them. It is clear that these values and this consciousness were in no way affected by the *terraferma* or the maritime empire, both of which were essentially part of a qualitatively separate spirit, the branches and fruit to which the root alone could give life.[119] Religious and astral beliefs and, above all, an understanding of history[120] certainly prevented the Venetians from considering their city to be actually immortal. But how many other attributes it had! – glorious, 'hymned throughout the whole world', 'famous and eternally memorable', 'sublime', 'worthy', rich, superb, wonderful, rare, etc.[121] If it were to decline, would it not be necessary to 'make another like it – if that were possible – because all of Italy and all the world would suffer for the lack of it'?[122] Within that privileged space, moreover, any citizen whatsoever could reach out and touch what, elsewhere, it was only permitted to desire, a real projection of supernal beatitude: 'whoever lived and stayed there seemed to be in an earthly paradise, without any tumult of war or suspicion of enemies, nor would he look to suffer misfortune or fear any mental perturbation, the city having endured and stood so long, for so many hundreds of years, in peace, quiet and repose; and whoever wished to live in peace and quiet and expect to go about his business peacefully could not stay nor live in a quieter or more peaceful place than the city of Venice; and he would not cause trouble or offence, nor would he be offended there, because the city was free and without factions; nor in any other city in the world could he be quieter or more peaceful because no offence or harm was done, and he could make and dispose of what was his own as he pleased; nor would violence be done, nor injustice; nor would what was his be taken by force; so that one could say: "non est vivere extra Venetiis".'[123]

There is no doubt that this both touchy and complacent sense of uniqueness – which was not, indeed, without some justification – had helped prevent the fusion of Venice with the 'stato da mar', still more with the *terraferma*, or any real sense of an overriding common identity. The community of the lagoon was too different because after so many centuries its members, particularly the patricians who had created it, could not really put themselves in the place of others, whether strangers or their own subjects, however faithful.

VIII

Through the shared consciousness of being part of a wholly unusual political structure, this fundamental conviction of uniqueness was expressed in terms of another dimension, that of duration. Beyond the collective response to events,[124] beyond the use of time as a vitalizing medicine for the community,[125] beyond even the belief in the cosmic alternation of fortune and misfortune,[126] there was within the Venetian patrician class a faith in its own special and exceptional capacity to endure politically. It was not so much a matter of being aware that an opportune pause or a political negotiation could gain time for recovery,[127] nor of the belief – we have called it 'physiological' – that the Venetian organism could still endure.[128] It was a structural, a truly political conviction derived from associating the state's duration with the specific nature of the free and republican laws by which the city was governed.

'Time does much for republics', wrote Girolamo Priuli, 'because they never die.'[129] He was thinking, obviously, of his own: not merely because he belonged to and was particularly interested in it, but because Venice was 'more' republican than the others, the only true and valid one actually in existence. He even gave confirmation to this – albeit involuntarily, thanks to his irregular but intensely revealing style: 'The Venetian state, that is, republics, last a long time, and rulers, because they are human, must needs die.'[130] A lucid, though thoroughly spontaneous man, he did not only mean to stress that the Venetian ruling class possessed a potential continuity greatly superior to that of a princely state. On another occasion, in fact, he contrasted the nexus, republic and liberty with the dynastic succession of princes.[131] In the case of Venice, in other words, 'republic' was not purely and simply a synonym for 'state' nor a construction characterized by certain constitutional forms rather than others, but a community animated by the consciousness of a liberal regime created at a particular time and by its capacity for self-perpetuation. At the beginning of the *quattrocento* a cultivated functionary of the *Serenissima*, Lorenzo de' Monaci, had already pointed to the safeguarding of liberty as being the politically significant aspect of Venice's role in history.[132] The community of the lagoon had, in fact, known how to preserve itself not only from every kind of external enemy but – no less remarkably – also from internal plots, from those warring factions which are worse than conquest itself.[133] In this, it had shown itself superior even to Rome.[134] In the second half of the fifteenth century Bernardo Giustinian had extended this by now widespread theme, maintaining that freedom was the only true aim and ambition, past and present, of the Venetians: otherwise, especially now, they would not have had a sufficient motive for involving themselves in so much self-sacrifice.[135]

Certainly it could be true in general that 'time works for every republic'.[136] In fact, Venetians of the fifteenth and sixteenth centuries could see no other of any significance, none so unified and self-aware as their own. A young Venetian ambassador took care to say so to the world's most powerful monarch, on the eve of Lepanto: 'My lord, we are a republic of 1,200 years by the grace of the Lord God, so well established and united that even though we are much afflicted today and have lost what is ours and are in the way of losing even more, nonetheless what we have lost hitherto we can, given time and through those changes and vicissitudes which are the way of the world, finally regain, because our succession is of a kind which can never fail.'[137] In the search for a value that would guarantee collective perpetuity, something independent of site, even of longevity, even of fortune and celestial influences, and no longer able to think in terms of nation or *popolo*, Venetian sensibility became imbued with the notion of being free. 'We would live with liberty and in the proud manner left to us 1,200 years ago by our ancestors', the same Donà, together with L. Priuli, wrote shortly afterwards, 'whereas without liberty and that way of life, to a man we should choose to die; each one of us values that liberty and that condition above all the riches we possess privately.'[138]

Between the sense of the changefulness of all that is wordly and a fixed belief in the alternating and inexorable cosmic rhythm of the stars and of fortune, the Venetian patriciate as a whole inserted in this way a supra-personal, ever-lasting and ideal value of their own which formed a third temporal dimension: on a level neither individual nor cosmic but related to the historical duration of secular civilization in its entirety, it joined its fate to the indissoluble link between existence and freedom. At the beginning of the *quattrocento* a Venetian historian had indeed distinguished three ages in the life of the lagoon community. Two, childhood and adolescence, were very brief, and one much longer: youth.[139] The following century brought a distinct perception not only of the notion of maturity but also of obvious decay.[140] It was even possible to glimpse the moment when Venice would be nothing but a memory.[141] But the essence of Venice, its first claim to mobility, continued to be thought of – just as it had been by Lorenzo de' Monaci[142] – as having been the creation of a lasting relationship between social solidarity and independence, political regime and 'libertas'.

This liberty, seen as the guideline of the evolving Venetian state, was not abstract or idyllic but something hard-won, realized historically, at the expense now of some, now of others, as much within the area of the lagoon as outside it. It was, obviously, liberty conceived hierarchically, capable, that is, of allowing each internal group or subject community the type of activity which the patrician class considered legitimate in the stratified society it had shaped. Nevertheless, in the course of the *quattrocento* and *cinquecento*, the motivations behind this rigidly organized liberty took a sharply different direction, stressing on the one hand its function as a constant point of reference and throwing into relief on the other the critical and conscious interaction between these values and the actual course of events as they affected the *Serenissima*. In the fifteenth century liberty was still thought of, at intervals and from various viewpoints, as inseparably linked with the flourishing of maritime trade, whereas in the following century it assumed far more political and territorial forms. Bernardo Giustiniani, underlining Pepin's attempt to make Ravenna the real emporium of the Adriatic, maintained: 'illuc omnia negocia transitura, desertum autem iri portus omnes venetos et oppida; sublato autem mercaturae studio, quid reliqui supererat nisi servitutem subire morte peiorem?'[143] The famous historian gave credence on the other hand to the version according to which the conquest of the *terraferma* – where, he had previously maintained, the Venetians had not intervened for a millennium[144] – was justified by the hostile scheme of their Italian neighbours to silt up the lagoon and then march in and reduce the *Serenissima* to slavery.[145] His city had thus had a long struggle to safeguard its own basin and to create for itself frontiers capable of protecting it from the danger of losing both its port and its liberty.[146]

His contemporary, Poulo Morosini, explains even more explicitly the original constitutionalized connection which had always existed in Venice between the function of commerce and the defence of freedom: 'Nec inficiari quis Venetis legitime potest quod gerant commercia, cum, tutandae libertatis gratia, quam per duo et ultra millia annos illesam incontaminatamque servarunt, nullisque unquam servientes in illam extremi maris oram incultam omnique vivendi usu carentem, ne ullis iniuriam inferre viderentur, declinare decreverint, commerciisque vitam necessitate trahentes, libertatem, quam cunctis praetulerant opibus, tutari conati sunt.'[147] This, in his opinion, was also a choice: whether merely to refrain from offending neighbours on the *terraferma* through expansionist moves or to avoid the attractive dangers of mainland empire altogether.[148] The choice of liberty was also precise on the constitutional level, the power of the head of state being constantly circumscribed within limits fixed with the object of precluding tyranny over the citizens.[149]

And thus, in this context too, we return to the great theme of internal conflict which had characterized so much of the Venetian *quattrocento* and was to reach its critical stage in the first two decades of the following century. The dying Tommaso Mocenigo had already warned his countrymen that if they instituted a policy of conquest on the *terraferma*, they would face ruin. Now, in the examination of conscience forced by the need to analyse the sudden disaster of 1509, Girolamo Priuli, turning brutally on the other members of the patrician class, cried out to them: 'In peacetime you are lords and enjoy and show off what is yours; in wartime you are slaves and always in a state of trouble and suffering.'[150] The consciousness of being themselves unable – or of not knowing how – to take the destiny of their own Italian territories in hand, of having, for a whole gamut of reasons, to turn to others to defend them, represented a sort of revenge for the adversaries of expansion on the *terraferma*. For the nexus 'commerce and liberty', that of 'liberty and peace' was substituted in debate against the territorial drives of the *Serenissima*. Not because commerce – especially for a Priuli – could not still have been the real salvation of the city and the means of safeguarding its independence, but to the extent that to remain free Venice must now – even more on land than on the sea – avoid war entirely. To endure and to preserve its liberty it needed, first and foremost, peace. In place of new dimensions of space and power, argument was now couched in terms of ideals and values as constituting political programmes.

But there was more. Beyond the circumstantial, on the level of the slower structural evolution of the Venetian community and its growing self-awareness, the 'stato libero' meant, at the same time, a point of departure and a victory. Venice had been – as we have seen – a city, a 'terra' which had always felt isolated and unique. But the ancestral sense of pride and lordship inherited by the ruling patrician and even by the *cittadino* groups harboured (as has been indicated) a hidden yet keen sense of inferiority. On what consecrated ground could the *Serenissima* actually base its power? A glorious and extraordinary feat it undoubtedly was to have preserved its liberty for so many centuries. Nevertheless, in the eyes of the Venetians themselves it involuntarily appeared to be somehow anomalous. It was a privilege no different in kind from that of so many other medieval 'liberties', a prerogative which could not remain absolute, the legitimacy of which was always shadowed by uncertainty. Apart from proclaiming it the crucial value which identified the political nature of the community it had always been necessary to defend it. True, the ancient 'ducato' – in practice, a city, a commune – had been successfully established first as a *dominio* and then as a *signoria* and for some time the doge had been able to consider himself the equal, or almost, of other sovereigns. Between the *quattrocento* and *cinquecento*, moreover, Venice became liberated, as it were, from these perspectives and from this mental and political dimension, as it became a state among other states. This was the meaning behind the definition 'stato libero'. The one republic among so many princely states and empires, it achieved, just as its power reached a dangerous turning point, a definitive place among them in the international concert, with similar rights no longer as a privileged city but as a state. The shadow of the two medieval empires between which Venice had inserted its own secular autonomy finally vanished from its horizons – and from its hidden fears. In the new European order, the Venetian state was raised to the same status as the others – and was now freed from any danger of serious external claims upon it.

The fact of being a republic threw around Venice an aura not so much of particularism as of universal validity. In a Europe where liberty was taking on new shades of meaning in the face of the assertion of monarchical absolutism, the longstanding liberty of Venice assumed a new significance and fascination. While Venice was interpreting it as the most effective cause of its own political stability in the past and its organic survival into the future, Europe was making it a key point of reference, an ideal, and a myth. Thus after the dramatic events we have sought to illumine, Venetian liberty came to constitute a welding of past and present, a bridge between them.

NOTES

1. The image of the heart and other members was used by Girolamo Priuli in July 1509 with reference to the almost unprecedented withdrawal of the Venetian naval forces from the Levant to the Adriatic in order to ensure to the city – which was then exerting a crucial effort against the forces of the League of Cambrai – the greatest possible degree of protection from the sea: 'Dicte insule [Crete and Cyprus] heranno desproviste de armata maritima, la qual hera venuta versso Venetia perché dubitavanno da asedio in questa citade et per simel rispecto, per salvare il corre, haveanno abandonato li altri membri'; cf. *Diarii*, iii, 118 (in *R.I.S.* 2, xxiv, pt. iiia).

2. This problem has been underlined, even if in somewhat too rigid a manner and with certain perhaps premature judgements, in Giorgio Cracco's *Società e stato nel medioevo veneziano* (Florence, 1967), and in Angelo Ventura, *Nobiltà e popolo nella società veneta del 1400 e 1500* (Bari, 1964), a work about which I have expressed my reservations in *Studi Storici*, vii (1966) 401–408. In this connection it is worth quoting the impressions and conclusions of Girolamo Priuli in the critical moment of the summer of 1509: 'Donde che anchora il populo veneto, quale non si dovea experimentar per esser la magior parte forestieri che pocho stimanno piùi uno Signore cha l'altro, dimonstrasse fidellissimo et prumpto ad volerssi diffendere; tamen se dovea considerare che, dal governo in fuori dela citade et la nobeltade veneta et pochissimi citadini, tuto il resto heranno forestieri et pochissimi venetiani, et che non fusse sapienttia a metere una tanta citade in pericolo di asedio, in discrectione de vulgi, in libertade et arbitrio de populli...' (*Diarii*, iii, 101).

3. For an overall view of the general aspects of this period, see the collection *Venice au temps des galères*, ed. Jacques Goimard (Paris, 1968) with contributions by Maurice

Aynard, 'La Terre Ferme', 125–149, and Ugo Tucci, 'Dans le sillage de Marco Polo', 89–111. See also, especially for the articles bearing most directly on Venetian society, Frederic C. Lane, *Navires et constructeurs à Venise pendant la Renaissance* (Paris, 1965), together with the highly important studies collected in his *Venice and history* (Baltimore, 1966).

4. Cf. the *Renga de messer Thomado Mocenigo doxe alla Signoria*, in *Bilanci generali*, ser. II, vol. i, pt. i (Venice, 1912) 94–97 (R. Commissione per la pubblicazione dei documenti finanziari della Repubblica di Venezia); on differing opinions on political attitudes to the *terraferma*, see also Antonio Medin, *La storia della repubblica di Venezia nella poesia* (Milan, 1904) 100.

5. 'Voi Veneziani havete gran torto', said the duke of Milan, Galeazzo Maria, to the Venetian secretary Gonella in 1467, 'havendo 'l più bel stato d'Italia, a no vi contentar e turbar la pase e 'l stato d'altri. Se sapeste la mala volontà che tutti universalmente hanno contra de voi, vi se rizzeriano i capelli e lasceresti viver ogn'uno nel suo stato', in Domenico Malipiero, *Annali veneti dall'anno 1457 al 1500*, ed. Francesco Longo (Florence, 1843) ii, 216–217; the duke added: 'Havete un bel stato, e maggior entrata che potenzia d'Italia; no la sbaragliate: dubius est eventus belli'. Ibid., 218 (*A.S.I.*, vii, ser. Ia, pt. iia).

6. I may be permitted to refer to the brief article I published in collaboration with Corrado Vivanti, together with a map by Jacques Bertin, 'Le film d'un grand système de navigation; les galères marchandes vénitiennes: XIVe–XVIe siècles', in *Annales*, xvi (1961) 83–86.

7. Cf. the two excellent studies by Frederic C. Lane, 'Ritmo e rapidità di giro d'affari nel commercio veneziano del Quattrocento', in *Studi in onore di Gino Luzzatto* (Milan, 1950) i, 254–273, and 'Fleets and fairs: the functions of the Venetian Muda' in *Studi in onore di Armando Sapori* (Milan, 1957) i, 649–663, both reprinted in *Venice and history*.

8. 'La fama et la gloria del stato venetto', wrote Girolamo Priuli at the beginning of the sixteenth century, 'he procedutta et venuta per li viagij et per la riputatione del mare et questo senza dubio alchuno che, manchando la navigatione et il stato maritimo a Venetiani, mancherianno ettiam la riputatione et la gloria loro et in pochissimi anni se consumeranno a pocho a pocho', *Diarii*, iii, 14. The writer goes on to add: 'Se volemo descriver la veritate et non inganarsi, non he dubio alchuno che la citade veneta sia venuta ad tanta reputatione et famma, quanto ahora se atrova, solum per il mare, videlicet per li traffegi et navigatione continui che se fanno et per li viagij.' Ibid., 156.

9. 'Non hera alchuno citadino et nobelle, over populare, quali havessenno il modo, che non havesse comprato almancho una posessione et chaxa in terraferma, et maxime in Padoana et Trivixana, per essere lochi propinqui, per potere andar a solazo et ritornare in uno over duo giorni.' Ibid., iii, 50.

10. 'Li Padri veneti et tuta la citade heranno tantto inclinati et destinati a questa terraferma che piùi non se poteva dire, et abandonava li viagij maritimi rispecto a questa terraferma; et questo procedeva perché, essendo li nobelli et citadini veneti inrichiti, volevanno triumfare et vivere et atendere a darssi apiacere et delectatione et verdure in la terraferma et altri spassi assai, abandonando la navigatione et viagij maritimi quali heranno piùi fastidiosi et laboriossi: et tamen dal mare procedeva ogni bene.' Ibid.

11. 'Donde he seguitto che chadauno se ha atachatto a questi solazi, apiaceri et delichateze et morbini dela terraferma senza utilitade alchuna, et hanno abandonato il exercitio maritimo, le navigatione et li viagij, quali heranno de guadagno, de utilitade, de sparagno, perché li navichantti, considerando cum quanta faticha et cum quanto sudore se avadagnanno li danari per forza, restringenno le spexe superflue et convengonno sparagnar: et tanto he guadagnato, perché il sparagno fa le facultade grande . . . Ahora veramente li giovani nobelli et citadini venetti, che in principio dela sua etade solevanno atendere ale navigatione et ali guadagni, atendevanno ali solazi, apiaceri, a chaze et sparbieri, astori cum grandissima spexa, et de manchadantti diventavanno vilani senza experientia dele chosse del mondo.' Ibid.

12. 'Li Venetiani', he wrote after Agnadello, 'heranno molto piùi inclinati ala Terraferma, per essere piùi delectevole et piazevole, cha al mare suo antiquo et cagione de ogni loro gloria, amplitudine et honore.' Ibid., 49.

13. 'Essendo li duo terzi dele posesione et chasamenti del teritorio patavino deli nobelli et citadini veneti', wrote the banker (ibid., 243), who also put down an approximate estimate of his investments: 'Considerando maxime quante posessione et chaxe deli nobelli et citadini veneti se atrovanno in questi teritorij [above all from Padua and Treviso] per grande valuta de danari et, ut ita dicam, de duo milliona d'oro.' Ibid., 170.

14. As the height of insult, the epithet 'fishermen' was applied to the Venetians by the inhabitants of the Lombard plain, by Lodovico Sforza as well as by the citizens of Padua. (Cf. Priuli, *Diarii*, iii, 116.) This shows that around 1500 the Venetian patricians were still thought of as *parvenus* within the society of the Italian mainland.

15. The essential importance of money emerges as a considered judgement at least from the first half of the *quattrocento*. (Cf. for example, A.S.V., *Senato Misti*, reg. 59, f. 29, 11 Feb., 1434.) But affirmations of this sort become more marked above all in the second half of the fifteenth century (cf., for example, ibid., S.T., reg. 4, f. 76^v, 28 June, 1458; ibid., f. 112, 22 June, 1459; ibid., f. 125, 4 Oct., 1459; ibid., reg. 6, f. 107, 12 Oct., 1470; ibid., f. 168, 4 July, 1472; ibid., reg. 11, f. 97, 25 Jan., 1492, etc.).

16. *Diarii*, iii, 121.

17. Ibid.; cf. also ibid., 49 and i, 271.

18. Ibid., ii, 14.

19. Ibid., ii, 156.

20. Ibid., i, 196. As the writer warms to his theme, the time is reduced still further: 'in pochissimi giorni la cità veneta veneria al mancho'. Ibid., ii, 14.

21. Ibid., iii, 121.

22. Ibid., 49.

23. Ibid., 49–50.

24. Ibid., 14 e, S.S., reg. 42, f. 4.

25. *Diarii*, iii, 14.

26. Cf. A.S.V., S.T., reg. 6, f. 86, 8 Mar., 1470. After hearing the news of the fall of Negroponte, the Milanese ambassador to the *Signoria* had written: 'Tutta Venezia è presa dallo sgomento; gli abitanti, mezzo morti dalla paura, dicono che la perdita di tutti i possedimenti di Terraferma sarebbe stata un male minore.' Cf. F. Babinger, *Maometto il Conquistatore e il suo tempo* (2nd ed., Turin, 1967) ch. iv, 302.

27. Priuli, *Diarii*, iii, 51.

28. The Venetians had fixed its borders at the gulf of the Quarnaro, whence they considered their *terraferma* to begin; cf., for example, Priuli, *Diarii*, i, 136, and ii, 92 and 145.

29. D. Malipiero, *Annali*, pt. i, 40. On these and the Venetian–Turkish questions, cf. F. Babinger, op. cit.

30. D. Malipiero, *Annali*, pt. i, 39.

31. 'Et è sta' gran cosa che la Terra s'habbia contentà de far acordo con Turchi', commented Malipiero, 'senza quell'antica e nobile condicion, tanto apreziada da i nostri vechi, messa in tutte le capitolazion che se faseva con loro.' Ibid., pt. i, 43.

32. Ibid., 51 and 52.

33. Around 1464 Paolo Morosini expressed his fellow citizens' conviction thus: '. . . dum terra marique conatu maximo bellum intulimus, derelicti tantum impetum sustinere solique certare nunc cogimur'; cf. *De rebus ac forma reipublicae venetae Gregorio Heymburg, Germanorum doctori praeclarissimo*, in *Bibliotheca manuscripta ad S. Marci Venetiarum*, ed. Giuseppe Valentinelli (Venice, 1870) iii, 243. A few years later, at the height of the war, he expressed himself more emphatically: 'Quintus agitur annus quo Veneti Dalmatia, Albania, Graecia, Thessalia omnique ora maritima, soli, tanto eorum periculo ac impensa, hosti maximo occurrere compulsi sunt, nec adhuc belli finis aut

fidelium ulla praesidia expectantur'; cf. *Defensio Venetorum ad Europae principes contra obtrectatores*, ibid., 215.

34. Cf. for example, Priuli, *Diarii*, ii, 168.

35. Cf. S.T., reg. 6, f. 122, 1 Mar., 1471.

36. 'Non so come si potrà starli all'incontro, se no se farà manco stima del danaro de quel che se fa', one reads in the letter quoted from Girolamo Longo: 'e Dio no vogia che in pochi zorni no se perda quel che se ha acquistado in longo tempo'; cf. D. Malipiero, *Annali*, pt. ia, 49–50. 'Perso Negroponte, tutto 'l resto del Levante sarà in pericolo', Piero Dolfin wrote from Scio to Candian Bollani on 14 Feb., 1470, ibid., 47; 'se il si perde', G. Longo emphasized in the same connection, 'tutto 'l stado de Levante in fin Istria sarà perso.' Ibid., 52.

37. 'Adesso', noted Malipiero towards 1470, 'par ben che sia abbassada la grandezza veneziana et estinta la nostra superbia.' Ibid., 58–59.

38. 'Queste lettere', wrote Malipiero after the news of the taking of Negroponte, 'ha messo tutti in gran terror e se dubitava che, seguitando 'l Turco la vittoria, se perdesse tutto 'l stado.' Ibid., 58.

39. 'Li ministri della Signoria in Levante', reported Malipiero in 1474, 'teme grande-mente del fin della guerra per la grandezza del Turco e per la poca reputazion de i nostri soldati e del nostro governo. Ne chiamano homeni imperiti, impotenti, imbelli, desprovisti, senza capitani, senza essercito, senza arme, senza obedientia e senza alcun presidio.' Ibid., 107–108.

40. 'L'isola di Candia è in grandissimo timor de Turchi per no haver fortezza onde redurse; e i villani, per esser desarmadi, cegna de fuggir a la montagna e lassar l'isola abandonada. Rethimo e la Canea no fa provision alcuna; el borgo de Candia no è in fortezza, perché i fossi è munidi e i borghisani ha tumultuado davanti 'l Rezimento.' Ibid., 109.

41. 'Era quasi la metà dell'autunno, quando appresso 'l tramontar del sol una squadra de Turchi comparse su le rive del fiume Lisonzo; e già cominciavano a passar, quando i sudditi della signoria i scovrirno . . .' Ibid., 77.

42. 'Di queste cosse de Constantinopoli', Priuli confessed in January, 'rare volte se intende la veritade et dicessi molto piùj assaj di quello he, over che die esser.' *Diarii*, i, 15. Indeed, D. Malipiero had noted two years earlier that, for example, 'A' 6 de fevrer se dubitava che 'l Turco no mandasse fuora armada grossa a tempo nuovo: e fo preso de armar in la Terra 20 galie, 4 in Dalmazia e 6 in Candia.' *Annali*, pt. ia, 142.

43. Extensive and bitter comments in this connection can be found in the *Diarii* of G. Priuli and Marino Sanuto. Cf. also D. Malipiero, *Annali*, 179, and A. Tenenti, 'I corsari in Mediterraneo all'inizio del Cinquecento', in *Riv. Stor. Ital.*, lxxii (1960) 251.

44. An echo of overt criticism can be found in: 'Li Senatori veneti, prudentissimi, meritanno grande reprensione in questa imprexa, perché, considerando et cognoscendo per fermo che in questa cità de Modom consiste et he la chiave del loro stato contra il Turcho, dovea et hera conveniente et debito loro aver neli tempi preteriti fortifichato, munita et tal tamen posta in forteza questa degna citade che per alchuno tempo mai havessenno habudo paura del signor Turcho né dela sua potentia, quanto grande la fusse.' *Diarii*, ii, 26–27.

45. 'Tutta la citade rimase morta et quasi, ut dicam, desperatti, iudichando et dubi-tando questo esser il principio dela ruina del Stato veneto; et per tutta la citade se facevanno grandissimi pianti et lamentatione.' Ibid., ii, 38.

46. Cf. D. Malipiero, *Annali*, ia, 183 (comment of Louis XII to the ambassador Antonio Loredan).

47. Ibid., 195.

48. *Diarii*, i, 183; cf. ibid., 198 and 270.

49. Ibid., 203.

50. Ibid., 178.

51. 'Li Venetiani immediate spazoronno uno gripo a la volta de mar sopra tute le marine, che per tuto si dovesse far fochi et ffeste dela obtenuta victoria del stato de Milanno et in armata etiam se dovesse far feste, azioché questa nova dovesse pervenir ale orechie del gram Turcho, el qual vedendo la ruina del signor Lodovico, che hera quello che lo havea facto prender le arme contra Venetiani, dovesse alquanto temer et soprastar de andar piùj avantti.' Ibid., 177.

52. 'Cognoscevanno certissimo che non heranno bastanti per loro solli a poter contrastar a tanta grande potenzia et rabia de questo Signor Turcho, che faceva tremar tuto il mondo.' Ibid., ii, 14; cf. also ibid., 38, 87, 183, 202 and 245.

53. 'Anchora che fosse tuto mandato indarno et ad uno corpo che he senza pulso', wrote Priuli *a propos* the reinforcements sent to Modone, 'nichil minus non se die restar sempre de far ogni provisione fino che la natura manchi.' Ibid., 19.

54. Ibid., 166.

55. 'Li poveri signori Venetiani', wrote the diarist at the beginning of 1502, 'intendendo questa nova, heranno in disperatione, judichando, se 'l Turcho uscirà questo anno cum armata potente, de dover perder tuto il resto del stato maritimo, et non sapevanno che fare.' Ibid., 200. The outlook was more gloomy still in April of 1503 (ibid., 257). Such fears were to last until the summer of 1503.

56. Ibid., 199, 202, 245 and 269.

57. Ibid., 269.

58. Ibid., 250.

59. 'Cum verità la citade veneta per questa guera turchescha hera condictionata talmente che, chui desiderava il bene dela republica veneta, dovea desiderar che li signori Venetiani dovessenno star in pace . . .' Ibid., 254.

60. 'Molte volte non abbiamo avuto altra speranza che in Dio e nel tempo, e l'uno e l'altro ci ha conservati', Machiavelli makes the men of Sarzana say when pleading their cause against Florentine domination. Cf. *Istorie fiorentine*, ed. Franco Gaeta (Milan, 1962) lib. v, ch. xi, 344.

61. Priuli, *Diarii*, ii, 250. As a way of defying destiny and puncturing the wall of every shade of scepticism, Priuli summed up: 'Quando conoscesse certissimo che il signor Turcho non la dovesse mantenire [la pace], io volevo averlla conclussa per benefitio del stato veneto, perché il tempo fa per quello grandemente.' Ibid., 269.

62. . . . Dulceis parare amicos
    Dum studeo, atque viris iuvat innotescere doctis:
        Furtim inter ista pigrum
    Obrepsit senium, et subito segnescere vireis
        Mirorque sentioque,
    Vixque mihi spatium iam defluxisse valentis
        Persuadeo iuventae'
Op. cit. (Gorlitz, 1595) f. Biii.

63. Cf. Fernand Braudel, *La Méditerranée et le monde méditerranéen à l'époque de Philippe II* (2nd ed., Paris, 1966) pt. iia, vol. ii, 4.

64. It is enough to refer to the unpublished *copialettere* cited by Freddy Thiriet,' Les lettres commerciales des Bembo et le commerce vénitien dans l'Empire ottoman à la fin du XVe siècle', in *Studi in onore di Armando Sapori* (Milan, 1957) ii, 911–933.

65. 'Questa deliberatione nel Senatto veneto hebe balote 128, che significha la voluntade de tuti, possendo, de metere infidelli in Ittallia et di voler vedere la ruina de altri avantti la sua' G. Priuli, *Diarii*, iii, 188.

66. 'Li sui citadini et nobelli et Senatori heranno tanto intimiditi et invilitti et im-pauriti che molti havenno mandato fuori dela citade le sue robe et arzentti et danari et zoglie, et molti etiam abscondevanno le predicte sue robe, mobile, danari, zoglie et arzentti in li monasterij de monache et scondevanno li danari soto terra et mandavanno ettiam assai il suo in le citade maritime propinque, Capo de Istria, idest Justinopolis,

et Zarra et altre citade maritime, per poter ali bisogni condure il tuto in Turchia.' Ibid., iii, 26.

67. 'Niuno', wrote Priuli in this connection, 'se die tagliar il membro virile per fare iniuria alla sua consorte.' Ibid., 398.

68. Cf. for example, ibid., ii, 14, 32, 163, and iii, 141.

69. 'Da ogni parte se comfinava il statto venetto cum quello del signor Turcho', wrote Priuli in 1504, 'ne se poteva muovere il signor Turcho da niuna parte cum gente d'arme et altro che 'l non facesse grandissimo damno ala republica veneta et ali sui teritorij.' Ibid., ii, 344.

70. Cf. for example, the dispatch sent by Leonardo Donà and Lorenzo Priuli to the Senate on 17 Apr., 1573, in *Corrispondenza da Madrid di Leonardo Donà*, ed. Mario Brunetti and Eligio Vitale (Venice–Rome, 1963) ii, 678.

71. Thus Leonardo Donà represented Corfu and Dalmatia to Philip II as the 'porte' of Apulia and of the Kingdom of Naples; ibid., i, 229 (dispatch from Madrid to the Senate, dated 11 Mar., 1571).

72. '. . . Vedendosi che, quanto noi perdemo et di stato et di forze, tutto passa nelle mani de turchi et augumenta le loro forze in maggior danno della christianità et di sua Maestà medesimo, pareva che il continuar nella guerra fusse appunto un voler ingrandir l'inimico e dargli adito, con il mezzo dell'occupazione del nostro stato, all'invasione di quello delli altri et specialmente di quelli istessi di sua Maestà propria . . . Con giustissima et evidentissima ragione poteva la Serenità vostra temere che quella parte del nostro che non è solennissimamente fortificata dovesse con facilità capitare nella sue mani, et a questo modo esser la rovina d'Italia.' Ibid., 679, the dispatch cited above of 17 Apr., 1573.

73. See in this connection Ruggiero Romano, 'Aspetti economici degli armamenti navali veneziani del secolo XVI', *Riv. Stor. Ital.*, lxvi (1954), 39–67.

74. I may be allowed to refer to my book on *Cristoforo da Canal: La marine vénitienne avant Lépante* (Paris, 1962), and, for the following period, to my other work, *Piracy and the decline of Venice: 1580–1615* (London, 1967).

75. 'Nei tempi andati', lamented Cristoforo Da Canal in his treatise *Della milizia marittima*, 'quelle parti della Dalmatia et della Grecia di che ella era donna, tutte erano piene di gente che supplivano molto bene al bisogno che havevamo; al presente (com' esser puo' palese a ciascuno) quei paesi non tengono la quinta anzi pure la decima parte de loro cittadini'; op. cit., ed. Mario Nani Mocenigo (Rome, 1930) pt. iia, 174.

76. Cf. the *Relazione di Cristoforo Da Canal* as *provveditore dell'armata*, A.S.V., S.S., ser. *Relazioni*, busta 55. The work dates from 1558.

77. Cf. the *Relazione* of Alessandro Contarini of 8 Jan., 1541 (ibid., *busta* 61).

78. Cf. in particular, besides the previously cited *Relazione di provveditore dell'armata* of Cristoforo Da Canal, the dispatch he sent in connection with his official duties; *Provveditori da terra e da mar, filze* 1194–1197.

79. 'Il popolo [of Venice] . . . è al presente talmente comodo dei beni della fortuna che altro che uno importantissimo bisogno non lo farebbe mai entrar volontario sulle galee'; cf. C. Da Canal, *Della milizia marittima*, pt. iia, 174.

80. Cf. in this connection the second and third parts of the work by A. Tenenti on *Cristoforo Da Canal* . . . (Paris, 1962) already cited.

81. *Le navigazioni atlantiche di Alvise da Ca' da Mosto*, ed. Rinaldo Caddeo (2nd ed., Milan, 1929) 159. But, though unawares, he was answered by his contemporary Bernardo Giustinian, who expressed the firm conviction of the Venice of that time: 'Ne sono da esser giudicate parti del mondo le grandi solitudini ed arene o gli ingegni più tosto ferini che umani. Quelle sono proprie parti del mondo, le quali sotto più piacevole contrada del cielo sono habitate degli huomini, non tanto menando la vita a uso di fiere quanto pieni d'humanità et di ragione naturale.' In *Historia dell'origine di Venetia* (Venice, 1608) lib. ii, 43.

82. *Le navigazioni atlantiche*, 168.

83. Sanuto, iv, 69 and 99. Cf. also G. Priuli, *Diarii*, ii, 156.

84. For the beginning of the sixteenth century it is enough to cite the three positive testimonies to a Venetian presence in India which can be derived from Sanuto, iv, 545, 546 and 665.

85. Ibid., iv, 99.

86. Among those who were incredulous in the beginning was, in spite of his experience, Priuli; 'io non li presto autenthica fede', he wrote in August of 1501 (*Diarii*, ii, 152), though he soon came to change his mind. Not only in 1502 (ibid., 242), but as late as 1506 some of the leading senators were still refusing to face the situation; cf. ibid., 428: 'Tamen anchora ne heranno alchuni, et dico de li senatori venetti de grande sentimento, che non volevanno per chossa alchuna persuadersi che questo viazo potesse durarre et continuare.'

87. Ibid., 242.

88. Cf. for example, ibid., 156, 171, 174, 364, 385, 422, etc.

89. Ibid., ii, 155 and 156; cf. also ibid., 423.

90. Ibid., 156.

91. Ibid., 153.

92. 'Saria meglior nova', Priuli wrote in the summer of 1509 with reference to news of the setbacks and difficulties encountered by the Portuguese, 'ala citade veneta che ahora recuperar il sttato di terraferma perduto perché, avendo li trafegi et li viagij aperti et le spetiarie, et non mancherianno li danari cum li quali se potria facilmente recuperar il stato perduto.' Ibid., iii, 247; also see ibid., 52.

93. 'Il re di Portogallo avea facto et fazeva intender continuamente al dominio venetto che lui hera presto fargli ogni partito et darli queste spetie et che dovessenno mandar le loro galie a Portogallo a levar le spetie. Tamen li sapienti Padri, che volevanno maturo consiglio sopra simil materia de tanta importantia, et maxime che ne heranno molti indurati de opinione che questo viazo de l'India non potesse durarre, et non volevanno lassar li viazi soliti dela Soria et antiqui per prendere uno altro viazo novo et senza praticha, dil che deliberonno di soprastar a questa materia, et star a vedere le provixione farà il signor Soldam.' Ibid., ii, 352; cf. Sanuto, iv, 101 and 201.

94. Sanuto, v, 319. See, for the whole question of Portuguese spices, the recent work of Vitorino Magalhaes-Godinho, *L'économie de l'empire portugais aux XVe et XVIe siècles* (Paris, 1969), unfortunately without indices of names and subjects.

95. G. Priuli, *Diarii*, ii, 418 (May, 1506). In connection with those who remained obdurate, Priuli noted in August of 1504: 'Altri obstinati, come sempre achadde, non lo volevanno credere anchora cum tanti avixi, perche li pareva chossa mal al proposito et molto damnossa ala citade veneta.' Ibid., 352.

96. Ibid., 364 (Nov., 1504). About a year later, the writer reported: 'Questa nova fece rimaner morti tuta la citade venetta, zoé li marchadanti et altri veramente, che consideravanno il futuro et de quanto danno fusse . . .' Ibid., 359. On this question see the excellent study by Ugo Tucci, 'Alle origini dello spirito capitalistico a Venezio. La previsione economica', in *Studi in onore di Amintore Fanfani* (Milan, 1962) iii, 545–557.

97. 'Tamen questi heran pronostici prusumptuosi', Priuli had initially written, 'perché li cielli potranno disponer altramente.' Ibid., ii, 171.

98. 'Li marchadanti veneti, visto li viagij restrecti et senza spetie et cum pocha utilitade, se sonno ritirati dali viagij et li loro danari posti in posesione, cum sit che 'l fusse meglio aver ogni picola utillitade cha niente et tenire li danari mortti.' Ibid., iii, 52.

99. Ibid., 317.

100. Ibid., 52.

101. 'Avendossi visto li padri veneti per il tempo passatto sopra tanta et si bella rota de fortuna, che veramente per tuto il mondo heranno aprexiati et reputati cum fama eterna et non consuetti mai a perdere, lasso a considerar a chadauno se doveanno aver

43

fastidio et malinchonia, che ne haveanno legittima cauxa', wrote Priuli after the loss of Modone: cf. *Diarii*, ii, 44; see also ibid., 54.

102. Cf. ibid., iii, 54, 67, etc.

103. 'Quale citade veramente non heranno fortifichate molto né le potevanno mantenire, come di sopra he dechiarito, et questo perché se reputavanno fussenno in centro civitatis Venetiarum, essendo chussi propinque et che sempre ali bisogni se potessenno socorerre; né se pensava d'alchuno che le se potessero perdere et per questa cagione non furonno fortifichate.' Ibid., 55.

104. Sanuto, viii, 338; cf., G. Priuli, *Diarii*, iii, 27, 29, etc.

105. And Priuli goes on to list excellent reasons for this: 'per le grande forze, per la grande potentia, per il stato grande, per la grande reputatione, per il grande nome, per la grande richeza, per la grande et tanto nominata sapientia deli padri et senatori venetti.' *Diarii*, iii, 136.

106. In justification, Priuli explained that 'l'hera grande vergogna et vituperio ad uno nobille et citadino tenire arme in la sua abitatione, et heranno quasi deluxi da tutti, non judichando dovesse devenire simel ochassione: donde che in pochissime et rarissime chaxe de Venetia se atrovavanno arme né mancho armature da persona.' Ibid., 274.

107. Ibid., 289

108. 'Dubitavanno molto non essere siguri in dicta citade, considerando essere cossa molto pericolossa stare in discretione de populi et de vulgi.' Ibid., 97.

109. Ibid., 338.

110. Ibid., 26. 'Vero he', added the writer further on, 'che se li nobelli, citadini et populli venetti volessenno cum bonno chorre et animo diffendere la citade predicta, non haverebonno paura ne stimarebenno tuto il mondo per il mirabille et divino sycto dela citade.' Ibid., 101.

111. Ibid., 132; cf. ibid., 186.

112. Ibid., 186.

113. 'Veramente mirabile citade per il suo mirabile sycto', which provided it with abundant supplies in the full tide of war; ibid., 307. 'Hic pax, hic securitas vel a continenti vel a mari', Bernardo Giustinian had written, for example, after narrating the failure of the French attack, in his *De origine urbis gentisque Venetorum historiae;* 'maenibus non indigere, non portis, paludium munitionem inaccessibilem inexpugnabilemque, expertos esse quanto tutiores sint insulae littoribus.' Ibid., lib. xv, col. 165, *Thesaurus antiquitatum et historiarum Italiae* (Leiden, 1722) v, pt. la. Gasparo Contarini echoed this in the *proemio* to his celebrated treatise *De magistratibus et republica venetorum*: 'Venetiarum situs divino potius quodam consilio quam humana industria praeter fidem eorum omnium qui eam civitatem non videre, cum ab omni impetu terra marique tutissimus est tum etiam aptissimus omnium ad cujusque rei copiam sive ex mari sive ex continente civibus suggerendam atque ad commercia omnis generis mercium cum omnibus pene nationibus habendam', in *Thesaurus . . .*, lib. i, col. 2. Cf. also Antonio Medin, op. cit., 40.

114. G. Priuli, *Diarii*, iii, 325.

115. Ibid., 240.

116. Ibid., 315. 'Majores nostri', Bernardo Giustinian, for example, had already written, 'salutis libertatisque causa in ea stagna commigravere.' *De origine . . .*, lib. xv, col. 155.

117. Cf. for example, G. Priuli, *Diarii*, iii, 326. Also, Cristoforo Da Canal, *Della milizia marittima*, lib. i, 32; Leonardo Donà, *Corrispondenza . . .*, i, 244. Even in the *quattrocento* Bernardo Giustinian had written: 'Io non mi reco non meno a vergogna il non sapere l'origine della mia patria che s'io non sapessi rispondere a chi mi domandasse del mio nascimento.' *Historia . . .*, lib. i, 6.

118. G. Priuli, *Diarii*, iii, 12.

119. Ibid., 84.

120. 'Considerando ettiam che ogni chossa facta over procreatta he necessario che tandem habia il fine, pensando ettiam ali grandi signori Romani che furono signori del mondo et tandem anchora loro hanno habuto fine dipoj molte persequctione et travagli.' Ibid., 136; cf. ibid., 367, and B. Giustinian, *Historia* . . ., lib. i, 24.

121. G. Priuli, *Diarii*, i, 14 and 165; iii, 273, 282 and 326.

122. Ibid., iii, 399.

123. Ibid., 331. These themes were already clearly sketched in the *trecento*, as the passage from Fra' Enrico da Rimini (placed at the beginning of the fifteenth century by Lorenzo de' Monaci in his *Chronicon*) shows: 'Haec autem Venetorum gens tanta pace ac securitate fruitur, quod nullus unquam inde intuitu partis expellitur. Advenientes et profugi ibi tute servantur; nullus alterius oppressor, nullus alieni habitaculi est invasor: secura sunt omnia . . .' Ibid. (Venice, 1758), lib. iii, 32. Cf. ibid., 27.

124. We can quote the Venetian saying: 'Segondo li tempi il valente marinaro die navichare' (G. Priuli, *Diarii*, iii, 361); but no less significant is the habitual coupling of time and opportunity (cf. for example, ibid., iii, 364: 'aspectando tempo et ochassione', and Leonardo Donà, *Corrispondenza* . . ., ii, 605: 'per non perder il tempo et l'occasione.').

125. 'Et in fine', wrote Priuli with reference to the problem of 1509, 'se die fare ogni chossa, sia quale se voglia, per non morire et vivere, se l'he possibelle, perché chui ha tempo ha vita.' *Diarii*, iii, 396. Leonardo Donà and Lorenzo Priuli were to echo this in a dispatch from Madrid of 9 May, 1573: cf. *Corrispondenza* . . ., ii, 709.

126. 'Bisognava fare come se poteva, ponendo tempo de medio, et lassare scorrere queste influentie celeste contrarie et liberare una volta la republica veneta da pericolo et sperando cum il tempo che tutto dovesse prendere qualche bonno setamento et partito', G. Priuli, *Diarii*, iii, 203. 'Cosi ha convenuto far la Serenità vostra in queste sue tribulazioni', wrote L. Donà and L. Priuli in the dispatch of 9th May, 1573, cited above, 'ciò è metter tempo di mezzo, rimediar alla piena et al diluvio che di presente le soprasta sperando poi che la vicissitudine che è propria del mondo potrà anche riparar alle future [tribulations] . . .' *Corrispondenza* . . ., ii, 709. Immediately before this the ambassadors had had recourse to this no less significant expression: '. . . quella speranza che il tempo et la variatione delle cose potrebbe in miglior congiuntura apportare.' Ibid.

127. 'Sperando poi', wrote, again, L. Donà and L. Priuli in another dispatch of 20th Apr., 1573, 'che il tempo et li infiniti accidenti che possono occorrere sia per rimediare all'avvenire.' *Corrispondenza* . . ., ii, 688. 'Il fondamento veneto', in 1509 was, according to Priuli, 'conservare la loro citade et dare tempo a la fortuna.' *Diarii*, iii, 101.

128. 'Il tempo faceva molto per li Signori Venetiani nel termine et condictione che si atrovanno', Priuli remarked. *Diarii*, iii, 132.

129. Ibid., ii, 267.

130. Ibid., iii, 398.

131. 'Chussi ettiam hera necessario fare a Venetiani per conservare la republica et la libertade loro, et dare tempo ale chosse loro, sperando cum il tempo recuperare il perduto, perché le republice sempre vivenno et li Signori morenno.' Ibid., 405. On the liberty-permanence connection cf. also Antonio Medin, op. cit., 10.

132. 'Reor non fuisse sine caelesti providentia et singulari ope Dei quod haec [Venetiarum civitas] ex omnibus ante et post se conditis sola, et quod mirabilius est, sine campis, pratis et vineis, libertatem, in qua fundata fuit, ultra annos mille integram, invicta dominatione servaverit', in *Chronicon*, lib. i, 3. It was Monaci, again, whose work referred to the precedents for this argument, quoting, for example, Fra' Enrico da Rimini: 'Nulli omnino subdi patitur dicta gens, summa gaudens libertate . . .' Ibid., lib. ii, 33.

133. Ibid.

134. Ibid.

135. 'Hoc adigebat eos ad caetera contemnenda, quae prima mortales extimant. Praesertim cum viderent quantis in malis, qui illa concupiscerent, versarentur. Adepta siquidem libertate, quis tot navigationum, commerciorum peregrinationumque labores sine ulla intermissione subeat? Nihil habeat ubi interdum animum remittatur. His quoque temporibus si libertatem sustuleris, vix quenquam reperias praeter ordines humiliores, qui in hac alga et arundinibus vitam duceret. Nemo siquidem post laborem requiem non appetit. Libertas illis securusque suis cum familiis status pro requie succedebat.' *De origine* . . ., lib. v, col. 58.

136. G. Priuli, *Diarii*, iii, 433.

137. *Corrispondenza da Madrid di Leonardo Donà*, i, 244, 22 Mar., 1571.

138. Ibid., ii, 709, 9 May, 1573. In a dispatch of 2 Dec., 1572, signed by L. Donà and L. Priuli, the Venetian patricians are described as 'gentil homeni liberi et invecchiati in una Signoria de mille e ducent'anni.' Ibid., 605.

139. 'Si quis, ut Lucii Flori verbis utar, populum Venetiarum ut hominem consideret, tres in eo gradus sive progressus inveniet: infantiam, adolescentiam, juventutem, quae usque nunc divina miseratione floret in augmento. Haec civitas suam produxit infantiam usque ad initium regni Longobardorum. . . . Juventus Venetiarum initium habuit quando lares focique Methamauci thronusque ducatus fuerunt in Rivoaltum, antescripta causa impellente, translata.' Lorenzo de' Monaci, *Chronicon*, lib. i, 10 and lib. iii, 27.

140. Among the copious evidence which could illustrate this, see for example G. Priuli, *Diarii*, i, 225; ibid., ii, 168; iii, 36, etc.

141. Consuetudine antiquissima dela republica veneta, che per ogni libra de grossi se intendeva ducati diexe; et questo descrivo per intelligentia deli successori nostri fino a molti anni, ché facilmente, come credo, si muterà ogni cossa et di monede et di altra sorte de ducati et altra sorta di moneda, et questo solum fazo azioché ali tempi futuri se possia cognoscer et veder quello valevanno li danari et la condictione di quelli ali nostri tempi', Ibid., ii, 213–214. Cf. above, n. 120.

142. 'Generalis [nobilitas] . . . provenit ab unitate civium antiquata in jure et regimine suae civitatis, nulla subjectione libertatem interrumpente. . . . Nulla alia civitas diutius in unitate, dignitate et libertate, communi jure et continua dominatione permansit, nulla suam politiam tam diu ad insignes posteros tanta felicitate transmisit.' *Chronicon*, lib. iii, 30.

143. *De origine* . . ., lib. xiv, col. 155.

144. Ibid., lib. x, col. 103.

145. Ibid.

146. Ibid., col. 104.

147. *De rebus ac forma* . . ., 247.

148. 'Qui ergo libertatem ceteris praeferendam decrevere, vitamque potius commerciis agitationibusque per orbem tutari, sola sic necessitate cogente, quam leniori praediorum amoenitate devicti in servitutem tyrannidemque suam suorumque vitam dedere, his locis, his libertatis legibus degendum sibi suisque statuerunt, nulli scilicet injuriam ferre, sibi suisque suo labore cavere.' *Defensio* . . ., 196.

149. 'Fuit pariter principatus ac libertatis adeo constans institutio ut nunquam suae nobilitati insignis princeps deesse videretur, et qui tempore fuerit eligendus, adeo aequis firmatisque sponsionibus principatum assumeret, ut nusquam ab aequissimis suis legibus recedendo libertatem amitterent cives, nec ipse in tyrannidem declinaret, quod in hanc diem, bonorum omnium auctore favente, deductum est.' Ibid., 194.

150. G. Priuli, *Diarii*, iii, 343.

II

STANLEY CHOJNACKI

In Search of the Venetian Patriciate:
Families and Factions in the Fourteenth Century*

I

This paper is an attempt to reconstruct the Venetian patriciate on the eve of the Renaissance, to identify the class's membership and to determine patterns of differentiation within the class. Among the aristocracies of *trecento* Italy, Venice's has traditionally enjoyed a reputation for distinctiveness. While elsewhere in the area of the communes the experience of the upper class seems to have been for all practical purposes a struggle among rival claimants to aristocratic status, in Venice, historians seem agreed, the identity of the patriciate was never in doubt.[1] In Venice, according to a long tradition, there was no continuing struggle between magnates and *popolo grasso*, no influx of *gente nuova* into the upper class, no contention between rural nobles and urban merchants.[2] *Trecento* Venice may have had its economic and diplomatic problems, and even some internal political difficulties. But at least the Venetians did not have to worry about who the members of the ruling class were.

In the traditional view the critical moment in the development of a fixed patriciate had come at the end of the *duecento*, in the famous closing of the Venetian Great Council, the *Maggior Consiglio*. A series of legislative measures in the late 1290s had established and progressively elaborated two principles: that the existing political class – specifically those families whose members were sitting or had recently sat in the Great Council – would henceforth exercise a monopoly over political activity in Venice and that this monopoly would be hereditary.[3] Historians have disagreed on the significance of the *Serrata del Maggior Consiglio* in the context of thirteenth-century Venetian politics.[4] But there is general agreement on its main effect, the restriction of aristocratic – in Venice called noble – status to those families which had achieved political prominence by the late thirteenth century.[5] There would be occasional relaxa-

* Part of the research on which this paper is based was supported by a grant from the All-University Research Fund of Michigan State University.

47

tions of this restriction in moments of exceptional governmental need or aristocratic magnanimity, notably in 1381 and again in the seventeenth and eighteenth centuries.[6] But the main tendency from the late *duecento* on was to maintain patrician 'purity' by avoiding 'contamination' by recruits of non-patrician origin.[7] Indeed, along with Venetian internal stability and slow decadence in the seventeenth and eighteenth centuries, the conception of the patriciate's fixed composition stands as one of the sacred conventions of Venetian history.

Another historiographical tendency, rather less hallowed but increasingly prevalent in recent decades, adds a further dimension to this convention. It has to do with political conflict in Venice and it is especially significant because of its focus on the fourteenth century. If the *Serrata* had had repercussions of the kind which might be expected to follow an upper class's erection of barriers around itself, they normally would have occurred in its immediate aftermath. Yet while elsewhere in Italy aristocracies were contending with pressures from below, political conflict in Venice – to the extent that historians have admitted there was such a thing – seems characteristically to have been an intra-patrician phenomenon.[8] Indeed for one recent student of Venetian political and social history, Giorgio Cracco, the Venetian *popolo* by the end of the *trecento* was reacting to events like a *'corpo morto'*.[9] This patriciocentric orientation of recent investigators of fourteenth-century politics is altogether consistent with the venerable tradition of a fixed post-*Serrata* class composition. In fact by making political energy an exclusive patrician preserve it deepens it. Despite the originality of Roberto Cessi's highly suggestive analyses of political and economic groups in the patriciate; despite the intelligence of Giorgio Cracco in his avowedly revisionist approach to medieval Venetian history, the basic premise underlying their studies remains the time-honoured one of an un-changing patriciate's utter monopoly of Venetian politics and society.[10]

Yet if studies such as those of Cessi, Cracco and others ultimately buttress the traditional patrician orientation, they have also contributed to a questioning of another hoary tradition in Venetian historiography, the *mito di Venezia*. Professor Bouwsma's and Professor Gilbert's very recent studies provide thorough and wide-ranging discussions of the myth and its fortunes in Italian intellectual and constitutional circles during the Renaissance, and there is no need to go into it at length here.[11] But it is worth noting that in its *trecento* application one of the myth's essential elements, the civic loyalty and class solidarity of the patriciate, is seriously questioned by the writings of Cessi, Cracco *et al.* – if it is not thrown out altogether.[12] In these writings the idea of patrician civic loyalty becomes problematic precisely because the idea of class solidarity is rejected.

The most forceful statement of this interpretation is Roberto Cessi's 'Intro-duzione storica' to *La regolazione delle entrate e delle spese (Sec. XIII–XIV)*. Here and elsewhere, Cessi viewed the Venetian government's fiscal measures in the late Middle Ages as expressions of the ascendancy of one or another interest group within the patriciate.[13] Thus for him the critical issue in fourteenth-century Venetian politics was the success or failure of 'aspirations to economic dominance (*prepotenza*)' of a 'strong monopolizing aristocracy' possessing 'superior liquid wealth'.[14] Deriving their wealth from Venice's Levantine trade, these 'monopolistic groups' sought to direct Venetian policy toward protection of their commercial interests by fiscal measures and toward commitment of the state's resources to the advancement of the Venetian economic and political presence in the Levant. Because these objectives were not universally endorsed within the patriciate, because, specifically, they frequently entailed great hardship for the less affluent sectors, the monopolists had to wage a bitter struggle to dominate the policy-making machinery of the government.[15] It is in this political dimension of the struggle, involving above all the Venetian Senate and the various *ad hoc* councils that were commissioned frequently in the *trecento*, that Cessi was most interested and his imaginative use of legislative records most effective.

This configuration of *trecento* Venetian politics has been extremely influential. Relying almost exclusively on Cessi's work, Giovanni Pillinini has suggested that the famous attempt by the Doge Marin Falier to overthrow the government of the Republic in 1355 was itself one phase of the monopolists' campaign to take control of the state.[16] And Giorgio Cracco has recently reformulated Cessi's interpretation in strict dialectical terms and, extending it, has used it to configure the subversion of the open, inclusive governmental system of the twelfth-century Venetian commune in the course of the thirteenth and fourteenth centuries.[17]

Although these interpretations are original in important ways, their common thesis, that the patriciate was not a coherent bloc but actually consisted of different, contending interests, is not entirely without precedent. As far back as the late fifteenth century – the years of the myth's full blooming – the patrician annalist Domenico Malipiero reported that in Venice, 'as in many other places', there were two factions, which in 1486 disputed the election of a successor to the recently deceased doge, Marco Barbarigo.[18] The factions to which Malipiero was referring, and which subsequent generations of writers have continued to note, were divided not by economic interest, as in the works of Cessi and his recent followers, but by genealogy. In this configuration there were two identifiable – indeed, identified – groups of families with different degrees of antiquity in the Venetian past. The *case vecchie* traced their origins to the first dim days of Venice's history, some claiming descent from the Roman nobles who had settled in the Venetian lagoon after fleeing the Huns and the Lombards. Ranged opposite the *case vecchie* were the *case nuove*, a larger group of families which in the twelfth and thirteenth centuries had acquired wealth and political experience sufficient to earn inclusion in the nobility at the time of its closing in 1297.[19] Whatever the contemporary significance of these genealogical niceties in a late-medieval context, later observers have discerned rivalry between the two groups. The main bone of contention seems to have been the

D   *49*

dogeship itself, to which in fact no member of a *casa vecchia* was elected between 1382 and 1620; the passage in Malipiero's *Annali* deals with this issue.[20] Although the rivalry between *case vecchie* and *case nuove* seems to be a *quattrocento* phenomenon, the essential genealogical distinction was a reality even in the fourteenth century, as the chronicle attributed to Piero Giustinian attests.[21] In any case the distinction does add another caveat to the view of the patriciate as a homogeneous, harmonious bloc. At the same time, however, it fortifies the patriciocentric view of Venetian history in the period after the *Serrata*.

Out of these various approaches there emerges a fairly neat formula to describe Venetian politics in the *trecento*: within a clearly defined and firmly entrenched aristocracy, contending sub-groups engaged in a series of policy struggles with economic, political and diplomatic ramifications. The formula can be made to fit all the major developments of the century. Thus the 1310 conspiracy led by Baiamonte Tiepolo and Marco Querini takes the form of an attempt by patrician victims of a 'subtle policy of discrimination' within the ruling class to destroy a 'totalitarian regime', as Giorgio Cracco sees it; or, alternatively, it was the plot of a 'secessionist nobility' – some eager to 'avenge presumed wrongs they had unjustly been made to suffer', but others, 'moved by ambition', desirous of obtaining 'domination over the government' for themselves – to oust the existing governmental personnel, which is Cessi's view.[22] In a similar way the various measures taken by the government to respond to commercial difficulties by restricting imports through the *Ufficio dei Naviganti* is seen by Cessi as an effort by 'particular merchant groups, the major ones', to increase their profits by 'eliminating competion and becoming arbiters of the market' at the expense of the 'general economy', including less wealthy patricians.[23] Closely related to this is the view which sees in the debate in the early 1350s over the question of going to war with Genoa a struggle between, on one side, wealthy merchants anxious to protect Venice's eastern interests at all costs and, on the other, less affluent particians who desired a period of recovery after the economic setbacks of the late 1340s.[24] Although the Venetian *popolo* appears occasionally in these configurations it is characteristically in the capacity of instruments of one or other of the noble factions.[25] The important interests and actions in all these critical moments of the Venetian *trecento* are patrician interests and actions.

Yet despite its plausibility in each instance, despite the interpretative ingenuity that often accompanies its application, and despite the immense weight of tradition behind it, the formula suffers from a fundamental weakness: no one ever systematically identifies the patriciate. To be sure there is a fairly large group of families or clans with unimpeachable patrician credentials. Their names appear prominently not only in the *trecento* but throughout Venetian history, and they are readily recognized: Dandolo, Contarini, Gradenigo, Morosini, Corner, Giustinian, Falier, Querini, Sanuto and so on, all of whom are *case vecchie*. Among the *case nuove* there are equally familiar names: Donà, Mocenigo, Barbarigo, Loredan, Venier, to list only a few. One could put together a composite list of the twenty-four *case vecchie*, and the sixteen *case nuove* said to have been party to the conspiracy to deny the *vecchie* the dogeship, and the result would include nearly all the readily recognizable Venetian patrician names.[26] Yet those forty names – representing both sides in the *vecchie–nuove* rivalry – would account for only 22 per cent of the 181 families whose members held political office – a patrician prerogative – in the 1350s and 1360s.[27] Were the other 141 office-holding families all on the side of the *case nuove*? This may indeed be a plausible hypothesis, but it cannot be tested without at the very least some regard to who the others were. In the same way, in their discussions of the struggle between the 'monopolistic oligarchs' and the moderate patricians in the mid-*trecento*, Cessi and Pillinini together mention thirty-three patrician family names – again representing both sides of the issue – while there are 152 names in the office-holder lists for the years 1349–1352 alone.[28] What role did the 119 unmentioned families play in this 'dramatic moment, such as has rarely been registered in the annals of Venetian constitutional life'?[29] And on a more general level, what was it that gave the thirty to forty most prominent families their prominence? Why is it that their names and not the names of the other patricians are the readily recognizable ones? The answers to these questions are vague at best.

Yet on them depends an effective understanding of fourteenth-century Venetian politics and, ultimately, of the relationship between the patriciate and the state in Venice. If in fact there were a few powerful families which dominated politics and economic life, then patrician class solidarity, traditionally regarded as focusing on the common good, might really have amounted to nothing more than a discipline imposed by an oligarchy on the larger mass of the patriciate.[30] Whether such a discipline aimed indeed at the general well-being of the Venetian polity or conformed more narrowly to the interests of the oligarchy, the result is still to question the significance of the patriciate's 'veneration of the Republic'.[31]

For these reasons it is important to try to obtain a clearer view of the *trecento* patriciate's composition and of the distinctions that may have existed within the class. In the following pages I would like to essay something of a quantitative approach toward this clearer view. The investigation involves two major steps. It is necessary, to begin with, that we have some idea of who belonged to the patriciate. The question to be answered is, was the class's membership indeed as fixed as has traditionally been thought? Our object here is not to take up the matter of the size of the Great Council's membership after the introduction of the hereditary principle in the wake of the *Serrata*. It seems clear that it did increase.[32] What occupies our attention rather are the families which made up the class. Were there as many of them some decades after the *Serrata* as there had been in 1297, and were they the same ones? On the answer to these questions hinges an evaluation of the *Serrata*'s real effect in fixing once and for all, at the end of the *duecento*, the composition of the ruling class. Our second step is to determine whether there were families or groups within the class which might have possessed the means to establish their predominance. This step impinges on the question of a powerful oligarchy within the larger body of the patriciate. Did some patrician families possess a disproportionate share of wealth or political influence?[33]

In attempting to answer these fundamental questions I have tried to use the most systematic documentation of patrician activities available. However that fact itself indicates that the conclusions here must be considered tentative. A fuller knowledge of the patrician experience in the *trecento* is available in sources whose riches still await reduction to systematic order.[34] The lines of attack employed here might usefully be followed in exploitation of them. As for the chronological scope of this investigation, I have concentrated on the period 1293–1379. The last decade of the *duecento* is a logical choice; it was then that the *Serrata* took place, then that the patriciate acquired its juridicial definition. The choice of the second date, 1379, requires a bit more explanation. In 1379 the fourth war with Genoa reached a critical point for Venice. Historians refer to it as the War of Chioggia because of the siege to which Venice was subjected by the Genoese fleet massed around Chioggia, at the south-western end of the Venetian littoral. The success of the Venetians in breaking the siege meant the survival of Venice. It was a dramatic political moment. The experience of the war also produced certain significant socio-economic effects within Venice. Withstanding the Genoese had required an enormous fiscal effort, one result of which was, in the view of many historians, 'a real upheaval in fortunes and social situations'.[35] Whether or not this upheaval was indeed as extensive and permanent as it has been made out to be, it seems clear that the pressures of the war were deeply felt. From the perspective of patrician development, another important result of the war was the induction into the ruling class of thirty *popolani*, rewarded for their great contributions to the war effort.[36] For these reasons – the momentous experience of the siege and its economic and social effects – the War of Chioggia seems a milestone, and a valid terminal point for a discussion of the patriciate in the period after the closing of the Great Council.[37]

II

The intentions of the patriciate regarding class membership in the decades after the *Serrata* are pretty clearly demonstrated in the measures enacted to evaluate claims to membership in the Great Council. As early as 1307, just ten years after the *Serrata*, the patriciate seemed to be having second thoughts about the numbers of Venetians eligible under the new system: there was a lot of talk of the cheapening of patrician status as a result of the way in which the new regulations governing membership in the Great Council were being applied.[38] In addition to formulating the essential provisions that all who had sat there in the years 1293–1297 would continue to be members of it, and that this right would be hereditary, the legislation of 1297–1299 had established procedures for letting in otherwise qualified men who had not in fact been in the Council during the crucial quadrennium.[39] At first this involved a favourable vote of twelve members of the Council of the Quarantia in a session with at least twenty members voting, the vote to be taken upon the recommendation of four members of the Ducal Council. In 1300 the requirement was reduced to a simple majority of the Quarantia, that is, only eleven votes in a quorum of twenty councillors. But in 1307 the procedure was revised to require the favourable disposition of five ducal councillors instead of four and of twenty-five members of the Quarantia. This constituted a sharp change, since the Quarantia requirement now jumped from eleven favourable votes to twenty-five.[40]

Yet even these measures were not adequate. In 1310 another measure raised the Quarantia requirement to thirty favourable votes and introduced a majority vote of the Great Council itself as an additional requirement. Five years later the necessary Great Council majority was raised to two-thirds. Apparently, however, even these accumulated obstacles were not enough to discourage unqualified aspirants. In 1316, responding to large numbers of applications by men unable to satisfy the requirements, the government passed a law assessing a fine of 300 lire to any applicant who failed to win approval.[41] Finally, in 1319 the *avogadori di comun*, Venice's public prosecutors, were given the charge of investigating all claims to patrician status.[42] Apparently the elaborate rules governing admission had only produced greater subtlety on the part of aspirants with less than persuasive claims. As a result, full-fledged investigations were to be undertaken by the government, in the form of the *avogadori di comun*, who from that point on maintained surveillance over patrician purity.[43]

These indications of the patriciate's jealousy of its status prompt a couple of reflections. In the first place, they suggest that well after 1297 the work of the *Serrata* was still unfinished. There were still men seeking – and some presumably finding – their way into the ruling class, men whose right to do so was at best questionable. This in turn suggests that the patriciate was not yet a clearly defined, universally recognized group of families whose distinctiveness *vis-à-vis* the rest of Venetian society was acknowledged and accepted by all. At the same time these measures indicate that the patriciate's own conception of what it meant to belong to the class, a conception expressed in the progressively defined requirements for admission, was not fully established but developed in response to the importunings of men of questionable qualifications.[44] In this sense it may be argued that the *Serrata* itself constituted merely the opening phase in an extended process of class definition. The principle of hereditary, defined ruling class was solidly established in the 1290s. But applying it in the concrete, deciding who constituted the class, took a great deal longer. Indeed, there are grounds for arguing that it took at least into the ninth decade of the *trecento*.

The problem of defining the patriciate was not, however, confined to preventing inward seepage. Complicating the patriciate's concern to keep out unqualified men – and to define what the qualifications were – was outward seepage in the fourteenth century. The proposal in 1403 by members of the Quarantia to accord patrician status to a non-noble family each time a patrician family died out reflects high-level concern over extinction of noble families.[45] The assumption of thirty new families into the ruling class in 1381 may similarly represent a response to the demographic toll of the *trecento* as well as a desire to reward certain citizens for their particularly generous contribution to the defeat of the Genoese at Chioggia.[46] And measures to permit young patricians to enter into public life at an earlier age than had previously been the case offers a clue to understanding the class's concern over depletion of its manpower resources: it simply took a lot of men to run the Venetian government.[47] In a process complementing that of the *Serrata*, the patriciate in the thirteenth and fourteenth centuries steadily tightened its hold on all the offices and councils of the state. This was done by making the Great Council the matrix of all other offices: elections to them were held in the Great Council and candidates for them were chosen from the Great Council's membership.[48] The result was patrician domination of the entire structure of government; but the enjoyment of it required the availability of patricians to fill the offices. For that reason the extinction of noble families was a problem to which a solution had to be found.

Thus social stability in the Venetian patriciate was a sword that cut both ways. Too great an influx of new men would frustrate the aim of the *Serrata*; too strict a policy of exclusion might involve an incapacity to man the government. At least so the foregoing indications suggest. But was there indeed an alteration in the class's composition in the eighty years following the *Serrata*? Is there any substance to the foregoing inferences that new men were coming in and old families were dying out?

Analysis of some thirteenth and fourteenth-century lists of patricians indicates that this was very much the case. According to the evidence yielded by a comparison of these sources, not only did the composition of the patriciate change; it changed very significantly indeed during the period 1293–1379. First, some gross statistics might convey a sense of the dimensions of alteration in the class's membership. Of 244 families whose patricians status can be established with near-certainty, at least at some point during those years, just under a third, 32 per cent, either died out before 1379 or made their first appearance as patricians only after 1300.[49] (This computation, it is important to note, does not include the thirty families inducted into the patriciate in 1381.) Table 1 illustrates the manner in which the changes occurred. Category 1 represents families which were patrician in the 1290s and survived past 1379. Categories 2 and 3 are actually one group: those families which were patrician in the late thirteenth century but which died out before 1379. Category 4 includes only families with members in political office in the mid-*trecento*, but no evidence either of patrician status before 1300 or of survival as late as 1379. Category 5 represents families which demonstrated patrician status no earlier than the fourteenth century and which survived beyond 1379. Category 6 includes families of whose patrician status there is no record earlier than 1379 but which then continued to appear in the records as patricians after that date. It should be clear that although a substantial majority of the patriciate gave the class a constancy of composition throughout the period, even a conservative computation reveals significant changes in the course of it, changes which question the judgement that there was fixed class composition after the *Serrata*.

There is another, clearer way of stating the tendencies represented in Table 1. And it is one that reveals some very interesting trends. Adopting the perspective of the *terminus a quo* we may observe that over one-fifth (21 per cent) of the 210 families whose patrician status in the 1290s (i.e., Categories 1–3) seems well established were extinct by 1379.[51] By contrast the opposite perspective, that of 1379, reveals that newcomers into the patriciate were less numerous: nearly nine-tenths, 87.7 per cent, of the 187 families extant in 1379 had been patrician in the late thirteenth century. (This figure of course excludes those thirteen families which made their first appearances as patricians after 1300 but did not last till 1379.) However if we add to the 1379 totals the thirty families admitted into the patriciate in 1381 we obtain an interesting result. The total number of patrician families in 1381 rises to 217, approximately what it had been in the

Table 1

CHANGES IN PATRICIAN COMPOSITION, 1293–1379[50]

Categories	*No. and % of families*
1. 1290s–1379	166 (68%)
2. 1290s–1350s/1360s	16 (6.6%)
3. 1290s–extinct in *trecento*	28 (11.5%)
4. Extant in *trecento* only	13 (5.3%)
5. Extant in *trecento* and 1379	13 (5.3%)
6. Extant in 1379, not before	8 (3.3%)
	244 (100%)

1290s.[52] And among these 217 the percentage of new families (i.e., appearing as patrician only after 1300) in the 1380s rises to 23.5 per cent, effectively counterbalancing the percentage of older families which had died out between 1300 and 1379.

What this curious consistency suggests is that although in 1403 the government may not have wanted to adopt the principle of creating a new patrician family for each one that died out, in fact the practice was to do precisely that. What this meant in demographic terms is not quite so clear, since families varied greatly in size, as we shall see below. However it seems reasonable to argue that in the process of replacing extinct families with newly-ennobled families a one-for-one rate of exchange would prevail. By definition a family becomes extinct when the male line defaults, so a dying family was a small family.[53] On the other hand, creation of new patricians generally involved only one male and his direct descendants; a new patrician family would also be a small family. Thus it is entirely possible that replacing families could also be a fairly precise means of keeping up personnel strength, reckoned in individual adult males.

But there is another dimension to the patriciate's composition between the late thirteenth century and 1379. It has to do with the pool of potential patricians from which new members were recruited to maintain class strength. It is useful in this connection to note that of the at least 244 patrician families extant at some point during this period, only 166 had been represented in the Great Council during the crucial quadrennium, 1293–1297.[54] Where did the other seventy-eight, nearly a third of the total, come from? An answer to this question would throw some additional light on the principle underlying co-option of new members into the patriciate and, for that reason, on the patriciate's conception of itself in the *trecento*.

Some of the families missing in 1293–1297 were veterans of earlier Great Council sessions whose members simply had not been elected during the 1290s. Presumably it was for the cases they represented that the procedures for additional admissions had been set up at the time of the *Serrata*. In this group were such well-known names as Foscari, Celsi, Zulian, Emo. Altogether there were 41 families whose members had sat in the Great Council in the 1260s, 1270s, or 1280s and which would be extant in the fourteenth century, but which were not represented from 1293–1297.[55] Indeed, this group of 41 families and the 166 families present in the Great Council during the 1290s account together for rather more than four-fifths (84.8 per cent) of the 244 families which sent members to the Great Council during the last four decades of the thirteenth century. Since another twelve of these thirteenth-century families apparently died out before 1300, all but slightly more than one-tenth (10.3 per cent) of all the extant Great Council families of the late thirteenth century were in the post-*Serrata* aristocracy.[56] On this basis alone it can be – and has been – argued that the *Serrata* was an act less of exclusion than of inclusion.[57]

But if the thirteenth-century Great Council families account for 207 of the 244 patrician families extant between 1293 and 1379, what of the remaining 37? What was the origin of their claims to patrician status? In the cases of fifteen of them the documents contain specific references to their admission to the patriciate.[58] Four others appear, on the basis of indications in the sources, to have been Venetians of some significance before 1300.[59] Eight more were acknowledged as noble by the mid fourteenth-century patrician chronicler, Piero Giustinian, an indication that there was no doubt of their status by that time.[60] Of the remaining ten families, the patrician status of three is not altogether solidly established.[61] That leaves seven patrician families, less than 3 per cent of the total of 244, whose origins and claims to their status is unclear. But there is another statistic that emerges from this analysis. Of these same mysterious 37 families, seven had had business dealings with patricians before 1300, some as early as the twelfth century.[62] Two of the others had been brought into the patriciate in the 1290s upon their settling in Venice after the fall of Acre. As residents of Acre they very likely had had business dealings with Venetian merchants there; their settling in Venice indicates in itself familiarity and sympathy with things Venetian.[63] That leaves 28 families, 11.5 per cent of the total, about whom I was unable to find indications of business involvement with other patricians before the *Serrata*.

What all this clearly suggests is two fundamental characteristics of the patriciate's composition in the decades after the *Serrata*. Although the view that the patriciate was fixed by the *Serrata* must be modified in the light of substantial movement in and out of the class during the *trecento*, it is fairly clear that the inward motion favoured families with previously established ties to the existing ruling class. This hypothesis can be tested by examining the thirty families awarded patrician status in 1381. Although there is no doubt about their non-noble status before 1381 – the chronicler Caresino, who was one of them, specifically calls them *populares* – thirteen of them, more than two-fifths, bore names of extant patrician families. They may have belonged to colonial branches of patrician families which had failed to register with the *Avogadori di Comun* as the law required; this is strongly suggested in the case of Marco Pasqualigo 'de Candida'.[64] Or they may have been the issue of contaminated liaisons, of the kind to which contemporary legislation made clear reference.[65] Or is it possible that they coincidentally bore names that happened also to belong to patricians. Still the implication is clear: even in this exceptional instance of wholesale induction of *popolani* into the patriciate, the ruling class still tended toward the familiar. Indeed the impulse seems much the same as had operated on the Quarantia in 1307, when Andrea Pisani was admitted to the Great Council because his brother had been in it before 1297.[66]

As for the other new patricians of 1381, they reflect the other impulse behind the awarding of patrician status in the *trecento*: to reward *popolani* for services rendered the state. In the case of the War of Chioggia the government's motivation was clearly expressed. In an attempt to inspire patriotic munificence the government had committed itself in 1379 to elevate to the patriciate thirty individuals who would be particularly conspicuous by their contributions to the war effort. The natural result was the induction of economically substantial families into the patriciate.[67] The same principle had operated seventy years earlier, when fourteen individuals, many bearing patrician names, were ennobled for their part in putting down the conspiracy of Baiamonte Tiepolo in 1310.[68] In the one case the service rendered was strictly political, in the other financial. But in both instances the reward for distinguished contributions to the public well-being was membership in the patriciate.

On the basis of this analysis we may hazard some tentative conclusions about the patriciate's composition in the *trecento*. In the first place, the class was not a static bloc. The patriciate that effected the *Serrata* was not the same as the class that would emerge from the War of Chioggia some eight decades later. By the latter date many thirteenth-century patrician families had died out and new families had emerged to take their places. However, though the composition of the class did change, the change was governed by certain principles which ensured continuity. One was that patrician status was somehow involved with political or financial service to – and by implication a commitment to – Venice.

The ruling class was associated with the well-being of the Venetian polity. The other principle, less clearly articulated but powerfully operative in the patrician experience, was that as the class continued to form and define itself in the course of the *trecento* it sought to do so by resorting to familiar names in its recruitment of new members.[69] New patricians should come from old families, whether non-noble branches of existing patrician families or old, rich, 'popular' families.[70] There were foreigners inducted in the course of the century, but their ennoblement seems to have been more honorific than substantive.[71] When the award of patrician status promised to involve the participation of a new family in the full orbit of patrician life, the tendency was to find it among the old Venetian families. In this sense the experience of the fourteenth century was a rounding-up of the juridically defined class, a process of working into the class all its potential members.

From this perspective the *Serrata* can be viewed as a long process, lasting nearly till the end of the *trecento*, of forming the patriciate. The essential principle had been laid down in the 1290s, but its application and even the articulation of its concrete social significance were not fully accomplished till after many decades. Many factors operated to effect its completion: demographic losses, pressures from aspirants to patrician status, the obligations of manning the government. But it took more than the act of one year, or even the accumulated legislation of two decades, to complete the *Serrata*. The patriciate did not reach its final form till close to the end of the *trecento*.

III

The two means by which Venetian families might ascend into the patriciate, and which at bottom constituted the bases of nobility of the most ancient patrician families as well, also underlie the rivalries which various writers have detected within the fourteenth-century aristocracy. Long-standing and active membership in Venetian society appears to have been a requirement for post-*Serrata* recruits into the patriciate; it also was what distinguished the *case vecchie* from the *case nuove*. Again, political and economic distinction, expressed in the service of the Venetian polity, was another way of attaining patrician status. But once achieved it could also provide ambitious factions of oligarchic disposition with the means of achieving their objectives at the expense of the rest of the class. In our attempt to reconstruct the fourteenth-century patriciate it is essential to consider its internal configuration as well as its composition. Indeed in a number of ways the significance of the changes in the families which made up the class is inextricably bound up with the existence of distinct groups within it. The class whose old members died out and were replaced according to certain developing principles must have been influenced in applying those principles by the way in which power and wealth were distributed within the class. And on a deeper level, the patriciate's self-conception, which seems to have developed at least in part as a function of the class's structural formation in the *trecento*, would be profoundly affected by power struggles as intense as those described by Cessi, Cracco and Pillinini.

However, reconstruction of the interplay of forces within the patriciate is an enormously complex task. Partly the difficulty stems from the class's size and variety. The writers who have ventured interpretations of this interplay underscore the complexity by confining themselves to the most prominent families without a great deal of attention to the relations between these families and the rest of the class.[72] In part also the difficulty lies in the subsidiary questions which need to be answered. The first, essential question to be considered before any attempt to define the patriciate internally can be ventured has to do with the units into which the class was divided, its families. What was the patrician family? And more precisely, what was the significance of a common family name in relations among patricians?

Determinining the role of the patrician family begins with answering two related questions: how large was it, and what were the relations among its various members?[73] The importance of the second question depends on the answer to the first. To illustrate these points let us look at four of the 156 patrician families represented in the fiscal census, the *estimo*, carried out by the government as part of its programme to beat back the Genoese threat in 1379.[74] The four families are the Morosini, the Loredan, the Ghisi and the Babilonio. All four had long histories in Venice; all four had been represented in the Great Council in the 1290s and earlier; all four had served in public office in the 1350s and 1360s. In a word they seem classic examples of established Venetian patrician families, the backbone of the class.[75] Yet although alike in many ways, the four families were unlike in another, critically important respect. For in the *estimo* of 1379 there were fifty-nine Morosini, sixteen Loredan, five Ghisi, and one Babilonio. The vast disparity in sizes of families is further illustrated by statistics from the *estimo*. The average number of *stimati* per patrician family was 7.1, yet there were thirty-five families with ten or more, thirteen families with twenty or more *stimati*.[76] Considering this vast range of family sizes the validity of using the family as a unit of measurement is open to question. If a document should tell us what position, say, Nicoletto Babilonio took on a question of governmental policy we should feel pretty sure that we knew the sentiment of the Babilonio family on that issue. The same holds true of the other thirty-three males who were the only representatives of their families in the *estimo*.[77] But a firm statement of policy by a Contarini, one of at least fifty-six males with that name, a Morosini, one of fifty, a Giustinian, one of thirty, or even a Barbaro or a Memmo, each of them one of seven males *stimati* – how representative it would be of the family's sentiment is problematic. The heading 'family' in Venice clearly covers a wide range of extensions.[77a]

The problem of generalizing about Venetian patrician families is further complicated by the question of distinct branches, which in some cases seem to be different clans altogether. The Morosini, for example, one of the largest and most venerable patrician clans, seem really to have been two families. One had its origin in ancient Mantua – according to one tradition the Morosini of this line were descendants of Virgil – the other came from Slavonia; as both families had become Venetian in Venice's early centuries their original names were transformed into Morosini.[78] Several other families present similar genealogical variety with origins in the distant past.[79] Others, like the Donà and the Da Molin, had internal distinctions of more recent origin.[80] It may be that in the one case the antique distinctions no longer prevailed, in the other the divisions were only apparent. Still, the fact that contemporaries were aware of them adds another cautionary consideration in contemplating generalization about members of families.

Caution is counselled also by two other kinds of differences among homonymous individuals. The first is disparity of wealth. Looking again at the *estimo* of 1379 we find that the individual estimates within families varied widely indeed. Among the Dandolo, for example, there were estimates as low as 300 lire and as high as 20,000; among the Corner they ranged from 500 to 60,000; among the Giustinian, again 300 to 20,000; among the Malipiero, 400 to 20,000. These were families with large numbers of *stimati*.[81] However even among families with smaller representations in the *estimo* there were wide variations. The estimates of the three Arimondo, for example, ranged from 1,500 to 16,000 lire; of the two Dalla Frascada, from 500 to 5,000; of the four Zulian, from 300 to 6,000.[82] As Gino Luzzatto has pointed out, the *estimi* figures themselves are not altogether adequate gauges of wealth since they do not take into account liquid wealth.[83] Yet though limited they do provide a consistent set of economic data on the patriciate, so for purposes of relative evaluation they are useful.

The other indication that urges caution against too ready generalization about family unity is geographical location. The households of patrician families were spread out in every corner of the city. Of the 156 patrician families in the *estimo*, 110 had members living in at least two of Venice's six *sestieri*; of these, 68 were represented in three or more *sestieri*. Considering that 34 of the 156 families had only one representative on the list this is a very high degree of dispersion indeed: over 98 per cent of those who could appear in multiple *sestieri* did so, and altogether 76.9 per cent of all the patrician families in the fiscal census were represented in more than one *sestiere*. This is remarkably different from the situation apparently prevailing in contemporary Florence.[84]

Yet despite all these caveats against too ready use of the family as an effective unit of the patriciate, it would be hasty to dismiss family solidarity altogether as a factor in the ruling class's internal articulation. Frederic Lane has shown in a number of studies that in the fifteenth and even the sixteenth century the patrician businessman's family still constituted the main source of his associates.[85] Contemporaries also expressed their consciousness of the family as a unit. The mid-*trecento* chronicler Piero Giustinian's generalizations about the origins of individual families are echoed in those of Marino Sanuto more than a century and a half later. For both these writers the clan was still the determining factor in patrician identity.[86] The dispute between *case vecchie* and *case nuove* itself, whatever its actual substance may have been, also testifies to the conception of a certain identity belonging to each member of a patrician family by reason of the name he bore. This consciousness also took official form in governmental policy. After quelling the uprising of patrician colonials on Crete in 1363, for example, the government punished some of the rebels by ordering them never again to leave Venice; they were to remain in the custody of their families in Venice. The family tie was thus apparently considered to extend across the seas, even in the case of branches long established in Venetian colonies.[87] Office-holding restrictions based on the family also testify to family-consciousness, although it is not clear to how many degrees they extended.[88]

Even geographical and economic divisions within families that we noted above do not in themselves indicate the severance – or non-existence – of close intra-clan ties. Two examples from the Morosini family may serve to illustrate this point. Michele di Fantin Morosini of the parish of S. Maria Formosa, who was to become doge in 1382, was rated in the *estimo* of 1379 at 38,000 lire, a very high sum. His only son, Giovanni, who also lived at S. Maria Formosa at this time, was rated at only 1,500. Yet when Michele died Giovanni's inheritance was obviously a handsome one; the economic discrepancy in the *estimo* was in this case only apparent.[89] Giovanni also apparently lived for a time in the parish of S. Casciano, in the *sestiere* of S. Croce, clear across town from S. Maria Formosa, which was in the *sestiere* of Castello. Eventually he moved back to what was apparently the main palace of his branch of the family, at S. Maria Formosa; but his son Andrea lived in S. Giovanni Laterano, and his grandson, Giovanni di Piero di Giovanni, eventually ended up residing in the parish of S. Salvador, in the *sestiere* of S. Marco.[90] The effective spanning of apparent geographical and economic gaps is also demonstrated in the case of the three sons – Giovanni, Domenico and Tomaso – of Marino di Giovanni Morosini of S. Antonin, in the *sestiere* of Castello. By 1379, Marino had died, but his sons were still living in S. Antonin. In the *estimo* Dominico was rated at 13,700 lire, his brothers at 3,700 each.[91] By 1387 they had left S. Antonin and were residing in the splendid Palazzo Morosini at S. Giovanni Grisostomo, near Rialto, in the *sestiere* of Cannaregio. But they had not cut their ties with S. Antonin. They were still renting – and contemplating selling – their property there to a cousin, Bernardo Morosini, who was himself rated in the *estimo* at 12,000 lire. Moreover by 1397 they had entered also into the inheritance of their father's brother, Renier Morosini of S. Antonin, an inheritance which may have included a property on the island of Murano. Renier, it should be noted, had been rated in the *estimo* at an impressive 37,000 lire, a far greater sum than the 3,700 lire estimates of his nephews, who nevertheless came to share in his wealth.[92]

These two examples indicate that disparities in wealth within families could in at least some cases be simply temporary generation gaps which would be closed when wills were read. They also show that living on different sides of town did not necessarily mean the dissolution of ties among relatives. The fact that in the 1290s only 69 of the 166 families represented in the Great Council from 1293–1297 had members living in more than one *sestiere* – 41.6 per cent compared with 76.9 per cent in 1379 – suggests that large-scale dispersion throughout the city was still a developing trend in the *trecento*.[93] If in later centuries it might have signified, or promoted, the fraying of intra-clan ties, it certainly seems not to have done so by 1379.

It seems fair to say, then, that though it would be misleading to picture the patrician family as a single-minded, solidly united clan of the tower-family variety encountered earlier in other Italian cities, it would be just as inaccurate to dismiss out of hand the effects of a common tradition and a common name on individuals' conceptions of their natural associates within the class. Naturally one feels more secure in treating the less numerous families as units than in doing so in the case of great sprawling clans like the Contarini, the Morosini, the Venier, the Giustinian and so on. Yet even these seem to have had a sense of community among their many branches. In his deposition to the police after having received a mortal wound in a fight in 1364 with Piero di Zanetto Lando, Naufosio Morosini said that the violence began with an insult by Piero against 'Ca' Morosini' – it is difficult to imagine that someone hurling a family insult of this kind would distinguish among Morosini branches, or that the offended patrician might himself differentiate before reacting. The same generic family reference was still being made a century later, as in the case of the Cardinal Piero Morosini, who in his will specified that his library 'should remain in Ca' Morosini'.[94]

Whether such demonstrations of family solidarity were consistently translated into common policy in economic and political matters is a question that must await full-dress studies of the experience of individual families for a satisfactory answer. Nevertheless their testimony does offer grounds for regarding family ties as the basis of enduring association among patricians. If a particular question of policy might unite in common cause, say, an individual Dolfin, or Lion, or Zane with an individual Grimani, Mocenigo, Gradenigo or Corner, over the long run these individuals would still tend to find strength, trust and consistent support within their individual clans. And the interest of the clan on other issues might well induce its members to counterbalance such momentary extra-clan alliances by the forging of others with different allies.[95] With this in mind we may proceed to an examination of the families which made up the particiate in the *trecento*, in an attempt to see if within the class there were some families or groups of families which stood above their fellows in political and economic prominence.

The examination involves seeking answers to three questions: Were there within the patriciate a number of politically and economically prominent families? Did such families enjoy their prominence permanently and in all areas of Venetian life? Did they constitute an oligarchy, dominating the class and the state in their own interests? The first question can be answered with a forthright affirmative. The second evokes a more temporizing response. And the third demands considerable discussion and definition. Let us consider them individually in turn.

The first question has to do with the distribution of power and wealth within the class. Both these substances are elusive in every society, but they are especially hard to pin down in the case of late-medieval Venice, where complete and systematic documentation of patrician activities is very scarce. And the scarcity is even greater in the case of documentation of the relative status of patricians. However if we cannot know exactly who was wealthy and who was powerful within the patriciate, we can put our hands on sources which provide at least an approximate picture of the distribution of wealth and power. Three such sources are the records of the Great Council's membership in the late thirteenth century, lists of elected officials in the mid fourteenth century, and the fiscal estimate of 1379 – to which we have already turned. In the cases of the first and third sources we must content ourselves with later copies of official records, with all the uncertainties that that implies.[96] Moreover the three are not uniform; they differ from one another both chronologically and topically. However while these dissimilarities mean that their validity for comparative analysis is circumscribed, they do have the virtue of permitting us different perspectives. Finally, they are fairly comprehensive. If the Great Council's membership lists and the rosters of mid-*trecento* office holders necessarily exclude patricians who were not politically active, at least they indicate to us nearly everyone who was, even to a modest degree.[97] And given the political nature of patrician status in Venice it seems fair to assume that very few patricians indeed were not represented on these lists. The same is true of the *estimo* of 1379. By definition the poorest nobles, or those whose wealth was invested in forms other than the immovables with which the *estimo* was concerned, were not on the list. There were at least seventeen noble families extant and active in 1379 but not represented on it.[98] Yet it can be safely assumed that their role in Venice's economic life was not a determining one.[99] On the whole the *estimo* can be considered a representative picture of relative patrician wealth in Venice.

In view of the chronological and topical differences among the three sources, their unanimity on the distribution of power is striking. In all three cases a small minority of the patriciate dominates. Whether the dominance was over the Great Council in the 1290s, the structure of government in the 1350s and 1360s, or immovable wealth in the late 1370s, a group of some forty families commanded the lion's share. And among those forty families there was in each case a considerably smaller group of families whose presence was especially formidable. The consistency of this tendency toward concentration of political activity and wealth can be clearly illustrated in tabular form.

Table 2 represents the distribution among families of the Great Council's membership, 1293–1297. My procedure was to rank the 166 families represented in the Council during those years according to the numbers of councillors each contributed. I then divided the Council's membership into three approximately equal parts. The third step was to see how many of the most highly represented families it took to fill one-third of the total Council membership; the result was Group 1 in the table. I then moved down the next ranks of families till I had accounted for another third of the Council's membership during the quadrennium; this was Group 2. The remaining families, who contributed the remaining one-third of the councillors, constitute Group 3. The results are indicated below:

Table 2
GREAT COUNCIL MEMBERSHIP, 1293–1297[100]

Group	No. and % of councillors	No. and % of families
1	343 (34%)	11 (6.6%)
2	346 (34.3%)	32 (19.3%)
3	319 (31.7%)	123 (74.1%)
	1008 (100%)	166 (100%)

The procedure for analysing the distribution of political offices among families in the mid *trecento* was somewhat different. After selecting the years 1349–52 and 1362–65 as the sample period, I focused on the most important offices in the governmental system. The principle was to determine whether a few families had a preponderant share of the critical policy-making councils of the Venetian state. The offices were the Senate, the Quarantia, the Ducal Council, the Council of Ten, and, for 1351–52, the special commission of *savi* appointed to oversee the war against Genoa. The remaining steps in the analysis were the same as in the case of the Great Council's membership: ranking the families by the number of officials they contributed, dividing the total number of officials into three equal parts, assigning the three parts to groups of families according to their rank. The result follows:[101]

Table 3
HOLDERS OF IMPORTANT OFFICES, 1349–52, 1362–65

Group	No. and % of offices	No. and % of families
1	572 (33.6%)	14 (9.2%)
2	557 (32.7%)	29 (18.9%)
3	573 (33.7%)	110 (71.9%)
	1702 (100%)	153 (100%)

The consistency between the results of the analyses represented by Tables 2 and 3 is striking, especially when allowance is made for the differences between the sources from which they are derived. Domination of the government by a bit more than one-quarter of the politically active patriciate seems a solidly established tendency during both the period of the *Serrata* and its extended aftermath. And the same pattern of concentration is true of wealth, as indicated in the *estimo* of 1379.[102] Here the procedure was twofold. The first step, represented in Table 4a, imitated the analyses in Tables 2 and 3: ranking families according to the totals of their members' estimates, dividing the total of the 156 patrician families' estimates into three equal parts, constructing three groups of families. However in view of the results of Tables 2 and 3 it seemed useful also to make an additional division of the patriciate into three groups more or less numerically comparable with the three which had emerged from the previous analyses. Accordingly, Table 4b represents the following steps: I totalled the estimates for the fifteen wealthiest families, designated Group 1, then I did the same for the next thirty families (Group 2). The remaining families constitute Group 3. Then next to each group I entered its collective wealth, as indicated in the *estimo*.

Table 4a
DISTRIBUTION OF WEALTH, *Estimo* OF 1379

Group	Amount and % of wealth	No. and % of families
1	Lire 1,327,191 (34.2%)	7 (4.5%)
2	„ 1,309,915 (33.8%)	22 (14.1%)
3	„ 1,234,262 (32%)	127 (81.4%)
	Lire 3,871,368 (100%)	156 (100%)

Table 4b
DISTRIBUTION OF WEALTH, *Estimo* OF 1379

Ranks and % of families		Amount and % of wealth
Families 1–15	(9.6%)	Lire 1,970,456 (50.9%)
Families 16–45	(19.2%)	„ 1,172,763 (30.3%)
Families 46–156	(71.2%)	„ 728,149 (18.8%)
Families 1–156	(100%)	Lire 3,871,368 (100%)

It seems clear from the collective testimony of the three sources that power and wealth – or at least numerical domination of the government and of immovable wealth – were concentrated in about one-quarter of the patrician families. However taken by itself this evidence indicates only an oligarchical structure. Before we can conclude that in fact *trecento* Venice was in the hands of a restricted group of families we have to ask two more questions. And the first, obvious one is, were the leading forty-odd families in each list the same ones in all three lists? Did the same families maintain their prominence from the 1290s through the 1360s, and in both political activity and wealth? In fact, quite a few of them did. Out of the sixty-seven families which appeared in

Groups 1–2 in at least one of the family lists we have analysed, twenty-six enjoyed that prominence in all three. Table 5 illustrates the breakdown of the sixty-seven families' participation in the lists:

Table 5

LEADING FAMILIES, 1293–1379[103]

Lists	No. and % of families
1. Great Council – offices – *estimo*	26 (38.8%)
2. Great Council – offices only	3 (4.5%)
3. Great Council – *estimo* only	— —
4. Offices – *estimo* only	9 (13.4%)
5. Great Council only	14 (20.9%)
6. Offices only	5 (7.5%)
7. *Estimo* only	10 (14.9%)
	67 (100%)

The figures in Table 5 indicate that almost two-thirds of the leading families in the Great Council during the 1290s (i.e. two-thirds of the 43 families represented in categories 1, 2, 3 and 5 of Table 5) continued to be politically significant for the next six decades at least, and that in just about nine cases out of ten continued political prominence went hand-in-hand with economic prominence. At the same time they show a fairly close general relationship between political prominence and economic prominence. Four out of every five politically significant families in the mid-*trecento* – and this includes families not among the most highly represented in the Great Council, 1293–1297 – were economically prominent, at least according to the *estimo*.[104] But in fact the consistency of family prominence was even greater than the table suggests. If we were to take the families in Categories 2–7 of Table 5 and include them among the leading families in those lists where they are not now among the leaders, provided that they are among the top one-third of those lists' families (computed by rank), then almost half of our sixty-seven families would appear among the leaders in all three lists.[105]

Yet despite a significant consistency among the families fleshing out the oligarchic structure we have been studying, the fact remains that more than half of the leading families were not always among the leading families. It is true that of all sixty-seven families only one, the Lion, had not been represented at all in the Great Council during the period 1261–1297, and even the Lion appear to have been accepted into the patriciate before 1297.[106] It is also true that in thirty-three of the seventy-one cases in which one of the sixty-seven families was not in Groups 1 or 2 in one of the lists, the family was still among the top one-half of all the families in the list. Nevertheless it remains true that there were intra-class changes, with some families enjoying prominence in one area or at one time, but not in the other. This indicates a certain measure of mobility within the patriciate in the period after the *Serrata*; as such it constitutes an intra-class complement to the changes in the class's composition we noted in earlier pages. It also indicates that the correlation between political distinction and wealth was not hard and fast. Together these indications reveal that in the decades after the *Serrata* the patriciate was still in a process of formation, internally as well as externally.

But if the changes involved in this process did occur among the leading one-quarter or so of the class, they left a more exclusive nucleus untouched. Among the twenty families who rank in Group 1 on one or more of our lists, all but three appear at least within Group 2 on all of the lists.[107] And fourteen of them consistently rank among the leading twenty families in the Great Council in the 1290s, in the important political offices in the mid-*trecento* and in the *estimo* of 1379.[108] These fourteen are clearly the very heart of the class. Together they account for a third both of the Great Council's membership in the 1290s and of the important office holders in the mid *trecento*; together they possessed nearly half of the immovable patrician wealth in the *estimo*.[109] If an oligarchy did indeed exist in fourteenth-century Venice, these fourteen families would surely have figured in it. Particularly in the light of the changes we have just noted at the lower ranks of the leading families, the influence of these fourteen looms even greater by reason of their consistent prominence.

Were they, or any of them, indeed part of an oligarchy? Here we have reached our final question regarding political and economic prominence within the fourteenth-century patriciate. For an answer, two points must be considered: how these fourteen, and more generally, how all the leading families attained their significance; and whether the indications of prominence we have seen are supported by other kinds of evidence.

On the first point, another look at the *estimo* of 1379 reveals that a strikingly close correlation exists between the number of males registered for each family and that family's political and economic prominence as we have observed it. The fourteen families which we have consistently encountered at the head of the patriciate are also all among the first twenty families in numbers of males mentioned in the *estimo*. Of the remaining twelve of the twenty-six families which also appeared consistently in Groups 1–2 in Tables 2, 3, and 4b, nine were among the first thirty-four in numbers of males, the other three were among the eighteen families tied for fiftieth place. Moreover seven of the nine families which demonstrated prominence only in the fourteenth century (i.e., the families in Category 4 of Table 5) ranked among the forty-nine families with the greatest number of males; the other two were also among those tied for fiftieth place. Thus, focusing only on the later *trecento* – the period for which the *estimo* has most validity as a patrician census – thirty of the thirty-five families which were both politically and economically prominent at that time were among the forty-nine with the largest number of male members, and the other five all had only one male less.[110] Going further down the ranks of families, the correlations were not quite so close between size on one hand and wealth and political prominence on the other. Tables 6a and 6b show the tendencies. The column at the left in each table represents a breakdown of the families in the *estimo* into three groups: the families with most males; the families with somewhat fewer males; the families with least males.[111] The columns on the right represent a similar breakdown of the families whose members held important political offices in the mid-*trecento*, ranked according to the number of offices the family held (in Table 6a) and of the families in the *estimo*, according to total family estimates (in Table 6b).

Table 6a
FAMILY SIZE AND NUMBER OF IMPORTANT OFFICES
Rank by no. important offices

Rank by no. males	Families 1–50	Families 51–97	Families 98–153	None
Families 1–49	38	6	3	2
Families 50–100	12	19	16	4
Families 101–152	—	14	17	21
None	—	8	20	—

Table 6b
FAMILY SIZE AND TOTAL FAMILY ESTIMATED WEALTH
Rank by total estimated wealth

Rank by no. males	Families 1–49	Families 50–100	Families 101–156
Families 1–49	39	9	1
Families 50–100	10	29	12
Families 101–152	—	13	39
None	—	—	4

Despite a greater tendency among the lower ranks for families to break out of the close correlation patterns between family size and degree of wealth and political activity, there is still a neat balance at all levels. But the greatest significance in the patterns lies in the fact that the correspondence holds firmest at the highest levels. The lion's share of wealth and political offices belonged to the families with the lion's share of nobles. Whether or not this still constituted concentration, it appears to have proven a preferable alternative to allowing certain smaller families to achieve a disproportionate concentration of wealth and power in their favour. The principle seems clear: a family's political and economic prominence depended upon its size.

But although this raises some important questions about the substance of power, as opposed to purely numerical prominence, it still does not exclude the possibility that these large families still dominated the class for their own particularist benefit. Indeed their very size could have given them an irresistible means of mastery over the rest of the patriciate. Yet again, the evidence seems to state that this was not the case.

Among the various gauges of prominence we have analysed, election to key political positions is an obviously crucial one. We have seen that in the councils in which the critical decisions of internal and external policy were made, the wealthiest, most enduring and largest families predominated. However, scrutinizing the totality of office holders during the sample years 1349–52, 1362–65, we find that the same large, prominent families were just as active in the more modest offices in the government as they were in the important councils. The same Alvise Dandolo who was a senator in 1363–64 had taken his turn as a supervisor of meat sales earlier in 1363. The same Marco Boezio Querini was *podestà* at Conegliano in 1349, *signore di notte* in 1351 and one of the twenty-five *savi* for the war with Genoa during the latter year.[112] And this was consistently true. Just as a family's size determined the number of important offices its members would occupy, it also indicated the number of minor posts the family would be obliged to fill. Among the twenty families which occupied the greatest number of important offices, nineteen were also among the busiest twenty families with respect to all office holding. Of the leading thirty-five families among important office holders, thirty-two stood in an identical group among holders of all offices. And the correspondence is true all down the line.[113] Clearly, the leading families' domination of the major governmental councils was an indication less of oligarchical monopoly than of a more general imperative of political participation, of bearing their share of the patrician responsibility to man the government.[114] Their share was determined by their size. And a further sign that the big families did not monopolize government is the corollary of what we have just seen. The smaller families had their fair share of the important offices. Indeed, in some cases their share could be more than fair. At one point during the 1353–54 session of the Council of Ten, there were sitting in the Council men from each of the following numerical ranks of families: 2, 4, 11, 14, 39, 67, 74, 92, 103 and 126.[115]

If the leading families did not monopolize a disproportionate share of the great offices, neither did they dominate private wealth as thoroughly as might seem the case at first glance. Although Tables 4a and 4b revealed a tremendous concentration of wealth among a relatively few families, a closer look reveals that the size of the families must be taken into account for a complete picture of the distribution of wealth. For example, of the twenty wealthiest patrician families in the *estimo* – computed by their estimate totals – only three were among the leading twenty families in a ranking by *average* estimate within the family. The Contarini ranked second in total estimates with a collective estimate of 288,141 lire; but among the sixty-eight Contarini individually estimated the average was 4,250 lire, only the thirty-second highest average. In the same way the Giustinian ranked seventh in total estimates, but forty-third in average estimate. Altogether seventeen of the thirty-five families with the highest estimate totals ranked from thirty-sixth downward with respect to average estimate.[116] It is true that the endurance of family solidarity would constitute for the members of the large families an additional source of economic strength. It is also true that powerful families might be better situated to effect lower estimates for themselves – although the hardships apparently experienced by some wealthy patricians as a result of the forced loans levied on the basis of the *estimo* during the War of Chioggia would suggest that such finagling was not always successful – if indeed it ever was.[117] Still the lack of correspondence between a family's ranks by total estimated wealth and by average estimated wealth is reason to believe that the great families were not exploiting their numbers to significant economic advantage.

Indeed the cumulative results of all the foregoing analyses indicate that while a relatively small percentage of patrician families dominated numerically both in government and in the ownership of immovable wealth, they did not translate their numerical preponderance into particularist advantage. The reason is not hard to find: they had no single particularist interest. Among the leading thirty-five families of the later *trecento*, among even the most prominent fourteen which dominate in all aspects of Venetian life throughout our entire period, there were both *case vecchie* and *case nuove*, both proponents of war with Genoa and members of the peace party. Those thirty-five families included nineteen *case vecchie* and seven of the principal *case nuove*.[118] Similarly, four of the thirty-five are represented among the group which Giovanni Pillinini classifies as 'intransigent' in their commitment to war with Genoa in the 1350s, four others are named among the proponents of accommodation with the Ligurian republic and four more – including the Giustinian, one of whom is tagged as an intransigent – are characterized by Pillinini as wavering between the two extremes.[119]

The essential, indeed the sole common characteristic setting these great families apart from the mass of the patriciate was their size and the prominence which was a result of their size. On the issues of political moment in *trecento* Venice they ranged themselves into opposing camps. And because they did it was impossible for any one faction within the patriciate to attain unchallenged supremacy. The articulation of internal struggle in *trecento* Venice, the alignments within the patriciate upon the important questions, were such that no one side could conquer: because the alignments cut right through the ranks of the great families, the opposing sides were too strong to crush. The result was an equilibrium of countervailing forces, face to face. If such an equilibrium was not yet a positive commitment, universally held within the patriciate, to the well-being of Venice – a commitment of a kind which would be celebrated a century later by writers on Venice – at least it provided the conditions within which such a commitment might develop. At least it prevented Venice from going the factional way of other Italian states.

IV

Writing in the seventeenth century, the patrician scholar Giannantonio Muazzo observed that the period from the *Serrata* to the middle of the fifteenth century was a distinct phase in the evolution of the Venetian constitution, at the end of which the formative period of Venice's institutional development was over.[120] He might have said the same, with some chronological adjustments at the end, of Venice's social evolution as well. With respect both to its composition and to the relative degrees of strength among its component families, the patriciate remained in a process of formation at least through the seven or eight decades which followed the *Serrata*.

The demographic vicissitudes of the *trecento* and the personnel requirements of running the government, as well as the lack, throughout at least the first part of the *trecento*, of a clear definition of the qualifications for patrician status, led to constant alterations in the class's composition. The result was that the patriciate of 1381 was considerably different from the patriciate of the 1290s. Very likely the class's constant confrontation of the extinction of old families and the entry of new ones played a significant role in the ultimate elaboration of patrician self-consciousness. It was well into the *trecento* that legislation on the requirements for admission to the class began insisting on the worthiness of both of the candidate's parents, not just on the father's nobility.[121] The fact of such legislation – which continued well into the next century and culminated in the establishment of the *Libro d'Oro* of the nobility in the early sixteenth century[122] – long after the *Serrata*, suggests that the conception of nobility in Venice, like the composition of the nobility, far from attaining definitude at the end of the thirteenth century, continued to develop throughout the *trecento*.

The patriciate's internal configuration also continued to develop. Some families of prominence in the late *duecento* no longer enjoyed that prominence by the later *trecento*. On the other hand newer families emerged in the latter period to take their place toward the top of the class. But this exchange was not true of the class as a whole. In the midst of the most prominent families at any point was a small number of families, some twenty-six, whose continued visibility and importance over the entire period 1293–1379 guaranteed a certain stability and consistency to the class as it underwent its post-*Serrata* elaboration. This restricted number of prominent families, dominated numerically in their turn by fourteen pre-eminent families, did not represent a single set of political principles or policies: they were to be found on all sides of the issues which concerned the Venetian polity during the fourteenth century. But they did represent a numerically unshakeable bulwark of the Venetian political tradition whose leading products they were.[123] It was the tradition embodied in this nucleus of families which provided continuity to the patriciate, and to the Venetian polity generally, through the period of the *Serrata*'s elaboration in the *trecento* and through the political difficulties which beset Venice during that century.

APPENDIX I

The following is a list of the 244 families whose existence and patrician status during the *trecento* are documented either in a single official source, a number of sources, official or private, or both. The families are grouped according to their categories as indicated in Table I.

Category 1. 1290s–1379

Abramo	Ciuran	Foscari	Mocenigo
Agadi	Cocco	Foscarini	Moro
Alberto	Contarini	Foscolo	Morosini
Arimondo	Coppo	Fradello	Mudazzo
Babilonio	Corner	Gabriel	Nadal
Badoer	Correr	Ghisi	Nani
Baffo	Costantino	Girardo	Navagero
Balastro	Da Canal	Giustinian	Nicola
Balbi	D'Equilo	Gossoni	Orio
Barbarigo	Da Fano	Gradenigo	Paradiso
Barbaro	Dalla Fontana	Grimani	Pasqualigo
Barbo	Dalla Frascada	Grioni	Pino
Barozzi	Da Lezze	Grissoni	Pisani
Basadona	De Mezzo	Gritti	Pizzamano
Baseggio	Da Molin	Grusoni	Polani
Bellegno	Da Mosto	Istrigo	Polo
Bembo	Da Mula	Lando	Premarin
Benedetto	Da Pesaro	Lion	Priuli
Bernardo	Da Ponte	Lombardo	Querini
Bocasso	Da Riva	Longo	Quintavalle
Boldù	Dandolo	Loredan	Romano
Bollani	Darduin	Magno	Rosso
Bon	Darmer	Malipiero	Ruzzier
Bondemiro	Darpino	Manolesso	Ruzzini
Boninsegna	Davanzago	Marcello	Sagredo
Bonzi	Davidor	Marino	Salamon
Bragadin	Diedo	Marion	Sanuto
Bredani	Dolfin	Massolo	Sesendolo
Cabriel	Donà	Mazaman	Signolo
Calbo	Dono	Megano	Silvo
Caotorta	Doro	Memmo	Soranzo
Capello	Duodo	Mengolo	Steno
Caravello	Emo	Miani	Storlado
Caroso	Erizzo	Michiel	Suriano
Cavalier	Falier	Minio	Tagiapera
Celsi	Ferro	Minoto	Tiepolo

Category 1. 1290s–1379

Tomado	Vendelino	Vitturi	Zeno
Trevisan	Venier	Volpe	Zorzi
Tron	Viadro	Zancani	Zulian
Valaresso	Vidal	Zancaruol	Zusto
Valier	Vielmo	Zane	
Veglia	Vioni	Zantani	

Category 2. 1290s–1350s/1360s

Albizzo	Biaqua	De Lorenzo	Staniario
Amizo	Bonomo	Leucari	Tanoligo
Aventurado	Brizi	Marango	Viari
Barisan	Businago	Savonario	Ziani

Category 3. 1290s, extinct in trecento

Acotanto	Briosso	Gradelon	Mazaruol
Aicardo	Carazacanevo	Lugnano	Mussolino
Ardizon	Da Camino	Madeo	Secogolo
Barbeta	Dalla Scala	Maistrorso	Tonisto
Betani	Dalla Sevella	Malaza	Totula
Bordone	Donzorzi	Marconi	Trainanti
Brazolan	Gambarino	Martinazzo	Zanasi

Category 4. Extant in trecento only

Balestrieri	Dal Sol	Guatardo	Sclavo
De Malis	Da Verardo	Pianega	Stornello
Da Mare	Gomberto	Pollini	Tolonigo
Di Pigli			

Category 5. Extant in trecento and 1379

Adoldo	De Renier	Ghezzo	Lanzolo
Arian	Dente	Guoro	Onoradi
Avonal	Diesolo	Lambardo	Papacizza
Dalle Boccole			

Category 6. Extant in 1379, not before

Avogardo	Battaglia	D'Anselmo	Da Zara
Balduin	Buora	Dalla Fornase	Galina

APPENDIX II

The following is a comparative list of the leading patrician families, 1293–1379. It consists of the first 43 families in the Great Council, 1293–1297 (Column I); the first 43 families among the holders of important offices, 1349–53 and

1362–65 (Column 2); and the first 45 families, in terms of total family wealth, in the *estimo* of 1379 (Column 3). The numbers next to the family names indicate each family's rank in the list represented in the column. Capital letters indicate that the family was in Group 1 – as this classification was used in the tables in the text – in the list represented in the column. Family names in parentheses indicate that those families were not among the leading families on that list, but that because they are among the leaders on at least one other list their rank on the list in question might be useful for purposes of comparison.

Great Council, 1290s	*Offices, mid-1300s*	*Estimo, 1379*
CONTARINI – 1	CONTARINI – 1	CONTARINI – 2
MOROSINI – 4	MOROSINI – 2	MOROSINI – 1
QUERINI – 3	QUERINI – 10	QUERINI – 11
DANDOLO – 2	DANDOLO – 5	DANDOLO – 10
MICHIEL – 6	MICHIEL – 12	MICHIEL – 14
DOLFIN – 8	DOLFIN – 9	DOLFIN – 8
GRADENIGO – 5	Gradenigo – 17	GRADENIGO – 15
VENIER – 9	VENIER – 3	Venier – 19
DA MOLIN – 7	Da Molin – 15	Da Molin – 9
Soranzo – 16	SORANZO – 3	SORANZO – 4
Giustinian – 19	GIUSTINIAN – 6	GIUSTINIAN – 7
Corner – 13	CORNER – 8	CORNER – 3
Zorzi – 36	ZORZI – 11	ZORZI – 13
(Trevisan – 66)	TREVISAN – 13	TREVISAN – 6
ZENO – 9	Zeno – 23	Zeno – 34
FOSCARINI – 11	Foscarini – 17	Foscarini – 23
Loredan – 15	LOREDAN – 6	Loredan – 17
Zane – 19	Zane – 30	ZANE – 4
(Bragadin – 44)	BRAGADIN – 14	Bragadin – 25
———	Lion – 24	LION – 12
Falier – 17	Falier – 15	Falier – 16
Badoer – 19	Badoer – 21	Badoer – 31
Viadro – 23	Viadro – 36	Viadro – 38
Donà – 26	Donà – 26	Donà – 20
Barbarigo – 27	Barbarigo – 20	Barbarigo – 30
Malipiero – 30	Malipiero – 41	Malipiero – 29
Mocenigo – 30	Mocenigo – 32	Mocenigo – 22
Sanuto – 30	Sanuto – 36	Sanuto – 39
Baseggio – 13	Baseggio – 34	Baseggio – 40
Tiepolo – 18	Tiepolo – 43	(Tiepolo – 85)
Polani – 19	Polani – 30	(Polani – 61)
Dalla Fontana – 36	Dalla Fontana – 26	(Dalla Fontana – 105)
(Bembo – 44)	Bembo – 22	Bembo – 26

Great Council, 1290s	Offices, mid-1300s	Estimo, 1379
(Barbaro – 95)	Barbaro – 24	Barbaro – 32
(Priuli – 123)	Priuli – 28	Priuli – 18
(Da Mosto – 52)	Da Mosto – 33	Da Mosto – 27
(Memmo – 95)	Memmo – 38	Memmo – 41
(Nani – 52)	Nani – 41	Nani – 45
Da Canal – 12	(Da Canal – 63)	(Da Canal – 131)
Premarin – 23	(Premarin – 61)	(Premarin – 68)
Tron – 23	(Tron – 98)	(Tron – 59)
Nadal – 28	(Nadal – 136)	(Nadal – 89)
Barozzi – 28	(Barozzi – 124)	(Barozzi – 68)
Bellegno – 30	(Bellegno – 44)	(Bellegno – 53)
Boldù – 30	(Boldù – 57)	(Boldù – 71)
Ghisi – 30	(Ghisi – 57)	(Ghisi – 92)
Balastro – 36	(Balastro – 87)	——
Caotorta – 36	(Caotorta – 51)	(Caotorta – 156)
Caroso – 36	(Caroso – 63)	——
Sesendolo – 36	(Sesendolo – 79)	(Sesendolo – 154)
Signolo – 36	(Signolo – 136)	(Signolo – 94)
Zantani – 36	——	(Zantani – 98)
(Marcello – 52)	Marcello – 19	(Marcello – 51)
(Diedo – 95)	Diedo – 28	(Diedo – 65)
(Ciuran – 95)	Civran – 33	(Civran – 65)
(Gritti – 123)	Gritti – 38	(Gritti – 49)
(Cocco – 123)	Cocco – 38	(Cocco – 97)
(Barbo – 44)	(Barbo – 79)	Barbo – 21
(Moro – 52)	(Moro – 44)	Moro – 24
(Grimani – 123)	(Grimani – 63)	Grimani – 28
(Minio – 52)	(Minio – 63)	Minio – 33
(Bondemiro – 95)	(Bondemiro – 51)	Bondemiro – 35
(Capello – 123)	(Capello – 72)	Capello – 36
(De Mezzo – 66)	(De Mezzo – 124)	De Mezzo – 37
——	(Cabriel – 98)	Cabriel – 42
——	(Rosso – 87)	Rosso – 43
(Pisani – 80)	(Pisani – 44)	Pisani – 44

NOTES

1. Philip Jones's configuration is paradigmatic: 'In a few towns, notably Venice, this [communal] patrician regime survived unchallenged for as long as the commune lasted; but in most places, from about 1200, it began to break up. On the one hand the governing class fell apart into rival factions; on the other hand the *populus* or *popolo*, enriched by trade and enlarged by urban immigration, began to rebel against magnate domination,

and in the course of the thirteenth century secured a share, and in places control, of the communal government.' 'Communes and despots: the city state in late-medieval Italy', *Royal Historical Society, Transactions*, ser. v, xv (1965) 75. Venice's distinctiveness among Italian states has been accepted by most writers, who have consequently treated the Venetian experience in the late Middle Ages without significant reference to the forces influencing events in mainland Italy. A recent effort, highly original yet not altogether convincing, to reverse this tendency is G. Cracco, *Società e stato nel medioevo veneziano* (Florence, 1967); see especially 103–106, 211–213, 290–291. Cracco's formulation of Venetian history has been strongly influenced by the writings of E. Sestan, particularly 'Le origini delle signorie cittadine: un problema storico esaurito?', *Bullettino dell' Istituto Storico Italiano per il Medio Evo*, lxxiii (1961) 41–69, even though Sestan's argument focuses on the feudal aristocracy, whose existence in Venice is at the very least problematic. See esp. 56–57.

2. The corporate bodies into which rival factions elsewhere organized themselves did not have their counterparts in Venice. Particularly notable for its absence was an organization of the *popolo*, clearly distinguished from and engaged in a struggle with families of more ancient prominence. See, for a single example, the delineation of this division in E. Cristiani, *Nobiltà e popolo nel comune di Pisa* (Naples, 1962) ch. 1, esp. 22 seq.; also, more generally, Jones, 'Communes and despots', 76. Among the leading families of thirteenth-century Venice a distinction was made between *nobiles* and *antiqui populares*, but it was not canonized in juridical form. For some discussion of the thirteenth-century currents see M. Merores, 'Der grosse Rat von Venedig und die sogenannte Serrata vom Jahre 1297', *Vierteljahrschrift für Sozial- und Wirtschaftsgeschichte*, xxi (1928) esp. 57–63; H. Kretschmayr, *Geschichte von Venedig*, 3 vols. (Gotha, 1905–1934) ii, 70–71; Cracco, *Società e stato*, 106–134. Although these and other authors detect differences between the two groups, they agree that by the end of the thirteenth century nearly all of the prominent citizens, whatever their origins, had been absorbed into one ruling class.

3. There are convenient accounts of the legislation involved in this process in Merores, 'Der grosse Rat . . .', 75–81; and G. Maranini, *La costituzione di Venezia dalle origini alla Serrata del Maggior Consiglio* (Florence, 1927) 335–351. The essential point of this legislation was that membership in the Great Council was tantamount to nobility; consequently limiting the nobility's membership meant restricting access to the Great Council, which simultaneously became the source of the personnel of the other offices in the government.

4. Margarete Merores interprets it as the final step in a process of including all prominent Venetians in an enlarged, comprehensive ruling class: 'Diese Verschmelzung von nobilis vir und antiquus popularis ist, wie ich glaube, die wichstigste Tatsache der Sozialgeschichte Venedigs im 13. Jahrh . . .', 'Der grosse Rat . . .', 61. For Roberto Cessi, on the other hand, the *Serrata* represented a procedural expedient: in order to preserve the integrity of an already formed aristocracy against the 'aspirazioni di una ristretta clientela a un dominio oligarchico', it was necessary to prevent this small group from exploiting the Great Council's existing electoral procedures and filling the Council with its partisans from the lower classes. The solution was to do away with elections. 'Politica ed economia veneziana del Trecento', in *Politica ed economia di Venezia nel Trecento. Saggi* (Rome, 1952) 9–11. Cessi developed this idea in a number of other writings. Resembling Cessi's view is that of G. Maranini, op. cit., 29–31, who gives particular emphasis to factional struggles between groups among the leading families. An aristocratic view of the *Serrata* is that of the fifteenth century chronicler, Pietro (?) Dolfin, quoted by his slightly later fellow patrician, Marino Sanuto: 'La città di Venezia vedendo, che alcuni Plebei e gente vile proposero di farsi prendere e avere ufizi e magistrati e reggimenti, come se fossero gentiluomini naturali per lungo tempo, i veri Patrizi tra loro trattarono in segreto di ragionare di provedere a questo e di voler serrar il gran Consiglio . . .' *Le Vite de'duchi di Venezia*, R.I.S., xxii, col. 583. See also P. Molmenti, *La storia di Venezia nella vita privata*, 3 vols. (7th ed., Bergamo, 1927) i, 65. To these citations must now be added one to

the important recent article of F. C. Lane, 'The enlargement of the Great Council of Venice', in *Florilegium Historiale, Essays presented to Wallace K. Ferguson*, eds. J. G. Rowe and W. H. Stockdale (Toronto, 1971), 237–273. This article appeared too late for me to incorporate Lane's findings into my work. Its title, however, gives some suggestion of similarities of interpretation with the present study.

5. See the metaphor of Merores: 'Der grosse Rat . . . dem im 13. Jahrh. alles zuströmte was sich genug Macht und Ansehen zuschrieb, um die Aufnahme zu erlangen, die Geschlechter der Nobiles und des Popolo grasso, die antiqui populares, er war der Schmelztiegel geworden, aus dem um die Wende des 13. Jahr. zum 14. der soziale Kern der venezianischen Republik, die Aristokratie, sich herauskristallisierte . . .' 'Der grosse Rat . . .', 109.

6. For later entrants see B. Cecchetti, 'I nobili e il popolo di Venezia', *A.V.*, iii (1872) 427; J. C. Davis, *The decline of the Venetian nobility as a ruling class* (Baltimore, 1962) 18, 106–125. On the entrants of 1381, see above, p. 57.

7. For some general observations on this impulse to maintain patrician *purezza*, see Cecchetti, 'I nobili e il popolo', 429.

8. There are two main exceptions. One is the plot of Marin Bocconio and his followers, who in 1300 sought to enter the Great Council by force, apparently embittered by their exclusion from it by reason of the recent legislation. On the Bocconio plot, see the description in Sanuto, *Vite de' duchi*, cols. 581–584, and the interpretations of Kretschmayr, *Geschichte*, ii, 71; Cracco, *Società e stato*, 355–356; and Romanin, iii, 5–6. The other important instance of conflict with significant popular involvement is the conspiracy of the Doge Marin Falier in 1355. See the detailed account of V. Lazzarini, *Marino Faliero* (Florence, 1963) 157–164 and passim.

9. 'I sudditi reagiscono . . . da corpo morto, ormai estraneo al processo storico; il popolo frapponeva tra sè e lo stato le barriere del servilismo, dell'ossequio interessato, oppure della rassegnazione, dell' indifferenza, o talora, sporadicamente, dell'osilità . . .', *Società e stato*, 454.

10. On Cessi and Cracco, see notes below.

11. W. J. Bouwsma, *Venice and the defense of republican liberty* (Berkeley and Los Angeles, 1968) 63–67 and passim; F. Gilbert, 'The Venetian constitution in Florentine political thought', in *Florentine Studies. Politics and society in Renaissance Florence*, ed. N. Rubinstein (London, 1968) 466–472. See also on the myth, G. Fasoli, 'Nascita di un mito', in *Studi storici in onore di Gioacchino Volpe*, 2 vols. (Florence, 1958) i, 445–479; F. Gaeta, 'Alcune considerazioni sul mito di Venezia', *Bibliothèque d'Humanisme et Renaissance*, xxiii (1961) 58–75.

12. Although the myth's formal elaboration took place in the late fifteenth–early sixteenth centuries, its essential terms were current among European observers at an earlier date. According to the fourteenth-century Venetian chronicler Lorenzo de' Monaci, Albertus Magnus observed that '. . . de gentis Venetorum potentia, circumspectione, providentia, unitate civium et concordia et amore totius iustitiae cum clementia, omnibus fere nationibus iam [est] notum', quoted in Fasoli, 'Nascita', 467–468. For a humanistic viewpoint on the virtues of the Venetian nobility, see Cristoforo Landino's arguments about the liberalizing effects of commerce, which distinguish the Venetian patricians from the Neapolitan nobility, quoted in E. Garin, *L'umanesimo italiano* (paperback ed., Bari, 1965), 104–105, esp. 105, n. 8.

13. *La regolazione delle entrate e delle spese (sec. XIII–XIV)*. R. Accademia dei Lincei, *Documenti finanziari della Repubblica di Venezia*, ser. I, vol. ii, pt. i (Padua, 1925). Other writings in which Cessi developed this theme with different emphases have been gathered together in the previously cited *Politica ed economia di Venezia nel Trecento. Saggi*. Of particular importance are: ' "L'officium de navigantibus" e i sistemi della politica commerciale veneziana nel sec. XIV', in ibid., 23–61; and 'Le relazioni commerciali tra Venezia e le Fiandre nel sec. XIV', ibid., 71–172. Cessi's important contributions to

Venetian historical scholarship have been integrated into his synthetic *Storia della Repubblica di Venezia*, first published in the mid-1940s but now in a new, significantly revised edition: 2 vols. (Milan–Messina, 1968). The second half of vol. i deals with the questions considered here.

14. 'Per quanto nella classe mercantile non sia ancora [in the second decade of the *trecento*] chiaramente differenziata una forte aristocrazia monopolizzatrice, tuttavia s'appalesano non indubbi sintomi di aspirazioni di prepotere economico di alcuni gruppi esponenti della maggior ricchezza mobiliare.' *La regolazione*, p. xlii. Cessi also ties this group to that element of the patriciate against whose machinations the *Serrata* had been instituted (see above, n. 4). Referring to attempts at fiscal reform through the raising of duties on the Levantine trade, he observes that such a policy 'non dovesse non destare apprensioni ed opposizioni in coloro che aveano visto fallire i tentativi di instaurazione di un governo più consono ai loro ideali politici ed economici . . .', ibid., pp. xlii–xliii.

15. *La regolazione*, pp. xlii, l–li, lxiv–lxv, lxxii–lxxiii, cxlv seq. Cessi's account is a *tour de force* of imaginative reconstruction. In their desire to promote their Levantine interests at all costs, the wealthy monopolists both advocated war with Genoa, Venice's main rival in the Levant, and opposed fiscal measures – necessary to improve the government's financial condition – which, while they might aid the war effort, might also encroach on the monopolists' commercial profits. Both policies engendered opposition among a majority of the Senate, but the monopolists' shrewd manoeuvring in other councils of government enabled them to prevail, at least temporarily. Cessi leaves unanswered the question of how the monopolists succeeded in obtaining majority votes in the Great Council. But see the section dealing with the manoeuvrings preparatory to the war with Genoa, ibid., pp. clii–clxxi. For a later conflict involving Levantine interests in a different context, see the accounts of the early-*quattrocento* debate between the proponents of mainland expansion, associated with Francesco Foscari, and the traditionalists, who insisted on cultivating Venice's eastern interests and the profits they brought, associated with Tomaso Mocenigo. H. Baron, *The crisis of the early Italian Renaissance* rev. ed., (Princeton, 1966) 390–392; Cessi, *Storia della Repubblica*, i, 362–367; Kretschmayr, *Geschichte*, ii, 278–280.

16. G. Pillinini, 'Marino Falier e la crisi economica e politica della metà del '300 a Venezia', *A.V.*, ser. V, xcix (1968) 45–71. According to Pillinini, the doge was the scapegoat of a group of patricians who were 'cercando di restringere il sistema della collegialità larga a vantaggio di una ristretta' – the language itself echoes Cessi's – 70. When their attempt to take over the government failed it was necessary to sacrifice the doge, 'che si era esposto e avrebbe potuto diventare motivo di scandalo . . .', 70–71.

17. *Società e stato*, passim. For Cracco the entire period from the later thirteenth through the fourteenth century was a period of 'lunga decadenza', in which the vigorous and broadly-based political society of the 'primo comune' in the twelfth century was subverted by an increasingly narrow ruling group, which finally issued into the oligarchy of the Renaissance. Thus for Cracco, 'La Venezia del Rinascimento e del "mito" era, insomma, la Venezia che incarnava e sublimava, esasperandoli, i termini di una crisi colossale (una crisi iniziata nel tardo Duecento); e che già portava in sè, e quasi nutriva, i germi della propria decadenza', 458.

18. *Annali veneti di Domenico Malipiero*, ed. F. Longo, in *A.S.I.*, vii (1844), pt. 2, 681–683. According to Malipiero, the bitterness of this controversy led not only to intrigues over elections to important offices in the government, but even spread as far as Milan, where Lodovico Sforza il Moro twitted the Venetian ambassador about it, saying, in Malipiero's account, 'che'l vede la ruina de questa Terra, e che i Principi comenzerà a far nuovi pensieri de i fatti nostri', ibid., 682.

19. The *case vecchie* were: Badoer, Baseggio, Barozzi, Bragadin, Bembo, Contarini, Corner, Dandolo, Dolfin, Falier, Giustinian, Gradenigo, Memmo, Michiel, Morosini, Polani, Querini, Salamon, Sanuto, Soranzo, Tiepolo, Zane, Zeno and Zorzi. The leading

case nuove were: Barbarigo, Donà, Foscari, Grimani, Gritti, Lando, Loredan, Malipiero, Marcello, Mocenigo, Moro, Priuli, Trevisan, Tron, Vendramin and Venier. Romanin, iv, 421, n. 2. It is interesting to compare these lists, on the basis of which Venetians split into factions in the *quattrocento*, with the three thirteenth-century categories devised by Merores, who considers the *vecchi-nuovi* distinction worthless; see 'Der grosse Rat . . .', 65–69.

20. In 1450, according to one tradition, 'congiurarono insieme 16 Casate nuove delle principali di non lasciare ascendere al Dogado alcuno di casa Vecchia, mà sempre uno delle nuove . . .' The writer adds that these 16 conspiratorial families came in consequence of this action to be called '*case ducali*', distinguishing them from the rest of the *case nuove*. *Distinzioni segrete che corrono tra le casate nobili di Venezia*, B.M.V., MSS italiani, cl. VII, 1531 (7638), f. 3. This anonymous seventeenth-century ms has been attributed to Marc'Antonio Giustinian (member of a *casa vecchia*) by E. A. Cicogna, *Delle iscrizioni veneziane*, 6 vols. (Venice, 1824–53) iv, 495. For a later ramification of the *vecchi-nuovi* distinction, see G. Cozzi, *Il doge Nicolò Contarini. Ricerche sul patriziato veneziano agli inizi del Seicento* (Venice–Rome, 1958) 4–6.

21. *Venetiarum historia vulgo Petro Iustiniano Iustiniani filio adiudicata*, eds. R. Cessi and F. Bennato. Deputazione di Storia Patria per le Venezie, *Monumenti Storici*, n.s., xviii (Venice, 1964). This chronicle contains, on 255–276, a section called 'Proles Venetorum', in which the geographical and chronological origins of noble families, past and present, are indicated. The section concludes (276) with a list of the 25 most ancient families. The list is the same as that of the *case vecchie* enumerated above, n. 19, except that the Bragadin and Salamon are absent from this list and the Ziani, the Bellegno and the Gauli are present. According to the editors the chronicle was written by 1358, that is, long before the conspiracy to exclude the *vecchi* from the dogeship; see pp. xvii–xx. On the Giustinian chronicle and this edition of it, see A. Carile, 'Note di cronachistica veneziana: Piero Giustinian e Nicolò Trevisan', *Studi Veneziani*, ix (1967) esp. 109, n. 17.

22. Cessi, *Storia della Repubblica*, i, 286; Cracco, *Società e stato*, 365. Cracco's perspective, which emphasizes the wrongs allegedly perpetrated by the government on the conspirators, fits into an old tradition which sees the Tiepolo–Querini conspiracy as the last gasp of democracy after the Serrata. In this configuration Baiamonte Tiepolo was the champion of the disenfranchised classes. See P. Daru, *Histoire de la République de Venise* (2nd ed., Paris, 1821) i, 549 seq. On this view of Baiamonte, see Romanin, iii, 49–50.

23. Cessi, 'Officium de navigantibus', 26–27. The function of the *Ufficiali dei Naviganti*, established first in 1324 and then decommissioned and resurrected at various points during the *trecento*, was 'ristabilire l'equilibrio nel commercio della piazza di Venezia colpita da crisi pletorica. Le importazioni erano cresciute e soverchiavano le esportazioni, e sopravanzavano il limite normale di assorbimento della piazza medesima, in modo che la merce giaceva nei fondachi, con grave danno dei grandi trafficanti, che dovevano subire la concorrenza, spesso fortunata, dei minori, aiutati dal capitale o dal credito straniero. Era però un equilibrio, che doveva risolversi a vantaggio di gruppi mercantili particolari, e i maggiori, non dell'economia generale. Poichè, se era vero che la nuova legge mirava a eliminare il disagio prodotto da un eccesso di importazione, col ridurla automaticamente, e favorendo l'esportazione sia col beneficio di esenzione della recente linea di Fiandra, sia col promuovere lo sviluppo della marina mercantile, era però altrettanto vero che questa artificiosa restrizione ritornava a vantaggio del grosso capitale, che avrebbe potuto sostenere senza gravi conseguenze gli effetti di qualche aggravio temporaneo, mentre, eliminando la concorrenza e diventando arbitro del mercato, sarebbe stato facilmente compensato da maggiori lucri', ibid. See also Cracco, *Società e stato*, 373–384.

24. 'Questa guerra è all'origine di una serie di tensioni che turbano la classe dirigente veneziana. Ed è proprio il nesso tra guerra ed economia, cioè in definitiva tra politica ed economia, che sta alla base dell'alternativa, di fronte a cui la classe dirigente veneziana

viene a trovarsi. La guerra poteva essere il mezzo con cui superare la crisi eliminando la concorrenza genovese, ma contribuiva, almeno fino a un certo punto, ad aggravare la crisi stessa, in quanto il suo costo veniva ad incidere sull'economia', Pillinini, 'Marino Falier e la crisi', 55. See also Cessi, *La regolazione*, pp. cxlv–ccx.

25. According to Cessi, in the Tiepolo–Querini plot of 1310, '. . . serve di strumento gente di popolo, lusingata forse dal desiderio di preda più che da ideale politico', *Storia della Repubblica*, i, 286. For Cracco too the patrician conspirators '. . . potevano anche sperare che la sommossa trascinasse perfino il popolo artigiano e minuto, se non altro perchè esasperato, trasformando un'azione ristretta in urto plebiscitario, dell'intera città, contro il governo', *Società e stato*, 369. Cracco sees this same tendency present in the Falier conspiracy of 1355, in which discontented patricians sought '. . . alleanze (presso la gente di mare, presso gli artigiani) . . .', ibid., 440.

26. See above, n. 19.

27. A.S.V., *Segretario alle voci, Misti* (henceforth abbreviated *Voci, Misti*), reg. 1 (1349–53), reg. 2 (1362–67), passim. These registers list the holders of all elective offices for the years indicated. The figure 181 represents all the families mentioned at least once in the registers. It consequently does not include other families which may have been represented in the government during the other years of those two decades, for which the *Voci* lists have not survived.

28. Cessi, *La regolazione*, passim; Pillinini, 'Marino Falier e la crisi', passim. *Voci, Misti*, reg. i, 1–40, 61–62. All office-holders elected for the years 1349–1351 have been included; in addition there are some whose tenures extended into 1352, such as the members of the Senate elected to serve from mid-1351 to mid-1352 (f. 62).

29. Cessi, *La regolazione*, p. clv. According to Cessi the 'prepotenti' succeeded, once war with Genoa seemed inevitable, in creating support for their policies among the mass of the patriciate by focusing on national honour and playing down the economic ramifications of the situation. His argumentation, however, is not altogether convincing, nor does he document the force of this sentiment among the patriciate.

30. See, for example, Cracco's discussion of the effects of the events of the later *trecento*: '. . . la quasi totalità del patriziato vide livellarsi la sua forza economica a tutto vantaggio di poche famiglie – circa una dozzina – che invece emergevano con patrimoni favolosi. Ne derivava uno strutturarsi gerarchico della nobiltà, che aveva i suoi riflessi immediati sul piano politico e della distribuzione degli *honores*: prima venivano i Potenti, poi i "mezzani", che erano i più, indi la piccola nobiltà . . .', *Società e stato*, 450–451. The dozen 'Potenti' are not named.

31. Fasoli, 'Nascita di un mito', 478. Discussing fourteenth and fifteenth-century Venetian writers on Venetian politics, she comments: 'Non c'è differenza sostanziale tra Lorenzo de'Monaci e Paolo Morosini, che scrisse tre quarti di secolo dopo, poiché l'uno e l'altro si rifanno alla tradizionale interpretazione della storia veneziana, alla loro coscienza di cittadini tradizionalmente educati nella venerazione della Repubblica.'

32. The membership of the Council was 589 in 1297, the year of the *Serrata*, but rose steadily in the following years, reaching the figure of 1,150 in 1314, according to later chroniclers: Merores, 'Der grosse Rat . . .', 90. See also Molmenti, *Storia*, i, 104: '. . . s'inganna chi crede che il Consiglio si chiudesse ad un tratto in una rigida immobilità'. The important question, however, is not whether additional *individuals* entered the Council after 1297, but to what extent new *families* did so. On this entire matter, see now Lane, 'The enlargement of the Great Council . . .', esp. 245–48, 257.

33. See the classic statement by Gino Luzzatto of the tradition, which contradicts to some extent the views on oligarchy of Cracco and Cessi, that in Venice no individuals were allowed to acquire too much wealth or power: remarking that Venetians were never among the most active professional lenders, Luzzatto explains, 'La raison de cette différence [between Venetians and others more active in lending] . . . doit être recherchée . . . dans la diversité des situations politiques, et dans la solidité de structure de l'État

vénitien, qui jamais – à partir du moins du XIIIe siècle, – ne permit aux capitalistes, soit isolés, soit groupés, d'occuper cette position dominante, si favorable à leurs intérêts privés, que conquirent par example, à Florence, les compagnies de l' "Arte di Calimala". A Venise, l'État, au moyen de sa complexe division des pouvoirs, du caractère collégial et temporaire de ses offices, de ses nombreux et puissants organes de contrôle, exerce une rigide fonction de nivellement'. 'Les activités économiques du Patriciat vénitien (X^e– XIVe siècles)', in *Studi di storia economica veneziana* (Padua, 1954) 145. See also Bouwsma, *Venice and the defense*, 66–67.

34. Among the sources housed in A.S.V. which contain material on inter- and intra-familial intercourse, on relative degrees of wealth, real and liquid, among nobles and on the endurance of family solidarity over the course of generations, some of the richest are the following: notarial protocols, divided into the *buste* of the *Cancelleria inferiore*, which contain the generality of notarized acts, and the *Testamenti*, or wills; the *commissarie* (estate records) of deceased Venetians, administered by the procurators of St. Mark; the records of the various civil courts, notably the *Curia di petizion*, which exercised juris-diction in commercial disputes. All three sources are fairly well ordered; the *commissarie* have recently undergone a significant reordering. However the data in the sources are varied and scattered. Consequently large-scale exploitation of significant amounts of the data must be preceded by the development of a systematic methodology.

35. 'É un vero rivolgimento di fortune e di situazioni sociali', which created 'accanto alla vecchia nobiltà, notevolmente diminuita ed in parte stremata di forze, una categoria abbastanza numerosa ed agguerrita di nuovi ricchi, che deve aver avuto larga parte nella più rapida espansione capitalistica della società veneziana nel secolo successivo', G. Luzzatto, 'Introduzione', *I prestiti della Repubblica di Venezia, sec. XII–XV*. R. Accademia dei Lincei, *Documenti finanziari della Repubblica di Venezia*, ser. III, vol. i, pt. i (Padua, 1929) clxx, with an extended discussion on pp. clxix–clxxv. Much of Luzzatto's discussion is more accessible in his *Storia economica di Venezia dall' XI al XVI secolo* (Venice, 1961) 140–145. See also R. Cessi, 'La finanza veneziana al tempo della Guerra di Chioggia', in *Politica ed economia*, 195: Writing of the heavy imposts of the war Cessi observes that '. . . è questo . . . il momento, in cui . . . è preparato . . . uno spostamento più sensibile di ricchezza'. Despite evidence of hardship experienced by significant numbers of patricians in the wake of the war, the extent of this 'social revolution' is still an open question and needs a thorough investigation; Cessi, ibid, 192.

36. A list of the 30 can be found in *Raphayni de Caresinis chronica*, ed. E. Pastorello, *R.I.S.* 2, xii, pt. 2, 57. The significance of these admissions has been interpreted in various ways. See Luzzatto, *I prestiti*, p. clxx; Cracco, *Società e stato*, 450, n. 3.

37. It strikes me that the entire period from the War of Chioggia through the first wave of acquistions on the Italian mainland during the early *quattrocento* can be viewed as a distinct phase of Venetian history, characterized by a dynamism built upon a founda-tion laid in the decades after the *Serrata* and preparatory to the stability of the Venetian Renaissance.

38. '. . . si mormorava per la città che ne entravano tanti huomeni nuovi nel Gran Cons° avanti el serrar di questo in sei anni, quanto il Cons° de XLta ne' haveva accetati in quattro mesi', *Registro delle aggregazioni alla nobiltà veneta dalla Serrata del Maggior Consiglio cioè dal 1296 fino al 1404*, B.M.V., ital. VII, 199 (8511), f. 39v. This seventeenth-century ms is one of several at the Marciana dealing with post-*Serrata* admissions to the patriciate and the measures designed to regulate such admissions. Another is B.M.V., ital. VII, 935 (7428). Similar mss in A.S.V. contain the same material; see, for example, *Parti prese nel dare la nobiltà veneta a diverse famiglie, Miscellanca Codici*, I, *Storia veneta*, 44.

39. See the accounts of the legislation in Merores, 'Der grosse Rat . . .', 75–81; and Maranini, *La costituzione . . . dalle origini*. A good resumé in English can be found in F. C. Hodgson, *Venice in the thirteenth and fourteenth centuries* (London, 1910) 192–196.

40. G. A. Muazzo, *Patritiorum*, B.M.V., ital. VII, 196 (8578), f. 2v. This ms by the

seventeenth-century patrician scholar is a compendium of various materials on the patriciate. On Muazzo, see now A. Lombardo, 'Storia e ordinamenti delle magistrature veneziane in un manoscritto inedito del sec. XVII', in *Studi in onore di Riccardo Filangieri*, 3 vols. (Naples, 1959) ii, 619–688. I would like to thank Professor David Jacoby for the reference to this article.

41. Muazzo, *Patritiorum*, f. 3.

42. Muazzo, *Patritiorum*, f. 3v–4.

43. For a discussion of later heraldic measures, including the famous *Libro d'Oro*, see Cecchetti, 'I nobili e il popolo', 428–436.

44. As late as 1376 it took three roll-call votes of the Great Council to effect passage of a measure forbidding entry to the Great Council – and thus the patriciate – to anyone born out of wedlock. This measure was designed to put an end to a practice which 'pluries est occursum', by which patricians would have children 'de mulieribus debilis et vilis condicionis' whom they would marry *post partum* in order to get the sons into the Great Council. *Parti in materia araldica*, A.S.V., *Avogaria di Comun*, reg. 14, f. 9.

45. Cecchetti, 'I nobili e il popolo', 434–435; Davis, *Decline of the Venetian nobility*, 18–19. As if to give force to this concern, the doge in 1403, Michele Steno, was the last of his family, which thus became extinct at his death in 1413. Marino Sanuto, *Le vite dei dogi*, R.I.S. 2, xxii, pt. 4, 42. I wish to thank Professor Frederic C. Lane for this reference. I shall refer to this edition of Sanuto as *Le Vite dei dogi*. References to the earlier edition (first cited above, n. 4) are to *Vite de' duchi*. I regret any confusion, and offer the explanation that the second edition does not include those sections cited earlier.

46. *Caresinis chronica*, 56: 'Summa ducalis providentia, considerans statum patriae notanter consistere in potentia felicis armatae, ut hostes, aut forti pugna, aut constanti obsidione vincantur, quamvis universi cives, a maiori usque minimum, alacriter forent dispositi vitam et bona exponere pro defensione patriae et propriae libertatis, tamen . . . statuit in consilio Sapientum Guerrae, 1379 . . . ut cives de promptis fierent promptiores, quod, adveniente tempore pacis, consiliarij Venetiarum et capita de xl^ta . . . tenerentur infra xv dies solenniter congregare Consilium Rogatorum et Additionis, ac Sapientum Guerrae, et in eo scrutinium celebrare, in quo quilibet de Consilio possit unum nominare, qui videatur dignus honore Maioris Consilij, probando electos singulos; et illi qui plures ballotas haberent, aggregentur Maiori Consilio cum heredibus suis'. According to the most liberal calculation as many as 147 patrician families might have died out between 1297 and 1379. The main source for this figure is Marino Sanuto's list of patrician families, which includes his dates for the extinction of those no longer extant in 1522, when he compiled the list. *Vite dei dogi*, 17–47. I am inclined to view this figure as inflated; see below, n. 49.

47. In 1319 the Great Council instituted the *Barbarella*, so named because each year, according to the act's provision, on 4th Dec. (St. Barbara's Day), the names of all young men whose eligibility for membership in the Great Council had been proven were put into a vessel. As many were withdrawn as there were vacant seats in the Council, although it is not clear how this latter figure was arrived at. The young men whose names were drawn were then permitted to assume their seats before the previous statutory age of 25. Moreover by this same act all 25-year-old sons of patricians – whose eligibility had been established – automatically took their seats in the Council. Muazzo, *Patritiorum*, f. 4rv. Early in 1320 (1319 *more veneto*) a further measure provided that if the Quarantia intended to present the names of candidates to the Great Council *de gratia* – by special privilege – they must do so before the mid-year elections to various governmental offices, an indication that the electors were desirous of more candidates. Ibid., f. 4v. On the Barbarella, see G. Maranini, *La costituzione di Venezia* . . . (Florence and Venice, 1931) 42 seq. For a description of its observance in the late *quattrocento*, see Marino Sanuto, *Cronachetta*, ed. R. Fulin (Venice, 1880) 220–222.

48. See Cessi, *Storia della Repubblica*, i, 271 seq. for a description of the system of offices

and councils over which the Great Council presided at the end of the thirteenth century. For a discussion of the evolution of the Council's authority during that century, see Merores, 'Der grosse Rat . . .', 35–42.

49. This and subsequent figures are based on systematic exploitation of systematic sources. However this one in particular is a sort of best guess. The criteria I have used most consistently in trying to determine whether a given family did or did not exist in the *trecento* are (1) official mention and (2) multiple mention. There is little doubt, for example, about the existence and patrician status of families mentioned in the mid-*trecento* lists of office holders in *Voci, Misti*, regs. 1 and 2. However the other two main sources, the lists of members of the Great Council during the years 1261–1297, printed in R. Cessi, ed., *Deliberazioni del Maggior Consiglio di Venezia*, Accademia Nazionale dei Lincei, Atti delle assemblee costituzionali italiane dal Medio Evo al 1831, ser. 3, section 1 (Bologna, 1950) i, 269–362; and the fiscal census or *estimo* of 1379, printed in Luzzatto, *I prestiti*, doc. 165, 138–195, are both Mss from centuries later than the subject matter with which they are concerned. Moreover, neither membership in the Great Council between 1261 and 1297 nor the presence of 'ser' before a name in the *estimo* of 1379 necessarily meant patrician status between 1300 and 1379 for a family. Hence I have tried to limit attribution of that status to families of whom there are multiple indications that they were patrician, considering indications of office holding activity in the following sources: F. Zago, ed., *Consiglio dei Dieci: deliberazioni miste, Registri I–II (1310–1324)*, Fonti per la storia di Venezia, Sez. I, Archivi pubblici (Venice 1962) and Ibid., *Registri III–IV (1325–1335)* . . . (Venice, 1968); A. Lombardo, ed., *Le deliberazioni del Consiglio dei XL della Repubblica di Venezia*, i, 1342–1344, Deputazione di Storia Patria per le Venezie, *Monumenti storici*, n.s., ix (Venice, 1957) ii; 1347–1350, *Mon. stor.*, n.s., xii (Venice, 1958); R. Cessi and P. Sambin, eds., *Le deliberazioni del Consiglio dei Rogati, serie 'Mixtorum'*, i, libri I–XIV, Dep. di Stor. Pat. per le Venezie, *Monumenti storici*, n.s., xv (Venice, 1960) and R. Cessi and M. Brunetti, eds., *Le deliberazioni del Consiglio dei Rogati, serie 'Mixtorum'*, vol. ii, libri xv–xvi, *Mon. stor.*, n.s., xvi (Venice, 1961).

In particular I have imposed the multiple-mention rule on the names mentioned by Marino Sanuto, *Le vite dei dogi*, 17–47, as belonging to families which became extinct during the *trecento*. Because of some errors of Sanuto (see, e.g., 47, n. 5) I have adopted only those names from his list which appear in other *trecento* sources.

50. Sources: Cessi, *Deliberazioni del Maggior Consiglio*, 269–362; Luzzatto, *I prestiti*, 138–195; *Voci, Misti*, regs. 1, 2, 3 (1383–1387); Sanuto, *Le vite*, 2nd ed., 17–47; A.S.V., *Misc. Cod.*, I, *Storia veneta*, 44, f. 1rv; B.M.V., ital. VII, 199 (8511). *Voci, Misti*, reg. 3, covering the 1380s, was used to verify the existence after 1379 of families encountered earlier in other sources. The two Mss, one from A.S.V., the other from B.M.V., give lists of men ennobled during the fourteenth century; these were used for Category 4. Again, Category 6 does not include the patricians ennobled in 1381 as a reward for their contributions to the defence against the Genoese, even though they are indicated as 'ser', along with pre-1381 patricians. The families in the various categories are listed in Appendix I, pp. 72–3.

51. The figure was arrived at by including all the families represented in the Great Council, 1293–1297 (Cessi, *Deliberazioni del Maggior Consiglio*, 341–362); all those mentioned as having been in the Great Council earlier in the century, but not in the 1290s, which then appeared again as patrician in the fourteenth century (Cessi, *Delib. Mag. Cons.*, 269–341; *Voci, Misti*, regs. 1, 2, 3; Luzzatto, *I prestiti*, 138–195); and, finally, all families represented in the Great Council between 1261 and 1284 and then mentioned by Sanuto as having become extinct in the fourteenth century (Cessi, loc. cit., Sanuto, *Le vite dei dogi*, 17–47).

52. These figures do not take into account the extinctions of the Pino and Tomado families, which Sanuto indicates occurred in 1388 and 1383, respectively (*Le vite*, 39, 44). Sanuto's dates are often incorrect; I attribute this to a tendency on his part to cite the

date of the last mention of a family in the documents he consulted, even though this date may have preceded the death of the last of the line by some years. As an example, he unaccountably indicates the year 1407 as the date of the Steno family's extinction, even though Michele Steno continued as doge till 1413. Ibid., 42: 'Sten ... manchò per misier Michiel Sten, doxe – 1407.'

53. This seems borne out by the examples of the 16 families represented in the Great Council in the 1290s and in the *Voci, Misti* registers for the 1350s and/or 1360s, but then apparently extinct by 1379. Their representation in the lists of office holders in the mid-*trecento* is sparse: 11 of them had only one individual in office; two had two males representing them, but of these one of the families sent only one member to office in the 1360s and the other sent no members in the 1360s. The remaining three families each had three members among the office holders, but two of the families only had one representative in the 1360s, the other had two. In all 16 cases the male line seems to be dwindling in the 1360s.

54. Cessi, *Delib. Mag. Cons.*, 341–362.

55. Cessi, *Delib. Mag. Cons.*, 269–362.

56. The 12 families are: Ardizon, Belli, Betani, Briosso, Campolo, Carazacanevo, Gambarino, Maistrorso, Stati, Timodeo, Vasano, Vido: Sanuto, *Le vite*, 18, 22, 23, 25, 26, 31, 36, 42, 45. The discrepancy between the total of 207 families in the Great Council in the later thirteenth century and in the *trecento* patriciate indicated here and the figure of 210 reached by adding categories 1, 2, 3 in Table 1 is explained by the presence in Table 1 of three families, Boninsegna, Lion and Suriano, not represented in the Great Council lists but reported as having been among the fugitive families from Acre given membership in the Great Council upon their arrival in Venice in the 1290s. See Sanuto, *Le vite*, 23, 33, 41; also *Historia Iustiniano adiudicata*, 272–273, where all three families are mentioned, but only the Boninsegna and the Lion indicated as having come from Acre. The other families from Acre are all mentioned in the Great Council lists for the 1290s.

57. Merores, 'Der grosse Rat . . .', 90; Molmenti, *Storia*, i, 104; F. C. Lane, 'At the roots of republicanism' in *Venice and history* (Baltimore, 1966) 525.

58. The three from Acre; see above, n. 56; 12 others whose admission to the class is recorded in the early fourteenth century: Adoldo, Balestrieri, Dente, Pollini, Papacizza, Stornello, Dal Sol, Di Pigli, Da Verardo, Sclavo, Pianega, Guataro: A.S.V., *Misc. Cod.*, I, *Storia veneta*, 44, ff. 11v; B.M.V., ital., VII, 199 (1511), ff. 9–29.

59. Avonal, Balduin, De Renier, Guoro – all of whom were associated with patricians in business before 1300. R. Morozzo della Rocca and A. Lombardo, eds., *Documenti del commercio veneziano nei secoli XI–XIII*. Documenti e Studi per la Storia del Commercio e del Diritto Commerciale Italiano, XIX–XX, 2 vols. (Turin, 1940), i, 52, 138, 259; ii, 113.

60. Dalle Boccole, Da Mare, Diesolo, Ghezzo, Lambardo, Lanzolo, Onoradi, Gomberto: *Historia Iustiniano adiudicata*, 271–273. In thirteenth- and fourteenth-century documents the names 'Lambardo' and 'Lombardo' both appear. The chronicler Giustinian, cited above, mentions only the latter; thus there is some initial reason to suppose that these are two renderings of the same name. However Sanuto, *Le vite*, indicates that two distinct families were extant at the time he compiled his list in 1522 (32–33). I have thus included both in these calculations. (The Lombardo were represented in the Great Council in the 1290s; e.g., Cessi, *Delib. Mag. Cons.*, 351.)

61. Nicolò Arian was one of the officials supervizing the duty on wine in 1363 – *Voci, Misti*, reg. 2, f. 12 – even though Lazzarini, *Marino Faliero*, 250, notes that Antonio Arian, 'di antica e ricca famiglia', was a *popolano* so embittered by his family's exclusion from the Great Council at the time of the *Serrata* that in his will of 1361 he forbade his children to marry patrician spouses. There are two D'Anselmo referred to as 'ser' in the *estimo* of 1379 – Luzzatto, *I prestiti*, 155–156 – but most sources refer to the D'Anselmo as having been awarded noble status in the early *quattrocento*: *Misc. Cod.*, I, *Storia veneta*, 44, f. 2v; Sanuto, *Le vite*, 19. Finally, although the Dalla Fornase are among the 30

families admitted into the patriciate in 1381, the member of the family in Caresini's list (*Caresinis chronica*, 57) has a different given name than the Dalla Fornase mentioned as 'ser Jacomello' in the *estimo* of 1379 – Luzzatto, *I prestiti*, 174. Hence I am disinclined to exclude the latter from the pre-1381 patriciate.

62. See the reference above, n. 59; also Adoldo, Balestrieri, Suriano. Morozzo della Rocca-Lombardo, *Documenti del commercio*, i, 30, 326; ii, 327. Note that the Suriano family, indicated as one of the fugitive families from Acre, had had prior business connections in Venice.

63. Lion, Boninsegna; see above, n. 56.

64. *Caresinis chronica*, 57. The nobly named new patricians were: Paolo and Giacomello Trevisan, Antonio and Giovanni Darduin, Nicolò Polo, Francesco Girardo, Marco Pasqualigo da Candia, Nicolò Longo, Francesco de Mezzo, Paolo Nani, Nicolò Tagiapera, Nicolò de Renier, Alvise dalla Fornase.

65. See above, n. 44.

66. B.M.V., ital. VII, 199 (8511), f. 24v.

67. See the quotation from *Caresinis chronica*, above, n. 46. Ten of the families elevated in 1381 without patrician names appear in the *estimo* of 1379. If these families are added to the 156 patrician families in the *estimo*, making a total of 166, three of them would be among the wealthiest one-third of the class in terms of total family wealth (De'Garzoni would rank 14th, Zaccaria would rank 41st and Lippomano would rank 50th), and altogether seven of them would be in the wealthier half of the patriciate (Vendramin – 55th, Paruta and Stornado, tied for 56th, and Condulmer – 76th): Luzzatto, *I prestiti*, 138–195, passim.

68. A.S.V. *Misc. Cod.*, I, *Storica veneta*, 44, f. 1. See also Sanuto, *Vite de'duchi*, 1st ed., cols. 592–599.

69. Among the individuals whose entry into the patriciate between 1300 and 1379 is documented in *Misc. Cod.*, I, 44, f. 11v, are 11 whose names are the same as those of families represented in the Great Council between 1294 and 1297: Caotorta, Ferro, Agadi, Caroso, Gossoni, Mengolo, Quintavalle, Sesendolo, Donà, Moro, Barisan.

70. The 41 families in the Great Council in the 1260s, 1270s and/or 1280s which were not in the Council during the crucial years of the 1290s but which appeared again as patricians during the *trecento* fall into this category, even though there is no record of their being awarded patrician status. See above, p. 56.

71. See the lists in Sanuto, *Le vite*, 2nd ed., 48 seq., and esp 48, n. 6.

72. Pillinini, 'Marino Falier e la crisi', is particularly given to such locutions as '. . . Bertuccio Grimani e Bertuccio Falier, ad esempio . . .' (55); 'Il gruppo . . . è costituito fra gli altri da Giovanni Dolfin . . .' etc. (57); '. . . uomini come . . .' (67, 70). The names of the spokesmen for various policies are important, indeed crucial for the kind of analysis of legislative records that provides the basis of Pillinini's and Cessi's approach. However the relative degrees of strength of opposing sides in policy disputes cannot be conveyed by such references. Indications of intimacy or at least of frequency of association, of the kind to be found in notarial documents, must be adduced to acquire a picture of patterns of groupings within the patriciate.

73. The following observations scarcely scratch the surface of this complex problem, which is, however, as important as it is complex. In order to plumb a bit more deeply I am engaged in a detailed study of one patrician clan, the Morosini, from the late thirteenth to the early fifteenth century. For one dimension of the difficulties such a study involves, see the reconstruction of the Ghisi family's genealogy of R.-J. Loenertz, 'Généalogie des Ghisi, dynastes vénitiens (1207–1390) dans l'Archipel', *Orientalia Christiana Periodica*, xxviii (1962) 121–172, 322–335. My thanks to Professor David Jacoby for this reference.

74. For a description of the role of the *estimo*, and of the system of forced loans, or *prestiti*, in which it figured, during the War of Chioggia, see Luzzatto, *I prestiti*, cxxxiv

seq.; Cessi, 'La finanza veneziana al tempo della Guerra di Chioggia', passim; F. C. Lane, 'The funded debt of the Venetian Republic, 1262–1484', in *Venice and history*, 87–98.

75. All four families had been represented in the Great Council consistently throughout the period 1261–1297. See, for their representation in the 1261–1262 session, Cessi, *Delib. Mag. Cons.*, 269–271.

76. Luzzatto, *I prestiti*, 138–195. See also above, pp. 67–8.

77. The males that figure in these calculations are not necessarily adults, nor are they themselves necessarily *stimati* as individuals. I have simply counted all the males mentioned for each family in the *estimo*.

77a. In this discussion I use the word 'family' in the Venetian sense of 'house' (*casata*). In fact this terminology is vague. For a large family, such as the Morosini, the anthropological terms 'sib' or 'clan' seem more appropriate. See, for example, G. P. Murdock, *Social Structure* (New York–London, 1949), ch. 3–4. However to avoid going into this issue too deeply in the present study, I shall simply employ 'family' to mean a 'consanguineal kinship unit that may include a large number of households.

78. G. A. Cappellari Vivaro, *Il campidoglio veneto*, 4 vols., iii, B.M.V., ital. VII, 17 (8306), ff. 117 seq.; B. Bembo, *Cronaca (ossia origini) delle famiglie patrizie venete*, B.M.V., ital. VII, 14 (7418), ff. 203rv.

79. Sanuto, *Le vite*, 47–48, lists the families which had at least two different coats-of-arms and which had undergone changes of scutcheon during the centuries. See also *Historia Iustiniano adiudicata*, 255 seq. for the genealogical coincidence of distinct families in the early centuries of Venice.

80. According to Sanuto, the Donà dalle Rose branch was ennobled as late as 1311; the Da Molin with the golden windmill on their scutcheon had come to Venice from Acre. *Le vite*, 27, 34. Other branches of both families had been consistently represented in the Great Council from 1261–1297.

81. The Dandolo, with 22 *stimati*, had an average estimate of 3,700 lire, a median estimate of 1,150 lire. The Corner: 29 *stimati*; average – 6,600 lire; median – 2,000 lire. The Giustinian: 30 *stimati*; average – 3,700; median – 3,000. The Malipiero: 10 *stimati*; average – 3,900; median – 2,000. Luzzatto, *I prestiti*, 138–195, passim.

82. Arimondo: average – 6,500 lire; median – 2,000 lire. Dalla Fornase: average – 2,750; median – 2,750. Zulian: average – 3,000; median – 2,800. Ibid.

83. Luzzatto estimates that the figures in the *estimo* corresponded to about one-fourth of the *stimati*'s total wealth. See *Storia economica di Venezia*, 141; also G. Luzzatto, 'Sull' attendibilità di alcune statistiche economiche medievali', in *Studi di storia economica veneziana*, 280–281.

84. See, on Florence, G. A. Brucker, *Florentine politics and society, 1343–1378* (Princeton, 1962) 28–29; R. A. Goldthwaite, *Private wealth in Renaissance Florence* (Princeton, 1968) 258–59, and passim. The continued tendency of members of Florentine families to live in the same quarter of the city in the fifteenth century can be seen by a glance at the 'Appendices' in N. Rubinstein, *The government of Florence under the Medici (1434–1494)* (Oxford, 1966) 236–315, which list, by quarter, the members of various Florentine councils during that century.

85. F. C. Lane, 'Family partnerships and joint ventures in the Venetian Republic', in *Venice and history*, 36–55; also his *Andrea Barbarigo, merchant of Venice, 1418–1449* (Baltimore, 1944) esp. ch. 1.

86. *Historia Iustiniano adiudicata*, 255–276; Sanuto, *Le vite*, 17–47. Although he makes distinctions among the branches of families, it is clear that Sanuto, writing in the early sixteenth century, conceives of patrician families as units whose cement spans branch lines. The same is true of such later antiquarian-genealogists as Cappellari, *Campidoglio*, and Marco Barbaro, *Arbori de'Patritii Veneti, Misc. Cod.*, I, *Storia veneta*, 21.

87. R. Predelli, ed., *I libri commemoriali della Repubblica di Venezia. A.S.V. regesti.* Deputazione Veneta di Storia Patria, *Monumenti storici*, ser. 1, vols. i, iii, vii, viii (Venice,

1876–1914) vii. Commenting on this uprising, the chronicler Caresini declared that the noble rebels '. . . demeruerunt a tam egregijs stirpibus appellari, quae semper produxerunt cives famosissimos', *Caresinis chronica*, 14. For an example of the way family ties could spano the eastern Mediterranean, see Loenertz, 'Généalogie des Ghisi', 126–143, which deals with one branch of the Ghisi.

88. The *quattrocento* chronicler, Giorgio Dolfin, relates that when, in 1412, the Senate established a special council to oversee the war then going on with Hungary, it was specifically noted that 'potesseno esser 4 per chaxada' on the council, *Cronaca di Giorgio Dolfin*, B.M.V., ital. VII, 794 (8503), f. 284. The question of degrees to which such restrictions extended is a thorny one. See, in the context of the thirteenth-century Great Council, the observations of Merores, 'Der grosse Rat . . .', 60–61.

89. Both Michele's and Giovanni's estimates are in Luzzatto, *I prestiti*, 145. For the genealogy of Michele's family, see Barbaro, *Arbori*, v. f. 339. Giovanni's wealth by the 1390s is documented in the account book of his estate: A.S.V., *Procuratori di S. Marco, Commissarie miste*, B. 2.

90. Giovanni di Michele's residence in S. Cassan is mentioned in Barbaro, *Arbori*, *v*, f. 339; Giovanni di Piero di Giovanni's in S. Salvador, in ibid., f. 346. Andrea di Giovanni is mentioned as living in S. Giovanni Laterano – which is also in Castello – in *Voci*, *Misti*, reg. 4, f. 105v.

91. The genealogy of these Morosini is in Barbaro, *Arbori*, v, f. 293. Their estimates are in Luzzatto, *I prestiti*, 142.

92. The palace at S. Giovanni Grisostomo, which looks out on the old Fondaco dei Tedeschi, now Venice's central post office, was built by the three men's father, Marino di Giovanni. Most of this information is to be found in wills. The will of the father, Marino di Giovanni, dated 1369, is in Museo Civico-Correr (Venice), MSS Michiel, P.D., cod. 1268. Domenico di Marino's will, dated 1387, is in A.S.V., Archivio Notarile, *Testamenti*, B. 1255, notary Pietro Zane, f. 12v–13v. Giovanni di Marino's, written in 1397, is in ibid., B. 571, notary Giorgio Gibellino, no. 106. Renier's and Bernardo's estimates are in Luzzatto, *I prestiti*, 142.

93. Both the Great Council's list and the *estimo* indicate the *sestiere* and parish of each individual on them.

94. '. . . perpetuo remaneat in cha mauroceno . . .', A.S.V., Notarile, *Testamenti*, B. 986, notary Francesco Rogeri, no. 110. Cardinal Piero's will is dated Aug. 3, 1450. The deposition of the moribund Naufosio is in A.S.V., *Signori di Notte al Criminal, Processi*, reg. 8, ff. 50–52.

95. These six are among the ' "grandi" della finanza' who, according to Pillinini, sought to take control of the government in the mid–*trecento*. 'Marino Falier e la crisi', 56–57.

96. On the source of the lists of Great Council members in the later thirteenth century, see Merores, 'Der grosse Rat . . .', 58, n. 34. On the source with the *estimo*, see M. Merores, 'Der venezianische Steuerkataster von 1379', *Vierteljahrschrift für Sozial- und Wirtschaftsgeschichte* xvi (1922) 415–416. The *Voci*, *Misti* registers are contemporary public records.

97. By the later thirteenth century the process by which the Great Council became the fount of all office holders was nearly complete. See Merores, 'Der grosse Rat . . .', 35–42. The *Voci*, *Misti* records contain the holders of nearly all – if not absolutely of all – the many offices in the Venetian governmental system, both internal and external, administrative, judicial and political.

98. The following families appear among the office holders in the 1360s (*Voci*, *Misti*, reg. 2) and in the 1380s (*Voci*, *Misti*, reg. 3), but not in the *estimo*: Balastro, Bocasso, Caroso, Coppo, D'Equilo, Davanzago, Dente, Dono, Erizzo, Gabriel, Gossoni, Lanzolo, Nicola, Pizzamano, Romano, Sagredo and Vielmo.

99. The general policy of the government was to restrict the volume of an individual's

international commercial activity to the level of the wealth at which he was assessed for forced loans. See Cessi, 'Officium de navigantibus', 23–25 and passim; Luzzatto, *Storia economica*, 123–126.

100. Source: Cessi, *Delib. Mag. Cons.*, 341–362. A similar procedure for 11 selected conciliar sessions of the 1260s ,1270s and 1280s reveals the same kind of concentration as appears in Table 2. Adding the councillors from these sessions to those of the 1290s, a total of 5,543 members of the Great Council results. 237 families are represented among these councillors. (The difference between this figure and that of 244 indicated above, p. 56, as representing the Great Council families 1261–1297 is made up of families which did not appear in the sample sessions analysed here.) Analysis reveals that 43 families (25.9%) contributed 3,780 (66.4%) of the 5,543 councillors. Moreover 36 of these families are also among Groups 1 and 2 in Table 2. This indicates a considerable measure of consistency throughout the later thirteenth century. Ibid., 269–362, passim.

101. Sources: *Voci, Misti*, reg. 1, ff. 1–62; reg. 2, ff. 1–39. For a brief discussion of the various offices and their functions, see Cessi, *Storia della Repubblica*, i, 271–275. A more extended treatment is Maranini, *Costituzione dopo la Serrata*. See also the extended extract from the *Historia del Governo antico e presente della Repubblica di Venetia* of the seventeenth-century patrician G. A. Muazzo in Lombardo, 'Storia e ordinamenti', 662–688.

102. I have excluded from this analysis ten families indicated as noble in the *estimo* (men called 'ser') but clearly owing their patrician status to the act of 1381, after the *estimo* had been drawn up. I have also subtracted their estimates from the total figures.

103. These 67 families include all families which were among the first 43 of the Great Council families of the 1290s, among the first 43 families of important office holders in the 1350s–1360s and/or among the first 45 in terms of total family wealth in the 1379 estimate. See Appendix II, for a schematic list of these 67 families.

104. The correlation might even be higher were we to know the other assets – cash, stocks of goods, foreign investments – of the estimated families. Logic suggests that the politically prominent families would be most likely to have diversified, internationally wide-ranging investments.

105. The following table illustrates this result. The seven categories are the same as in Table 5. The top one-third among families in the Great Council in the 1290s would be families 1–51 (14 families are tied for 52nd place). The top one-third among the important office holding families are families 1–50 (6 families are tied for 51st place). The top one-third of estimated families, in terms of total family estimates, are families 1–52.

Categories	No. and % of families
1	33 (49.3%)
2	4 (5.9%)
3	2 (3.0%)
4	8 (11.9%)
5	12 (17.9%)
6	3 (4.5%)
7	5 (7.5%)
	67 (100%)

106. The Lion were among the families inducted into the patriciate in the 1290s following their flight from Acre after its fall to the Mamelukes in 1291. Sanuto, *Le vite*, 20. Two others of the 67 leading families, the Cabriel and the Rosso, were not in the Great Council in the 1290s, but had been in it during the three preceding decades. See Cessi, *Delib. Mag. Cons.*, 270, 284.

107. The other three are the Lion, the Trevisan and the Bragadin. All three are absent from Groups 1 and 2 among the Great Council families of the 1290s. In the case of the

Lion this involved total absence from the Council (see preceding note). The other two were not far from the level of the families in Group 2 for the 1290s: the Trevisan ranked 66th, the Bragadin ranked 44th.

108. The 14 families are: Contarini, Corner, Da Molin, Dandolo, Dolfin, Falier, Giustinian, Gradenigo, Loredan, Michiel, Morosini, Querini, Soranzo and Venier.

109. That is, they held 379 (37.6%) of the Great Council seats in the 1290s; 562 (33%) of the important offices analysed in the 1350s and 1360s; 1,748,706 lire (45.2%) of the total patrician wealth in the *estimo*.

110. The families which shared the 44th–49th places all had six males in the *estimo*; the families which shared the 50th–67th places all had five. The 35 families mentioned here correspond to Categories 1 and 4 of Table 5.

111. It should be noted that of the 156 patrician families included in the *estimo*, four did not have any males. Thus the discrepancy between the two sets of figures in Table 6b, both dealing with the *estimo*.

112. For Alvise, *Voci, Misti*, reg. 2, ff. 14v, 33v. For Marco, *Voci, Misti*, reg. 1, ff. 13, 24v, 38.

113. The correspondence is illustrated in the following table:

	All office ranks		
Major Office ranks	*Families 1–50*	*Families 51–97*	*Families 98–172*
Families 1–50	46	4	—
Families 51–97	3	32	12
Families 98–153	1	10	45

114. On the office holding requirements that are a feature of the patrician experience in Venice from at least the twelfth century, see V. Lazzarini, 'Obbligo di assumere pubblici uffici nelle antiche leggi veneziane', in *Proprietà e feudi, offizi, garzoni, carcerati in antiche leggi veneziane. Saggi* (Rome, 1960) 49–60, reprinted from *A.V.*, xix (1936). More recently, D. E. Queller, 'The civic irresponsibility of the Venetian nobility', in D. Herlihy, et al., eds., *Economy, society, and government in medieval Italy. Essays in memory of Robert L. Reynolds* (Kent, Ohio, 1969) 223–235.

115. These ranks are from the list of holders of all offices. The families to which they correspond are: Contarini, Loredan, Soranzo, Trevisan, Vitturi, Barbo, Da Pesaro, Balastro, Darpino, Bernardo. *Voci, Misti*, reg. 1, f. 61.

116. In making these calculations I have used all the estimates of each family, not simply those for the males, since the total family wealth is at issue.

117. Despite Luzzatto's examples of such hardships as a result of the wartime exactions, it is not clear that they were of a permanent nature. The foremost example of a 'ruined' formerly wealthy patrician, that of Federico Corner, who was so reduced that he had to request permission from the government to delay his *prestiti* payments, is not completely convincing, since his son, Giovanni di Federico Corner was apparently able to put the family back on its feet within two decades. On Federico after the War of Chioggia and on the debilitated patricians generally, see Luzzatto, *I prestiti*, pp. cxliv seq. On the Corner recovery in the 1390s, see G. Luzzatto, 'Capitalismo coloniale nel Trecento', in *Studi di storia economica veneziana*, 122–123. Cracco seems to me to overstate the extent of the reversal of economic fortunes during the war, basing himself on these few examples of hardship cited by Luzzatto; see Cracco, *Società e stato*, 450–451.

118. M. A. Giustinian, attrib., *Distinzioni segrete*, B.M.V., ital. VII, 1531 (7638), ff. 1–3. See also above, n. 19, for the *case vecchie* and the principal *case nuove*, and below, Appendix II, for the first 35 families. It should be noted that the remaining nine families are also *case nuove*, by reason of their not being *case vecchie*.

119. According to Pillinini, the intransigents among the 35 included a Giustinian, a Memmo, a Gradenigo and a Zane. The moderates included a Lion, a Mocenigo, a

Bragadin and a Falier. The waverers included another Giustinian, a Corner, a Sanuto and a Morosini. 'Marino Falier e la crisi', 70–71.

120. '. . . il quarto [and last of the 'tempi' of the government's development] sarà nel mille quattrocento e cinquanta, nel qual tempo può dirsi che si formasse il presente Governo della Repubblica, poichè trattane la regolatione del Consiglio di Dieci, non si videro esentiali mutationi', printed in Lombardo, 'Storia e ordinamenti', 664. The third 'tempo' went up to the *Serrata*, in Muazzo's scheme.

121. See above, n. 44.

122. Cecchetti, 'I nobili e il popolo', 428–432.

123. See Lane, 'At the roots of republicanism', 524–526; Bouwsma, *Venice and the defense*, ch. 2; Fasoli, 'Nascita di un mito', passim.

III

DAVID HERLIHY

The Population of Verona
in the First Century of Venetian Rule*

Of all the disciplines which might be considered ancillary to history, the demography of past societies has attracted over the past generation perhaps the most intense interest, and has surely enjoyed the most remarkable growth. Through the skills developed by this servant science, historians now know better than they have ever known the human dimensions of the societies they study, and the changes – often extraordinarily violent – which those communities experienced at various epochs of their history. But the new discipline has achieved its most spectacular successes not so much in estimating aggregate populations of the past, but in investigating the humble but still vital events – the births, marriages and deaths – which ceaselessly shaped and reshaped the separate households and the total societies which they constituted. Today, the results of these novel inquiries exert an influence well beyond properly demographic or even economic concerns. The historian is now learning how and in what circumstances men and women married in the past, managed their homes, reared their children, aged, and met with death; he can therefore better appreciate how they lived, how they organized their institutions, and what they valued.

It is therefore appropriate in a collection of studies dedicated to Venice and Venetian civilization to include an essay on the demography of the city, or at least of the region she dominated economically and politically. Unfortunately, however, before the late sixteenth century, our data on the Venetian population are irreparably scattered and unreliable.[1] This dearth of knowledge is the more regrettable as Venice once must have possessed extraordinary documents. According to the Belgian demographic historian, Roger Mols, she was the first city in all western Europe to undertake comprehensive censuses of her people.[2]

As early as 978, perhaps in imitation of the Byzantines, Venice was compiling

* The author would like to express his gratitude to Dott. Giulio Sancassani, director of the State Archives of Verona, and to Prof. Egidio Rossini, for their generous help and guidance in working with the Veronese *estimi*. Computer time used in the analysis of the data was made available through a grant from the American National Science Foundation.

partial lists of her population.[3] Over the subsequent centuries the sources repeatedly allude to similar records, which named adults who did, could or should pay certain taxes, take certain oaths, or bear arms for the city. From the end of the thirteenth century, a specialized statistical office served the Venetian government, and collected for it data on the population both within the city and in overseas possessions. That office undertook an early, perhaps the first complete census of the city in 1338. This *anagrafe major*, as it was called, bore, perhaps significantly, a name of Greek or Byzantine derivation. Simultaneously, the Venetian government was developing its system of direct taxation, the *estimo*. Efficiency in taxation required that the city identify those among its citizens who could afford to pay, without ruining them or the economy. Liabilities as well as assets had to be considered, and prominent among a family's obligations, at Venice as in any society, were the children it supported. By the early fifteenth century, those responsible for setting the tax assessment were inquiring into the size and structure of households, in order to determine relative ability to pay. According to the regulations of the Venetian Senate, dated 1411, the tax assessors (twelve 'wise' men, the *savi tassatori*) were to evaluate in *lire di grossi* all the movable possessions of the Venetian citizens, whether in cash, merchandise, precious metals or stones, and loans extended to the state.[4] Real property too was assessed on the basis of rent received, on the assumption that eleven lire of rent represented a capitalized value of 1,000 lire – a return of 9.9 per cent. However, the house inhabited by the taxpayer's family was not to be assessed. From the total value of the taxpayer's property, the assessors were to deduct 200 lire for every minor son, daughter, nephew, niece or grandchild, whom he was supporting.

These regulations bear close similarities with the later Florentine tax system, the *catasto*, first introduced in 1427.[5] Evidently Florence, together probably with other Italian cities, was learning from Venetian practice. But in spite of the energy and apparent skill with which the Venetians surveyed their own wealth and numbers, the archives of the city today preserve almost nothing of the results of their labours. Not even a partial census of Venice has survived until 1509, and even in that late year we have only a fragment, describing the total population of three of the city's six *sestieri*. Only from the late sixteenth century can we analyse with any detail or accuracy the composition by age or sex of the Venetian population.

Sadly then, it is easy to summarize what little is known of Venetian demographic development before the sixteenth century. In 1338, according to the *Chronicon Justiniani*, the men in the city able to bear arms, 'from twenty years through sixty years', numbered 30,000.[6] At nearly the same time (1336–38), according to the chronicler Giovanni Villani, Florence could marshal about 25,000 of its citizens able to bear arms, from a broader range of the population (between fifteen and seventy years of age).[7] To estimate the total population from these numbers of adult males, perhaps we can use the age distribution of an urban population, that of Florence in 1427, to determine our multipliers.[8]

If age distributions in all these populations were roughly equivalent, then Florence in 1336–38 would have had 89,000 persons (Villani himself says that the city had 90,000 mouths), and Venice would have claimed a population of 120,000. In 1338, she was probably also close to her peak medieval size, before the Black Death of 1347–48 decimated her numbers.

Unfortunately, we have not even a rough estimate of the tolls claimed by the plague and the disasters which followed it, but the population seems to have slid in the late fourteenth century to 100,000 or less.[9] Much later, the historian Marino Sanuto (d. 1536) published a string of statistics supposedly describing the population and resources of Venice in ca. 1422. He attributed to the city a population of 190,000 persons.[10] The most prominent of modern historians of Italy's population, Julius Beloch, rejected the figure as fanciful. It is larger than the number registered in any subsequent census, from 1509 until the twentieth century, and it does not correspond with Sanuto's own figures regarding grain consumption.[11] On the basis of the quantities of wheat needed to feed the urban population, Beloch calculated a population of about 84,000 for Venice in ca. 1422. But it was a growing city. In 1509 (still according to Beloch's estimates), it reached 102,000 and was still gaining rapidly. By 1563, it attained the highest figure ever recorded before the twentieth century – 168,627 persons. Thereafter, the city registers a slow, but also slowly accelerating, decline. When abundant records finally dispel the darkness surrounding Venice's demographic history, the *Serenissima* was already past her age of most rapid growth and most brilliant prosperity.

Daniele Beltrami has already catalogued the symptoms of demographic decadence which accompanied the city's economic and political decline.[12] The population grew older, passing from a median age of 30 years in the seventeenth century to 34 in the eighteenth. (At Florence in 1427, and at Verona in 1502, the median age was 22 years.)[13] Venice was having difficulty holding or attracting the young. From the middle seventeenth century the sex ratio also shifted in favour of women, as young men in search of furtune shunned the city. Those males who remained, married at an older age, and had fewer children. The balance of life tipped in favour of deaths over births. In sum, the city in its years of decline came to support proportionately larger numbers of women, the elderly, the economically inactive. The character of the population faithfully reflected Venice's stagnant economy and placed additional burdens upon it.

This then is the sketchy picture we possess of Venice's demographic history. After the population plunge accompanying and following the Black Death, the city entered a period of expansion, which seems to have been most rapid in the late fifteenth and early sixteenth centuries. Her rate of growth seems also to have been quite vigorous for the age. In 1336–38, for example, Venice was larger than Florence by perhaps a third. In 1562–63, she was 2.8 times the size of the Tuscan capital.[14]

What factors sustained this considerable expansion, and how did it affect the character of the Venetian population? Here, unfortunately, our sources fail us. But if we know little of the structure of the Venetian population in its period of most rapid growth, we are much better informed in regard to the neighbouring, smaller cities of the lower Lombard plain – Padua, Verona, Vicenza and Brescia. These cities in the early fifteenth century also became part of the Venetian territorial state. Of course, we could hardly contend that the demographic or economic history of the towns of the Venetian *terraferma* paralleled exactly the experiences of their capital. But it is difficult to conceive that the subject cities, tied so closely one to the others by geography, trade and government, could have followed radically different courses of growth or decline. On the contrary, demographic historians and geographers now stress that geographic regions tended in the Middle Ages to develop and maintain certain stable patterns of population distribution.[15] The regional populations were characteristically divided among a large metropolis which dominated the area, several secondary cities of moderate size, and numerous rural villages and hamlets. The communities tended to maintain a fairly stable balance among themselves, even when the total population was growing or declining.

If this concept of a regionally defined and reasonably stable pattern of settlement has any validity, then the experience of the smaller towns might help confirm or refute what our much sketchier evidence tells us concerning Venice itself. And even if the hypothesis of a stable balance in regional settlement is unacceptable, this much at least may be affirmed. The second cities of the Veneto were economically dependent upon the trade routes of which Venice was the hub, and their fortunes are a good indication of the levels of prosperity within the regional economy. So also, the demographic trends in the subject cities can show the social impact of Venetian rule, and the consequences following upon the establishment of the Venetian territorial state. To know Venice in the fifteenth and sixteenth centuries, we should do as the Venetians were doing in this their most brilliant epoch: we should pay close attention to the *terraferma*.

Two towns seem to have consistently rivalled each other for position as the second city of the Veneto – Padua and Verona. Padua, some twenty-five miles west of Venice and a Venetian dependency from 1405, possesses a census from 1320 and a tax survey (*estimo*) of 1430.[16] The city, in ca. 1300, seems to have had a population of 35-40,000, and it ruled a *contado* of perhaps 57,000 persons. It seems to have been probably a third the size of Venice, and roughly the size of Verona.[17]

Of all the cities of the Veneto, Verona seems to have preserved the richest series of demographic records. Like Padua, Verona was a Venetian dependency from 1405. On the Adige river seventy miles west of Venice, guarding the approaches to the Brenner pass, she has traditionally served as the gateway to Italy and has traditionally benefited from trade with Germany to the north. On topographical grounds Luigi Simeoni estimated that the city already possessed 10,000 inhabitants at the end of the eleventh century.[18] In 1254, in one of the largest communal oaths to survive from the thirteenth century,

6,464 Veronesi swore to uphold a treaty with Vicenza and Padua.[19] This suggests that Verona was larger than Pisa in 1228 (4,271 Pisans are registered in an oath of that year), or Pistoia and Bologna in 1219 (3,206 men from the former city and 2,187 from the latter then swore to maintain a treaty).[20] If we may assume that all adult males participated, Verona in 1254 would have had a population of 20–25,000 persons.[21] But the city was growing, and probably reached, like Padua, 35–40,000 inhabitants at the time it was enclosed by its third circle of medieval walls (1324–25). By then too, Verona was doubtlessly close to her maximum medieval size before the Black Death.

In the fifteenth century, our knowledge of Verona's population grows immeasurably richer. The State Archives of the city have preserved a series of twenty-four urban surveys (*estimi*), redacted between 1409 and 1635. No less than twelve of these *estimi* were drawn up within the first century of Venetian rule, and are dated 1409, 1418, 1425, 1433, 1443, 1447, 1456, 1465, 1473, 1482, 1492 and 1502.[22] These surveys list for each of the approximately fifty districts or *contrade* of the city the names of the household heads and their tax assessment, expressed in Veronese pounds.[23] In association with these *estimi*, the Archives have also preserved a series of census records used in their preparation. These are the *anagrafi* – a name apparently borrowed from Venetian usage.[24] Each *contrada* of the city had its own separate *anagrafi*; physically, they are contained in distinct fascicules or 'little books of mouths' (*libretti di bocche* or *descriptiones personarum*, as contemporaries called them).

To illustrate the character of these documents, the *estimo* of 1425 for the *contrada* of Avesa gives as the first name mentioned: 'Ansuixius bracentus Zampetri extimatus in novem solidi. lib. o sol. viiii den. o'. The *anagrafi* of this *contrada* have been preserved, and in them we find the same household described in detail:[25]

Ansuixio di Zuanpero bracento	agni xxxiiii	
Veronexa soa muiere	agni xxv	
Lorenço so fiolo	agni ii	mexi vi
Iachomo so fiolo	agni	mexi i
Dionixo fradelo del predito	agni xxvi	
Dona madre di scritti	agni lxv	

Unfortunately, many of the *anagrafi* have been lost, especially for the early surveys of the fifteenth century. The first surviving 'books of mouths' were drawn up in connection with the *estimo* of 1425. We have them for twelve of the forty-eight *contrade*, which contain 1,084 of the 3,386 households of the city (about one-third of the total). By 1502, *anagrafi* from thirty-three of fifty-one *contrade*, containing 4,126 out of 7,142 households (about 58 per cent), have reached us. Although we do not have complete 'descriptiones personarum' for any of these early *estimi*, nonetheless sufficient numbers have survived to give us a representative sample of the urban population.

David Herlihy

Recently, Amelio Tagliaferri has examined the economic development of Verona from 1409 to 1635 on the basis of six of these *estimi* (those of 1409, 1456, 1502, 1545, 1605 and 1635 respectively).[26] His study contains a wealth of information, both economic and demographic, and is now indispensable reading for scholars working in Veronese history or utilizing the fiscal archives of the city. But his treatment of demographic themes was intended as an introduction to Verona's economic history, and not as the object of his principal attention. His picture, therefore, especially of the fifteenth century, allows for some corrections and considerable additions. In estimating household size and the total population of Verona on the basis of the *estimo* of 1409, he assumed that the average household contained five persons. He did not consider the evidence offered by the earliest surviving *anagrafi*, those of 1425, which rather give a figure of 3.68 persons per household. He thus probably overestimated the city's population in 1409. At all events, he did not realize how small Verona had become by 1425, and he underestimated the dimensions of its subsequent growth in the later fifteenth century. And he did not attempt to consider changes in the age distribution or sex ratios of the population, or in the structure of its households.

Within the limits of a short study, we cannot ourselves attempt a truly systematic and exhaustive analysis of these rich documents, even for the fifteenth century. Rather, we shall try through samples to illustrate some of the remarkable changes occurring in the Veronese population during the first century of Venetian rule (1405–1502). While making use of the data already collected by Tagliaferri, we shall single out for special analysis the *estimi* and *anagrafi* of 1425 and 1502 respectively. For 1425, we shall include in our analysis all the surviving *anagrafi* from twelve *contrade* of the city (the names of the *contrade* are listed in Table 2). For 1502, we shall study eleven of thirty-three *contrade* from which *anagrafi* have survived. Ten of the eleven are the same *contrade* which we shall examine for 1425; the eleventh, San Vitale, is a *contrada* from which a fragmentary 'description of persons' has survived from the earlier year.[27] Our two samples, in other words, are drawn from substantially the same neighbourhoods of the city, and this should assure that the contrasts between the two groups reflect actual changes in the urban population and not the accidents of survival.

Information from the *estimi* and *anagrafi* were coded and punched on to cards, according to a format developed for the analysis of the Florentine *catasto* of 1427.[28] (For the past several years, the author has been collaborating with the *Centre de Recherches Historiques* at Paris to analyse the *catasto* by computer.) Fortunately, the Florentine *catasto* and the Veronese *estimi* and *anagrafi* are similar enough in character for methods of editing the data, and computer programs to analyse it, which were originally designed for the former document, to work with success when applied to the Veronese material. This of course permitted a considerable saving in time and effort.

The interpretation of our data from Verona still requires, however, some knowledge of the administrative procedures by which this information was collected, and this in turn makes necessary a brief consideration of the history of the Veronese *estimo*, or system of direct taxation. The oldest surviving statutes of the communal government, dated 1228, already allude to a system of direct taxation, which functioned both in the city and in the countryside.[29] Although the Statutes do not offer a detailed description of this *datia larium* or hearth tax, we can discern some of its prominent features. The city governmen imposed a total assessment upon both the rural villages and the urban *contrade* (called *waite* in the Statutes). The basis of the assessment was probably the number of households in the village or neighbourhood, with no consideration taken of relative wealth.[30] However, in subdividing the assessment among their own residents, the villages and the *contrade* seem to have been required to proceed on the basis of an *estimo*, that is, to distribute the tax burden according to relative wealth and ability to pay.[31] Certain groups were, however, exempt from the hearth tax – the nobles (called *gentiles homines*) and others who were maintaining horses for the communal army, and recent immigrants from outside the Veronese district who were granted an immunity for four years. The resident who believed that he had been excessively charged by his neighbours could appeal to the communal government, but was first required to pay according to his assessment. Residence in the city seems to have conferred a tax advantage, as the Statutes of 1228 require that those who moved from the countryside to the city still had to pay the tax in their rural homes for five years. No one, moreover, could be considered an urban resident unless he lived with his wife and family in the city for at least eight months of every year.

Unfortunately, the Statutes of 1228 do not say who precisely made the assessment, whether the assessors considered both fixed and movable assets, or whether deductions were allowed for the amount of debts or the number of dependents. Nor do the Statutes tell us how exactly the tax was imposed and collected. Presumably, the communal government imposed on the villages and *contrade* a flat charge per household, even though the total sum was then redistributed proportionately among the households according to ability to pay.

The more extensive Statutes of 1276 (with additions to 1323) describe in considerably more detail, if still not comprehensively, how the Veronese hearth tax functioned. Upon assuming office, the *podestà* was to undertake the redaction of a complete list of the households (*lares*) of the Veronese district.[32] Within each village, two to eight men, called *massarii*, were publicly to announce that all household heads, both men and women, were to appear before them for registration. Within the city, the same task was fulfilled by officials known as the *iurati guaitarum*. Those who did not declare themselves were to be deprived of all civil rights and placed outside the protection of the law. The *massarii* or *iurati* were then to draw up before a notary a list containing the names of all 'who maintain an independent household' (*qui stat per se in focolario*). Although the Statutes are not consistent on this point, the nobles and knights seem to have lost their exemptions in the late thirteenth century.[33] Even priests were to be taxed for their personal possessions, but doctors and troubadours (*ioculatores*),

G   97

for unaccountable reasons, were exempted from the hearth tax during part at least of this period.[34]

The *podestà* compiled the separate lists into two identical volumes, retained one himself, and delivered the other to the 'sacristy', presumably of the cathedral, which served as the government's archives and repository of important documents. Since the *podestà* had in his possession only a list of names and not an assessment of wealth, presumably the government was distributing tax assessments among its villages and *contrade* on the basis of their size alone. The volumes which this procedure produced must have been very similar to the oldest surviving survey we possess of a large rural area, the *Liber focorum* of the countryside of Pistoia.[35] Redacted probably about 1244, this Book of Hearths names the household heads for the entire rural population, but gives no indication of their relative wealth.

At Verona (and doubtlessly also at Pistoia), the duty of redacting a local *estimo*, and thus distributing the tax burden in proportion to relative wealth, was left to the *massarii* or *iurati*, and was in fact required of them.[36] These officials were to elect 'by ballot or by bean' (*ad brevia vel ad fabam*) six assessors, two from among the richer residents, two from the poorer, and two from those neither rich nor poor (in the contemporary terms, from the *maiores*, *minores* and *mezani*). Within ten days, these men were to assess all residents of their communities. They could demand from them a sworn statement of their 'properties, possessions and *iura*', the last term probably signifying credits. According to an addition of 1302, the *estimo* of a village or *contrada* could be changed only if it pleased a majority of its people and only with the permission of the *podestà*.[37]

The Statutes of 1276 still give no hint that the assessors were regularly considering the size or structure of households in order to determine ability to pay. But clearly, even at this early date, some kinds of demographic information were being collected. For example, the Statutes complain at length that some urban dwellers were fraudulently listing peasants as their personal servants, and thus removing them from the rural *estimi*.[38] To prevent this, the *podestà* was to summon all urban residents who maintained dependents in the countryside. They were to name them and swear that they were authentically servants. Clearly, the *podestà* had no 'lists of mouths' at his disposal, as he could have learned from them who were and were not servants. On the other hand, the government was already coming to consider the composition of households, in distributing the tax burden.

In 1324, in order to ring the city with its third circle of fortifications, Can Grande della Scala imposed a tax of 20 solidi (or one pound) per pound of assessment in the city, and 16 solidi per pound in the countryside.[39] In 1325, both city and countryside were taxed at the rate of 16 solidi per pound.[40] These impositions show beyond doubt that the government now not only possessed 'books of hearths' listing the heads of households; it also knew the total assessments of city and countryside, as it could not otherwise have estimated how much a particular tax rate would return. Almost certainly, the commune was now setting the sum of the assessment, and distributing it among its citizens. In 1332, as we have mentioned, the city was assigned an assessment of 6,000 pounds, which compared with a like assessment of 6,000 pounds for Padua, and 3,000 for Vicenza and Treviso – the other large cities of the Della Scala territories.[41] This suggests in turn that the government was exerting a much closer supervision over the assessment procedures, and perhaps had supplanted the local *massarii* and *iurati* in evaluating the wealth of each household. In 1409, according to the first surviving *estimo*, the city was supporting the same assessment of 6,000 pounds which it bore in 1332.[42] The tax system thus seems to have achieved a certain stability already at the time of Can Grande della Scala. But, unfortunately, the available sources tell us almost nothing about the development of the *estimo* in the fourteenth century; in particular, we do not know when precisely the redaction of the *anagrafi* became an integral part of the assessment procedures.

Apparently the earliest properly administrative record we possess relating to the direct tax system is a 'extimum terrarum et villarum districtus Verone', dated 13th May, 1397.[43] It gives the total assessments in pounds and solidi for 272 rural communes, grouped into seven regions. The total assessment of the district was only 376 pounds, 11 solidi and 6 denarii. Many within the population, however, were exempt from the tax, and the total assessment with exemptions deducted was 289 pounds 16 solidi 6 denarii, which compares with the 6,000 pounds borne by the city. The exiguous amount of the rural assessment, and the large number of exemptions allowed, suggest that the wars of the last years of Della Scala rule had massively devastated and depopulated the countryside.

When the Venetians assumed dominion over Verona in 1405, they made no immediate changes in the communal institutions. They named the chief officials, including the *podestà*, and frequently insisted that the commune pay subventions, extend loans, or support soldiers. But to meet these demands, Verona continued to rely on her established methods of taxation, including the *estimo*.

The first surviving *estimo*, as we have mentioned, is dated 1409, and it describes 4,020 households in forty-eight neighbourhoods or *contrade*. With the third *estimo* of 1425, we also have, for twelve *contrade*, the *anagrafi* describing the composition of the households. In redacting these documents, the commune seems to have followed traditional procedures. It set a figure of 6,000 pounds, which had to be distributed among the *contrade* and the households according to their relative wealth. In making this distribution, two operations had become clearly distinct by the early fifteenth century. It was first necessary to collect the relevant information concerning the wealth of the household and its obligations. On the basis of this information, a judgment then had to be made concerning the assessment which the household should bear.

In 1425, two *raxonerii* and a *iurato* in each *contrada* seem to have been responsible for collecting the needed information.[44] It is certain that they surveyed nearly everyone in their neighbourhood, even apparent paupers. The logic of the assessment was such that the paupers themselves could not be identified until all the information had been collected, and at all events every householder in the city was ultimately responsible for some assessment.[45] Exempt categories seem to have included only foreign mercenaries, Venetian officials, or foreign religious – provided they owned no property in the city. These surveyors collected in separate *libretti* information on the composition of the household (the *anagrafi*) and upon its possessions. Some few surviving fragments in Verona's fiscal archives contain lists of cattle owned or grain and other food products possessed.[46] Undoubtedly similar lists were prepared describing real property; none of these, however, seems to have survived.

These separate *libretti* were delivered to the communal government, and the second phase of the work, the actual assessment, could begin. The government selected a body of forty-five assessors (*aestimatores*), which was to include rich men, poor men, and those in between.[47] This body of forty-five was in turn divided into five commissions (*mude*) of nine members each. These commissions worked independently of one another, but considered the same data preserved in the *libretti*. The five commissions each calculated an assessment for every household in the city, on the basis of wealth, the weight of family responsibilities, and the age, health and skills of the household head. The government collected the five assessments, and at once excluded the lowest and the highest figures. It then took an average of the remaining three, and this figure was entered into the official and final copy of the *estimo*. To discourage litigation and perhaps also reprisals against the assessors, the *libretti*, with the exception only of the *anagrafi*, were probably systematically destroyed.

The Veronese *estimo* was considerably less sophisticated than the contemporary systems of tax assessment then functioning at Venice or Florence. Rather than relying on five separate assessments, these latter cities sought to calculate with rigour and precision the true worth of a family's patrimony. For example, they inventoried exactly all property owned and rents received; to determine the property's value, they capitalized the worth of the rent at a fixed rate (7 per cent at Florence). Florence at least made every effort to preserve the preparatory documents associated with the assessment, and this shows considerable confidence in the fairness and accuracy of the procedures. The Veronese *estimi* are thus much smaller and considerably less revealing than the *catasto* archives at Florence. In particular, they tell us almost nothing concerning the wealth of the household apart from its relative ability to pay; unlike the *catasto* they give no information on the value of merchandise held, business investments, loans to the government, or outstanding liabilities.

How good are the Veronese *anagrafi* as census records? In primitive censuses, it is usually possible to discern salient omissions from a consideration of the age pyramid. The group most likely to be under-reported are young children, especially girls. Table 1 shows the structure of the Veronese population in 1425 and 1502 respectively, according to age and sex. In neither census are there evident distortions. The largest age category in 1425 also contained the youngest persons (ages 0 to 4). In 1502, the largest category was the interval of ages 5 to 9, but because of the influx of young servants into the city, this is not an abnormal situation. The high sex ratio for the youngest years (122.0 in 1425 and 111.1 in 1502) does suggest an under-reporting of female babies, especially in the earlier census. But the distortion is not of major proportions. In sum, the *anagrafi* present a good picture of the numbers and approximate ages of the Veronese citizens. This undoubtedly reflects the character of the assessment system.

Table 1
THE DISTRIBUTION OF AGES AT VERONA, 1425 AND 1502

Age	1425			1502		
Interval	Men	Women	Perc. Total	Men	Women	Perc. Total
0–4	217	180	11.0	612	548	11.2
5–9	169	147	8.6	664	610	12.3
10–14	181	164	9.0	677	560	11.8
15–19	145	161	8.1	465	578	10.1
20–24	135	147	7.9	470	540	9.8
25–29	111	112	6.2	392	368	7.4
30–34	153	135	7.9	392	346	7.2
35–39	89	93	5.0	266	271	5.2
40–44	141	132	7.8	361	327	6.6
45–49	88	70	4.2	193	186	3.7
50–54	101	120	6.1	277	252	5.2
55–59	59	52	3.2	101	110	2.1
60–64	93	133	6.4	200	162	3.5
65–69	46	37	2.4	51	54	1.1
70–74	54	68	3.6	81	93	1.7
75–79	12	9	0.6	22	17	0.4
80–84	18	34	1.6	33	29	0.6
85–89	1	0	0.0	5	4	0.1
90–94	4	9	0.4	4	3	0.03
95–99	4	2	0.2	1	1	0.02
Totals	1,821	1,805		5,267	5,059	

Sources: twelve *contrade* of Verona in 1425, eleven in 1502. See names in Table 2.

Children and other dependents, such as the aged, conferred a tax advantage on the families which supported them, and the household heads had every reason to declare their numbers accurately.

One further feature of the Veronese *anagrafi* which render them of particular value is their registration of servants in the household which they served. In the Florentine *catasto*, on the other hand, servants were not considered members of their master's household; young servants were placed with their natural parents, who often were living in the countryside, and adults were considered household heads in their own right. At least as regards servants, the Veronese *anagrafi* give us a truer picture of the actual household than the otherwise much richer Florentine *catasto*.

How well did the people of Verona know their own ages? Many report them with a *circa*, and there is in nearly all censuses a tendency to avoid odd numbers not divisible by five, and to favour those ages which end in two, four, five, six, eight or zero. Demographers have devised a method for measuring this tendency to favour ages divisible by two or five. Under conditions of perfect reporting, those in the unpreferred ages (those ending in one, three, seven and nine) should constitute approximately 40 per cent of the population. We can calculate for any given census the number who should report these unpreferred ages (40 per cent of the total) and then count those who do report them. The ratio of observed numbers to estimated numbers (with 100.0 given for perfect reporting) gives us an index showing the amount of rounding present in the reporting of ages.

In 1425, the Veronese score a remarkably low 37.8.[48] This is much below the scores of such Tuscan cities in 1427 as Florence (62.0), Pistoia (54.4) or Arezzo (48.7), and is only slightly better than the score in 1427 of the rural population of Arezzo (35.7).[49] On the other hand, the Veronese greatly improved their score by 1502, as in the census of that year they attained the rating of 55.0.[50] As the accuracy of age reporting reflects the cultural level of the population, the Veronese by 1502 seem to have overcome the confusion and disarray which marked their community in 1425. As we shall presently see, there are other indications too that the city had experienced profound changes between the two censuses.

Particularly in 1425, many Veronese were guessing at their ages, or not reporting them precisely. But this distortion is largely characteristic of the older age levels, especially age 40 and beyond. Even with pronounced rounding, we can discern with confidence the relative importance of children, young adults and the aged within the population.

In Table 2, I have presented a comparison of our two populations on the basis of individual *contrade*. To estimate the population size of these *contrade* and then of the city, I have proceeded in the following way. I have counted for each *contrada* the number of households for which *anagrafi* have survived, and entered this number in the column labelled 'Complete Households' in the table. In the columns labelled 'Persons' I have given the number of persons named for these complete households in the *anagrafi*. The average household size was then calculated, and this figure was used to estimate the population of the incomplete households, for which we have no *anagrafi*. This estimate, added to the numbers actually listed by the *anagrafi*, gave us the estimated population for the *contrada*. The average household size calculated on the basis of all our complete households was used to estimate the total urban population. In 1502, however, rather

Table 2

The Growth of Veronese Contrade, 1425–1502

Contrade	1425					1502					Percentage Increase
	Households	Complete Households	Persons	Average Size	Estimated Population	Households	Complete Households	Persons	Average Size	Estimated Population	
S. Quirico	86	82	398	4.85	417	150	123	763	6.20	930	125
S. Cecilia	34	34	188	5.53	188	67	56	547	9.77	655	248
S. Agnese Foris	39	36	124	3.44	134	111	98	507	5.17	575	329
Torselle–Tomba	14	13	67	5.15	72	33	33	179	5.42	179	150
Ognisanti	125	125	397	3.18	397	227	216	1,194	5.53	1,255	215
Avesa	45	45	200	4.44	200	68	65	466	7.17	488	144
S. Stefano	145	137	480	3.50	508	287	257	1,537	5.98	1,717	238
Isola di Sopra	57	54	205	3.80	216	122	113	665	5.88	718	232
Isola di Sotto	105	98	426	4.35	456	143	126	802	6.37	910	101
S. Nazario	239	203	587	2.89	691	506	440	2,330	5.30	2,365	242
Totals	889	827	3,072	3.71	3,115	1,714	1,527	8,990	5.87	9,792	214
Chiavica	62	61	277	4.54	282						
S. Giorgio	133	131	406	3.10	412						
S. Vitale						362	302	1,684	5.58	2,018	
Totals	1,084	1,019	3,755	3.68	3,809	2,076	1,829	10,674	5.82	11,810	

Estimated population for city in 1425, 3,866 Households, 3.68 persons per Household, is 14,225.
Estimated population for city in 1502, 7,142 Households, 5.89 persons per Household, is 42,000.

than taking the figure of 5.87 which derives from our sample, I have used the slightly higher figure of 5.89, which represents, according to Tagliaferri, the average household size for all surviving *anagrafi* from thirty-three urban *contrade*.

Table 2 shows several remarkable changes in the urban population of Verona between 1425 and 1502. In the ten *contrade* from which we have *anagrafi* from both dates, the population seems to have increased by a substantial 214 per cent over these seventy-seven years. If these neighbourhoods are typical (and they represent a generous sampling of the city), then Verona must have tripled in size between the two dates.

Table 3 illustrates more precisely when this striking expansion seems to have occurred.

Table 3

AVERAGE ANNUAL GROWTH RATES AT VERONA, 1425–1502

	1409	*1425*	*1456*	*1502*
Households	4,020	3,866	4,078	7,142
Average Size	3.68	3.68	5.20	5.89
Estimated Population	14,800	14,225	20,800	42,000
Average Annual Change*	—	−0.24	+1.49	+2.28

* Simple average yearly increase in relation to total of previous census.

Source: Figures for 1456 are taken from Tagliaferri, *Economia veronese*, 44. Multiplier of 3.68 is based on the *anagrafi* of 1425, and used for the *estimo* of 1409.

If the estimates calculated in Table 3 are approximately correct, the population of Verona reached its lowest point at approximately 1425, but thereafter began to expand. The period of most rapid growth occurred after 1456, and strongly suggests that the Peace of Lodi (1454) and the political stability established by it were highly favourable to Verona's economic fortunes. The praise which historians such as Francesco Guicciardini bestowed on the prosperity of Italy before the French invasions (1494) seems well merited, if we may judge from Verona's experience.[51] At Verona and in the Veneto, peaceful and presumably prosperous times continued even after 1494, and lasted until the invasion of the Veneto provoked by the League of Cambrai (1509).

These records further give us the chance of observing how this growth was reflected in the separate movement of two basic variables: number of households and average household size. Initially, the expansion brought about not so much a growth in the number of households, but an increase in average household size. Between 1425 and 1456, average household size grew by 41 per cent (from 3.68 to 5.20 persons), and the number of households increased by only 5.5 per cent (from 3,866 to 4,078). But after 1456, the number of households, rather than average size, became the more dynamic variable. Households grew by 75.4 per cent between 1456 and 1502, but average size by only 13.5 per cent.

Although average household size grew less rapidly after 1456, nevertheless the Veronese household was much different in 1502 from what it had been in 1425. I have illustrated these contrasts through four graphs, drawn by computer. Graph 1 and Graph 2 show the distribution of households in the two censuses according to their size; they illustrate what percentage of households possessed only one person, what percentage only two, and so forth. Graphs 3 and 4 show for the same years where the population was living in terms of households, that is, what percentage of the people resided in households of only one person, what percentage in households of two persons, and so on.

The most apparent contrast between the two censuses is the startling increase in the numbers of large households, and in the percentage of the urban population residing in them. With an average of only 3.68 persons, the Veronese household of 1425 was quite small, but it is worth noting that minute size seems characteristic of all Italian households of which we have records from the same epoch. The average size of households at the city of Florence in 1427 was only 3.8; at Arezzo in the same year, 3.5; at Pistoia, 3.6; and at Prato, 3.7.[52] At Bologna in 1395, the household was again only 3.5 persons on the average.[53] The distribution of households according to number of members seems to show a similar pattern in all these cities. At Verona in 1425, Arezzo in 1427, or Bologna in 1395, the most common household consisted of only two persons, and in all these cities households of this sort comprised approximately 30 per cent of the total (27 per cent at Verona, 28 per cent at Arezzo, 30 per cent at Bologna). As Graph 3 further shows, in 1425 households of only three members contained the largest single group of the population – 18 per cent.

By 1502, this pattern had almost completely changed at Verona. Households with two members fell from nearly 30 to only 10 per cent of the total. Huge households of twelve and more persons included 18 per cent of the population – the largest single group. Elsewhere in Italy too, there is a tendency for households to grow larger in the late fifteenth century, but historians have been slow to investigate the precise reasons for this fundamental social change.[54]

Did location or wealth affect the amount of this growth? Did rich households, for example, grow proportionately more in average size than in numbers, and poor households more in numbers than in average size? And how did the internal structure of the household change during this period of pronounced growth?

To the first question, the evidence from Verona points to a negative response: no, neither wealth nor location in a poorer or richer neighbourhood seems to have influenced the average growth in household size. We are able, with the aid of the computer, to investigate this problem with a certain statistical rigour. If richer households grew proportionately faster in size than the poorer, we would expect a stronger correlation between wealth and household size in 1502 than in 1425. One principal means by which statisticians investigate the relationship between variables is the product-moment correlation coefficient.[55] In this measure, a correlation of 1.0 represents absolute dependence of one variable

Graph 1

DISTRIBUTION OF HOUSEHOLDS ACCORDING TO
NUMBER OF PERSONS, 1425

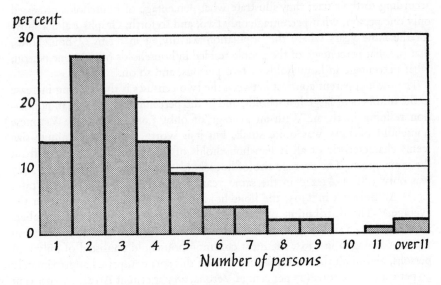

Graph 2

DISTRIBUTION OF POPULATION ACCORDING TO
NUMBER OF PERSONS, 1502

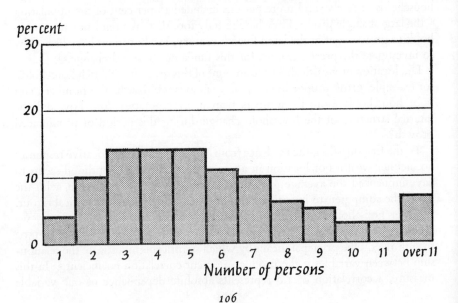

The Population of Verona in the First Century of Venetian Rule

Graph 3

DISTRIBUTION OF HOUSEHOLDS ACCORDING TO SIZE OF HOUSEHOLDS, 1425

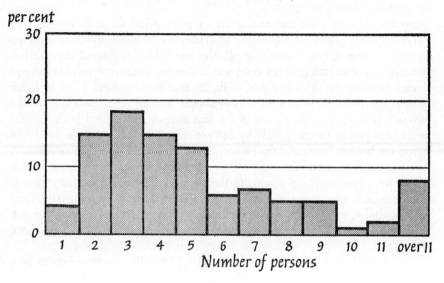

Graph 4

DISTRIBUTION OF POPULATION ACCORDING TO SIZE OF HOUSEHOLDS, 1502

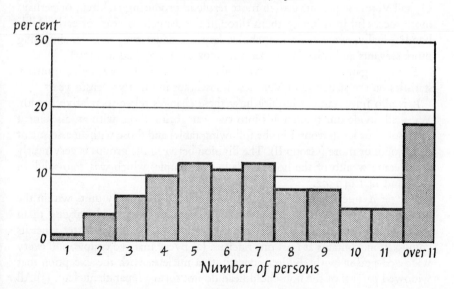

upon another, and 0.0 represents complete independence of one from the other. If we correlate wealth and household size in 1425, the resulting coefficient is 0.564 and in 1502 it is 0.575. In both years, the rich were maintaining perceptibly larger households than the poor, but the contrasts between them was no sharper in 1502 than it was in 1425.

So also, it is very difficult to discern a topographical factor influencing the increases whether in total population or in numbers of households or in average household size. Of our nine *contrade*, the one which registered the greatest increase in population (329 per cent) was S. Agnese, a suburban neighbourhood located outside the third circle of walls. Its average assessment of 16.26 solidi was nearly identical to that of all the sample *contrade* (16.61 solidi). But the *contrada* of S. Cecilia, the richest of the nine *contrade* and located in the central and oldest part of the city, grew by 248 per cent. The two islands in the Adige river, the Isola di Sopra and the Isola di Sotto, in spite of their close proximity, grew at quite different rates – the Isola di Sopra by 232 per cent and the Isola di Sotto by a modest 101 per cent. In these and in all the nine *contrade*, there is no perceptible pattern governing the increase in average size, relative to numbers of households, relative to gains in the total population. All households, the rich and the poor, were both bigger and more numerous in 1502 than they had been in 1425.

But were their internal structures changing? Here the answer seems to be a firm yes, and here wealth and social position did exert a marked influence.

In studying the changes in the internal structure of Veronese households, there are three factors which deserve principal attention. Was the growth in average household size to an important degree due to an increase in the number of joint or combined households, including more than a single married couple? Or had Veronese parents grown more fertile in producing children, or perhaps more successful in bringing them through the dangerous years of early childhood? Finally, were their households larger because they were maintaining more servants and other dependents in 1502 than they had in 1427?

To investigate such problems, we shall first present, in Table 4, some summary statistics on the structure of Veronese households in our two census years.

It is also important to inquire how these changes relate to relative wealth. We shall divide our households into two categories, those with an assessment of 16 solidi or less (Group I in the following table) and those with an assessment of 17 solidi or more (Group II). The division between the groups is very nearly the average wealth of the households in our sample, which was 16.6 solidi in 1425 and 14.1 in 1502.

The term 'nucleus' used in these tables refers to the family units within the household. These are not always readily discernible, and in identifying them we have followed these conventions: (1) Every household, no matter what its composition, contains at least one nucleus. (2) Every married couple, and every widowed person with children, constitute a nucleus, with the exception that widowed parents of the household head do not form a separate nucleus. (3) All

Table 4

THE STRUCTURE OF HOUSEHOLDS AT VERONA, 1425 AND 1502

	1425	1502
Households	1,084	2,076
Complete Households	1,019	1,829
Persons	3,755	10,674
Average household size	3.68	5.82
Number of nuclei	1,146	2,232
Average per household	1.12	1.22
Persons per nucleus	3.27	4.78
Number of households with only one nucleus	907	1,552
Per cent of total	89.0	84.8
Number of households with woman head	166	175
Per cent of total	16.2	9.6
Number of households with immigrant head	279	599
Per cent of total	26.6	28.9
Number of children, age 0–15	1,119	3,917
Average per household	1.10	2.15
Average per nucleus	0.97	1.85
Number of servants	313	1,311
Average per household	0.37	0.72
Per cent of population	7.00	12.3

Source: twelve *contrade* of Verona in 1425, eleven in 1502; ten *contrade* are the same for both years.

Table 5

WEALTH AND THE STRUCTURE OF VERONESE HOUSEHOLDS, 1425 AND 1502

	Group I		Group II	
	1425	1502	1425	1502
Complete households	830	1,607	189	222
Nuclei	908	1,880	238	339
Average per household	1.09	1.17	1.26	1.60
Children, age 0–15	652	3,226	467	691
Average per nucleus	0.72	1.72	1.96	2.05
Servants	80	491	233	820
Average per household	0.10	0.31	1.23	3.87
Children, age 0–4	273	977	124	182
Women, age 15–44	540	1,804	245	545
Ratio per woman	0.506	0.542	0.507	0.334
Married women, age 15–44	368	1,012	110	171
Ratio per married woman	0.742	0.964	1.013	1.062

Source: Same as Table 4.

single persons, or widowed persons without children, do not form a nucleus, unless they are identified as the head of the household.

As Table 4 illustrates, joint or combined households did not become significantly more numerous in 1502 from what they had been in 1425. In both years, the overwhelming majority of households (89.0 per cent in the earlier census and 84.8 in the later) included only a single nucleus. To the extent that combined households increased at all, that growth was limited to the richer part of the population, and was primarily due (although these tables do not show it) to the relatively greater number of married servants who lived within the home.

A factor of much greater weight in explaining the increase in average household size is the number of children the Veronese families were supporting. The average number of children, aged 0 to 15, per nucleus, which is nearly equivalent to the number of children per married couple, jumped from 0.97 in 1425 to 1.85 in 1502. But this substantial increase, approaching nearly 100 per cent, was not distributed evenly across all categories of wealth within the population. As shown in Table 5, the average number of children per nucleus more than doubled for the poorer levels of the population, but remained fairly constant, and high, for the richer. Evidently the poor were subject to much stronger fluctuations than the rich in their ability to breed, or to raise, children. We can illustrate this curious phenomenon by another means, through calculating both for 1425 and for 1502 the coefficient of correlation between wealth (as represented by the assessment figure) and the number of children aged 15 or under living in the households. From what we have already stated concerning the assessment procedures, it should be evident that such a correlation will necessarily be artificially lowered. The assessors considered the obligations of the household, including the number of children it was supporting, and lowered the assessment figure accordingly. In spite of this dampening influence, the correlation between assessment and number of children supported by the household remained high in 1425 – 0.434. But in 1502, that same coefficient of correlation drops to a very weak 0.199. Wealth, in other words, no longer was exerting as strong an influence over the number of children a family was supporting in 1502, as it had in 1425.

Unfortunately, the character of our documents does not allow us to judge the relative importance of fertility and infant mortality in determining the number of children in the households. One admittedly crude way of judging the relative fertility of women is through the 'child–woman ratio', which compares the number of children aged 0 to 4 in the population to women (sometimes only married women) of child-bearing age, often taken as 14 to 44. Table 5 gives these ratios, both for 1425 and 1502, both for all women of child-bearing age and for those who are married. The ratio is of course influenced not only by actual fertility, but also by the death of children before their fifth year and by the death of young women. In spite of these weaknesses as a measure of female fertility, it may have some value, at least for comparative purposes.

Perhaps the most spectacular shift evident in these ratios is the decline in the number of children per woman in the wealthier part of the population, but this is primarily due, as we shall presently see, to the multiplication of unmarried female servants within the household. We further note that for poorer, married women, the ratio shows a substantial increase, from 0.742 to 0.964. Here too, the assumption must be that poorer women had become in the interval between our censuses remarkably more successful in rearing children. Although the child–woman ratio offers no rigorous proof, it does appear that the birth-rate of the poor had improved across the seven decades. It would at all events be difficult to believe that infant mortality among the poor had declined so substantially in the closing years of the fifteenth century.

These Veronese censuses at least suggest some interesting conclusions concerning the influence exerted by wealth upon the number of children produced, or at least successfully reared, by Italian families of the Renaissance. In the Tuscan cities illuminated by the *catasto* of 1427, richer families unmistakably were rearing more children than the poorer, and this is true also for the city of Verona in 1425.[56] By 1502, at least at Verona, the poorer households came close to equalling the wealthy in the numbers of children they were supporting. At Verona, in other words, and presumably in other Italian areas, poorer households were much more sensitive than the wealthy to economic conditions and to the influence they exerted on family size. The children of the wealthy were almost equally numerous in the troubled economic times of ca. 1425, and in the high prosperity of ca. 1502. This does not mean that the wealthy in both periods were reproducing their numbers at equally high rates. But characteristically, they seem to have controlled their own fertility by limiting or delaying the marriage of their young. The poor, in contrast, by methods which are far from clear to us now, seem to have curtailed their own numbers by producing relatively fewer children within marriage, especially in periods of economic distress. This may appear entirely contrary to modern experience, but it seems to be the conclusion which at least at present best fits our data.

Thus, the great increase in average size of Verona's poorer households between 1425 and 1502 is primarily to be explained by the increased numbers of children they were supporting. But the wealthy households were also growing in average size, without any comparable increase in their numbers of children. To what is their growth primarily attributable? Table 4 already proposes an answer: between the two dates, the number of servants in the censuses increases substantially. Servants become more common even within the poorer households, but of course, it is among the rich that the increase is most evident. Again, we can investigate the relationship of wealth and number of household servants rather rigorously, through coefficients of correlation. In 1425, the correlation between the assessment and the number of servants was already high, 0.552. It is of course hardly surprising that the rich had more servants than the poor. But in 1502, the correlation grows even stronger, reaching 0.752. This means that the wealthy were supporting proportionately

David Herlihy

more servants in 1502 than they had in 1425, and by a substantial amount.

This proliferation of servants in the population (nearly 12 per cent of all Veronesi were in household service by 1502) further indicates, we would suggest, a change in the quality of life at Verona, among the wealthier classes. Families served by staffs of fifteen or more servants, unknown in 1425, were not uncommon by 1502.[57] The maintenance of such numbers of retainers must have required much larger houses and palaces. The servants performed many specialized services, and frequently included a tutor to train the children of the master.[58] The growth in household service inevitably meant that the rich were enjoying a more elegant, comfortable and perhaps refined life in 1502 than they had in 1425. In a traditional view, the Renaissance brought with it a new social affluence and a new graciousness in the arts of living. This formula, although often abused and justifiably attacked, seems to retain a certain validity when applied to social change at Verona in the late fifteenth century.

Table 6
SEX RATIOS AT VERONA, 1425 and 1502

	1425	1502
Ages 0–15		
Men	602	2,074
Women	517	1,851
Ratio	116.3	112.3
Ages 16–60		
Men	1,069	2,953
Women	1,119	2,990
Ratio	95.4	98.7
Ages 61 and over		
Men	150	240
Women	169	218
Ratio	88.2	110.0
Totals*		
Men	1,821	5,267
Women	1,805	5,059
Ratio	101.2	104.0

* Includes only persons of stated sex and age.

Source: same as Table 4.

There are several other changes which occurred between our two censuses, and which help fill out our picture of the interaction between demography, economics and, in some measure, culture at Verona. The city by 1502 had become relatively more attractive to men than to women. Table 6, which gives the sex ratios of the population according to age, illustrates this shift.

Fewer in the total population in 1502, women are even less in evidence as heads of households; the percentage of lady household heads declines from 16.2 per cent in 1425 to 9.6 in the later census, as shown in Table 4. In spite of the attractions of household service, the urban industries were drawing substantial numbers of men in 1502, and this again indicates a high level of prosperity. The percentage of household heads who are immigrants to the city also grows slightly from 26.6 to 28.9 between the two censuses, as Table 4 indicates. Although the shift in sex ratios is not of dramatic proportions, nevertheless the city by 1502 had come to include a larger proportion of economically active males.

Much more dramatic is the change in the average and median ages of the two populations, as Table 7 shows.

Table 7

AVERAGE AND MEDIAN AGES AT VERONA, 1425 AND 1502

	1425		1502	
	Men	*Women*	*Men*	*Women*
Average age	29.6	31.9	25.8	25.9
Median age	28	29	22	22

Verona's population was, on the average, younger by nearly five years in 1502 than it had been in 1425. The city's inability in the earlier period to hold or to attract the young is a further reflection of its economic plight. At Florence, for example, in 1427, the average age of males was 26.0 years and the median age was 22. Florentine women in the same year averaged 27.3 years of age, and similarly show a median age of 22. These are the characteristics of an industrially active population – the characteristics which Verona herself shows in the prosperous year of 1502.

Not only do the Veronese *anagrafi* offer us the chance to observe the reactions of a population to different economic conditions; but they also show us some more lasting customs of the city or of the region governing marriage and family life. One of the most influential of such customs is the usual age of marriage for men and women. At Florence, for example, in 1427 girls married very young (their average age at marriage was only 17.6 years), and they married men much older than themselves (by 13 years).[59] Those urban girls who did not marry by the age of 20 seem to have been consigned to convents. The society of the city was almost without unmarried women in their twenties, and it abounded with single young men. This affected, in numerous ways, urban society and culture. The large number of unmarried males offered a favourable milieu for the practice of prostitution and perhaps also for sodomy, for which the Tuscan towns were especially notorious. Within the household, Florentine mothers were young, and fathers quite advanced in years, when they welcomed their children into the world. Mothers in the Florentine census with babies less than a year show an average age of 26.5 years; new fathers were, on the average, 39.8 years old. This too affected the character of the domestic milieu, the training given Florentine children, and the values they absorbed.

Were such customs governing age of marriage exclusively Florentine or Tuscan, or were they characteristic of other Italian areas, including Verona? Table 8 summarizes some basic data concerning marriage at Verona from our two censuses.

At Verona in 1425, the average age difference between married couples, seven years, was considerable, but also considerably less than the thirteen years characteristic of Florence at the same epoch. Moreover, at Verona, girls married later, and men sooner, than at Florence. In the age category 18 to 22, 84.3 per cent of Florentine girls were already married, compared to 39.9 per cent at Verona in 1425. Half of Verona's men in the age category 23 to 27 were married, and only 23.1 at Florence. Single girls in their twenties were not as rare in Veronese households as they were at Florence, and unmarried young

Table 8
MARRIAGE AT VERONA, 1425 AND 1502

	1425		1502	
	Men	*Women*	*Men*	*Women*
Per cent married				
13–17 years	1.6	6.2	0.2	1.0
18–22	11.6	39.9	6.2	20.8
23–27	50.0	93.8	32.5	57.5
28–32	63.6	94.5	61.9	77.4
33–37	84.4	94.3	72.5	87.9
Average age of married persons	46.2	39.3	44.0	38.3
Average age difference between spouses	7.0		5.8	
Average age of new parents	37.7	28.5	35.9	30.4

Source: Same as Table 4.

men were not as numerous in urban society. So also, mothers of new babies at Verona were two years older than the Florentine, and the fathers two years younger.

These figures show some interesting changes in the census of 1502. The percentage of married persons at almost every age level falls, but this is primarily attributable to the greater numbers of household servants, most of whom remained single. Under favourable economic conditions, those men who did take a spouse married younger by probably two years (to judge from the drop in the average age of married men). Women married younger too, but the fall in age of marriage for males was more substantial. Age difference between the spouses declines to 5.8 years. The fathers of new babies were younger, but the mothers are older. This latter figure seems to reflect the heightened fertility of married women, especially in the poorer classes.

These statistics thus indicate wide differences in the domestic and social situations between Verona and Florence, and probably also between the Veneto and Tuscany. In age of marriage, age difference between the partners, age of parenthood, and so forth, the data from Verona do not show, even in 1425, the extreme values characteristic of Florence. This is not the place to explore at length the social and cultural implications of these figures, but they should be noted in our continuing investigations of the urban communities of Renaissance Italy.

We have so far considered what our two censuses show concerning the changes in Verona's population over the first century of Venetian rule. To complete our picture of this social change, we should also review what they say concerning the development of the urban economy over the same period. Tagliaferri, through studying the professions of household heads in the *estimi* of 1409, 1456 and 1502, has already pointed out some evident contrasts as well as continuities.[60] The principal industry, employing in its various operations about a third of the city's active population, was the manufacture of wool cloth, and its relative importance seems to have neither grown nor declined over the course of the fifteenth century. (An important speciality did, however, develop in the wool industry; this was the manufacture of woollen hats. In our own sample *contrade*, for example, the number of *birettai* who appear as head of households grow from 0 in 1425 to 32 in 1502.) The manufacture of other textiles – linen, cotton and silk – show a similar stability. The production of silk cloth, destined for great development in the sixteenth century, as yet shows no sign of its future growth.

Verona's prosperity, in other words, seems founded on the vigorous recovery of traditional trades rather than the introduction of entirely new industries. Nevertheless, there are some occupations which register substantial gains. The most important seems to have been household service, and the communal government also increased its staff. As we have mentioned, nearly 12 per cent of the population in our sample *contrade* – better than one out of ten people – were household servants in 1502. At the same time, still in our sample *contrade*, household heads employed by the commune grew from 11 to 56, and officials serving churches and hospitals increased from 3 to 16.

A second, clearly growing sector of the economy was trade and transport. The number of sailors in our *contrade* grew from 3 to 18, and porters from 10 to 39. Many of these are identified as *portitores vini*, and their presence in the *estimi* suggests that Verona was developing an important commerce involving her now famous wines from the Soave valley and the Valpolicella. This is perhaps indicated also by the expansion of coopers (*bottarii*) from 6 to 34 household heads between the two censuses. Professions serving a luxury market also register an increase. Goldsmiths gain from 6 to 11, and painters (many of them from Tuscany) move from 4 to 14. Teachers of letters, if we may put them in the same category, increase from 1 to 5, and many wealthy families were, as we have mentioned, maintaining private tutors for their children. Life for the rich does seem to have grown more comfortable in the late fifteenth century.

These then are the principal demographic and economic changes at Verona which our two surveys reveal during the first century of Venetian rule. After the destructive wars of the late fourteenth century, Verona entered a period of considerable demographic expansion, which was based on an equally vigorous economic recovery. It would seem a safe assumption that the remarkable prosperity of the late fifteenth century, so evident at Verona, touched the entire Veneto and its capital, Venice. It seems equally likely that, as our sparse evidence already indicates, Venice too was enjoying a strong demographic expansion in the same period. A city one-third larger than Florence in the early fourteenth century, surpassed in size the Tuscan capital by three times in the middle 1500s. At the same time, Venice was pre-empting much of the cultural leadership of the Renaissance, once exercised by the Florentines. Did servants at Venice, as at Verona, become distinctly more numerous over this century, and domestic and social life distinctly more elegant and more refined? Did Venetian society, like the Veronese, follow customs governing marriage and family life markedly different from the Florentine? The scanty evidence so far collected suggests here too an affirmative answer, but more research is needed to offer confirmation.[61] Still, one reason for studying small but well-illumined towns such as Verona is to learn the questions we should be asking concerning the great metropolitan centres of Renaissance Italy.

NOTES

1. The most extensive survey of the history of the Venetian population was substantially written 70 years ago by Karl Julius Beloch, *Bevölkerungsgeschichte Italiens*, iii: *Die Bevölkerung der Republik Venedig, des Herzogtums Mailand, Piemonts, Genuas, Corsicas und Sardiniens. Die gesamtbevölkerung Italiens* (Berlin, 1961), 1–68. The data therein contained essentially reflect the results of the author's earlier studies 'La popolazione di Venezia nei secoli XVI e XVII', *N.A.V.*, n.s. iii (1902) 5–49, and 'Bevölkerungsgeschichte der Republik Venedig', *Jahrbuch für Nationalökonomie und Statistik*, 3rd ser. xviii (1899) 1–49. Recently, the late Daniele Beltrami studied the population in considerably more detail than Beloch, but only from the late sixteenth century. See his *Storia della popolazione di Venezia dalla fine del secolo XVI alla caduta della Repubblica* (Collana Cà Foscari. Istituto di Storia Economica, i; Padua, 1954).

2. *Introduction à la démographie historique des villes d'Europe du XIVe au XVIIIe siècle*, i (Louvain, 1954) 18.

3. For a detailed history of Venetian demographic records, see especially Aldo Contento, 'Il censimento della popolazione sotto la repubblica veneta', *N.A.V.*, xix (1900) 179–240. Mols, *Démographie historique*, i, 19, discusses, with bibliography, the possible Byzantine origins of the Venetian census practices.

4. *R. Commissione per la pubblicazione dei documenti finanziari della Repubblica di Venezia. Serie Secundo. Bilanci generali*, i, pt. i, *Origini delle gravezze e dei dazi principali (976–1579)* (Venice, 1912) clxxvi.

5. The Florentines similarly exempted from the assessment the house which the tax-payer's family inhabited, and calculated the value of other properties on the basis of rents received, on the assumption that the rents represented 7 per cent of the land's value. They also allowed a deduction for residents of the city of 200 florins per family member. For the *catasto* regulations, see Otto Karmin, *La legge del Catasto fiorentino del 1427 (Testo, introduzione e note)* (Florence, 1906), and the analysis of the rural *catasti* by Elio Conti, *I catasti agrari della Repubblica fiorentina e il catasto particellare toscano* (La formazione della struttura agraria moderna nel contado fiorentino, iii, pt. i; Rome: Istituto storico italiano per il medioevo, 1966).

6. Cited by Beloch, *Bevölkerungsgeschichte*, iii, 3.

7. *Cronica di Giovanni Villani* (Florence: Magheri, 1823) vi, 184. 'Troviamo diligente-mente che in questi tempi avea in Firenze circa venticinquemila uomini da portare arme da quindici anni infino in settanta, tutti cittadini . . .'

8. Of 36,196 Florentines for whom ages are reported in the *catasto* of 1427, 10,570 were males between the ages of 20 and 60, and 11,614 were between the ages of 15 and 70 inclusive. The respective multipliers would thus be 3.38 for the former and 3.10 for the latter.

9. The plague, which struck Venice in 1347, is reported to have wiped out 50 noble familes. A partial *estimo*, including only household heads with an assessment of 300 pounds or more, has survived from 1379. It lists 2,170 households, of which 1,209 are noble and 919 are 'citizens'. In 1586, there were in the population 1,747 noble houses. Beloch, *Bevölkerungsgeschichte*, iii, 4, therefore concludes that the population in 1379 was about 100,000.

10. *Diarii*, viii, 414, cited by Beloch, *Bevölkerungsgeschichte*, iii, 5.

11. As late as 1906, the Venetian population was only 170,000. Sanuto further says that the city consumed 335,000 *staia* of wheat per year, which in Beloch's view would have fed less than half the population he claims was present.

12. *Popolazione*, cited in n. 1 above.

13. Ibid., 97. On the Venetian *terraferma*, the median age was 21.5 years in 1630, and 25 in 1780. For Verona's age structure, see below, Table 7. The Florentine data are taken from the *catasto* of 1427.

14. In 1562, the city of Florence contained according to the Medici census of that year 59,216 (Beloch, *Bevölkerungsgeschichte*, iii, 141).

15. See especially J. C. Russell, 'The metropolitan city region of the Middle Ages', *The Journal of Regional Science*, ii (1960) 55–70, and 'Thirteenth century Tuscany as a region', *Texas Agricultural and Industrial University Studies*, i (1968), especially the biblio-graphy on 43–44. For a geographic treatment of regions, see E. L. Ullman, *Readings in urban geography*, ed. H. M. Mayer and C. F. Kohn (Chicago, 1959). Russell goes so far as to affirm that the types of communities within the region consistently included approximately the same percentages of the population. (For example, in most regions, 1.5 per cent of the people lived in the metropolitan capital.) Given, however, the great varieties of regions, and the paucity of our knowledge concerning their populations in the Middle Ages, it is hard to judge the validity of this assumption.

16. On the dating and character of the urban census of 1320, see especially J. K. Hyde, *Padua in the age of Dante* (New York, 1966) 32–37. There has also survived a rural survey from 1281, listing the number of households in the Paduan *contado*. Gino Luzzatto, 'La popolazione del territorio padovano nel 1281', *N.A.V.*, n.s. iii (1902), 373–84, estimated that the 12,660 hearths in the survey contained a population of 63,000 persons, on the assumption of five persons per hearth, but Hyde favours the smaller multiplier of 4.5. For the *estimo* of 1430, see Beloch, *Bevölkerungsgeschichte*, i, 6–7. Mols, *Démographie*, iii, 5, gives a bibliography of the still not numerous studies devoted to the cities of the Venetian *terraferma*.

17. In 1332, under a *collecta* or direct tax imposed by the Della Scala of Verona, Padua

and Verona were each assessed 6,000 pounds. Since the *collecta* or *estimo* seems to have been based on numbers of households, as will presently be discussed, it is likely that the two cities were nearly equal in size. Vicenza and Treviso, which also formed part of the Della Scala domains, were each assessed 3,000 pounds. For the figures, see Hyde, *Padua*, 37, n. 1.

18. 'La popolazione di Verona alla fine del secolo XI', *Studi su Verona nel Medioevo*, i (Studi Storici Veronesi, 8–9; Verona, 1959) 35–39. Simeoni attempted to determine what *contrade* or districts of the city were settled and established in the late eleventh century, and then he attributed to them the population they possessed in the fifteenth century. Evidently, therefore, his estimate does not rest on especially firm foundations.

19. The full text of the oath is unfortunately still unpublished, and is contained on large parchments in the Archivio di Stato of Cremona, A.S.C. 1772–90 and 1793–94. The totals given here are taken from Simeoni, 'L'amministrazione del Distretto veronese sotto gli Scaligeri', *Studi su Verona* (Verona, 1959) 277. I am indebted to Prof. Egidio Rossini for calling my attention to this remarkable document.

20. For these oaths, see David Herlihy, *Medieval and Renaissance Pistoia. The social history of an Italian town, 1200–1430* (New Haven, 1967) 73.

21. If we use the multiplier of 3.4 based on the distribution of ages at Florence in 1427, the population of Verona would be 22,000. For the multiplier, see above, n. 8.

22. The *estimi* are now preserved in the Archivio di Stato of Verona (henceforth A.S.Ver.), *Antico Archivio del Comune di Verona* (henceforth, A.A. *Comune*), vols. 249–260. For a complete list of all the *estimi* through 1625, see Amelio Tagliaferri, *L' economia veronese secondo gli estimi dal 1409 al 1635* (Biblioteca della rivista Economia e Storia, 17; Milan, 1966) 20.

23. There are slight differences in the number of *contrade* from one survey to another. For the development of these *contrade*, see Egidio Rossini, 'Evoluzione dell' impianto contradale di Verona nei secoli XIII e XIV', *Atti e Memorie della Accademia di Agricoltura Scienze e Lettere di Verona*, ser. 6, xix (1967–68) 1–25.

24. The *anagrafi* are also preserved in the A.S.Ver., A.A. *Comune*, and in another deposit, the *Deputazione Provinciale di Verona* (henceforth, *Provinciale*).

25. A.S.Ver., A.A. *Comune*, 26.

26. *Economia*, cited in n. 22 above.

27. A.S.Ver., *Provinciale*, 773bis, containing only one folio and listing the members of only four out of 229 families. The data from this *contrada* for 1502 had been collected before the fragmentary nature of the comparable *anagrafi* of 1425 was realized. It seemed advantageous to retain the data in our sample from 1502, as this helped make the sample more representative of the entire urban population.

28. A code book describing the format of the data and the conventions followed in coding is available at the Social Science Data and Program Library Service of the Data and Computation Center, University of Wisconsin. The magnetic tape containing the data is also available to scholars at the same Center.

29. *Liber iuris civilis urbis Veronae . . . quem Wilielmus Calvus notarius anno domini MCCXXVIII scripsit*, ed. Bartolomeus Campagnola (Verona, 1728), especially chaps. 140, 190, 209 and 211.

30. According to the Statutes of 1276, the city government kept a record of the number of households and the names of the household heads for both the city and countryside, but had no information concerning their relative wealth (see below, n. 32). The only data, in other words, available to the government for setting the assessments were the number of households in the *contrade* and villages.

31. This seems implied by the *Liber iuris*, 163, which stipulates that the 'podere' or possessions of the taxpayer 'extimetur per illos de Waita illa, in qua habitant'. The later Statutes of 1276 are still more explicit. *Gli Statuti veronesi del 1276 colle correzioni e le aggiunte fino al 1323*, ed. Gino Sandri (Monumenti storici pubbl. dalla R. Deputazione di

Storia Patria per le Venezie, n.s. iii; Venice, 1940–59) i, 175, 'Ut omnis dacia ponatur per libram in villis'.

32. *Statuti del 1276*, ed. Sandri, i, 167, 'Ut omnes lares villarum districtus Verone scribantur et de dacia solvenda'. In a subsequent addition, the same requirement of listing all households was being applied to the city as well, that is, to the 'laribus guaytarum civitatis et burgorum Verone'.

33. Ibid., i, 224, provision dated 1276 requiring that the *gentiles* or nobles pay taxes with the rural villages or with the city. Those residing in the city had to 'eligere guaitam in qua stare voluerint et ibi se facere scribi in extimum et focolariis'. This particular provision was later cancelled, but in the numerous if scattered references to the *estimo* from the early fourteenth century there is no evidence that these exemptions were being respected.

34. Ibid., i, 176, stipulating that the clergy were to be taxed for their own but not for the Church's possessions; ibid., i, 189–90, for exemptions of doctors and *ioculatores*.

35. *Liber focorum districtus Pistorii (a. 1226). Liber finium districtus Pistorii (a. 1255)*, ed. Q. Santoli (Fonti per la Storia d'Italia, 93; Rome, 1956). For the date of the *Liber focorum*, which Santoli makes too early, see Herlihy, *Pistila*, 59–61.

36. For what follows, see *Statuti del 1276*, ed. Sandri, ii, 42–45.

37. Ibid., i, 180.

38. Ibid., i, 173, and ii, 124.

39. *Chronicon veronense ab anno 1117 usque 1278 auctore Parisio de Cereta ab aliis vero continuatum ad annum 1375, R.I.S.*, viii (Milan, 1726) 644.

40. Ibid., 644. 'Et eo anno primo Iunii posita fuit datia in civitate et villis Veronae de XVI solidis per libram.'

41. Hyde, *Padua*, 37, n. 1. See above, n. 17.

42. The total assessment of the *estimo* of 1409 was 115,750 solidi, or very nearly 6,000 pounds (5,787.5 pounds). See Tagliaferri, *Economia*, 61, Table 14, for the totals of six *estimi*. Tagliaferri (p. 35) cites a regulation of 1442 which set 4,000 pounds (80,000 solidi) as the base figure for the city, but this is much below the totals of the six *estimi*. It appears therefore that the city must quickly have restored and rather consistently utilized the figure of 6,000 pounds as the tax base.

43. A.S.Ver., A.A. *Comune*, 247.

44. A.S.Ver., A.A. *Comune*, 26. 'De Avexa. Boche schrite e produte per Bernardo e per Berno di Avexa raxonerii de la dita chontrada e per Iacomo di Biaxio iurato.'

45. In 1409 and 1425 for example, the 'miserabiles' and 'nihil habentes' were still given an assessment, usually of 5 solidi for males and 2 solidi for widows. Tagliaferri, *Economia*, 27–40, discusses the methods by which the *estimi* were made and affirms the comprehensive character of the surveys, even for the poorest classes of the population.

46. For a 'Descriptio pecudum et agnellorum' of 1424–25, see A.S.Ver., A.A. *Comune*, 29, for the *contrada* of Torreselle-Tomba. For an inventory of 'grani e legumi', see ibid., 720, dated 1415, for the *contrada* of Mercato Nuovo.

47. Tagliaferri, *Economia*, 34–35.

48. At Verona in 1425, 549 out of 3,626 persons are reported in the unpreferred age categories.

49. For Arezzo and Pistoia, see Christiane Klapisch, 'Fiscalité et démographie en Toscane (1427–1430)', *Annales-Economies-Sociétés-Civilisations*, xxiv (1969) 1326. At Florence, 8,989 out of 36,235 persons who report their ages are in the unpreferred categories.

50. That is, 2,278 out of 10,326 persons for 11 *contrade* of the city.

51. Cf. Francesco Guicciardini, *Storia d'Italia*, ed. C. Panigada (Bari, 1929) i, 2.

52. See Klapisch, 'Fiscalité', 1330, for Florence, Arezzo and Pistoia. For Prato, see Enrico Fiumi, *Demografia, movimento urbanistico e classi sociali in Prato dall' età comunale ai tempi moderni* (Biblioteca storica toscana, 14; Florence, 1968) 111.

53. Paolo Montanari, *Documenti sulla popolazione di Bologna alla fine del trecento* (Fonti per la storia di Bologna, Testi, 1; Bologna, 1966) 6.

54. At Florence, for example, in the quarter of San Giovanni, the average household size was 3.7 persons in 1380, 4.6 in 1469–70, 6.4 in 1551, and 7.3 in 1561. Cf. Mols, *Démographie*, ii, 133. At Palermo, the average also gains from 4.9 in 1479 to 6.8 in 1591.

55. This measure of association was first devised by Karl Pearson, and mathematical explanations of its character are now common in introductory statistical texts. See, for example, Hubert M. Blalock, Jr. *Social Statistics* (New York, 1960) 285–301. In calculating the coefficients for the Veronese data, the logarithm of the assessment figure, rather than the figure itself, was used. This transformation is commonly used in social analysis in order to limit the influence of a few extreme values (in our case, the very few, but extremely wealthy families).

56. See my comments in 'Vieillir à Florence au Quattrocento', *Annales-Economies-Sociétés-Civilisations*, xxiv (1969) 1349–50.

57. For example, in the *contrada* of St. Cecilia, the household of Thomasius Milei had 18 servants in 1502; that of Iohannes Alexandri Peregrini had 17; that of Bernardus Hieronymi Salerni had 13; and so forth (A.S.Ver., *Provinciale*, 157).

58. Cf. A.S.Ver., *Provinciale*, 676, *contrada* of San Quirico, household of Cosemo Morando, 'Albertino pedante in casa anni 25'. Most of the servants are described as 'massarie' for women and 'famegi' for men, but other common names are 'gastaldi' (stewards of country estates, almost always married), 'donzeli', 'faxili a stabulo', 'famelio a la villa', and so forth.

59. For further comment, see Herlihy, 'Vieillir au Quattrocento', 1345–50.

60. *Economia*, 180–95.

61. Beltrami, *Popolazione*, 180, cites the figure of 28.8 as the average age of marriage for women at Venice in the eighteenth century. This is much older than the age of marriage for women in contemporary Florence, and suggests that quite divergent customs governed the arrangement of marriages in the two societies.

IV

MICHAEL MALLETT

Venice and its Condottieri, 1404-54

In May 1458 Bartolomeo Colleoni came to Venice to receive his baton as captain general of the Venetian army from the hands of the new doge, Pasquale Malipiero. He had already been captain general for three years but as his *condotta* had now been renewed and as Malipiero had only recently replaced Francesco Foscari, it was the moment for a double celebration. Colleoni had not been to Venice since he had returned to Venetian service in 1454; he had received the baton for the first time in the main square in Brescia from the hands of the *provveditori*, the senior Venetian nobles attached to the army. Now the installation of a new doge and the greeting of a relatively new captain general were the occasions for one of the more famous Venetian festivals of the century.[1]

Colleoni was met at Marghera by a fleet of boats including no less than three bucentaurs. He was escorted in great state down the whole length of the Grand Canal to the monastery of San Giorgio which was traditionally used as a sort of anteroom to St. Mark's and the doge's palace. On 24th May in a solemn ceremony in St. Mark's he received the baton, and there followed three days of jousts and tournaments in Piazza San Marco to mark the occasion. Tournaments were a traditional form of public spectacle in Venice, which may seem surprising for a merchant republic but perhaps tells us something about Venetian attitudes which is important to the theme of this essay. The installation of a new doge was usually accompanied by a tournament, as were moments of great national rejoicing for a victory.[2] On this occasion Colleoni had brought with him nearly all the commanders of the Venetian army, *condottieri* some of whom had joined Venetian service as much as twenty years earlier and who were now entering a fifth year of peace, since the Peace of Lodi and the end of the Milanese wars, in that service. Amongst those who followed Colleoni in the procession to St. Mark's, and who took part both in the individual jousting and in the great staged mock battle which concluded the festivities, were

Diotesalvi Lupi, a Venetian infantry commander for over thirty years, many of the Da Martinengo family linked to Colleoni by ties of marriage and to Venice by long habit of service, Bertoldo d'Este, the son of one of Venice's most faithful soldiers, Taddeo d'Este, and Carlo Fortebracci, Orso Orsini, Ludovico Malvezzi, Antonello della Corna and many others. These men represented a new phenomenon in Italian fifteenth-century warfare, the faithful *condottiere*; Colleoni, although he had twice spectacularly abandoned Venetian service, was, with his forty-four years spent in that service, a part of this phenomenon. He also represented a distinguished succession of captain generals who had led the Venetian armies in the first half of the fifteenth century and whose status had changed considerably during that period. Finally the jousting and the Ventian interest in it represents in a symbolic way Venice's attitude towards and involvement with her soldiers. These are the three themes which I want to develop in this essay; the long serving *condottieri*, the role of the captain general, and Venice's dealings with both.

The beginning of the fifteenth century did not mark a dramatic turning point in Venetian military history any more than it brought a sudden interest in and commitment to mainland Italy. Venice had made use of mercenary commanders, both foreign and Italian, in her occasional fourteenth-century wars on the mainland, and also in her empire overseas. Pietro de' Rossi had commanded the large joint Florentine–Venetian army against the Della Scala in the late 1330s. The war against the Carrara in 1372 had brought Rinieri del Guasco, Francesco degli Ordelaffi (who received a state funeral after his death in Venice) and Giberto da Correggio into Venetian service. Giberto was made a member of the Great Council as reward for his services. The War of Chioggia had brought fighting to Venice's own doorstep; mercenaries and mercenary captains became a common spectacle in the city, and one of them, Roberto da Recanati, was hanged between the columns for his treachery to the state. Another, Jacopo de' Cavalli, was elected to the Great Council and later laid to rest beneath an imposing funerary monument in SS. Giovanni e Paolo. Similarly in the empire several members of the Romagnol Brandolini family had given distinguished service, and the suppression of the revolt of Candia was entrusted to Luchino dal Verme with a mercenary army.

However the greater degree of Venetian involvement in Italian affairs and in mainland possessions after 1404, and particularly the long series of wars against Milan after 1425, led to a marked intensification of her military commitments, and brought the problems of the relationships between the *condottieri* and the Venetian state into the foreground of public debate.

During the period 1404–54 Venice was seriously at war for approximately twenty-five years.[3] At first the wars were intermittent. 1404–5 saw the overthrow of the Carrara and the occupation of Vicenza, Verona and Padua. Two campaigns against the Hungarians followed in 1411–12 and 1418–20. Then from 1426 to 1454 war with Milan was, if not continuous, certainly a continuous possibility. The frontier was gradually pushed westwards, creating an ever larger state to defend and an ever larger recruiting ground for soldiers. At the same time inevitably the army tended to increase in size. While the Carrara and the Hungarians had been fought with armies of around 10 to 12,000 men, the Milanese wars produced a steady increase in Venetian military strength.[4] The league of December 1425 with Florence committed Venice to maintaining an army of 8,000 cavalry and 3,000 infantry in time of war; but this was a minimum strength in the following years.[5] In 1439 Venice was reported to have 16,000 cavalry alone on her books, and in the following year this figure rose to 20,000. In 1447 and 1448 the strength of the army was estimated at about 17,000 in all, and between 1450 and 1454 it numbered around 20,000.[6]

What was of even greater significance than these numbers, which must be considered merely approximate, was the growing permanence of the army. Again the 1425 league had provided for peacetime forces of at least 3,000 cavalry, and the continuous tension of the succeeding years ensured that even during relatively long periods of truce the standing forces remained stronger than that. The league with Naples in 1450 bound Venice to maintain 6,000 cavalry and 4,000 infantry during times of peace.[7] But the emergence of a standing army was not just the result of the tensions of the post-1425 period; it had been a clear feature since the beginning of the century. Between 1405 and 1411 a permanent force of 1,500 cavalry was stationed in fortified camps near the main *terraferma* cities.[8] This was in addition to the numerous infantry garrisons and was commanded by a permanent captain, Taddeo dal Verme, who had proved his loyalty and effectiveness in the Paduan war. Between 1413 and 1418 Pandolfo Malatesta, who had successfully conducted the latter stages of the war against the Hungarians, was retained with the rank of captain general. This was partly a diplomatic measure, as Malatesta was lord of Brescia and as such served as a buffer between Venice and Milan. His *condotta* from Venice was theoretically for 1,000 lances *in aspetto*, but in practice while 600 of these lances were on call in Brescia, the remaining 400 were stationed in Verona on full pay commanded by Martino da Faenza.[9] Nor were these the only permanent cavalry forces employed by Venice during the five-year truce with the Hungarians. There were also a number of lesser *condottieri* stationed at various strategic points in the *terraferma*. Between 1421 and 1425 the permanent army was about 2,000 cavalry and the senior commander after the death of Filippo Arcelli in 1421 was Taddeo d'Este.[10] It was at this juncture that the Senate declared 'that it is always our policy to have good men available in both peace and war'. By early 1424, two years before Venice actually declared war on Milan, an intense build-up of military strength was in progress. A number of ex-Bracceschi *condottieri* were employed, and Guidantonio da Montefeltro was made captain general *in aspetto* after considerable discussion about which of the leading *condottieri* of the day should command Venice's army.[11]

It is the emergence of this permanent force which was the most significant feature of Venetian military history in the first half of the fifteenth century. Permanent forces were a solution to the problems of handling mercenary companies and maintaining political strength towards which all the major Italian states were moving, but Venice with its greater internal political unity seems to have led the way. At the same time the changes which were taking place dictated a steady reorientation of the traditional relationship between the state and its *condottieri*.[12]

The *condotta in aspetto* was the normal method of providing some sort of military defence for an Italian state in peacetime.[13] In that it did not demand the continuous presence of the *condottiere* and his troops such an arrangement was particularly suited to the growing numbers of independent *condottiere* rulers who had established bases for themselves in southern Lombardy, Emilia, Romagna and the Marches. Venice was particularly concerned to build up a clientele of such satellite states as a means of protecting her new frontiers. Ottobuono Terzo, Gabrino Fondulo and Pandolfo Malatesta in Parma, Cremona and Brescia respectively, the Este in Ferrara and the Gonzaga in Mantua, and the Malatesta and the Manfredi in the Romagna, were all tied to Venice by diplomatic, financial or military agreements. The *condotta in aspetto* was by no means the only device for creating this protective screen round the growing Venetian state. These *condottiere* princes tended to be included in Venice's alliances with the other major Italian states as confederates and 'adherents'; their diplomatic interests were tended by Venetian ambassadors; they received pensions, loans and sometimes direct military aid from Venice; Venice sent representatives and presents to their weddings and stood as godfather to their children. In 1412 when Pandolfo Malatesta came to fight for Venice against the Hungarians, Jacopo Soriano was sent to Brescia to govern the city in the absence of its lord.[14] In 1409 when Ottobuono Terzo was killed, a Venetian *provveditore* was sent to pay his troops and to protect the position of his children in Parma.[15]

Most of Venice's leading commanders in the first part of the century came from this group of *signori*. Malatesta de' Malatesti and Francesco Gonzaga fought in the Paduan war;[16] Pandolfo Malatesta succeeded Carlo Malatesta as captain general in 1412. Later Gianfrancesco Gonzaga commanded the Venetian army in Lombardy from 1432 to 1437, while first Niccolò d'Este and then Guidantonio Manfredi were 'lieutenants beyond the Po' between 1426 and 1434. In 1448 it was to Sigismondo Malatesta that Venice turned to retrieve her damaged fortunes after Caravaggio and the disgrace of Michele Attendolo.

However, the dramatic defection of Gianfrancesco Gonzaga in 1438 was a symptom of a changing relationship between Venice and the independent *condottiere* rulers.[17] Gonzaga's was a diplomatic volte-face rather than a military betrayal as his *condotta* had expired and he had for some months expressed his determination to leave Venetian service.[18] It was not only the result of growing distrust of him in Venice, but also a symptom of a realization on the part of the *signori* that as Venice became increasingly committed to mainland policies their independence under her aegis was likely to become threatened. The departure of Gonzaga to Milanese service was accompanied by a distinct cooling in relations between Niccolò d'Este and Venice, and by the gradual ousting of

Guidantonio Manfredi, who was encouraged to take service with Florence and was subsequently refused a *condotta* by Venice on the grounds of suspected ill-faith.[19]

Although the independent satellite ruler continued to be a factor in Venetian policy, particularly in the Romagna, his military role was increasingly being taken over by the long-serving *condottiere* totally attached to Venice. The existence of a group of 'Marcheschi' *condottieri* whose continuous service for Venice was in marked contrast to the normal pattern of relationships between *condottieri* and the Italian states has been often noted by military historians. But the full extent of this system, the number and the prestige of the men involved, together with the variety of ways in which they were tempted to remain in Venetian service are questions which have not been fully explored.

Some of these men were natives of the *terraferma* cities: such were Bianchino da Feltre who served Venice for at least eleven years between 1422 and 1433, and Ventura da Rovigo in the same period.[20] More significant was Alvise dal Verme, the Veronese noble who served Venice from 1425 until 1435 before becoming irked by the restrictions which permanent allegiance to Venice implied and departing to fight for Milan.[21] Also amongst this group, Cesare da Martinengo, a Bergamasco, is of particular interest.[22] He was already in Venetian service in 1430, was captured at Castel Bolognese in 1434 and for at least four years Venetian diplomacy intrigued for his release while his company was kept in being in Venetian service. Then, after periods of service with René of Anjou and Milan, he returned to spend his later years fighting under the banner of St. Mark from 1447 to 1452. The Da Martinengo family were closely connected with Colleoni who, as a Bergamasco and a man who spent most of his military career in Venetian service was the archetype of this group of soldiers. Two men who figured prominently amongst these local captains may have been Venetians; Bernardo Morosini had a *condotta* in both Hungarian wars and in 1426, and in the mid-1430s was commander of the mercenary garrison in Zara;[23] Michele Gritti fought at Castel Bolognese in 1434, had a *condotta* for 100 lances in 1437, was captured at Chiari in 1438, and after a period as a Milanese prisoner returned to Venetian service in the early 1440s.[24]

However, most of the *Marcheschi* were men who came into Venetian service from outside, proved their worth, and were subsequently given every encouragement to remain. A brief survey of the careers of some of these men will give an idea of the extent of this tendency.

The most striking example was Taddeo d'Este who first appeared in Venetian service in 1414.[25] He was much praised for his part in the fighting in Friuli and Istria against the Hungarians in 1419–20, and became senior Venetian commander on the death of Filippo Arcelli, his brother-in-law. Subsequently he fought at Maclodio (1427), Castel Bolognese (1434), Monte Lauro (1443) and Casalmaggiore (1446), and was the commander of the mercenary garrison in the siege of Brescia. He was twice captured by the Milanese and on each occasion his release was treated as a matter of urgent priority by Venice. In 1443 he was described as 'persona pratica, intelligentissima, et nobis fidatissima' and frequently commanded large detachments of the army although he never reached supreme command.[26] By 1448 when he was killed defending Mozzanica he had a *condotta* for 1,000 cavalry. His funeral in Brescia where he was regarded with deep respect and gratitude was said to have been attended by more people than had ever been seen at a funeral in the city.[27] His son Bertoldo continued to serve Venice both in Italy and overseas until he was killed at the siege of Corinth in 1463.[28]

A less distinguished but no less faithful soldier was Scariotto da Faenza who defended Cividale against the Hungarians in 1419. He fought at Maclodio and continued in Venetian service with repeated references to his outstanding loyalty until at least 1443.[29] In his case also his son, Giovantonio, continued to fight for Venice until the war of Ferrara.

Guido Rangoni, a Bolognese, joined Venetain service on the recommendation of Gattamelata in 1434. Four years later he declared that 'he was ready to live and die' in Venetian service and moved his wife and family to Padua where they were given a house and a pension.[30] Rangoni was a particularly useful man because of his Bolognese connections and in the 1440s he was frequently detached to protect Venetian interests in that city. He fought at Monte Lauro, Casalmaggiore and Caravaggio, and in 1454 was still in Venetian service with a *condotta* for 700 cavalry.

Two captains who joined Venice in the late 1430s were Cristoforo Mauruzzi da Tolentino and Giovanni de' Conti. Cristoforo da Tolentino, the son of Niccolò da Tolentino, had distinguished himself at Fiordimonte in 1435 and was already a *condottiere* of some standing and considerable ambitions when he was taken into Venetian service in 1437.[31] But despite rows with Venice over the inefficiency of his cavalry, and despite little increase in his *condotta* during the twenty years of his service, he remained faithful.[32] Giovanni de' Conti was described on different occasions as being both a good soldier and one of the most licentious and violent of Venice's captains.[33] In 1454, after at least fourteen years in Venetian service, his release from a Milanese prison was bought by Venice offering Colleoni's wife and daughter in exchange. He eventually left Venetian service about 1459 to join the papal army.

Then there were the 'Gatteschi', the companions of Gattamelata who entered Venetian service in 1434. Gattamelata himself was already an old man by this time but he remained faithful to Venice until his enforced retirement in 1440. His brother in arms, Brandolino Brandolini, retired in 1437, but Brandolino's son Tiberto, who was married to Gattamelata's beautiful daughter Polissena, served Venice from 1434 to 1452. He fought in all the major battles of the 1440s and is often thought to have been mainly responsible for the Venetian decision to attack at Caravaggio. By this time he had increased his *condotta* to 800 cavalry, but with little prospect of further advancement in Venetian service he turned to Milan in 1452.[34]

One of the reasons for the desertion of both Colleoni in 1451 and Tiberto

Brandolini in 1452 was Venice's decision to make Gentile da Leonessa supreme commander. Gentile de Leonessa was related by marriage to Gattamelata and had inherited command of his troops. This and his obvious fidelity, rather than any notable military achievements, seemed to give him the edge in Venetian eyes when in 1451 they were looking round for a captain general. He spent all his military career in Venetian service and was one of the very few who rose to supreme command in that service.[35]

The list of the *Marcheschi* does not end with these men; there were others who served Venice for continuous periods of ten years or more during the first half of the fifteenth century. Jacopo Catalano, Giovanni de' Malavolti, Piero della Testa, Piero Gianpaolo Orsini, Giovanni di Marino, Cavalcabò de' Cavalcabò, Carlo Fortebracci, Ludovico Malvezzi, and Guerriero da Marsciano were other examples of *condottieri* who received great encouragement to remain in Venetian service and who made up a core of permanent commanders.[36] Some spent all their lives in Venetian pay, being picked out by the *provveditori* when serving as squadron commanders under one of the established *condottieri* and offered their own *condotte*. On other occasions the son or relative of a *Marchesco* was encouraged to take over his father's company and continue a family tradition in Venetian service. Tiberto Brandolini, Bertoldo d'Este and Giovanantonio di Gattamelata were brought forward in this way.[37]

Nor were all the *Marcheschi* cavalry leaders; some of the most faithful soldiers whom Venice had were her infantry captains. Diotesalvi Lupi is the best known example, a man who rose from being an obscure captain of infantry in Carmagnola's company to governor general of Venetian infantry. He served Venice for over thirty years and was knighted by Michele Attendolo in the name of the Republic at the gates of Milan in 1447.[38] One of his predecessors as commander of the infantry was Quarantotto da Ripamortorio, who had been one of the first to enter Padua in 1405, fought with distinction in both the Hungarian wars, and was leading infantry captain in Carmagnola's army at Maclodio in 1427.[39]

How was this surprising degree of fidelity and permanence created by Venice when advancement in her service tended to be slow and when she was dealing with men notorious for their unscrupulousness and self-interest? That it was deliberate policy and not just a chance consequence of a long period of wars is suggested by a Senate statement in 1433: 'Quia factum gentium nostrarum est maximae importantiae et in eo procedendum cum matura deliberatione et maxime attento que infrascripti conductores non ut stipendiarii sed partialiter nobis serviverunt et honorem et statum nostrum sustinerunt . . .'[40] The advantages of service with Venice were not high rates of pay or possibilities of rapid advancement, but security, long-term contracts, and above all a series of rewards which linked the chosen *condottieri* to the state.

Niccolò Piccinino was reported to have said that he would like to serve Venice rather than Milan because the duke of Milan was mortal whereas Venice would never die,[41] and this feeling of permanence was reflected in the links which tied the captains to her. The most honorific yet in a certain sense the emptiest of the rewards used was election to the Great Council and inclusion in the ranks of the Venetian nobility. Of the forty foreigners elected to the Great Council between 1404 and 1454, thirteen were *condottieri* in Venetian service.[42] Most of the captain generals of the period were given this honour which was extended to their heirs. It was certainly not expected that the family so honoured would participate in political life, but it did place them under the protection of the state and this protection was frequently invoked even by *condottieri* and their families who had long since ceased effectively to serve Venice. Together with a seat on the Great Council frequently went the grant of a palace in Venice. Pandolfo Malatesta was given a palace on the Grand Canal near S. Eustachio in 1413, and this palace was subsequently awarded to Carmagnola after Malatesta's death.[43] Gianfrancesco Gonzaga was also rewarded with a palace in San Pantalon on the site of the present Ca' Foscari. After his desertion the palace was given to Francesco Sforza.[44] Alvise dal Verme had inherited a palace in Campo San Polo which after his defection was given to Gattamelata.[45] This policy of awarding palaces was again something of a formality as there is little evidence of any of these men being encouraged to make much use of them, while they were freely and extensively used by Venice to entertain important visitors. However, Malatesta's palace cost Venice 6,000 ducats, and Gonzaga's 6,500 when it was bought from the Giustiniani in 1430, so the gifts were something more than a formality in terms of cost to the state.

More immediately lucrative and, at least in theory, no less permanent were the pensions freely given by the Senate to faithful *condottieri*. It was sometimes the case that the pension was only paid for as long as the *condottiere* continued to serve Venice, but more usually it did not have this condition attached; indeed sometimes it was extended to heirs and successors in perpetuity. Many of the captains received rewards of this nature ranging from the pensions of 1,000 ducats a year given to men like Pandolfo Malatesta and Gattamelata to the 150 ducats a year offered to Diotesalvi Lupi in 1438. Sometimes cash was given in the form of a lump sum bonus for some particular feat of arms. Pensions were also given to the wives and families of *condottieri* if they took up residence within Venetian frontiers. The twenty ducats a month which Giovanni de' Conti's wife received when she came to live in Vicenza was a standard marriage allowance for Venetian *condottieri*. The wife of Cristoforo da Tolentino was in fact receiving two pensions in 1455, one in Treviso and one in Padua. This was an error which was quickly rectified, but it meant that for a time she was receiving 1800 *lire* a year in addition to her husband's *condotta*.[46]

The easiest way to confer an annual pension on a *condottiere* was by giving him estates which yielded the desired sum in income. Here Venice was at an advantage over the other Italian states in that the steady expansion of her frontiers in this period made available to the state a considerable number of estates of political opponents and rebels. These were often given or, in less deserving cases, sold to *condottieri*. In this way the soldier was not only given his reward, but was tied in a physical way to the state and encouraged to settle with his family within, and often close to, the frontiers. The most complete and effective form of this type of reward was the concession of a fief or, as it was picturesquely called, a 'nest'. By granting a position of semi-independence in, and legal jurisdiction over, a certain area Venice was satisfying to some extent the *condottiere* desire for a state. The formal obligations to the Republic of the feudatories were minimal and do not seem to have included an automatic commitment to fight; but the strategic placing of the main fiefs granted to *condottieri* ensured that they were readily available for service.

The degree of independence which a fief gave to a feudatory varied depending on the prestige of the *condottiere* and the extent to which Venice wished to reward him. A captain general's fief usually meant complete jurisdiction and the exemption of his fief from all taxes except the salt tax. In the lesser fiefs, however, criminal jurisdiction tended to remain in the hands of the nearest Venetian rectors, and in some cases the fief remained subject to the *estimo*. In all cases the feudatory had to swear not to harbour Venetian rebels, and to pay an annual tribute in wax candles to the basilica of St. Mark.[47]

The enfeoffing of Carmagnola with Chiari, Cesare da Martinengo with Orzi Vecchi, Piero Gianpaolo Orsini with Bariata, Gattamelata and Brandolini with Valmareno, and Michele Attendolo with Castelfranco were all early examples of a custom which reached its clearest expression in the position established by Colleoni at Malpaga. In 1451–2 Guido Rangoni, Cristoforo da Tolentino, Giovanni de' Conti and Gentile da Leonessa were all added to the list of feudatories in quick succession. One of the best known of the fiefs was that of Sanguinetto which was held successively by Carmagnola, Alvise dal Verme, and Gentile da Leonessa. Sanguinetto dominated an important frontier angle between Mantua and the Po and guarded the southeastern approaches to Verona, and so it was particularly important to ensure that it was in strong and faithful hands.[48] On the death of Gentile da Leonessa it remained with the *Gatteschi*, first with Bertoldo d'Este who had married one of Gentile's illegitimate daughters, and then with Antonio di Ranuccio, count of Marsciano, who was married to Todeschina, daughter of Gattamelata.[49]

With all these rewards, both of cash and estates, great care had to be taken to avoid creating jealousies amongst the *condottieri*. A reward was frequently accompanied by a request to the recipient to keep quiet about it, or the grant was sometimes postponed until the winter season when the army had been dispersed to quarters.

Nor was Venice's recognition of the services of her soldiers confined to their lifetimes, although there was certainly an element of restraint in the honours allowed to dead heroes. The state funeral accorded to Paolo Savelli and the great equestrian monument set up in his honour in the Frari were a little exceptional,[50] and it seems that both the more famous monuments to Gattamelata and Colleoni were commissioned by the families of the *condottieri*, although formally permitted by Venice.[51] Venice did however spend 250 ducats on Gattamelata's funeral, and generous provisions were made for the bereaved families of *condottieri* who died in Venetian service.

Inevitably this move towards a permanent military establishment had its effect on the *condotta* system normally used for mercenaries in fifteenth-century Italy. The common practice was for the state to issue *condotte* as needed for limited periods and for specific numbers of men. The duration of the *condotta* was divided into two periods: the *ferma* which was the initial period of service binding on both employer and *condottiere*, and the *ad beneplacitum* or *di rispetto* which was the subsequent period in which the employer had an option on the *condottiere*'s services. The *condottiere* had to be told a certain time before the end of the *ferma* whether he was required for the second half of the *condotta* or not. In the first years of the fifteenth century *condotte* were normally of short duration and a *ferma* of three months was very common. This made it possible to dispense with the services of the companies during the winter season when active campaigning was rare.

In this period the numerical strength called for by the *condotta* was always specified, and there was usually an elaborate system of inspections which could be enforced by the employer to ensure that these numbers were maintained. It was also usual for the rates of pay per lance to be stated in the contract, and the *condottiere* and his officers divided up a set proportion of the pay of the company, known as the *caposoldo*. The more senior *condottieri* could usually negotiate for themselves payment over and above the *caposoldo*, i.e. a *provvisione*, out of which they were expected to maintain a retinue of personal followers.

One of the great problems is to determine how *condottiere* troops actually were paid and what control the employing state had over the payment of individual soldiers. This short-term *condotta* system with its stipulations about rates of pay and frequent inspections implied a fairly close control, although it seems more likely that the paymasters paid the soldiers in squadrons rather than individually. However, in the fifteenth century a different system which allowed greater independence to the *condottiere* was becoming more common. The practice of giving *provvisioni*, which had originated as a means of conferring additional prestige on a commander-in-chief, gradually and inevitably spread downwards. At the same time pressure from the increasingly powerful *condottieri* coupled with protracted periods of war and the trend towards greater permanence in *condottiere* armies produced a tendency to make monthly payments only to the *condottieri* and leave them responsible for paying the troops. In such a situation the control of the state became eroded, inspections were less justifiable and less easy to enforce, rates of pay became less standardized.

The two pay systems seem to have existed side by side in the Venetian army in the fifteenth century. After 1450 it was usual for captain generals at least to be paid lump sums for their troops, but the development of this method was not just the result of the growing prestige of the *condottieri* or the pressure which they were able to exert on their civilian employers. It was one aspect of wider changes which were taking place in the *condotta* system with the emergence of permanent forces.

In 1419 Venice, with a group of trusted *condottieri* already forming and the Hungarian threat looming, chose to increase her forces not by seeking new *condottieri* but by offering an increase of *condotte* to the men already under contract.[52] This was a device which was used frequently during the 1420s and 1430s and served the practical purpose of avoiding taking on new and untried commanders as well as that of rewarding, and in a sense promoting, those already employed. It amounted to a change in the terms of the original contract but the *condottieri* were unlikely to object until the process was reversed. This however was the inevitable corollary of the system; when peace was signed Venice insisted on a proportional decrease in all the *condotte*. But as some of the less satisfactory *condottieri* would be paid off altogether, the others usually allowed themselves to be persuaded that they were lucky to be retained in service at all and accepted this fluctuating system. In 1433 there was the most striking example of how the system worked. Peace with Milan was signed on 26th April, and early in June the Senate decreed a reduction of forces by over half to 5,000 cavalry.[53] It followed this up by deciding on a list of the most trusted and useful *condottieri* who were to be retained with their companies reduced to half strength.[54] In the event this was too great a reduction for the *condottieri* to suffer passively and their outspoken resentment caused the Senate to revise its figures and allow them two-thirds of their original companies.[55] In fact it was clear that so arbitrary a system was not a satisfactory solution to the problem, and by the early 1440s the fluctuations in size between the wartime army and the peacetime army had been formalized by the introduction of a new type of *condotta* which laid down from the outset two numerical strengths for the company. Guido Rangoni's new *condotta* in 1441 was one of the first in which the new formula was used; his *condotta* was to be for 700 cavalry in time of war and 500 in time of peace.[56] At the same time throughout this period the lengths of the *condotte* were being extended. By the 1440s one or even two years was the usual length of the *ferma* for even the junior *condottieri*.

These changes in the nature of *condottiere* service clearly had their effect on the issues of state control and methods of pay. In February 1427 Carmagnola set out the two alternative systems of hiring troops in a letter to the Senate and strongly advised that the system of paying all the money to the *condottieri* themselves was preferable as it gave the *condottiere* a personal interest in seeing that he had good troops.[57] Carmagnola was implying here, and indeed stated elsewhere, that he wanted to see the end of inspections by the civilian officials as a corollary to the change in methods of pay, and this was a standard *condottiere* line of argument. However, if the *condotta* contracts themselves are any guide, Venice seems to have adopted its new system spasmodically. Particular *condottieri* were occasionally given complete responsibility for the payment of their troops; as early as 1404 Malatesta de' Malatesti was specifically given this privilege, and there are indications that Gianfrancesco Gonzaga had it. However, the first *condotte* in which the total amount due to the whole company was expressed in a lump sum to be paid to the *condottiere* were those of Francesco Sforza as captain general of the league in the 1430s.[59] These were exceptional *condotte*, and the lump sum payment only appeared in Venetian contracts with that agreed with Jacopo Piccinino in 1450 when he was offered 90,000 ducats a year for 1,000 lances.[60] Colleoni in 1454 was offered 100,000 ducats a year for an 'appropriate' but unspecified number of troops and this was to be the standard form for most of the *condotte* of captain generals in the second half of the century.[61] Also in 1450 there were clear indications that all the *condottieri* were being paid lump sums for their companies but this may well have been because at that moment they were dispersed in quarters throughout Venetian territory.[62] By this time the main responsibility for paying the *condottieri* lay with the treasuries of the *terraferma* cities, and each company was allotted to a particular treasury.

It is clear that the growing habit of dispersing the army to quarters not just in winter but sometimes for two or three years inevitably had its effect on the way in which the army was controlled. In such a situation the type of *condotta* which gave a lump sum to the *condottiere* and left him to distribute it was more convenient and became more common. At the same time rates of pay became more flexible; there had always been a tendency to pay less in winter, but now Venice sought to impose special low rates in peacetime, and at one stage there was a move to cut rates in autumn when food supplies were cheaper.[63] It also became the practice to have different rates of pay for different parts of the *terraferma*; rates of pay in Friuli were lower than those in Verona or Brescia.

Another way in which permanent forces were changing the *condotta* system was in the matter of advances. It had always been the custom to give the *condottiere* an advance of two or three months' pay for his troops to enable him to meet the expenses of reaching his new employer. As this could sometimes mean marching the length of Italy the advance was necessary, and it was paid off by reducing the pay over the first few months of the contract. The extension of the lengths of contracts was making the advance less frequent, and at the same time Venice's permanent *condottieri* were finding themselves put to considerable expense at times of mobilization. They therefore began to demand advances during a contract period particularly in the spring before taking the field. Venice at first resisted these demands as being unjustified innovations, but by the 1440s it had again accepted that times had changed and that there were new circumstances in which advances at moments other than that of signing a contract were appropriate.[64]

Venice had clear regulations for the employment and the control of *condottieri*. These were laid down in fifty-six articles covering recruitment, lodgings, inspections, oaths to be sworn, protection of the civilian population, etc.[65] In order to ensure that the *condottieri* observed the regulations and paid fines for breaches of them, Venice insisted on financial guarantors being named by new *condottieri*, and even on occasions demanded hostages from amongst a *condottiere*'s family. It also imposed taxes on the *condottieri*, both a proportion of their income known as the *onoranza di San Marco*, and one-tenth of the booty which they took in its service. That some discipline could be maintained is suggested by a number of cases in which *condottieri* were arrested for misdemeanours. Jacopo d'Ariano was arrested for robbing a German merchant in Friuli in 1412,[66] and Sigismondo Malatesta was dismissed in 1450 when he was accused of being responsible for the rape of the Duchess of Bavaria on her way to the Roman Jubilee.[67] In 1435 when Antonuccio de' Camponischi dall' Aquila, having taken an advance failed to turn up for service, commercial reprisals were initiated against Aquila to recover the sum advanced.[68] There is even some evidence of the establishment of a special provost corps when Carlo Malatesta was authorized to create a unit directly responsible to him for discipline in the army.[69]

Given all this emphasis on securing the permanent services of chosen *condottieri* and creating a standing force, it is not surprising that Venice took it particularly hard when one of the *Marcheschi* deserted. While the execution of Carmagnola must be seen as an isolated incident of a different nature, the defections of men like Alvise dal Verme in 1435, Colleoni in 1443 and Tiberto Brandolini in 1452 had considerable repercussions. The reasons were largely the same; in the emerging Venetian system the ambitious man inevitably felt restricted as growth in the size of his *condotta* was controlled and even on occasions reversed. The immediate cause of the defection of both Dal Verme and Colleoni was the attempt to reduce their *condotte* in peacetime, and it is perhaps surprising that defections were so few. Venice did seem to have found a way of satisfying the majority of the *condottieri* whose ambitions and pretensions were perhaps not so great as has sometimes been thought.

The fact that an expanding army needed an overall commander-in-chief was not always appreciated in Venice, and it was by no means accepted at any time during the first half of the fifteenth century that there should always be a captain general. The main problem which directed men's minds towards the need for a single commander was that of order and discipline within the army, and for this reason the commander-in-chief's jurisdictional powers were more clearly defined than his freedom to make military decisions. That it was by no means clearly established that a single famous *condottiere* should be made commander-in-chief is suggested by the frequent debates on the subject. In 1411, after a proposal to offer the command to Carlo Malatesta had been defeated in the Senate, it was suggested by Antonio Contarini that a Venetian noble should be elected to command the army.[70] The suggestion received little support as did another to appoint a kind of super-*provveditore*, but this was not the only time that the idea of a Venetian commander was raised.[71] Another alternative to the single *condottiere* commander was command by committee. The army which was conducting the siege of Verona in 1404–5 was directed in this way by a committee comprising Francesco Gonzaga and Jacopo dal Verme, the two leading *condottieri*, together with the *provveditori* and Gabriele Emo who held the rank of *governatore*.[72] Later in the period immediately after the execution of Carmagnola when the former second-in-command, Gianfrancesco Gonzaga, was understandably reluctant to accept the post of captain general, the idea was suggested again. This time it was proposed that a committee of the two *provveditori* and the three leading *condottieri*, Guidantonio Manfredi, Luigi da Sanseverino and Piero Gianpaolo Orsini, should decide policy while the three *condottieri* would take it in turns for a month each to have tactical command of the army.[73] The committee element was in fact always present in Venetian military control; the commander-in-chief was usually bound to consult with the *provveditori*, although it was also clearly stated that he alone 'disponat, regulet et gubernet exercitum nostrum et gentes nostras'.[74] He was also expected to consult with the senior *condottieri* who were given the rank of marshals of the army. However, the formal constitution of a supreme committee was clearly not a practical alternative to the single commander-in-chief, although it was not necessarily accepted that the single commander should have the title of captain general. This title carried both immense prestige and a high salary, and there were many reasons why it was given with reluctance. In the early years of the century this reluctance was less marked; Malatesta de' Malatesti, Paolo Savelli and Galeazzo da Mantua held the post in turn in the Paduan war,[75] and Pandolfo Malatesta succeeded Carlo Malatesta as captain general in the first Hungarian war when the latter was wounded at Motta. However, in 1419–20 Filippo Arcelli had to be content with the title of governor general. Whether this was because the army was smaller than in the previous wars, or whether because of some particular animosity towards Arcelli himself is not clear. Arcelli certainly seems to have been one of the least appreciated of Venice's commanders despite his considerable successes in 1420 in clearing the Hungarians out of the Conegliano–Belluno–Sacile area.[76] By 1426 Carmagnola with his great reputation could scarcely be denied the title of captain general although there was at first considerable distrust of him. After his death there was little doubt that Gonzaga was the most suitable man. But following the retirement of Gonzaga late in 1437, Gattamelata was only offered the title of governor general.[77] On this occasion there was the hope that Gonzaga might return, and also the possibility that Francesco Sforza, who was captain general of the league of Venice, Florence and the pope, would come to Lombardy and take over command of the Venetian army. So there was some justification for Venice's reluctance to commit herself to Gattamelata, and indeed even the offer which was made had to be discreet, as Guidantonio Manfredi, who was senior to Gattamelata, was still in Venetian service, and the announcement of Gattamelata's promotion was delayed until Manfredi had left. Only after his successful retreat from Brescia was Gattamelata honoured with the supreme title.[78]

By the time of Gattamelata's retirement Francesco Sforza had appeared on the scene and it was pressure from him which forced the Senate to offer the post of captain general to his cousin Michele Attendolo in 1441.[79] Sigismondo Malatesta was governor general for a year after the disgrace of Attendolo before he succeeded in persuading the Senate to make him captain general. His dismissal placed Venice in the position of having to choose a commander-in-chief from among three of her senior *condottieri*. Colleoni was probably the most experienced but he had already deserted Venice once; Jacopo Piccinino had the largest *condotta* but he had only recently joined Venetian service; so the choice fell on the least distinguished but most faithful of the three, Gentile da Leonessa. However, he was only given the title of governor general, perhaps in an attempt to avoid antagonizing his rivals too much. After Gentile's death at the siege of Manerbio in 1453 Piccinino took over the title of governor general.

The relationship between the commander-in-chief and the government in Venice was clearly closer than that of the other *condottieri*. When he took up his post he was given a public reception and was presented with the baton either by the doge himself or by the *provveditori* if for some reason it was not convenient to hold the ceremony in Venice. He received the major rewards of membership of the Great Council and a palace in Venice. He was always treated with great circumspection; he received a full briefing on the political situation and on Venice's strategic aims at the beginning of each campaign, and the Senate always took care to keep him informed of diplomatic as well as military developments.

But it is the recriminations and distrust which marked Venice's dealings with her captain generals rather than the rewards and consideration which she bestowed upon them that are remembered. While it was inevitable that Carmagnola and Francesco Sforza, both of whom had long-standing connections with Milan, should play prominent parts in the diplomacy of the period, and indeed were encouraged by Venice to do so, it was also soon clear that they were more inclined to negotiate for themselves than for their employers. Nor was suspicion of treachery the only basis of conflict. Disputes over the treatment of prisoners, the replacement of lost horses, and the timing of the dispersal of the army into quarters were all common. Carlo Malatesta protested continuously about shortage of troops; Carmagnola and Francesco Sforza fought out with Venice the issue of inspections of *condottiere* forces by the civilians.[80] But above all it was over the actual conduct of the campaigns that government and soldier found it hardest to see eye to eye. The intermediary in all these disputes was the *provveditore* and it is now time to turn to a consideration of this official and the other civilians who frequented the Venetian camps.

The *provveditori* were the senior representatives of the government in the camp and were always nobles elected in the Senate; they transmitted instructions and advice from Venice to the captain general; they reported back on the whole conduct of the army; they supervised the activities of the civilian paymasters and quartermasters; they advised the captain general who had an obligation to consult with them. The *provveditore* received 100–200 ducats a month in pay and expenses which was a fairly high rate by Venetian standards; he was expected to have a small retinue of servants, notaries and other assistants; he often also had command of a force of lances which acted as a bodyguard and gave him added prestige in the camp.[81]

The damaging effect of these civilian officials who accompanied the armies of Renaissance Italy has often been commented on. Ricotti remarked that they were 'inconvenient, and often dangerous, in any active campaign, and seemed more fitted to spying and punishing failures, than to facilitating victories'.[82] There is indeed plenty of evidence of clashes between Venetian captains and their *provveditori*; the Carmagnola affair was sometimes seen both at the time and later as primarily a clash of personalities between the count and his *provveditori*, particularly Giorgio Corner.[83] Gonzaga certainly was on bad terms with his *provveditori*.[84] At the same time the *provveditori* have often been accused of promoting rash moves and were blamed by some reporters for the fatal decision to attack at Caravaggio.[85]

It was certainly true that the interests of the government and those of the *condottieri* were by no means always the same. Venice wanted dramatic victories and conquests, particularly when peace negotiations were imminent. The *condottieri* were professionals who had both their reputations and their limited forces to protect. They were always reluctant to commit themselves to battle unless all the circumstances were favourable and they frequently tended to be over-cautious in following up a victory. At the same time it is clear that the times on which the captain general was plagued by detailed instructions on military policy from Venice were probably more than offset by the times when he was given a comparatively free hand. Pandolfo Malatesta's policy in 1412 of keeping his army together and harassing the advancing Hungarians rather than defending the towns piecemeal was for a time very unpopular in Venice, and the Senate attempted to overrule Malatesta and break the army up into garrisons.[86] But Malatesta got his way in the end and the campaign was successful. Indeed so successful was it that exactly the same tactics were subsequently recommended by the Senate to Gentile da Leonessa when he was under great Milanese pressure in 1451.[87] In this context it is perhaps worth noting that instructions sent from Venice were by no means imperative or necessarily uninformed. A standard device was to send two different sets of advice geared to two different possible situations, and to ask the *provveditori* to pass on the letter which was most appropriate to the military situation when they received it.[88]

But above all it is an oversimplification to see the *provveditori* only as civilian spies and mindless functionaries of a civil government out of touch with military realities. The Venetian *provveditori* came mostly from a small group of men who developed considerable military expertise and experience. The Venetian nobility were in any case no strangers to the military arts; all had training as crossbowmen, and many had served on the galleys. Even if one discounts some of the more exaggerated claims for the military abilities and significance of the *provveditori* made by Venetian chroniclers, the *provveditori* were clearly a group apart. There were many occasions when they commanded small detachments in the field, and it was not uncommon for them to take over command of the whole army in the temporary absence of the captain general.[89] Men like Carlo Zeno, hero of the Chioggia war and *provveditore* in 1404–5, Francesco Bembo who commanded a force against the Austrians in 1413 and the Po fleet against Milan in 1426, Francesco Barbaro, the hero of the siege of Brescia, and Pietro Loredan who commanded the army in the absence of Carmagnola in 1428 and was one of Venice's most distinguished admirals, were *provveditori* on many occasions.[90] They were accompanied by others with less obvious military reputations but considerable experience of life in the camps. Fantino Michiel was *provveditore* on at least seven occasions; Giorgio Corner held the post almost continuously between 1426 and 1432; Federico Contarini, Gherardo Dandolo and Jacopo Antonio Marcello were constantly in the camp between 1436 and 1453.[91] Even Pasquale Malipiero, who when he succeeded Francesco Foscari as doge was regarded as a man of peace, had had considerable experience as *provveditore*. He had even commanded the army briefly in 1450 and therefore in 1458 he was no stranger to the soldier kneeling before him to receive the baton of captain general. It would seem inevitable that such men would develop some degree of sympathy for and understanding of the problems and attitudes of the *condottieri*. Indeed Carmagnola specifically asked for one of his *provveditori*, Tommaso Malipiero, to be allowed to remain at his post after his term had expired,[92] and conversely Gattamelata was reputed to have the confidence of the *provveditori*. It has been argued, with particular reference to Andrea Giuliano, another Venetian who had prolonged experience in this field, that the *provveditori* helped to moderate the aggressiveness of the Foscari regime and established a real working relationship with some of the *condottieri*.[93] Obviously there were also exceptions to this interpretation, but it seems on the whole a more accurate one than the traditional view of permanent conflict between the soldiers and the attached civilian officials.

The *provveditori* were not the only civilians in the camp, but as the fifteenth century advanced there was a decline in the number of temporary elected civilian officials attached to the army, and the growth of a permanent military administration. In the early part of the century Venetians often held the post of *governatore* which implied control over the administration of the camp and discipline in the army. Gabriele Emo held this position in the army besieging Verona in 1404–5, but in subsequent campaigns the *governatore* was usually a *condottiere*. On the other hand the elected civilian paymasters remained a feature of the organization, but their activities were increasingly co-ordinated and controlled by the permanent officials of whom the most important was the *collaterale*.

In the early years the post of *collaterale* was also usually filled by a Venetian noble elected for a short period. He supervised the recruiting and paying of the troops and was particularly responsible for preventing desertions. He was empowered to employ spies in the companies to report any potential deserters.[94]

It soon became apparent however that these were tasks which required permanent officials and not rotating elected nobles, and so the group of professional military administrators began to emerge. The outstanding example of this type of official was the Vicentine, Belpetro Manelmi, who was a Venetian *collaterale* for at least thirty-five years from 1418 to 1455, and *collaterale generale* of the army from 1431 onwards.[95] He was the man who was responsible for the practical supervision of the *condotta* system; he carried out inspections, arranged the minor *condotte*, kept the *libro delle condotte*, in which records of all the contracts and of the state of the companies were entered, and organized the reductions and increases of the *condotte*.[96] He had an even more direct responsibility for infantry recruiting, and he worked closely with the *provveditori* and the captain general in all administrative matters connected with the army. He was very unpopular with the *condottieri* and there was in 1434 a move to oust him because it was said that he was so hated that his very presence discouraged *condottieri* from taking service with Venice.[97] But he was clearly too useful a man to be dispensed with easily, and for a further twenty one years he presided over the administration of the Venetian army. Under him were five *vice-collaterali* each with his headquarters in one of the *terraferma* cities and each responsible for a number of the companies. Among these men was another Vincentine, Chierighino Chiericati, who subsequently took charge of the administration of the papal army under Paul II, and wrote a brief military treatise which very much sums up the attitudes of these administrators.[98]

Manelmi was therefore the leader of a group of professional military advisers and administrators whom Venice employed during this period. These men were sometimes ex-*condottieri* and acted as fortress commanders, recruiting officers, inspectors, *collaterali*, and special advisers on military affairs. Many of them were *cittadini originali* of Venice; others were natives of the *terraferma* cities, like Frignano da Sesso from Verona who ended his service as commander of the citadel in Verona,[99] Antonio di Facino da Vicenza who as a recruiting officer travelled the length and breadth of Italy in the 1420s and 1430s,[100] and Paolo di Leone da Padova who was the Senate's special adviser to Pandolfo Malatesta in 1412, and appeared in Urbino in 1417 preparing a report for the Senate on the recruiting possibilities in that area.[101] Here then was another essential feature of the growing permanence of Venice's military forces, the essential professional figures on the fringes of the changing mercenary system.

The renewal of Bartolomeo Colleoni's *condotta* in 1457 was for three years *ferma* followed by two *di rispetto*. He received 100,000 ducats a year to employ as many lances as seemed appropriate, and an appropriate following both in terms of the pay which this sum represented and in terms of comparison with the strength of other *condottieri* would have been at least 1,000 lances. He had already been promised large estates and prospects of achieving personal glory.[102] All this compares dramatically with the agreement reached with Malatesta de' Malatesti, Venice's first captain general of the century. He received a *condotta* for four months *ferma* and two *di rispetto* with provision for 300 lances. Although, exceptionally, he was authorized to pay his own troops, his personal salary of 1,000 ducats a month was clearly distinguished from this pay. There was no mention of rewards or estates.[103]

But an even greater contrast existed between the armies which these two men commanded. Malatesta's army was an heterogeneous gathering of *condottiere* companies collected for the occasion from all over Italy. Amongst them was the Company of the Rose, one of the last relics of the free companies of the fourteenth century.[104] The army which Colleoni rejoined in 1454 and which he rapidly came to command was in many respects a permanent army. Its captains were mostly men who had been in Venetian service for many years, and its administration was already a smooth running machine.

Much of this change was clearly the result of the long wars since 1425 and the increasing prestige of the *condottiere* in Italian society. The other Italian states were moving in the same direction by the middle of the fifteenth century. The Visconti force of *familiares ad arma*, a sort of household cavalry, in the 1420s,[105] and Florence's permanent relationship with Hawkwood were both early examples of the same trend. However, Milan during the wars after 1425 seems to have made little use of any permanent elite corps, although the relationships between the Visconti and their *condottieri* show many of the same features as can be observed in Venice. On the other hand after Hawkwood's death Florence never seemed to establish the same sort of liaison with another *condottiere* and was always reluctant to grant estates or rich rewards to its soldiers. It was in Naples under Alfonso V in the 1440s that there was clear indication of an attempt to create a permanent military force,[106] and the Neapolitan military theorists of the latter half of the century, Diomede Carafa and Orso Orsini, wrote in terms of a permanent army.[107] Similarly after 1450 evidence of a growing permanence in Sforza and papal military organization is clear.[108]

However, the emergence of a permanent system in Venice before 1425 and the acceptance, and indeed positive direction, of what was happening by the Venetian Senate, placed Venice ahead of the other Italian states in these developments. This was perhaps the natural result of a more advanced degree of political unity and organization, but there were also other particular factors at work. The military threats to Venice were not just from Milan; the northern and eastern frontiers required constant vigilance throughout the century. Furthermore Venice because of her position had peculiar recruiting problems, particularly in the first quarter of the century when most Italian fighting took place in south and central Italy. *Condottieri* had to be brought by galley from Trani and Bari; they had to be lured overland from the Abruzzi, Perugia and Urbino.

But perhaps more important than these military problems were the attitudes in Venice towards war and warriors in the fifteenth century. These were a compound of the physical security of the city against its own armies, the traditional military role of the Venetian patriciate, and the new aggressiveness discernible in the Foscari regime. Venice found herself with a permanent army by the middle of the fifteenth century not just by chance but also by choice.

NOTES

1. A. Angelucci, *Ricordi e documenti di uomini e trovati italiani per servire alla storia militare* (Turin, 1866) 77–9; B. Belotti, *Vita di Bartolomeo Colleoni* (Bergamo, 1931) 277–80.

2. The wedding of Jacopo Foscari, son of the doge, in 1441 was also the occasion for a great joust led by Francesco Sforza; M. Sanuto, *Vite de' duchi di Venezia, R.I.S.*, xxii, 1101.

3. Apart from the standard histories of Venice there is a small group of secondary works on the wars of this period: I. Raulich, *La caduta dei Carraresi, signori di Padova* (Padua, 1890); idem., 'La prima guerra fra i veneziani e Filippo Visconti', *Riv. Stor. Ital.*, v (1888); C. Tarducci, 'L'alleanza Visconti-Gonzaga del 1438 contro la repubblica veneta', *Archivio Storico Lombardo*, iii, xi (1899); G. Soranzo, 'L'ultima campagna del Gattamelata al servizio della repubblica veneta (1438–40)', *A.V.*, lx–lxi (1957); L. Rossi, 'Firenze e Venezia dopo la battaglia di Caravaggio', *A.S.I.*, xxxiv (1904). For the early wars one of the most useful contemporary accounts is that in 'Cronachetta veneziana del 1402–15', ed. V. Joppi, *A.V.*, xvii (1879).

4. Even Sanuto, who is normally the main source for military statistics, gives little indication of the size and composition of the armies before 1425. These estimates have been arrived at from indications in A.S.V., S.S., particularly reg. 2, 89 (4 Feb., 1405) 99 (21 Mar., 1405) and 153 (25 Sept., 1405); 4, 231v (17 Jan., 1412); 7, 81 (7 June, 1419). See also for the army in 1404–5: B.M.V., mss. It. VII, 794, *Cronica di Zorzi Dolfin*, 270v.

5. S.S., reg. 9, 54v–57v (3 Dec., 1425).

6. Apart from the well-known Venetian army lists for 1426–7 and 1439 published by E. Ricotti in *Storia delle compagnie di ventura* (2nd ed., Turin, 1893) ii, 445–6 and 453–4 from Sanuto, there are a number of other lists of Venetian *condottieri* and their respective strengths:

   1429   S.S., reg. 11, 21r–v (14 July).
   1431   Sanuto, *Vite de' duchi*, cit., 1015–6.
   1433   S.S., reg. 12, 190v (29 July).
   1434   Carlo d'Arco, *Nuovi studi intorno alla economia politica del municipio di Mantova* (Mantua, 1847) 250.
   1447   Cristoforo da Soldo, *Cronaca*, ed. G. Buzzolara, *R.I.S.* 2, xxi, pt. 3, 77.
   1450   Ibid., 98.
   1450   S.S., reg. 18, 205v (20 July).

7. *Libri commemoriali*, xiv, 77 (24 Oct., 1450), summarized in R. Predelli (ed.), *I libri commemoriali della Repubblica di Venezia, Regesti*, iii–v (*Monumenti storici pubblicati dalla r. dep. veneta di storia patria*, I, *Documenti*, vii, viii, x) at v, 55.

8. S.S., reg. 3, 4 (11 Mar., 1406).

9. For the series of renewals of Malatesta's *condotta* see S.S., reg. 5, 155 (5 Oct., 1413) and 183r–v (6 May, 1414); reg. 6, 15 (19 Oct., 1414), 44v (4 Apr., 1415), 76 (21 Nov., 1415) and 85v (17 Feb., 1416). See also Predelli, iii, 365 and 373. A good deal of information on Pandolfo Malatesta's troops during this period can be found in the Archivio di Stato, Fano: *Codici Malatestiani*, esp. nos. 54 and 56. The Italian lance in this period consisted of three men: a heavily armed 'corporal', an attendant man-at-arms, and a mounted page. The *condotta in aspetto* was a more or less long-term contract for a *condottiere* to produce his company when called upon. He received only half pay or less for

his troops but he was free to take up other contracts as long as they did not conflict with his *aspetto* commitments.

10. S.S., reg. 8, 54v (19 May, 1422).
11. Predelli, op. cit., iv, 52 (29 Jan., 1424).
12. For further remarks on the comparative aspects of this problem, see below, p. 139.
13. The most useful works on the *condotta* system are: Ricotti, op. cit.; G. Canestrini, 'Documenti per servire alla storia della milizia italiana', *A.S.I.*, i, xv (1850); W. Block, *Die Condottieri* (Historische Studien, 110, Berlin, 1913); P. Pieri, *Il rinascimento e la crisi militare italiana* (2nd ed., Turin, 1952); C. C. Bayley, *War and society in Renaissance Florence* (Toronto, 1961) 3–58. An old-fashioned, inaccurate, but occasionally useful biographical dictionary is C. Argegni, *Condottieri, capitani e tribuni (Enciclopedia biografica e bibliografica italiana*, xix Milan, 1936).
14. S.S., reg. 5, 50 (26 July, 1412).
15. Ibid., 4, 21v and 26v (1 and 12 June, 1409).
16. Not Pandolfo Malatesta as in Romanin, iv, 19.
17. Tarducci, 'L'alleanza Visconti-Gonzaga', cit., 283.
18. S.S., reg. 14, 66 (27 Oct., 1437) and 84 (28 Dec., 1437). See also Cristoforo da Soldo, cit., *Cronaca*, 3–5.
19. S.S., reg. 14, 74v (29 Nov., 1437) and 81v (17 Dec., 1437).
20. References to individual *condottieri* which follow are far from complete; they are intended to serve only as an indication of the material available. For Bianchino da Feltre see an early *condotta* in Predelli, op. cit., iv, 40 (18 Feb., 1422), and the reference to his long service in S.S., 12, 190v (29 July, 1433). Ventura da Rovigo was mentioned in the same Senate minute.
21. Only two *condotte* for Alvise survive in Predelli, op. cit., iv, 70 and 154; but his retirement from Venetian service caused much discussion in 1435–6 (S.S., reg. 13, 189v, 26 Nov., 1435 and 228, 4 May, 1436).
22. His first period of service is not documented in the *commemoriali* and this has led Belotti to ignore it. However the evidence in S.S. is clear, and Sanuto lists him amongst Venetian *condottieri* in 1431. For later *condotte* see Predelli, op. cit., v, 7, 19, 41 and 49.
23. Sanuto, *Vite de' duchi*, 870 (1412) and 990 (1426); S.S., reg. 7, 121v (19 Nov., 1419); Predelli, op. cit., iv, 183.
24. There are only two *condotte* for Gritti in the *commemoriali* (Predelli, op. cit., iv, 247 and 276), but frequent references in S.S. in the 1430s.
25. The complete absence of any *condotte* for Taddeo d'Este in the *commemoriali* is an indication of the inadequate nature of this source, as his continuous service is clearly documented both in Sanuto and in S.S. He was elected to the Great Council in 1435.
26. S.S., reg. 16, 36v (5 Sept., 1443).
27. Cristoforo da Soldo, *Cronaca*, cit., 79: 'Alli 24, lo giorno di Sto. Zoan Battista fu fatte le sue exequiee portato a Sto. Franceso com grandissimo honore. Fu alle sue exequie tutto lo chieregato di Bressa; tutti quanti li battuti; tutto quanto lo popolo, picenni e grandi, donne e femine. Non fu mai veduto tanta gente a un corpo; e questo, per lo amor portava lo popolo di Bressa al ditto Thadeo perche fu lui che li governo in lo assedio grande che ho scritto piu avanti.'
28. Angelucci, *Ricordi e documenti*, cit., 86.
29. Scariotto was particularly commended for over twenty years' service in S.S., reg. 14, 83 (23 Dec., 1437).
30. Ibid., 159v (23 Oct., 1438); for his *condotte* see Predelli, op. cit., iv, 85; v, 20, 41 and 57.
31. His first *condotta* is in Predelli, op. cit., iv, 214 (15 Dec., 1437), but there are seven others recorded in the same source with the last in 1457.
32. S.S., reg. 14, 234 (31 Oct., 1439).
33. For praise of him see S.S., reg. 15, 107 (19 Dec., 1441); criticism came from

Marco Foscarini in a letter to Francesco Barbaro. Angelo Maria Querini, ed., *Francisci Barbari et aliorum ad ipsum epistolae* (Brescia, 1743) 248.

34. Annibale Brandolini d'Adda, *I Brandolini di Bagnacavallo; storia di una famiglia di condottieri* (Venice, 1942) 61–79. Many of the *condotte* of Tiberto are recorded in the *commemoriali*.

35. On Gentile, see P. Guerrini, 'Il testamento di Gentile da Leonessa', *Archivio veneto-tridentino*, iv (1923); he also is well documented in the *commemoriali* and was described by Foscarini (see above) as 'Gentilis cui tempori brevitas saeviendi desiderium praestitit'. Even as late as 1476 there were still 100 lances in the Venetian army known as 'lanze spezzate gattesche' commanded by Antonio, count of Marsciano, the son-in-law of Gattamelata; Biblioteca Ambrosiana, Milan, ms Z.226, sup., fasc. 1.

36. For Cavalcabò, see A. Cavalcabò, 'Un condottiero del '400 e la presa della Rochetta di San Luca di Cremona (17–18 Oct., 1431)', *Bollettino Storico Cremonese*, i (1931).

37. The company of Guerriero da Marsciano, who was killed about 1440, was kept in being for some years until his son was old enough to take command of it (S.S., reg. 15, 22, 18 May, 1440).

38. A. Mazzi, 'L'atto divisionale delle sostanze di Diotesalvi Lupi, condottiero della fanteria veneziana', *Bollettino della civica biblioteca di Bergamo (Bergamum)*, iv (1910); M. Lupi, 'Memorie per servire alla vita di Diotesalvi Lupi', *Miscellanea di storia italiana*, vi (1865).

39. For early references, see Sanuto, *Vite de' duchi*, cit., 809 and 828–9; Quarantotto's seniority was later emphasized in S.S., reg. 4, 192v (1 Sept., 1411) and 7, 122 (22 Nov., 1419).

40. S.S., reg. 12, 181 (4 June, 1433).

41. Ibid., 15, 117v (5 Apr., 1442).

42. Sanuto, *Vite de' duchi*, 443–4.

43. Ibid., 880 and 893; for the award to Carmagnola see Predelli, op. cit., iv, 121. For more details of this and other *condottiere* palaces see G. Tassini, *Curiosità veneziane* (Venice, 1897) 670.

44. Sanuto, *Vite de' duchi*, 1003 and 1103; Tassini, op. cit., 280.

45. Sanuto, *Vite de' duchi*, 434 and 1045; Tassini, op. cit., 196.

46. On Giovanni de' Conti's family see S.T. reg. 2, 200 (11 July, 1451); for the pensions to Cristoforo da Tolentino's wife see S.T. reg. 3, 151v (13 Mar., 1455).

47. Most of the grants of major fiefs are recorded in the *commemoriali*. For the variety of jurisdiction involved, see the grant of Chiari to Carmagnola; *libri commemoriali*, xii, 65, summarized in Predelli, op. cit., iv, 152–3, and published in A. Battistella, *Il Conte Carmagnola* (Genoa, 1889) 491–2, and that of Casteldidone to Cavalcabò de' Cavalcabò (*libri commemoriali*, xii, 98, summarized in Predelli, op. cit., iv, 166, and published in Cavalcabò op. cit., 59–60). On the question of different degrees of jurisdiction in Milanese enfeudations see Bueno de Mesquita, 'Ludovico Sforza and his vassals', *Italian Renaissance Studies*, ed. E. F. Jacob (London, 1960) 204–5.

48. When Sanguinetto was granted to Gentile da Leonessa in 1452 (Predelli, op. cit., v, 74) it was described as having been previously in the hands of Alvise dal Verme. For Carmagnola's possession of it, see M. Caffi, 'La tomba del Carmagnola', *A.S.I.* (1869) 171.

49. Sanuto, *Vite de' duchi*, 1147 and Argegni, op. cit., iii, 36.

50. Savelli died of plague while convalescing from wounds received in the final stages of the siege of Padua in 1405, so his funeral came at a moment of considerable euphoria in Venice. On the monument, see W. Valentiner, 'The equestrian statue of Paolo Savelli in the Frari', *Art Quarterly*, xvi (1953).

51. G. von Grävenitz, *Gattamelata und Colleoni und ihre Beziehungen zur Kunst* (Leipzig, 1906); C. Milanesi, 'Della statua di Erasmo da Narni, detto il Gattamelata', *A.S.I.*, ns. ii (1855) reprinted in G. Eroli, *Erasmo Gattamelata da Narni, suoi monumenti e*

sua famiglia (Rome, 1876) app. I. And see H. W. Jenson, 'The equestrian monument from Congrande della Scala to Peter the Great', in *Aspects of the Renaissance*, ed. Archibald R. Lewis (U. of Texas, 1967) esp. 82.

52. S.S., reg. 7, 108v (26 Sept., 1419). For subsequent examples of the same process, see ibid., 8, 54v (19 May, 1422) and 11, 163 (14 Feb., 1431).

53. S.S., reg. 12, 181 (4 June, 1433).

54. Ibid., 190v (29 July, 1433).

55. Ibid., 13, 8 (26 Sept., 1433).

56. Predelli, op. cit., iv, 261 (5 Nov., 1441). For evidence of the use of similar 'double' contracts in Milanese armies, see E. C. Visconti, 'Ordine dell' esercito ducale sforzesco, 1472–4', *Archivio Storico Lombardo*, iii (1876) docs. xiv and xix.

57. S.S., reg. 10, 18 (10 Feb., 1427).

58. For Malatesta de' Malatesti's *condotta* see Predelli, op. cit., iii, 299–300.

59. Canestrini, 'Documenti . . .', cit., 146–55; S.S., reg. 13, 117v–118r (28 Oct., 1434) and 14, 186–187r (28 Feb., 1439).

60. Predelli, op. cit., v, 47.

61. Belotti, *Bartolomeo Colleoni*, cit., 603–4.

62. S.S., reg. 18, 205v (20 July, 1450).

63. Ibid., 11, 145 (29 Oct., 1430).

64. Ibid., 19, 44v (24 Feb., 1451).

65. *Libri commemoriali*, xii, 135, summarized in Predelli, op. cit., iv, 186–7. These regulations were revised and reduced in number in 1441 (*libro commemoriali*, xiii, 106v, summarized in Predelli, iv, 256). Another copy of the Venetian standing orders for *condottieri*, dated 5 Dec., 1433, is to be found in Archivio di Stato, Milan: *Archivio Ducale, Visconteo*, 20.

66. Predelli, op. cit., iii, 360.

67. Sanuto, *Vite de' duchi*, 1137 and L. Rossi, 'Un nuovo documento su di un delitto di Sigismondo Malatesta, Signore di Rimini', *Rivista di Scienze Storiche* (1910).

68. Predelli, op. cit., iv, 187.

69. Ibid., iii, 357.

70. S.S., reg. 4, 217v (12 Dec., 1411).

71. In 1432 and again in 1434 the same suggestion was made: ibid., 12, 91 (12 June, 1432) and 13, 76v (7 June, 1434).

72. Ibid., 2, 61v (2 Oct., 1404).

73. Ibid., 12, 95 (21 June, 1432).

74. See, amongst others, the *condotta* of Malatesta de' Malatesti in 1404 (*libri commemoriali*, ix, 162v, summarized in Predelli, op. cit., iii, 299–300). There was not always this insistence on consultation with the *provveditori*; Carlo Malatesta in 1412 was told that secret military plans need not be discussed with the *provveditori* (*libri commemoriali*, x, 116, summarized in Predelli, iii, 357), and Gattamelata was authorized 'di fare come a lui pareva e piaceva e non guardasse ad alcuno ricordo de' provveditori sia chi si voglia' (Sanuto, *Vite de' duchi*, 1074).

75. Galeazzo da Mantua has been variously identified as Galeazzo Gonzaga and Galeazzo di Cataneo de' Grumelli. The latter seems to be more plausible.

76. Filippo Arcelli was notorious for his brutality and rapacity after taking a city and the *provveditori* were instructed to try and control him (S.S., reg. 7, 160, 19 June, 1420). For an account of his successful campaign, see H. Kretschmayr, *Geschichte von Venedig* (Gotha, 1905–34) ii, 267–8.

77. S.S., reg. 14, 82 (17 Dec., 1437). Brandolino Brandolini's retirement about this time has sometimes been attributed to jealousy that his colleague had been preferred to him, but it seems that Brandolini's decision had been taken before that of the Senate to appoint Gattamelata (Ibid., 14, 74, 30 Nov., 1437).

78. For further discussion of Gattamelata's position vis-à-vis Venice and the *provve-*

ditori, see the author's contribution, 'Gattamelata e Venezia', to the proceedings of the *Convegno sulle compagnie di ventura nella storia d'Italia e d'Europa* held in Narni, 31 May–2 June, 1970, and due to be published shortly.

79. Many of the account books of Michele Attendolo's company for the period of his service with Venice, and the preceding fifteen years, have recently been discovered, and some of the results of their examination will be published shortly by Mario del Treppo.

80. The whole question of the areas of conflict between the state and its *condottieri* is one which is too large for this essay. Venice's problems and the issues involved were shared by other Italian states, and discussion of these must be postponed to another occasion.

81. Typical of the many examples of elections of *provveditori* recorded in S.S. is that of Pietro Loredan in April 1437. He was to receive 160 ducats a month and take fifteen mounted followers including a notary. He was also given command of the company of Cesare da Martinengo which was still in Venetian service although Cesare had been a Milanese prisoner for nearly three years (14, 28v).

82. Ricotti, *Storia della compagnie di ventura*, cit., ii, 18.

83. The bibliography on the Carmagnola affair is immense and this is not the place to examine it in detail. However, a letter of Pietro del Monte in July 1432 (published by I. Carini in the periodical *Muratori*, ii, fascs. 7–10) is a good example of the view that Carmagnola's abusive and violent treatment of his *provveditori* was his principal crime. It was also held in Florence at the time that the conflict between Carmagnola and the *provveditori* was the main issue (G. Bustelli, *Sulla decollazione di Francesco Bussone, Conte Carmagnola* [Cesena, 1887] 20–6 and 58–9).

84. Tarducci, 'L'alleanza Visconti-Gonzaga', cit., 267–8.

85. Ricotti, op. cit., ii, 82, takes this view on the evidence of Cristoforo da Soldo and Navagero.

86. S.S., reg. 5, 85v (27 Nov., 1412) and 90 (13 Dec., 1312).

87. Ibid., reg. 19, 108v–110 (30 Dec., 1451).

88. See particularly S.S., reg. 12, 14 (10 Sept., 1431) and 14, 49 (6 Aug., 1437) when this device was used. For discussion of the first occasion, see S. Troilo, *Andrea Giuliano: politico e letterato veneziano del Quattrocento* (Biblioteca dell' Archivum Romanicum, ser. 1, xvi–xviii, 1931–2) 86–7.

89. Carlo Zeno took over command during a temporary absence of Malatesta de' Malatesti in 1404 (S.S., reg. 2, 45v, 22 Aug., 1404); Pietro Loredan similarly commanded the army when Carmagnola was taking the waters in 1428 (ibid., 10, 170, 23 Aug., 1428); and Giorgio Corner and Andrea Giuliano directed the campaign in the Valtellina after the execution of Carmagnola (Troilo, op. cit., 96).

90. The career of Pietro Loredan was one of almost continuous military service; captain of the Gulf (1411), commander of the fleet on the Livenza and generally regarded in Venice as the hero of the battle of La Motta (1412), *provveditore* in Dalmatia (1414), victor at Gallipoli (1416), captain of the Gulf (1420), *provveditore* with Carmagnola (1426–8), victor at Rapallo (1431), wounded fighting in Corfù (1432), commander of the Po fleet (1438). See Argegni, op. cit., ii, 106.

91. The activity of these men as *provveditori* can be traced through S.S. where they appear constantly. Fantino Michiel was *provveditore* in 1405, 1411, 1412, 1426, 1427, 1431 and 1432. Corner spent seven years in a Milanese prison after his capture in the field in 1432. Contarini was *provveditore* in 1436, 1437, 1438, 1439, 1445 and 1448; he was for some time a prisoner of the Milanese, and died in the field on the eve of Caravaggio after being bitten by a rabid dog. Dandolo directed the siege of Lizana in 1439, and was a friend of Alvise dal Verme who maintained contact with Venice through him. Marcello was *provveditore* in 1438, 1439, 1445–6, 1447, 1448, 1450, 1452, 1453 and 1463.

92. S.S., reg. 9, 142v (8 July, 1426).

93. Troilo, *Andrea Giuliano*, cit., 101. Giuliano was given command of 25 lances in

1414, and between 1425 and 1447 was *provveditore* on a number of occasions. He was a friend of Luigi da Sanseverino whose interests he represented in the Senate on two or three occasions.

94. S.S., reg. 2, 95v (8 Mar., 1405) and 7, 72v (2 May, 1419). The *collaterale* received ¼ ducat for each lance he enrolled (A.S.V., *Notatorio del Collegio*, v, 116, 27 May, 1419).

95. For the first seven years of this period Belpetro Manelmi was *collaterale* in Verona and I am indebted to Mr. John Law for showing me many references to him in this capacity (see Archivio di Stato, Verona, *Antico archivio del comune: registrum litterarum ducalium*, ix, ff. 45, 101, 116v, 131v, 145v). By 1427 he was *collaterale* with the army (Predelli, op. cit., 82), and by 1431 *collaterale generale* (for a letter to Doge Foscari, see F. C. Pellegrini, *Appendice di documenti sulla repubblica fiorentina* [Pisa, 1891] p. xxviii). His continued activities in the 1450s are attested by S.T., reg. 2, 171 (8 Feb., 1451) and S.S., reg. 19, 62v (31 May, 1451). His death in office is documented in S.T. reg. 3, 154v (8 Mar., 1455). One of his daughters was married to a Morosini; E. Manelmi, *Commentariolum . . . de obsidione Bresciae*, ed. G. A. Astezati (Brescia, 1728) p. iii.

96. For his particular activity in connection with the *condotte*, see S.S., reg. 12, 63v (23 Feb., 1432) and 181 (4 June, 1433); 13, 183 (1 Oct., 1435).

97. Ibid., 63v (17 Apr., 1434): '. . . est ingratus et odiosus omnibus nostris gentibus armigeris.'

98. G. Zorzi, 'Un vincentino alla corte di Paolo II; Chierighino Chiericati e il suo trattatello della milizia', *Nuovo archivio veneto*, ns. XXX (1915).

99. A.S.V., *Senato, Misti*, reg. 54, 88. For his part in the 1404–5 war, see S.S., reg. 2, 96 and 108v. He was also one of a committee of experts called in to advise on the digging of the Livenza fortifications in 1411 (ibid., 4, 192v). See *Notatorio del Collegio*, passim, for this period, for the elections to minor military posts.

100. S.S., reg. 3, 52v (20 Jan., 1407); 9, 132 (19 June, 1426) and 11, 189v (7 May, 1431).

101. Ibid., 5, 56 (12 Aug., 1412); 6, 137 (15 Mar., 1417); he also arranged the *condotta in aspetto* with Pandolfo Malatesta (5, 124v, 28 Apr., 1413). On Paolo, see also B.M.V., mss. It. VII, 167–8, P. Gradenigo, *Memorie istoriche dei generali di terra ch' erano all serviggio della serenissima Repubblica di Venezia*, i, f. 38.

102. Belotti, *Bartolomeo Colleoni*, cit., 277 and 603–4.

103. *Libri commemoriali*, ix, 162v, summarized in Predelli, op. cit., iii, 299–300.

104. S.S., reg. 2, 32 (16 July, 1404).

105. Fondazione Treccani, *Storia di Milano*, vi, 517.

106. Ricotti, op. cit., ii, 95; P. Gentile, 'Lo stato napoletano sotto Alfonso I d'Aragona', *Archivio storico per le provincie napoletane*, n.s., xxiii–xxiv (1937–8) 11–12.

107. P. Pieri, 'Il "Governo et exercitio de la militia" di Orso degli Orsini e i "Memoriali" di Diomede Caraffa', *Archivio storico per le provincie napoletane*, n.s. xix (1933). Orso Orsini was himself in Venetian service from 1450 to 1459, and frequently refers to Venetian experience and practice in his treatise.

108. Visconti, 'Ordini dell' esercito ducale sforzesco', cit.; A. Da Mosto, 'Ordinamento militari delle soldatesche dello Stato Romano dal 1430 al 1470', *Quellen und Forschungen aus den italienischen Archiven und Bibliotheken*, v (1902). Further discussion of the growth of permanent armies in Italy must be postponed to the author's *Warfare in Renaissance Italy* to be published shortly.

V

FREDERIC C. LANE

Naval actions and fleet organization, 1499-1502

I

In 1499 Venice lost its maritime supremacy, which had not been seriously challenged since the War of Chioggia ended in 1381. The story of the fleet actions in 1499 has been told with attention mainly to the degree of blame of individual commanders.[1] The personalities involved make the story more dramatic, but equally important in determining the outcome were the composition and the organization of the Venetian fleet. Examination of this aspect suggests that Venetian failures were due less to the 'decay of ancient virtues' than to the persistence of old habits in the face of new situations. The history of events opens the door to an understanding of structural changes.

New conditions in naval warfare, calling for creative responses, arose from the development of cannon and of better-rigged, big round ships. The Venetians had been alerted to the damage that cannon could do to ships during the Turkish siege of Constantinople in 1453. Not only had Turkish cannon breached the walls of the city; they had sunk Venetian vessels trying to run past the fort which the Turks built on the Bosphorus, and had almost forced the Venetian fleet to abandon its anchorage within the Golden Horn.[2] Later, in 1470, when the Turks took Negroponte, the most reasonable and contemporary explanation of the failure of the Venetian admiral to relieve the city was his fear of the big Turkish guns on shore.[3] Cannonading battles between large fleets at sea were becoming a possibility but had not yet been experienced in 1499. The Venetian–Spanish victory at Lepanto was to show in 1571 in a limited way how cannon-fire could be employed effectively in a clash of galleys. Late in the sixteenth century Elizabethan seamen fighting Spain mastered the tactics that made gunfire decisive in combat between 'round ships' that depended entirely on sails for manoeuvring and locomotion. For nearly a century previously, however, the adjustment of naval tactics to gunfire was a problem full of unknowns.

Various solutions tried involved a mixture of two types of ships, galleys and round ships. The latter rose in the esteem of naval commanders because they had a greater gun-carrying capacity. At the same time changes in naval architecture and in rigging associated with the type called the carrack made them more manageable. The 'full-rigged' carrack had three or four masts and five to seven sails, some of them lateen but mostly square. They were bigger than the cogs they displaced, with even higher castles at prow and stern. The carracks as big as 1,200 to 2,000 metric tons burden which were built for commercial use could quickly be loaded with men and cannon for battle. Almost as large, but faster because of their sleeker lines, were the *barze* which were the speciality of Leonardo Bressan, the foreman of the shipwrights in Venice's state arsenal in the last decade of the fifteenth century.[4]

Fleet actions and naval administration for the war of 1499–1503 are reported by exceptionally well informed sources. One of the undersecretaries of the marine (*savii ai ordeni*) was the industrious historian and indefatigable reporter, Marino Sanuto. He not only reports day by day events in Venice, including his own participation in the preparation of the warfleets, even down to the selection of the crossbowmen at the butts; he includes summaries or complete texts of letters from the fleets.[5] Even more competent in strictly nautical matters is Domenico Malipiero who was a squadron commander, 1496–1500.[6] A third version comes from a merchant-banker, Girolamo Priuli, who set down the news of the Rialto in rambling fashion with cynical comments concerning the senatorial in-group to which his revered father belonged.[7] Details brought out in the prosecution of unsuccessful commanders are more fully recorded by Pietro Dolfin.[8] These contemporaries provide highlights and shading not to be found in official records.

To them Venetian naval power seemed at its peak on the eve of the Turkish war of 1499. Venice's contest with her traditional rival, Genoa, had lapsed because of Genoese discord and subjection to Milan or France, but in the last encounters between Genoese and Venetian fleets, at Modon in 1404 and Porto-fino in 1431 the Venetians had been victorious. Spain and France had not yet proved themselves serious rivals. The Ottoman emperor had inflicted a severe humiliation, to be sure, when he sent a fleet from Constantinople to Negro-ponte in 1470 to assist in the capture of that Venetian base in the northern Aegean. And the Ottoman fleet had returned safely to Constantinople. But there it stayed protected by batteries for the eight subsequent years of war while the Venetian fleet ranged at will over the Aegean, sacking cities and conducting slave raids which might be viewed as some compensation for the burning and slave raiding of Turkish troops in Friuli. The loss of Negroponte had been written off as an episode that could be blamed on the Venetian commander, calling him more a man of letters than a seaman.[9] It did not shatter the confidence of Venetians in their control of the seas.

They could feel the more self-satisfaction at the beginning of 1499 because of their successful use of naval power during the war begun in 1495 to expel from Italy the French whom Charles VIII had led to the conquest of the kingdom of Naples. Venice waged that war at sea by sending a fleet of more than twenty galleys to take cities in Apulia from the French, while other galleys were patrolling in more eastern waters. After mastering Apulia, Venice sent fleets west to assist operations against the French at Naples and at Genoa. One of the western fleets, under Domenico Malipiero, then became a main support of the Pisans in their struggle against Florence for freedom. But after the expulsion of the French, Venice dismantled most of the fleet armed for that occasion: the total of war galleys at sea fell from about thirty-five in 1495 to about thirteen in 1498.[10]

The campaigns of 1495–1498 left Venice so deeply entangled in Italy that she did not give full attention to a new Turkish threat. Venice was intent on keeping possession of the recently acquired Apulian cities and persisted in defending Pisa against the Florentines. As these moves turned Milan and other Italian states against her, she encouraged the new king of France, Louis XII, to undertake an invasion of Milan. By this sensational reversal of alliances Venice was to acquire Cremona. Venice's growing strength within Italy and her alliance with the French, who habitually talked of a new crusade to retake Constantinople, gave the Turk cause for alarm, a feeling which the threatened duke of Milan did his best to stimulate. The Turk was sworn to peace, but during the winter of 1498–1499 reports began reaching Venice that the sultan was preparing a great armada in his arsenals at Constantinople. It might be used in the Black Sea, it might be directed against Venice; it seemed for a time to be designed for an assault on the island of Rhodes held by the Knights Hospitallers of St. John. Not until June was it clear that its destination was the Venetian possessions in Greece and the Ionian Sea.[11]

While hoping it would go elsewhere and leave them free to devote their wealth to the war against Milan, the Venetians had begun as early as December to organize an opposing fleet, and in April 1499 elected to command it a captain general of the sea, who had sweeping authority over all Venetian ships and overseas possessions in order to wage war if necessary.[12]

The man chosen was Antonio Grimani, a self-made man, whose reputation for shrewdness was so high that all the Rialto was accustomed to try to find out what he was buying or selling and follow his lead. Left fatherless at the age of four, he had made his fortune by trade and travel in Syria and Egypt and then won high political office because of the respect inspired by his wealth and intelligence. He had no noble relatives on his mother's side, she having been a commoner. His military reputation was based on his having been elected in 1495 at the age of sixty-one to the command of the fleet which conquered some key cities in Apulia. After a few months with the fleet, during which he obtained possession of as much territory there as the diplomatic situation made advisable, he was relieved at his request, received a hero's welcome on his return, and was elected procurator, the post of highest honour next to the dogeship, which he seemed obviously to be aspiring to (and was indeed ultimately to obtain).[13]

Grimani's first problem was to complete the manning and outfitting of the ships being armed for the occasion and collect those that were cruising on various missions between Pisa and Cyprus. Some details about how this was done will be examined later; their significance will be clearer after an account of the course of events when the opposing fleets made contact. Suffice it here to say that Grimani succeeded brilliantly in this first part of his task. In July he had near Modon the most formidable armada which had ever up to that time been collected under the flag of St. Mark's winged lion. It was notably diversified: 44 light galleys, the standard type of trireme built for battle and patrol; 12 great galleys, larger, slower, heavier triremes built primarily for trade but equipped for battle; 4 very large round ships, *barze* or carracks, each of 1,200 tons at least (2,000 *botti*) with a crew of 300 or more; 10 large round ships, *barze* or carracks of 300 to 700 *botti*, armed at Venice with 90–200 men each; 14 other large ships, of 300 *botti* to 900 *botti*, diverted from commercial voyages or armed in the colonies, including one ship full of pilgrims, many of them nobles, who volunteered for the battle; 11 much smaller vessels; making a total of 95 in all.

More than a score of other vessels, most but not all of them small, were on their way from Venice to join him. Since a full galley crew normally numbered about 200 and Grimani had been sent some additional soldiers, his total force was reckoned as 20,000 to 25,000 men.[14] All the bigger ships were armed with cannon but unfortunately there is little information on their size or range.

As the Turkish fleet worked its way down the eastern side of the Morea, thousands of the Greeks who formed a large part of its crews escaped and informed Grimani that it was headed for either Corfu, the key Venetian base at the entrance to the Adriatic, or Lepanto, a Venetian stronghold on the gulf of the same name in central Greece. When a large Turkish army arrived under the walls of Lepanto, it became clear that the mission of the Turkish admiral was to join that army, bringing it cannon and other equipment for a siege.[15] Transport of cannon through the mountainous Balkans was so difficult that the Turks had often cast their cannon at the place where it was to be used.[16] The mission of the Turkish fleet in 1499, like that of the Spanish armada in the English channel in 1588, was not to seek to destroy an enemy fleet, but to beat off attack and make a juncture with a waiting army. In spite of the contrasts in detail and in results, the general pattern of the resulting actions has accordingly some similarity to those against the Spanish armada.

From the reports of the deserters from the Ottoman fleet and from his scouts Grimani learned that the opposing fleet numbered 260 sail, also highly variegated, as follows: 60 light galleys, triremes; 30 *fuste* or *galeote*, light long ships with only two men to a bench; 3 great galleys or *galeazze* somewhat bigger than the Venetian great galleys and each carrying beside its rowers 200 Janissaries, the Ottoman crack troops; 2 very big round ships, one, with 1,000 men on board, mostly Janissaries, even bigger than the biggest of the Venetian vessels; 18 medium sized round ships, 200 to 500 *botti*; 127 smaller vessels:

supply ships, despatch boats and such auxiliaries. He estimated the total man-power of his opponent as 37,000.[17]

Although he was outnumbered in both men and ships, Grimani's letters to the Senate expressed confidence that he would gain a victory. He had a superior number of heavy vessels. As the two fleets came close to each other the Turkish admiral proceeded cautiously as if he too was fearful of the large number of big ships in the Venetian fleet.

Given these odds, Grimani sought to join battle in such a way as to make maximum use of his great galleys and big round ships. A tactical principle that had been employed in naval battles for hundreds of years was to put the heavier vessels in front so that they would disrupt the enemy battle line, while the lighter, faster vessels came into action later as reinforcements and in pursuit. With many cannon on the round ships and great galleys, those tactics would be all the more effective, as was to be proved in 1571 in the battle of Lepanto. It was natural therefore that Grimani should call on his biggest round ships and his great galleys to lead his attack.

The wind, however, was an essential in such an attack. Even the great galleys, although they could be rowed, could not come to battle with opposing light galleys unless they had a favourable wind or were towed. Moreover, Grimani counted on the weight of his big ships to smash and sink many of the multitude of Turkish small craft, which they might well do if they had wind in their sails.[18]

In fact the weather was unreliable but not unfavourable. In that season in those waters, the off-shore night wind usually dies in the morning but before noon an onshore breeze springs up and lasts till sunset.[19] As the Turkish fleet began proceeding up the western side of the Morea, Grimani kept his sailing ships out to sea so that when the on-shore wind began they would have the weather-gauge and could attack with the wind astern. Sometimes that wind was strong enough to advance his plans, sometimes not.

The first encounter of the two fleets was on 24th or 28th July in the waters between Coron and Modon. For four hours they sailed on parallel courses five to six miles apart and then the Venetian round ships and great galleys having the weather-gauge began to bear down towards the Turkish fleet. Instead of welcoming combat, the Turkish admiral withdrew his fleet into the harbour of Porto Longo on the island of Sapienza, which lies just south of Modon. Reasoning that a battle at sea would enable him to make better use of the kind of superiority which he had, and perhaps with a thought of the reinforcements on the way, Grimani made no attempt to attack the Turks in the harbour, but he showed his confidence by keeping his round ships and great galleys cruising off the port.

When northerly winds eight days later made it more difficult for that blockading squadron to hold its position, Grimani instructed them to beat to the north and anchor off the island of Proti.[20] There they were quite sure to be to windward of the Turks, able to fall upon them as they worked their way

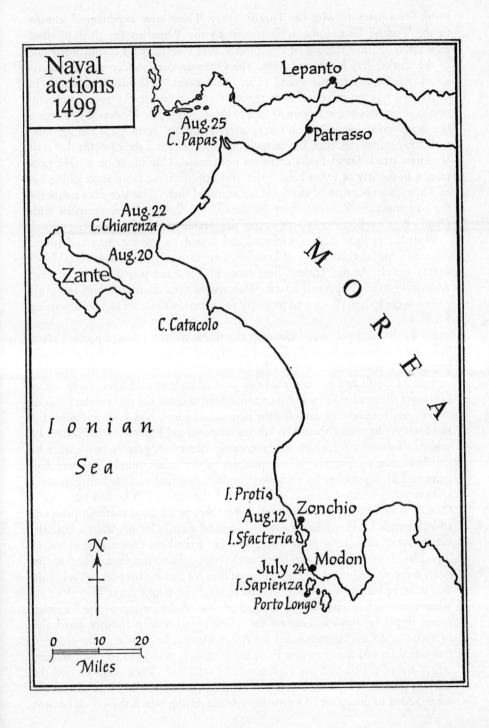

Naval
actions
1499

Lepanto

Aug. 25
C. Papas

Patrasso

Aug. 22
C. Chiarenza

Aug. 20

Zante

C. Catacolo

MOREA

Ionian

Sea

I. Protio

Aug. 12

Zonchio

I. Sfacteria

Modon

July 24

I. Sapienza

Porto Longo

N

0   10   20
Miles

north for a juncture with the Turkish army. There were experienced seamen in the Turkish fleet, some well known to the Venetians for their piratical exploits. The most famous of the 'pirates' was Camalì, who commanded one of the Turks' very big round ships. The Ottoman commander was an experienced general and former grand vizir, Daud Pasha.[21] He advanced slowly in order to keep the gangling fleet together and to enable the more powerful vessels to protect the many small supply ships. Once past Modon they hugged the shore where local Turkish forces offered support. Some ships ran aground and many sailors deserted, but in spite of these losses and the constant threat of Venetian attack Daud Pasha crept on northward. One night he sought protection in the bay of Pylos behind the island of Sfacteria, familiar to all readers of Thucydides because of the Spartans captured there. The Venetian name for the bay was then Zonchio, later Navarino, and their main engagement with Daud's fleet has become known as the 'deplorable battle of Zonchio'.

With his 44 light galleys, Grimani had joined his great galleys and round ships off Proti, slightly north of Zonchio. Late arrivals had raised his total force to 123 vessels. As the Turkish fleet came up the coast past Zonchio on 12th August he ordered a general attack. With wind astern the round ships and great galleys were to lead; it seemed precisely the situation Grimani had been waiting for.

Just as the trumpets were sounding the signal for the attack, up sailed some light reinforcements from Corfu led by Andrea Loredan, an experienced and popular naval commander who had been charged by the Senate with the defence of Corfu and had accepted that post when it seemed likely to be a post of danger. Persuaded in early August that Lepanto, not Corfu, was the point of attack, Andrea Loredan gathered the best fighting men on Corfu and sailed for the fleet. As he told Grimani to whom he presented himself on his arrival he wished to share in the glory of the coming victory. A year or two earlier he had been the commander of a squadron of Venetian round ships and had enhanced his reputation by combining a discipline that excluded all gambling and swearing with extreme popularity with the crews. But he had not caught Camalì whom he had been hunting. Now there was a great battle in prospect, and although his commission ordered him to guard Corfu, Andrea Loredan was too chivalric a spirit to obey. On his arrival an enthusiastic shout of 'Loredan, Loredan' went up from crews throughout the fleet. The captain general received him coldly and reproved him for leaving his post but told him that since he had arrived at that crucial moment he might prove his valour on whatever vessel he chose. Loredan picked one of the largest of the Venetian round ships, the *Pandora*. Leading the attack together with another vessel also of about 1,200 tons commanded by Alban Damer, he assaulted the strongest individual unit in the opposing fleet, the 1,800 ton vessel full of crack soldiers which Loredan believed was commanded by Camalì. These ships carried the heaviest guns in the fleet and many of them. An unprecedented roar of cannonading added to the terror of a four-hour battle during which the vessels became chained together. The powder on the Turkish ship was set afire and all three were consumed in flames (Plate A).

Meanwhile the rest of the fleet did next to nothing. The flagship of the Venetian carracks collided with one of the Venetian great galleys, captured or sank one of the lighter Turkish vessels, then luffed and stood out to sea. Almost all the great galleys also turned into the wind and away from the battle, so disgracefully cowardly an action that everyone began shouting, 'Hang them, hang them'. The Turks made no attempt at counter-attack but they rescued their men from the burning big ships, while only two Venetian vessels attempted even that, and thus the loss of brave men was greater for the Venetians than for the Turks. One Venetian round ship, of 400 tons (600 *botti*), was sunk by cannon fire. A Dalmatian light galley rescued part of its crew but there is no report of the light galleys making any other rescues or indeed taking any part in the action in any way.[22]

The Turks on their side had suffered considerable damage from the few Venetian ships that were engaged, especially from the one great galley that did attack. Under Vicenzo Polani it successfully fought off a swarm of Turkish light galleys. Moreover the Turks had lost their very best ship, which they had thought invincible, and indeed the Venetians had seemed to be winning that battle of the big ships before all three went up in flames.[23] The Turkish admiral proceeded on his way more cautiously than ever and fortified his ships next to the shore at the next approach of the Christian fleet.

In material terms the 'battle of Zonchio' was not a defeat for Venice; it was merely a victory missed. But the effect on the morale of the Venetian fleet of the cowardice and disobedience which had been displayed was disastrous, especially since Grimani took no immediate steps to punish anyone, not even removing from command those most responsible for the failure to engage fully. To be sure the first example of disobedience he had faced was that of Andrea Loredan in leaving his post at Corfu, and Loredan was now being hailed for having died a hero's death. It was rumoured in the fleet that Grimani had failed personally to support Loredan's attack because of fear lest the credit for the victory go to him, a rival for the dogeship.[24] Whether true or false, such a rumour deepened the demoralization.

The week after the encounter at Zonchio was spent by the Venetians re-assembling at Zante. There they were joined by four galleys and eighteen other ships sent to support them by the king of France. The combined Christian force now numbered more than 170 sails and was still in a position, if properly led, to destroy or at least scatter the Turkish fleet.

Instead of attacking the Turks in their fortified anchorage, where they had land troops nearby for support, the Christian commanders decided to drive them out with fireships. These did no damage but the Turks put to sea again and new skirmishes followed on August 20th and 22nd opposite Castel Tornese. Again the Venetian great galleys failed to attack as ordered, most of the Christian fleet was stationed too far out to sea, and a scirocco wind favoured the Turks, they rounded Cape Chiarenza with loss of only three galleys, one bireme and some smaller vessels. A final attempt to block their passage was made on 25th August at Cape Papas as they were turning into the Gulf of Lepanto. There the French and Venetian round ships exchanged cannon shots with the Turks for some time but seemed afraid to try to board the enemy, perhaps remembering the fate on 12th August of the big ships held together by grappling irons. The French, seeing that the Venetians held back, did likewise. Finally the Venetian galleys attacked the tail-end of the Turkish fleet and destroyed several galleys as most of that armada limped safely into the Gulf of Lepanto.[25]

Grimani had written earlier to the Senate that they need not fear for Lepanto for it could not be taken without artillery and the artillery was on the fleet he was about to destroy. When the Venetians in Lepanto discovered that the fleet they saw approaching was not their own, coming to their relief as they expected, but the enemy's bringing his artillery, they hastily surrendered.[26]

In Venice meanwhile news of a great victory was being confidently expected, indeed even celebrated with bonfires and the ringing of bells on the basis of false rumours. Grimani's earlier descriptions of how he had assembled his fleet caused Girolamo Priuli to praise him as a second Alexander, or an equal of Julius Caesar. When news of the fiasco arrived not only in his letters but in many from other officers of the fleet, he was damned with equal fervour. From fear that their palace would be sacked by a mob, his sons emptied it of its fine furnishings and sent to monasteries the merchandise stored there, including thousands of ducats worth of spices. The Senate voted to appoint a new captain general of the sea and ordered Antonio Grimani to return, not in honour in his own galley, but in disgrace in a smaller vessel. Anticipating formal orders, he started home in his galley before his successor arrived. When word of that reached Venice he was ordered to present himself in chains to the *avogadori di comun* for imprisonment until trial, and one member of the *Signoria* moved that if he was so defiantly disobedient as to tie up off the Piazzatta in his own galley, as if in honour, he should within three days be beheaded between the two columns in that same Piazzetta.[27] Fearing for his life, his son met him in Istria and since none of the officials there was willing to humiliate Antonio Grimani by putting him in chains, his son himself fastened them to his father's legs. He arrived at the Piazzetta in a pilot boat and was met there by another son, the cardinal for whom he had recently obtained the patriarchate of Aquileia. Being in chains, he had to be carried by four servants across to the Ducal Palace. He was taken down into the 'strong prison' amid the curses of spectators.[28] Only six months earlier he had crossed the Piazzetta confidently dressed in crimson velvet, accompanied by the doge and foreign ambassadors, as he bore to his galley the flag of command conferred on him at the altar in St. Mark's.

II

What had gone wrong? His trial and that of other commanders hardly provided a fair answer, for it became a political football in which factional rivalries and personal ambitions led to his conviction and to that of Alvise Marcello, the commander of the round ships, while other commanders were acquitted, and the chief prosecutor obtained his goal of taking over the honour of procurator of St. Mark's, after Grimani had been stripped of it.[29]

Reflecting public opinion, Girolamo Priuli said that Grimani had been brave as a lion until he saw the Turkish fleet and then was out of his wits with fear.[30] But when he had been captain general earlier, in 1495 attacking Monopoli in Apulia, Antonio Grimani had shown no physical fear. When the large round ship which had been expected to lead the attack on the city's walls was becalmed, Grimani took the lead in his galley, ran it ashore and personally directed the attack while under fire.[31] Of course, the cannonades from the Turkish fleet off Zonchio were far more terrifying, but he could well argue that there was another more decisive difference. If when off Zonchio he had led his light galleys past the round ships into the centre of the mass of Turkish vessels he would have thrown away all the advantage to be expected from the guns, castles, and men of those big ships and would have run a great risk of leading his whole fleet to destruction.

Grimani's own version was simply that his orders had not been obeyed because of the cowardice and disloyalty of the subordinate commanders. Of disobedience and many signs of cowardice there is no doubt. For example, one subordinate clearly at fault was Alvise Marcello who had been assigned command of all the round ships. He took the *barza* which was his flagship far enough into the battle for him to be wounded in the leg before turning into the wind and thus tacking away from the action. His letter written just after the battle claims of course that he and his ship had fought valiantly but it also dwells on the impact, both physical and moral, of the Turkish artillery hurling 150 pound stones that killed two of his staff on the sterncastle and penetrated even into his cabin.[32]

Men full of fear might have obeyed orders nevertheless if the orders had been clear and made sense, inspiring confidence in those giving the orders. Marcello's chief explanation of the failure of his squadron of round ships to perform as it should have was that the battle orders he had given were all countermanded by Grimani's chief of staff (*armiraio*) at the last moment.[33] Domenico Malipiero, the best of the commanders present, also criticized Grimani for defects in the way he organized his fleet.[34] Skilled as Grimani was in business and politics he had not had as much experience at sea as many other Venetians. Nor had the staff officers of his selection. At his request the Council of Ten had granted leave of absence from their regular duties to two key members of his staff, one an accountant, the other the director of silver coinage at the Mint.[35] They no doubt gave efficient help in the rapid mobilization, but traditionally the captain general's chief of staff was a skilled navigator experienced in naval warfare. Grimani's selection for that post of the mint-master, Giorgio della Moneta, suggests that he had his mind more on the problems of financial administration than on battle action. No Venetian fleet commander had previously faced Grimani's problem, however. Never had a fleet of such size containing such diverse vessels as light galleys, great galleys, and *barze* or carracks been organized so that they were all brought into play and their fighting power used to best advantage, especially their fire power. No simple formula for solving the problem had been worked out (or ever was), at least not for engagements between large fleets.

In retrospect it is easy to see weaknesses in the chains of command through which he tried to operate. The three commanders who were highest in rank next to himself, the three *provveditori*, were each placed in charge of a squadron of light galleys and told to serve one on each side and one behind the central squadron of light galleys which was led by Grimani himself.[36] The great galleys were under two commanders who alternated in leading that group.[37] The round ships were organized by Alvise Marcello into four squadrons, each led by the largest vessel in the group.[38] While it is relatively easy to draw an organization chart of this plan, it is impossible to tell from the battle orders where the different units were, or were supposed to be, in relation to each other when proceeding into battle. From what happened it seems that the round ships should have been in front, the great galleys behind them, or possibly at their flanks, and the light galleys in the rear. If that was the case, Marcello's disposal of the round ships seems faulty. He had ordered one of the very biggest, the *Pandora*, to be flagship of the squadron stationed to windward ('sopra vento'). In view of the general plan of attacking downwind, that would put it in a relatively useless rear position, behind smaller round ships but in the way of the light galleys. Perhaps that was the reason why Grimani's chief of staff was reversing Marcello's orders at the last moment. Or it may have been because of the disruptive effect of Loredan's last minute arrival.

Another difficulty with the plan was that it placed all the highest officers in the rear. The time was passing when a general was expected himself to lead his troops into action, like Alexander charging at the head of his cavalry, but it had not yet passed. For Grimani to have gained that moral advantage he would have had to give up the tactical advantage of having his heavier ships lead the attack, or else he would have had to leave the light galley, which because of its speed was the standard ship of battle and traditional flagship, and carry his flag into one of the round ships. That would have meant displacing Marcello almost entirely. Within a year galleys that were heavier but also fast were being built for use by commanding officers (*galie bastarde*) but none is mentioned in 1499.[39] Another difficulty with Grimani's organization was that under it the light galleys could not move with any flexibility to support the heavier vessels; their orders told them to stay with the *provveditori* commanding their squadron.[40]

In short the development of gunpowder and the carrack had created problems which could not be solved within the framework of Venice's traditional schemes of fleet organization. We will see that so much of that traditional scheme was determined by the Senate that Grimani is hardly to be blamed for not having remedied its deficiencies before the encounter at Zonchio.

The cases of cowardly disobedience in that battle gave him a chance, however, which a man of different temperament would have seized, to make changes both in personnel and structure. The appropriate steps were indicated by the offer which Domenico Malipiero made that he would assume command of all the round ships if one of the other *provveditori* would take charge of the great galleys. To have done so would have put some top commanders in the front line. Malipiero was ready to assume the danger and the glory of action like that of Andrea Loredan at Zonchio. If Grimani had done so himself, he might have restored morale. But such a change would have involved deposing in disgrace the men who had been elected by the Great Council to high positions of command. The other *provveditori* said nothing immediately when Malipiero made his proposal in a council of war, but they later told the secretary to cut that out of the minutes for they did not wish to dishonour anyone ('tuor l'onor a nisun').[41]

Grimani himself was equally reluctant to impugn anyone's honour. He was an ambitious politician intent on winning the ducal election that was to occur soon and he was anxious not to make enemies. This was the reason for his failure to punish the disobedient, according to Girolamo Priuli.[42] The records of his trial show that he was trying to place on the *provveditori* the onus of any 'breaking' of officers. They threw the responsibility back on him. Grimani's high-priced Paduan lawyer argued that he lacked authority to dismiss or punish without the consent of the *provveditori*. The state attorneys said he had.[43] The orders he issued officially contained harsh threats of death for any failure to attack when ordered,[44] but noble officers probably realized that such passages were merely traditional rhetorical flourishes – at least so they proved in practice – although when Grimani ordered the under-officers, who were commoners, to attack when he ordered, even if it meant killing their noble commanders, threatening otherwise to hang them, they took it seriously enough to be even more demoralized.[45]

Hesitation about removing officers from their commands is all the more understandable in view of the way they obtained their ranks and assignments. The *capitanio generale del mar* was chosen only in the event of a major mobilization and had such great authority that he was often compared to a Roman dictator. (I have avoided calling him an 'admiral' because the similar Venetian term, *armiraio* or *admiratus*, referred to the highest non-noble officer in the fleet, whom I have referred to as captain general's chief of staff.) The *provveditori* were not only squadron commanders but councillors of the captain general. They formed with him the council of war that could decide what to do with the fleet, but he had full powers in executing the decisions of the council.[46] A number of *capitani* had authority limited to particular squadrons. There were normally *capitani* for each fleet of merchant galleys; for example the *capitanio al trafego* commanded the fleet trading between Tunis and Alexandria. A man chosen *capitanio delle navi* had previously commanded only the few especially large round ships built by the government but the title carried with it presumed command of all the round ships in the fleet, which meant in this case more than a score. Individual ships were commanded either by *sopracomiti* if they were light galleys or by *patroni* if they were great galleys or round ships. Below the above ranks, all of which were reserved for nobles, were those commonly if not exclusively held by non-nobles, whom we might call non-commissioned officers. Each *capitanio* had an *armiraio* whom he selected and who was generally much more competent technically in nautical matters than the noble for whom he worked, but all the higher ranks of the non-commissioned officers had to be approved by committees formed by the nobles concerned with naval admin-istration, and such committees chose the gunners and the deck officers individually for many specific ships.[47]

The *sopracomiti* who commanded the galleys normally armed for patrolling or minor wars were elected by one of the governing councils of the Republic, as were also all the higher commanders, the *provveditori* or *capitani*. Sometimes the honour of election as *sopracomito* preceded by many years the assignment to an actual command, that is, the ordering by the *Signoria* that a galley be taken from the arsenal for him, and that cash be provided to a paymaster so that the elected *sopracomito* might set up a hiring bench on the Molo between the Ducal Palace and the lagoon and make the advance payments on wages which were the essentials of enrolling a crew. The *sopracomiti* who 'armed' in 1498 and early 1499 had almost all been elected in February, 1493.[48] Traditionally it was the Great Council, as the sovereign fount of honour, which elected *sopracomiti*, *provveditori*, and *capitani*. As in so many matters, the Senate or its steering committee, the *Collegio*, or the Council of Ten tried to control selections.[49] Solicitation of such offices was so repeatedly forbidden that it must have been widely practised, and the jockeying between different councils over making the selections suggests how much the positions were sought after and how much any commander would have resented having taken from him while in service the honour which he had won by votes in the Senate or Great Council.

The *patroni* of the great galleys obtained their posts by a different method and one which in 1499 affected selections in much of the rest of the fleet. These *patroni* gained their positions by making the highest bid for the galleys when the government put up to auction the charter for their operation on specified commercial routes. Because the Turkish intentions were doubtful all through the spring, in 1499 the great galleys had been auctioned for the usual voyages. The *patroni* who had bid them in could not be installed until they were approved by the Senate as meeting requirements of age, general fitness, and especially of adequate financial backing. Once approved, they set up their hiring benches in front of the Ducal Palace and began giving out the advances in pay, totalling about 1,000 ducats a galley, that were necessary to enroll a crew. They could of course claim compensation for being diverted from their money-making voyages to service in the war fleet, but would collect for that from the government only much later.[50] Manning the galleys through private enterprise, as this method might be called, had the great advantage, as the banker Priuli remarked, that the more it was used the more the government could man a fleet without dispensing its own cash.

For that reason probably, and because the contemporaneous war in Lombardy left the government very short of cash, it accepted offers from other commanders to finance the hiring of crews. In regard to most of the round ships there was no thought of the government paying out coin immediately because it rented ships from owners who supplied not only the vessel but its master and a crew of specified size. For example, the *Pandora* had been rented from the Pesaro of London, who supplied Stefano Ottobon as *patron* and 300 men for 1,500 ducats a month to be paid in three years. The other privately owned round ships were rented on comparable terms, but the other three largest ships were already owned by the government. Their *patroni* were elected, except that to provide for manning the flag ship of the *capitanio delle nave*, Alvise Marcello, there was competitive bidding for a contract to engage and pay the crew, with reimbursement later. The contractor could name the *patron* who would, of course, be subject to the *capitanio*. The lowest bid was from one of the chiefs of the Ten, who named his son as *patron*. Alban d'Armer, the elected *patron* of another big ship, already partly manned, then asked and received similar terms, although Sanuto thought it a steal. Even some of the *sopracomiti* asked to be allowed to establish claims for future repayments by hiring their own crews – which suggests that some people thought there was money to be made out of these arrangements.[51] It was generally the case that a *sopracomito* who wanted a good crew had to pay out some coin himself for bonuses and hope to recover later from the government. Some of the galley commanders may have wanted to take over more of the paymasters' functions just in order to get a better crew to do themselves honour.

The latter was presumably the main motivation of Antonio Grimani in advancing as he did a large part of the cost of manning the fleet. When the Senate voted in April that a captain general should be elected, Grimani, while saying he did not wish the high command, offered to provide funds to arm ten galleys. In effect he was calling attention to his availability and his capacity to ease the financial strain.[52] Venice was in the middle of a severe banking crisis. Of its three leading banks, one had failed in February and another collapsed in May.[53] But when Grimani ceremonially began enlisting crews on 20th April, dressed in scarlet behind the hiring bench, he and the naval paymasters had five mountains of coins in front of them from which to pay men who signed on – 30,000 to 40,000 ducats, rumour said. He personally advanced 16,000 ducats; in return the Council of Ten obligated funds from the Salt Office to repay him in less than a year.[54] When the state treasurers diverted to other purposes some of the coin which his son had brought them, he protested violently in the

Senate, even saying 'he wanted his own money or he wouldn't go'.[55] He speeded arming in Crete by writing to officials there that in case of need they could draw on him personally for the money that would be required.[56] At his trial Grimani pleaded among his past services that he had spent 20,000 ducats getting the fleet manned quickly.[57]

A tempting explanation of the fiasco at Zonchio is to blame it on the number of converted merchantmen in the fleet. On the other hand, it might be pointed out that some merchantmen were among the few ships that gave a good account of themselves and that some regularly elected officers on government vessels were among those most clearly delinquent. But any attempt at a clear distinction between regular military navy and merchant marine is anachronistic in view of the methods of manning and selecting officers just described, and of the extent to which commanders of trading fleets normally moved up to high commands in the battle fleets.

In regard to the crews there is more basis for a distinction between warship and merchantman. On both, the crews were free men, volunteers – so Venetians proudly boasted at a time when slaves were increasingly used in all the other Mediterranean fleets.[58] None was chained to his bench and all received pay for their services. Warships were very largely manned in the colonies, however, and the *galeotti* from the colonies were partly conscripts or substitutes hired as replacement for draftees. The light galleys in the fleet in 1499 were manned as follows:[59] 13 in Dalmatia or Istria; 11 in Crete; 18 in Venice itself; 4 in Apulia; 2 in Corfu. They were commanded by *sopracomiti* chosen where the crew was collected, although the vessels themselves came from the Venetian arsenal and Venice sent out cash to assure crews.[60] Those classified as 'manned in Venice (armate in questa terra)' regularly went to Dalmatia to 'interzare', that is, to enlist a third man for each bench. Some *sopracomiti* found that costly; but captain general Grimani took conscription rolls with him and filled out his crew at little expense.[61] The number added in Dalmatia was sometimes much more than a third; *provveditore* Simon Guoro left Venice with only forty-five, counting on getting the rest in Dalmatia.[62]

In Venice crews had been conscripted for thirteenth and fourteenth-century wars,[63] but in the fifteenth century the government depended on wages and 'fringe benefits' to attract volunteers to warships as well as to trading vessels. Wages for merchant seamen are known only for the galleys of trade. The lowest wage there, that of the oarsmen, was fixed by law at 8 or 9 lire.[64] These must have been relatively good jobs because it seemed necessary repeatedly to make regulations against the receipt by the *patroni* of 'kickbacks' from the men they favoured by hiring them.[65] Eight lire a month, less than 16 ducats a year, was not very high pay (an ordinary master shipwright in the arsenal made about 50 ducats a year) but the 'fringe benefits' of a crewman on a merchant galley were considerable. His post gave him the right to carry some merchandise between the world's best markets with high security without paying freight on it, and gave such good opportunities for smuggling that it seemed only practical to give *galeotti* a legal right to bring into Venice some things scot free.[66] On the war galleys terms of employment were different. The base pay was 12 lire a month for oarsmen. The fringe benefits (aside from chances to smuggle, which were not negligible even on war galleys) consisted mainly of a share in any booty. On the other hand there were legitimate deductions from the 12 lire, as for weapons, clothing, and medical and priestly services, and there were kickbacks, legal and illegal, to paymasters and to officers. When in the spring of 1499 oarsmen refused to enroll on the great galleys at 8 lire because they expected to be sent into the fleet, and demanded 12, they were cajoled into signing on partly by threats of no future jobs and partly by being told that on the war galleys one-third of the pay was eaten up by such deductions.[67]

The status of the seamen within Venice is graphically revealed by several incidents. At the end of 1494 when about 300 men, the crew of the *barza* which had been armed by the government, were being paid off, an attempt was made to deduct about a third of what was due them as a kind of withholding tax, comparable to that which was being held back from salaried employees. Infuriated they rushed through the Ducal Palace to the door of the room where the Senate was meeting, demanding to speak to the doge and the *Signoria*. They brushed aside secretaries and broke down the first of the two doors to the Senate chamber before the chiefs of the Council of Ten succeeded in quieting them. Half a dozen were arrested but were let go six days later because, as Malipiero commented in describing the incident, the government feared otherwise not to have crews when they were needed and because their uprising was only in order to get the wages they had earned and had been promised to them.[68] Also significant is what happened in 1500 when oarsmen were again asked to enroll for only 8 lire on great galleys that were almost certainly going into the battle fleet. They refused and kept on refusing in spite of threats until the government gave in and agreed to pay 12 lire.[69] As these instances illustrate, the crews were indeed free to withhold their services and free to protest when paid otherwise than as promised, as frequently happened, and were allowed considerable licence as to the form of their protests. Most commonly they simply stood on the staircase within the Ducal Palace crying out demands for pay – to be heard by senators, councillors and foreign ambassadors until the government was shamed into paying them. Once they protested by sacking the bread stores and went unpunished.[70]

In the incident of 1494 it is significant that Malipiero refers to the protesters as 'galioti della barza'. In calling them *galeotti* he did not mean to identify them as oarsmen, for the *barza* was a round ship not a galley, nor as sailors, for no such large number was needed to handle the sails and tiller. Most of them had been hired as marines and in calling them *galeotti* he was identifying them as fighting men of the fleet. Like other volunteers or mercenary soldiers in an age famous for such incidents as the sack of Rome in 1527, Venice's *galeotti* showed most enthusiasm in their fighting when inspired by prospect of loot,[71] but there

L

were no complaints of their behaviour in the face of the Turkish fleet off Zonchio and certainly no evidence that crews of converted merchantmen behaved any differently than crews of war galleys. The charges of cowardice and disobedience were all directed at the officers.

New crews, however, became difficult to recruit after that battle. Seamen were considered in short supply in Venice already in the winter of 1498–99. With the navy adding its demands for men to those of the merchant marine many had to be recruited elsewhere in the Adriatic. At least one galley went from Venice to Ancona to find a crew, and several joined the fleet short-handed.[72] In spite of difficulties, about 20 light galleys, 15 great galleys, and 15 large round ships were listed as 'manned in Venice'. Allowing for some filling up at other Adriatic ports, that meant 5,000 to 7,000 men from Venice or between one quarter and one-third of the 20,000 men in Grimani's fleet. Since the total population of the Venetian lagoons was about 150,000, even 5,000 men was more than one-tenth of its men of military age. To recruit any such high proportion of Venetians for prolonged service in a war fleet was becoming less and less practical.

III

Under Grimani's successors, only a little progress was made towards new solutions of the three problems we have outlined: combining for effective battle action round ships, great galleys, and light galleys; enforcing discipline on elected officials; and recruiting adequate crews for large war fleets.

To succeed Grimani, the Senate and Great Council picked his rival Marchisio Trevisan, who had had the good fortune to be with the land forces which were successful that summer in acquiring Cremona. He tried to raise spirits by conquering Cephalonia in the winter months of 1498–1500. It looked easy but he failed to take it. An epidemic, together with discontent with new, fire-eating commanders sent out from Venice, intensified the demoralization and decimation of his crews. His letters became a monotonous cry for more men, more money, fresh ships – always for more men.[73]

Meanwhile the Turks were preparing a new armada and outfitting it within what Venice considered their own waters, the Ionian Sea. The campaign of 1499 had from a strictly naval point of view ended in a draw: both fleets had been rendered incapable of further action that year. Who would control the Ionian Sea was yet to be decided. The Ottoman emperor recruited new crews in Anatolia and Constantinople. At his newly acquired port of Lepanto he repaired the fleet that had survived the battle of Zonchio. He built new vessels there and also near Prevesa and Valona where good timber supplies were available.[74] For the first time the Turk was outfitting a fleet within the Ionian Sea, almost within the Adriatic, to challenge Venice in its home waters.

In response to Trevisan's appeals and the Turkish preparations, the Senate voted additional reinforcements. It had more money available because of successes in the war in Lombardy.[75] But it could not find volunteers to go to the disease-ridden camps and ships at Corfu and Cephalonia. Veterans were dissatisfied because they had not been promptly paid.[76] Venice began conscripting men from the lagoons and enlisting volunteers from the subject cities on northern Italy. Some *galeotti* had been recruited from Verona in time to serve under Grimani, and the doge proposed levying 10,000 men from the *terraferma*, taking one man from every four households, but the action taken in 1500 was a relatively mild call for volunteers. In February 1500 the administrators on the *terraferma* were ordered to find 2,000 who would serve for six months, receiving 3 months' pay in advance and two years' exemption from taxes.[77] When these replacements began reaching the fleet in May 1500 the captain general began a long series of unfavourable reports. The 'Lombards' died or ran away or were no good because they did not know how to behave at sea.[78]

For conscription within Venice, instead of returning to the parish organization which had been used in previous centuries, the government used the industrial and fraternal organizations embracing the artisans and shopkeepers. Naturally the first to be drafted were the gondoliers and other boatmen who were organized according to the ferries (*traghetti*) in which they worked. As early as July, 1499, it was decreed that the ferrying should be done only by men over forty or fifty so that the younger men would have to enlist in the fleet in order to earn their living.[79] Then thirty at least were called from each *traghetto*.[80] About the same time the five *scuole grandi* were called on to furnish each 100 men.[81] In September all the guilds were called on to supply men.[82] All these measures still left the fleet short of men throughout 1500 and 1501.[83]

New ships were sent to Trevisan to replace those sent home for dismantling or repair and they were a mixture, as in the past, of round ships, great galleys, and light galleys.[84] Trevisan's capacity to operate ships of such diverse qualities as a single fleet was never put to the test. He was so short of men that he did not feel strong enough to challenge the Turkish fleet, not even when it was divided. He failed to prevent the fleet refitted at Lepanto from joining in June at Prevesa with the new ships built there. He died while following the combined Turkish fleet as it then sailed south to support the army that was besieging Modon.[85]

To act in place of a captain general until a new one was chosen in Venice, the *sopracomiti* in the fleet elected Girolamo Contarini, then one of the *provveditori*.[86] He had been a leader in the conquests in Apulia.[87] More than any other Venetian commander at this time, Girolamo Contarini was alert to the changes that gunfire was making in naval warfare. He expressed his faith in cannon in describing in 1495 a chase in which he almost caught Camalì – would have caught him, he said, if only two Dalmatian galleys that were his consorts had obeyed orders. Camalì had lots of men on light fast ships, but Contarini had faith in the superior guns in the Venetian galleys. Now as fleet commander he issued general battle orders that distinguished between signals directing his fleet to start bombardment of the enemy and signals directing them to close for boarding.[88] Also, he envisaged his fleet proceeding in a line rather than in a column of squadrons. He was an enthusiastic, brave commander inclined to overestimate his own cannon and underestimate those of the enemy.

His courage and optimism and the desperate need of some feat of arms if Modon were to be saved led him into what might be called the Second Battle of Zonchio, 24th July, 1500. Trailing a Turkish fleet, which he reported as 230 sail including 60 light galleys, he brought his own fleet of 34 light galleys, 13 great galleys, and 20 round ships to the anchorage off Proti. A scouting galley reported that the enemy galleys were within the bay of Navarino (Zonchio) and all the Turkish big round ships were further south at Sapienza. The wind was light and uncertain but Contarini hoped it would increase enough to bring his own round ships and great galleys into action, while preventing the Turkish ships from coming up from Sapienza. In fact, a Venetian caulker, who was a prisoner at the time on one of the Turkish round ships, later described Camali and other Ottoman commanders on those square-rigged vessels as pulling out their beards with frustration, unable to join in the battle, as they watched the Venetian great and light galleys falling on Turkish vessels coming out of the bay. But the Venetian round ships also lacked enough wind to get into the action. The great galleys led the Venetian attack and were at first successful, but four of them deserted the fight at a crucial moment and two of them were cut off and surrounded by a multitude of smaller Turkish vessels. While he was leading his light galleys to their support Contarini's galley was hit in the stern by a cannon ball that passed clean through the captain's cabin carrying away six frames on one side of the hull and four on the other, so that his galley began to sink, and he was forced to retire.[89] After a long fight, the two great galleys succumbed. One was scuttled, the other was taken to Constantinople and used as a model in the Turkish arsenal. The captured banners were displayed at Modon to discourage its defenders' hopes of relief.[90]

A gallant attempt later to relieve Modon was equally ill fated. The ships got in, but while the defenders were unloading the much needed munitions they left the walls so lightly guarded that the besiegers stormed into the city.

Modon had been the main Venetian base south of Corfu and the most important Venetian stronghold in the Morea. Its fall was portentous. Nearby Coron and Zonchio also fell, and the Turkish army moved on to Nauplia on the other side of the Morea, the one remaining Venetian strong point in Greece. Since the Turks had demonstrated naval control of the Ionian Sea they might be expected to attack its islands next. The inhabitants of Zante began sending women and children to Dalmatia. But seapower had quite different meanings to the Turks and to the Venetians. Disasters caused the Venetians to send more reinforcements to the fleet. Success was for the Ottoman emperor an opportunity to withdraw his forces. He had achieved the main objective of the campaign – the conquest of territory that eliminated Venetian power in Greece, and he had many land frontiers to worry about. Hungary was threatening.

The Turkish army and navy returned to Constantinople in August or September without even stopping to make a real assault on Nauplia.[91]

Because of the Turkish withdrawal, Venice's next captain general of the sea, Benedetto Pesaro, never had to direct in a battle between fleets the heterogeneous collection of vessels of which he took command. This Pesaro was an experienced seaman, known as Pesaro of London, who had been fleet commander of the Flemish galleys. Also, he had served in the most authoritative positions in the government, as ducal councillor and more recently as a chief of the Council of Ten. He was considered a stern man of few words, 'luxurious and libidinous', always wanting a woman with him, which was considered by Priuli especially shameful in a man of Pesaro's seventy years. Some men suggested for the command in 1500 indicated they did not want the post in view of its grave difficulties, but Pesaro sought it and accepted it gladly.[92]

When he took over, the Venetian ships were trailing the Turks into the Aegean. Pesaro organized the pursuit and complained that the slowness of his round ships seemed likely to prevent him from catching the Turks before they were protected by the batteries at the Dardenelles. Perhaps that was bluff. He refreshed the spirit of his crews by letting them loot everything they could find within two miles of the shore on the Aegean island of Mytilene. He conceived his main task, however, to be the firm establishment of Venetian control of the Ionian Sea in spite of the loss of Modon. The fall of Modon had alerted other Christian powers to a possible power vacuum in that area and Spain, France, and Portugal all sent fleets. With the aid of the Spaniards, Pesaro took Cephalonia. Later, Venetian forces alone in 1502 took Santa Maura (Levkas), so that all the Ionian Islands were in Venetian hands. Pesaro penetrated the Gulf of Arta and captured the ships the Turks were building there. A similar effort in the Vojussa River near Valona failed but the Turks were prevented from building a substantial naval base anywhere in the Ionian or Adriatic Seas. Merchant fleets were safely convoyed to Syria and Egypt and great galleys resumed their trading voyages to both east and west; in fact they were under way before the end of 1500.[93]

These achievements were enough to give Pesaro a reputation as a man to be feared. He increased that reputation when a pirate named Enrichi fell into his hands and he put him to death by roasting him for three hours. The torture was revenge for Enrichi's roasting of a Venetian noble with whom he had quarrelled over payments for protection.[94]

Among Venetians also, Pesaro built a reputation as a man to be feared, because of the way he disciplined his noble subordinates. He demoted some and beheaded two for surrendering forts they were ordered to defend, even though one of those beheaded was Marco Loredan, a *provveditore* elected by the Senate, a relative of the newly elected doge, Leonardo Loredan, and the son of Alvise Loredan, a distinguished captain general of the mid-century.

While such boldness in enforcing discipline increased Pesaro's general popularity, the aftermath illustrates why commanders careful about their political careers might hesitate to imitate Pesaro. After he had taken Santa Maura, his secretary, Marco Rizo, was summoned home under arrest charged with various kinds of extortion or fraud, especially in connection with treasure which had been found in the castle at Santa Maura. The state attorney who was pressing the charge was a Loredan and Doge Leonardo Loredan was said also to hold against the secretary the beheading of Marco.[95] After Benedetto Pesaro's death in August, 1503, he himself was accused of having taken about half of the treasure. The defence put up by his heirs turned on the extent of his rights as captain general to booty seized in battle. They and his clerk-accountant were accused of falsifying the books. In a general attack on Pesaro, official auditors asserted also that he had made a 14 per cent profit in cashing bills of exchange sent him, had recorded as paid ninety men on one ship that had only two, and so on.[96] But his heirs escaped any criminal persecution, and Marco Rizo, although subjected to torture, was cleared completely in 1506 and restored to high rank in the ducal chancery. His brother was the priest in charge of the parish of San Moisè. This debarred Marco from functioning as secretary of the *Collegio* when papal relations were under consideration but it may have helped to prevent his being railroaded.[97] Benedetto Pesaro's son, a senator, who was serving as *capitanio* of the galleys of Flanders when the charges were made, on his return intervened in a discussion of the next Flemish voyage to defend his father.[98]

The captain general may have felt he deserved a good part of those 16,000 ducats; it does not seem out of character. He had a reputation for being free-handed, and to raise morale after he first took command he ordered his share of booty to be added to that of the crews. But his luck or foresight in seizing Santa Maura before the gold which the sultan had sent there to provide for fortifying it had yet been spent for that purpose presented a special temptation. Half of 16,000 ducats was enough to dower several daughters; the legal limit on dowries was set in 1505 at 5,000.[99]

Pesaro's recognition that the crew needed booty to supplement their meagre wages made him popular with his men. After the raid on Prevesa in which large quantities of cordage, anchors and other naval stores were captured, he spoke for his crews in claiming that it was booty from which a share should be credited to their accounts.[100] Recruitment improved under his leadership but he felt his operations much limited by the lack of men and the worthlessness of the conscripts from northern Italy. For the raid on Prevesa and Vojussa he took all the crews off five or six galleys in order to man adequately the eight or ten he took with him.[101] Repeatedly he deplored the 'Lombardi' as worthless; one galley of 'Schiavoni' was worth twenty of 'Lombardi' he asserted; the latter were always sick and no medicine would cure them, not even money.[102]

Pesaro's leadership in the fleet, like that of Andrea Gritti in the recapture and defence of Padua in 1509, may be considered turning points in the military morale of Venice. Years later, in permitting Antonio Grimani to return to his city in honour when his connections at the papal court were needed, and in elevating him to the dogeship in 1521, the Venetians were recognizing that the deplorable outcome of the battle of Zonchio had not been due to his cowardice or criminal negligence. Also they recalled that other admirals had been condemned and later honoured, most notably Vettor Pisani in the War of Chioggia. There had been charges of cowardice and insubordination after almost every naval encounter that was not an overwhelming success.[103] The conviction of Antonio Grimani and his rehabilitation and elevation to the dogeship is only an extreme case.

Grimani's career epitomizes the fact that diplomatic and financial ability were gaining priority over naval service in determining political success in Venice. This change in priorities was one factor in the decline of Venetian sea power. The deficiencies in the way the crews were recruited and the officers selected also contributed. At least, such concomitants of Venetian social structure are to be considered more decisive than any circumstances affecting the outcome of particular battles, such as superior weapons or the personalities of commanders. On the other hand, the growths of the Ottoman and Spanish empires during the first decades of the sixteenth century raised the demands of sea power to new dimensions. Within three decades after the battle of Zonchio, the Ottoman Turk had ousted the Knights of St. John from Rhodes and turned it into the base for a Moslem fleet, conquered all Syria, Palestine, and Egypt, and made an alliance with the Barbary pirates which placed much of the naval resources of North Africa at his command. During the same decades, the Spanish conquered other parts of North Africa, added Naples to Sicily, and by hiring Andrea Doria put the navy of Genoa also at their disposal. Squeezed between these two giants, Venice's empire, which had once seemed large, looked puny. The growth of such rivals within the Mediterranean explains Venice's decline in naval power more than does any backsliding on her part. To keep up she would have had to make extraordinary achievements in superior organization. In shipbuilding she did so and matched her rivals in numbers of ships. But she could not match them in fighting men and her efforts to do so were handicapped by the weaknesses revealed in 1499 in her ways of obtaining crews and officers.

NOTES

1. Luigi Fincati, 'La deplorabile battaglia del Zonchio (1499)' in *Rivista marittima* (1883) 185 seq., and in *A.V.*, xxv (1883) 415 seq. is excellent on the setting and the general nature of the action but as pointed out by Cecchetti, ib., 415 Admiral Fincato saw only a small part of the available evidence. The account by Camillo Manfroni in *Storia della marina italiana dalla caduta di Costantinopoli alla battaglia di Lepanto* (Rome, 1897) 214–220 puts less blame on Grimani personally, more on poor morale generally. G. Cogo, 'La guerra di Venezia contro i Turchi, 1499–1501' in *N.A.V.*, xviii (1899) 5–76, 348–421 and xix (1900) 81 seq. gives the general background, some documents, and good detail on events in Venice. Ester Zille, 'Il processo Grimani', *A.V.*, ser. V, xxxvi

(1945-46) 137-194, adds much on internal political aspects, being the first to use the chronicle of Pietro Dolfin, cited below, edited meanwhile by Cessi and Sambin. On the other hand, Sydney N. Fisher, *The foreign relations of Turkey, 1481-1512* (Urbana, Ill., 1948) keeps the Turks in the centre of the story although depending mainly on material in Sanuto's *Diarii*. Turkish sources were used by J. Hammer, *Histoire de l'empire ottoman depuis son origine jusqu'à nos jours*, tr. J. J. Hellert, iv (Paris, 1836).

2. Franz Babinger, *Mahomet II le Conquérant et son temps, 1423-1481* (Paris, 1954) 98-102; Nicolò Barbaro, *Cronaca dell' assedio e della presa di Costantinopoli, 1453*, ed. E. Cornet (Vienna, 1856) 31, 35-39.

3. F. L. Polidori, ed., 'Due ritmi e una narrazione in prosa di autori contemporanei intorno alla presa di Negroponte fatta dai Turchi . . . 1470', *A.S.I.*, Appendice, vol. ix (1853) 439. See also the reference to the superiority of Turkish guns at that time over those on Venetian ships in the letter in *A.S.I.*, ser. i, vii (1843) 49-52.

4. Frederic C. Lane, *Venetian ships and shipbuilders of the Renaissance* (Baltimore, 1934) 41-51, 60, or rev. ed., *Navires et constructeurs à Venise pendant la Renaissance* (Paris, 1965) 37-47, 56.

5. Marino Sanuto, *Diarii*.

6. Domenico Malipiero, *Annali veneti dell'anno 1457 al 1500*, eds. Tommaso Gar and Agostino Sagredo, *A.S.I.*, ser. i, vii (Florence, 1843). Malipiero's high qualities as a person and commander are evidenced by the comments of several officials who worked with him and the unwillingness of his crews to have him leave them at Pisa. Sanuto, i, 578, 1062, 1086-7, 1093; ii, 264; iii, 1267. See also n. 34 below. But the *Annali* attributed to Malipiero were rearranged by Francesco Longo (d. 1584) who had inherited his notes or rough draft and who may have altered or added, perhaps drawing on various kinds of materials. Some carelessness of Longo in reworking a diary and a collection of letters and rough drafts might explain such contradictions as Malipiero's statement given in the first person, 551, that he returned from Pisa to Venice in April, 1498, whereas other passages, 506, 509 report him still in Pisa in July, and innumerable letters in Sanuto's *Diarii* later in the year report him there, and having in February, 1499, been 'out' for 32 months (Sanuto, ii, 498) as do official records in A.S.V., S.S., reg. 37, f. 85. Doubts about what Longo had done to Malipiero's draft were expressed by the editor, pp. xxi, xxiv and by Rinaldo Fulin, *Diarii e diaristi veneziani* (Venice, 1881) pp. vi-vii.

7. Girolamo Priuli, *I diarii*, in *R.I.S.* 2, xxiv, pt. iii, vol. i, ed. Arturo Segrè (Città di Castello, 1912), vols. ii and iv, ed. Roberto Cessi (Bologna, 1933, 1938).

8. Petri Delphini, *Annalium Venetorum*, pars quarta, eds. Roberto Cessi and Paolo Sambin, in *Diarii veneziani del secolo decimosesto*, i, fasc. i (Venice: Istituto Veneto di Scienze, Lettere ed Arti, 1943).

9. The use which the Venetians made of their absolute command of the sea during the later years of the war was so contrary to nineteenth-century conceptions of a glorious naval tradition that it is underplayed by both Luigi Fincati, 'L'armata di Venezia dal 1470 al 1474', *A.V.*, xxxiv (1887) and Camillo Manfroni, 'La campagna navale di Pietro Mocenigo', 1470-74, *Rivista marittima* (1912) pt. 2, 473 seq., and in his *Storia* above cited, chaps. vi and vii.

10. Manfroni, *Storia*, chap. xiv; Malipiero, pt. 2; Marino Sanuto, *La spedizione di Carlo VIII in Italia*, ed. R. Fulin as supplement to *A.V.*, 1873. For size of fleets, ibid., 360, 415, 416; and Sanuto, i, 744, 690; ii, 224.

11. It was 21 June before Sanuto wrote: 'al presente si è certificati esso Turcho venir a nostro danno'. *Diarii*, ii, 839-840.

12. Sanuto, ii, 224, 336.

13. Andrea da Mosto, *I dogi di Venezia* (Milan, 1960) 227-236; Priuli, i, 220-221, Sanuto, *Spedizione di Carlo VIII*, 495-7, 634, 650; *Diarii*, i, 746-8, 810.

14. Lists and totals at various dates in Sanuto, ii, 1126, 1241-1260; Priuli, i, 168.

15. Fisher, op. cit., 67-9; Sanuto, ii, 1127, 1141-2.

16. Babinger, op. cit., 444.

17. Sanuto, ii, 1250, 1054–6; Priuli, i, 150; Malipiero, 173–5. Totals vary but in unimportant ways.

18. Priuli, i, 157; Malipiero, 172, and frequent references to the wind in letters from the fleet, e.g., Sanuto, ii, 1123–4, 1230.

19. Fincati as cited in *Rivista marittima* (1881) pt. 1, 194. In the accounts cited below of actions in that area there are also many references to the 'provenza' which is identified as 'vento di maestro' (N.W.) by Cristoforo da Canal, *Della milizia marittima*, ed. Maria Nani Mocenigo (Rome, 1930) 206, 224.

20. Malipiero, 172; Sanuto, ii, 1122, 1141–2, 1148.

21. Hammer, op. cit., iv, 56; Fisher, 18, 38, 67–9. On Camalì, and also on the importance of the naval actions of 1499 in connection with piracy, see Alberto Tenenti, 'I corsari in Mediterraneo all' inizio del Cinquecento', *Riv. Stor. Ital.*, lxxii (1960) 234–287.

22. The clearest reliable account of the actions in August seems to be the summary inserted in Sanuto, ii, 1290–1294, probably written by Sanuto himself on the basis of the letters from the captain general and other reports which he only partially reported earlier. The most detailed of these is the highly emotional and partisan letter of Girolamo Cesoto, Antonio Grimani's chaplain, to Vincenzo, Antonio's son, which reached Venice ahead of the official dispatches. Sanuto, ii, 1224, 1230–1241. The account in Malipiero's *Annali* is in a letter (175–9), probably one that Malipiero sent to the *Signoria*. It is somewhat confusing in reporting twice the burning of the big ships. Priuli's account, *Diarii*, i, 181–5 adds some details and much indignant lamentation. Details can be gleaned from the account of the trial in Dolfin, 59–79. Differing only in some minor details is the account written later by Donado da Lezze, *Historia Turchesca*, ed. I. Ursu (Bucharest, Editunea Academici Romane, 1909) 226–9. Expressing more succinctly the same attitudes as Girolamo Priuli but more precise on some matters is the account in a chronicle from which large excerpts are given in [Giacomo] Nani's 'Memorie pour servire alla storia militare maritima della Repubblica di Venezia tratte in gran parte di MSS contemporanee . . .', ms no. 161, Biblioteca della Università di Padova, ii, paras. 2944–8.

23. Hammer, iv, 56, says the Turkish commander of their biggest ship himself set it on fire in despair.

24. Malipiero, 185.

25. In addition to the accounts above cited, Grimani's letter in Sanuto, ii, 1286 and Marcello's in ibid., ii, 1325.

26. Sanuto, ii, 1141–2, 1291; Priuli, i, 197, 206.

27. S.S., reg. 37, f. 142.

28. Sanuto, iii, 46–8; Priuli, i, 164, 220–1; Cogo as cited in *N.A.V.* (1899) 37–76.

29. Zille, as cited in (*A.V.* 1945–6).

30. Priuli, i, 164, 167.

31. Sanuto, *Spedizione di Carlo VIII*, 492–7; Malipiero, 372–6.

32. Sanuto, ii, 1258; Malipiero, 176–7. On his trial and wounds, Dolfin, 69, 92–3, 239–241 and Zille, as cited in *A.V.* (1945–6) 192–3. When finally brought to trial he had already been in prison many months. He was the only noble officer condemned besides Grimani. Although not beheaded as the *avogadori* asked, he was sentenced to permanent exile in Canea.

33. Sanuto, ii, 1257–9; iii, 83. Malipiero, 176 and Priuli, i, 181, also suggest last minute reorganization associated with Loredan's arrival so that he and Damer could lead the attack.

34. Malipiero, 175. Dolfin, 66, reports his testimony at Grimani's trial as 'molto reservato e degno' and critical of Grimani for his 'poco ordene e governo', especially in two respects: one was 'non dar gli ordeni de bataglia avanti el fato d'arme'. The other was in raising a banner with the crucifix instead of flying the golden banner to which Venetians habitually responded, the banner with which Grimani had been invested with

command at the ceremony in St. Mark's before his departure. For moves to make Malipiero captain general later, see Dolfin, 108 and Sanuto, iii, 551. While Malipiero was subject to an inquest by the *avogadori*, as were all the *provveditori*, he came home still in command of his galley, the only top commander to do so. S.S., reg. 37, ff. 141, 143. The vote making him ineligible for election as captain general went through the Great Council by the narrow margin of 673 to 517. A.S.V., S.M., reg. 15, f. 26. On his service as *capitanio delle navi*, and *vice capitanio generale del mar* in the war of Ferrara; see Malipiero, *Annali*, pp. xix-xx and 291-295; Manfroni, *Storia*, 121-2.

35. A.S.V., *Consiglio di Dieci, Miste*, reg. 28, f. 8 (Apr. 27, 1499).

36. Copies of the orders to be observed in attacking the Turkish fleet issued by the captain general on 28 July are given in Sanuto, ii, 1124-1126; Malipiero, 174-5; and partially in Priuli, i, 155-6, but they apply only to the light galleys.

37. In July there were 12 great galleys in the fleet, in August, 17; Sanuto, ii, 1243-1250. Those that were intended for trading voyages along Africa were given extra bulwarks, and their *capitani* elected for these voyages, *Barbaria* and *al trafego*, were to take turns commanding all great galleys; Malipiero, 172. Priuli, i, 157, says that each had command of 8 great galleys, but Andrea Baxadona, *capitanio delle galee di Barbaria*, accused of disobedience and cowardice, defended himself successfully by claiming that except for the weeks when he was in command his responsibilities were only those of a galley master, a *patrono*. Dolfin, 254-5. Their battle orders, none too clear, are in Sanuto, ii, 1292.

38. Priuli, i, 157 says three squadrons, but Alvise Marcello's letter in Sanuto, ii, 1257 says four and specifies the flagships.

39. *Galie bastarde* were built in 1500 (S.M., reg. 15, f. 26; Sanuto, iii, 561, 1642) and during the first part of the fifteenth century (Lane, *Venetian ships*, 58) but not in 1498-9.

40. Malipiero, 171, indicates that an entirely different combination of light and heavy galleys was contemplated for the earlier attempt to engage in July.

41. Dolfin, 67, 74.

42. Priuli, i, 326. Donado da Lezze, whose brother Marin da Lezze was a *sopracomito* in the fleet, wrote in his *Historia* above cited, 229: 'altra cossa è ad esser mercante et altra a governar stati et Armate, ne mai si vidde ne s'intese, ch'un uomo misero facesse cosa che fosse buono, salvo che in acquistar denari'. That probably reflected the opinions of those Venetians who had spent more of their lives in the fleet than on the Rialto. But Grimani's reluctance to punish was probably more a result of political calculation than of mercantile habits. His ultimate vindication by his election as doge in 1521 proves that his calculation was correct in a way. In the long run bitter personal enemies might have hampered his career more than did the immediate general hostility and disgrace.

43. Dolfin, 67, 74, 76. For Grimani's effort to place on the *provveditori* the blame for his failure to punish, see also Sanuto, iii, 322; Priuli, i, 326, 328. For the terms in which his commission gave him *imperium* see S.S., reg. 37, f. 89.

44. Malipiero, 175; Sanuto, ii, 1124.

45. According to Grimani's chaplain, he feared lest the *comiti* and *paròn iurati* (the high non-noble officers in direct command of the actions of the crew) would fail to attack and then blame their superior officers. To prevent that he sent orders that if the noble commanders *patroni* and *sopracomiti* did not attack when ordered, the *comiti* and *patroni* should kill them, otherwise they would be hanged themselves. The chaplain says this left them all 'sbigotiti'; Sanuto, ii, 1238-9. Indeed, his battle orders, as given by Sanuto, ii, 1126, said that the *comiti* who did not obey the captain general and *provveditori* but 'vorano far al modo de soi patroni, siano spicati per la gola non investando'. See also Priuli, i, 155-6. There was a similar clause in the later orders of Pesaro, but not in those of Trevisan or Contarini, on which see n. 88 below.

46. Camillo Manfront, 'Cenni sugli ordinamenti delle marine italiane nel Medioevo', *Rivista marittima* (1898) pt. 4, 476-9, 489; Cogo, as cited in *N.A.V.* (1900) doc. vii, p. 108.

47. Manfroni, *Rivista marittima* (1898) pt. 4, 474-483. Sanuto's diary is full of refer-

ences to his personal participation in the selection of bowmen and deck officers (e.g., ii, 467, 491, 869) and those for merchant galleys are recorded as actions of the *Collegio* in its *Notatorio.*

48. Compare the list in Sanuto, ii, 1241–1242 with that in A.S.V., *Segretaria alle voci,* reg. 8, f. 113.

49. Dolfin, 7, 23; Sanuto, ii, 613, 634, 650, 654, 667; iii, 201, 209, 211, 274, 285, 1253; vi, 22, 358; xxxvi, 582, 590; xxxvii, 151, 188; S.S., reg. 37, f. 85; S.M., reg. 19, ff. 117–8; reg. 20, ff. 8, 9, 125. Some *sopracomiti* other than those listed in *Segretaria alle voci,* reg. 6, ff. 87–88 and reg. 8, f. 113 are mentioned in *Notatorio di Collegio,* reg. 15, ff. 2, 20, 25, 62.

50. Alberto Sacerdoti, 'Note sulle galere da mercato veneziane nel XV secolo', *B.I.S.,* iv (1962) 95–7, 87–90; Sanuto, ii, 526, 578, 835, 837, 840, 844, 884.

51. Priuli, i, 122; Sanuto, ii, 452, 464, 508, 628–9, 637, 666–7, 672–5, 718, 751, 771; iii, 114; *S.M.,* reg. 14, f. 181r–v where provision is made to assign to them additional funds 'non essendo satisfacti in termine di anni tre'; also, ibid., ff. 183–9, 192, 193, 198, 206.

52. Sanuto, ii, 613, 819–20; S.S., reg. 37, f. 85, 12 April, 1499.

53. Lane, *Venice and history,* 72.

54. Ibid., ii, 637; Priuli, i, 118; Sanuto, ii, 631; *Consiglio di Dieci, Misti,* reg. 28, f. 8, 26 Apr., 1499.

55. Sanuto, ii, 650 'che voleva li soi propri danari aliter non anderia'.

56. Sanuto, ii, 858.

57. Priuli, i, 331.

58. Marino Sanuto, *Cronachetta,* ed. R. Fulin (Venice, 1880, per nozze Papadopoli-Hellenbach) 185.

59. Sanuto, ii, 1241–3; plans in ibid., ii, 336; Priuli, i, 121.

60. S.S., reg. 37, f. 189, 190; and Crete: Sanuto, ii, 570, 628, 755, 783, 812, 872, 918; Apulia: ibid., ii, 224, 436, 557; Dalmatia: ibid., ii, 629, 884; iii, 38.

61. Sanuto, ii, 376, 610, 710, 625, 640, 657, 662; Alberto Tenenti, *Cristoforo da Canal: La marine vénitienne avant Lépante* (Paris, 1962) 68–70; S.S., reg. 37, ff. 88–90.

62. Sanuto, ii, 101, 125, 400–1.

63. Romanin, ii, 332, 393; V. Lazzarini, 'Frammento di registro del tempo della guerra di Chioggia', *A.V.,* ser. V, xxi (1937) 126–129; Mario Brunetti, 'Contributo alla storia delle relazioni veneto–genovesi dal 1248 al 1350', in *Miscellanea di storia veneta* (Venice: Deputazione Veneta di Storia Patria, ser. III, ix, 1916) 65–6, 91–2.

64. A.S.V., *Senato, Deliberazioni, Incanti Galere,* reg. 1, ff. 66, 68, 89, 92, 114.

65. Ibid., f. 108; Priuli, i, 325; ii, 274–5; Marino Sanuto, *Cronachetta,* 90–91.

66. Sacerdoti, as cited in *B.I.S.* (1962) 93, *Incanti Galere,* reg. i, f. 92; A.S.V., *Compilazione leggi, busta* 27.

67. A.S.V., *Senato, Commissioni, Formulari,* reg. 4, f. 7; *Compilazione leggi, buste* 25, 27; Sanuto, ii, 844–5; Malipiero, 167.

68. Malipiero, 694.

69. Dolfin, 30; Sanuto, iii, 251–254, 259, 266; Priuli, i, 319; S.M., reg. 15, f. 12–13, 11 May, 1500.

70. Priuli, ii, 125; Sanuto, iv, 27.

71. Malipiero, 372–376; Contarini's letter. Sanuto also refers to the *zurme* for a *barza*; ii, 988. The Senate concerned itself with making sure that commanders gave crews their share of the booty 'che se pur i galeoti vano in armada non volevo exponer la vita ad pericolo per non haver alcuna utilità', S.M., reg. 15, ff. 17–18.

72. Sanuto, ii, 631, 648, 650, 685, 690, 696.

73. Priuli, i, 190, 193, 217, 228–9; Sanuto, ii, 1297, 1348; iii, 39–40, 54–70, 78–83, 93, 105, 109, 112–114, 122, 125, 126–7, 138, 150–1, 156, 181–2, 211, 236, 251, 253, 280, 303, 333–6, 362; Malipiero, 189, 190, 197; Dolfin, 12.

74. Hammer, iv, 62; Dolfin, 16; Priuli, i, 320; Sanuto, iii, 177–8, 256, 320, 336, 600.

75. Priuli, i, 304–9, 317; Sanuto, iii, 228–9 and below n. 78.

76. For difficulties over the payment of wages due and reinstating men who had fled the epidemic: Priuli, i, 125, 291, 301, 303; i, 125; Sanuto, iii, 251, 322, 367, 483, 1560; Dolfin, 30; S.M., reg. 15, ff. 17–18, 25, 33–4.

77. Sanuto, ii, 685–6, 690, 743, 784; iii, 119. A.S.V., S.M., reg. 14, ff. 205–6, 18 Feb., 1499–1500, for the offer to volunteers from the *terraferma*; and ibid., reg. 15, ff. 100, 135 for galleys armed from the Lago di Garda; Sanuto, iii, 142, 155, 336, 783; Priuli, i, 291; Dolfin, 33; Malipiero, 197.

78. Sanuto, ii, 783–4; iii, 336, 1394; Dolfin, 241; Priuli, ii, 110.

79. Priuli, i, 134; Sanuto, ii, 658.

80. Malipiero, 167–80.

81. Sanuto, ii, 873; *Consiglio di Dieci, Miste*, 28, f. 16, 28 June, 1499.

82. Priuli, i, 199; Sanuto, ii, 1348, 24 Sept., 1499, but I failed to find record of action at that date in the records of the *Collegio*, Senate, or Ten

83. Fisher, op. cit., 79; Sanuto, iii, 425, 444–5, 517–8, 1585.

84. Sanuto, ii, 260, 285, 263–6, 319, 324, 365, 396, 403, 410; Priuli, i, 303–9.

85. Sanuto, iii, 425, 446, 486–504, 517–8, 561, 583, 584; Dolfin, 109, 113.

86. Sanuto, ii, 599.

87. Malipiero, 148–151, 372–6.

88. From Grimani there is no record of orders to the fleet as a whole. His orders for light galleys are in Sanuto, ii, 1124–5. A brief order by the joint captains of the great galleys is in ibid., ii, 1292; and an order issued by the French and Venetian commanders to the whole combined fleets on 21 Aug., 1499, is in ibid., ii, 1292–4. This latter specified for all kinds of vessels which Turkish ships they should attack ('investir', i.e. board). The disposition is not explicit but implies a column of six squadrons. Trevisan's orders, ibid., iii, 604–6, which never went into effect, specified attack first by the round ships, then by the great galleys, and then by three squadrons of light galleys of which his would be the last – the same plan as Grimani seems to have had in mind for the first battle of Zonchio. Summarizing and commenting on it, Dolfin, 102, remarked that placing his own squadron as the last to attack 'indica poco animo del General'. Contarini's more imaginative orders are in Sanuto, iii, 613–4. Those of Pesaro issued 17 Sept., 1500, ibid., iii, 814–7, and never put into action (see above, p. 165), envisaged the same plan as Trevisan's but are more detailed. Texts of the fleet orders are also given in the above cited Nani's 'Memorie', Padua, ms no. 161, ii.

89. Dolfin, 124–132; Sanuto, iii, 584, 599, 600, 610–12, 622–3, 949–950. The commanders of the round ships and great galleys blamed their failure to support Contarini on the wind, or lack of it, and blamed him for attacking against such odds. Ibid., iii, 614, 668–9, 1078. Contarini accused them of not following orders and claimed if they had supported him, Modon would not have been lost. Ibid., iii, 722, 726. Da Lezze, who had a brother on one of the great galleys, blamed the Venetian defeat on the fact that the wind failed at a crucial moment. *Historia*, 251.

90. Sanuto, iii, 950, 1223; Dolfin, 141.

91. Fisher, op. cit., 75–79. On fears at Zante: Cogo, as cited in *A.V.* (1900) 117 and Sanuto, iii, 719, 810.

92. Priuli, ii, 19–20, 287; Sanuto, iii, 550, 553–4, 558.

93. Fisher, op. cit., 76–80; Cogo, as cited in *A.V.* (1899), 348–421; and the dispatches of Benedetto Pesaro in Sanuto, iii and iv (Index).

94. Priuli, ii, 191; Sanuto, iii, 205–6.

95. Sanuto, iv, 87, 231; v, 56–7, 126, 892–3; Priuli, ii, 195, 277–8, 281, 287; Dolfin, 198.

96. Priuli, ii, 287, 407, 419–420; Sanuto, v, 1054–5; vi, 320, 349–350.

97. Sanuto, v, 492–3; vi, 180–1, 301, 543; A.S.V., *Avvogaria, Raspe*, reg. 3660/20, ff. 134–5 (18 Feb., 1506).

98. Sanuto, vi, 61, 323. The son, Girolamo, had been elected to the Senate when only 30 at the time when his father's popularity was at its peak. Dolfin, 242.

99. Priuli, ii, 392.

100. Priuli, ii, 100, 172; Sanuto, iii, 1419; Dolfin, 237.

101. Sanuto, iii, 1416, 1581, 1585.

102. Sanuto, iii, 1394, 1419, 1544–7, 1581.

103. For 1299, see *Deliberazioni del Maggior Consiglio*, ed. R. Cessi in *Atti delle assemblee costituzionali italiane dal Medio Evo al 1831*, R. Accademia dei Lincei, ser. III, sect. i (Bologna, 1934), iii, 446. After Carlo Zeno's victory in 1404, Zeno complained that not all galley commanders had done their duty and asked that the *avogadori* prosecute. Cappelletti, *Storia di Venezia* (Venice, 1850), v, 256–7; C. Manfroni, 'Lo scontro di Modone', in *Rivista marittima* (1897) 326–7.

VI

DONALD E. QUELLER

The development of Ambassadorial Relazioni[1]

Since the rise of modern historical scholarship in the nineteenth century the *relazioni* of Venetian ambassadors have enjoyed a just renown as informative and reliable sources. Only Venice with its patriciate and bureaucracy uniquely qualified for diplomatic affairs produced documents of this sort. Yet for all its long-standing fame the genre requires further examination. Scholars have not been sufficiently aware of its evolution, its change over time, but have tended to accept the *relazioni* of the sixteenth century as prototypal, viewing the genus in Aristotelian rather than Darwinian terms.[2] In particular, little is known of the pre-history of the *relazioni*, but it has been assumed that a large collection of invaluable earlier documents of the sixteenth-century sort were destroyed in the fires of the 1570s in the palace of the doge. In fact much can be known and still more can be reasonably speculated to enable us to place the historical development of the *relazioni* upon a firmer base.

One need not join the false cult of adulation of Venetian patriotism and statecraft to find in the *relazioni*, as does Francesca Antonibon, a kind of document *sui generis*, not only among diplomatic documents, but among literary types.[3] Some scholars less familiar with Venetian *relazioni* have taken the word in a generic sense and have found *relazioni* delivered by ambassadors of other states, although Venetian precedence and pre-eminence are generally conceded. Maulde La Clavière claimed Florentine *relazioni*, and there does exist in the Archivio di Stato at Florence a large collection labelled *Rapporti e relazioni di oratori*. A closer examination, however, reveals no distinction between Florentine *relazioni* and *rapporti*, neither of which resembles the Venetian product. The Florentine documents are merely final reports upon specific missions.[4] Many of them, especially those referring to mandates in which a number of tasks were assigned, simply list in order the outcome of the mission in regard to each item: *Primo . . ., secondo . . ., terzo . . .*, etc. A glance at the collection of instructions to orators confirms that what was required in

Florence was just a final report of 'what you have done in this matter', *viva voce* and occasionally also in writing.[5] From the second half of the sixteenth century Romolo Quazza also claims Mantuan *relazioni* similar to those of Venice.[6] Only one of these has been published, that of Annibale Litolfi on England in 1557. It is a strange miscellany at the other end of the spectrum from the itemized Florentine reports. In addition to some of the usual material of a *relazione* on the geography of England, its ports and cities, its commerce, its militia and arms, we find descriptions of English legal education and English architecture. Litolfi also describes the English at some length: they have no sense of honour, are heavy eaters, love comfort, but are brave and warlike. He tells about the dress of women, their freedom, and the punishment for infidelity. We are interested to learn that 'luoghi pubblici di disonesta non ci sono'. There is no account of the income and expenses of the English government or of the character and appearance of the king and his councillors – these would be virtually indispensable to a Venetian *relazione*. A remark that the ambassador will postpone writing of Parliament until another time reveals that this so-called *relazione* is probably an extremely chatty dispatch.[7] Other examples given as *relazioni* in Quazza's index also turn out to be dispatches.

We may concede that simulations of Venetian *relazioni* appeared from time to time. J. E. Neale found one, Sir George Carew's relation of the state of France in 1609, avowedly an imitation of the Venetian genre and due solely to Carew's own initiative.[8] Also, Carlo Morandi has published a small collection of Savoyard and Genoese as well as Venetian *relazioni* from 1693 to 1713, and these also follow the Venetian pattern.[9]

A fully developed Venetian *relazione* of the sixteenth century or later was quite different from a final report on the conduct and outcome of a mission. The *relazione* provided a broad and comprehensive synthesis, periodically brought up to date by successive ambassadors, of the political, military, economic and social conditions of the country visited.[10] Already before the end of the sixteenth century the historian Scipio Ammirato, writing under Medici patronage, valued the uniqueness of the Venetian *relazioni*, which told of 'the customs of the prince, of the site, the riches, the fertility, and other qualities of places and of men'. Venetian ambassadors performed their duty so well, in his opinion, that they often showed a firmer grasp of these matters than men of the host country itself.[11] Abraham de Wiquefort, the celebrated authority on international law a century later, also appreciated the difference between ordinary reports made by all ambassadors and Venetian *relazioni*.[12]

That the *relazione* was no place to repeat the sort of news that would be found in dispatches was also a commonplace to Venetian ambassadors by the 1530s. The words of Niccolò Tiepolo in 1532 are an echo heard again and again: '. . . everyone who returns from any mission comes to this most wise Senate, not to render account of his actions to it (which can be clearly grasped from the letters written by him from time to time), but to report if he has learned anything of the country from which he comes worthy of being heard and pondered by prudent senators for the benefit of the fatherland'.[13] In recent decades there has been some tendency among historians to exalt the importance of *dispacci* at the expense of *relazioni*. Dispatches provide a simple, full and almost spontaneous account of what was happening and the impressions of the moment.[14] All to the good – but over a century ago Baschet pointed out that *dispacci* were useful for one purpose, *relazioni* for another. Of the dispatches one can ask the gradual and daily course of events, description of facts, momentary interpretations, immediate impressions, conversations with ministers, audiences with princes, current rumours. In his *relazione*, on the other hand, the ambassador was not a mere chronicler of events, but the painter of a political tableau in broad terms; he depicted the characters of princes and ministers, the attitudes and sentiments of peoples, the strengths and weaknesses of states.[15] Valuable though they are, there is not much extraordinary about Venetian dispatches. The *relazioni*, on the other hand, with the exceptions noted previously, are unique.

The rulers of Venice were avid for knowledge of foreign lands that might be useful in the formation of policies, and the *relazione* was a stylized device for providing information concerning 'the power and disposition of all great lords and princes of the world as well as of the condition of lands and of the people who dwell in them'.[16] This was an essential part of the duty of a Venetian ambassador, along with following his instructions and reporting frequently on the results of his mission.[17] Marino Cavalli, just returned from the court of Ferdinand of Habsburg in 1543, recalled that he had conscientiously reported everything in his dispatches, 'but I could not then communicate that which it is more important to know, that is, the causes, the counsels, with what intentions and with what means things have been done, and what goal they may have had. To my mind this is not of minor importance, nor will it be of minor utility to the most prudent government of this most serene dominion when it is a matter of dealing with anything concerning Germany . . .' Some may think, according to Cavalli, that knowing a few generalities is enough, but only an exact knowledge and understanding of the forces, the method of governing, the amount of reliance one can place upon other states, can prevent errors in policy.[18] Knowledge of the past provided by the *relazioni* was the best guide to decision-making in the present.[19] The anonymous French *Traité du gouvernement de Venise* tells with approval how newly-appointed Venetian ambassadors sought out in the archives the *relazioni* of their predecessors in order to undertake their missions well informed.[20]

In the course of the sixteenth century the fame of the Venetian *relazioni* spread far and wide and copies were sold abroad at good prices, not only to governments, but also to erudite collectors.[21] Venetian noble families kept among their own papers examples of the genre, especially those by which a member of the clan had brought honour upon the house. From these sources came the copies that are now scattered among various libraries and archives.[22] Repeated legislation from 1401 on was directed toward the acquisition by the government of all public papers in the possession of returning diplomats and the restriction of access to these documents to a limited group, but to no avail.[23] Great concern over the circulation of *relazioni* cannot have existed, however, until the sixteenth century, for some material contained in the early extant *relazioni* would have been extremely embarrassing to the Republic if it were known to foreign governments. Zaccaria Contarini, for example, in 1492 named French pensioners susceptible to Venetian bribery and also delivered himself of a famous and utterly uncomplimentary description of Charles VIII, while Francesco Donato in 1504 called the queen of Aragon ugly and deformed.[24] Marino Sanuto, moreover, had ready access to the archives, as we may assume did other members of the patriciate. In the course of the sixteenth century, however, the *relazioni* gained international renown, and concern for security grew. Unless control could be exercised, Venetians feared 'the ill effect of either sealing their envoys' lips or divulging to the public what ought to be kept secret'.[25] At no time, however, do the efforts to achieve security seem to have been very successful, and, although this was unfortunate for Venetian government, it is the great good fortune of the modern historian, for to the scattered copies we owe many of the extant *relazioni*, especially the earliest.

As sixteenth-century diplomats, statesmen and literati instructed themselves through the *relazioni*, so, in the nineteenth and twentieth centuries, historical scholars have discovered rich sources of instruction. The Swiss historian Johann von Müller is credited with discovering the historical value of the *relazioni*, but their high renown is due largely to Leopold von Ranke, who relied heavily upon them for his *Fürsten und Völker von Süd-Europa*, *Die römischen Papste*, and other works. He it was who first gained permission (with great difficulty, after first having been refused) to study the *relazioni* preserved in the Archivio di Stato, where he worked happily for five months late in 1830.[26] Since Ranke's day the *relazioni* have been renowned among the sources for early modern history and their lack for medieval history has been deplored.[27]

Although a few *relazioni*, known from unofficial and often adulterated copies scattered about various libraries, archives and private collections, were printed in the sixteenth and seventeenth centuries, only after Ranke began to publicize them did the great collections, especially the fifteen volumes edited by Eugenio Albèri, begin to appear. Even these collections are inadequate to the needs of modern scholarship, as Arnaldo Segarizzi saw, although he died before he was able to make more than limited progress toward a modern critical edition.[28] A current effort does not undertake to provide the needed critical edition, but merely to reprint in one collection the best texts previously published.[29]

What has especially fascinated Ranke and his followers is the biographical detail in the *relazioni* on the protagonists of European history – above all the colourful portraits in words, like Zaccaria Contarini's description of Charles VIII of France:

'The Majesty of the King of France is twenty-two years of age, small and badly formed in his person, ugly of face, with eyes great and white and much

M

more apt to see too little than enough, an aquiline nose much larger and fatter than it ought to be, also fat lips, which he continually holds open, and he has some spasmodic movements of hand which appear very ugly, and he is slow in speech. According to my opinion, which could be quite wrong, I hold certainly that he is not worth very much either in body or in natural capacity.'[30]

Even the most recent editor in 1965 emphasizes the innumerable portraits of eminent personages.[31]

Certainly these were invaluable, but that vein has been thoroughly mined. Portraits of princes, moreover, are not the stuff of most modern historical writing. The *relazioni* include whatever information ambassadors considered profitable for the government, and, since these ambassadors were generally able statesmen, this same matter is also profitable to the modern historian. Accounts of the income and expenses of governments, the state of their military and naval forces, occasional population figures, and many other pieces of valuable information remain to be fully exploited. In his *relazione* the ambassador was not the slave of the moment and of events; here he presented a considered picture of the court, a political tableau painted judiciously, a synthesis upon the country and especially the government to which he had been assigned. Willy Andreas has expressed surprise that Burckhardt did not turn to the Venetian *relazioni* as a prime source for 'The state as a work of art'. He urges that the light of the *relazioni* should be turned upon Venice itself and the views, wishes and objectives prevalent there. He has done this himself with some success, though much remains to be done.[32]

It is possible, perhaps, to wax too enthusiastic over the experience, training, judgment and insight of those who served St. Mark as ambassadors and composed the *relazioni*.[33] They were, however, drawn from a relatively small and, from the mid-sixteenth century, a shrinking class upon which all responsibilities of state devolved, and so were far from amateurs in political affairs.[34] Many of them had served on more than one embassy. The greater part and the more important of the *relazioni* extant, moreover, were written by resident ambassadors, who had spent many months at their posts. Each was assisted by a competent staff headed by a secretary, and within the secretariat there were available men trained in the languages of all the countries with which Venice had relations.[35] The qualifications, opportunities and resources of Venetian ambassadors enabled them to produce a unique type of report, not more important than others, perhaps, but highly useful.

The nature of the Senate as the body before which the classical *relazioni* of the sixteenth century were delivered also contributed to moulding the genre. The audience were members of the merchant oligarchy upon whom political responsibility rested, many of them rich in experience of affairs of state, all well informed.[36] The presentation of a *relazione* in the Senate was an occasion of great solemnity, and was regarded by ambassadors and senators alike as an event of considerable importance.[37] Especially if the ambassador were an experienced man known for his ability as observer and speaker, the senators would anticipate with pleasure hearing him.[38] By this means the younger and less experienced members of the Senate were instructed, and even outstanding senior members added to their store of useful information. The ambassador was challenged, therefore, to add to their wisdom by informing them more fully than a mere report would allow of the land whence he had just returned. If he succeeded, he would be praised by the doge before the College and the Senate, by which, says the *Traité*, the gentlemen of Venice set great store.[39] This opportunity to display one's worth before the Senate might compensate for the physical and financial hardships of the ambassadorial office, for it could open the way to the highest political posts, such as the Small Council or the dogeship itself.

It is too commonly assumed, however, that from the very beginning *relazioni* were invariably delivered in the Senate.[40] An act of 1296 points out that ambassadors had slipped into the habit of reporting only before the doge and his Small Council, and it reaffirmed their duty to report before those councils in which their commissions had been issued.[41] An act of 1401 notes that ambassadors believed that they had fulfilled their duties by reporting in the College, and the requirement of 1296 was repeated.[42] At the end of the thirteenth century, and through the fourteenth and even the fifteenth, although the Senate's jurisdiction was increasing, it had not acquired a monopoly over Venetian diplomacy. Ambassadors were despatched and commissions issued in various councils, such as the Great Council, the Forty and the Ten. By about 1500, it is true, ambassadors were normally under the jurisdiction of the Senate.[43] The fully developed *relazione* of the sixteenth century was delivered (not necessarily in identical form) both in the College and in the Senate. This is mentioned in an important act on *relazioni* of 1425, and Sanuto indicates that in the last decade of the fifteenth century it was done. The *Traité* adds that, if there were two or several Ambassadors were despatched and commissions issued in various councils, such practice of delivering a succinct report in the more restricted College and a full-dress *relazione* in the Senate remained the custom.[45]

Although Andreas regards the *relazioni* themselves, as well as the state reflected in them, as at least approaching works of art, it is the art of the statesman, not that of the *littérateur* or humanist. Even though they are sometimes adorned moderately with classical, scriptural and other allusions and quotations, they are in general very businesslike, as befits the words of Venetian patricians, few of whom claimed literary eminence.[46] The chief source of information was what the ambassador himself had been able to learn in the course of his mission from his own observations, from local public officials, from other ambassadors, or through espionage.[47] Francesco Morosini, sent to congratulate Henry of Valois on his election as king of Poland, declined to discuss that country, since he had not been there, but he did describe the new king and discussed the form of government and the king's authority, material which he had obtained 'with much diligence' from Poles at the court of France.[48] Trafficking in news with other ambassadors was a favourite diplomatic pastime.[49] Whenever possible, Venetian ambassadors liked to base their information upon official documents of the host country, financial records, perhaps, above all.[50] The ambassador or his secretary often kept a set of notes to provide a basis for his eventual *relazione*.[51] We do know that some ambassadors also culled information from the books of both ancient and modern authors.[52] We even know of one, Marco Foscari, who informed himself concerning the Florentine government by having a description of it written for him by a secretary of the Tuscan republic. When he finally composed his written *relazione* he relied heavily upon his Florentine informant.[53] Venetian ambassadors also often borrowed freely from the *relazioni* of their predecessors, especially in those parts dealing with the land and the people. The more general remarks and even statistics were simply copied from one *relazione* to the next by those ambassadors who took their responsibilities less seriously than they should. Such borrowing, however, was in some circumstances quite understandable and justifiable, since the returning ambassador was required to present his *relazione* regardless of the breadth or depth of the knowledge he could be expected to possess. What of the ambassador extraordinary who was sent on a mission of congratulation or condolence lasting only a few days at a court where Venice maintained informed and informative resident ambassadors year after year? His original contribution could certainly not be great, yet the general rule that each one should report on certain subjects had its strengths. If ambassadors returning from England informed the Senate *ad nauseam* that 'Great Britain was an island off the northwest coast of Europe, with Scotland in the north and England in the south, and with another island called Ireland further west', there remained the virtue that the infrequent ambassadors to less well-known lands, like Russia and Poland, were also bound by the customary format to provide information less well known to the Senate.[54]

While an outline of the contents of the classical *relazioni* of the sixteenth century can be drawn from the documents themselves, and some ambassadors conveniently outline in their prefaces what they are going to include, we are also fortunate to possess several documents of a more typological character.[55] One is the *Traité du gouvernement de Venise*, which provides an outline of a typical *relazione*. The ambassador speaks first of the events of his embassy; this represents the basic report common to ambassadors everywhere. Then, however, he goes on to speak of the ruler and his family, the attitude of the ruler toward Venice and other states, his ordinary and extraordinary revenues and expenses in time of peace and war, the council and other influential people, and the nobles and their relations with the ruler. This is quite a simple format.[56]

From the pamphlet, *De legato*, first published in 1566 by the Venetian lawyer-humanist-diplomat, Ottaviano Maggi, we draw a similar outline of the typical *relazione*. Upon the legate's return it was his duty to report diligently to his prince what he had done and observed in his legation. 'Afterwards, he should set forth the strengths and power; the jurisdiction and authority; the taxes and treasury; the relationships and marriage relationships; the form of administration; the nature and customs of the prince before whom he conducted his embassy; and the attitude of that prince toward other princes'.[57]

A much more elaborate outline revealing humanistic influence appears in a sixteenth-century document. These things, it declares, are to be examined in making a *relazione*. First, the orator should discuss the site, giving the ancient and modern names of the place, its boundaries and subdivisions, its most important cities, famous ports, fortresses, episcopal sees, principal rivers, mountains and forests. He should then proceed to deal with the climate, temperature and rainfall, fertility of the land, its mineral resources, the animals found there, the distribution of population, mountains, plains, woods and swamps, and any other noteworthy effects of nature. The people should also be described at length, their customs and habits, their appearance and stature, their attitudes and religion, their organization and preparation for war by land and sea, their crafts, commerce, exports and imports, and the riches of nobility and people. Finally, of course, he must not forget the prince, his ancestry, his person, his life and customs, whether he is loved by his subjects, his income and expenses, the guard that he keeps, the grandeur of his court, and with what princes he has friendships and enmities.[58] Baschet called these 'puerile instructions'.[59] At any rate, they are pedantic.

None of these outlines was actually followed consistently, for, although strong custom sanctioned the treatment of certain topics, every ambassador quite properly retained great freedom concerning the form of his *relazione*. The outlines do provide, however, an idea of the range of subjects covered by *relazioni* from the simplest to the most elaborate.

The form and content of *relazioni*, in fact, differed considerably, although certain items – the *Traité* provides a basic list – were generally considered essential. Beyond these fundamentals, the contents vary according to the personality, interests and expertise of the envoy, and according to the circumstances of the mission. A more extensive, well-informed and original *relazione* could be expected of a returning resident ambassador than of an ambassador extraordinary whose mission was more limited in time and scope. Among extraordinary ambassadors, also, different sorts of information might be provided by those assigned substantial tasks and those sent on ceremonial occasions. *Relazioni* were usually quite lengthy discourses. Exceptional, however, was Pietro Duodo's *relazione* on France in 1598, which required two days for its reading and occupies 175 pages in print.[60] An extraordinary ambassador having only a ceremonial mission was likely to be considerably more brief. Marcantonio da Mula, who had been sent to congratulate Philip II on the Treaty of Cateau-Cambrésis, protested 'that a short legation does not require a long relation', especially since a detailed account had recently been given by Michele Surian. Da Mula, nonetheless, proceeded to cover briefly the customary items.[61] Returning from an extraordinary mission in 1538, Francesco Giustinian remarked that the *Signoria* only a few days before had heard a *relazione* on France by Gioan Basadona. If he, Giustinian, were now required to take up in order 'the revenues, the expenses, the government, the character of the most Christian King and of his kingdom (as is the custom of orators when they return from their ordinary missions)', he would do injury to the *Signoria*, to Basadona, and to himself. His dispatches, moreover, had kept them informed on the course of the mission, so he would now speak only of the underlying reasons why peace had not been achieved.[62] Girolamo Lippomano thought that a short mission to Don Juan of Austria at Naples in 1575 would require only a simple account of what he had done, but when additional tasks were assigned him requiring a nine months' stay rather than the two anticipated, he decided to give a full *relazione*.[63] Lorenzo Bernardo, on the other hand, who had been *bailo* in Constantinople four years earlier, was sent again to bring his successor back for trial (the latter jumped overboard and drowned when they came in sight of Venice); although Bernardo had given a *relazione* of four or five hours' duration at the conclusion of his previous assignment, he now delivered another lengthy one. The importance of Venetian relations with the Porte, the death of the *bailo*, and the presence of senators not members of that body four years earlier provided justification.[64]

Although Venetian *relazioni* were generally straightforward, businesslike, and only very moderately given to literary adornment, exceptions to this general rule do exist. Marco Foscari's *relazione* on Florence, written in its final form in 1533, may owe its remarkable character to the lapse of five years after its first presentation. The final version (a small book in length) has an introduction of four printed pages on the duties of a Venetian, who ought to love the *patria* as a dog loves his master. The body of the document is full of learned allusions: the commission of Romans supposed to have been sent to study the laws of Solon before the drafting of the Twelve Tables, Virgil, Ovid, Pliny, Livy, Tacitus, Aristotle, Christ, the Digest, Bartolus, Ptolemy of Lucca, Dante, Biondo, Machiavelli, Leonardo Bruni and others. He dares to criticize Bruni's Latin. The conclusion is a paean to his own accomplishments. Yet, for all its pretentiousness, Foscari's *relazione* is full of good material on the usual subjects.[65]

A curious document translated in the mid-nineteenth century as *A Relation, or rather a true account, of the Island of England; with sundry particulars of the customs of these people, and of the royal revenues, under King Henry the Seventh, about the year 1500* contains an extraordinary mélange of information and mis-information. It clearly is not typical of *relazioni*, and contains much information of general interest, but of no obvious value for Venetian diplomacy. English beer and ale, for example, are 'most agreeable to the palate, when a person is by some chance rather heated', which is true enough, but scarcely vital information. Amid this miscellany of impressions we learn some English history (with Edward I and Edward III confused), and we hear of English hospitality and ethno-centrism. Later we are told that 'one must necessarily conclude, either that the English are the most discreet lovers in the world, or that they are in-capable of love. I say this of the men, for I understand it is quite the contrary with the women, who are very violent in their passions. Howbeit the English keep a very jealous guard over their wives, though everything may be compensated in the end, by the power of money'. The author provides a harsh description of English apprenticeship, to which he appends remarks upon the scandalous

custom of a widow remarrying the most desirable of her late husband's appren-
tices, 'who was probably not *displeasing* to her in the lifetime of her husband'.
We have also a description of the splendour of the tombs of Edward the Confessor
and St. Thomas of Canterbury. Much of the matter that would go into a typical
relazione is here, but there is also much more as irrelevant to it as the examples
cited above.[66] The document in question is almost certainly not a true diplomatic
relazione.[67] Such scraps of information, however, do crop up from time to time
in those which are undoubted and official. Lodovico Falier, for example, reporting on England in 1531, spoke of English beer, 'which makes a man drunk, as
would the strongest wine, if he drinks too much of it'.[68] German drinking habits
seem to have been a favourite subject of Venetian ambassadors. Alvise Mocenigo
reported in 1548 that Germans were almost always drunk, partly because they
drank more wine than necessary, but partly because, having been raised on
water and beer, only a little wine made them inebriated. They were even more
devoted to wine than to Martin Luther. The princes hold drunkenness for a
virtue, rather than a vice, believing that a man who refuses to get drunk is
trying to hide his evil thoughts. They sometimes conclude difficult negotiations
while drunk, finding agreement by making concessions which would otherwise
be impossible. The bishop of Trent once told Mocenigo that he would rather
be able to drink half a bottle of wine with a meal, in discussing religious differences with German princes, than know all the texts of St. Luke and St. Matthew
by heart, because then he would hope to gain their agreement. Dr. Eck once
said that the German princes were able to negotiate soberly only for one or two
hours in the morning.[69] Federigo Badoer remarked of the Germans in 1557
that they were very excessive in eating and even more in drinking, so that a
sober German was considered to be sick. The men were as cold in sex as hot for
wine, so the women were accustomed to chastity.[70] Vincenzo Querini in 1506
found both men and women of Burgundy frigid and far from sensual.[71]

The variations among the classical sixteenth-century *relazioni* indicated above
were due to personalities and circumstances, but there was also a pattern of
change through time. Carlo Morandi has pointed out that the *relazioni* of 1693–
1713 studied by him differ significantly from those of the sixteenth century.
Behind the foreground of princes and courts, there was greater consciousness of
lands and peoples. Curiosities came to abound, sometimes to the point of abuse.
Relazioni acquired a more erudite and bookish character, less dependent upon
the immediate experience of the ambassador. There was more ordered and
patient analysis. Geographical information was abundant, in part for its own
sake, in part in relation to its economic, military and ethnic importance. There
was a stronger interest in commercial resources and in social classes. *Relazioni*
became increasingly generalized essays on the country from which the ambassador had returned.[72]

Scholarly opinion is divided concerning the earliest surviving *relazione*. Some
have held for a report by Marsiglio Zorzi, *bailo* in Syria, 1240–1243.[73] I do not
regard this as a *relazione*, certainly not in the sense in which a Venetian *relazione*

is something unique. The headnote itself reads 'Marsilius Georgius, *bailo* of the Venetians in Syria, narrates in order many things done in that place', and this is precisely what Zorzi proceeds to do. It is a final report of his negotiations over the privileges of the Venetians in Syria, followed by a list of the rights of the Venetians in Tyre, a selection from the chronicle of William of Tyre, and another list of the rights of the Venetians in Cyprus. It does not possess the general and didactic character of the sixteenth-century *relazioni*, which discuss princes, councillors, armies, finances, geography, the people, and other matters of a more general interest. It antedates by a quarter of a century the law of 1268 which contains the first suggestion that matters discovered along the way to the profit and honour of Venice should be added to the customary final report.[74] In a very limited way, perhaps, the two lists of Venetian rights and the excerpt from William of Tyre may anticipate the requirement of 1268, but I view them as addenda more directly related to his specific mission.[75] Other scholars accept as the first extant *relazione* that of Zaccaria Contarini on France in 1492, and I concur in this judgment.[76] Contarini includes the 'comings and goings' of his legation, and this practice never completely died away, but he also spoke more broadly of the persons of the king and queen, the grandeur of the kingdom, the government, its income and expenses, armies and other preparations for war, the enmities that the king had and the means he possessed for freeing himself of them, and the factions and enmities that prevailed at the court. These are the things we have come to expect in the *relazioni*.

Although we do not possess any *relazioni* prior to 1492 (unless we accept the report by Zorzi of 1243), Girolamo Donato in 1499 referred to his own *relazione* on Rome as conforming to 'the ancient and laudable custom'.[77] It is well known that Marino Sanuto's *Diarii* contain summaries of many *relazioni*, a number of them from the last decade of the fifteenth century, but none prior to that of Contarini.[78] In the hope that similar, but earlier summaries of *relazioni* might be found, I have examined – somewhat superficially and with very little success – other narrative sources for Venetian history. They are not very helpful, for chroniclers, when they deal with the missions of ambassadors at all, are concerned with the bare outlines of objectives and results – and this is not the stuff of *relazioni*.[79] I had also especially hoped that the short treatise, *De officio legati*, written at the end of the fifteenth century by the humanist-diplomat Ermolao Barbaro might say something of the origins of the *relazioni* – or at least something concerning those of his own day. This hope, too, was frustrated.[80]

There do exist, however, slight traces of *relazioni* before 1492. Malipiero, in describing Polo Ognibene's report on his mission to Persia in 1475, states that the ambassador *referisse*, a verb which authors of sixteenth-century *relazioni* employ to describe what they are doing.[81] Malipiero also records a report of Nicolò Cocco on Constantinople in 1481, using of it the verb *referir* and the noun *relazion*, although he does not provide enough information for satisfactory comparison with sixteenth-century *relazioni*.[82] Even though the contents of Ognibene's speech in 1475 do not much resemble those of a classical *relazione* and what Cocco said is almost entirely unknown, I believe that Malipiero gives us here two examples of 'the ancient and laudable custom'. They may fall short of the classical form of the sixteenth century, or Malipiero may have reported them inaccurately or selectively; the verb *referir*, however, at least as Sanuto uses it, is contrasted to *reportar* in such a way as to prove that a distinction existed between a mere report and a *relazione*.[83]

Two tentative identifications of *relazioni* in the 1470s and 1480s, however, provide very inadequate evidence of the 'ancient and laudable custom' of 1499, and we can only speculate concerning the evolution of the genre prior to that time. *Relazioni* were first required by an act of the Great Council of 23rd December, 1268. Venetian ambassadors returning to Venice were to place in writing within fifteen days the responses that they received to their embassy 'and whatever they may have known and may have heard said on the way that they believe to be to the profit and honour of the Venetians . . .'[84] This act is well known, but apparently seldom read. From one another and ultimately from the sixteenth-century repertory of Venetian laws by Bartolomeo Zamberti various authorities have taken the summary, *Oratores in reditu dent in nota ea quae sunt utilia dominio*.[85] These words do not appear in the act itself, as it appears in *Fractus*, to which Zamberti refers, or in *Comunis I*, either in the register or as published by Cessi. Nor do they appear in the headnotes to any of the above. Scholars should know that the humanistic word *orator*, designating an ambassador, signifies a date later than the thirteenth century. Using this summary in place of the act itself, several scholars interpret the law as requiring only an oral report, while the act itself and the headnote specifically state *facere poni in scriptis* and *facere scribi*.[86] Everyone, moreover, who converts the date does so incorrectly, either being ignorant of the meaning of *exeunte decembri* or else blindly following a mistaken leader.[87] Carefully read, the act of 1268 places a deadline upon the long customary final report, requires that it be written, and provides for the addition of material not strictly related to the specific mission, thus introducing the stuff of which the later *relazioni* are composed.

Some scholars find the origin of the *relazioni* in an act of 24th July, 1296, which complains that ambassadors had recently failed to conform to the custom that they should report upon their missions in the councils in which they had been commissioned, but had contented themselves with reporting before the doge and his councillors. Henceforth they must report in the council which had appointed them, and that council must hear them within fifteen days.[88] This act is not concerned with the character of the report, but only with the place in which it should be delivered. Those who find here the beginning of the requirement of a *relazione* are not giving adequate weight to the act of 1268, and are misunderstanding the intention of the Great Council in 1296.[89]

The law of 1268 requiring that miscellaneous matter pertaining to the profit and honour of Venice be added to the ambassador's report on the response to his mission suggests that the classical *relazioni* of the sixteenth century evolved from the ordinary final report. We have no way of knowing how soon ambassadors actually did begin customarily to supplement their reports with more didactic information. We can, however, perceive traces of the ancient report on a mission in the *relazioni* of the fifteenth century. A requirement of 1401 that ambassadors ought to present *relationes et ambaxiatas suas* lends credence to the contention that *relazioni* evolved from the ordinary final reports of ambassadors, and that the two remained intertwined at the beginning of the fifteenth century.[90] Polo Ognibene's account in 1475 of his mission to Persia, as given by Malipiero, also dealt very largely with an account of his mission, very little with the more general matter of the classical *relazioni*. Ognibene described his journey and his audience with Uzun Hasan, the ally of Venice against the Turks. He told of the arrival of a Venetian merchant who had been despoiled by robbers, and of the king's kindness to him. He reported a Turkish defeat at the hands of the Vlachs. Finally, he gave some details upon the military preparations of Persia against the common enemy. Much of the nature of the common final report thus survived in 1475.[91] Even Contarini's *relazione* of 1492, the first one extant, begins: 'My duty . . . is to refer to your Sublimity all the comings and goings of this our legation', although he does add later the intelligence on the prince and the government that we regard as essential to the classical *relazione* of the sixteenth century.[92] This mixed character is shared by the *relazioni* of many of his successors.[93] The so-called *relazione* of Francesco Bernardo in 1497, moreover, which we possess in full, merely recounts the course of the mission without the more didactic and general material.[94] The evidence is clear, therefore, that the classical *relazione* evolved only very gradually out of the customary final report on the mission, and that this evolution was by no means complete by the end of the fifteenth century.[95]

If only *relazioni* had been written as required by the Great Council in 1268 we could trace the evolution. There is little doubt that *relazioni* of some sort were presented verbally. Sixteenth-century ambassadors professed to be following 'an ancient custom observed by all other ambassadors until the present day'.[96] An act on *relazioni* of 1524 also notes that the obligation of presenting a verbal *relazione* was not often shirked.[97]

There is no evidence of written *relazioni*, however, until the end of the fifteenth century. An act of the Senate of 31st May, 1425, states clearly in its preface that 'of the said *relazioni* nothing is afterward possessed in writing', so that much knowledge useful to the Senate was lost. The law of 1268 was evidently not being obeyed – but the repetitiousness of much Venetian legislation reveals that a great many laws were not obeyed. The act of 1425 again required that *relazioni* must be given in writing.[98] It also ordained that they must be registered in the chancellery in a book devoted especially to that purpose – a new requirement. This register should begin with the *relazione* of Polo Corario on Milan, 'which he ought to give in writing, and it should be placed in the aforesaid book'.[99] It would be surprising if these specific and immediate instructions were not carried out, at least for a short time, although no evidence of such a register has been found.

Even after 1425, it seems, ambassadors continued to ignore the requirement of a written *relazione*, for a senatorial act of 1524 protests that much of value to the city is lost because those who heard the *relazioni* could not remember what had been said. Within fifteen days after the oral presentation, therefore, ambassadors and others will be obliged to place their *relazioni* in writing *ne le cose substanziali*. Thus the act of 1524 represents a modest relaxation of the disregarded decree of 1425. The written *relazioni* should be registered in one of two secret books in the chancellery, one for the *relazioni* of rectors and syndics, the other for those of *baili, provveditori* and ambassadors.[100]

After 1524, also, the law continued to be ignored, for an act (presumably that of 1524) was read in the Senate in 1533 repeating the old requirements. Marco Foscari, an experienced and distinguished statesman and diplomat, confessed that before hearing this law read he had been unaware that his *relazioni* on Rome in 1526 and on Florence in 1528 had to be given in writing. He made it clear also that many others were equally deficient.[101] Antonio Suriano, another diplomat of long experience and high standing, was also stimulated to submit tardily two *relazioni* in writing in 1533.[102] From 1533 until the end of the Republic of St. Mark we do possess numerous *relazioni*, although by no means a full series in registers, as we should if the law had been obeyed.[103]

Yet we do possess written *relazioni* prior to 1533, although they are few and late, and we know that some, at least, were registered. The *Traité*, which is supposed to have been written about 1500, reports that 'many times' *relazioni* were written and registered.[104] Not 'always' or 'customarily', but 'many times'. Even the sixteenth-century *relazioni* which we possess in written form are not drawn consistently from registers, but from *filze* in the Archivio di Stato, family archives, patriarchal archives, foreign archives and libraries, and a variety of other depositories.[105] We may conclude that *relazioni* were customarily delivered orally through the thirteenth, fourteenth and fifteenth centuries. Toward the end of the fifteenth century, it appears, some of them began to be written, as required by law, but as late as 1533 this was not the prevalent practice. There is no evidence of the required registers. It has been supposed that the *relazioni* of centuries were destroyed by burning or lost in the confusion resulting from the fires in the Ducal Palace in 1574 and 1577.[106] If only we possessed the reports of the grand chancellor to the Council of Ten on the losses sustained in these disasters, we should at least know what it is that we are lacking. It is clear that the damage was great.[107] The evidence presented above, however, indicates that the Venetian archives did not possess at that time a large and systematic collection of *relazioni* antedating the 1530s.[108]

A hard look at the *relazioni* as an evolving form leaves intact much of the old view made popular by Ranke, their uniqueness and their value to Venetian statecraft and to modern historiography. They do not, it is true, provide the sort of information found in dispatches, but history is much the richer for their use and valuable veins remain to be exploited even after almost a century and a half of mining. Scholars may cease to lament, however, the loss of rich resources for the history of the thirteenth, fourteenth and fifteenth centuries. Even though the seed was planted, the classical *relazione* did not emerge mature and fully armed from the head of the Great Council in 1268, but was the fruit of a long period of gestation. It began as an occasional offshoot of the ordinary final report, which over the centuries gradually displaced its parent. In spite of the efforts of legislators, it was not customarily delivered in writing and preserved in the archives. No great collection of *relazioni* existed to be consumed in the fires of 1574 and 1577.

NOTES

1. I wish to express my appreciation to Dr. Luigi Lanfranchi and Dr. Maria Francesca Tiepolo of the Archivio di Stato, Venice, who assisted me greatly in clarifying several points which I was not able to check in the archives myself. I also wish to thank my research assistant, George Stow, for suggesting a thorough rearrangement of my first draft, which, in my opinion, has been an improvement. In an earlier and abbreviated form, this paper was read at the Southern California Renaissance Conference, 11 May, 1968. Since this paper was written there has appeared *Pursuit of Power: Venetian Ambassadors' Reports on Spain, Turkey, and France in the Age of Philip II, 1560–1600*, ed. by James C. Davis (New York, Evanston, and London, 1970). Davis's introduction is traditional in outlook and not concerned with the origins of the genre. It is only with proofs of the present essay before me, that I have obtained *Relations des ambassadeurs vénitiens*, selected and introduced by Franco Gaeta, trans. by Jean Chuzeville (Paris, 1969). Gaeta's introduction is admirable, although I differ from him on some points.

2. See above, p. 183.

3. Francesca Antonibon, *Le relazioni a stampa di ambasciatori veneti* (Padua, 1939) 17.

4. M. A. R. de Maulde La Clavière, *La diplomatie au temps de Machiavel*, 3 vols. (Paris, 1892–93) iii, 366–388; Archivio di Stato, Florence: *Signori – Carteggi – Rapporti e relazioni di oratori.* E.g., i, f. 1 and iii, ff. 2rv.

5. Archivio di Stato, Florence: *Signori – Carteggi – Missive – Legazioni e commissarie – Elezioni e istruzioni a oratori*, xxi, ff. 6, 100 [101], 104v [105v]. Similarly the *relatione* mentioned by Cicco Simonetta in 1473 was merely a Milanese ambassador's account of what the king of Naples and the duchess of Calabria wanted him to report to Galeazzo Maria Sforza; *I diarii di Cicco Simonetta*, ed. Alfio Rosario Natale (Milan, 1962) 61. French 'relations' under Louis XI had a character similar to the Florentine reports, concentrating upon the course of negotiations; Antoine Degert, 'Louis XI et ses ambassadeurs', *Revue Historique*, cliv (1927) 17–18. 'Relations' of the age of Louis XIV combined many of the characteristics of a classical Venetian *relazione* with those of an ordinary final report; William J. Roosen, *The ambassador's craft: a study of the functioning of French ambassadors under Louis XIV* (Ph.D. dissertation, University of Southern California, 1967) 92–94.

6. Romolo Quazza, *La diplomazia gonzaghesca* (Milan, n.d.) 32.

7. Ibid., 57–70.

8. J. E. Neale, 'The diplomatic envoy', *History*, xiii (1928–1929) 216.

9. Carlo Morandi, *Relazioni di ambasciatori sabaudi, genovesi e veneti durante il periodo della Grande Alleanza e della successione di Spagna (1693–1713)* (Bologna, 1935) p. xxi. See, for example, the outline provided for his Savoyard *relazione* on the court at Vienna by Count San Martino di Baldissero, 89. Gaeta, op. cit., p. vi, cites Spanish imitations of the end of the sixteenth century.

10. Antonibon, 13–14. Baschet said that the difference was absolute. Armand Baschet; *Les archives de Venise: Histoire de la chancellerie secrète* (Paris, 1870) 332–333. Perhaps it *became* absolute, although I am not sure even of that. On the one hand, Marcantonio Barbaro, returning from duty as *bailo* at Constantinople in 1573, delivered one typical *relazione*, then later reported in the *Signoria* on the details of his negotiations for peace; Albèri, *Le relazioni degli ambasciatori veneti al Senato durante il secolo XVI* (15 vols., Florence, 1539–63) ser. III, i, 299–346 and Appendice, xv, 387–415; on the other, Jacopo Ragazzoni, secretary to Barbaro, mixes the two: ibid., ser. III, ii, 77–102. He narrates his negotiations during a period when Barbaro was a prisoner, 79–97, then adds the more general material distinguishing a *relazione*, 97–102.

11. Marco Foscarini, *Della letteratura veneziana* (Venice, 1854) 488, n. 3; Albèri, I, iii, p. iii, and Appendice, xv, p. xii; Armand Baschet, *La diplomatie vénitienne et les princes de l'Europe au seizième siècle* (Paris, 1862) 31–32. Foscarini also cites the testimony of Gabriel Naudè, secretary to Cardinal Mazarin, 489, n. 1.

12. Abraham de Wiquefort, *L'ambassadeur et ses fonctions*, 2 vols. (The Hague, 1680–81) ii, 403. 'Tous les Ambassadeurs font rapport; mais il y en a si peu qui fassent une relation pertinente de l'Estat, où ils ont residé, qu'il semble que cela soit particulier a ceux de Venise . . .'

13. Albèri, I, i, 33–34. Another example, ibid., I, i, 147. Andreas relates the development of the didactic *relazione* to the institution of the resident ambassador; Willy Andreas, *Staatskunst und Diplomatie der Venezianer im Spiegel ihrer Gesandtenberichte* (Leipzig, 1943) 67–68. On the change of emphasis from negotiating to information gathering with the evolution of the resident ambassador, see Donald E. Queller, *The office of the ambassador in the Middle Ages* (Princeton, 1967) 88. Sanuto offers a different slant: Marino Giorgio (Zorzi) includes in his *relazione* things that he has not written in his letters, for 'many things happen which should not be written'; Sanuto, xxiv, 84. This may be atypical. See n. 14.

14. Andrea da Mosto, *L'Archivio di Stato di Venezia*, 2 vols. (Rome, 1937–40) ii, 25; *Relazioni di ambasciatori veneti al Senato*, ed. by Luigi Firpo, vol. i, *Inghilterra* (Turin, 1965) 23. Firpo argues that *dispacci* were read only before the doge and a small number of others, and, thus, being more confidential, could reveal material better left unsaid in *relazioni*. It appears, however, that dispatches were customarily read before the Senate; see Baschet, *Les archives . . .*, 266. Also, senatorial replies to *dispacci* are common in the registers of that body, and many reveal a knowledge of the *dispacci*, sometimes by an item by item response. Publication of the dispatches has been announced by the *Deputazione di Storia Patria per le Venezie*; *A.V.* ser. V, lxxxv (1968) 178–9. I have not yet seen the paper in which the plan of publication is described. Incidentally, medieval *dispacci*, like *relazioni*, are not extant, except for scattered examples in family archives and the like, but many can be reconstructed from these senatorial replies.

15. Baschet, *Archives*, 361. See also Antonibon, 13, n. 2, and the authorities cited there. Machiavelli, however, urged the inclusion in dispatches of some of the matter that distinguished the Venetian *relazioni*. 'Memoriale a Raffaello Girolami quando ai 23 d'ottobre partì per Spagna all'imperatore', in *Tutte le opere di Niccolò Machiavelli*, ed. Francesco Flora and Carlo Cordié (2nd ed., Milan, 1960) ii, 517–518.

16. Vincenzo Querini's *relazione* on the Empire, 1506; Albèri, I, i, 3. The Senate's desire for interchange of information on foreign affairs is indicated by the admission to the Senate of every ambassador between the time of his election and his departure and, upon his return, until the next St. Michael's day (29 Sept.); Da Mosto, i, 35.

17. Albèri, I, iii, 31 and II, iii, 369.

18. Ibid., I, iii, 91–92.

19. Ibid., II, v, 75 and II, iv, 298. Ottaviano Maggi, *De legato* (Hanover, 1596) 71–73.

20. *Traité du gouvernement de la cité et seigneurie de Venise*, in P.-M. Perret, *Relations de la France avec Venise*, 2 vols. (Paris, 1896) ii, 292. The *Traité* is thought to have been com-

posed about 1500. This passage on the reading of the *relazioni* in the archives leads me to suspect that it is later, for I find no evidence that originals or registers were kept so early, and considerable evidence that they were not; cf. above, pp. 186–7. I wish someone better informed on Venetian constitutional history than I would examine this interesting document closely with a view to dating it.

21. See the informative discussions by Baschet, *Archives*, 348–352, and *Diplomatie*, 39–53. The value of *relazioni* in the market place held up in subsequent centuries. Alvise Molin reported in 1661 that they were not only commonly sold in Vienna, but were forged for sale. *Die Relationen der venezianischer Botschafter über Deutschland und Österreich im siebzehnten Jahrhundert*, ed. Joseph Fiedler, 2 vols. in *Fontes rerum austriacarum*, pt. ii, vols. xvi–xvii (Vienna, 1866–67) ii, 43–44. Rawdon Brown recounts how *relazioni* were eagerly bought in Rome in 1713. *Calendar of State Papers, Venetian*, i, pp. xliii–xlv.

22. Andreas, 276.

23. *Early Venetian legislation on ambassadors*, ed. Donald E. Queller (Geneva, 1967) 82, no. 43. See also Alfred von Reumont, *Della diplomazia italiana dal secolo XIII al XVI* (Florence, 1857) 71–72, and Brown, *Calendar of State Papers, Venetian*, i, p. xvii. Baschet, *Archives*, 168, n. 1, publishes an act of 1596, recapitulating earlier acts of 1518 and 1558. This provides another example of repetitious legislation in a futile effort to obtain compliance. Giovanni Priuli reported in 1722 that he discovered many *relazioni* on the Empire in the imperial library and in private hands. It seems that another legislative attempt to keep *relazioni* secret had recently been made; *Die Relationen der Botschafter Venedigs über Deutschland und Österreich im achtzehnten Jahrhundert*, ed. Alfred Ritter von Arneth, in *Fontes rerum austriacarum*, pt. ii, vol. xii (Vienna, 1863) 42.

24. Albèri, I, iv, 15 and 21; Sanuto, vi, 428.

25. *Calendar of State Papers, Venetian*, i, pp. xliii–xlv.

26. Leopold von Ranke, *Die Verschwörung gegen Venedig im Jahre 1618*, in *Sämmtliche Werke*, xlii (Leipzig, 1878) 175. Baschet, *Archives*, 36–37, has an excellent description of Ranke's work in the Venetian Archives.

27. As long ago as 1874 Charles Yriarte wrote: 'Tout a été dit et bien dit sur les *Relazioni* des ambassadeurs vénitiens'. *La vie d'un patricien de Venise: Marcantonio Barbaro* (Paris, 1874) 126.

28. Arnaldo Segarizzi, *Relazioni degli ambasciatori veneti al Senato*, 3 vols. in 4 (Bari, 1912–16); Firpo. *Relazioni*, i, pp. vi–vii. Baschet, in *Diplomatie*, 53–102, provides a fine bibliographical essay on the *relazioni*.

29. Firpo, *Relazioni*.

30. Albèri, I, iv, 15. Contarini's unfavourable portrait of the French king is confirmed by Francesco Guicciardini, *Storia d'Italia*, ed. Constantino Panigada (Bari, 1929) i, 68. Sometimes Venetian ambassadors likened themselves to portrait painters. Alvise Mocenigo, returning from the Empire in 1548, wrote: '. . . sforzandomi di rapresentare in parole alla presentia di Vostra Serenita et di Vostre Eccellentissime Signorie uno ritratto del corpo, del animo et delle dispositioni di Cesare quanto piu simile potrò, et imitando in questo li buoni pittori, li quali volendo ben trazer un corpo dal naturale, studiano nella pittura sua non ommetter cosa, che in quel corpo si veda, accioche'l ritratto suo pari piu simile . . .' *Die Relationen der Botschafter Venedigs über Deutschland und Österreich im sechzehnten Jahrhundert*, in *Fontes rerum austriacarum*, pt. ii, vol. xxx (Vienna, 1870) 12. Giovanni Correr wrote in 1566: '. . . servendomi delle parole in luogo di pennello, cercherò di rappresentare a Vostra Serenità un ritratto di quel Sig. Duca (of Savoy) . . .' Albèri, II, v, 3. Sixteenth century Venetian statesmen were believers in the false science of physiognomy. Pius V possessed 'il naso aquilino che denota animo generoso ed atto a regnare . . .' Ibid., II, iv, 200. Baschet also, for example, was primarily interested in these word portraits. *Archives*, 360, and *Diplomatie*, 13.

31. Firpo, *Relazioni*, i, p. v.

32. Andreas, 73–82.

33. The words of Albèri and Baschet, for example, glow with admiration. Albèri, Appendice, xv, pp. vii–viii; Baschet, *Diplomatie*, 398–399.

34. James C. Davis, *The decline of the Venetian nobility as a ruling class* (Baltimore, 1962) 54–74.

35. *Traité*, 279.

36. Neale believed that such a series could not exist 'without that form of audience for a returning ambassador which was peculiar to Venice'. Loc. cit., 216.

37. On the ceremonial garb worn on these occasions, see Lazari, in Albèri, III, iii, pp. xix–xx. A crimson robe seems to have been customary for an ambassador, but in the three paintings of Carpaccio's St. Ursula cycle depicting ambassadors, considerable variety in dress is indicated. Sanuto occasionally indicates a black robe, once explaining that the ambassador was in mourning; iii, 1286 and xxii, 164.

38. Baschet, *Diplomatie*, 416–417.

39. *Traité*, 292. Sanuto often mentions the praise by the doge. E.g., i, 615. Once he mentions, '. . . fo laudato *de more* . . .', ii, 923. Another time, although the *relazione* was given very ineptly, '. . . il Serenissimo, iusta el solito, lo laudoe', i, 103.

40. Romanin, viii, 392–393.

41. *Deliberazioni del Maggior Consiglio di Venezia*, ed. Roberto Cessi, 3 vols. (Bologna, 1931–50) iii, 403; 'Die ältesten Verordnungen der Venezianer für auswärtige Angelegenheiten', *Abhandlungen des philosophisch-philologischen Classe der Königlich Bayerischen Akademie der Wissenschaften*, xiii (1875) 107.

42. Queller, *Early Venetian legislation*, 82, no. 43.

43. '. . . li nostri savi e buoni progenitori abbiano nella repubblica nostra posto per costume, che tutti li ambasciatori che de diversi parti del mondo ritornano nella patria, diano notizia al senato di quel principe appresso del quale si hanno trovato in legazione . . .', *Relazione* of Vincenzo Querini, 1506. Albèri, I, i, 3.

44. Queller, *Early Venetian legislation*, 86, no. 49; Sanuto, i, 216, 615; ii, 923, 1043; *Traité*, 292. Sanuto mentions that the youngest of four ambassadors to Rome reported in the College in 1523; xxiv, 139. Marc'Antonio Barbaro in 1573 and 1574 delivered different versions of his *relazione* in the Senate and the *Signoria*; Yriarte, 225 and n. 3. Alvise Manenti in 1500 and Alvise Buonrizzo in 1582 reported to the *capi* of the Council of Ten, as well as to the Senate. Very secret matters, after a while, were not given in the Senate; Sanuto, iii, 179; Segarizzi, *Relazioni*, III, ii, 31–35.

45. Vincenzo Lazzari, in Albèri, III, iii, p. xx. E.g., Alvise Sagredo's *relazione* of 1665, as described by Antonibon, 58.

46. Andreas, 87–89; Albèri, I, i, p. xii. Explicit disclaimers of literary artifice are not rare among the *relazioni*. E.g., Michele Suriano in 1562: 'E benchè non penso dilettar chi legge nè con la vaghezza della materia, che è in grand parte lacrimabile, nè con lo splendore e ornamento delle parole (che non ho molto studio in questo) . . .' Ibid., I, iv, 106. Matteo Dandolo in 1542: '. . . nella prima sarà la descrizione della Francia, non secondo Giulio Cesare, ma secondo che sua maestà la possiede . . .' Ibid., I, iv, 29–30. Bernardo Navagero in 1546: '. . . ma a me pare che avendo rispetto alle altre occupazioni di questo illustrissimo consiglio, debito mio sia di dire, e di vostra serenità desiderio di udire, solamente quelle cose dalla cognizione delle quali ne possa venire in chiaro lume alle eccellentissime signorie vostre nelle sue deliberazioni occorenti, e con questo quella utilità per la quale io credo che principalmente sia stato instituto che tutti gli ambasciatori nel suo ritorno riferiscono alle eccellentissime signorie vostre'. Ibid., I, i, 291.

47. Recently Charles H. Carter has severely criticized Venetian *relazioni* on the grounds that Venetian ambassadors were not in a position to obtain solid information and, in fact, passed along without *caveat* rumours, government handouts and misinformation planted on them by other ambassadors. 'The ambassadors of early modern Europe: patterns of diplomatic representation in the early seventeenth century', in *From the Renaissance to the Counter-Reformation: essays in honor of Garrett Mattingly*, ed. Charles H. Carter (New

York, 1965) 279–280. I should be pleased to join Carter's assault upon the myth of Venetian government, but, on balance and in the context of the times, I think the evidence will not sustain so severe an attack. Wiquefort and Lord Chesterfield believed Venetian ambassadors to be remarkably well informed. Wiquefort, i, 176; Philip Dormer Stanhope, fourth Earl of Chesterfield, *Letters to his son*, 13th ed., 4 vols. (London, 1821) ii, 144, no. CLXXVII. Quazza has pointed out that Mantuan ambassadors prided themselves on being so well informed that even Venetian ambassadors sometimes sought information from them; *La diplomazia gonzaghesca*, 27. See also above, n. 21, on the sale of Venetian *relazioni* abroad. Alvise Molin noted that the false *relazioni* forged for sale 'sono forse le più nocive, perche con imprudenza, et inesperienza formate, e dalle voci di piazza trahendo la loro sostanza . . .' Fiedler, *Die Relationen . . . im siebzehnten Jahrhundert*, ii, 43. He believed the genuine *relazioni* to be more soundly based.

48. Albèri, I, vi, 251.

49. Queller, *Ambassador*, 89–90.

50. Girolamo Ramusio, secretary in Naples, reported to the doge that he had seen the official royal ledger for 1594. Albèri, Appendice, xv, 348.

51. Baschet published excerpts from the *carnets* of Leonardo Donato on Rome in 1592, believing that they formed the basis of his later *relazione*. *Diplomatie*, 206–211.

52. Ramusio, for example, tells us: '. . . toccando le cose curiose e importanti raccontate dalle antiche istorie e scritti da' moderni autori . . .' Albèri, Appendice, xv, 299–300. In the course of the *relazione* he refers to his readings on such subjects as the Norman *Regno*, the Donation of Charlemagne, and Naples as a Greek colony, sometimes stating that the writers held differing opinions. There is a lot of history, fairly detailed and sometimes wrong. See also the *relazione* of Marco Foscari above, p. 182.

53. Segarizzi, *Relazioni*, III, ii, 227. Also, and including identification of the Florentine secretary as Iacopo Nardi, Demetrio Marzi, *La cancelleria della repubblica fiorentina* (Rocca San Casciano, 1910) 329–334.

54. The criticism is Carter's, loc. cit., 279–280.

55. For outlines given by the ambassadors in their introductions, see Albèri, I, i, 289, and iii, 4; Appendice, xv, 300–301. A very simple outline, ibid., I, ii, 11. See also Fiedler, *Die Relationen . . . im sechzehnten Jahrhundert*, 11.

56. *Traité*, 292.

57. Ottaviano Maggi, *De legato*, 70–71. On Maggi, see Garrett Mattingly, *Renaissance diplomacy* (New York, 1955) 212.

58. Segarizzi, *Relazioni*, i, 285, n. 3. I have recently republished this document along with the previously unpublished document to which it is appended. "How to succeed as an ambassador: a sixteenth century Venetian document," in *Post Scripta: essays on medieval law and the emergence of the European state in honor of Gaines Post*, ed. by Joseph R. Strayer and Donald E. Queller (=*Studia Gratiana*, vol. XV), Rome, 1972, pp. 653–671.

59. *Diplomatie*, 30–31.

60. Albèri, appendice, xv, 75–250.

61. Albèri, I, iii, 393–408. Giacomo Soranzo, ambassador extraordinary to congratulate Murad III upon his succession, wrote: '. . . non aspettino da me un lungo discorso intorno la potenza, forza e stato di sultano Amurat imperatore dei Turchi, come cose e per lettere intese da vostra serenità, ed a piennο refertegli altre volte da suoi clarissimi baili; ma aspettino che sommariamente e più brevemente che io potrò, ragioni di due cose principalmente per le quali è stato istituito il referire, e la quale daranno gran lume, al creder mio, a vostre signorie illustrissime. L'una, e prima, è sopra la natura e qualità del Gran Signore, e di quelli che sono più principali a quella Porta, e delle forze sue. La seconda, come si trovi esso Gran Signore disposto verso gli altri principi del mondo, ed in concetto ha ciascuno; il toccar il quale dei passi reputo cosa non solo utile, ma necessaria'. Ibid., III, ii, 195.

62. Ibid., I, i, 199–200. In his *relazione* on France in 1492 Zaccaria Contarini does not

comment upon the duchy of Milan, where he stopped, for resident ambassadors regularly supplied information of which he was ignorant, but he did supply a brief section on Savoy, where Venice did not have a resident. Ibid., I, iv, 7–9.

63. Ibid., II, ii, 268.

64. Ibid., III, ii, 321–426.

65. Segarizzi, Relazioni, III, i, 3–96.

66. A Relation, or rather a true account, of the Island of England; with sundry particulars of the customs of these people, and of the royal revenues, under King Henry the Seventh, about the year 1500, trans. from the Italian with notes by Charlotte Augusta Sneyd (London, 1847). Reprinted in Firpo, Relazioni, i.

67. It is believed that the author may have been a secretary of an ambassador. Sneyd, Relation, p. v; Reumont, Diplomazia, 76–77; Firpo, Relazioni, i, p. x. Antonibon (75) believes that Sanuto's summary of Andrea Trevisan's relazione of 1498 (Diarii, i, col. 978) may have this document as its original. This cannot be, since there is absolutely no correspondence. The Relation could be a secretary's notes intended to provide raw material for an ambassador's eventual relazione.

68. Albèri, I, iii, 12.

69. Fiedler, Die Relationen . . . im sechzehnten Jahrhundert, 123–124.

70. Albèri, I, iii, 183.

71. Ibid., I, i, 14. Baschet remarks that Venetian ambassadors speak very little of the mistresses of Francis I, although indications of them do appear in the account of expenses for the king's small pleasures. Diplomatie, 410.

72. Morandi, pp. xxii–xxiii. Also Andreas, 120–121.

73. Urkunden zur älteren Handels-und Staatsgeschichte der Republik Venedig ed. G. L. Fr. Tafeland G. M. Thomas, 3 vols., in Fontes rerum austriacarum, pt. ii, vols. xii–xiv (1st ed. 1856–57, reprinted Amsterdam, 1964) ii, 351–398; Romanin, viii, 393, no. 2; Giuseppe Volpi, La repubblica di Venezia e i suoi ambasciatori, 50; Nicola Nicolini, Il consolato generale veneto nel regno di Napoli (1257–1495) (Naples, 1928) 60; Vittorio Lazzarini, 'Marsilio Zorzi conte di Curzola e Meleda', A.V., xxx (1942) 86 and n. 2 (n. 2 contains a description of the earlier ms in the Querini-Stampalia library at Venice including an extract from William of Tyre and a list of Venetian rights in Cyprus); Paolo Selmi, L'inizio ed il primo sviluppo della diplomazia stabile della Repubblica di Venezia (thesis, University of Padua, 1960) 13, kindly lent to me by Dr. Selmi. Romanin attributed the origin of the relazioni to the twelfth century, but without documentation; viii, 392–393.

74. Above, p. 185.

75. In any case, it is not strictly an ambassadorial relazione, for Zorzi was bailo at Constantinople. See my argument that the bailo was not an ambassador. Queller, Ambassador, 80–82.

76. Albèri, I, iv, 1–26. In support of its priority: Alfred von Reumont, Dei diplomati italiani e delle relazioni diplomatiche italiane dal 1260 al 1500 (Padua, 1850) 53, and Diplomazia, 71 and 76; Albèri, I, iv, 2; Baschet, Diplomatie, 100; Andreas, 66 and 83; François L. Ganshof, Le Moyen Age, vol. i, in Histoire des relations internationales, gen. ed., Pierre Renouvin (Paris, 1953) 278–279.

77. Sanuto, ii, 835.

78. Some of the summaries in Sanuto listed by Antonibon as relazioni appear to me to be only reports of the ordinary kind, reporting to the principal the outcome of the mission but lack the distinguishing characteristics of the classical Venetian relazioni. E.g., Sanuto, i, 735–736, and 858–859. It is perhaps appropriate to include them in such a list, but they do indicate that the classical relazione was not yet firmly formed.

79. Nothing of use was found in the following: Martino da Canale, La cronaca dei Veneziani dall' origine della città, in A.S.I., viii (1845) 268–766; Jacopo Zen, Vita Caroli Zeni, ed. G. Zonta, in R.I.S. 2, xix, pt. vi and (1334–1418) in R.I.S., xix; Andrea

Navagero, *Historia veneta*, in *R.I.S.*, xxiii; Rafaino Caresino, *Chronica a. 1343–1388*, ed. E. Pastorello, in *R.I.S.* 2, xii, pt. ii, and *R.I.S.*, xii (disappointing, since Caresino himself had considerable diplomatic experience); Andrea Dandolo, *Ducis Venetiarum chronica per extensum escripta a. 46–1280 D.C.*, ed. E. Pastorello, in *R.I.S.* 2, xii, pt. i, and *R.I.S.*, xii (to 1339 – this also disappointing); Marin Sanuto, *Le vite dei dogi*, vol. I, ed. G. Monticolo, in *R.I.S.* 2, xxii, pt. iv, and *R.I.S.*, xxii.

80. Hermolaus Barbarus, *De officio legati*, in *De legatis et legationibus tractatus varii*, ed. Vladimir E. Hrabar (Dorpat, 1906) 65–70. Since Barbaro was a humanist, scholar, lawyer, diplomat and son of a diplomat, I had especially hoped to find something useful. See Mattingly, loc. cit., 108.

81. Domenico Malipiero, *Annali veneti dall' anno 1457 al 1500*, arranged and abbreviated by Senator Francesco Longo, ed. Agostino Sagredo *A.S.I.* (1843–44), vii, 110.

82. Ibid., 132. He also gives a *relazione* of Alvise Sagondino, secretary returned from Constantinople in 1496, again without sufficient detail. Ibid., 153.

83. 'A di 23 april. In collegio. Vene sier Marin Zorzi el dotor, venuta zà quasi molti mexi orator di Napoli, et per esser sta amalato non havia referito, e si reportò al pregadi, tamen non referite mai . . . et per principi fo laudato et ditta in *reliquis* referira al pregadi'. Sanuto, ii, 643.

84. Cessi, *Maggior Consiglio*, ii, 102.

85. Bartolomeo Zamberti, A.S.V. ex-Brera, m. 241–242, cod. 242, p. 122. The six-teenth-century repertory is quoted instead of the act by Foscarini, 488, n. 3; Alfred von Reumont, *Diplomazia*, 66; Baschet, *Archives*, 347; Antonibon, 13; Andreas, 65, no. 2. The authentic text of the Chancellery is A.S.V., *Maggior Consiglio, Fractus*, 82. Cessi published the contemporary copy made for the Quarantia. A.S.V., *Maggior Consiglio, Comunis*, I. f. 79. I am indebted to Dr. Lanfranchi for assistance in locating the source of the error and in distinguishing the versions of the act.

86. Baschet bases a lengthy description of the evolution of the *relazioni* upon this false interpretation; *Archives*, 346–348. See also Antonibon, 13. Rawdon Brown, generally so informative, misleads us by reporting that this law required the *Signoria* 'to supply them with a clerk to write out the narrative'; *Calendar of State Papers, Venetian*, i, p. xliii. The part of the law which he quotes in n. 1, however, has reference not to the *relazioni* of returning Venetian ambassadors but to the petitions of visiting ambassadors and the response made to them by the doge and his small council. Cessi's edition of the act furthers this misapprehension by expanding 'ambaxator venec' ('venec' also in *Fractus*) as *ambaxatores Veneciarum*, whereas the context clearly shows that it must be 'quando-cumque aliquis vel aliqui solempnes ambaxatores Veneciam venerint ab aliqua parte, debeant poni in scriptis petitiones eorum et responsiones eis facte per dominum Ducem et eius Consilium . . .' For citations, see above, n. 84 and n. 85.

87. Reumont, *Diplomazia*, 66; Arneth, *Die Relationen*, xii; Giulio Cesare Buzzati, 'Diritto diplomatico veneziano del sec. XIII', in *Studi giuridici dedicati a Francesco Schupfer*, vol. ii (Turin, 1898) 227; Segarizzi, *Relazioni*, i, 283; Andreas, 65. Brown was familiar with the *consuetudo Bononiensis* of counting backward from the end of the month for its second half, but counted one day too many, arriving at 22 Dec. *Calendar of State Papers, Venetian*, i, p. xlii.

88. Cessi, *Maggior Consiglio*, iii, 403. Also in Georg Martin Thomas, see above, n. 41.

89. Antonibon, 13, n. 1; Firpo, *Relazioni*, i, pp. v–vi. Selmi and Firpo also believe that only an oral presentation was required until 1425, which is incorrect. For additional acts trying to halt the custom of reporting only before the doge and a restricted body, see Queller, *Early Venetian legislation*, 67–68, no. 25; 71, no. 28; and 82, no. 43.

90. Queller, *Early Venetian legislation*, 82, no. 43.

91. Malipiero, 110. We must keep in mind, however, that a chronicler would be likely to report the part on the substance of the mission, while omitting the more general part.

92. Albèri, I, iv, 3. In contrast to the classical *relazioni* of the sixteenth century Baschet regards Contarini's effort as a museum piece. *Diplomatie*, 306–307.

93. At least as summarized by Sanuto, the following contain much of the character of a common report. *Diarii*, i, 405–408 and 438; 735–736; 858–859. All three were delivered before 1500. Andrea Gritti's *relazione* on the Turk in 1503 was of mixed character. 'Questo, Serenissimo Principe, è stato tutto l'ordine del negozio che, ambasciator di Vostra Serenità, ho avuto a Costantinopoli, il qual ha convenuto riferir particolarmente, e forse tediosamente, a questo sapientissimo Senato per la difficoltà grande che ho avuto di poternela avvisar di tempo in tempo, come era mio debito e desiderio . . . Mi resta dir a Vostra Serenità alcune poche cose dell' animo del Gransignore verso questa Seren-issima Repubblica, della disposizion de' magnifici bassà, e delli ordini dati a D. Lunardo Bembo eletto per me vice bailo'. Albèri, III, iii, 1–44. Piero Zen gave his *relazione* on Constantinople 17 and 18 Nov., 1530. The first sitting was devoted to the 'comings and goings' of his mission, the second to the general and didactic matter. Sanuto, liv, cols. 116–117. Andreas (pp. 67 and 83) believes that the *relazione* received its classical form about 1500.

94. Malipiero, 636–640.

95. Albèri, Appendice, xv, p. vi; Antonibon, 14. Not only the *Traité*, but Maggi's *De legato* of 1566 give a report on the mission as the first part of a *relazione*. See above, p. 180.

96. Albèri, I, i, 3. Again: '. . . gli antichi progenitori nostri hanno prudentissamente o per legge statuito, o per lunga e laudata consuetudine introdotto ed observato, che ciascheduno che ritorni . . .' Ibid., I, i, 33–34.

97. 'Tra le altri laudabili forme e istituzioni circa il governo del Stato nostro è sta' sempre da li sapientissimi maiori nostri observata questa inviolabilmente e per principale: che tutti i ministri suoi venuti de qui alla presenzia del serenissimo Prencipe nostro, ed *etiam* alcuni a questo senato, referiscono del rezimento over officio e magistrato suo . . .' Segarizzi, *Relazioni*, i, 284. Sanuto gives examples from 1497 and 1498 when ambassadors apologized for tardiness in giving their *relazioni* because of sickness. *Diarii*, i, 460; ii, 643. Recognition of the obligation to present a *relazione* is also indicated by the submission of a written *relazione* when an ambassador was transferred from one post to another without returning to Venice, as in the case of Nicolò Foscarini, transferred from Savoy at the beginning of 1498 to become *capitanio* of Verona. Ibid., i, 858–859. An example of 1601; Albèri, II, v, 232. Another example of 1744; Arneth, *Die Relationen*, xl–xli. See Baschet, *Diplomatie*, 5.

98. Most authorities, not having read the act of 1268, hold that the act of 1425 first required *relazioni* to be in writing. Reumont, *Diplomati italiani*, 51, and *Diplomazia*, 71. Baschet, *Archives*, 346–347; Yriarte, 130, no. 1; Buzzati, 227; Antonibon, 13; Andreas, 65; Selmi, 16; Firpo, *Relazioni*, i, pp. v–vi. Apart from misdating the act of 1268 as 9 Dec., Segarizzi is precisely right on the contents of the acts of 1268 and 1425. *Relazioni*, i, 283.

99. Queller, *Early Venetian legislation*, 86, no. 49.

100. Segarizzi, *Relazioni*, i, 284. The manuscript reads Nov. 15, not, as Segarizzi has it, Nov. 10. The *relazione* is described in the act as a mere report, although we have by this time rather numerous examples containing the more generalized matter.

101. 'Essendo stato letta nell' eccellentissimo consiglio dei Pregadi la parte, che obbliga tutti gli oratori ed altri ministri publici a presentare in iscritto in cancelleria le loro relazioni; e fatto intendere che tutti quelli che non le hanno date, le debbono dare in esecuzione di detta parte: pertanto io Marco Foscari . . . essendo venuto nel 1526 oratore da Roma, e non avendo data in iscritto la relazione che allora feci nell' eccellentissimo consiglio dei Pregadi (perchè non aveva notizia di detta parte); ancorachè, per la lunghezza del tempo, tutto sia alterato e mutato, e quelle trattazioni mi siano uscite di memoria, tuttavia, per non essere inobediente, dichiaro colla presente scrittura le infra-

scritte particularità'. Albèri, II, iii, 137. 'Non avendo avuto notizia de la lege, quando io feci la relazion mia de la legazion di fiorenza, che fo de 1528, del mese di marzo, io non la deti altramenti *in scriptis*. Ma ora, essendo sta' letta la parte e fatto intender a tutti quelli che non hano dato la sua relazione *in scriptis*, la debano dare; ancora che tutte le cose alora occorevano siano al tutto mutate, *tamen*, per esser obediente, per la presente scrittura declaro le infrascritte particularità, che con fatica mi ho redutto a memoria . . .' Segarizzi, *Relazioni*, III, i, 97–98. See Tommaso Gar on these two *relazioni* in Albèri, II, iii, 123–124.

102. Suriano does not state the facts as plainly as Foscari, but see Gar in Albèri, II, iii, pp. ii–iii and 275–276. It is clear from Suriano's own words that his *relazione* on Florence followed hard upon that of Foscari, and it was undoubtedly also stimulated by the effort to enforce the law in 1533. Segarizzi, *Relazioni*, III, i, 99. It is possible that Gasparo Contarini's *relazione* on Rome was another of those submitted in writing only in 1533. Albèri, II, iii, 274.

103. Arneth was able to discover only ten *relazioni* for the twenty-seven ambassadors to Germany in the eighteenth century, and he considered it more probable that this reflected non-compliance with the law than subsequent loss of the documents. *Die Relationen*, xvi. In 1722 Giovanni Priuli, returning from the Empire, remarked that he was honoured to deliver his *relazioni* 'doppo tanti anni da che un tale antico e prudente costume era già andata in disuso'. Ibid., 42. There were at least *relazioni* from the Congress of Utrecht and from Rome in 1713, from the Empire in 1708. Antonibon, 90, 107 and 73, respectively.

104. *Traité*, 292. See also the specific *request* that the *relazione* of Gianjacopo Caroldo, resident secretary in Milan, be placed in writing. Albèri, II, v, 301. Mattingly (p. 113) believed that some time in the fifteenth century the Senate recognized exceptional *relazioni* by having them written down, and that later this exceptional recognition became the rule. This does not take account, however, of the earlier legislation, even though not obeyed, requiring written *relazioni*. Mattingly plausibly believed that in the course of the fifteenth century noteworthy *relazioni* were specifically ordered to be recorded and preserved, a practice which became in time habitual. Some of those written before 1500 were given in that form for special reasons, such as the transfer of the ambassador to another post without returning to Venice. Even these were read in the Senate. Sanuto, i, 858–859.

105. Rawdon Brown indicates that the Negri Index, compiled in 1669, showed only a few *relazioni* preserved in the secret chamber at that time. *Calendar of State Papers, Venetian*, i, pp. xliii–xlv.

106. Baschet, *Diplomatie*, 11; Albèri, Appendice xv, p. viii. Rawdon Brown provides a detailed account of the fires and the confusion of the Chancellery resulting from them. Loc. cit., i, pp. xxii–xxvi.

107. Baschet, *Archives*, 164–165; Brown, ibid., xxiv.

108. Until recently I accepted the customary interpretation. *Early Venetian legislation*, 48–49; *Ambassador*, 142. Reumont believed that the collection of *relazioni* began only in the sixteenth century. *Diplomazia*, 71 and 76–77.

VII

NICOLAI RUBINSTEIN

Italian reactions to Terraferma expansion in the fifteenth century

---

One of the constantly recurring themes in Italian politics during the second half of the fifteenth century was that Venice was aiming at the *imperio d'Italia*.[1] In the first years of the sixteenth century, reaction to Venetian 'imperialism' contributed to the diplomatic developments leading up to the League of Cambrai and the concerted attack on Venice in 1509.[2] These developments were triggered off by the Venetian occupation of a large part of the Romagna, which had previously been ruled by Cesare Borgia, after the death of Alexander VI in 1503. Niccolò Machiavelli was at the time in Rome on a mission for the Florentine republic, and together with Cardinal Francesco Soderini tried to persuade the new pope, Julius II, to take energetic measures against Venice's occupation of territories belonging to the Papal States, an occupation which had brought the Venetians to the northern frontier of the Florentine state. 'If the others',write the Ten of War to Machiavelli on 15th November, 1503, on the eve of the capitulation of Faenza, 'tolerate that the Venetians carry on with a campaign which is leading them to the monarchy of Italy, we shall look after our own interests, and shall take the decisions that seem to us best';[3] and Machiavelli writes to them on the 24th: 'One finds here a universal hatred of them . . . and to sum up, one draws the conclusion that the campaign of the Venetians against Faenza will either throw open to them the whole of Italy, or lead to their ruin'.[4]

The immediate cause of this *odio universale*, in so far as it in fact existed in Rome and the Papal States, was the Venetian occupation of the Romagna. At the same time, Florence, which saw her interests vitally affected by that occupation,[5] had every reason both to exaggerate and foster the fear of Venetian imperialism in order to induce the pope to take a strong stand against Venice. Venetian territorial expansion and anti-Venetian propaganda formed the two major aspects of the growth, in the preceding century, of the notion of the *imperio veneto* of Italy. It will be argued in this study that while Venetian *terraferma* policy was bound to create anti-Venetian feelings, the view that that

197

policy was ultimately aiming at the *monarchia d' Italia* was the effect of diplomatic action and propaganda.

The Venetian *terraferma* state of the fifteenth century was founded after the death of Giangaleazzo Visconti, when Venice acquired the eastern Lombard territories which had been previously ruled by him, as well as Padua; but it must not be forgotten that these were not the beginnings of her expansionist policy on the Italian mainland. As early as 1308, Venice had tried, albeit unsuccessfully, to obtain control of Ferrara;[6] and in 1339, she succeeded in acquiring, from Mastino della Scala, Treviso with its territory, which she kept until the end of the War of Chioggia and recovered in 1389. In the fourteenth century, Venice's main concerns on the Italian mainland were economic, and in particular related to her food and salt supplies and to the safety of her trade routes;[7] but even then she was not past taking advantage of the difficulties of her neighbours in order to extend her jurisdiction. This was the case in 1339, when she profited from the break up of the Scala dominions after Mastino's defeat at the hands of an Italian league, and again in 1402, when Giangaleazzo Visconti's dominions disintegrated after his death, although an additional, and probably decisive, factor was now the danger of the lord of Padua, Francesco Novello da Carrara, creating a powerful territorial state on the mainland opposite Venice by taking over the Visconti possessions in eastern Lombardy.[8]

Accordingly, contemporary Italian opinion does not seem to have regarded the Venetian initiative, which led to the acquisition of Verona, Vicenza, and Padua itself, and which came later to be seen as a turning point in Venetian and Italian history,[9] as a new departure in Venetian policy, and even less as marking the beginning of imperialist ambitions in Italy. Such ambitions were, at the time, associated with Giangaleazzo Visconti. Venice's acquisitions on the *terraferma*, made when the dangers from Milan's aggrandizement to the independence of northern Italian states was still fresh in the minds of Italians, could be seen as a defensive action designed to prevent the restoration of Visconti control in eastern Lombardy, or its replacement by that of the Da Carrara. They were evidently of a different order from Giangaleazzo's real or alleged aim to create an Italian kingdom.

Coluccio Salutati, the chancellor of Florence from 1375 to 1406, had done his best to show that this was the ultimate aim of the duke of Milan, 'qui se regem facere cupit';[10] but Florentine propaganda was not alone in drawing attention to such objectives,[11] for the existence of which Giangaleazzo's actions and successes could in fact appear to provide ample evidence. They left a lasting, and to some extent traumatic, mark on the Florentines, who had been close to becoming the victims of Milan's aggrandizement, and who naturally enough remained highly sensitive to any subsequent signs of imperialist ambitions. This is shown in the reaction of the Florentines to the advance of Ladislas of Naples into the Papal States and Tuscany in 1408 and 1409, a reaction which culminated in the assertion that the king of Naples was plotting to subdue all Italy.[12] There was, as far as we can see, no such response in Florence to the advance of Venice into eastern Lombardy. One reason for this was no doubt that the Venetian advance did not constitute any danger to Florentine political independence or territorial interests. Another was that the acquisition, by fair means or foul, of neighbouring city-states was, and had been for a long time, considered an entirely legitimate aspiration of communal politics. It was often justified in terms of security, as providing protection for one's own *libertas* against real or hypothetical attacks, and this argument, however specious it may have often been, evidently assumed greater force after the threats by Giangaleazzo Visconti to the independence of Florence and of Tuscany. It was precisely on such grounds that Florentines justified, almost contemporaneously with the Venetian *terraferma* conquests, their own acquisition of Pisa, which was equally the result of the collapse of the Visconti state. Coluccio Salutati accused the Pisans of having waged war against Florence jointly with Milan for fifteen years,[13] and Gregorio Dati wrote, shortly after the final capitulation of Pisa in 1406, that the Florentines had bought that city from Giangaleazzo's natural son, Gabriele Maria, 'remembering how many injuries they had suffered in the past through the Pisans, how many wars and defeats . . . knowing how much honour and greatness would ensue to the Florentines, if they acquired Pisa and became her rulers, how profitable and convenient it would be for their commerce, how much security it would offer them never again to be besieged . . .'[14] It is not surprising that Dati could say of Venice's conquest of the Da Carrara dominions that 'it has been a great and splendid acquisition for the Venetians, and they were allowed to make it because of the grave sins of that lord of Padua'.[15] True, Florence had tried to assist Francesco Novello, who had many friends in Florence, by way of diplomatic protests; but, as another contemporary Florentine writes, 'he remained alone . . . no one ever decided to come to his help'.[16]

As we have already observed, the Florentines, despite their experiences with Visconti expansionism, had their special reasons for not objecting more forcefully to Venice's spectacular acquisition of extensive possessions on the *terraferma*. A stronger reaction could have been expected from the cities that were directly affected by Venetian expansion, and especially from Milan. Andrea Biglia, for one, in the *History of Milan* he wrote around 1430, limits himself to the terse comment on the fall of the Da Carrara that 'ita Veneti, quod nunquam antea paene . . . speraverant, maritimo imperio terrestrem quoque dominatum e nostris cladibus adiecere'.[17]

This *dominatus* the Venetians succeeded in extending further, first in Friuli, Istria, and Dalmatia, and then, once more at the expense of Milan, in Lombardy during the first of the wars they waged as Florence's allies against the duke of Milan, Filippo Maria Visconti: in the peace of 1428, they definitively acquired Bergamo and Brescia with their territories.[18] The Florentines, who had made great efforts to persuade Venice to ally with them against renewed Visconti expansion, could hardly blame her for making territorial acquisitions as a result of that alliance. Yet there were in Florence, naturally enough, misgivings about these Venetian successes, which sharply contrasted with Florence's own failure to conquer Lucca between 1430 and 1433; and as early as 1428 Florentines were apparently beginning to ask themselves whether the Venetians were not nourishing much more ambitious hopes of conquering the Milanese duchy itself.[19] Such apprehensions did not, however, affect the relations between the two states until after the death, on 13th August, 1447, of Filippo Maria Visconti.

At that time, the Florentines were greatly concerned about Alfonso of Aragon's designs in Tuscany.[20] The king of Naples had been allied with Filippo Maria Visconti since 1435;[21] moreover, he had been helping Pope Eugenius IV to expel Francesco Sforza from the March of Ancona, and Florence had become involved in this lengthy war against her *condottiere*.[22] In December 1446, Alfonso had sent her an ultimatum demanding that she desist from giving help to Francesco Sforza; he told his council at Naples that he would now be able to deal a decisive blow to his enemies, after which he could impose his will on the whole of Italy, 'daria ley a tota Ytalia'.[23] The ultimatum was not followed up, but after Filippo Maria's death, Alfonso advanced with his army into Tuscany. Having prevailed on Siena to grant him passage, he entered Florentine territory in November, occupied a few places, but then turned to the coast, where he captured Castiglione della Pescaia at the beginning of December. He failed, however, to gain possession of Piombino, whose lord, Rinaldo Orsini, was a protégé of Florence, and in June 1448 laid siege to that town, whose great strategic importance was appreciated by him as much as by the Florentines.[24]

On 13th August, 1447, the Florentine *Signoria* instructed their ambassador in Venice to appeal for military assistance in view of the news that the king of Naples was advancing with large forces in order to invade Tuscany and stage an offensive against Florence;[25] in October, they warned the Sienese, in terms that recall Coluccio Salutati's state letters against Giangaleazzo Visconti, that Florence was only the first objective of Alfonso's campaign: the Sienese could be certain 'that the aim of that prince is none other than to oppress all the free republics [*tutte le libertà*] of Italy and reduce them to serfdom under his rule'; he had no other reason for his aggression against Florence than his 'ambition to rule and to expand his dominions [*dilatare il suo imperio*]'. The Sienese should recall the invasion of Tuscany by another king of Naples, Ladislas, who had come to conquer Siena and Florence, and of their glorious and successful joint resistance against his vast army in the defence of their freedom.[26] The insistence on Alfonso's imperialist plans was evidently designed to back Florentine appeals for military assistance to her Venetian ally, and for Sienese rejection of Alfonso's overtures. However, suspicions of Alfonso's ultimate objectives were also voiced in Florence in the secret debates of the government's advisory commissions: after Alfonso had, in August 1447, proposed a truce to the Florentines, the *pratica* advised the *Signoria* that his only motive for doing so was 'to enable him to succeed to the rule over Lombardy'.[27]

One of Alfonso of Aragon's immediate aims, in the summer of 1447, was in fact the succession to the Milanese duchy, and thus of the *dominio di Lombardia*, but his Tuscan campaign, whatever its immediate origins, could well appear to be indicative of even more ambitious plans. In his opening speech to the Venetian *Signoria*, Giannozzo Manetti, who was sent to Venice in August 1448 to persuade her to support the projected expedition of René of Anjou against the king of Naples, described Alfonso's ultimate objective as 'Italie imperium'.[28] Roman history provided humanist statesmen with terms that could lend themselves to describing contemporary events and institutions; but such classicizing usage was liable to be based on superficial analogies. In his *Decades*, Flavio Biondo sounded a warning against the indiscriminate use of classical terms for modern institutions, and exemplified its pitfalls in the word *imperator*.[29] In the case of *imperium*, there were the additional difficulties in that the term had, in medieval public law, been pre-empted by the Holy Roman Empire, and that its precise meaning in Roman constitutional history was not always easy to define.[30] Yet it may have been the very ambivalence of the term in later Roman usage which made it particularly suitable for conditions in which the boundaries between immediate jurisdiction and political hegemony were liable to be blurred. Not only had *imperium*, which originally denoted the power bestowed on the highest Roman magistracies for the enforcement of their authority, acquired a subsidiary territorial significance,[31] the notion of the *Romanum imperium* could be defined by St. Augustine in terms of direct subjection as well as of alliance.[32] Italian humanists, in their turn, could use *imperium* as interchangeable with *dominium*, to describe Italian territorial states;[33] but the term could also be used to describe the kind of political ascendancy in Italy the king of Naples was alleged to be aspiring to. For Giannozzo Manetti, the classical precedent of his imperialist ambitions was Hannibal: just as Hannibal had fought Rome over the 'imperium orbis terrarum', so Alfonso was aiming, through war, at the 'imperium Italiae'.

It was in this atmosphere of growing suspicion of Alfonso of Naples' ultimate objectives that the expansionist policy which Venice adopted in eastern Lombardy after the death of Filippo Maria could in its turn give rise to the belief that Venice too was harbouring imperialist plans, whose realization would extend her power far beyond the present boundaries. The notion that Venice was aiming at the *imperio d'Italia*, which played so important a role in Italian political opinion at the close of the fifteenth century, began to take roots during the months and years following on the death of Filippo Maria Visconti. During this period, the fate of Francesco Sforza's claims to the succession of the duchy of Milan on the ground of his marriage to Filippo Maria's daughter, depended largely on the attitude of the Venetian government. Francesco Sforza and his able envoys, foremost among them Nicodemo Tranchedini from Pontremoli, sought to counter Venice's opposition to Sforza's claims by persuading her Florentine ally that her real aim was the acquisition of the duchy and thus of control over Lombardy, and that her ultimate objective was rule over Italy.

Their task seemed to be facilitated from the start by Francesco Sforza's powerful supporter in Florence. Four days after Filippo Maria Visconti's death, on 17th August, 1447, Nicodemo Tranchedini reported from Florence, where Francesco had sent him a few months earlier,[34] that Cosimo de' Medici was advising

Francesco Sforza to seek the support of the king of Naples for his claims to the Milanese duchy, 'and that the king would give it to him, in order to prevent the Venetians from lording it over Italy': Cosimo was holding out hope of success, 'as all Italy dislikes the prosperity of the Venetians'.[35] According to Nicodemo, Cosimo told the *pratica*, on the same day, that it was not in the interest of Florence that Venice should acquire the late duke's dominions, *el stato del Duca*.[36] On the 28th of the same month, he wrote his master that the Florentine *Signoria* had asked Venice to conclude peace with the new Milanese republic, but that the Venetian orator, Ermolao Donato, had rejoined that his government would be content to do so as long as the Milanese territory (*ducato*) came under Venetian jurisdiction: for as long as Milan possessed this territory, she constituted a constant threat to Italy. Nicodemo concluded that in this way, the Venetian ambassador 'provided conclusive evidence of the Venetian desire for the *monarchia de Ytalia*'; and he added that 'these words did not fall on deaf ears'.[37] He was too optimistic; in February 1448, he wrote to Francesco Sforza that Cosimo had told him that 'it would be most difficult to obtain [from the Florentines] approval for abandoning the Venetians . . . except in the case of greatest necessity'.[38]

What was the truth behind these allegations against Venice? Conditions in the Milanese territory after the death of Filippo Maria Visconti offered Venice once more opportunities for territorial aggrandizement which she was eager to seize. Just as, after the death of Giangaleazzo Visconti, Vicenza had placed herself under Venice, so now Piacenza and Lodi submitted to her.[39] These were her first substantial acquisitions from Milan since 1428, and carried her power beyond the Adda river, but they could still be seen as a logical continuation of the westward advance of her *terraferma* frontier which had come to a virtual standstill in that year. To take over the Milanese duchy itself would have constituted an entirely new departure, whose realization would have decisively changed the distribution of power not only in Lombardy but also in Italy as a whole. Was such a project being seriously considered in Venice?

There may well have been a group in Venice who in 1447 and 1448 favoured such a course of action,[40] but there is no evidence that it ever became official policy. A report the Venetian ambassador to Naples gave in Florence, in December 1447, of Alfonso's accusations against Venice, to the effect that she intended to usurp the rule over Milan which rightfully belonged to him, has been wrongly referred to as proof of such intention.[41] In fact, the Senate had, on receipt of the news of Filippo Maria's death, immediately sent an envoy to Milan to encourage its citizens 'ad reducendam eam civitatem in libertate' and to offer them help 'ad illam conservandam': Venice had not waged war against Milan but against its duke.[42] However, a few days later the captain general of the Venetian troops, Micheletto Attendolo, was ordered to take Crema or Cremona.[43] In a letter written during those days to the procurator of St. Mark, Federigo Contarini, the Venetian statesman Francesco Barbaro sharply criticized attempts to take advantage of the present weakness of Milan in order to extend the Venetian frontiers west of the Adda, but does not mention a project to absorb Milan itself. The war against Filippo Maria Visconti, he says, had not been undertaken 'dominandi libidine . . ., sed ut vim vi repelleremus'; now Milan was again a free republic, it was preferable 'auctoritate et aequitate consociare vires Galliae [i.e. of Lombardy] nobis quam armis dissociare'.[44]

Francesco Barbaro's advice was not heeded, and during the following years Venice not only tried to secure the Adda frontier by mopping up the remaining Milanese possessions east of the river and establishing bridgeheads on its western bank, but also to extend her rule west of it. That she was far less successful than could at first have been expected was due to Francesco Sforza, who used his military exploits to establish his own authority in parts of the Milanese territory. Although bitterly disappointed at being deprived, for the time being, of the coveted prize of the Milanese duchy by the proclamation of the republic, he had agreed to serve the new government as captain general (30th August, 1447); as early as November 1447, he took Piacenza from Venice, and in the following year threw the Venetians back east of the Adda; in September 1448, he inflicted a crushing defeat on their troops at Caravaggio.[45] As a result of this defeat, the Venetians came to terms with him, promised to help him acquire the Milanese duchy, and reduced their territorial demands: while in the unsuccessful negotiations with the Ambrosian republic they had insisted on the acquisition of Lodi, Crema, and Cremona, they now declared themselves satisfied with that of Crema and the Ghiaradadda.[46] When Venice finally concluded peace with the Ambrosian republic in September 1449, the Venetians even accepted the restoration to Milan of Lodi, which had recently been acquired by Francesco Sforza, while they received Crema and the Ghiaradadda. Crema was their only major territorial acquisition since August 1447, and together with the Ghiaradadda would have rounded off the Venetian possessions east of the Adda and north of Cremona. The peace treaty declared that river the frontier between the two states,[47] but in order to continue it down to the river Po, Cremona and its territory would have to be added to the *terraferma* state, and their acquisition remained Venice's major territorial objective. Thus under the pressure of military and political reverses, Venice reduced her territorial demands at the expense of Milan to the acquisition of a 'natural frontier'. Even after the reversal of alliances in consequence of Francesco Sforza's accession to the Milanese duchy in February 1450, when Venice was no longer obliged to make substantial concessions, her only major demand was Cremona which was, together with all the lands east of the Adda, allotted to her in the treaty of alliance which she concluded in October of that year with Alfonso of Aragon against the new duke of Milan.[48] When during the abortive peace negotiations in 1451 Francesco Sforza demanded the restitution of Milanese lands east of the Adda and the passages (*passi*) over that river, the Venetian ambassadors retorted that Venice had acquired them 'iusto et honestissimo bello', and that these acquisitions 'non ulla ambitione seu desiderio ampliandi dominii, sed pro securitate sua tenere et conservare intendit, sicut omni iure debet'.[49]

In the circumstances, the claims of Francesco Sforza and his envoys that Venice was aiming at the *imperio* of Lombardy or even of Italy, had an air of unreality. One might have expected the Milanese to have made them their own, but their main preoccupation appears to have been with the territorial ambitions of Venice at their expense. To the Venetian offer of support and non-aggression, the Milanese government replied in August 1447 that Venice's deeds did not bear out her words, as was shown by the acquisition of Piacenza and Lodi, 'and the other places they had taken, and were attempting to take'.[50] Early in 1448, the Milanese rejected the Venetian peace conditions, according to which Lodi, Crema, and Cremona were to come under Venetian rule;[51] a Milanese ambassador stated in Florence in March that 'as the Venetians are so powerful, as their appetite was by now well known, and as they want now to reserve for themselves the gateways to Milan, a peace of this sort would mean to be at their discretion'.[52]

The Florentines too were at that time concerned at the prospect of their Venetian ally exploiting the situation in Lombardy to expand her territory. In appealing, in September 1447, to the Venetian government to conclude peace with Milan, they suggested that the Milanese should be told that the victorious league was not *'cupida di crescere imperio,* but willing to give the defeated an honourable peace'.[53] It was in order to elicit increased Venetian assistance against the king of Naples that the Florentine *Signoria* made a special point of conveying to the Venetians Alfonso's complaints against them. Alfonso accused them of having tried to usurp the Milanese duchy, of which he was the rightful heir, after Filippo Maria's death. If they succeeded in doing so and acquired Lombardy, he was no longer safe in his own realm, for 'once the Venetians are lords of Milan, they can drive him from his kingdom with a stroke of the pen'. He accordingly insisted that his Tuscan campaign was ultimately directed against Venice, and that he had only begun with Florence 'as the weaker of the allies and the one which is closest to him'.[54] Similarly, the *Signoria* instructed their ambassadors in Venice to inform the Venetian government of the Milanese complaints about Venice – that 'while the duke was alive, they had always been preaching peace', but that as soon as he was dead they had taken Milanese lands; and that both Milan and Florence were victims of expansionist policies.[55]

Nicodemo Tranchedini may have been right that, on the news of Filippo Maria Visconti's death, Cosimo had given the *pratica* to understand 'that it was not in the interest of the Florentines that the Venetians rule the *stato* of the duke', and that only Francesco Sforza could possess it without danger to Florence.[56] In those early days, there may have been a genuine fear in Florence, kindled by the Sforza agent, that Venice would try to take over Milan.[57] In the following months, criticism of Venetian policy in the *pratiche* centred, more realistically, on Venice's selfish attempts to extend her territory at the expense of Milan, which contrasted with her failure to give Florence adequate help against Alfonso. The Venetians 'ita rem suam gessisse', says Girolamo Machiavelli in a *pratica* of April 1448, 'ut semper imperium propagaverint, cum nos magno damno affecti sumus', while Cosimo de' Medici argued that it would have been their duty, with all the military power they possessed, 'magis parti laboranti [i.e. Florence] succurrere, quam victoriae imperioque propagando intendere'.[58] Florence's alliance with Venice, reiterates Girolamo Machiavelli in a *pratica* of November 1449, 'semper eis imperium accrevisse, nobis vero fuisse dannosam',[59] and Cosimo declares in December: 'societatem ... Venetum duo afferre, que semper sapientibus fuerunt repudiata, damnum scilicet et ignominiam.'[60] 'It is also common opinion', write the Florentine *Signori* to their ambassadors in Venice in May 1448, 'that if that Illustrious *Signoria* had been willing to restore Lodi to the Milanese, peace between them would have been concluded a long time ago ... for the sake of Lodi, the entire league has to face great expense and danger, and all Italy is thrown into confusion ...'.[61]

It was not Cosimo de' Medici but Francesco Sforza and his envoy Nicodemo Tranchedini who time and again harped on the wider imperialist theme in Venice's policy. When in February 1448, during the peace negotiations between Venice and the Ambrosian republic, Cosimo observed on a proposal of a separate alliance between Florence, Milan, and Francesco Sforza, 'that it would be most difficult to obtain approval [in Florence] for abandoning the Venetians ... except in the case of greatest necessity', Nicodemo advised Francesco Sforza to go on inciting (*inanimire*) Cosimo, and adds that he is sure that in the end Cosimo will take courage (*pigliarà animo*) to bring about a decision in Sforza's favour, for he will be compelled to do so by 'necessity, as he will see ... that the Venetians have partitioned Italy with the king of Aragon'.[62] And after the conclusion of the peace treaty between the Milanese republic and Venice in September 1449, Francesco Sforza instructed his ambassador in Florence to tell Cosimo that it was in Cosimo's and Florence's interest to give him financial and diplomatic support 'in order to prevent the Venetians from becoming lords of Milan and of Lombardy', and to insist that it was 'the intention of the Venetians to take possession of Milan ... and that once they were lords of Milan, one could say that they were lords of the whole of Italy'.[63]

After Milan's surrender to Francesco Sforza, Venice did everything in her power to deprive him again of the duchy; in July 1450, she concluded peace with Alfonso of Naples, and in October an alliance with him against Francesco Sforza.[64] Not surprisingly, Sforza propaganda against Venice, as well as against her new ally, now reached unprecedented heights, and the imperialist theme played a leading role in it, with the Venetians being compared to the ancient Romans. The Venetians, writes Francesco Sforza to Nicodemo Tranchedini in Rome in February 1451, for the benefit of the pope and the cardinals, have never accepted our peace offers, 'for they are constantly greedy for power and for the possessions of all their neighbours, in order to satisfy their ambition to dominate Italy, and then to extend their rule beyond Italy, as the Romans had done; for they believe that they can compare themselves to the Romans of the days when they were powerful'.[65] Nicodemo did not need to be instructed how to blacken Venice's reputation in Italy, but he surely surpassed himself when he told

Nicholas V in December 1451 that the Venetians were 'diabolical men who had neither honour nor conscience nor the fear of God, and who wanted to conquer Italy'.[66] If in Rome the Venetians were represented as godless conquerors, Venetian 'imperialism' was given a somewhat different slant at the courts of Italian despots. The marquess of Mantua knows, writes Cecco Simonetta to Nicodemo Tranchedini on 30th May, 1451, 'the greed of the Venetians', which is 'nothing else but to try to extirpate and uproot all the *signori* and feudal lords of Italy, as they have done to a number of them in the past, and to try to subject what remains of the Italian republics'.[67]

Such accusations did not fall on deaf ears. According to the Sforza ambassador at Ferrara, in March 1451 Borso d'Este told the Neapolitan ambassador, who had invited him to join the alliance against Francesco Sforza, that he was dismayed at Alfonso's support for Venice: in doing this he was preparing 'the destruction of his son and of all the remaining rulers [*signori*] of Italy . . . for once the Venetians are in possession of Cremona' and Alfonso or Francesco Sforza is dead, 'the Venetians, who are immortal, will without difficulty become rulers of Italy'.[68] The marquess of Ferrara had genuine reasons for being apprehensive of Venetian aggrandizement; but the imperialist argument he uses comes too close to the anti-Venetian propaganda of the Sforza not to have been influenced by it.

Much the same was true of Florence. On 1st June, 1451, the Venetian government and the king of Naples expelled the Florentine merchants from their territories; on 30th July, Florence concluded an alliance with Francesco Sforza.[69] In the changed circumstances, Sforza propaganda on Venice's Italian imperialism at last began to bear fruit in Florence. On 18th June, Francesco Sforza wrote to his ambassador in Rome, Nicodemo Tranchedini, that the expulsion of the Florentine merchants by Venice and Alfonso showed clearly 'their ambition to dominate Italy', and that he had written about this to the Florentine *Signoria* and suggested remedies.[70] On the 28th of that month, the *Signoria*, in an attempt to detach Alfonso from Venice, instructed their ambassador to the king to impress on him that if he wished to preserve the kingdoms he had acquired in Italy and hand them over to his successors, it was not expedient for him to back the expansionism (*appetito*) of the Venetian government. This *appetito* of the Venetians, as could be plainly seen by their actions before, and especially after the death of the duke, was 'nothing less than the desire to take possession (*insignorirsi*) of Lombardy and of neighbouring regions, and subsequently of the *imperio d'Italia*'.[71] Conversely, in the instructions which the *Dieci* gave the ambassador to the king of France in September, the Venetians were accused of contesting Francesco Sforza the rightful possession of the duchy of Milan because they were planning to occupy Lombardy, 'and in time *lo imperio di Italia*', and of having, in the meantime, partitioned Italy with Alfonso.[72] And after the attack of the Venetian forces on Francesco Sforza's troops in May 1452, which ended the period of the 'cold war', the Florentine *Dieci* instructed the ambassador to Perugia to explain to the Perugians that the Venetians' military and diplomatic actions during the past years, and even before Filippo Maria's death, provided ample evidence 'that the Venetian government had for a long time been planning to dominate the whole of Lombardy, and after that the whole of Italy . . .'[73]

Once peace negotiations were seriously under way, these far-fetched accusations were dropped; what was now, more realistically, at stake was the frontier between Venice and Milan: was the Adda to remain the frontier, under Venetian control, was Venice to keep the acquisitions she had made at the expense of Milan since 1447?[74] The Peace of Lodi of 9th April, 1454, settled these questions for the time being, and led to the conclusion of an Italian league, designed to secure, for twenty-five years, the territorial integrity of the Italian states.[75] The war was over, but the anti-Venetian propaganda of the war years left a deep mark on Italian views on Venetian political objectives during and after the war. In his semi-official *History of Florence*, which he completed shortly after the Peace of Lodi,[76] the Florentine chancellor Poggio Bracciolini states that the war had been caused 'Venetorum ambitione simul et Alphonsi ampliandi imperii cupiditate', and that it had been her alliance with Francesco Sforza, concluded 'auctore et suasore Cosimo', which had saved Florence; for had she remained Venice's ally, the new duke would doubtless have succumbed to Venetian power, 'ex quo et nobis postmodum illorum arbitrio parandum erat'.[77] Poggio's successor in the Florentine chancery, Benedetto Accolti, further stressed Cosimo's decisive role in persuading the Florentines to abandon the alliance with Venice for that with Francesco Sforza, 'quia intelligebat, Philippo sine successore mortuo, Venetos facile totius Galliae dominatum habituros; quod si evenisset, minime dubium erat, quin postea universis Italiae populis imperassent'.[78] To have saved Florence and Italy from Venetian domination, became part of the historical image of Cosimo; if after Filippo Maria's death, Venice had occupied his duchy, says Cristoforo Landino around 1475, 'in gravissimum periculum veniebat universa Italia' to be subjected to Venetian power, which 'pernitiosam pestem' Cosimo alone foresaw and forestalled.[79] Much the same point is made, around the same time, by Benedetto Dei in his scurrilous attack on Venice: if Venice had annexed Milan, from which she was prevented by Cosimo, she would have become 'queen of Italy'.[80] Nor were the Florentines alone in remaining wedded to this 'imperialist' interpretation of Venice's objectives after 1447. Pius II, who had his own reasons for being critical of Venetian policy, says in his *Commentaries* that Florence had come to Francesco Sforza's aid, 'fearing that the Venetians, if they once got possession of Milan, would attack all Italy', and repeated the accusation that Venice was bent on founding a new monarchy in Italy.[81]

The Venetians would react to, or try to forestall, such accusations by emphasizing their traditional defence of liberty, and by asserting their refusal to take advantage of their neighbours' plight. 'All Italy should know', writes Ludovico Foscarini to Francesco Barbaro after the conclusion, in September 1449, of the peace treaty between Venice and the Milanese republic, *maximam animi ingenuitatem* of the Venetians, who, while exerting themselves for the liberation of

Italy, are content with their present jurisdiction, although they would be capable of extending it, 'cum possumus nostrum prorogare imperium'.[82] Under the leadership of Francesco Foscari, says Bernardo Giustinian, in 1457, in his funeral oration on the doge, Venice had been resisting the ambitions of Filippo Maria Visconti, who 'flagrabat italici regni cupiditate'.[83] She had been forced 'by necessity' to repulse 'force by force', 'vim vi', in order that 'imperium libertasque a maioribus relicta incolumis servaretur'. Conversely, accusations of imperialist designs could be directed against other Italian powers as well, and even against Florence: thus in December 1450, the Senate instructed their envoy in Lucca, which Venice was trying to win over, to tell the Lucchese that Francesco Sforza and Florence had agreed to partition Lombardy and Tuscany between them: the duke of Milan was to retain all captured lands in Lombardy, 'omnes vero civitates . . . Tuscie esse debant Florentinorum'.[84]

During the years following the conclusion of the Peace of Lodi, which confirmed her failure to annex Cremona and lands west of the Adda, Venice was in fact primarily concerned with ensuring the safety of her existing *terraferma* possessions. Thus during the Pazzi War (1478–80), the Venetian government was constantly apprehensive lest military operations be carried into the Romagna, and when Florence and Milan concluded a separate peace and alliance with the king of Naples and the pope in 1480, Venetians feared that this would result in war in the Romagna.[85] However, Venice's war against Duke Ercole d'Este in 1482, whose immediate causes, or pretexts, were infringements of Venetian rights in Ferrara and boundary disputes, could hardly be justified on grounds of security alone,[86] and it was not surprising that it should be seen abroad as yet another confirmation of her imperialist ambitions in Italy at large. 'De libertate nobis videtur agi totius Italiae, non de principatu modo ferrariensi', writes the Florentine *Signoria* to the Bolognese on receipt of the news of the Venetian attack on the duke of Ferrara; 'neccesse est . . . opponamus arma nostra eorum armis, qui deglutire atque absorbere Italiae libertates parant'.[87]

The events following the expedition of Charles VIII to Italy in 1494 offered Venice unprecedented opportunities for extending her control outside her *terraferma* possessions. After the conclusion of the league against the French king in March 1495, and the collapse of French power in the kingdom of Naples, Venice retained a number of ports in Apulia;[88] and, nominally on behalf of the league, she sent troops to Pisa to assist the Pisans in their war against Florence, whose rule they had shaken off after Charles VIII's entry. In the course of military operations against Florence, she occupied Bibbiena in the Casentino, thus threatening Florence from two directions.[89] Now at last there appeared to be a genuine cause for alarm at Venice's imperialist ambitions in Italy, and it was only to be expected that the assertion that Venice was aiming at the *imperio d'Italia* would receive a new lease of life in anti-Venetian propaganda.[90] The notion had become by now so stereotyped as to amount to a political creed. What is striking is how little it had changed since the days of Francesco Sforza and Nicodemo Tranchedini. Venice's unbounded desire to dominate, her ambition to extend her rule over the whole of Italy, and even beyond the Alps, her dream of a new Venetian *monarchia* in imitation of the ancient Roman Empire: these accusations, which had been so insistently formulated by Sforza propaganda from 1447 onwards, are now used by the Florentines in their anti-Venetian diplomacy.[91] During the long war against Pisa, which was not concluded until 1509, with the surrender of that town, the fear of Venetian imperialism became almost an obsession with the Florentines. In Francesco Guicciardini's *History of Florence*, which was written at the time of the League of Cambrai,[92] Venetian striving after the *imperio d'Italia* forms one of the few continuous threads in the narrative of the relations between Italian States after the middle of the fifteenth century.[93] In retrospect, the disastrous defeats of Venice at the hands of the League could thus appear almost as nemesis for past hubris. Shortly afterwards, the Venetian patrician Girolamo Priuli in his turn placed much of the blame for the crisis that had overtaken Venice on her expansion policy, but with a telling difference: his censures were not aimed at any ambitions for a Venetian *imperio d'Italia*, but at the Venetians' excessive care for their *terraferma* dominions at the expense of their sea power, which according to Priuli formed the real basis of Venice's greatness.[94] Even so outspoken a critic of Venice's *terraferma* policy as Priuli did not depart from the traditional Venetian argument that for whatever immediate reasons that policy was pursued at the time, expansion on the mainland served to safeguard and strengthen the security of the Venetian state, and was thus in keeping with the normal patterns of territorial aggrandizement in Italy. Even at this moment of truth, Venetians would still insist, in contrast to their critics and enemies, on the limited objectives of their *terraferma* policy.

NOTES

1. See Gina Fasoli, 'Nascita di un mito', in *Studi storici in onore di Gioacchino Volpe* (Florence, 1958) i, 472 seq.; N. Valeri, 'Venezia nella crisi italiana del Rinascimento', in *La civiltà veneziana del Quattrocento* (Florence, 1957) 35–47. There is no detailed study of the polemic against Venice in the second half of the century.

2. See F. Seneca, *Venezia e Papa Giulio II* (Padua, 1962) ch. 1.

3. Niccolò Machiavelli, *Legazioni e Commissarie*, ed. S. Bertelli (Milan, 1964) ii, 638: 'sopportando li altri a' Viniziani una tale impresa che li conduce alla monarchia di Italia, noi cercheremo il fatto nostro, et piglieréno quelli partiti che ci paranno migliori.'

4. Ibid., 676: 'Si vede qua un odio universale contra di loro ... e fassi in summa questo iudizio, che la impresa che e' Viniziani hanno fatta di Faenza, o la sarà una porta, che apriria loro tutta Italia, o la fia la ruina loro.' See also *Dieci* to Machiavelli, 20 Nov., 1503, ibid., 659: 'importa alla libertà nostra il tenere Viniziani discosto a' confini nostri.'

5. In the *pratica* of 21 Nov., 1503, these apprehensions were clearly formulated by the spokesman of the Ten of War, the *Dieci*, Filippo dell' Antella (Archivio di Stato di Firenze [=A.S.F.], *Consulte e Pratiche*, 67, f. 216): what had been feared had happened in the Romagna, 'chè vi sono entrati e Viniziani, e quali non lasciano cosa che piglino ... et che è da considerare che siamo vicini a' Viniziani, et che volendo offendere, possono facilmente, et che la loro volontà è insaziabile ...'

6. See G. Soranzo, *La guerra fra Venezia e la S. Sede per il dominio di Ferrara (1308–1313)* (Città di Castello, 1905) 76 seq.

7. For Venetian economic policy on the mainland before the conquest of the *terraferma*, see G. Luzzatto, *Storia economica di Venezia dall' XI al XVI secolo* (Venice, 1961) 50 seq.

8. R. Cessi, *Storia della Repubblica di Venezia* (Milan–Messina, 1944) i, 345; F. Cognasso, in *Storia di Milano*, vi (Milan, 1955) 111.

9. Cf. e.g. Bernardo Rucellai and Girolamo Priuli, quo. below, notes 91 and 94. See also Luzzatto, op. cit., 155 seq.

10. See H. Baron, *The crisis of the early Italian Renaissance*, revised ed. (Princeton, 1966) 28–9, 470, and P. Herde, 'Politik und Rhetorik in Florenz am Vorabend der Renaissance', *Archiv für Kulturgeschichte*, xlvii (1965) 198 seq.

11. On pro-Visconti views on Giangaleazzo as future ruler of the Italian kingdom, see D. M. Bueno de Mesquita, *Giangaleazzo Visconti, duke of Milan (1351–1402)* (Cambridge, 1941) 308–10, and Baron, op. cit., 37–8.

12. Ibid., 366–7.

13. Quoted by Herde, op. cit., 217.

14. Gregorio Dati, *Istoria di Firenze*, ed. L. Pratesi (Norcia, 1902) 100–101: 'ricordandosi... quante offese hanno aute per colpa e cagione de' Pisani ne' passati tempi, quante guerre e sconfitte... conoscendo quanto onore e esaltazione seguirebbe a' Fiorentini se acquistassono Pisa e fussono signori, quanto destro e acconcio e utilità n'arebbono nel lato delle mercatanzie, quanta sicurtà sarebbe in perpetuo di non potere essere mai più assediati ...' On the date of composition of the *Istoria*, see Baron, *Humanistic and political literature in Florence and Venice at the beginning of the Quattrocento* (Cambridge, Mass., 1955) 63 seq. Cf. also Giovanni di Pagolo Morelli, *Ricordi*, ed. V. Branca (Florence, 1956) 447. On the loss of the fortress of Pisa in September 1405, after the rising of the Pisans against Florence, Morelli comments: 'tutti i veri fiorentini in quel puncto addolorarono e mai dimenticarono questa perdita... e mai si dimenticherà, se non fia fatto la vendetta compitente, e quella fia nell' acquisto di Pisa. Allora presumeremo Dio abbia promesso quello...'

15. Op. cit., 88: 'è stato uno grande e bello acquisto per li Viniziani, ed è venuto loro fatto per la gravezza dello peccato di quello signore di Padova.'

16. Morelli, op. cit., 434: 'rimase solo... niuno diliberò mai aitarlo.' Early in 1404, the *Signoria* considered diplomatic intervention at Venice in favour of Francesco Novello da Carrara, but on 2 May the *pratica* advised that such a démarche should be moderate in tone: 'Venetias mittantur oratores... cum commissione limitata quod non possint nisi dolere de inceptis et de impresa Venetorum, rogando quod desistere debeant ...' (A.S.F., *Cons. e Prat.*, 37, f. 50). There is no reference to such an embassy in the register of the *Signoria* for 1404, A.S.F., *Signori e Collegi, Legazioni e Commissarie*, 3.

17. *Rerum Mediolanensium Historiae*, in *R.I.S.*, xix, col. 24.

18. Romanin, iv, 128–30; C. Cipolla, *Storia delle signorie italiane dal 1313 al 1530* (Milan, 1881) 342–4.

19. See G. Cavalcanti, *Storie fiorentine*, ed. F. Polidori (Florence, 1838–39) i, 252–4: the proposal to conclude peace with the duke of Milan found acceptance in Florence on the grounds that 'se il Duca perdesse il suo stato, i Veneziani conviene l'acquistino'. Those in favour of peace were saying: ' "Non vedete voi, che di qua niente abbiamo acquistato, e di là l'acquisto che è facto, è aggiunto alle Veneziane forze? Se noi seguitiamo la guerra, il Duca conviene che perda la Signoria: chi ci assicura che, vinto lui, e' non si rivolgano a noi?".'

20. On Alfonso of Aragon's Tuscan policy after 1446, see A. Ryder, 'La politica italiana di Alfonso d'Aragona (1442–1458)', *Archivio storico per le province napoletane*, n.s., xxxix (1960) 238 seq.

21. See Ryder, op. cit., ibid., n.s., xxxviii (1959) 53–4; *Storia di Milano*, cit., 348–9. The treaty of 1442 constituted a renewal of the alliance of 1435.

22. See C. M. Ady, *A History of Milan under the Sforza* (London, 1907) 25–30.

23. Ryder, op. cit., n.s., xxxix, 238.

24. Ibid., 267–75.

25. A.S.F., *Signori e Collegi, Legazioni e Commissarie*, 12, ff. 33–34v, to Neri Capponi: Alfonso was advancing with large forces 'per passare in Toscana alli danni nostri'.

26. Ibid., ff. 47–48v, instructions for Paolo da Ghiaceto, ambassador to Siena, 14 Oct., 1447: 'il desiderio di quel principe non essere altro se none opprimere tucte le libertà d'Italia et ridurre quelle a servitù sotto il suo dominio'. According to the *Signoria*, the chief difference between Ladislas and Alfonso was that the former 'combatteva per gloria d'Italia', the latter 'per volere opprimere il nome italico'. That Alfonso of Aragon was a foreign ruler was an important element in Florentine propaganda against him.

27. '. . . per potere succeder al dominio di Lombardia' (A.S.F., *Cons. e Prat.*, 52, f. 23v, 2 Sept., 1447; report of Giannozzo Pitti and Luca degli Albizzi).

28. Manetti's oration is published by H. W. Wittschier, *Giannozzo Manetti: das Corpus der Orationes* (Graz, 1968) 166–75 (see 170); it is summarized in the account of his embassy to Venice by his secretary, Griso di Giovanni Griselli, which has been published by N. Lerz in *A.S.I.*, cxvii (1949) 247–78 (see 262).

29. *Historiarum ab inclinatione Romanorum libri XXXI, decadis* III, lib. i (Basel, 1531) 393: 'Ut enim pauca de multis dicam, eum qui omnibus in bello praeest, . . . si more vetusto imperatorem dixero, in aequivocum incido illius, quem Caesaris loco habemus.' He points out that 'vocabulorum mutatio talis est facta, ut si vetusta illis exponendis attulero, mea ipse relegens scripta non intelligam.'

30. Cf. articles 'Imperium', by Rosenberg in Pauly-Wissowa, *Real-Encyclopädie der Altertumswissenschaft*, ix, pt. 2 (Stuttgart, 1916), and by J. Bleicken in *Der kleine Pauly*, ii (Stuttgart, 1967); R. Koebner, *Imperium* (Cambridge, 1961) 5 seq.

31. Cf. Mommsen, *Römisches Staatsrecht* (3rd ed., Leipzig, 1887–8) iii, 826–9 ('*imperium*, welches eigentlich die magistralische Amtsgewalt bezeichnet, aber häufig auch für das Amtsgebiet gesetzt wird').

32. *De civitate Dei*, 3, 1: 'quod ad Romam pertinet Romanumque imperium . . . id est ad ipsam proprie civitatem et quaecumque illi terrarum vel societate coniunctae vel conditione subiectae sunt.'

33. Leonardo Bruni, in his *Rerum suo tempore gestarum commentarious*, in *R.I.S.2*, xix, pt. 3, 429, describes Giangaleazzo's conquests of Verona and Padua as 'ad imperium additae'; Andrea Biglia uses *imperium* and *dominatus* as interchangeable terms for Venice's dominions (see above, 199). For Venetian usage of *imperium* for the *terraferma* possessions, see e.g. the quotations from Ludovico Foscarini and Bernardo Giustinian above, 207–8. For a later example, cf. Marcantonio Sabellico's account of the Venetian conquests on the mainland after 1402 (*Rerum Venetarum ab urbe condita libri XXXIII*, (Venice, 1718, 1, 458): 'Ex tam clara victoria, Vincentia, Verona, Colonia, Feltrum, Belunnum, ac novissime Patavium ipsum cum suis finibus Veneto imperio cessere.' But examples could be easily multiplied. See also Koebner, 47–50.

34. F. Sacchi, 'Cosimo de' Medici e Firenze nell' acquisto di Milano allo Sforza', *Rivista di scienze storiche*, ii (1905) 278.

35. Ed. ibid., 396–7, doc. 3, from Archivio di Stato, Milan, *Archivio del Conte Francesco Sforza*, 32 (in this, as in the following quotations from the same source [below, n. 36 and 37], the published text has been corrected on the basis of the archival documents): '. . . e deveràlo fare el Re, sì perchè Venetiani non signoregino Italia, e ancora perchè la S.V. habi qua manegiare altrove che a casa sua . . . dolendo et rencrescendo a tucta Italia la prosperità dei Venetiani, ve verrà facto ogni cosa da bene . . .' Both this and the following letter are in code, but are accompanied by contemporary decoded copies.

36. Ed. ibid., 397–8, doc. 4: '. . . essendose questa sera facta pratica alla Signoria de quanto sia da fare, Cosimo alla scoperta ha consigliato che si imprenda da li loro maiori, li quali a la morte del Duca vechio se sforzarono che 'l stato suo pervenne alle mano de . . . [in code, not decoded], adciochè quella potentia si dividesse; e favellò per uno modo che alla scoperta [*ed.* Signoria] ognuno intende non faza per loro che Venetiani

habbiano el stato del Duca, anci dimostrò per circuitione [*ed.* conventione] che solo la S.V. era quella che'l divea [*sic*] e potea havere senza pericolo e mancamento' of Florence. There are no minutes in *Consulte e Pratiche*, 52, which covers Aug. 1447, of a debate in the *pratica* on that day.

37. Ed. Sacchi, op. cit., 399–400, doc. 6 (this letter is partly in code, and not decoded): the *Signoria* had written to Venice 'che saria bene deponere le arme e confortare Milanesi a libertà . . . ad che Misser Almoro [Donato] . . . per migliorare el facto vostro, disse che la sua Signoria intendia questo medesimo, pur che el corpo de Milano havesse libertà, ma che'l ducato suo fosse sotto a Venitiani, imperhochè Milano col ducato suo saria sempre suffitiente ad mettere Ytalia sottosopra; et più altre parole usò circa ciò, in modo che fece evidente demostratione che Venitiani appetischano la monarchia de Ytalia; et non cadero queste parole in terra . . .'

38. See below, n. 62.

39. Romanin, iv, 214.

40. See Francesco Barbaro's letter quoted below. In the letter of Nicodemo Tranchedini of 22 Feb., 1448 (see n. 62), Nicodemo says that the Florentine ambassador Luca degli Albizzi had returned from Venice, where he had come to the conclusion that the Venetians 'sono tanto passionati in sul sottometere Lombardia, che non attendono nè rasonano, senon como potessero dividere Milanesi' from Francesco Sforza, 'reputando che vuy solo gli tagliate la corona de Lombardia et de Ytalia . . .'

41. See above, 204 and n. 54. A. Desjardins, *Négociations diplomatiques de la France avec la Toscane*, vol. I (Paris, 1859), p. 61.

42. The decision of the Senate is ed. by Romanin, cit., 522–3 (doc. 3). The envoy was the secretary of the *Signoria*, Bertucio Negro.

43. Ibid., 214.

44. Ed. R. Sabbadini, *Centotrenta lettere inedite di Francesco Barbaro* (Salerno, 1884) 130–2, doc. 129 (19 Aug., 1447). See also P. Gothein, *Francesco Barbaro* . . . (Berlin, 1932) 272–4.

45. *Storia di Milano*, cit., 411–13, 418–420.

46. Ibid., 422–4; Romanin, 215, 219. The treaty of Rivoltella of 18 Oct., 1448, is ed. in Dumont, *Corps universel diplomatique*, iii, pt. 1 (Amsterdam, 1726) 169–72.

47. *Storia di Milano*, cit., 439–41. The definitive treaty was signed on 24 Dec. See also G. Zippel, 'Ludovico Foscarini ambasciatore a Genova, nella crisi dell'espansione veneziana sulla terraferma (1449–1450)', *Bullettino dell' Istituto Storico Italiano per il medio evo*, lxxi (1959), 191 seq.

48. See R. Predelli, *I Libri Commemoriali della Repubblica di Venezia*, vol. v, in *Monumenti storici pubbl. dalla R. Deputazione veneta di storia patria*, ser 1, x (1901) 55–6.

49. Paris, *Bibliothèque nationale, manuscrits italiens*, 1585, ff. 200–208 (f. 201v).

50. Niccolò Guarna to Francesco Sforza, Milan, 27 Aug., 1447 (Paris, *Bibliothèque nationale, manuscrits italiens*, 1584, f. 273): the 'Presidenti' had told him that the Venetian *Signoria* had conveyed to them their 'singulare piacere de la libertade chiamata da questa cittade, et di ciò commendava et offereva etc., et che ex nunc hariano proveduto . . . che da alcuna soa gente non fosse offeso lo terreno e iuridicione de Milano . . .', on condition that the Milanese did the same in Venetian territory. To this they had replied that 'ad la parte del levare de le offese, questa comunitade restava contenta', but had reminded the Venetians 'che per volere effectualmente fare quello che per loro se offereva in parole, non gli pariva se tenesseno quelli modi che bisognaria; et questo dicevano per rispecto de Lodi e de Piasenza e de le altre cose prese, e che temptavano de pigliare, le quali spectavano ad questa I. Comunitade', either because they had belonged to the late duke, or because, as in the case of Lodi, the town 'subito dopo la morte del prelibato quondam Signore fece fedeltà et obedientia . . .'

51. Romanin, iv., 215; *Storia di Milano*, cit., 415.

52. *Signori* to Neri Capponi and Luca degli Albizzi, ambassadors to Venice, 26 Mar., 1448 (A.S.F., *Signori, Missive, la Cancelleria* (=*Miss.*), 37, ff. 88v–89): the Milanese were

prepared to reach a settlement, 'ma che essendo i Viniziani della gran potenzia che sono, e conosciuto il loro appetito, chè horamai l'anno inteso, e volendosi riserbare le porti di Milano, che questa sarebbe una pace da stare a discretione di Venetiani, e non sarebbe niuna.'

53. *Signori* to Bernardo Giugni, ambassador to Venice, 6 Sept., 1447 (A.S.F., *Signori e Collegi, Legaz. e Commiss.*, 12, f. 42): '. . . Monstrando a' Melanesi quanto commodo seguirà per questo alla cità loro . . . Veggendosi la lega victoriosa, non essere cupida di crescere imperio, ma dare honesta pace alli vincti, anzi non solamente pace ma libertà, amicitia et collegatione . . .' They had written to the ambassadors on 19 Aug., immediately on receipt of the news of Filippo Maria's death (ibid., ff. 38v–39v) that 'sentendo i Melanesi e questi popoli essere tucti sollevati per tal morte a vivere a libertà', the League should offer them peace and help. On Florentine relations with Milan and Venice between 1447 and 1450, see Sacchi, op. cit., and É. Jordan, 'Florence et la succession lombarde (1447–1450)', in *École Française de Rome, Mélanges d'archéologie et d'histoire*, ix (1889) 93–119.

54. *Signori* to Guglielmino Tanaglia and Luca degli Albizzi, ambassadors to Venice, 27 Dec., 1447 (A.S.F., *Signori, Miss.*, 37, ff. 39v–41): '. . . quello che più gli doleva era che essendo morto il ducha, vedeva come egli erano a ordine di farsi signori di quella signoria, la quale apparteneva a llui, et che obtenendo quella potevano poi con le lettere spacciare lui del suo reame . . .' At the end of the letter, Alfonso's complaint is spelled out once more, for greater emphasis, and in particular his argument that 'ogni volta che i Viniziani fussero signori di Milano, con le lettere sole potrebbono cacciare del reame'; and the *Signoria* add that this 'parte ci pare molto da considerare', for the king did not hide 'la sua intima intentione, che è fare guerra a noi solo per diminuire la potentia della lega e per impedire ogni grandeza' of Venice. The ambassadors are instructed to stress at Venice ('la fate gustare bene costà') that Alfonso's Tuscan campaign had accordingly to be seen as directed principally against Venice, and that he had 'cominciato a noi come a membro più debole et perchè ci truova prima'. In this way the Venetian *Signoria* was to be urged 'ad essere promptissima a darci . . . soccorsi', as 'per loro cagione noi siamo così offesi e trovarci in sì gran periculi e affanni'.

55. *Signori* to the same, 20 Jan., 1448 (ibid., ff. 55v–56v). These complaints had been made to the *Signoria* by the Milanese ambassadors to Alfonso who had interrupted their return journey at Florence: '. . . soggiunsono che i Viniziani nella vita del Duca sempre avevano predicato la pace, et che dipoi incontinenti dopo la morte d'esso Duca tractando quel medesimo, s'avevano prese le terre etc.; et che nè per noi nè per loro si faceva la guerra, perchè e loro e noi eravamo quelli di cui si tractava la perdita, e tutti gli altri tractavano di farsi grandi sulle perdite nostre . . .'

56. See above, n. 36.

57. See above, n. 40.

58. A.S.F., *Cons. e Prat.*, 52, ff. 38v, 39v. In the *pratica* of 13 May, 1448, ibid., f. 44, Guglielmino Tanaglia complained about Venice's constant failure to send Florence help, as well as to engage in serious peace negotiations; cf. Jordan, op. cit., 108.

59. A.S.F., *Cons. e Prat.*, 52, f. 86v, 11 Nov. He adds: 'scire tamen Venetos omnia ad eorum utilitatem petituros . . .'

60. Ibid., f. 91, 1 Dec., 1449.

61. To Neri Capponi and Dietisalvi Neroni, 1 May (A.S.F., *Signori, Miss.*, 37, ff. 104v–105): 'Egli è pur comune opinione che se cotesta I. S.a avesse voluto rendere Lodi a' Milanesi, la pace tra lloro sarebbe stata già più tempo conchiusa . . . per Lodi si viene a mettere tutta la lega in spese e affanni e pericoli gravissimi, e tutta Italia in gran confusione . . .' Much the same sentiments are expressed by Poggio, who in a letter from Rome to the Florentine chancellor Carlo Marsuppini of 13 June, ascribes the present deplorable conditions of Florence partly 'Venetorum immoderatae dominandi cupiditati, qui si quid de ambitione et superbia detraxissent, iamdudum et Italia pace optata frueretur

et hic hostis [*scil.* Alfonso of Naples] olim evanuisset.' (*Epistolae*, ix, 28, ed. T. de' Tonelli [Florence, 1832–61] ii, 361–2).

62. Ed. B. Buser, *Die Beziehungen der Mediceer zu Frankreich während der Jahre 1434–1494* (Leipzig, 1879) 362–3, 22 Feb., 1448: '. . . che saria dificilissimo che qui se obtenisse lassare li Venetiani . . . senon in caso di grandissima necessità . . . Parmi la I.V.S. debia inanimire, et presto, et ancora da se medesimo: so certo [Cosimo] pigliarà animo, perchè ce è constructo da necessità, vedendo li emuli soi grilare, et li Venetiani haversi partita la Italia con el Re de Raghona'. See also n. 40.

63. Ed. Buser, op. cit., 366–7 (23 Oct., 1449): 'che per quella comunità et per Cosmo faza de darmi adiuto et favore de qua, per fare che Venetiani non se fazano Segnori de Milano et de Lombardia . . . Et far etiamdio questa conclusione, che la intentione de' Venetiani è de havere Milano, et che . . . essendo loro S.ri de Milano, se porria dire essere S.ri de tutta Italia'.

64. See L. Rossi, 'Niccolò V e le potenze d'Italia dal maggio del 1447 al dicembre del 1451', *Rivista di scienze storiche*, iii, pt. 1 (1906) 246–8; F. Catalano, in *Storia di Milano*, vii (Milan, 1956) 28, n. 3.

65. L. Rossi, 'Venezia e il re di Napoli, Firenze e Francesco Sforza dal novembre del 1450 al giugno del 1451', *N.A.V.*, n.s., x (1905) 281–2 (App. A, doc. 1): '. . . e Veneziani non gli hanno mai dal canto loro voluto condescendere, come quelli che stanno obstinati e induriti e semper con la bocha aperta per acquistar Signoria e usurpare quello de tucti soi vicini per adimpire l'apetito de li animi soi de dominar Italia, e poi più oltra, como fecero li Romani, credendo de compararsi ad Romani in quello tempo ch'erano in stato . . .' Such strictures contrast with the comparisons between Roman and Venetian institutions drawn by admirers of the Venetian constitution: see F. Gilbert, 'The Venetian constitution in Florentine political thought', in *Florentine studies*, ed. N. Rubinstein (London, 1968) 476, and cf. below, n. 78.

66. See Rossi, 'Niccolò V e le potenze d'Italia', 419, and doc. 26 (4 Dec., 1451): '. . . io dissi che sono homini diabolici et che non hano honore, conscientia, nè Dio inanti agli ochii, che cercano di conquistare l'Italia.' In view of the considerable measure of ecclesiastical autonomy claimed by Venice (see W. J. Bouwsma, *Venice and the defense of republican liberty* [Berkeley and Los Angeles, 1968] 71–83), the Venetians were evidently considered by Nicodemo Tranchedini to be particularly vulnerable in Rome to charges of impiety.

67. Ed. Rossi, 'Niccolò V e le potenze d'Italia', *Rivista di scienze storiche*, iii, pt. 2 (1906) 180–1 (30 May, 1451): '. . . la sete e apetito de' Veneziani, che cossi volesse che tutti li altri S.ri e comunitate de Italia lo cognoscessero . . . cosi bene como fa lui . . . l'apetito e voluntà de' Venetiani non è in altro che cerchare d'estirpare et exradicare tuti S.ri e gentili homini de Italia, como se vede che hano facto a li altri S. per lo passato, e cercare de sottomettersi tutto l'avanzo de le comunità de Italia.'

68. Antonio da Trezzo to Francesco Sforza, 2 Apr., 1451, ed. Rossi, 'Venezia e il re di Napoli', cit., 289: '. . . dice che cum molte rasone ha detestato questa opinione del Re in volere tanto exaltare el facto de' Veneciani e opprimere la S.V., cum dirli che questo non è a dire altro se non aparecchiare la disfactione de suo figliolo e de tutto el resto de tuti signori d'Italia . . . perchè avendo Veneciani Cremona e morendo la Maestà sua o la S.V., essi Veneciani, che sono immortali, senza difficultà se farano Segnori de Italia . . .' The notion of the 'immortality' of republics, in contrast to the mortality of *Signori*, was not uncommon in the *quattrocento*; cf. e.g. Gregorio Dati, *Istoria di Firenze*, cit., 97.

69. *Storia di Milano*, vii, 24; Rossi, 'Venezia e il re di Napoli', 31–2.

70. Ed. Rossi, 'Niccolò V e le potenze d'Italia', *Rivista di scienze storiche*, iii, pt. 2, 188: '. . . facilmente se può comprendere la loro mala despositione et voluntà et l'ambitione che hanno de dominare Italia. Nui havimo scripto ad Signori Fiorentini multo amplamente sopra questo facto.'

71. Instructions for Giannozzo Pitti, ed. Rossi, 'Venezia e il re di Napoli', 354: '. . . se

la Sua. Ser.tà desidera conservare li regni acquistati in Italia a lei et successori d'essa, non intendiam essere utile ad tale fine di seguire l'appetito del governo venetiano, il quale, come s'è veduto apertamente per li loro processi et innanzi et maximamente dopo la morte del duca, non è altro che d'insignorirsi di Lombardia e dell'altre parti vicine et successivamente poi dello imperio di Italia . . .' Cf. Antonio da Trezzo's letter of 2 Apr. quo. n. 68, in which the identical argument is used in order to detach Alfonso from Venice.

72. The instructions for Angelo Acciaiuoli's first embassy to France after the beginning of hostilities with Venice, of 10 Sept., is now ed. in *Dispatches with related documents of Milanese ambassadors in France and Burgundy, 1450–1483*, ed. P. M. Kendall and V. Ilardi, i (Athens, Ohio, 1970) 3–19. See 9: 'essendo l'animo de Vinitiani d'occupare Lombardia et col tempo lo 'mperio di Italia . . . queste due potentie . . . si congiunsero con lega et intelligentia, et tanto più volentieri quanto avevano già divisa Italia, della quale la Lombardia toccava a' Vinitiani et l'altre parti al Re . . .' Angelo Acciaiuoli's Latin oration to the French king, which he appears to have delivered on arrival at the court during his third embassy to France, in March or April 1453 (ed. P.-M. Perret, 'Le discours d'Angelo Acciaiuoli au roi de France (1453)', *Bibliothèque de l'École des Chartes*, liii [1892] 426–37) follows much the same lines: 'Bellum quod rex Aragonum ac Veneti . . . inferunt . . . solumodo duabus de causis procedit: altera est propter ambitionem quam sibi dominandi Italie proposuerunt . . . Scire insuper debet Vestra Maiestas quoniam pacto inter se universalem Italiam partiti sint.' (434).

73. Instructions for Matteo Palmieri, 17 June, 1452 (A.S.F., *Dieci, Legazioni e Commissarie*, 4, ff. 23–24v, 26–27): '. . . Per le quali cose manifestamente s'è compreso e comprende quel dominio Veniziano avere facto già lungo tempo concepto di volere dominare a tutta Lombardia, e di poi a tutta Italia, come chiaramente dimostrano anchora i modi tenuti per loro etiandio prima della morte del duca Filippo, chè volendo noi attendere a la pace co' Milanesi e a la salveza di questa città in libertà, nonne vollono udire alcuna cosa, anzi attesono a lografrgli con la spesa e con la guerra perchè venisse loro nelle mani. Et dipoi per volersi pure ritenere il dominio di Lodi, non vollono mai pace co' Milanesi, attendendo a defendere Piacenza e a cerchare del continuo il dominio di Lombardia.' Cf. n. 61.

74. On the negotiations preceding the peace of Lodi, see C. Canetta, 'La pace di Lodi (9 aprile 1454)', *Riv. Stor. Ital.*, ii (1885), 516–64; F. Antonini, 'La pace di Lodi ed i segreti maneggi che la preparono', *A.S.L.*, lvii (1930) 233–96, and *Storia di Milano*, vii, 56–61.

75. See G. Soranzo, *Le lega italica (1454–1455)* (Milan, s.d.). At the beginning of May, Cosimo de' Medici told Nicodemo Tranchedini that the Italian League, 'quando bene se havesse ad fare, seria da farla ad difesa de li stati in Ytalia, e contra qualunche de le parti la volesse perturbare tantum; et che forsi seria meglio cercare la fermeza e stabilità de la pace, e non cercare più inanti al presente . . .' (Nicodemo Tranchedini to Francesco Sforza, 6 May, 1454, Paris, *Bibliothèque Nationale, manuscrits italiens*, 1586, f. 277.)

76. *Historia florentina*, ed. J. B. Recanati (Venice, 1715); cf. my article on 'Poggio Bracciolini, cancelliere e storico di Firenze', in *Atti e Memorie della Accademia Petrarca di Lettere, Arti e Scienze*, n.s., xxxvii (1958–64) 215–39.

77. 366,371.

78. *Dialogus de praestantia virorum sui aevi*, ed. G. C. Galletti in Filippo Villani, *Liber de civitatis Florentiae famosis civibus* (Florence, 1847) 119. Accolti's criticism of Venice's 'imperialist' policy does not affect his admiration for the Venetian constitution: see ibid., 119–20. This ambivalent attitude towards Venice is later shared by Guicciardini and Machiavelli. See also G. Fasoli's observations on what she aptly calls the 'mito bifronte' of Venice, 'Nascita di un mito', 472 seq. On Florentine views on the Venetian constitution, see F. Gilbert, 'The Venetian constitution in Florentine political thought', 472 seq.

79. *De vera nobilitate*, partly ed. by E. Garin, *Testi inediti e rari di Cristoforo Landino e Francesco Filelfo* (Florence, 1949) 15. On humanist idealization of Cosimo, see Alison M.

Brown, 'The humanist portrait of Cosimo de' Medici, Pater Patriae', *Journal of the Warburg and Courtauld Institutes*, xxiv (1961) 186–221.

80. In his 'lettera mandata a' Viniziani', which forms part of his *Cronaca* and has been re-edited by G. degli Azzi in *A.S.I.*, cx (1952) 103–13 (it had been previously published by G. F. Pagnini, *Della Decima* . . . [Lisbon and Lucca, 1765–6] ii, 235–45): '. . . non ti richord' egli che lla Signoria tua di Vinegia aveva istretto Milano . . . e chome a ogni ora del giorno vo' aspettavate d'essernne signori? . . . vo' sapete a punto che Chosimo de' Medici vi levò di mano tal chosa . . . Cierto, no' chonfessiamo e rafermiamo che, se lla Signoria di Vinegia piglava la città del Duchato di Milano, ella si facèa reina d'Italia . . .' (105). Dei's 'letter to the Venetians' is generally quoted as principal, or sole evidence of anti-Venetian polemic during the second half of the fifteenth century (see in particular Valeri, 'Venezia nella crisi italiana', 35–45).

81. *Commentaries*, tr. F. A. Gragg with commentary by C. C. Gabel, *Smith College studies in history*, xxxv (1939–40) 22; xliii (1957) 743–4. On Pius II's anti-Venetian sentiments, due largely to Venice's failure to give the desired support to his crusading project, see G. B. Picotti, *La dieta di Mantova e la politica de' Veneziani* in *Miscellanea di storia veneta*, ser. 3, iv (Venice, 1912) 212–14, 277.

82. Ed. Zippel, 'Ludovico Foscarini ambasciatore', 229: 'Cognoscet omnis Italia maximam animi nostri ingenuitatem, qui curas vigiliasque nostras in liberanda Italia colimus, ditione nostra contenti, cum possumus nostrum prorogare imperium'. See ibid., 192–7.

83. In *Orazioni, elogi e vite scritte da letterati veneti patrizi in lode di Dogi* . . ., 2nd ed. (Venice, 1798) i, 31–2. On this funeral oration, cf. Patricia H. Labalme, *Bernardo Giustiniani* . . . (Rome, 1969) 114–25.

84. To Pino de' Pinucci, 31 Dec., 1450, A.S.V., *Secreta Senatus*, xix, ff. 110v–111: '. . . non videtur nobis alienum a necessitate rerum occurentium sibi [*scil*. the Lucchese] memorare quo . . . facta est liga et confederatio inter Florentinos, Comitem Franciscum et Ianuenses non ad ullam quietem Italie, sed potius ad inquietationem . . . omnium bene et quiete vivere cupientium. Et inter cetera capitula lige predictorum eos dominos Lucenses certos esse volumus esse unum capitulum, quod predicti collegati secretum tenere conati sunt, huius effectus et continentie, videlicet quod omnia que in Lombardia acquirerentur (quod absit), esse debeat Comitis Francisci et omnia loca maritima Ianuensium, omnes vero civitates et comunitates Tuscie esse debeant Florentinorum, ex quo aptissime apparet voluntas et ambitio predictorum colligatorum.' The Lucchese had special reasons to be watchful – 'quibus per experientiam rerum et temporum preteritorum nota et manifesta satis esse debet voluntas et animus Florentinorum erga eos, qui Florentini nichil quid fieri posset licite vel illicite pretermitterent pro occupanda dominatione et libertate sua . . .'

85. See F. Fossati, 'Sulle relazioni tra Venezia e Milano durante gli ultimi negoziati per la pace del 13 Marzo 1480', *N.A.V.*, n.s., x (1905) 236, n. 2.

86. Marino Sanuto, in his *Commentarii della guerra di Ferrara* composed in 1484 (Venice, 1829) 6–7, and Domenico Malipiero in his *Annali veneti* (*A.S.I.*, vii, pt. 1 [1843] 253–5) record the Venetian grievances against Ercole d'Este. In trying, at the end of 1481, to counter the complaints that Venice was disturbing the peace of Italy, the Venetian Senate somewhat disingenuously expressed the hope that 'neminem in Italia esse credimus qui dicere audeat cogitasse nos nedum esse molitos aliquid novi quod pacem et quietem Italie ledere potuerit', but insisted at the same time that Ercole recognize 'veros et vetustissimos terminos ducatus nostri' (to Francesco Diedo, ambassador in Rome, 21 Dec., *Secreta Senatus*, xxxi, f. 54v). Accordingly, the war against Ercole was proclaimed by the Doge in May 1482 as 'justissimun et honestissimun bellum' (Sanuto, op. cit., 12). According to Sigismondo de' Conti (*Le storie de' suoi tempi* [Rome, 1883] i, 118–9), Girolamo Riario had, in Sept. 1481, proposed to the Senate on Sixtus IV's behalf that Venice occupy Ferrara, which it could then keep as a papal fief. See also Romanin, iv, 401 seq.

87. A.S.F., *Signori, Miss.*, 49, ff. 107v–108 (11 May, 1482). Shortly afterwads, Vespasiano

da Bisticci wrote in his Life of Federigo da Montefeltro – *Vite di uomini illustri del secolo XV*, ed. P. d'Ancona and E. Aeschlimann (Milan, 1951) 203 – that Florence and Milan were trying to prevent 'che al Duca di Ferrara non fusse tolto lo stato, perchè era il principio a volersi insignorire del resto d'Italia'. According to Vespasiano, also in the Colleoni War against Florence (1467–68), the Venetians 'andavano pensando a tutte quelle cose per le quali eglino potessino ottenere quello che avevano lungo tempo desiderato, e questo era d'avere lo 'mperio d'Italia' (ibid., 193; see also 195).

88. By her treaty with King Ferrante II of Naples of 21 Jan., 1496 (in Malipiero, *Annali veneti*, 419–22; cf. 418–19), Venice received Brindisi, Trani, and Otranto as pledges 'per segurtà, e satisfattion delle spese', in exchange for Venetian protection.

89. Francesco Guicciardini, *Storie fiorentine dal 1378 al 1509*, ed. R. Palmarocchi (Bari, 1931) 120–21, 167.

90. Once more, the nature and extent of Venice's objectives were no doubt greatly exaggerated by her critics and enemies. The occupation of the Apulian ports, for one, has to be seen as part of her attempts of long standing to control the Adriatic. In her negotiations with Louis XII in 1498, she insisted, in conformity with the policy pursued after 1447, on the acquisition of bridgeheads on the western bank of the Adda, as well as on that of the remaining territories east of that river (cf. P. Pieri, 'Intorno alla politica estera di Venezia al principio del Cinquecento', republished in his *Scritti vari* [Turin, 1966] 127–8); in the end, she only received Cremona, which had been a major objective of those years, and the Ghiaradadda.

91. On 5 July, 1498, the *Dieci* wrote to the Florentine ambassadors at Milan, Francesco Pepi and Guidantonio Vespucci (A.S.F., *Dieci, Missive*, 23, f. 47) that it was important to explain to Louis XII 'la natura et ambitione de' Vinitiani, lo inordinato appetito loro del dominare, cerchando non solum subiugare Italia, ma di ampliare per ogni via lo stato loro, aspirando alla monarchia per lo exemplo de' Romani . . .' I owe this quotation to Professor Sergio Bertelli, who will discuss the relations between Florence and Venice after 1494 in his forthcoming book on the foreign policy of Florence between 1494 and 1512. Cf. also Bernardo Rucellai's history of Charles VIII's expedition, *De bello italico* (London, 1733) 3: 'Satis constat ab hinc supra centesimum annum, statum [ed. Senatum] Venetum terra marique eo magnitudinis processisse, ut reliquis Italiae populis regibusque formidolosus foret.'

92. On the date of composition of the *Storie fiorentine*, see my article on 'The *Storie fiorentine* and the *Memorie di famiglia* by Francesco Guicciardini', in *Rinascimento*, iv (1953) 172–8.

93. See *Storie fiorentine*, 6, 55, 57, 127.

94. *I Diarii*, ed. R. Cessi, R.I.S. 2, xxiv, pt. 3, vol. iv, 49: 'Et in anni cento over pocho mancho, che queste citade di terraferma sonno state soto lo imperio veneto, se puol considerare veramente il grande numero de danari spexi . . . Et questo procedeva, perchè questi Senatori Venetti heranno tanto inebriatti et obffuschatti in questo Stado italico, che non guardavanno danari nè a spexa alchuna per fortificharlo et munirlo . . .' (cf. 49–53).

VIII

VITTORE BRANCA

Ermolao Barbaro and late quattrocento Venetian humanism

As Venetian rule spread across the *terraferma*, and, in particular, to Padua and Verona, the humanistic tone characteristic of the two cities tended increasingly to fall under the intellectual spell of the *Serenissima* as well. The Paduan *studio* became the official university of the Republic, Venice's *quartier latin*, as Renan put it. The teaching of certain scholars – from Biagio Pelacani and Gaetano da Thiene to Nicoletto Vernia and then to Pietro Pomponazzi – encouraged the philosophical, especially the Aristotelian interests of a number of Venetian patricians who had studied at the university of Padua. And, on the other hand, the pedagogical views which had left their mark on Veronese humanism, through men like Barzizza and Guarino (who had, before Vittorino da Feltre, run flourishing schools at Venice), nourished the concern for the formation of human character, the emphatic concentration on the moral aspects of life and of individual actions that come to distinguish Venetian humanism at its apogee, that is, towards the end of the *quattrocento*. For behind the leading humanists of the first half of the century, Andrea Giuliano, Leonardo Giustiniani, Francesco Barbaro, can be clearly discerned the presence of Barzizza, who in 1407 introduced to Venice the practice of giving private tuition to young aristocrats; above all, there was the presence of Guarino who, during the five years (1414 to 1419) he spent in Venice, not only consolidated the humanistic tradition there but put the study of Greek on a firm foundation.

It was chiefly thanks to Guarino that in the third and fourth decade of the *quattrocento* there emerged within the ruling aristocracy of Venice a group of highly cultivated young men who became part of the humanistic movement that was then triumphing throughout the peninsula – and in an influential but highly individual manner. They did not form, as in Medicean Florence, an academic circle; they did not resemble a curial-academic circle such as that in papal Rome or those in Visconti and Sforza Milan and Aragonese Naples, which represented a union between chancery officials and courtiers. They were influential patricians, morally as well as materially independent, who almost always put their literary activities second to public service and dedicated to the humanities the time left to them after serving the state at home or, through diplomatic missions, abroad. Perhaps they possessed less literary refinement, but they brought to their cultural interests a solider, a more realistic understanding not only of the individual but of human nature at large. It was, moreover, their status, the mark they made on society, that in the last decade of the *quattrocento* put Venice among the leaders of the Italian humanistic movement as a whole.[1]

On the one hand, this was the time which brought to maturity Lauro Quirini's Hellenistic enthusiasm and his devotion to Bessarion, and the fervent anti-quarianism of Jacopo Zen, of Pietro Barbo (the future Pope Paul II) and of Cyriac of Ancona's patrician admirers, such as the doge Francesco Foscari, who stimulated an archaeological fervour witnessed not only by collections of note but by allusive yet definite references in the works of the Bellini and their school. And on the other hand this was also the time when Bernardo Giustiniani, procurator of St. Mark, in addition to the highest flights of Latin oratory produced the model – in the vein of a Biondo – of a measured and stringent historiography markedly at odds with popular tradition or a naif search for origins, a model later refined by Sabellico; a time, moreover, when Bernardo Bembo, senator and ambassador, passionate antiquarian and subtle bibliophile (yet by no means insensitive to the appeal of the *volgare*, especially in terms of his revered Dante), fostered the active traffic between the Medicean and Venetian worlds that characterized the last twenty years of the century.[2]

It was precisely from this environment, among a cultivated but politically committed patriciate, that the impulse came to establish a permanent school which would be open to all and which would have a clearly humanist tone. Up till then the only non-private instruction available was that conscientiously given in logic and natural philosophy at the Rialto school which had been founded at the wish of and with the aid of a bequest from Tomà Talenti, one of the four 'averroisti' who in 1367 had attacked Petrarch and his humanist culture. This closed with the distinguished teaching career of Paolo della Pergola, the teacher of Vernia, but its place came to be taken by the Venetian college of doctors of arts and medicine, founded in 1434. Barzizza, Guarino and Vittorino da Feltre taught, but privately. In 1443 the Great Council decided to set aside ten gold ducats a year for twelve youths to be taught grammar and rhetoric (among other things) as a way of preparing them for service in the chancery. The youths thus supported, however, accepted their scholarships without applying themselves to study, and it was doubtless the failure of this scheme that led to the setting up of a real school of grammar and rhetoric attached to the chancery of St. Mark's.

This was certainly functioning by 1450, when Giampietro Vitali d'Avenza, an undistinguished pupil of Vittorino and Guarino, was teaching there. He was succeeded by two true humanists, both natives of Rimini, Pietro Perleoni and Filippo di Federighini, who brought it into line with the literary trend that was then characterizing the humanistic culture of the day, and this tendency was energetically pursued and intensified by Benedetto Brugnoli da Legnano (a pupil of Vitali and – in Greek – of Ognibene da Lonigo) who directed the school for thirty-six years, from 1466 to 1502, and produced such notable scholars as Giovanni Querini and Egnazio, the last of the humanists who publicly taught 'le umanità' in Venice. Other professional teachers, moreover, were during the same period giving instruction in a second chair, sponsored by the Senate in 1460. This chair bore witness to the weight the public authorities gave to the practical value of the new culture and the prestige Venice was to attain by entering into competition with the other leading cultural centres of Italy. The chair was occupied first by Mario Filelfo, then by George of Trebizond. Their successor was Giorgio Merula whose eighteen-year tenure (1464 to 1482) introduced to Venice the impressive new philological method derived from Lorenzo Valla, partly through his polemic against Calderini's superficiality, partly through his own commentaries and, above all, through his most important work, the *Emendationes in Virgilium et Plinium* (1471).[3]

The renovating role of the school of St. Mark's–especially through its Graeco-Latin methodology – was concurrently strengthened by the establishment of a public library which was to take the lead from those already in existence, such as the important collections of S. Giorgio and SS. Giovanni e Paolo. On 13th May, 1468, Cardinal Bessarion donated his collection of books to the basilica of St. Mark's. This splendid emblem of the meeting between East and West brought to the city an extremely rich library of Greek and Latin codices and even though for some years the collection was not suitably arranged and was inconvenient to use, it exercised a decisive influence on the Hellenism that characterized and reinvigorated Venetian culture in the last years of the *quattrocento*.[4] It was then that patrician humanism in Venice reached its marvellous zenith, when members of the Great Council, procurators of St. Mark and ambassadors of the Republic became teachers at Padua and Venice, avidly studied philology and philosophy and collaborated with, as well as stimulated, the extraordinary flowering of the hundred and fifty printing establishments that made Venice the crossroads of European humanist culture (no fewer than 4,000 titles were published between 1469 and 1501, mainly in the humanities).[5]

The impressive development of the school of St. Mark's, the protection and nourishment afforded by the libraries, the renewed vigour with which philological studies were pursued (which involved the cult of and the primacy of poetry), the sweeping triumph of printing: these were the pre-conditions which allowed Venetian humanism to reach its peak in the last two decades of the *quattrocento*, a time when Venice challenged the leadership of Florence itself. This climactic period, with its specifically patrician tone and its philological triumphs derived its values and its sense of direction, however, above all from the endeavours of the greatest of Venetian humanists, Ermolao Barbaro.[6]

His work was, indeed, acknowledged in the Medicean circle as a pillar of scholarship and literature, as solid and tall as that erected by Politian. Through Aristotelian translations and commentaries, through treatises on moral philosophy and civic values, through orations and through masterly models of the epistolary art, above all through his searching philological studies, Ermolao, notwithstanding the brevity of his career, made a fundamental impact on European culture. Even men of the time of Erasmus and Budé looked to him as one of the greatest masters of the preceding generation, as bringing to maturity the brilliant philological tradition begun by the genius of Petrarch and systematically developed by Lorenzo Valla.

More than anything else it was the genius underlying their approach to philology that caused and continued to cause Italy and Europe to acknowledge Barbaro and Politian as the unchallenged Dioscuri of a new culture.

As is well known, the crucial spur to the orientation of thought and the direction of creativity was – without postulating an abrupt breach with medieval civilization – a steady effort to reconstruct and at the same time accurately to interpret the classical world. Only through philology, understood in its widest sense as including history and antiquarianism, could a really exact, complete and illuminating grasp of that exemplary world be obtained. Only by determining to come to grips with and fully understand the 'word' as the supreme expression of the man, as the 'copula' between men (if, as in Ficino's concept, man is the 'copula' of the world) and to recover the 'word' and every 'word' – hence every phrase, every verbal witness to man – in its most authentic form could the treasury of ancient wisdom be opened in all its splendour. Hence the search for and the recovery of the works of antiquity, hence the painstaking labour of purging texts of errors, hence research into orthography, grammar and style, hence the annotations, the commentaries and the translations. The effort required to release the beauty and clarity of thought of Graeco–Latin literature from the soil which had obscured or buried it was immense and was mythologized in the image, dear to the humanists (and given visual form by a number of artists before Dürer himself) of Hercules combatting the monsters (cf. Barbaro, *Ep.* ix, s.d., viii, etc.). This task of understanding fully, of stating with unfailing precision, of assimilating the past with confidence and grace, this, as Garin has said, was indeed 'the impulse that gave life and energy to the creative side of humanism in the original sense of the word'. And, we may note in parenthesis, it is the chief glory and the highest hope of our own tormented age as well, straining – in a massive historical and philological exercise in recall – to catch and combine the voices of past civilizations in order to blend the human values they express into the substance of our own.

In its finest form, that is, in textual criticism, this philological movement languished after the time of Petrarch and Valla and by the mid-*quattrocento* was in a stagnant and unpromising state. Dominant was on the one hand an ostentatious parade of luxuriant and frequently undiscriminating learning, and, on the other, a mania for correcting and hypothesizing based on the most fragile evidence, on mere *divinatio* or assumed grammatical constants and sometimes expressing itself in etymologies that either could not be checked against others or were pure guesswork. Too often those who worked on texts were hardly more than amateurs, now over-cautious, now too bold; neither the collation of texts nor their historical-linguistic reconstruction was systematically pursued. For this period in Venice it is enough to recall the superficial and misleading work achieved by Sabellico, in spite of his wide culture and deep knowledge of Latin, or to turn to the dense and endless commentaries on the classics of Calderini's school.[7]

Ermolao, the pupil of Pomponio Leto and of the foremost philologist of his day, Giorgio Merula, as well as a devoted follower of Gaza as far as Greek language and culture were concerned, was to conduct a long and intimate correspondence and exchange of views with Politian. It was under Barbaro's guidance that in 1480 Politian consulted the city's precious manuscripts and was encouraged to pursue the philosophical-philological method. Sensitive as were few others to every form of poetry (from that of antiquity to the popular style of Giustiniani and to the heretical and macaronic experiments of the Odasi), responsive, too, to the full range of art, including the innovating and allusion-filled works of Carpaccio and Giorgione, he made a decisive intervention into this philological realm of the approximation and the guess.

We still lack systematic studies in depth of our humanist philology. We lack, leaving aside certain approaches to Livy and Cicero, the textual history of the medieval and humanist periods even for the greatest Greek and Latin classics. We lack, that is, a chapter in our civilization which is essential to a grasp of the value and the sense of continuity and renewal which the classical tradition contributed to modern history. The philological work of Lorenzo Valla, of Merula, Politian, Barbaro, Aldus, Beroaldo, then of Vettori and so many others really constitutes the foundation of the intellectual and cultivated community of the west. Without their labours there would have been no trace of that *Koiné* which allowed and which still allows ideas to circulate easily throughout the atmosphere of all civilized Europe, facilitating a civilized dialogue among men as distant in space as divergent in their modes of life.

Situated so poorly, we can say little, and that only in very general terms, about the motives underlying Barbaro's approach to philological studies.[8] From his first tentative labours – between his twenties and thirties – on Themistius and on Aristotelian texts, he moved on to his master works: the *Castigationes* and the annotations to Dioscorides, Pomponio Mela and above all to Pliny: taken together, the greatest achievement of Venetian humanist culture and one of the major philological monuments of Europe. He began by setting aside the facile and fantastic conjectures of his contemporaries based on etymology and grammar or on the uncritical acceptance of suggestions made in antiquity itself ('aliud est aliena castigare aliud sua prodere: in alienis maiore cura quam iudicio, in nostris maiore iudicio quam cura opus est'. *Ep.* cii). He based his approach on the reasoned – though neither systematic nor chronological – comparison of codices and other forms of evidence, direct and indirect, which he evaluated with a critical zeal which never flagged. He approached the reconstruction of language not through grammatical *schemata* but through a rigorous literary and historical documentation and a rare semantic sensibility which expressed itself through the identification of sources, either explicit or implicit, used by his authors and through an evaluation of them. It was a philological approach which drew on a wide and inter-resonating culture and on a budding sense of history. And for his work on Pliny and Dioscorides he added a well-developed scientific sense which he brought to bear directly and experimentally on the problems investigated by these naturalists of antiquity. It is not for nothing that Ermolao is looked on as one of the precursors of the experimental method.

It is above all in the *Castigationes Plinianae* that Barbaro reveals the true stature of his new philology, a combination of weighty rigour and an acuteness of textual criticism which could be rivalled by no one beyond the Alps and, within Italy, only by Politian.

If my own limited and modest investigations permit me to see aright, Ermolao had at his disposal a group of codices included in the so-called *ordo recentiorum* according to modern classifications (related to the present Paris 6795 and the Leiden VII-Lipsius).[9] All the same, in spite of this disadvantage, he succeeded in amending in this text (which remained bristling with difficulties in spite of the efforts of a veritable crowd of humanists from Guarino on) nearly six thousand passages, in contrast to the hundred-odd conjectures (often fantastic) offered a few years previously by Sabellico.[10] His success depended on his bringing to bear on the passages he chose for discussion evidence drawn from analogous passages, from phonetics and metrics and above all from texts earlier than or contemporaneous with Pliny, and from inscriptions and coins, evidence evaluated not individually but mutually and historically. And at the heart of this massive work of restoration was a clear and profound belief in the decisive importance which the Plinian encyclopaedia held for the new culture. 'In tanta librorum non iactura sed naufragio non clade sed interitu', Ermolao wrote in 1491–2 to Pico (*Ep.* s.d., viii), 'non sumus ominino diis odiosi quando superstes est Plinius: sustentat ille nos utcumque mutilus, decurtatus, lacer. Nisi extaret, actum esset . . . Nunc eo duce, quamquam semianimi et exangui, vivimus . . . Alii rem latinam iuverunt, ille ipse nobis est Latium'.

I give only a few examples, but diverse and characteristic ones. In book ii (102, 242) Pliny speaks of the distance between India and the Columns of Hercules. The then current text had 'octoginta quinque . . . milia passuum' which was unacceptable as suggesting an impossibly low figure. Utilizing Macrobius and Ptolemy, Sabellico had substituted 'stadium' for 'passuum', unaware that this was to increase the distance beyond all likelihood. Barbaro discerned (c. f 2) that Ptolemy and Macrobius were later than Pliny and were quite possibly dependent on him. They had, thus, no independent value as authorities. Through a spirited inquiry into ancient geographers and their linguistic usages, Ermolao discovered the cause of the error to lie in the substitution of a numeral for the multiplier, of the 'facilior' *octoginta* for the 'difficilior' *octuagies* (i.e., not 85,000 *passus* but 80 times 5,000 *passus*, or 400,000 *passus*). In similar vein, thanks to his sharp-eyed and thorough reading of Greek sources (in this case Pausanias) dealing with Praxiteles, he was able to exclude (c. I 4r) Pliny's reference to the Athenian sculptor in book xxxv (12, 156); he made the authoritive emendation 'Pasitelem'. Indeed, his amazing command of Greek language and literature enabled him both repeatedly to correct Plinian quotations and transcriptions from Greek texts and to emend what had become to all intents and purposes naturalized, if humorous, corruptions. He showed, for instance, that the unfortunate 'pelamydes in alica coctae' was simply 'pelamydes in apolectos' (i.e. a sub-species of that fish; ix 15, 48, cf. 32, 150) and condemned to the limbo of ghosts that mysterious character 'Nicomaco' (c. H 6v) who appeared in book xxxv (8, 57) in place of the Greek adverb 'iconicos'. With his precise geographical knowledge he was able to return (c. f 2r) the 'maëdi' to Epirus from Asia Minor whither, thanks to a confusion with 'Medi', they had been exiled. He transformed back into its own shape a city that had been turned into a lake – not 'lacus Pandosia' but 'locus Pandosia' (iv, 1, 4; c. f 2r). With his understanding of the historical evolution of Greek mythology and its terminology he prevented the 'nobiles Bacchas' from being identified as cows (xxxv, 10, 109). With his wide-ranging knowledge of natural history he diverted fantasies about elephants which boasted shining silken backs into the realm of the lemurs, and quashed belief in the lynx (c. x 5v) which had double toes before and behind (not 'lynx' but 'iynx'; xi, 47, 256). His feeling for semantics banished the phantom poet Euthymus (not 'Euthymus poeta' but 'Euthymus pycta'; vii, 47, 152; cf. c. r 5v). And so one could go on through more than five thousand instances.

For the rest it must suffice to compare the text of Pliny as Barbaro found it (as in the editions of 1469 and 1472, for example) with what he left as its 'vulgate' – the edition, for instance of Venice, 1499 – to understand what led Politian to proclaim Ermolao as the *imperator* of philology. ('Si Hermolai mii dentur decem sub quibus meream, facile sperem literas cum graecas tum latinas e barbaria media receptum iri'; *Ep*. xii, 7). Politian, indeed, not only welcomed the *Castigationes* with such lively enthusiasm as to read them right through in one prodigious night, but praised and used them constantly in his last work, the 'centuria secunda' of his *Miscellanea*. In its last pages, referring to the Plinian labours of his lately deceased friend, he hailed them as a noble and almost emblematic example of the new course which philology was taking, notwithstanding the differences in their approach.[11]

In his *Castigationes* Barbaro provided, as did Politian in the *Miscellanea*, an example of a total philology, among the most searching and complete between the work of Petrarch and Valla and that of Lachmann. It was the approach that made possible the advanced and irreversible influence throughout Europe of Aldus' editorial work, the first steps of which were actually guided by Barbaro and his friends. It was for this that twenty years later the great founder of classical studies in France, Guillaume Budé, lauded Barbaro as 'vir ille magnus . . . longe ingenio nobis doctrinaque multiplici praestans'.

It was a philology both rigorously systematic and at the same time completely accessible, drawing its force not simply from erudition, however immense, nor simply from critical acumen, however brilliant, but above all through a deep and never failing conviction of the enduring value of words, of every word as a spiritual fact and an expression of man's nature.

This same conviction dominated the work of Ermolao's most devoted fellow soldiers in the philological campaign of his last decade, Giorgio Valla and Girolamo Donato. Taught Greek by Lascaris and philosophy by Marliani, nominated through Barbaro's influence to the second chair of humanities at St. Mark's as Merula's successor and rival to the methods of the Rialto and the Paduans, Valla devoted himself to preparing editions of Averroes and versions of Alexander of Aphrodisias, Psellus, Atenagoras and Euclid.[12] But the period of humanist translations was drawing to a close; the Greek text itself came to the fore. Between 1495 and 1498 appeared the Aldine Aristotelian *corpus* in the original Greek. In 1497 Leonico Tomeo – a follower of Barbaro's teachings – was elected reader in the Greek works of Aristotle at Padua. Valla's generation was now overtaken; when he stopped teaching in 1500 he was succeeded by a protégé of Bernardo Bembo's, Augurello.

What was happening was certainly apparent to Girolamo Donato, the *gran signore* and refined Hellenist, philosopher, theologian and musicologist, Barbaro's closest friend and among the first to be admitted by Politian into the circle which comprised the *quadrumviri litterarii* – Pico, Donato, Barbaro and Politian himself.[13] He was as convinced of the superiority of Greek over Latin literature as he was of the pre-eminence of Latin religious thought and theology over Greek. Accordingly, while he translated Chrysostom, St. John Damascene, the pseudo-Dionysius the Areopagite and Alexander of Aphrodisias, he also composed treatises in support of papal supremacy and the Latin doctrine concerning the Procession of the Holy Spirit. In the time left free from numerous and onerous public offices (which included the important Roman legation of 1509–11, during which he died) he entertained – as Egnazio records – the masters of the *Studio* in his Paduan palace and in particular discussed with them the immortality of the soul, a theme given a new direction by familiarity with the work of Alexander of Aphrodisias.[14] It was a subject that also preoccupied Pietro Barozzi, patrician, humanist, a great bibliophile and at that time bishop of Padua; preoccupied him, indeed, to such an extent that in 1489 he forbade any discussion of the unity of the intellect throughout his diocese, under penalty of excommunication. It was an attitude determined – and it can be found in certain treatises and letters of Barbaro and Donato – by the same ascetic and religious strain in humanistic thought which informed the Venice of Lodovico Barbo and St. Lorenzo Giustiniani and later had as its major exponents the great reformers, Paolo Giustiniani, Vincenzo Querini and Gasparo Contarini.[15]

The philological approach of Barbaro and his circle was, then, so strenuous and reinvigorating, so sincere and humane because their vision of the world and of man was sincere and humane and deeply religious. More than a century earlier, Petrarch, in his Venetian palace on the Riva degli Schiavoni began to bring together his *rime* while at the same time emending and annotating Martial and Apuleius and, perhaps for the first time, reading Homer. After one prophetic night he had meditated on three truths which he later – in polemic against the 'sophistry of the moderns' – bequeathed to the cultural atmosphere of Venice through his *De ignorantia*: the necessity of rediscovering and studying Plato and Aristotle directly rather than as maimed by commentators; the value of eloquence and poetry as supreme forms of human expression, truth in the shape of beauty; a consciousness that the Christian message constitutes a harmonious completion of that of antiquity as well as a triumph over it.

Over a century later, these three truths seemed to have been taken up again in Venice, in spirit if not in tone, by Barbaro. As writer and teacher, Ermolao's overriding effort was precisely to clear away the equivocations involved in the method of studying and interpreting Aristotle which dominated Padua University and the teaching of Vernia himself. From the very start he had been determined on a frontal assault on the rigid and closed peripateticism of the Paduan school: he responded eagerly to the appeal of 'divinus ille Plato' whom he had already hymned in the treatise *De coelibatu* as early as in his eighteenth year: 'tanta vir praestantia fuit ut non minus ingenii quam doctrinae desiderari nihil in eo homine possit' (ii, 2). And twelve years later, notwithstanding the diffidence characteristically felt in Venice towards Platonism and Neoplatonism (exaggerated by a whole critical tradition), he declared himself in a letter to Pico to be a reader of both Plato and Aristotle because 'no one can teach and expound Aristotle if he wishes to separate Aristotle from Plato almost as if they stood at opposite poles'. (*Ep.*, lxviii, and cf. also lxxxi.)

Having thoroughly examined Averroes and the untrustworthy medieval translations of Aristotle and having penetrated the neglected world of the Stagirite's Greek commentators (Alexander of Aphrodisias, Themistius, Simplicius) Ermolao, when little more than twenty, issued a bold challenge to the professional Aristotelian *cadre* of Padua. He was not motivated by contempt for the glorious university whose student he vaunted himself on being. He cherished the memory of his experience there, especially his contact with Vernia – to whom he explained, firmly but respectfully, the reasons underlying his new point of view and novel methods. (*Ep.* xxxi, lxii, lxx.)[16] But he wanted to win over to the new humanistic ideas the university of Padua itself, as the citadel, the very emblem of the peripatetic approach, an approach sealed off from the new sensibility. Ermolao undertook the Latin paraphrase of Themistius (published later, in 1481, in Treviso) not simply to underline the misunderstandings and scant originality of Averroes but to show that an exact understanding of Aristotelian texts led to conclusions quite at variance with those of the university lecturers of the old school. Through the philological restoration of Aristotle's text, in fact, he looked to a radical reform of Aristotelianism.

So against the conservative attitude of those who still chose to study the *Physics* through Averroes (rather than through Buridan or Marsilius of Inghen, etc.) a revitalizing movement began to take shape among Venetian scholars, such as Barbaro and Donato, who turned to fresh texts and prepared commentaries to support the new attitude. Between 1474 and 1485, at Padua and in Venice, Ermolao developed his grand project: to translate and comment on the whole range of Aristotelian writings. In 1480 he wrote to Girolamo Donato, who was also burdened by public offices and embassies (he followed Barbaro, in fact, in Milan and Rome): 'Would to heaven that it were possible to amend totally or at least diminish the errors of all those who call themselves good Peripatetics, for they can neither reason nor expound, knowing neither Latin nor Greek: rather than followers of Aristotle they resemble those who lived many centuries before Aristotle ... As for me, all my life until now, all that God will still grant me I will dedicate to this one task: as far as lies within a man, to restore the harmony between the natural sciences and humane studies'. (*Ep.* xii.) And four years later, in his inaugural lecture of 1484 he declared 'The philosophers of today read the commentators with great attention but ignore Aristotle ... out of his hundred and twenty five volumes they read and comment on six or seven at the most. I think I can promise you two things. First: to read to you and comment on the whole work of Aristotle within three or at the most four years, dialectic, natural philosophy, metaphysics, morals, rhetoric and poetics ... Secondly: to endeavour to the utmost of my ability to ensure that nothing in Aristotle, however difficult and obscure, remains incomprehensible to you'. (*Oratio* iii.) At once a grandiose and a polemically flavoured programme – above all a revealing one! (Cf. also *Ep.* lxi, lxii, lxxii, lxxvi.) Just as four years previously he had put forward as his ideal goal a harmony between the sciences and philosophy and the humanities, so now Ermolao was the first to give pride of place in his course on Aristotle to rhetoric and poetics; to those aspects of philosophy that is, which were altogether neglected at Padua, where not only were they neither read not commented on but they were entirely excluded from the Aristotelian corpus' At most they were admitted, on the lines of the Ciceronian tradition, as parts of the 'pratica', and at Padua were found room for within dialectic or logic in accordance with a syllabus that endured anachronistically until Bagolin's edition of the mid-*cinquecento*.[17] Thus a deep and strongly polemical awareness of a close harmony between philosophy and poetry, between truth and beauty brought back to life, after an interval of more than a century, the very ideal Petrarch had expressed in his dispute with the Venetian 'Averroists'. It prompted for Politian himself, during his Venetian sojourn of 1480, the growth of an awareness of the indissoluble links between philosophy and philogy (*Lamia*).

It was, indeed, from the Aristotelian texts, restored to their original form, that Barbaro, through a disciplined and forceful exercise in philology, was able to counter the arguments against poetry and eloquence repeated in 1485 by Pico with a far greater subtlety and vigour than had been mustered by Petrarch's four accusers. The dispute about the primacy of dialectic (or some other 'science') over poetry had by now lasted for some century and a half and, with Guarino,

Ermolao Barbaro the elder, Lodovico Foscarini and other humanists, had taken a turn in the Veneto which deserves fuller investigation.[18]

In taking up the defence of the subtle dialectics of the 'manner of Paris', Pico was to some extent following the argument of his master Elia dal Medico, a professor at Padua: as long as thought obeys the perfect mechanics of logic nothing more is needed, neither form nor the humanities. It was an affirmation of the separateness of rational truth from all other types of truth, the negation of the humanist attitude which looks on truth as the expression not only of careful thought but the product of a harmonious co-operation of every human faculty. In Barbaro's reply to Pico (*Ep.* lxxxi) as well as in many letters and lectures to his pupils, one dominating conviction was hammered home time and again: *humanitas* is not a matter simply of externals, of ornament; it is a spiritual entity which produces in man the true man, the citizen, man in his totality (one catches the echo of Guarino and Vittorino, of the great moral tradition of the Veneto); and *humanitas* reveals itself most fully in the word which, in turn, can never be detached from its root, the thought. 'Whoever seeks to separate philosophical thinking from the perfect means of expression', Ermolao declared, 'can be no more than a common little philosopher, a philosopher of wood, in fact'. (*Ep.* xii.)

Thus taking up the philological approach of Lorenzo Valla (he even quoted him explicitly; *Ep.* xlix), though more systematically, Ermolao proclaimed the inescapable connection between 'word' and 'thing', between *verba* and *res* (cf. also *Ep.* s.d. viii). That is, he denied – and Girolamo Donato was in full accord with him[19] – that there could be good ideas badly expressed. 'Aristotle and Plato, whom we follow in method and teaching, were great writers, so much so that there is no prose sweeter, purer, richer than theirs. Whoever therefore opposes philosophy to eloquence . . . clearly propagates a slander, a falsehood'. (*Ep.* lxxxi.) Like Petrarch and Valla, Barbaro is not arguing in favour of rhetorical ornament and artifice but defending the great classical tradition, Latin and Christian ('Optarem quidem sed non requiro cultum et elegantiam, requiro sententias', he wrote to Vernia in *Ep.* xxxi). It is a defence of clarity, of the communicability of thought, of the *humanitas* which is not only acuteness of thought but the complete and complex human intelligence. It is a demonstration of the impossibility of having 'knowledge' without 'wisdom', the absurdity of severing the world of nature from that of the spirit.

In this way Ermolao himself, who – with his translations of Greek mathematicians and of Dioscorides, with commentaries on Pliny the Elder and Pomponius Mela, with the historic founding of the world's first botanical garden at Padua – was one of the *quattrocento*'s most enlightened and energetic practitioners and promoters of the natural sciences, who was a precursor of the experimental method, whose European fame as a scientist was celebrated from Linacre to Linnaeus and Leibniz, fought energetically against the scientism and the preoccupation with technicalities that even then threatened on the academic horizon of Padua. We have seen how he emphasized to Donato the need to incorporate knowledge, *all knowledge,* within a framework that represented man in his full reality, both human and metaphysical (*Ep.* xii). As had Lorenzo Valla, he set up against the cult of a subject for its own sake, the aridness of a technical approach which claimed to package reality within a single discipline, the ideal of a truth which embraced human wisdom in its totality. When he debated with Dal Medico and Pico (*Ep.* lxviii, lxx, lxxx, lxxxi, lxxxiv) and in lordly fashion reduced to caricature the abstruse *calculationes* of the latest scholastic school,[20] he affirmed the communication of ideas to be the overriding need, far transcending esotericism or purely technical competence. He continued the Petrarchan and Albertian aim of understanding everything that was intelligible and translating it into a language that was fresh, clear and communicative, just as he deplored the mentality and the form of expression of certain of the Florentine Neoplatonist initiates. He believed that language, the *word* constituted the supreme manifestation, the supreme dignity of man, for it allowed the highest exercise of his spirit, the communication of his thoughts. It was precisely this activity, he declared, that made man resemble God. And from this deeply-felt and categorical belief followed the philological drive – the absolute need to define and to restore the true meaning of words, every word – and the humane and humanistic philosophy of Ermolao, so removed from that of a Vernia or a Pomponazzi which were completely indifferent to form, to the 'word', to the Ciceronian tradition as willingly to accept linguistic oddities and mongrel turns of phrase.

These key beliefs naturally led to an awareness of the limitations of thought and knowledge on their own. According to Barbaro, the science of truth must necessarily involve a clear understanding of the nature of behaviour, a sincere and absolute honesty of life, a profound humility. What I believe is the chief, the most important thing for those who wish to study philosophy, he told his pupils in 1484 (*Oratio* iii), what allows even the meanest intelligences to reach the summit of true wisdom is flight from all forms of voluptuousness. And in 1492: he whose mind is disposed towards wisdom 'wishes not to teach but always to be taught, hates passing judgement, is pleased to keep silent . . . this is that virtue lauded by Christians under the name of humility, which humility, while a most sure road to salvation and everlasting glory, is also every man's most needful companion, especially to the scholar, for without it we shall never be able to find the truth or form a prudent opinion'. (*Ep.* clvii.) And after having described the most absolute chastity, in the *De coelibatu*, as essential for the wise man and having repeated this advice in a letter to his friend Cotta (cxxix), he wrote his 'programme', as it were, in a moving poem addressed to his friend Pontico Faccino:

> . . . *Nec doctrina sat est, nisi sint probitasque fidesque*
> *Vitaque non ullis contaminata malis.*
> *Musa malos odit, Musae improbitate fugantur,*
> *Musas et vitium non capit una domus.*
> *Si mihi in alterutrum ius esse vel optio posset,*

229

> *Quamlibet indoctus quam malus esse velim.*
> *Simplicitas per se prodest: sine moribus artes*
> *Exitium multis perniciemque ferunt.*
> *Iudice me primum est bene vivere, scire secundum:*
> *Asseritur coelo, si quis utrumque potest.* (ix.)

These opinions are characteristic of Venetian humanism which had exhibited a puritan strain since Dominici's residence in San Giovanni e Paolo (1387–1399), and reflect the intense and austere spirituality which Antonio Corner and Gabriele Condulmer had brought to the reform of the monastery of San Giorgio in Alga early in the *quattrocento*, a reform of the utmost importance for humanist culture and spiritual life. And it was in this cultural environment, in the last decade of the century, that Aldo Manuzio, a pious man and a moralist, found his haven. In introducing his Latin grammar he wrote in a tone which paralleled that of Barbaro's verses: 'enitendum pro viribus ut et sanctos mores et bonas litteras simul edoceantur adulescentuli, quando alterum sine altero facere nullo modo licet. At si in altero peccandum foret, potior mihi ratio vivendi honeste quam vel optime discendi videretur. Malo enim eos nullas scire litteras ornatos moribus, quam omnia scire male moratos'.

In this awakened moral consciousness is rooted the knowledge that ancient wisdom, the lofty school of the classics, has its necessary and crowning comple-ment in the new Christian reality. Already in his first treatise, the *De coelibatu*, Ermolao had affirmed that all learning that did not look towards the praise of God is false, and that the superiority of the moderns over the ancients was due solely to the new wisdom preached by Christ. Thus, almost exactly anticipating the position taken by Aldus in his famous prefaces to Philostratus (1504) and Alexander of Aphrodisias (1513), he had written: 'Nam habuit aetas illa, quae post Socratem est subsequuta, maximos scelerum et libidinis fautores: quo fit ut mirari interdum soleam eos fuisse philosophos publice nuncupatos, qui a nulla re tantum quam a sapientia abhorrerent quique ab exoletis et ebrietate tantum haberentur ut studere nulli virtuti possent. Ut autem verbo complectar, usque adeo depravati illius temporis mores sunt, ut sive a Theodori scholis ... defluxisse ea vitia videantur, sive ab illo ipso Socrate praeceptore, ut minus culpa vacante, initium sumpserit voluptatis assertio, nihil minus a graecis expectetur quam virtutis et probitatis exemplum. Pudet referre quantum in perdocendo vitam cuiusque coinquinarit philosophorum impuritas, adeo nullus omnium vitio vacare et impietate visus est ... Quid erit tandem pertimescendum, aut quor non magno animo asseramus graecorum doctrinam, non mores, et verba, non facta, imitari oportere?' (ii, 3). And turning ten years later to the Flemish humanist Arnold of Bost he declared that 'duos agnosco dominos, Christum et litteras' (*Ep.* lxxvi), and writing to his friend Giorgio Merula in June 1492 from his Roman exile, during the months of unhappy solitude that followed his condemnation in Venice, he closely linked his eager and tenaciously pursued philological studies with Christian serenity and surrender to the will of Providence.

This was precisely the learned and Christian humanism which, on Erasmus's advice, Jacques Lefèvre d'Étaples came to Venice to seek in 1491. Ermolao's enthusiastic and pious correspondents Arnold of Bost and Josse Beissel (and their friend Robert Gaguin) had diffused Barbaro's humanistic message among the liveliest cultural circles in France, Flanders and Germany. Lefèvre d'Étaples's visit was no longer one designed to seek masters of the Latin language or learned grammarians in the tradition of Guarino and Perotti; he wanted to meet the representatives of a new way of thinking: 'videndi illectus amore Hermolai Barbari me glorior Italiam petisse', he wrote later to a correspondent. Franco Simone has rightly perceived that the text of Aristotle was the chief burden of his conversations with Barbaro,[21] a text that was on the way to being restored to an exact reading, stripped of Arab and scholastic commentaries; a text to be read, clearly enough, with the frame of mind induced by a spiritualized Christianity, but no longer circumscribed by Thomistic and scholastic *schemata*. With Ermolao, Lefèvre sought above all for the historical background to Aristotelian rationalism, brought into harmony with Plato's spiritualism and the message of the Gospels. This was the way of renewing Christian thought: through thinking afresh about its tradition in the light of classical sources. It was not by chance that Erasmus was to praise Ermolao 'quem nemo negat inter Italos, praeter summam morum innocentiam, eruditionis arcem tenuisse . . . absoluta diligentia'.[22]

The position taken by Petrarch which, over a century earlier had posted the highroads of Venetian humanism, was thus taken up again, explained and eloquently defended in the pages of one who in a sense set the seal on this crucial moment in the cultural and spiritual life of the *Serenissima*. Toffanin was right in noting that the words *homo*, *humanitas*, which in Pico's letter seem to have overtones almost of self-mocking and are pregnant with pre-Baconian significance, in Barbaro always carry a tone of reverence, of the classical-Christian tradition: the tone that some years later was to mark – and in the very circle of Venetian culture which had taken its cue from Barbaro – Marino Sanuto's use of the term 'humanista' for the great Aldo Manuzio.[23]

But besides the three leading motifs deriving from Petrarch which we have mentioned, other distinctive traditions within Venetian humanism seem to flow into Barbaro's work as if to their natural conclusion. There is, as we have seen, the belief that natural science cannot be excluded from a sound moral and metaphysical framework, from knowledge, that is, of both God and man, and that true human and humanist wisdom cannot allow the restrictions or the amputations required by the scientism of the false Aristotelians.

And on another hand there is the relationship between individual, family and state, established and felt in a sense different from that traditional to Tuscan humanism – though some notable echoes had sounded in Venice half a century before: it is enough to cite Francesco's *De re uxoria*. From his first treatise Ermolao had looked towards a life detached from all family ties as an ideal. In contrast to the rich tradition which saw the family as the harmonious and lofty complement of the individual (the works of Alberti, and Palmieri are but two examples), in Venice, where the state lay at the centre of things, where the omnipresence of the Republic dominated even family life, and where the new culture flourished and had its fulcrum among the political *élite* of an oligarchic patriciate, celibacy could be seen as an ideal, a state that could be identified with the highest wisdom, the most solid realism. As is clear from Barbaro's last treatise, the *De officio legati* (1489–90), the human space in which a man could realize himself was that of the state, not the family, a state whose sound and aristocratic oligarchical constitution and high ideal of liberty could truly offer conditions suited to the harmonious development of human dignity.

Thus the chief strands in the humanism of Venice and the Veneto, which had their highest and most systematic exposition in Barbaro, were firmly centred in the renewed consciousness of the dignity and vigour of the human spirit, in the attempt to find again in man an image of the universe's own harmony. In his famous dispute with Pico, when Ermolao pushed the arguments of the *litterae* to an extreme, he was not really doing more than defending his ideal of human dignity and wholeness, of an inner nobility reflected in an outward elegance. To deny this ideal seemed to him a denial of that very civilization and culture of which he and Politian were acclaimed as the greatest champions. This belief was not only justified and publicized but was almost made visible in his writings: in his continual search for a correspondence between inner reality and the external aspects of knowledge, between a pure harmony of the moral faculties and a fine decorum of bearing. To crown these writings Barbaro did not offer a merely abstract affirmation or conclusion, but clear and exemplary portraits of his ideal man.

This tendency in Barbaro is one which not only expresses his fundamental belief in the harmony between moral and intellectual gifts, between natural and metaphysical and poetic truths, but appears to represent a typically Venetian cultural tradition. It is a tradition which, beside the Florentine version *de hominis dignitate*, altogether committed to 'ragioni d'anima', develops along lines suggested by Guarino and Vittorino, a more concrete, down-to-earth vision of man in which the gesture, the reserve, the decorum are essential parts of this dignity, revealing an exceptional elevation of mind. Even before it developed in its full artistic and civic splendour, the humanists drew attention almost visually to the human and humanistic attractiveness of this Venetian 'decoro': from the fine description of Bernardo Bembo in Landino's *De nobilitate* to Galateo's well-known tribute to the 'nobiltà' of the Venetians in his *De educatione* (he had been a friend of Ermolao, in fact, during his Neapolitan days), and from the amazed respect recorded by Politian in his letters from Venice to the graceful portrait of Girolamo Donato in Paolo Cortese's *De cardinalatu* (1510 edition, 161v, 221v, 226v).

Those anticipations were, in Barbaro's case, expressed in terms of a thoroughly humanistic state of mind. The youthful but already well-defined views of the *De coelibatu* recur in the *Epistolae* and can be said to achieve their mature form fifteen years later in the more sober, but now sure and clear-cut lines of the *De officio legati*. Breaking decisively with the traditional technical and juridical treatises on ambassadors and embassies, Ermolao resolved the problems implicit in this theme through concrete instances: he describes in terms of the perfect ambassador his lofty ideal of a man whose every inner faculty responds to a measured decorum of personality and behaviour (it was, perhaps, for this reason that this little work appealed so much to Tasso).[24]

The marvellous 'portraits of inner life' of the greatest Venetian painting of this period – so closely involved, from Gentile and Giovanni Bellini to Carpaccio and Giorgione, with humanist culture and with Barbaro himself[25] – have tantalizing literary 'pendants' in these pages. These same pages, indeed, seem in some way to have contributed to the literary tradition which rarified the humanist ideal into the pure elegance of the 'cortegiano'. Its most refined and brilliant exemplars, indeed, glow from the pages of writers closely connected with Venetian culture and the humanist circle of Barbaro himself. Bembo, for example, Barbaro's pupil, who left a glowing and moving testimony to the humane quality of his learning in a well-known letter to Beroaldo, became the ideal successor to Barbaro's philological approach: lucid, open to every feeling about language.[26] Or Castiglione, pupil of one of Ermolao's closest friends, Giorgio Merula, and who as a boy possibly admired the famous Venetian diplomat at the court of Lodovico il Moro. Or, again, Della Casa who learned from Bembo to understand and to love the human quality in Barbaro's teaching. In fact four writers, for all of whom 'discretione' (in the Guicciardinian sense) was a common bond, all of them churchmen: bishops, patriarchs, cardinals. Theirs were minds which sought for intellectual and moral truth through the experience of human beings and which saw in the image of an ideal, a *total* man, both their beliefs and their hopes made real. These ideals, these 'portraits of inner life', expressed the experience of a culture which amid the political crisis of the Italian states 'had found shelter in the Church and, amid the crisis of the Church itself, maintained a by no means useless belief in persuasion and dialogue, in a classical sense of proportion and of the development of thought and word in time' – and beyond the immediate event.[27]

This was the spiritual and cultural experience which lay at the heart of the career of the man who, after the demise of the major humanists of the late *quattrocento* and during the height of the tragic crisis of Italy, set himself to preserve and continue the spirit and the labour of Barbaro, Donato and their great Tuscan colleagues. The name of Aldo Manuzio naturally occurred when we were speaking of Ermolao and his circle. It was Merula, Valla (whose major work he was to publish after his death) and, above all, Barbaro who had welcomed and encouraged him from 1488–90 (as his letter to Caterina Pio shows) in the new course which his publishing activities – recorded there in 1494 – was to take in Venice from about 1492.[28] It was a course that was to be decisive for Venetian culture. The bent he gave to philological studies was based above all on two convictions: on the one hand a belief in the value of the text for its own sake, fixed with unchallengeable accuracy (the result of a tireless search for the best codices and the most trustworthy editors) and freed from the fanciful clutter of commentaries which had burdened and obscured them, and on the other an understanding of the necessity for an interaction or, rather, a convergence between Greek and Latin culture as a means of comprehending the ancient world and its writings (his first catalogue, of 1498, contained only Greek texts). These were the very convictions that had inspired the approach to philology renewed and defended by Politian and Barbaro; many of his editions, indeed – and I mention *pour cause* the famous five volume edition of Aristotle, and that of Plato – represented nothing less than the realization of projects precisely outlined and looked forward to by Ermolao.

To this firm cultural foundation corresponded an equally resolute moral and religious stance – this too of a Venetian stamp – on the lines I have described. Apart from his distrust of hermetic and Neoplatonic and Neopythagorian trends, above all philosophical or scientific *libertinismo*, Aldus always insisted energetically on the necessary bond between true philosophical speculation and integrity of conduct and religious belief; in the heated debate between doctors and philosophers he appealed continually (as had Petrarch and Barbaro) to Christian orthodoxy, to the sound doctrines which no amount of speculation could impair.

These moral and religious demands also gave rise to the encyclopaedic ideal, serene and pacific, which had already appealed to Barbaro and Politian and which inspired Aldus' editorial activity. 'The heavens of religious belief and the moral law which appeared to so many of Aldus' contemporaries to be so distant and faint weighed on him', Dionisotti has perceptively noted, 'with an enrapturing immediacy. He firmly believed that books could make man better, but he was under no illusion that man's education would be easy . . . Hence the profound encyclopaedism of Aldus: a concern for a culture that could responsibly serve, *hic et nunc*, the whole society of men in their living and various reality'. It was a belief that led in 1500 to the printing, alongside the Greek and Latin classics, of St. Catherine's letters with a memorable and deeply-felt dedication to Cardinal Piccolomini, worthy of the austere pre-reform mood of Querini or Giustiniani, and that made him gather under his imprint the whole humanist tradition, Greek, Latin and vernacular, seeing the key to its organization not so much in philosophy as in literature.

It was clearly the wish to consolidate and in a way to extend his own influence through this movement of active and devout encyclopaedism that prompted the founding of his Academy. 'Aldus felt', Dionisotti goes on, 'that his solitary enterprise should become a common concern with other men, not only for the technical and practical assistance they were in a position to offer but for an exchange of views and discussion of the projects which, with their advice, he was planning to put into effect'. His enterprise had come as it were into the public domain and had acquired a European significance. Politian and Barbaro had prepared the way, help of various sorts was given by Ficino and Lascaris, Fra Giocondo and Bolzani, Bembo and Navagero, Linacre and Dukas, Carteromaco and Musuro, Aleandro and Egnazio. Humanists throughout Europe looked admiringly at his undertaking. There was even a move to set up an Aldine Academy on German soil, under the protection of the Emperor Maximilian. Linacre and Budé came to Venice in search of a retreat and cultural and spiritual enlightenment, as did Erasmus who stayed with Aldus himeslf, published a new edition of the *Adages* and probably collaborated in an edition of Plutarch's *Moralia*.[20] Amid the insistent clamour of arms, amid the ruin of Italian public and institutional life, between the apocalyptic invasion of Charles VIII and the disaster of Agnadello, Aldus, moved by a lofty moral purpose, continued and energetically renewed on a European scale the spiritual message of Venetian humanism. 'The independent Aldine Academy', Dionisotti could conclude, 'was, next to the great universities, the most important point of contact between the Italian humanistic tradition and the attitude which, with Italian inspiration, was becoming diffused among the other countries of Europe.'

There is, too, another plane on which the radical and mature humanism of Barbaro and Donato appears to extend its message on a European dimension and into the future. The tendency of the finest Venetian paintings – from Bellini and Carpaccio to Titian – to emphasize the solemnity of certain pictorial moments through the figures of thinkers or men of letters or to allude to the values of the new culture through certain choral scenes, seems to some extent to have been prompted by the personality of Ermolao himself and the cultural circle around him. It was an influence even more direct and exact than the one reflected, as we have noted, in the 'portraits of inner life'.[30]

In his *Venetia città nobilissima e singolare* (Venice, 1581, 132) Sansovino pointed out in his lively and minute description of a painting (Bellini? Carpaccio?) in the hall of the Great Council (destroyed in the fire of 1577) that there, too, according to Gentile Bellini's rough sketches, many of the figures were portraits of the great personalities of the time. And among the greatest captains and statesmen, he writes, were certain 'men of especial accomplishment in Greek and Latin letters and famed for their learning; . . . Angelo Poliziano, Hermolao Barbaro, and Hieronimo Donato dressed in gold with rich and splendid chains about their necks'. It is not difficult to imagine that the picture's aim was to provide a visual record of the place which *umane lettere* then held in the social setting of Venice.

But if this can be no more than a conjecture, however likely, the work of Carpaccio, which is still happily before our eyes, glowingly confirms the hypothesis. Indeed, in his paintings for the *Scuola* of St. Ursula – so closely linked to the patronage and Maecenatism of the Loredan and Barbaro families – he chose for the central figure of the most solemn and spectacular scene (the meeting with the pope) the very figure who was in a way the pivot about which the cultural life of Venice turned in that period and who had tragically died, at the age of thirty-nine, only a few months before. At precisely this time, moreover, Ermolao's philological masterpiece, the *Castigationes plinianae*, was republished in Venice. And as in the Ducal Palace, around Ermolao Barbaro – as if in an ideal school not of Athens but of Venice – it is possible that some of the other champions of the native humanism are portrayed, Marco Barbo, perhaps, Girolamo Donato, Domenico Grimani and still others, besides the painter himself.

Ten years later, in his cycle for San Giorgio degli Schiavoni, Carpaccio, still remaining faithful to these visual interpretations, portrayed St. Augustine against a background of bookshelves in the likeness of Bessarion, the devout and deeply erudite cardinal who had presented his splendid library to Venice.

Carpaccio's visualizations, these figures, real and ideal at the same time, both 'portraits of inner life' and symbols, emblems as it were of a new culture and the new spiritual life, continued to live, to develop and to become charged – possibly also through subtle and ambiguous Neoplatonic influences – with spiritual and allusive meanings in the great decades of Venetian painting which bridge the *quattro-* and the *cinquecento*. These were to be distinctive and characteristic elements of the most humanistic, most *rinascimentale*, most advanced art in Europe. From the early but confident examples of Gentile Bellini, from the gilded legend of St. Ursula and the powerful cycle of St. Jerome, by way of the highly diverse range of expression which can go under the name of Palma or the *Poliphilo*, we reach the summit: the Giorgionesque miracle of the Three Philosophers. Once again portraits of inner life and emblems are based on a vocabulary that is formal and allusive in the highest degree, once again, perhaps, the clear-cut and radiant profile of Ermolao Barbaro is chosen to represent the new culture, youthfully strong and spirited; and even if on the other hand we accept, with Nardi, that the youngest of the three philosophers represents Copernicus, or, with Calvesi and other scholars, Pythagoras or a scientist-philosopher, the general significance – emblematic and allusive – remains.[31]

Venetian humanism, as I have already had occasion to write, did not have, as did the Tuscan humanism of Politian, a grand poetic utterance. Its vitality and its worth emerge above all in the eager and confident taking up of its legacy to letters and to art in the succeeding age by a circle that was both Italian and firmly European. Its strenuous defence of the absolute value of word and form was to guide the lively linguistic sensibility and the rigorous grammatical systematization of the 'volgare' which began with Bembo and Fortunio and culminated in the *Prose della volgar lingua*. Its philosophy or, rather, its human and Christian wisdom, profoundly conscious of the limitation of any subject pursued only for its own sake, was to act as a leaven within the mighty ferments of Paolo Giustiniani's and Gasparo Contarini's religious renewal. Its deep conviction that the study of nature could not be divorced from the study of man was to find brilliant and positive testimony in the researches and intuitions of Luca Pacioli, a pupil of the Rialto school, (and much later was to be splendidly carried on in the work of Galileo, professor at the reformed university of Padua and powerfully affected by his contacts with Venice). Nor was there lacking, if we look carefully, a loftily poetic strain which entered the civilization of the succeeding centuries – and which still endures – in painting, for which Barbaro himself, taking up again the Horatian 'ut pictura poesis' had claimed a dignity and a function comparable to those of letters and of poetry.[32] The Venetian pictorial tradition from Carpaccio and Giorgione to Titian, so passionately turned towards man, so continuously devoted to visualizing inner life in terms of real or transfigured figures and landscapes: this is the most splendid and the most lasting poetic flowering that emerged from the soil of the so human literary civilization of *quattrocento* Venice.

NOTES

1. As is well known, there is no systematic history of Venetian humanism, even for its most significant period, the last quarter of the *quattrocento*. For basic information it is still necessary to refer to the great contributions of the eighteenth century: M. Foscarini, *Della letteratura veneziana* (Padua, 1752); G. Mazzuchelli, *Gli scrittori d'Italia* (Brescia, 1753); A. Zeno, *Dissertazioni vossiane* (Venice, 1753); G. degli Agostini, *Notizie istorico-critiche intorno la vita e le opere degli scrittori viniziani* (Venice, 1754); G. Tiraboschi, *Storia della letteratura italiana* (Milan, 1833, 1st ed. Modena, 1772); E. A. Cicogna, *Le iscrizioni veneziane* (Venice, 1824). More recent assessments of Venetian humanism are only to be found in works of a general nature, such as E. Renan, *Averroès et l'Averroisme* (Paris, 1903); V. Rossi, *Il Quattrocento* (3rd ed., Milan, 1949); G. Toffanin, *Storia dell' umanesimo* (3rd ed., Bologna, 1950); E. Garin, 'La letteratura degli umanisti' in *Il Quattrocento* (Milan, 1966). Essential, however, are the following: L. Lazzarini, *Paolo de Bernardo e i primordi dell'umanesimo in Venezia* (Florence, 1930); *La civiltà veneziana del Quattrocento* publ. for the Fondazione 'Giorgio Cini' (Florence, 1957); *Umanesimo europeo e umanesimo veneziano* ed. V. Branca (Florence, 1963); *Venezia e l'Oriente fra tardo Medioevo e Rinascimento* ed. A. Pertusi (Florence, 1966); *Rinascimento europeo e rinascimento veneziano*, ed. V. Branca (Florence, 1967). These last three volumes – all published for the Fondazione 'Giorgio Cini' – contain copious bibliographical material which is kept up to date in *Archivio Veneto* and *Studi Veneziani*. For Hellenic studies in Venice, cf. D. J. Geanakoplos, *Greek scholars in Venice* (Cambridge Mass., 1962).

2. It may be helpful to refer to a few of the works which can be used to give body to this rapid survey. For Lauro Quirini: A. Segarizzi, 'Lauro Quirini', *Mem. R.Acc. Scienze di Torino*, liv (1904) and particularly the forthcoming Fondazione Cini edition of his treatises *De republica* and *De nobilitate*, perpared by K. Krautter, P. O. Kristeller, H. Roob and C. Seno, which will include a very full introduction. For Jacopo Zen: L. Lazzarini, op. cit.; J. Zeno, *Vita Caroli Zeni*, in *R.I.S.*, 2, xix. For Pietro Barbo: R. Weiss, *Un umanista veneziano: Papa Paolo II* (Venice, 1958). For Cyriac, his relations with Venice and his patrician admirers, *Kyriaci Anconitani Itinerarium*, ed. L. Mehus (Florence, 1742); G. Bertalot and A. Campana, 'Gli scritti di Jacopo Zeno e il suo elogio di Ciriaco', *La Bibliofilia*, x li (1939); *La civiltà veneziana del Quattrocento*, cit., 137 seq. On the allusion in Bellini's work, cf. op. cit. n. 25. For Bernardo Giustiniani: E. Fueter, *Geschichte der*

neueren Historiographie (2nd ed., Berlin, 1925) 113 seq.; P. M. Labalme, *Bernardo Giustiniani* (Rome, 1969). For historiography: A. Carile, *La cronachistica veneziana* etc. (Florence, 1968); *La storiografia veneziana fino al sec. XVI*, ed. A. Pertusi (Florence, 1970). For Bernardo Bembo: V. Cian, 'Per Bernardo Bembo', *Giornale Storico della Letteratura Italiana*, xxviii (1896) and xxxi (1899); A. della Torre, 'La prima ambasceria di Bernardo Bembo a Firenze', ibid., xxxv (1900). For the interest in ancient art and archaeology: R. Weiss, *The Renaissance discovery of classical antiquity* (Oxford, 1969).

3. On the fortunes of schools in Venice – apart from general works and those dealing specifically with Barzizza, Guarini and Vittorino – cf. B. Cecchetiti, 'Libri, scuole, maestri . . . in Venezia nei secoli XIV e XV', *A.V.*, xxxii (1886); E. Bertanza and G. della Santa, *Maestri, scuole e scolari in Venezia fino al 1500* (Venice, 1907); V. Rossi, 'Maestri e scuole a Venezia verso la fine del Medioevo', *Scritti di critica letteraria*, iii (Florence, 1930: an article written in 1907); A. Segarizzi, 'Cenni sulle scuole pubbliche a Venezia nel sec. XV', *Atti R. Ist. Veneto Sc., Lett., Arti*, lxxv (1915–16); B. Nardi, 'La Scuola di Rialto e l'umanesimo veneziano' in *Umanesimo europeo*, cit. For Brugnoli: G. Mazzuchelli, *Scrittori*, cit., ii, 2134 seq.; for Mario Filelfo: G. Castellani, 'Documenti veneziani inediti relativi a Francesco e Mario Filelfo', *A.S.I.*, ser. V, xvii (1896); for George of Trebizond: G. Castellani, 'Giorgio di Trebisonda', *N.A.V.*, xi, 1896, P. Gothein, *Francesco Barbaro* (Berlin, 1932) 147 seq. and C. Vasoli, *La dialettica e la retorica dell'umanesimo* (Milan, 1968) 81 seq.; for Giorgio Merula: F. Gabotto and A. Badini Confalonieri, *Vita di Giorgio Merula* (Alessandria, 1894); M. Santoro, 'La polemica Poliziano-Merula', *Giornale Italiano di Filologia*, v (1952).

4. On this key episode cf. L. Mohler, *Kardinal Bessarion als Theologe, Humanist und Staatsmann* (Paderborn, 1923–1942); L. Labowsky, 'Bessarion Studies', *Mediaeval and Renaissance Studies*, v (1961) and 'Il cardinale Bessarione e gli inizi della Biblioteca Marciana', *Venezia e l'Oriente*, cit.; *Cento codici bessarionei*, ed. T. Gasparrini Leporace and E. Mioni (Venice, 1968).

5. Cf. in general S. Castellani, *La stampa in Venezia* (Venice, 1889); H. R. Brown, *The Venetian printing press* (London, 1891); F. Ongania, *L'arte della stampa nel Rinascimento italiano*, i, *Venezia* (Venice, 1894); E. Pastorello, *Bibliografia storico-analitica dell'arte della stampa in Venezia* (Venice, 1933).

6. It might be helpful, I think, to take this opportunity to note the essential biographical dates and the main activities of Ermolao as far as I have been able to determine them from his ample correspondence and from archival material: cf. Ermolao Barbaro, *Epistolae Orationes et Carmina, edizione critica*, ed. V. Branca (Florence, 1943); Ermolao Barbaro, *De coelibatu – De officio legati, edizione critica*, ed. V. Branca (Florence, 1969) especially 7, 17 seq., 20 seq., 24 seq. Specific, but fragmentary and frequently misleading details are given in the two monographs: T. Stickney, *De Hermolai Barbari vita atque ingenio* (Paris, 1903); A. Ferriguto, *Almorò Barbaro* (Venice, 1922).

Ermolao was born in Venice in 1453 or 1454. His father was Zaccaria, son of the great Francesco. He began his humanistic education around 1460 with his cousin Ermolao, bishop of Verona, a hagiographer and author of a *Contra poetas*. He completed it in Rome, at Ravenna and again in Verona as he accompanied his father on his various missions. At Verona, on 3 Dec., 1489, he obtained the laureateship for poetry from the Emperor Frederick III. From Oct. 1471 to Sept. 1473 he was in Naples while his father was in residence there as Venetian *oratore*, and made acquaintances within the Neapolitan humanist circle (Contrario, Pontano, Galateo): he wrote his treatise *De coelibatu*. Admitted to the Great Council 26 Sept., 1471, became *doctor artium* and *utriusque iuris* at Padua (23 Aug., 1474 and 17 Oct., 1477) where he professed philosophy and lectured on Aristotle's *Ethics* and *Politics* (1471–79). He came to know and established a deep friendship with Politian who lived in Venice in 1480, and supervised the publication of his *Themistius* (Treviso, 1481). After another stay in Rome (where his father was Venetian *oratore*) he was elected to the Senate in 1483 and to the *Rason Vecchie* in 1484. He did not, however, give up his humanistic studies and worked in especially close association with Giorgio Merula, Giorgio Valla and Girolamo Donato. In 1484 at Padua he read the Greek poets with a group of young nobles and, in addition, following his pronounced bent for scientific studies, founded the world's first botanic garden. In November, moreover, he began in Venice lectures and commentaries on Aristotle which drew large audiences (*oratio* III). He continued there in the following year before accompanying his father (once more *oratore* for the *Serenissima*) to Milan (Aug.–Sept. 1485). In 1486 he conducted the important polemic with Pico della Mirandola and went to Bruges as the republic's *oratore* to Frederick III and Maximilian (*oratio* iv). In Jan. 1488 he was elected *savio di terraferma* and then ambassador to Lodovico il Moro (Mar. 1488–Apr. 1489) and formed stimulating contacts within the humanistic circle in Milan (Merula, Antiquario, Calco). On returning to Venice he wrote the *De officio legati*, became an *avogador di comun* and was then appointed ambassador to the Holy See. On his way to Rome in May he stopped in Florence where he was given a warm welcome by Lorenzo the Magnificent and his court of humanists (Politian, Pico and Ficino were among his friends and admirers). On 6 Mar., 1491, he was nominated by Innocent VIII to the patriarchate of Aquileia without the approbation of the *Serenissima* and, stripped of his ambassadorship, he remained in exile in Rome where he completed the *Castigationes plinianae* and *In Pomponium Melam* (Rome, Eucharius Argenteus, 1493; G.W. 3340). He died of plague in July 1493.

His printed writings (apart from those already cited) were: *In Dioscoridem Corollari* (Venice, 1516); *Gilberti Porretani liber ... Hermolao Barbaro interprete* (Paris, 1541); *Rhetoricorum Aristotelis libri ... interprete Hermolao Barbaro* (Venice, 1544); *Compendium Ethicorum librorum* (Venice, 1544); *Compendium scientiae naturalis ex Aristotele* (Venice, 1545).

7. On the history of humanistic philology information of a general kind (necessarily not directly relevant to our present investigation) can be found in A. Bernardini and G. Righi, *Il concetto di filologia e di cultura classica* (Bari, 1947); G. Funaioli, *Studi di letteratura antica* (Bologna, 1949) i; C. Dionisotti, *Discorso sull'umanesimo italiano* (Verona, 1956). On Calderini and his approach there is now J. Dunston, 'Studies in D. Calderini' and C. Dionisotti, 'Calderini, Poliziano e altri', *Italia Medioevale e Umanistica*, xi (1968). And, especially for the final philological development of Politian and Barbaro, which shows them as motivated by the same ideals and employing a common methodology, V. Branca, 'La incompiuta Seconda Centuria dei *Miscellanea* di Angelo Poliziano', *Lettere Italiane*, xiii (1961); V. Branca and M. Pastore Stocchi, *Introduzione* to the critical edition of Politian's *Miscellaneorum Centuria Secunda* (Florence, 1972) Also cf. n. 9.

8. The conclusions that follow are documented and treated more fully – besides in the introductions and appendices cited in n. 6 – in my 'Un trattato inedito di Ermolao Barbaro', *Bibliothèque d'Humanisme et Renaissance*, xiv (1952); 'Una lettera in volgare di Ermolao Barbaro', *Miscellanea di studi offerta a Armando Balduino e Bianca Bianchi per le loro nozze* (Padua, 1962); 'Ermolao Barbaro in Francia', *Studi in onore di Carlo Pellegrini* (Turin, 1963); 'Ermolao Barbaro e l'umanesimo veneziano', *Umanesimo europeo e umanesimo veneziano*, cit.; 'Ermolao Barbaro poeta e la sua presentazione alla corte aragonese', *Classical Mediaeval and Renaissance Studies in honor of B. L. Ullman* (Rome, 1964); 'Un codice aragonese scritto dal Cinico', *Studi di bibliografia e di storia in onore di Tammaro De Marinis* (Verona, 1964); 'Fermezza cristiana e impegno filologico del Patriarca Ermolao Barbaro', *Miscellanea G.G. Meerseman* (Padua, 1971); 'Il metodo filologico del Poliziano', *Tra latino e volgare: per Carlo Dionisotti* (Padua, 1972). Also cf. G. Pozzi, 'Appunti sul Corollarium del Barbaro', ibid.

9. My principal debt here is to information kindly supplied by my friend P. Giovanni Pozzi, who together with his pupils has recently completed the critical and annotated edition of the *Castigationes plinianae* and *In P. Melam* (forthcoming from Autenore of Padua in the collection 'Thesaurus mundi'). In the introduction, which he has generously allowed me to read, a series of *lectiones veteres* from Barbaro which Mayhoff's *apparatus*

criticus supposes drawn from a restricted number of codices, is collated against thirteen mss. which have never before been taken into consideration by modern editors; the conclusion is that 'la situazione risulta estremamente instabile, sia considerando le varianti del Barbaro per rapporto all'apparato del Mayhoff, sia considerandole per rapporto alla nostra collazione. Il ms dell'apparato del Mayhoff che compare con più frequenza è il Par. lat. 6795 (E)', then Leiden IV, Riccardiano 488, Leiden VII (respectively A, R, and F² to the editors). 'Ora A è il codice più autorevole fra gli antichissimi, mentre R e F² appartengono fra i recenziori ad una famiglia diversa da E. Nessun orientamento concreto è possibile avere dall'esame delle varianti (da noi tentato anche in altri settori con lo stesso successo) . . . La speranza di ritrovare il codice o i codici pliniani usati dal Barbaro è dunque legata unicamente all'esame dei singoli manoscritti di Plinio oggi superstiti: ed a questo traguardo, nonostante degli sforzi parziali, non abbiamo avuto finora la fortuna di arrivare.'

This is clearly also due to the fact that Barbaro continually cast about for evidence from the most varied sources. Moreover, unlike Politian, he did not base his emendations primarily on the manuscript tradition and essayed no more than a rudimentary classification of them. He preferred to rely on parallel evidence. But for this difference between Barbaro's and Politian's method v. Branca, 'Il metodo filologico' etc., cit.

10. In 1488, to be precise, with the *Emendationes in Plinium* (Hain, 14059), and cf. Barbaro's Ep. cxviii, cit. On Sabellico cf. A. Zeno, *Degli istorici delle cose veneziane* etc. (Venice, 1718) i; on p. lxvii there is also a reference (among the unpublished works of Sabellico) to the *Apologia et recriminatio adversus Hermolaum Barbarum*; G. Mercati, *Ultimi contributi alla storia degli umanisti*, ii (Vatican City, 1939). On the Plinian tradition, cf. D. Detlefsen, *Die Beschreibung Italiens in des Naturales Historiae des Plinius* (Leipzig, 1901); K. Mayhoff, introduction to the Teubner ed. of the *Naturales Historiae* (3rd ed., Leipzig, 1967); E. de Saint-Denis, introduction to the Belles Lettres ed. of the *Naturalis Historia* (Paris, 1955).

11. A devoted pupil of Politian, Girolamo Amaseo, referred to this (mythical?) nocturnal perusal: 'in Plinium divina commentaria . . . ut ad se transferentur curavit, perlegitque nocte una totum librum'; cf. G. Pozzi, 'Da Padova a Firenze nel 1493', *Italia Medioevale e Umanistica*, ix (1966) 194. On the use made of the *Castigationes* in the *Centuria Secunda*, cf. V. Branca, 'Datazione della Seconda Centuria dei "Miscellanea" ', *Italian studies presented to E. R. Vincent* (Cambridge, 1962). In ch. 5, contrasting Barbaro's method with the mountainous and undiscriminating *filologia calderiniana*, Politian writes: 'Quae iam quantopere labes inoleverit satis, ut arbitror, Hermolaus Barbarus in plinianis emendationibus ostendit . . . fato functus . . . pro quanta, bone Deus, linquae utriusque, quanta bonarumque artium iactura. Erat enim Hermolaus amoeno ingenio, casta elegantia, doctrina varia, cura infinita, rerum verborumque ad rectum urbanus exactor, multumque et linquae et philosophiae et aliis bonis artibus collaturus, si non flore ipso aetatis intercidisset.' Cf. V. Branca and M. Pastore Stocchi, *Introduzione*, cit., 8 seq.

12. On Giorgio Valla, see J. L. Heiberg, *Beiträge zur Geschichte Giorgio Vallas und seine Bibliothek* (Leipzig, 1896); G. della Santa, 'Nuovi appunti sul processo di Giorgio Valla', *N.A.V.*, x (1896); E. Garin, 'La cultura milanese nella seconda metà del XV secolo', *Storia di Milano* (Milan, 1956) vii, 574 seq., 590; C. Vasoli, *La dialettica e la retorica dell'umanesimo* cit., 132 seq.

13. On this exclusive circle, formed in all probability during Poliziano's sojourn in Venice, it is enough to turn to Politian's correspondence, e.g., a deeply-felt letter to Antiquario (iii, 22) and above all to the exchange between the two friends (ii, 10, 11, 12, 13, 14, 15: Angeli Politiani, *Opera*, Venice, 1498). See also the moving ch. 90 of the *Miscellaneorum Centuria Prima* in which, as in Ep. ii, 15, the *quadrumviri litterarii* are evoked; in particular 'duo illi sed una devincti amoris copula, Veneti patricii, Hermolaus Barbarus . . . et Hieronymus Donatus, vir nescio utrum gravior an doctior an etiam humanior

certe omni lepore affluens, omni venustate'. Revealing, too, are the letters exchanged between Donato and Pico, cf. *Opera* (Venice, 1557) Ep. ix, xv, xxi, xxviii; and E. Garin, *La cultura filosifica del rinascimento italiano* (Florence, 1961) 257, 269 seq.; further, see the ms, letter to Lorenzo de' Medici which will soon be published by Dr. Paolo Rigo in a detailed monograph which will throw new light on the personality and on the work of this outstanding Venetian humanist. At present one can only cite Degli Agostini, op. cit., ii, 201–239; for the translations from Alexander of Aphrodisias, however, see E. Cranz, 'Alexander Aphrodisiensis', in *Catalogus translationum et commentariorum. Medieval and Renaissance Latin translations and commentaries* (Washington, 1960).

14. G. B. Egnazio, *De exemplis illustrium virorum venetae civitatis* (Paris, 1554) viii, 296. Cf. E. Garin, *La cultura*, cit., 93 seq., 267 seq.; E. Gilson, 'L'affaire de l'immortalité de l'âme', *Umanesimo europeo e umanesimo veneziano*, cit.; B. Nardi, *Saggi sull' aristotelismo padovano* (Florence, 1958) 365 seq. (also for Barbaro's translations) and *Studi su Pietro Pomponazzi* (Florence, 1965) 54 seq. and 149 seq.

15. Cf. M. Bolzonella, *Pietro Barozzi vescovo di Padova* (Padua, 1941); F. Gaeta, *Il vescovo Pietro Barozzi e il trattato 'De factionibus extinguendis'* (Venice, 1958). On Paolo Giustiniani, Vincenzo Querini and their circle, cf. H. Jedin, 'Vincenzo Querini und Pietro Bembo', *Miscellanea Giovanni Mercati* (Vatican City, 1948) and 'Contarini und Camaldoli', *Archivio Italiano per la Storia della pietà*, ii (1953); J. Leclercq, *Un humaniste ermite* (Rome, 1951); G. De Luca, *Letteratura di pietà a Venezia* (Florence, 1963); P. Giustiniani, *Trattati, lettere e frammenti*, ed. E. Massa (Rome, 1968); W. J. Bouwsma, *Venice and the defense of republican liberty* (Berkeley, 1968); J. B. Ross, 'Gasparo Contarini and his friends', *Studies in the Renaissance*, xvii (1970); G. Fragnito, 'Cultura umanistica e riforma religiosa', *Studi Veneziani*, xi (1970), as well, of course, as F. Dittrich's classic monograph G. *Contarini* (Braunsberg, 1881). Also we now have L. Pesce, *Ludovico Barbo* (Padua, 1969); G. Cozzi, 'Domenico Morosini e il "De bene instituta re publica"', *Studi Veneziani*, xii, 1971.

16. On Vernia and his relations with Barbaro and his circle, cf. P. Ragnisco, 'N. Vernia', *Atti R. Ist. Veneto Sc., Lett., Arti.*, ser. VII, xxxviii (1891); B. Kieszkowski, *Studi sul platonismo del Rinascimento* (Florence, 1936) 138 seq.; B. Nardi, op. cit., in n. 14; E. Garin, *La cultura*, cit., 293 seq.

17. L. Minio Paluello, 'Attività filosofico-editoriale aristotelica dell'Umanesimo', *Umanesimo europeo e umanesimo veneziano*, cit.

18. Pico's letter, checked against the ms., has now been edited with an excellent introduction and important restorations by E. Garin in his *Prosatori latini del Quattrocento* (Milan, 1952) 804 seq. For this controversy, its Petrarchan origin and its development in Venice, see in particular P. O. Kristeller, *Studies in Renaissance thought and letters* (Rome, 1956) 553 seq., and 'Il Petrarca, l'umanesimo e la scolastica a Venezia', *La civiltà veneziana del Trecento* (Florence, 1956); *La disputa delle arti nel Quattrocento*, ed. E. Garin (Florence, 1947); G. Ronconi, review of Francesco da Fiano 'Contra obloculores et detractores poetarum', *Studi sul Boccaccio*, iii (1965) and edition of the *Contra poetas* of Ermolao the Elder (Florence, 1972). For Ermolao the elder, cf. Degli Agostini, op. cit., i. 229 seq.; for Lodovico Foscarini, ibid., i, 45 seq.

19. See especially Donato's *praefatio* to the translation of Alexander of Aphrodisias' *De Anima* (Brescia, 1495) which has a particularly close relationship to the works of Barbaro cited above and with ep. lxviii.

20. Cf. Ep. c and ci of 1488: and C. Dionisotti, 'Ermolao Barbaro e la fortuna di Suiseth', *Medioevo e Rinascimento. Studi in onore di Bruno Nardi* (Florence, 1955).

21. F. Simone, 'Il contributo degli umanisti veneti al primo sviluppo dell'umanesimo francese', *Umanesimo europeo e umanesimo veneziano*, cit.; *Il Rinascimento francese* (Turin, 1961) 45 seq.; C. Vasoli, *La dialettica e la retorica dell'umanesimo* cit. 183 seq., The quotation is taken from Lefèvre's *Decem librorum moralium Aristotelis tres conversiones* (Paris, 1497) iv, 8. Other opinions to the same effect are in the preface to *Georgii Trapenzotii Dialectica*

(Paris, 1508); still others are cited by Girolamo da Pavia in *Duellum epistolare Galliae et Italiae* ([Venice], 1519) A. iiii[2].

22. *Adagiorum collectanea* (Paris, 1500) f. 8; *Epistolae*, ed. P. S. Allen (Oxford, 1906) i, 127.

23. G. Toffanin, *Storia dell'umanesimo*, cit., ii, 284; A. Campana, 'The origin of the word "humanist" ', *Journal of the Warburg and Courtauld Institutes*, ix (1946).

24. Cf. in general *De legatis et legationibus tractatus varii edidit* V. E. Grabar' (Tartu, 1905); G. Mattingly, *Renaissance diplomacy* (London, 1955), with a rich bibliography; and the reviews of the ed. cit. of the *De coelibatu* and of the *De officio legati* by G. Floriani in *Giornale Storico della Letteratura Italiana*, cli (1969) and by A. Manetti in *La Bibliofilia*, lxxiii (1971). On Tasso, see *Il Messaggiero*, 197–198.

25. This interpretation is now widely accepted and certain recent works have devoted particular attention to it: E. Wind, *Bellini's Feast of the Gods* (Cambridge, Mass., 1948); cf. C. Dionisotti, in *The Arts Bulletin*, xxxii (1950) 237 seq., xxxiii (1951) 70 seq.; A. Pallucchini, in *Arte veneta*, v (1951) 187 seq.; A. Chastel, 'Deux centres artistiques', *Bibliothèque d'Humanisme et Renaissance*, xii (1950); S. Bettini, 'Neoplatonismo fiorentino e averroismo veneto', *Memorie Acc. Patavina Sc., Lett., Arti*, lxviii (1955–56); E. Battisti, *Rinascimento e Barocco* (Turin, 1960) 146 seq.; R. Wittkower, 'L'Arcadia e il giorgionismo' and A. Chastel, 'Art et humanisme au Quattrocento', and G. Pozzi and L. A. Ciapponi, 'La cultura figurativa di F. Colonna e l'arte veneta', *Umanesimo europeo e umanesimo veneziano*, cit.; M. Bonicatti, *Aspetti dell'umanesimo nella pittura veneta dal 1455 al 1515* (Rome, 1964); F. Colonna, *Hypnerotomachia Poliphili*, ed. G. Pozzi and L. A. Ciapponi (Padua: 1964): cf. ii, introduction and commentary; P. Gauricus, *De sculptura*, ed. A. Chastel and R. Klein (Paris, 1969): as a whole, but especially introduction, 15 seq. It is worth noting that Gaurico does not seem to have used the *Castigationes Plinianae*. Cf. also E. H. Gombrich, *Symbolic images* (London, 1972).

26. Besides this letter, *Opera* (Venice, 1729) iv, 189, see the *De Virgili culice et Terentii fabulis liber*; in addition, the philological collaboration between Politian and the young Bembo, specially with regard to Terence should be borne in mind. Cf. in general C. Dionisotti, introduction to P. Bembo, *Prose e rime* (Turin, 1960).

27. C. Dionisotti, *Geografia e storia della letteratura italiana* (Turin, 1967) 71. The whole of the chapter 'Chierici e laici', 47 seq., is relevant here, as it is to what has been said about the circle of Paolo Giustiniani and Vincenzo Querini to which Bembo belonged. Among other insights, he acutely observes that 'Dietro di lui [Pietro Bembo], nella figura stessa del padre, è una tradizione quattrocentesca di alta cultura e insieme di alta responsabilità politica. Cultura e responsabilità laica, s'intende: a Venezia non esiste inframmettenza del clero nella politica dello Stato. Ma anche, dietro di lui c'era stata una frattura singola, ma in realtà decisiva, di quella tradizione ad opera dell'uomo che meglio l'aveva impersonata, Ermolao Barbaro, che a dispetto della Signoria aveva dimesso i panni di ambasciatore e vestito quelli di patriarca di Aquileia ed era perciò morto esule e in disgrazia della patria. Nel Bembo la frattura si ripete, attenuata nella forma ma non meno sostanzialmente netta, come, dopo altro intervallo di tempo, si ripeterà nel Contarini. Sono fratture operate da uomini maturi, non colpi di testa della giovinezza . . . Siamo di fronte non a una somma statistica di avventure individuali eterogenee, ma a una crisi che evidentemente impegna in un dato ambiente una generazione.'

28. It would be superfluous to cite the standard works on Manuzio: as syntheses and for their up-to-date information the two works by Ester Pastorello are extremely useful: *L'Epistolario manutiano. Inventario cronologico-analitico* (Venice, 1957) and *Inedita manutiana* (Venice, 1960). But these indications of Aldus' close relationship with the humanist *ambiente* in Venice are based above all on the rigorous (and vigorous) contribution by C. Dionisotti, 'Aldo Manuzio umanista', *Umanesimo europeo e umanesimo veneziano*, cit. For the Hellenism of Aldus and his Greek collaborators, cf. D. J. Geanakoplos, op. cit., as well, of course, as A. Firmin Didot, *Alde Manuce et l'Hellénisme* (Paris, 1884).

29. For Erasmus's stay in Venice: P. De Nolhac, *Erasme et l'Italie* (Paris, 1898) 26 seq.; A. Renaudet, *Erasme et l'Italie* (Geneva, 1954) 14 seq.; V. Branca, *Ermolao Barbaro in Francia*, cit.; and the previously cited works of Franco Simone.

30. What is suggested in the following paragraphs has been worked out in V. Branca and R. Weiss, 'Carpaccio e l'iconografia del più grande umanista veneziano', *Arte Veneta*, xvii (1963); it has been taken up and developed by a number of art historians, e.g. R. Pallucchini and G. Perocco, *I teleri del Carpaccio* (Milan, 1963); P. Zampetti, *Vittore Carpaccio* (Venice, 1966). See also M. Muraro, 'Vittore Carpaccio o il teatro in pittura', *Studi sul teatro veneto fra Rinascimento ed età barocca* (Florence, 1971).

31. Cf. A. Ferriguto, *Attraverso i misteri del Giorgione* (Castelfranco, 1933) – cf. R. Pallucchini in *Ateneo Veneto* (1934) – and 'Ancora dei soggetti di Giorgione', *Atti R. Ist. Veneto Sc. Lett. Arti*, xcviii and cii (1939 and 1943); R. Wischnitzer-Bernstein, 'The Three Philosophers', *Gazette des Beaux Arts* (1945); L. Baldass, 'Zu Giorgione Drei Philosophen', *Jahrbuch der Kunsthistorischen Sammlungen* (1953); B. Nardi, 'I tre filosofi di Giorgione', *Il Mondo*, 23 Aug. and 13 Sept., 1955; F. Rusk Shapley, 'A note on The Three Philosophers by Giorgione', *The Art Quarterly*, xxii (1959); A. Parronchi, 'Chi sono I tre Filosofi', *Arte Lombarda* (1965); M. Calvesi, 'La "morte di bacio". Saggio sull'ermetismo di Giorgione', *Storia dell'Arte*, 7–8 (1970).

32. See in general the article already cited by S. Bettini: and I. R. Spencer, 'Ut rhetorica pictura. A study in Quattrocento theory of painting', *Journal of the Warburg and Courtauld Institutes*, xx (1957); R. W. Lee, '*Ut pictura poesis'; the humanistic Theory of Painting* (New York, 1967); D. Rosand, 'Ut pictor poeta', *New Literary History*, III (1971–72).

IX

TERISIO PIGNATTI

The relationship between German and Venetian painting in the late quattrocento and early cinquecento

---

INTRODUCTION

There are moments in the history of art when it seems that fate wants to speed matters up, as it were, and sends a genius to contribute personally to the evolution of artistic forms. This could surely apply to the case of Albrecht Dürer with respect to the part he played in the development of art in northern Italy, in particular to the establishment of a highly important relationship between German and Venetian painting in the late *quattrocento* and the early *cinquecento*.

To get a proper grasp of this episode and to evaluate it with care requires the closest attention to be paid not only to its attendant circumstances but to the complex situation obtaining in the German and Venetian cultural worlds which came into contact – without a shadow of doubt profitably – through Dürer. In the first place the limits of the enquiry must be fixed, and none seem better than the time which elapsed between Dürer's first and second journeys to Venice (1494–1507). These are, in fact, the years in which the artistic traditions, completely different but capable of integration, of two of Europe's greatest cities, Nuremberg and Venice, were linked in a mutually advantageous exchange.[1] Then when considering the relationships between artists we must bear in mind the nature of that 'German element' which increasingly appears to have played an important role in the art of the Renaissance in northern Italy. Next the inquiry must throw light on two key aspects of the integration of the two cultures, German and Venetian: the youthful development of Dürer with respect to his contacts with Renaissance Italy, and the influence which he had in his turn on some of the greatest Venetians who were at work in the decade that spanned the two centuries, Giorgione, Lorenzo Lotto and Titian. Finally we should be able to see more clearly into the position of Jacopo de' Barbari who is alternately praised as Dürer's guide to the world of the Renaissance and disparaged as his less interesting fellow explorer or even as a mere dependent.

Just what the 'German element' amounted to has already been a subject of

244

intensive study among scholars in Germany. For Hetzer[2] 'das Deutsche Element' comprised a special response to the individuality of forms, often scattered and selective, which emerges within the traditional realistic vision of nature. Typical elements are the sense of movement in the drawing and its expressive energy, almost always brought to its highest level in the graphic arts. Hetzer points out that in Germany there was not the sort of stylistic continuity that gives the impression of unity to a period, nor a generally shared aesthetic point of view. Instead, the artist clung firmly to his own individuality when confronting the problems inherent in the work and when looking at natural phenomena, and the result is sharply 'anti-Renaissance' with respect to the ideological colour given that term by its use in reference to the art of Italy. This specific character appears most clearly in graphic art, in which the Germans excelled. Thus a print by the Master E. S. will tend to be worked out through highly individualized formal elements, often with the landscape predominating. Thus Schongauer creates a 'space' within his engravings which is not so much a 'form' as a 'motif,' that is, it bears witness to the *reality* of what appears to the eye rather than idealizes plastic or architectonic values in the Italian manner.

For Wölfflin[3] there was no better period in which to study the interplay between German and Italian 'forms' than the one in which Dürer worked. It was without any doubt through him that the encounter with the Italian Renaissance took place in a way that was destined to be immensely stimulating to the artistic conceptions of both schools, through his personality (that extraordinary German who was the first to seek a new world in the home of classicism rather than turning towards the culture of the Netherlands) that the 'German element' was expressed in such a way as to provide a remarkable reaction within Italian culture. And it is certainly not by chance that such a revolutionary process happened in a site open to the most diverse influences, in the meeting place for different civilizations that Venice had become in the late *quattrocento*.

Just how the chief components of that 'element' took hold I would prefer to trace stage by stage when considering the reactions of individual artists. But it might be useful briefly to anticipate the nature of this influence: realism with respect to nature, expressive values imparted to pictorial motifs, a dynamic quality in spatial and plastic relationships. Thus for the first time landscape is experienced as an 'organic' whole (Giorgione, Titian), while the portrait, from a simply psychological or decorative vision (following Pisanello) or analytical and descriptive (the Flemish–Bellinesque tradition), moved towards a realistic immediacy (Giorgione, Lotto and Titian). At the same time the drawing and the engraving diverge from the archaeologically motivated plastic emphasis of Mantegna and his followers down to Giovanni Bellini, towards the tenser and more suggestive mood of Titian's drawings. Finally, the whole aulic tradition of Bellinesque 'harmony' was suddenly charged with dialectical tension, an interdependence of spatial relationships which, with the young Titian's striking and otherwise inexplicable achievement (the frescoes in the *Scuola del Santo* in Padua) became a veritable 'dialogue'.

That the chief consequences of the 'German element' were due to Albrecht Dürer and challenged the artistic culture of Venice during his periods of residence in the city of the lagoon was believed implicitly by all German students, particularly by Tietze, Panofsky and Winkler.[4] And for all of them the Venetian experience was thought to be crucial, especially because it occurred at the most delicate moment in Dürer's development, between the end of the 'Wanderjähre' (1490–94) and his dogged, almost obsessional experiments with the proportions of the human body (1500–1505). But though paying attention to this side of the problem, with regard to which I shall for the most part follow or reconfirm the views expressed in the critical literature, I shall also hope to emphasize his importance among the younger Venetian artistic generation, those youngest fellow painters whose names Dürer never mentioned in the letters which referred to them as possible poisoners, as plagiarists, as jealous or wretched rivals doomed at last to fall silent before his own acknowledged greatness.

Seen from the Venetian side, the artistic problems raised by Dürer's providential visits to Venice acquire a more satisfactorily historical dimension and give body to surmises about the role of the 'German element' of which, as we have seen, he was the foremost agent.

DÜRER'S FIRST RESIDENCE IN VENICE (1494–5)

Few periods in an artist's life are so well documented, historically and pictorially, as are the two sojourns Dürer made in Venice in 1494–5 and 1505–7. From the artist's own pen we have documents, letters, diary entries and projects for paintings while a large body of dated or documented prints, drawings and paintings have survived from the period of these visits.[5]

If it is true that Dürer's first journey coincided with an outbreak of plague (commonly a reason for leaving its urban source and taking to the road for safety's sake), it is just as certain that there was an ideological motive behind Dürer's leaving Nuremberg in the September of 1494, only a few months after his marriage to Agnes Frey. Only an irresistible artistic vocation would have called the young German to Venice, one of the promised lands of Renaissance culture, 'twin city' of wealthy Nuremberg. Indeed, a considerable community of German merchants maintained a 'fondaco' there and played an extremely important part in Venice's economic and financial life; it is enough to mention the presence of the Fugger, the great Augsburg bankers. Moreover it was Venice that Dürer's closest friend, Willibald Pirckheimer, must have got to know well during the time he was studying in Padua (1488–91), before moving on to Pavia (until 1495) and thence home. The Nuremberg humanist's familiarity with Venice comes out clearly in the numerous inquiries which Dürer replied to in ten of his letters addressed to Pirckheimer during his second stay in the city in 1506–7.

Pirckheimer, as a student at Padua between the ages of eighteen and twenty-one, could only be seen as the direct link between Dürer and Italy if there were proof that they had been in touch before Dürer left Nuremberg. But between

1490 and 1494 the painter was also on his travels in Europe, so it is probably safer to think in terms of common points of contact, especially in terms of the members of the humanist, literary and publishing world of Nuremberg who later meant so much to both of them: the latinist Hermann Schedel, the poet Conrad Celtis, the merchant and Maecenas Sebald Schreyer. The latter had a private museum in his house in Nuremberg with two small rooms decorated with classicizing paintings whose subject matter (Apollo, the Muses, the Seven Sages, and portraits) points to an undoubted link with the art of Italy.[6]

But that Dürer was attracted to Italy as to an ideal environment specifically relevant to his art seems clear enough, especially if we take into account a certain unexpected thematic and formal shift in his work, fortunately copiously recorded and dated in his graphic work. That an artist with Dürer's temperament could suddenly change his style so profoundly implies that technical and formal change was accompanied by a deep inner conflict which clearly arose from the coming to maturity of an eager – one could almost say fated – desire to see Renaissance Italy face to face.

References to Latin and Greek literature, philosophical arguments, descriptions of paintings in Tuscany and in Padua and Venice, studies in the nature of the ancient world as recorded in its sculpture or revived in the study of human proportion, brought back into fashion by the four books of Vitruvius: these are certainly some of the many factors that affected Dürer's decision to turn to Italy, and it is curious that he must have grasped all of them through Padua and Venice, that is, through Mantegna and Bellini.

Dürer's style in 1493 can be clearly identified in terms of the portrait, landscape and the human figure. Let us look first at the *Self-Portrait with a Fleabane Flower* (in the Louvre). Though of undeniable expressive power, we are confronted with a 'variation on a theme', the theme of the traditional Flemish school of portraiture, which the artist could easily have seen on travels which had perhaps taken him as far north as to put him in direct contact with the work of Van Eyck, Van der Weyden and Bouts. The dark background from which the figure emerges in its strongly descriptive reality, the light which determines the modelling of details and concentrates attention on the expressive face and the lean hands while it glances rapidly over the changing greens of the coat, following the fluid brushwork of the carmine trim: they are all familiar recurring features in the main current of the northern tradition that had been the chief influence on German art in the mid-*quattrocento*.

It is enough to turn to the second self-portrait of 1498 (in the Prado) to gain a full understanding of the overwhelming effect of the Italian experience. It is no accident that the costume is now Venetian; the landscape, too, has an Italian feeling, recasting a record made during the journey of 1494–5 of lake Saint Christopher near Trent[7] but in softened forms which shade in clear blues away into the distance as in certain of Bellini's Madonnas – and one thinks of the Morelli Madonna in Bergamo, or the *Madonna of the Red Cherubim* in the Accademia in Venice. But what above all reveals the transformation in the artist is the unity in the rendering of space and light between the figure in the foreground and the distant view: one of those formal ideas alien to the German tradition but fundamental to the Italian approach from Piero della Francesca on, and firmly rooted in the Venetian school.

But where the contact between Dürer and the Veneto can be seen most openly is in his adherence to the conventions of Renaissance Padua as handled, for instance, by Mantegna. It is Panofsky who has thrown most light on this moment in Dürer's career and there is nothing to be gained by repeating the now classic comparison between Mantegna's prints, the *Bacchanal* and the *Sea Gods*, and the corresponding versions Dürer made of them in 1494 (Vienna, Albertina) (Plates 1, 2).[8] These drawings were probably done in Italy, and it is obvious that the German painter found in the Paduan prints the atmosphere of erudition and the classicism with which the traffic of ideas in Nuremberg had probably already familiarized him. Apart from the possibility of having met Pirckheimer, Dürer was certainly not unaware of the interests of his printer Schedel, who owned a 'book of antiquities' drawn by a pupil of Wolgemut (Dürer's own master from 1486–9); and it was Wolgemut who prepared a new edition of Petrarch's *Triumphs* and one of the Ferranese *Tarocchi* cards, some of which were copied by Dürer himself. And a similar interest prompted Dürer to copy Pollaiolo's famous engraving of nudes in his drawing of the *Rape of the Sabines* (1495, now at Bayonne).[9]

Dürer's copies are by no means slavish imitations, but that, surely, gives them their chief significance, for it confirms his long matured decision to enter the world of Renaissance Italy on his own terms. It is above all the drawing, the quality of the incisive and nervous line, the expressive force of the hatching which models the forms, that reveal Dürer's temperament though without sacrificing its specifically German character. We need only look closely at, for example, certain 'constructional' details inherent in Dürer's approach which can be seen in the nude female figure on the left of the Tritons to be convinced of his absolute stylistic independence and maturity when facing the Paduan model. Where the hatching in the Mantegna engraving has an abstract quality of 'chiaroscuro', with lines running rigidly parallel to one another, Dürer catches the actual nature of the surfaces because his hatching *models* the curves with subtle and persuasive realism. It is a fundamental difference, an ineradicable signature which draws on the whole German cultural tradition and makes his adoption of the new Renaissance formula – the monumental and geometrical proportion of the human body which he began to study with such determination – livelier, more deeply felt and thus more productive. But I shall return to this point later on.

Meanwhile, it would be worth noting other connections, hitherto apparently unnoticed, between Mantegnesque models and certain works by Dürer, interesting because they record an infection of motifs in independent works rather than in copies. This can be seen in the drawing in Hamburg of *The Death of Orpheus* (1494) where there can be no doubt that the figures of the scourging women, and their relationship to the unfortunate Orpheus at the composition's centre, derive from Mantegna's engraved *Flagellation* (H.8) (Plates 3, 4). It is not without interest, moreover, that on his first visit Dürer also turned to some of Mantegna's copyists, such as Giovanni da Brescia. There is a drawing of *Dancing Putti* in a private collection[10] which could almost be a copy of a print of the same subject by the Brescian engraver. And it is no accident that he later turned out to be one of the most assiduous forgers of Dürer's own prints.

Many other characteristic proofs of 'Italian influence' that Panofsky found for the years 1494–5, were drawings of marine animals (the *Crab* in Rotterdam, the *Lobster* in Berlin) certainly unique at the time for a striking truth to nature otherwise only reflected in the scientific spirit of a Leonardo. Again, in the ample range of watercolour landscapes that illustrate his journey across the valleys of the Adige and the Tyrol and back (Albertina, British Museum – formerly in Bremen), it is more than tempting to detect a pictorial approach which has become less Netherlandish than Italian, both in the use of perspective and the very lively feeling for colour. A similar note of truth to a colourful nature inspires the drawings of costume which come from the Venetian period, the *Woman* (1495) in the Albertina, for instance, or the *Circassian Girl* in Basel or the *Women of Venice and Nuremberg* in Frankfurt.

As I have said, however, contact between the cultures of Germany and Venice becomes closest and most creative in the treatment of the human figure. As Dürer was later to write in the introduction to the second book of his treatise *On Human Proportion*, when he was young and had no acquaintance with such a subject, the Venetian painter Jacopo De' Barbari 'showed me the figures of a man and a woman, which he had drawn according to a canon of proportions'. But as 'this Jacopo would not explain the principles upon which he went, he, having understood nothing of Jacopo's ideas, had begun to investigate the problem for himself, finding some guidance about the human figure from Vitruvius'. That is Dürer's explicit statement, and there is no reason to doubt it.[11] All the same, given that Dürer, writing in 1523, could refer to something that had happened either in 1494–5 or 1500–4 as having happened 'when I was young', the actual moment this refers to is uncertain; the reference to De' Barbari would fit either case. He could, indeed, have been in Nuremberg before Dürer left in 1494; he was certainly there after 1500 when he had come to the end of his labour on the *Plan of Venice*. It is not by chance that the first true study in human proportions – the famous *Nude Woman* with geometrical measurements in the British Museum – is dated 1500 (Plate 5).[12] But it might be felt that so late a development of an interest in the nude conflicts with the drawings from Mantegna's engravings of 1494 which already show his interest in the Renaissance problem of the human figure.

The solution to the problem probably lies in a clear understanding of what Dürer's nudes ('näckete Bilder') really meant to him. On the one hand there is his realistic conception of the nude and the special sensitivity which enabled him to approach its intrinsic beauty in this way (there is at least a trace here, however faint, of a classical taste, perhaps derived only from contacts with Nuremberg humanist circles). On the other are the problems and the aesthetic theory relating to the concordance of relationships between the parts of the human body with which he so insistently concerned himself in his search for ideal measurements. And here it is interesting to note that it was the most profound elements in the artist's consciousness, the German spirit, which triumphed in the end. After having studied the nude as an ideal example of harmonious proportion, in fact, he came gradually to grasp an increasing individuality even within a theoretical approach. So at the last, for the attempt to reduce the problem to a theoretical unity, Dürer substituted his notion of 'differential anthropometry' which became ever nearer to corresponding with the inexhaustible variety of nature.[13]

THE PROBLEM OF JACOPO DE' BARBARI

I confess that it still remains difficult to place the obviously important figure of De' Barbari in his correct place on this chess-board without some hesitation, even while accepting that it seems probable that his relationship with Dürer anticipated his first visit to Venice, if it had not begun before 1490.[14] However, from all Dürer's references to the personality of De' Barbari there is no doubt that an artistic relationship had been established between them at least from 1500 when the Venetian finally emigrated to Germany and Dürer was actively engaged on the problems of human proportion and producing numerous dated drawings. There remains, however, the unconvincing suggestion that the *Man and Wife* which so much impressed Dürer was somewhat akin to the nudes which figured in such engravings by De' Barbari as the *Victory and Fame*, *Mars and Venus* and in at least one drawing, his *Cleopatra*. Thus it it extremely difficult to know whether engravings by De' Barbari were or were not among the factors which turned Dürer towards the study of human proportions.

I do not believe that the Dürer–De' Barbari problem can be resolved, as has been attempted hitherto, simply by establishing the chronological relationship between De' Barbari's engravings and Dürer's works – mostly graphic – which seem to relate to them. Even if we could establish that with absolute certainty (and this is far from being the case) the fundamental problem would still remain: that is, when he did reflect certain of De' Barbari's nudes, did Dürer actually *intend* to give a Renaissance turn to his own ideas about the canon of proportions, or was he attracted simply by a casual interest in or sympathy for them or even, quite on the contrary, was he drawn to them because he saw them as being *more German* than the sculptural figures of Mantegna, or than the reliefs and classical statues which were then becoming more accessible in Venice through the collection which the Grimani were probably beginning to assemble.[15]

On the question of dating the thirty engravings by De' Barbari, scholars have come to widely differing conclusions, partly because it is closely wrapped up with their ideas about the importance of Jacopo's 'message' to Dürer. For

Kristeller,[16] who sees Jacopo as pioneering the northern Renaissance, the engravings are substantially divided into two groups, one typically Italian characterized by a heavily accented and clear-cut technique, strong in contrasts and of Mantegnesque inspiration. This would correspond to an earlier period in Jacopo's development in the Veneto before his meeting with Dürer, which is put towards 1495. In the earlier group Kristeller places the following engravings: the *Holy Family*, the *Madonna*, the great *Priapus*, the *Victory* and the *Victory and Fame*. These are judged to be 'early' because of the 'weaker and more faulty drawing' and the technique with its 'long oblique hatchings . . . with sharp contrasts of light and shadow' as well as the survival of a Schongauer-like refinement, the reflection of his contacts with the German scene.

To a second group would belong – still following Kristeller – the technically more accomplished engravings 'with finer, closer, more rounded hatching and cross-hatching' that shows 'much in common' with the young Lucas van Leyden. To this second group, which starts from 1509, the *Cleopatra* and the *Mars and Venus* would belong.

Panofsky, on the other hand, comes to the opposite view, in general seeing Dürer as following Jacopo in many of the themes that occur in his engravings between 1497 and 1504. His brilliant analysis of the *Apollo and Diana* (British Museum) is well known. Dürer had at first derived his Apollo from the famous statue in the garden of the Belvedere; later, having come upon De' Barbari's engraving of Apollo he altered the original design, changing the inscription SOL to APOLO, extending the luminous aureola and inserting the figure of Diana into the right-hand corner on the model of De' Barbari's work. The transformation from the copy from the antique (the Belvedere statue) to the imposing figure of Apollo thus would become a stage in the way to the 1504 engraving of Adam and Eve. It can be seen that this implies a date of at least some time before 1500 for De' Barbari's engraving.[17]

Again, Panofsky assigns earlier dates than does Kristeller to two more of De' Barbari's engravings, the *Victory and Fame*, which he sees as anticipating the drawing of nudes (dated 1505) in the Louvre and the *Adam and Eve* in the École des Beaux Arts in Paris and as an influence on the *Four Witches* of 1497; also *Mars and Venus*, which he suggests as the model for Dürer's *The Dream of the Doctor* (1497–8). We shall see later on how far these examples of precedence can be confirmed on iconographic and stylistic grounds.

Hind, too,[18] tends to see the influence of De' Barbari on many of Dürer's compositions, and placing their meeting in 1495, claims, though with all tentativeness (and also because the watermarks of the paper he used are almost all northern) that his greatest engravings can be assigned to his Venetian period, that is, 1495–1500.

There are, besides, yet other opinions which oppose interpretations such as these, which are substantially favourable to De' Barbari; opinions which run from Justi to Rosenberg[19] and which strictly limit Venetian influence on Dürer to his brush sketches of 1505–7.

To me, Kristeller's thesis, supported up to a point by a number of scholars, must be subjected to a very precise control. It does not seem in any way demonstrable that there are engravings by De' Barbari – such as those the German scholar puts in the 'second period' – which are indisputably late 'because they reveal analogies of form and technique' with the work of Lucas van Leyden. It is true that certain engravings with nudes by the talented and precocious Netherlands engraver can be dated around 1508, such as his *Adam and Eve*, but on seeing them in the overall context of his work it is clear that they have more in common with traditional German sources, like Schongauer, than with De' Barbari, and above all that their closest link is with Dürer, seen in terms of the strong descriptive temperament which bound him to Flemish realism. If there is a point of contact between De' Barbari and Lucas it is then to be looked for not in terms of any actual meeting so much as in their common debt to Schongauer, with his delicate, sinuous technique which models the shadows almost like a subtle spider's web of lines.

With the reference to Lucas firmly out of the way on account of its manifest absurdity, we should return to a few facts already recorded which concern De' Barbari's graphic work. Hind tells us that there are only three objective lines of evidence for a possible dating of the engravings.[20] The first is the chiefly northern provenances of the paper, which would place the pulling of the sheets (not necessarily the working of the plates) either before or after his period of residence in Venice – which can only be fixed with any certainty to the three years 1498–1500 when he was working on the plan of Venice. This leaves the whole question open and we must look to the second and third arguments: the date 1501 contained in an old inscription on the page of the great *Priapus* (H 23) in the Dresden *Kupferstichkabinett* and the insertion in a Schedel manuscript in the library of Munich, which was bound in 1504, of copies of the *Judith* (H 7), *St. Catherine* (H 8), *Mother and Child* (H 16), *Man with a Cradle* (H 17) and *Vanity* (H 18).

From all this the *terminus ante quem* which emerges serves only to establish that engravings in the style of the *Priapus* (clear and emphatic hatching, the lines mostly parallel, with a markedly abstract quality in the modelling and with distinct 'Paduan' reminiscences in the play of light over the anatomy) are earlier than 1501 (Plate 6). A conclusion which has been discounted, all the same, by almost all scholars.

Where I cannot fully agree, however, is in the assessment of the other group of engravings which, generally speaking, are identified on account of their dissimilarity to the *Priapus* group, engravings, that is, in which the hatching is more intricate, clinging to the modelling of the anatomy with a clearly realistic intention, sometimes subtly painterly with the 'cobweb' of lines obviously linked with Schongauer. Clearly, if together with *Priapus* we put in the first group the *Madonna* (H 2), the *Adoration of the Magi* (H 1), the *Guardian Angel* (H 12), the *Holy Family* (H 3 and 5), the *Apollo* (H 14) and the *Victory* (H 22) then around the *Mars and Venus* (H 13) must be grouped the *Victory and Fame* (H 26), the *Triton and Nereid* (H 22) and the *Cleopatra* (H 27). Now there is no doubt in my mind that in contrast to the former group, strongly oriented towards Mantegna and the Vivarini, the latter group is chiefly influenced by a number of 'Germanic' elements.

It is worth pursuing this point. Take for example the modelling of the nude in the engraving of *Mars and Venus* (Plate 7); it is achieved through an extremely delicate use (almost a web) of curving strokes, handled with unusual realism, following projections in the flesh with a curvilinear effect or deepening the shadows in the folds of the body with multiple cross-hatchings (Plate 8). If we take one of the few Schongauer engravings where we can study the nude (other than the *Crucifixion*) say, for example, the *Foolish Virgin* (B 87), here is the identical manner of modelling in the spider's web manner we have identified in the engravings of De' Barbari. To turn now to the *Victory and Fame*: here too the chief influence in the modelling of the anatomy is undeniably Schongauer's,[21] but it is even more noticeable in the 'rent' effect of the clothing or in *Fame's* great feathered wings, which are portrayed so realistically (Plates 9, 10). But it is also undeniable that there are also links with Dürer's engravings: the rumpled drapery is that of his *The Dream of the Doctor*, the *Fame* has the pose of the doctor's temptress (Plate 11), the *contrapposto* of the two figures is echoed in Dürer's drawing of *Adam and Eve* in the École des Beaux-Arts (Plate 12) and there is a further parallel between the two figures seen from the rear, the *Victory* and the *Eve*.

The so-called 'late' group shows the influence, then, above all of the pictorial language of Germany through Schongauer and a subsequent interest in Dürer, while the *Priapus* group looks to Mantegna and to Venice.

I would therefore propose a complete reversal of the dating (bringing forward the *Mars and Venus* group), running from the period of the hypothetical residence in Nuremberg to that of Dürer's first residence in Venice (1490–95). After that, De' Barbari did the engravings of the *Priapus* and the *Holy Family* groups, together with the 'Vivarinesque' paintings in Berlin and the Louvre, while he was in Venice, that is, between at least the years 1498 and 1500 (Plates 13, 14). In this way the few certain dates we have are included (as well as the not un-important chronological evidence of the northern papermarks) and the chrono-logy of the whole range of De' Barbari's prints takes a form which allows for most of Hind's and Panofsky's observations on the iconographic links with Dürer's graphic work.

This clears the way for a straightforward conclusion. Just as when he had been copying Mantegna's prints or Pollaiolo's drawings, when considering the suggestions offered by De' Barbari's works, Dürer critically selected the aspects which could be incorporated into his traditional vision, rather than those which would constitute the elements in the restructuring, as it were, of his own artistic personality on 'Renaissance' lines. That is the significance of the undoubted relationship between the *Mars and Venus* and *The Dream of the Doctor*, where the monumentality of Venus is certainly no less important than the figure's obvious expressive quality, with its almost anguished luminous passages, its nervous hints of northern witchcraft. And the same sort of adaptation is shown, as the soft gelatinous carnality of De' Barbari's *Victory and Fame* passed readily – if it was indeed the model – into the quivering sensuality of the line employed in the drawing of Adam and Eve. Nor should we forget with this masterpiece of Dürer's we come within the mood of the *Bathing Women* drawing in Bremen (1496) that was to end in the brutally marked realism of the *Four Witches* (Plates 15, 16). As yet there is no hint of any preoccupation with the canon of human proportions; on the contrary, we are still mired in the nerve-racked German preoccupation with the flesh: frustration, self-indulgence, bitter realism. And we recall that writing in 1523 the painter was to note that when he was working on the proportional drawing *Man and Woman* it was as foreign to him 'as if someone were telling him of another world'. Basically, the Dürer of the *Bathing Women* or the *Adam and Eve* had only made a tentative advance on the mood in which – in the Bayonne *Eve* (1493) and the Louvre *Nude* (1495) – he reacted to the female body in terms of a specific erotic perturbation, emphasizing the evocative shadows and modelling the forms with a constant sensual excitement, a mood which stressed the disturbing passage of time rather than the 'proportional harmony' of the human figure which had apparently not yet begun to concern him (Plate 17).

THE PROBLEM OF HUMAN PROPORTION (1500–1504)

One of the first drawings to observe the Vitruvian canon, measured off metrically in the form of a circle, is the one in the British Museum, containing a *Nude Woman* dated 1500 (Plate 5); the drawing of *Apollo and Diana*, also in the British Museum, is probably slightly later (Plate 18); the *Adam and Eve* in the Morgan Library, New York, dates from some time in 1504. These seem to define the period in which Dürer worked out the basic principles underlying the theorectical and formal problem presented by the human figure, but never without moments of uncertainty in which he reached back into the security of the German tradition. We need look at only three examples, chosen from among the artist's graphic masterpieces. In the *Sea Monster* (c. 1498) Dürer in all probability borrowed the female figure from Mantegna or from De' Barbari's *Victory*; in the *Hercules* he took the reclining figure and the scourging figures from Mantegna and the *Hercules* perhaps from Pollaiolo; in *The Large Fortune* (c. 1501-2) he plotted the massive figure of the flying Nemesis according to the 'canon of proportions' (the fat and the thin woman) in drawing no. 145 in the Dresden sketchbook (Plates 20-23).[22] But in all three prints he moves from his model to a pronouncedly realistic mood, at times sensual, at times brutally true to life, but never abstractly antiquarian, as De' Barbari became in the *Priapus* and similar prints. And it is enough to add the landscape passages, the foreshortened cliffs in the *Sea Monster*, the aerial view of Klausen in *The Large Fortune*, for us to be transported to the typical Nuremberg vein of views taken directly from nature from which emerged the first city views like the *Venice* of

Reuwich (1488) and Wolgemut (1493) and De' Barbari's *Plan of Venice* itself in 1500.

Between the *Nude* of 1500 and the *Adam and Eve* engraving lay only four years, but they are essential ones in the history of Dürer's development as far as the problem of human proportion is concerned, and thus his relationship to the Italian Renaissance. The Morgan Library drawing of *Adam and Eve* clearly shows how Dürer was adding a continuation of the impulse expressed in the British Museum *Apollo-Sol* (perhaps inspired in its turn by De' Barbari's *Apollo and Diana*) to his treatment of the male figures.[23] Just as Dürer extracted the maximum monumentality from the classical model of the Belvedere, with his *Eve* he restores to us a female form infinitely more stable and balanced than her predecessors in, for example, *The Dream of the Doctor*. However, the most important point is, I think, that in the drawing and above all in the engraving of 1504 the hatching becomes much less realistic, preparing for a novel engraving technique, that is, a somewhat more 'abstract' manner of giving the shadows than that used in the past, rendering the modelling by means of two absolutely concentric and equidistant systems of curves, which intersect like the meridians and parallels of a map. The effect was, in fact, to provide a 'finer grade of net, so to speak, to dissolve some of the lines into stipples, and to add a third series of curves which divide the spherical rhomboids into spherical triangles'.[24]

By 1504, then, Dürer seems to have brought his investigations into the theory of human proportion to maturity through a thoroughly deliberate acceptance of the canons worked out in Renaissance Italy, and this is especially evident in the sculptural and solid nature of his figures, released from their individuality and fleshliness as if under the influence of some charm.

But how long did this 'neo-Renaissance' state of grace last? The question is particularly apt when we confront his bulky but often apparently contradictory output for the decade 1495–1505, a period of amazing activity which added to the list of his graphic works such masterpieces as the *Apocalypse* series and those of the *Large Passion* and the *Life of Mary* together with pictures like the Pollaiolo-esque *Hercules* in Nuremberg (1500), the Bellinesque *Haller Madonna*,[25] now in Washington, the expressive *Portrait of Oswolt Krel* and the *Self-Portrait* (Munich, Alte Pinakothek) which seems to evoke certain Flemish figures of Christ in the light of a Leonardo-like power of suggestion. In 1504 Dürer seems to reach the highest point of his adherence to Renaissance norms with his *Adam and Eve* engraving. Yet at the same time he was painting the radically contrasting *Paumgärtner Altarpiece* in Munich, whose little clumps of donors in the central panel recall the most typical of mid-fifteenth century German paintings, and whose looming side panels present colossal standard bearers posed on the same diagonal in a quite 'placeless' space, unstable, nervously rhythmic and conveying a markedly 'Gothic' flavour with their shining armour, their flapping flags, their incisive portraits. In general terms it can be said that after the enthusiasm for things Italian that came with the first visit to Venice and the recementing of his friendship with Pirckheimer in the years around 1500, Dürer returned into the fold of the Germanic tradition to a noticeable extent.

All the same, on a new outbreak of plague occurring in Nuremberg in the autumn of 1505, we see him setting out once more for the south, his goal, naturally enough, being Venice. And it is appropriate to pause for a while to estimate the significance of this second visit and some of its chief episodes in order to see how far his return to Italy coincided with a revival of his interest in the Renaissance and, at the same time, to show how Dürer in his full maturity rather than entering the Venetian artistic circle largely as a learner, became in certain novel and highly intriguing ways one of its leaders.

The Second Visit to Venice (1505–1507)

When Dürer arrived in Venice, in all likelihood towards the end of 1505, and settled into the inn run by Peter Pander near the Fondaco dei Tedeschi he was a very different person from the young man who had come to the city of the lagoon eleven years earlier. This time he was preceded by a highly distinguished reputation, based above all on the diffusion of his prints. In addition he came under the happy auspices of a commission for the 'Rosenkranzfest' in the church of S. Bartolomeo, the *Feast of the Rose Garlands*, which had probably already been negotiated in Augsburg with influential members of the German merchant community in Venice (Plate 24).

We are fortunate in having what almost amounts to a diary in the form of ten letters to Pirckheimer written between 1506 and 1507; seven are now preserved in the Nuremberg library, one is in the British Museum, one in the possession of the Royal Society and the last formerly belonged to the antique dealer Heberle in Cologne. 'Here I am a gentleman, while at home I'm considered a parasite', Dürer declared, proudly assuming the role assigned to the artist in Renaissance Italy.[26] Even though settling down at once to preparing the panel for the *Rose Garlands* altarpiece he missed no opportunity of taking a part in Venetian life; like a veritable gentleman he mingled with men of letters, musicians, connoisseurs and aristocrats.[27] In these same years, and perhaps within the same intellectual circle, another artistic genius was at work: Giorgione. Many Venetian artists, however, showed their disdain for Dürer – not that this prevented them from copying his work – insinuating that he deserved little praise, because he lacked a true feeling for the 'antico'. A friend even warned him against eating and drinking in their company. Among all the painters in Venice he speaks of only one in terms of admiration and respect, Giovanni Bellini, who sought him out in his studio, praised his works and even went so far as to ask him for one. There is no doubt that he no longer derived any satisfaction from what had given him such pleasure eleven years before. There were now many painters of greater merit than Jacopo De' Barbari, who was in any case looked down on: it was said that if he had been a better artist he would

A. Naval Battle of Zonchio. Water-coloured woodcut, British Museum

1. MANTEGNA, Battle of Sea Gods (detail).
Engraving

2. DÜRER, Battle of Sea Gods (detail), 1494.
Vienna, Albertina. Drawing

3. DÜRER, The Death of Orpheus, 1494.
Hamburg, Kunsthalle. Drawing

4. After MANTEGNA, The Flagellation.
Engraving

5. DÜRER, Nude Woman, 1500. London, British Museum. Drawing

6. DE' BARBARI, the large Priapus.
Engraving

7. DE' BARBARI, Mars and Venus. Engraving

8. DE' BARBARI, Mars and Venus (detail). Engraving

9. SCHONGAUER, The Foolish Virgin. Engraving

10. DE' BARBARI, Victory and Fame. Engraving

11. DÜRER, The 'Dream of the Doctor',
Engraving

12. DÜRER, Adam and Eve. Paris, Ecole des
Beaux-Arts (Masson coll.). Drawing

15. DÜRER, Bathing Women, 1496. Bremen, Kunsthalle. Drawing

13. (*above left*) DE' BARBARI, The Holy Family. Engraving

14. (*below left*) DE' BARBARI, The Holy Family and Donor. Berlin-Dahlem, Staatliche Museen

16. DÜRER, The Four Witches, 1497.
Engraving

17. DÜRER, Nude Girl, 1493. Bayonne, Musée Bonnat.
Drawing

18. DÜRER, Apollo and Diana. London,
British Museum. Drawing

19. DE' BARBARI, Apollo and Diana. Engraving

20. DÜRER, Adam and Eve, 1504. Engraving

21. DÜRER, The 'Hercules'. Engraving

22. DÜRER, The Sea Monster.
Engraving

23. DÜRER, The 'large Fortune'. Engraving

24. (*above right*) DÜRER, The Feast of the Rose
Garlands, 1506. Prague, Narodni Galerie

25. (*below right*) GIOVANNI BELLINI, The
Madonna of the Doge Barbarigo, 1488.
Venice, St. Pietro Martire, Murano

26. DÜRER, Head of an Angel, 1506. Bremen, Kunsthalle. Drawing

27. CARPACCIO, Head of a
Martyr. Donnington
Priory, Gathorne Hardy
collection. Drawing

28. DÜRER, Head of the
Pope, 1506. Berlin-
Dahlem, Staatliche
Museen Kupferstich-
kabinett

29. GIORGIONE, Judith.
Leningrad, Hermitage

30. After GIORGIONE, Nude Woman, 1508. Etching

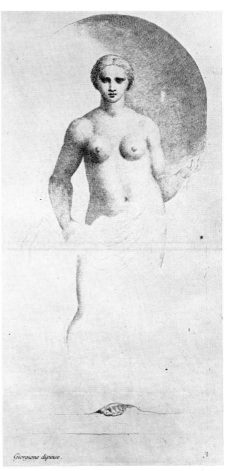

31. DÜRER, Nude Woman, 1506. Berlin-
Dahlem, Staatliche Museen
Kupferstichkabinett

32. GIORGIONE, Nude Woman (detail). Castelfranco Veneto, Casa Pellizzari Fresco.

33. GIORGIONE, Trial of Moses (detail). Florence, Uffizi

34. DÜRER, The Feast of the Rose Garlands (detail). Prague, Narodni Galerie

35. LOTTO, St. Jerome, 1506.
Paris, Louvre

36. DÜRER, St. Jerome. Engraving

37. LOTTO, Portrait of Bishop De Rossi.
Naples, Capodimonte

38. DÜRER, Portrait of a Young Woman.
Berlin-Dahlem, Staatliche Museen

39. LOTTO, Portrait of a Young Man.
Bergamo, Accademia Carrara

40. DÜRER, Head of a Girl.
Vienna, Albertina. Drawing

43. DÜRER, Eve, 1507. Madrid, Prado   44. RIZZO, Eve. Venice, Ducal Palace

41. (*above left*) LOTTO, Madonna with Saints, 1508. Rome, Borghese Gallery

42. (*below left*) DÜRER, Christ among the Doctors, 1506. Castagnola, Thyssen Collection

45. PALMA VECCHIO, Adam and Eve.
Brunswick, Herzog Anton Ulrich-Museen

46. DÜRER, Adam and Eve, 1510.
Vienna, Albertina. Drawing

47. TITIAN, Two Youths in a Landscape. Vienna,
Albertina. Drawing

48. DÜRER, The Rape of Europa (detail). Vienna, Albertina. Drawing

choſes en tous. j. Cor, xij,

Quant leaue deſtruyſoit la terre, la ſapien ce lea de rechief guerie, gouuernant le luſte par vng bois contemptible. Sap. x.

Venez, montons à la montaigne du Seigneur, & à la maiſon du Dieu de Iacob: & il nous enſeignera ſes voyes, & chemineron en ſes ſentiers. Venez, cheminõs en la lumiere de noſtre Dieu. Eſaie. ij, & Michee. iiij

Ceſte + eſt la voye, cheminez en icelle: & ne declinez ne à la dextre, ne à la ſeneſtre Eſa. xxx.

Abel, Adam, Eua

Toy, par le ſang de ton teſtament, as mene hors tes priſonniers de la foſſe ou il ny a point de eaue Zacharie. ix.

49. TITIAN, The Triumph of Faith (detail). Woodcut

50. DÜRER, The Bath House (detail).
Woodcut

51. TITIAN, The Miracle of the
New-born Child (detail).
Padua, Scuola del Santo.
Fresco

52. TITIAN, Portrait of 'Ariosto'. London, National Gallery

not have left Venice for Germany. Meanwhile Dürer began the sketches for the altarpiece.[28]

In spite of the formal commission from the Fondaco the Venetian painters continued their harassment. Many even pursued him home, forcing him to lock himself in.[29] Others denounced him to the *Collegio dei pittori* and got him fined by its magistrates for practising his art in Venice though a foreigner. But if he had not been occupied with the altarpiece he would have been loaded with commissions, for on all sides – except from that of the painters – he was welcomed and held in esteem.[30]

At last, in September, the altarpiece was finished. In addition to a self-portrait it bore his signature and the proud inscription 'Exegit quinquemestri spatio Albertus Durer Germanicus MDVI'. The doge and the patriarch came to see it and praised it highly. Such colours had never been seen in Venice; now he had stopped the mouths of those who had been saying that he was no painter but only a good engraver.[31]

In the wake of the altarpiece's success he painted another picture and some portraits; after his decision to return home he was forced to turn down commissions that would have brought him at least another two thousand ducats.[32] But first he went to Bologna for eight or ten days to learn something about perspective from the masters there. Meanwhile, the doge himself wanted him to stay in Venice and offered him a stipend of two hundred ducats a year. And yet he had to leave. How he would feel the cold on his return to the north![33]

Thanks to a final inscription, 'bought in 1507 in Venice', in a copy of Euclid's *Geometry* we know that his visit was in fact extended for a few more months.[34] Then, in February 1507, Dürer was back in Nuremberg.

It should be easier critically to evaluate Dürer's second residence than his first, above all thanks to the numerous and reliable data contained in his letters. Two remarkable features emerge with respect to the Venetian community of painters: on the one hand Dürer's devotion to Bellini, on the other the almost frenetic interest shown by Venetian artists who ended up by getting acutely on his nerves and who copied him without restraint. On this occasion Dürer was apparently not concerned with theories of the ideal; he openly made fun not only of De' Barbari but of those probably Mantegnesque works which had so enthused him eleven years previously.[35] On the contrary, all his admiration was now centred on Bellini whom he referred to in his letters as the greatest artist working in Venice. We shall soon see the effect of this change. Meanwhile, prepared by a closer acquaintance with German culture, especially through familiarity with prints, the most advanced Venetian milieu (the generation, that is, of Giorgione, Titian and Lorenzo Lotto) welcomed the new ideas transmitted by the great German painter.

But let us look at the composition of the 'Rosenkranzfest'. While keeping the figures down to 'half life-size' as was his custom the work (162 × 194.5 cm) differs in important respects from the Jabach and Paumgärtner altarpieces which had recently preceded it. These had kept to the polyptich form, with a central panel flanked by wings portraying saints and donors. In Venice, however, Dürer clearly saw himself as working within the Italian Renaissance tradition of respecting the principle of unity of space within a work of art. And in the second place, the space is clearly imagined from a frontal point of view, focusing vision on the figure of the Madonna, raised for the first time on a throne and forming an almost perfect pyramidal scheme in conjunction with the two kneeling figures in front of her. The traditional concept of pictorial space as being realized in terms of diagonal lines is thus contradicted in the interest of obtaining an enhanced animation and narrative effect. If the old formula is followed at all it is in the two sides of the painting, crowded with donors' portraits; these are arranged in receding tiers, in a way which draws on the greater credibility and realism so characteristic of the German style.

What Venetian elements affected Dürer in the meticulous planning that went into the composition of the 'Rosenkranzfest'? It would appear that they can be singled out from a number of Bellini's works.[36] Above all, the idea of the frontal composition worked out in terms of the pyramid comes from the great canvas of St. Peter Martyr in Murano, the 'Pala del doge Barbarigo' of 1488 (Plate 25). It is striking that though Dürer could have seen it during his first visit, he only made use of it now, but this confirms *in toto* his own words ('what pleased me eleven years ago no longer satisfies me') and fits the reconstruction I have attempted of his development as an artist, placing the peak of his 'neo-Renaissance' interest as late as 1504. As in the 'Pala Barbarigo' the Madonna sits on a throne which is raised from the ground on some sort of pedestal and she is cut off from the landscape by an awning. It is not surprising that landscape plays a far larger part in Dürer's work, occupying some four-fifths of the painting in contrast to the two-fifths left free in the Bellini. The Dürer, besides, lacks the architectural elements Bellini puts in to help locate his figures, the squared paving, the marble steps, the balustrade, the pole from which the awning is hung. Here again the German prefers natural features; two massive trees frame the scene (and it will be noted that Dürer, with a somewhat theatrical effect, has deliberately placed his self-portrait against one of them) while the awning and the magnificent crown are held aloft by cherubim who seem to have emerged from some 'Schnitzaltar' by Tilman Riemenschneider.

Yet for all the divergencies which at many points reveal a substantial difference in artistic *credo*, the debt to Bellini is beyond dispute and is deeply significant. It extends to individual features; the doge Barbarigo, for instance, is the exact prototype of Pope Julius II, who kneels on the left wrapped in a voluminous cope, nor is there any doubt that the angel playing the lute looks like a version of the violin-playing angel of the S. Zaccaria altarpiece.[37] It is curious that Dürer took so little from this masterpiece of Bellini's which was finished in the same year, 1505, but turned instead to the work of 1488. Yet bearing in mind how close the S. Zaccaria painting is to Giorgione in the melody it seems to carry and the extraordinary mote-haunted nature of the way the colour is applied, it is clear that Dürer chose to model himself on the 'Pala Barbarigo' because it represented a more 'solid' Bellini, a strongly graphic approach to painting which someone like Dürer would turn to most naturally.

For evidence of this taste for solid construction which always underlay Dürer's vision, we have but to turn to the numerous preparatory drawings for the 'Rosenkranzfest'. Take for instance the 'Angel's Head' in the Bremen museum, a pen drawing heightened with white on blue paper which investigates the effects of light glancing across the smooth surfaces of the face and in the soft curls of the hair (Plate 26). The technique, derived chiefly from Carpaccio and used habitually during his stay in Venice, was exploited for the purpose which came most naturally to Dürer: the search for startlingly realistic effects in solid forms (Plate 27).

Another unmistakable feature of the 'Rosenkranzfest' is the presence of portraits based on actual models; there are at least ten of them, representing individuals from the German community in Venice together with the artist and the German architect of the Fondaco. This crowd of real individuals within a religious painting was a striking novelty in Venice and we shall see its influence later, in the work of Lotto and Titian (Plate 28).

Taken as a whole, the impact of the 'Rosenkranzfest' on the Venetian artistic scene must have been considerable. So it is the easier to trust Dürer when he tells us that everyone acknowledged that they had never seen such colours and that they were deeply impressed by them. But even more than by the colours the painters must have been struck by the realistic way in which he was able to render landscape and the human figure, by the very qualities, that is, which they had already seen in his prints as distinguishing the German artist's work.

GIORGIONE

Probably the first Venetian to take an interest in Dürer was Giorgione, whose style, as the *cinquecento* opened, combined the influence of Bellini with others deriving from Flanders. Some of his youthful works, like the Benson *Holy Family* in the National Gallery, Washington and the *Madonna* in Bergamo clearly reflect the influence of Memlinc, who was known in Venice through works in private collections such as that of the Grimani. But the same paintings also reveal, especially in the draperies, a 'Gothic' influence that came from German prints, from Schongauer's to those of Dürer himself (*Madonna with the Monkey*).[38]

In addition, it is clear from one of his youthful masterpieces, the *Judith* in Leningrad, that from around 1504 Giorgione was taking an interest in human proportion that corresponded to Dürer's (Plate 29). Even though the heroine's body is clothed, it is not far-fetched to see it as influenced by the female nude in Dürer's *The Dream of the Doctor* – or by the *Fame* in De' Barbari's engraving. The movement of the hips is identical, so is the position of the left leg, revealed up to the thigh in Giorgione's painting with obvious poetic licence. Very similar, again, are the proportions of the body, such as the very small head, which recall the British Museum drawing with the Vitruvian *Female Nude* dated 1500. Finally, there is a straightforward reference to Dürer's (*The Dream of the Doctor*) and De' Barbari's (*Victory and Fame*) style of drawing in the curls of the drapery that makes a blood-red background to Holofernes' severed head and stands out against the green of the grass (Plates 11, 10).

As I have suggested elsewhere, there can hardly be any doubt that Giorgione continued to value Dürer's ideas about the human figure, especially in the period when he was preparing to decorate the Fondaco dei Tedeschi with frescoes which showed a series of nude figures of which only a single fragment remains, in the Venice Accademia.[39] And there is nothing arbitrary about linking Giorgione's *Nude* to – once more – prints by Dürer and De' Barbari (Plate 30). That Dürer was still deeply involved with the problem of the nude figure is proved by his numerous notebooks and perhaps still more pertinently by a number of independent drawings of extraordinary incisiveness, such as the *Nude seen from the Rear* in the Louvre (1505) and the *Female Nude* in Berlin (1505) (Plate 31). And there is a striking confirmation of Dürer's influence on Giorgione in the controversial 'fregio di Castelfranco' frescoes, where on an illusionistic scroll Giorgione has drawn a sketch of the nude which might be seen as the possible transition from Dürer's *Four Witches* to the *Nude* from the Fondaco (Plate 32).

Another and no less important link between Dürer and Giorgione can be found in their attitude to landscape. Though it is usual to see landscape in Italian painting as reflecting the influence of the arcadian poetry of the *quattrocento*, from Sannazaro to Bembo (if with a strong link to Flemish art),[40] to me there is an element in the conception of landscape in Venetian painting in the early *cinquecento*, from Bellini or Carpaccio, that is, to Titian, Giorgione and Lotto, which can be securely ascribed to German influence. Prints by Dürer such as the *Madonna with the Monkey* (c. 1498), the *Sea Monster* (c. 1498), *Hercules* (1498–9) or *The Large Fortune* (1501–2) allow ample provision for landscapes which could hardly have gone unobserved by young Venetian painters for whom neither the classicizing landscape of Bellini, which was still in humanistic vein, nor the scene-painting of Carpaccio could have remained wholly satisfying, especially when one takes into account the flowering of neo-realistic philosophy and the renewed interest in nature which accompanied it (Plates 21–23). Between 1504 and 1506, in fact, Giorgione began to produce 'landscapes with figures' which include the two 'Storiette' in the Uffizi (Plate 33), the Allendale *Adoration* in Washington and the lost *Finding of Paris* and which culminate with the lost *Aggression* and the *Tempest* in Venice. There is no doubt that this series constitutes a radical break with the traditional Venetian approach to landscape. Against the landscape scenes of a Bellini or a Carpaccio, always to some extent 'prefabricated' or intellectually assessed – though saved by the atmospheric use of colour, Giorgione set an 'organic' conception of nature and of man which could only have found its antecedents in the northern tradition and, in particular, in the work of Dürer (Plate 34). That landscapes of this sort could also arise through the work of engravers who copied Dürer's prints or, like Giulio Campagnola, adapted them to Venetian sensibility, does not affect this conclusion.[41]

Given such an atmosphere, the *Feast of the Rose Garlands*, seen publicly in 1506, could not have been without its effect. Is it possible not to imagine Giorgione as being among the first of the painters who besieged Dürer and among those who copied it? – even if he were later capable, as Dürer wrote, of remarking disparagingly to his 'philosopher' friends that the German's painting paid no attention to 'the antique', as distinguished, presumably, from the animistic theme of his own *Tempest* in Casa Vendramin or from the Praxitelean form of his *Venus* in Casa Marcello.

The influence of Dürer on Giorgione's portraits was, on the other hand, slighter; the models there were clearly Flemish until the crisis precipitated by his rivalry with Titian. The only definite resemblance, in fact, is between the *Old Woman* in the Accademia and Dürer's *Avarice* (painted in all likelihood in Venice) on the back of the Vienna *Portrait of a Man*, dated 1507. It has been pointed out that the x-ray investigation of the *Old Woman* reveals that Giorgione had originally imagined her with her breast uncovered, as in Dürer's *Avarice*, thus confirming the resemblance.[42] It is also well known that some scholars propose attributing the *Old Woman* to Titian in order to account for the somewhat sentimental 'terribilità' of the figure. While dissenting from this change of attribution I would, all the same, take the dramatic aspect of the *Old Woman* to reflect not the 'realism' of Dürer but one of the hallmarks of Giorgione's final manner, his effort – around 1510 – to meet the challenge of the soaring personality of Titian.[44]

LOTTO

In speaking of landscape, we have already referred to the influence of Dürer on Lorenzo Lotto. Above all it can be seen in the background of the 'pala di Asolo' (1505), which is almost identical with the 'Düreresque' landscape of Giorgione's Allendale *Adoration*, which perhaps formed the link between them. That at this very time Lotto was in the process of passing bag and baggage from the Belliniesque camp in which he had operated early in his career (the *Madonna* in the Naples gallery) towards that of landscape in the German manner seems to me proven by the *Allegory* which covered the portrait of De' Rossi, bishop of Treviso, finished probably during 1505, and the *Dream*, both in the Washington National Gallery. Moreover in 1506 comes the Louvre *St. Jerome* which is clearly a variation on Dürer's *St. Jerome* – the engraving of 1496 (Plates 35, 36).

The move from the Naples *Madonna* is remarkable; in the meantime came the experience of the years in Treviso in a literary atmosphere and one open, therefore, to influences of the most varied nature. It was an atmosphere analogous to that breathed by Giorgione in Venice and, because the places are so near, Lotto may well have come in contact with that as well. Certainly there was a

'Giorgionesque' element in Lotto's work at this time, though it was a matter of a common culture rather than of a shared style. From the Washington *Adoration*, imitated in the background of the 'pala di Asolo', to the *Tempest*, discernible in the De' Rossi *Allegory*[45] and the *Dream*, Lotto certainly was not unaware of the advances made by his near contemporary, Giorgione. But this correspondence had its common source in Dürer who early in the century in Venice played a fairly decisive role in modifying the lyrical naturalism of the approach of Bellini's followers towards a new feeling for landscape, an awareness of the organic significance of objects fused, as it were, into the glowing reality of their setting.

For Giorgione this was to mean the beginning of a transformation based on an appreciation of nature as it was and, by insisting on tonal modulation, bringing it within the great colouristic strain in Venetian art. The influence on Lotto was even more profound, forming the decisive element in his discovering a way of recording nature that, while it never fell into mere copying, consolidated and reinforced a native feeling for realism. He could thus articulate a form of narrative expression which seized on objects and on the accidents of light while extracting from them an intellectualized but poetic truth, and while reaffirming at the same time the note of firmly constructed plasticity sounded previously by Antonello.

That Lotto's paintings around 1506 were conceived and carried out under the influence of the sort of realism adopted by Dürer is in no way surprising if we bear in mind the possibility of direct contact between the two artists, deepening the stylistic bond which had certainly already been established through prints and which was to remain fundamental to the evolution of the Venetian painter's pictorial language. What Dürer stood for in Lotto's case was a warm invitation to an imaginative escape towards a poetic narrative based on an immediate and strenuous grasp of concrete appearances modulated through a religiosity at once opulent and ingenuous; at the same time he suggested to him opportunities for the exploitation of his underlying urge towards realism, opportunities he grasped in an almost polemical manner, flouting the academic idealization of Bellini and his school which tended to dissolve natural phenomena into a harmonious and dreamy key.

Hence Lotto's predilection for portraits. He found it easier to solve figurative problems when the real-life subject was at the centre of the poetic creation; he did not then have to impose on it a transforming and synthesizing process which he would later, in any case, come substantially to cancel.

The *Portrait of Bishop De' Rossi* (Plate 37) seems to have been painted in 1505, perhaps before he had had any personal contact with Dürer, though an instinctive rapport is expressed in the unusual acuteness of the characterization – achieved straightforwardly and with an impact so immediate as to have had the effect of a deliberate challenge in the Venice of that time.[46] The same absence of direct morphological correspondence – from drawing to drawing or painting to painting – reconfirms the resonance between their temperaments. So it is by no means extravagant to believe that if Lotto did, perhaps, actually meet the German, he must have seemed the very master he had been waiting for. Certainly there can be no doubt that Dürer's works of the Venetian period were an important stimulus to Lotto, confirming his use of a way of expressing himself that moved further and further from local tradition and the example of his earliest teachers.[47]

To use the years of Dürer's residence as a point of reference, moreover, is a way of finding a plausible explanation for a group of Lotto's paintings that have not hitherto been satisfactorily dated: the *Portrait of a Young Man* in the Accademia Carrara, the Onigo *Warriors* and the *Portrait of a Lady* in Dijon.

Take Dürer's two portraits of Venetian women (Berlin and Vienna) and above all the drawing with the head of 'Eve' (Albertina, no. 75) (Plates 38, 40). The visual language of the last work is surprisingly close to the little portrait in the Accademia Carrara (Plate 39). No youthful drawing by Lotto can be securely identified[48] but taking into account what can be learned from individual passages in his paintings we can say that his graphic vocabulary is remarkably close to Dürer's; a fine mesh of parallel or crossing strokes which give relief to the planes over which there is extremely sensitive play of light, heightened here, quenched there. Later on, colour was to distinguish the approaches of the two artists, but at this moment they had a great deal in common.[49]

With the little portrait in the Accademia Carrara dated around the time of the De' Rossi, we can in all likelihood associate with them in 1506 the Onigo frescoes in San Nicola in Treviso. The pictorial decoration of the tomb[50] comprises a large square of feigned marble enlivened by candelabra and branches in the Lombard style and a projecting support for the predellas of the warriors, a familiar enough scheme in Treviso where painted house fronts could still be numbered in dozens, though in this case the style is Venetian rather than provincial. The attribution of the little portrait in the Accademia Carrara to Lotto makes it easy to see this, too, as Lotto's work; it is enough to look at the faces, drawn and shaded with the 'Düreresque' technique we have already defined. And to whom other than to Lotto, one could well ask, could the strange and daring pose of the figures be attributed, their disequilibrium enhanced by a writhing movement in such sharp contrast with the column in the background? Again, the colour, bright and cool, recalls the characteristic play of light found in two other, equally impressive figures of Lotto's, the S. Liberale from the *S. Cristina* altarpiece and the *St. Vitus* in Recanati. And if still further evidence is needed we can turn to the two medallions in the fresco's cornice, until recently almost invisible:[51] the little figures of satyrs and marine deities in one of them are exactly similar to those in the Washington *Allegory*, dated 1505.

To add an actual portrait to this series, the sharply observed, almost bourgeoise *Woman* in Dijon – also very close, on many grounds, to the common source in Dürer – is to establish for Lotto a thoroughly mature approach to his art, based on a realistic immediacy which recognized neither academic nor traditional limits.

To the period of the Onigo *Warriors* towards the end of 1506 – with so many masterpieces certainly a decisive year for the artist – can confidently be added the commission for the *S. Cristina*. If he had not been at work on an important work in Treviso he would hardly have renewed the lease on his studio there while getting ready to go to Recanati in October 1506. And among the documents relating to the *S. Cristina* there is an order for the frame on 7th November, 1507, and the painting – then under legal sequestration – was paid for on 18th August, 1508.[52]

The *S. Cristina* is one of the artist's finest works. Troubled, it seems, by the demand for an impressive and traditionally conceived *sacra conversazione*, Lorenzo turned to the most authoritative models: Antonello's S. Cassiano panel and Bellini's altarpiece in S. Zaccaria. From Bellini he took the idea for his architectural setting, open at the sides with light flooding along a colonnade, beyond which the countryside is glimpsed. He also took the plan for the figures, with four saints grouped in a semicircle about the Virgin raised high on a pedestal. From Antonello he took the flowing plasticity of the colour; proof of this borrowing comes from the obvious derivation of the figures of S. Cristina, the Magdalen and S. Cassiano as well as of numerous features of the foreshortened hands. Bellini and Antonello: but the transcription is in fact quite autonomous, stamped by the absolutely personal manner he had derived from his contact with Dürer's realism. In comparison with these models, in fact, the first impression given by the altarpiece is of a contraction of the visual field which forces the figures into a more immediate dialogue with the spectator, the clearest exemplar of this relationship between painted and real men being the swift and ardent glance of S. Liberale who is distinguished from the other saints by a somewhat arrogant mein, comparable to that of the Onigo *Warriors*; this, too, is a portrait from the life. And the two pillar-like saints who form with the framing figures of Catherine and Lucy a sort of still nave about the music of the angel violin player: is this all that remains of the monumentality of Bellini, who constructed his figures as if they were elements in some splendid architectural scheme? In S. Zaccaria, the light dims as it falls on the planes of the figures, making drapery supple, softening the hollows carved into the shadows; it is an essentially musical presence. For Lotto on the other hand the light reflects shiveringly – one could say 'alla tedesca' – from the stiff swirls of drapery, randomly gleaming – a carefully studied effect of naturalism. Characteristic, too, is the affectionate, almost artisan-like modesty that breathes from the picture and leaves nothing unaccounted for, from the patterned Turkish carpet to the silk of the banner, from the metal of the arms to the saint's veil; no lyrical self-indulgence here: matters are controlled, almost grimly so, in Lotto's as yet too naked anxiety to depict, describe and narrate everything

Other paintings which also can definitely be attributed to this 'Düreresque' period are the *Marriage of St. Catherine* in Munich, the *Sacra Conversazione* in the Borghese gallery and the *Portrait of a Young Man with a Lantern* in Vienna.

Closest of these to the *S. Cristina* altarpiece is the painting in Munich, an example of the artist's characteristically graphic bent and of his indifference to the classical laws of balanced composition: the bearded old man in the back-ground looks, indeed, as though he was added after the work was finished for the pure pleasure of tilting at conventional figure drawing.

An extremely fine net of lines underlies the cool glaze of the colour in the Borghese *Sacra Conversazione* of 1508 (Plate 41). If corroborative evidence were needed in connection with Lotto's youthful drawings it could be found convincingly here, in the chiaroscuro of thin lines which can be seen beneath the skin of the old S. Onofrio, under the greyish face of S. Nicola or in the shadows of the clothes and beneath the clear flesh tones of Mary and the child. It is the drawing – analogous, again, to that of his real teacher, Dürer, in the figure of *Christ among the Doctors*[53] (Plate 42) – which allows this work to be compared with the *Young Man with a Lantern*, one of his finest creations and one which sums up all Lotto had learned in these first five years. The cold fury of Dürer's *Oswolt Krel* can be felt to such a degree as to suggest that Lotto was directly inspired by it.

THE CRISIS OF 1507

Let us now return to Dürer and to works that followed the *Feast of the Rose Garlands*. There were the numerous portraits mentioned in his letters, among which we can be content with recalling the so-called 'Burcardo' at Hampton Court and the *Young Man* in the Palazzo Rosso in Genoa dated 1506, the *Portrait of a Man* in Vienna (with the *Avarice* on its other side) and the *Young Girl* in Berlin dated 1507, and the *Portrait of a Lady* signed 'A D' also in Berlin. Apart from these, three Madonnas are of especial interest: the *Madonna with the Siskin* in Berlin (1506), the *Madonna of Bagnacavallo* and the *Madonna of the Mountain* in a private collection.[54]

The influence of Bellini can, in varying degrees, be traced in all three, notably in the *Madonna of the Mountain*, where the Virgin is shown on a balcony behind which drops away a bird's eye view of landscape as in many of Bellini's *Madonnas* of the 1480s; the seated child, too, seems very near to the child in the *Madonna with two Saints* in the Venice Accademia. The *Madonna of Bagnacavallo*, on the other hand, seems much closer to a German model, particularly – as Roberto Longhi pointed out – in the meticulous drawing of its spatial asymmetry: 'the wavering, groping yet empirical complexity of the Gothic world'. The Berlin *Madonna* stands somewhere in the middle, balancing between the rather feebly Bellini-like central figure (close, nevertheless, to the comparable figure in the *Feast of the Rose Garlands*) and a clearly German feeling for landscape. This can be seen in the background and again in the crowded figures which are un-certainly located in space, though this is made to seem more real by a number of essays in *verismo*, the homely detail of the cushion, for instance, or the book, or the stool and its scroll.

We have three works, then, which in different ways recognize the authority of the patriarch of Venetian painting and at the same time reveal a steadily watchful German imprint. From this period we have a portrait like the one signed 'A D' in Berlin which shows the full impact of Venice in the gentle gradations of its light and the suffused colouring of the parts that fall into shade.[55] Very close in time is the disturbing *Portrait of a Girl* in Berlin, dated 1507, the ambiguity of whose subject has even prompted its exegetes to discuss its sex. However, leaving the arcana of psychology on one side, what we have here is another example of the contradictory element we have found elsewhere in Dürer's work: the latent Germanic feeling coming irresistibly to the surface and pulling us into a realistic and expressive world of a most challenging immediacy.

In 1507, indeed, feeling the appeal of his own country, Dürer was at a stage far removed from his first enthusiasm for the Italian Renaissance. Certain anti-classical tendencies had pressed again to the surface of his approach to painting, visible in the almost truculent expressiveness of his forms and forcing him towards the verge of mannerist 'conflict'. As Panofsky justly divined, Dürer returned towards the end of his second stay in Venice to 'a Gothicizing way of expressing himself' best demonstrated by contrasting the engraving of *Adam and Eve* of 1504 with the *Adam and Eve* in the Prado, dated 1507 (Plate 43). These last figures can properly be characterized as 'an anticipation of Mannerism . . . [resulting] from a recrudescence of Gothic tendencies within the framework of an already classical style'.[56]

But with reference to the goals Dürer set himself in 1494 and 1495 to what extent can early *cinquecento* Venice be held responsible for so significant a crisis? The answer substantially lies in a phenomenon which mirrored one of the most specific features of its own artistic background which had kept intact (for all its apparent move towards the Renaissance style) a certain rootedness in Gothic culture which still flowered from time to time and was at once registered by Dürer's acute sensibility. And one thinks not so much of De' Barbari, who had probably been forgotten by now, as of the sculpture of Raverti, Bregno and Rizzo to be seen in the Ducal Palace and the Frari and doubtless significant for the 'Germanic' element in their work, the element which, in the last analysis, was closest to Dürer's way of thinking and to his deepest aspiration. We may think of the *Adam and Eve* attributed to the Lombard Matteo Raverti on the south-west corner of the Ducal Palace, above all of Rizzo's *Eve* in the same palace (Plate 44), an amazing masterpiece to emerge in the Venice of Antonello and Bellini with the splendid isolation of its dramatically northern accent – the Gothic note which Dürer's ear was first tuned to catch, though the descent here was through Lombard tradition.[57]

In confirmation of the sharp 'change of course' represented in the 1507 *Adam and Eve* by which Dürer re-established his independence, one can look at the first Venetian generation of the *cinquecento*. Following the shift towards monu-mentality exemplified by Giorgione's frescoes for the Fondaco, painters were more affected by Dürer's 'neo-Renaissance' phase than by his later works which looked increasingly toward his homeland. To take Palma Vecchio as an example: his *Adam and Eve* in Brunswick takes up the balanced, monumental stance of

Dürer's 1504 engraving and shows clearly enough that by around 1510 to 1515 the main appeal of the Germanic style had had its day (Plate 45). And it is worth recalling that it was in 1510 when Dürer, back in the German fold, played traitor most magisterially to his idealized version of 1504 and presented in the *Adam and Eve* in the Albertina one of the very finest of his pen drawings – and one that was already possessed by Mannerist agitation (Plate 46).

Dürer's Italian adventure comes, then, to an end in 1507 with a significant recovery of his independence as a painter derived in part from certain 'Gothicizing' elements in Venetian art itself. Extraordinary as it was, it would be difficult to point to any other lasting influence saving, of course, the spiritual enrichment it involved, especially in the field of artistic theory, as his lasting interest in perspective, geometry and human proportion was to prove. These interests come to the fore again much later, however, at the end of his life. And it is intriguing that as if by coincidence the composition of his last work, the *Four Apostles* in Munich (1526), irresistibly recalls Bellini; the distribution of the figures, with Sts. Peter and Mark closely together in the centre, and certain typological features resemble the four saints which Bellini, as far back as 1458, had placed at the sides of his *Frari Madonna*, certainly one of the pictures Dürer had most admired during his residences in Venice.[58] Despite its very different effect – one of an entirely Lutheran *terribilità* – the ideal and formal qualities of this masterpiece derive from an assonance with what must have been the most tenuous of memories.

TITIAN

In the 'dialogue for four' of the Munich Apostles, Dürer also seems to be echoing another famous Venetian work completed probably before 1511: Titian's altarpiece in the Salute, the *St. Mark with Four Saints*. As early as 1929 Hetzer drew attention to its connection with Dürer's metrics rather than with its Venetian antecedents.[59] He recognized in fact the revolutionary compositional fancy, the sense of movement, the unaccustomed exchange of spatial relationships which constituted the 'German element' in the artistic culture of Renaissance Italy. Certainly there is no simple explanation for the sudden flowering of the young Titian and it cannot be said that criticism has yet done much to follow the route suggested by Hetzer. On the other hand it is difficult to go with him all the way: he is certainly too sweeping in taking Titian as 'the most fruitful example of the meeting between Germanic fantasy and the Italian spirit'. That Titian came from the mountains and was thus 'almost German' is hardly a valid argument; moreover, it was not only the 'German element' that gave his landscapes their sense of being a true record, or his composition the air of being 'superbly ornamental, and no longer merely plastic,' which he discovered, for example, in the Salute altarpiece.[60] Other suggestions of Hetzer's are still less helpful. He sees an echo of Dürer in the tree trunk in *Sacred and Profane Love*; in Titian's costumes and their deep folds the Germanic 'sense of ornament'; in the *Member of the Calza* in the Fondaco an echo of Dürer's standard bearers; German inspiration behind the 'asymmetry' of the *Pesaro Madonna*; memories of the *Horseman of the Apocalypse* in *Bacchus and Ariadne* – and so it goes on for other, later, works.[61] For the most part all this is a matter of iconographic resemblances, often of an incidental or disputable nature, to which others could be added without throwing any real illumination on the opening phase of Titian's career.[62]

Nevertheless, Hetzer's notion of connecting the first surge of Titian's art with the Germanic element in early *cinquecento* Venice contained much that makes excellent sense. We can see it easily enough, for instance, in the correspondence between Titian's and Dürer's draughtsmanship, suggested by Hadeln before being amply demonstrated by Hetzer with reference to the woodcuts, more especially with the *Apocalypse* series.[63] In Titian's drawing of *Two Youths in a Landscape* (Vienna) (Plate 47) and *The Jealous Husband* (École des Beaux-Arts) – both earlier than 1511 – Pallucchini also recognizes that 'certain interrupted or jerky lines, certain notched outlines, especially in foliage, certain strokes of the pen which scratch deeply into the paper are elements typical of Dürer'.[64]

Titian also took hints from Dürer, as well as from Mantegna, Michelangelo and Raphael for the superb woodcut *The Triumph of Faith*, which is accepted as dating from around 1511. Rather than in the violently expressive angels who follow the cross or fly ahead of the procession, Dürer in my opinion is to be seen in the hulking figures of Adam and Eve in the front which exactly recall his woodcut technique in the 'a placca' shading of the musculature (as in the *Bath House*) or the typology of *The Large Fortune* itself (Plates 49, 50). Still with woodcuts in mind, I would suggest that if – as Tietze Conrat believed – the inspiration for the woodcut *Passage of the Red Sea* goes back to 1513,[65] the powerful groups of horses not only owe something to Leonardo but more probably have some connection with the horses depicted by Dürer in the *Apocalypse* group.

In general, then, I would agree that in the second decade of the century Titian's drawing comes to maturity chiefly through the influence of Dürer, whose authority helped him win free from the *sfumato* emphasis of the Giorgionesque school and to make a comparable escape in painting.[66] And if this seems to claim too much, we must nevertheless admit that the almost inexplicable presence on the walls of the *scuola* of the Santo in Padua of the three dramatic frescoes of the *Miracles of St. Antony* (1511) owes much to Titian's having intuitively realized the constructional potentiality of Dürer's line, which he could have grasped either from prints or from a few sketches he might have seen (perhaps against the German's wish) and absorbed with an eye always prompt to fasten on what was best in the art of his day (Plate 51). From a page from Dürer's sketchbook showing a *Rape of Europa* (Albertina) (Plate 48), for instance, which comes from Dürer's first residence in Venice – and which might have remained there for some time – the young Titian could have learned all that was to distinguish him from his teachers, Bellini and Giorgione: a vision of landscape so natural that the myths of Europe or of woodland deities could develop there dramatically and spontaneously (as in the youthful 'storiette' of 1505–1510 in

Padua and Bergamo, which develop Giorgione's 'landscape with figures' mood so forthrightly); a powerfully realistic treatment of the human figure, able to express the compacted animation of a gesture (the so-called *Portrait of Ariosto* in London) (Plate 52), a tale charged with sentiment (the Paduan frescoes) or a moment of high heroism (the Antwerp altarpiece).

Thus if the emphatic and incisive line of the German master underlay the tension within Titian's forms, it also passed into the body of his painting as a whole, urging it through powerful slashes of the brush to the potent vibrancy, the existential power, the amazing creative determination that was to make Titian, in the course of the few years between 1510 and 1515, the unchallenged renovator of Venetian painting in the Renaissance.[67]

NOTES

1. T. Hetzer, *Das Deutsche Element in der Italienischen Malerei des XVI Jahrhunderts* (Berlin, 1929) makes 1500 the turning point (*Wandlung*) in the Venetian art of the Renaissance.

2. Hetzer, op. cit., 49 seq.

3. H. Wölfflin, *Italien und das Deutsche Formgefühl* (Munich, 1931).

4. H. and E. Tietze, *Kritisches Verzeichnis der Werks Albrecht Dürer* (Augsburg–Basel–Leipzig, 1928 and 1938); E. Panofsky, *Albrecht Dürers* (Princeton, 1948); F. Winkler, *Albrecht Dürer* (Berlin, 1957). This essay, I should point out, was completed before the great Dürer exhibition of 1971; nor was I able to take advantage of Fedja Anzelewsky's fundamental monograph (Berlin, 1971).

5. Since the English edition of W. M. Conway, *Literary remains of Albrecht Dürer* (Cambridge, 1899); see also the anthology ed. A. Werner (New York, 1958) Dürer's writings have been published in a critical edition by H. Rupprich, *Dürer Schriftlicher Nachlass* (Berlin, 1956–69).

6. L. Grote, *Hier bin ich ein Herr* (Nuremberg, 1950) 46, would refer this work to Dürer himself as the payment for it was made between March and June 1495. But as Dürer was in Venice in 1494–5 there was surely too little time for its execution. Could it be instead the work of De' Barbari, who may then have been residing in Nuremberg? It would in fact be very odd that such a work had not be associated with Dürer's name if he was its author, especially as it was in the house of a humanist to whose circle he himself belonged.

7. I owe this identification to the kindness of Francesco Valcanover.

8. Panofsky, op. cit., 31.

9. Panofsky, op. cit., 31, 33. It is worth pointing out that drawings by Pollaiolo were available to Mantegna's circle in Padua. Indeed, his master Squarcione possessed one, containing nudes, which we know about through the documents of a lawsuit put in train by Squarcione against his pupil Giorgio da Sebenico, who had stolen it. See A. Lazzarini, *Documenti relativi alla pittura padovana* (Venice, 1908) 169.

10. Grote, op. cit., fig. 42.

11. Rupprich, op. cit., i, 101.

12. Winkler, op. cit., 145, fig. 72.

13. Panofsky, op. cit., 266–270.

14. Thus the hypothesis developed by De Hevesy in his *Jacopo de' Barbari* (Brussels, 1925) 10, where he suggests that the musician 'Jacopo Barbiria', sent from Nuremberg to the court of Hungary, was in fact De' Barbari himself. Neither can too much trust be

put in the connection which a number of writers make between Dürer's letter of 7 Jan., 1506, in which he says that 'the thing which so well pleased me eleven years ago pleases me no longer', and the work of de' Barbari, nor can we be certain that the two men met in Venice in 1495. As Rupprich makes clear (op. cit., i, 44), Dürer certainly alludes to more than a particular meeting with de' Barbari, perhaps to his works along with other Venetian paintings which had impressed him during his first stay, in all probability works in the style of Mantegna and the Vivarini, as can be seen clearly enough in the Dresden Madonna, painted immediately after his return to Nuremberg. The same conclusion was reached by R. Longhi, *Arte italiana e arte tedesca* (Florence, 1941) 21. For A. M. Hind, *Early Italian engraving* (London, 1948) ii, 143, the meeting took place in 1495.

15. On this last point see G. Pauli, 'Dürer, Italien und die Antike', in *Vortraege der Bibliothek Warburg* (1921–22) 51; K. Clark, *The Nude* (London, 1956) 367.

16. P. Kristeller, *Engravings and woodcuts by Jacopo de' Barbari* (Berlin, 1896) 2.

17. Panofsky, op. cit., 86.

18. Hind, op. cit., 141.

19. L. Justi, 'Jacopo de' Barbari und Albrecht Dürer', in *Repertorium für Kunstwissenschaft* (1898) 346, 439; J. Rosenberg, *Great draughtsmen* (Cambridge, 1959) 59.

20. Hind, op. cit., 144, 157.

21. This was accepted by Kristeller himself, op. cit., 3.

22. Rupprich, op. cit., pl. 30, fig. 95.

23. Panofsky, op. cit., 85, 87.

24. Panofsky, op. cit., 68.

25. The Haller Madonna seems to derive not so much from Bartolomeo or Alvise Vivarini, as many have supposed, as from one of the freshest of Bellini's masterpieces, the *Madonna degli Alberetti* of 1487 in the Venice Accademia. This is the source for the relationship between the verticals represented by the mother and child, emphasized by the gleaming colours of the hanging; this is the source for the solemn, almost hieratic pose and for the convention adopted for the face, with its reminiscence of Antonello's geometrical forms. Certainly Dürer added elements inseparable from his realism in the near foreground and in the little open window on the right which seems to have pushed forward and unbalanced the extremely lively *putto*.

26. Letter to Pirckheimer of 13 Oct., 1506, in Rupprich, op. cit., i, 58.

27. 6 Jan., 1506, in ibid., i, 41.

28. 7 Feb., 1506, in ibid., i, 43.

29. 28 Feb., 1506, in ibid., i, 43.

30. 2 Apr., 1506, in ibid., i, 48.

31. 8 Sept., 1506, in ibid., i, 54.

32. 25 Sept., 1506, in ibid., i, 56.

33. 13 Oct., 1506, in ibid., i, 58.

34. Ibid., i, 221.

35. According to Levey, *Dürer* (Bergamo, 1965) 75, it was Carpaccio's work that most appealed to him in 1495. In 1505, on the other hand, he expressed enthusiasm for Giovanni Bellini's altarpiece in S. Zaccaria. To the painters who no longer pleased Dürer on his second visit can perhaps be added Gentile Bellini who in 1495 held a strong interest for him, at least for his rendering of Venetian costume. Some of Dürer's drawings of Venetian costumes seem in fact to derive from Gentile's studies for his *Procession in Piazza San Marco*, now in the Accademia. See B. Degenhart, 'Ein Beitrag zu den Zeichnungen Gentile und Giovanni Bellini und Dürers ersten Aufenthalt in Venedig', in *Jahrbuch der Preussischen Kunstsammlungen* (1940) 37.

36. Levey, op. cit., 75. Panofsky (op. cit., 112) also points out the resemblance to Lochner's *Adoration of the Magi* in Cologne Cathedral which Dürer mentions in his Low Countries travel diary (1520). Dürer could of course have seen Lochner's painting during his 'Wanderjähre' (1490–93).

37. R. Pallucchini, *Catalogo della mostra di Giovanni Bellini* (Venice, 1949) 190.

38. T. Pignatti, *Giorgione* (Venice, 1969) 46, 48. The first to draw attention to the relationship between the German engravings and Giorgione appears to have been Hetzer, op. cit., 107.

39. T. Pignatti, op. cit., 63.

40. J. Burckhardt, *La civiltà del Rinascimento* (Florence, 1944) 361; A. R. Turner, *The vision of landscape in Italian art* (Princeton, 1966) 99, 134.

41. T. Pignatti, op. cit., 57. One of the few exceptions among the paintings of the older generation in Venice is the *Cavaliere* of Carpaccio in the Thyssen collection, where the minutely detailed botanical garden in the foreground, with the numerous animals playing in it, cannot but reflect a memory of engravings by Dürer like the *St. Eustace*, or drawings like the *Mary and Jesus* in the Albertina in Vienna (c. 1503, reproduced by Panofsky, op. cit., fig. 135). But this is a painting that is so exceptional in Carpaccio's *oeuvre* that it was in fact attributed to Dürer – an attribution everywhere discounted since the discovery of the signature and date (1510) on the *cartellino*.

42. A. Morassi, *Giorgione* (Milan, 1942) 103.

43. Most recently E. Panofsky, *Problems in Titian* (London, 1969) 90.

44. Pignatti, op. cit., 68.

45. It clearly is a storm, perhaps signifying the disasters that attend the sensual life (represented by the satyr) in contrast to the serene joys of the spiritual life (the mathematical *putto* on the left, where the soul ascends a path of light).

46. I see no object in comparing this portrait with such works of Bellini as the *Dandolo* in London or the *Condottiero* in Washington. These tend towards an abstract and idealized monumentality. In Lotto's portrait, on the other hand, the aggressively realistic intention, on the psychological plane, is obvious. I would refer again to a strong likeness to some of Dürer's drawings, for instance in the *Architect* in the Albertina (no. 76) done in Venice shortly afterwards. Also the manner of drawing hands used by the two painters is strikingly similar even to the same chiaroscuro technique of using parallel strokes as in an engraving. Dürer's many studies of hands (in the Albertina and in Berlin) certainly seem to have been known to Lotto.

47. To confirm how much Lotto owed to the influence of Dürer in the bent for narrative poetry which was the central feature of his approach to painting, a final note on his contacts with Dürer (which lasted throughout his life) will be helpful. The *St. Jerome* in the Borghese painting (1508) is derived from a figure in Dürer's *Christ among the Doctors* (1506); the angel's head in the Recanati picture appears to be that of drawing no. 79 in the Albertina, just as the drawing for the head of St. Vitus in the same polyptich could be the head in Dürer's drawing no. 75 in the Albertina. The device of crowding figures into superimposed planes, which is markedly Gothic, recurs frequently in Lotto, for example the old doctor in the 'second plane' of the *Marriage of St. Catherine* in Munich, in the figure of Joseph in the *Pietà* of the Recanati polyptich and that of the old man in the painting formerly in the Puslowski collection. All recall the compositional treatment of the old man in Dürer's *Christ among the Doctors*, painted in Venice in 1506. The same crowding together of superimposed planes is to be found in the *Sacra Conversazione* in the Rome National Gallery, the *Adultery* in Paris and in the *Crucifixion* of Monte S. Giusto. In 1514 Dürer published a print of St. Jerome in his study and shortly afterwards Lotto copied it literally, with so loving an attention to the play of light in it as to leave no doubt as to the depth of his interest, which went well beyond mere matters of iconography (in spite of the later alterations, I believe the little picture in the Zocca collection in Rome to be his. Repr. in L. Coletti, *Lorenzo Lotto* (Bergamo, 1953) 39. The same St. Peter and Paul in Ponteranica, with their billowing drapery and their flushed and trembling faces are themselves very close to the *Four Apostles* in Munich. The *Celana Assumption* is a reminiscence of the engraving of the lost *Assumption* of Dürer; the whole feeling that is so characteristic of Lotto's interiors is extremely close to Dürer;

this can be seen in the *Recanati Assumption*, which resembles engravings like the St. Jerome of 1511, or the light streaming in from some of the little square windows in the Borghese portrait. Thus we find a constant resort to the manner of the great German, aided as the years passed by his adopting approaches similar to those of Altdorfer, Grünewald and to the Flemings themselves, among them, for certain landscapes like the *pala dei Carmini*, Patinir.

48. And there are other comparisons: the *Head of a Woman* in the Accademia – H. and E. Tietze, *Venetian drawings* (New York, 1944) pl. 324 – is very close to drawing no. 75 in the Albertina; the *Bust of a Young Man* in the Stehli collection in Zurich (Vivarini, T.2249); the *Bust of a Young Man* in the Leipzig museum (Vivarini, T.2246); the *Bust of a Young Man* in the Staedel Institute in Frankfurt (Vivarini, T.2244); the *Portrait of a Young Man*, no. 84 in the Albertina (T.A.326, according to Previtali); the *Head of the Madonna* in the Rome National Gallery (L. Grassi, *Storia del disegno*, Rome, 1947, xviii).

49. Dating the Carrara portrait 'sul far del secolo' – A. Banti and A. Boschetto, *Lorenzo Lotto* (Florence, 1953) 73 – stresses perhaps too much the overall influence of Antonello to the detriment of the vibrant sentiment so typical of Lotto and already pronounced, as in the De' Rossi portrait, not to mention the Recanati *St. Vitus*, B. Berenson, *Lorenzo Lotto* (New York and London, 1895; 3rd ed. 1905) 35 and G. Frizzoni, 'Lorenzo Lotto' in *Archivio Storico per l'Arte* (1895) i, had, moreover, proposed a date around 1505–6, which fits the reconstruction of the artist's youth given here.

50. Dedicated by the three sons of Agostino Onigo: Angelo, Gerolamo and Pileo; the last mentioned died in 1502, thus giving the *ante quem* for the marble monument, but not necessarily for the fresco.

51. Reproduced in L. Coletti, *Treviso* (Inventari del Ministero P.I., 1935) 399, and in G. M. Richter, *Giorgio da Castelfranco, called Giorgione* (Chicago, 1937) pl. ix.

52. In G. Biscaro, 'Lorenzo Lotto a Treviso', in *L'Arte* (1898) 148.

53. See for example the *Head of Christ* in the Albertina no. 79: it is the same way of constructing the planes with undulating and parallel lines, then heightening them with patches of light and shade. And I shall not emphasize any further – even if it would serve a useful purpose – the Morellian parallels between the hair, the heavily shadowed mouth, the luminous eyes. On this painting see J. Bialostocky, in *Journal of the Warburg and Courtauld Institutes* (Jan.–June 1953) 17.

54. R. Longhi, 'Una Madonna del Dürer a Bagnacavallo', in *Paragone* (1961) no. 159, figs. 1 and 3.

55. M. Levey, 'Minor aspects of Dürer's interest in Venetian art', in *The Burlington Magazine* (1961) 512, proposes a Bellinesque model, possibly reflected in two drawings in the Vendramin album in the British Museum.

56. Panofsky, op. cit., 120.

57. Panofsky had already suggested the comparison with Rizzo's *Eve* (op. cit., 120).

58. As Levey has noticed (op. cit., 28). Also the previously mentioned central painting with an enthroned Madonna, an angel musician and various portraits seems full of Venetian echoes (drawing dated 1521 in the Louvre, ibid., pl. 76).

59. Hetzer, op. cit., 28.

60. Ibid., op. cit., 108.

61. Ibid., 110–118.

62. Rothschild, for example, discovered that Titian's *Madonna with the Cherries* in the Vienna museum has links with Dürer because it contains a young St. John copied from his *Madonna with the Goldfinch* in Berlin. 'Tizians Kirschenmadonna', in *Belvedere* (1932) 107.

63. D. von Hadeln, *Tizians Zeichnungen* (Berlin, 1924) 27; Hetzer, op. cit., 109, iii.

64. R. Pallucchini, *Tiziano* (Florence, 1969) 17.

65. E. Tietze-Conrat, 'La silografia di Tiziano "il passaggio del Mar Rosso" ', in *Arte Veneta* (1950) 110.

66. The influence of Dürer on Titian has been put forward again recently also by

Panofsky, who insists, however, on the fact that 'all these influences served only to nourish his originality' (op. cit., 1969, 13). See also my: *Über die Beziehungen zwischen Dürer und dem jungen Tizian*, in *Anzeiger des Germanischen Nationalmuseums Nürnberg* (1971–72), 61. Apparently no trace of these critical interpretations is to be found in the recent *Titian* by H. Wethey (London, 1969 and ff.).

67. The argument of this essay was treated in part during my teaching semester at the University of California, Berkeley (1966), in a Graduate Seminar in the Department of Art. I am glad to mention here the names of my students whose final papers were often very useful to me in this research: Lynn Brown, Elizabeth P. De Gall, Joan Hreben, Sheila McClure, Mary McMaster, Virginia Miller, Liesel Volwassen and Bruce A. Watson.

X

FELIX GILBERT

Venice in the crisis of the League of Cambrai

The battle of Agnadello was lost; three weeks later the Venetians were forced to abandon Padua. The only foothold which Venice was able to keep on the *terraferma* was Treviso. With the loss of most of its possessions in northern Italy the Venetian empire was confined to the sea.

For the Venetians the grim summer of 1509 invited reflections about the mutability of fortune. Indeed, in the pages of the diary which Girolamo Priuli kept, the report on the events of this summer is interspersed with meditations on the causes of this sudden fall of the Venetians from greatness and power. That this reversal was God's will was clear to Priuli as well as to all his contemporaries. The question which Priuli pondered was why God had found it necessary to mete out this cruel punishment to Venice.[1]

In his search for an answer Priuli discovered one reason after the other why Venice had aroused God's ire. First of all, there was the immoderate pride and arrogance of the Venetian ruling group, of the 'padri et senatori et nobelli veneti'. In their contempt and disregard for all those who did not belong to this group they neglected their foremost duty, the dispensation of justice. They were dilatory in granting people a hearing and in pronouncing judgments; consequently, court proceedings became protracted and as expenses increased many found it impossible to gain justice and maintain their rights. As administrators on the *terraferma* the Venetian nobles had lived in pomp and splendour. Because many of them could ill afford this life of luxury which they believed their exalted position required, they accepted bribes. And when complaints about their behaviour reached Venice, their families and friends defended them; and the support of influential patricians was exchanged for promises to vote for them. In consequence, accusations were disregarded, as justified as they might be, and it was easily comprehensible that, in despair, the population of the *terraferma* revolted against Venetian rule when the opportunity arose.

In other aspects of public life, too, the Venetian patricians had offended God by a disregard of their sworn duties. Despite vows to keep government business secret everyone knew almost immediately what had been said and decided in meetings of the Council of Ten or the Senate. Despite an oath to elect officials without letting anyone ever know for whom they voted, the electors signalled to the candidate whom they preferred how they would vote; those who refrained from such bargainings were kept out of office.

In Priuli's view mal-administration was only a particular aspect of a more general process: moral corruption was widespread. Many of the nunneries in the city were actually brothels. Because of the influence of those who frequented them – not only youths and foreigners but also older patricians in high positions – and because of the social status of the nuns who frequently came from noble families, all the measures which had been adopted to eradicate this evil remained ineffective.

Another sign of moral turpitude was the openness with which homosexuality was practised in Venice. Young men made themselves look like women: they wore jewels; they perfumed themselves; and their clothes exposed most of their naked bodies. Parents did not dare to discipline their sons, but let them go their own ways. Again, the reason was that high officials, members of the Senate, were practitioners of this vice. Even the Venetian noblewomen who in olden times had been distinguished by chastity and simplicity were now eager for all kinds of amusements and tried to appear and behave as seductive as possible. Again, there was no strict enforcement of the laws against luxury; a week after they were issued they were forgotten.

Priuli was convinced that these vices had not only provoked divine retribution but that the moral corruption of the Venetian ruling group was the direct cause of political mistakes which had resulted in the difficult, almost desperate, situation in which Venice found herself in 1509. The pope had become hostile because the greed of the Venetian patricians to reserve ecclesiastical benefices for themselves had violated papal rights. Because the Venetian nobles had become accustomed to a soft life they had neglected to take the appropriate measures for defence. 'The doge and the Venetian senators wanted both to remain quietly and comfortably at home and to sleep in their own beds but they also wanted to be victorious. To have these two things together is difficult, almost impossible.'[2] One could scarcely expect mercenaries and foreign soldiers to fight courageously and tenaciously if they were not commanded by men whose existence depended on the outcome of the battle. 'If the Venetian rulers wish to keep their Italian possessions they will have to learn the military art.'

For Priuli morals and politics were closely connected. Venice's fame and greatness was due to its overseas enterprises and these had required a hard and strenuous life. The expansion over the *terraferma* had been a mistake – the result of a search for a life in less arduous and more pleasant surroundings.

Priuli's outcry against the Venetian ruling group must be an expression of views widely held at the time; at least very similar complaints and criticisms can be found in the diary of Marino Sanuto four years later. Then the war was still going on with all the ups and downs and sudden changes of fortune characteristic of the military events of this period. Padua, whose loss Priuli had regarded as sealing the fate of Venice, had been reconquered in the July of 1509 and then Venice regained some of its possessions on the *terraferma*. The Venetians even succeeded in separating Julius II from the anti-Venetian coalition by surrendering to him the disputed territories and control over ecclesiastical appointments in their domain. The French and German armies in northern Italy remained formidable however, and after fighting and manoeuvring with alternating success, the French and Germans advanced far into the *terraferma* by the end of the summer of 1510. In the campaign of the following year the French and the Germans continued their advance and approached the lagoons. The pope and Venice realized the need for allies and in October they concluded a Holy League with Spain and England against France. The magnificent procession with which this event was celebrated showed the relief which the Venetians felt: 'Cessa i sospir, cessa li to pianto, che felice ti farò più ch'a inanti', was inscribed on the statue of St. Mark.[3]

The campaign of the summer of 1512 was full of sudden, dramatic changes. First the powers of the Holy League advanced, but then the French won the battle of Ravenna and northern and central Italy seemed to be at their feet. However, the losses with which the victory had been bought were high, and the French withdrew. At the end of May the Venetians were again in possession of most of the *terraferma*. But in Julius II's view the French remained a dangerous threat and he believed he could be secure only if he broke up the French alliance with the German emperor. Consequently the pope tried to pressure the Venetians to cede Verona, Vicenza and Brescia to Maximilian. The Venetians were unwilling to give up these towns and the result was a sudden reversal of alliances. On 23rd November, 1513 an alliance between Venice and France was signed. The event was greeted with the same enthusiasm with which the conclusion of the Holy League had been welcomed a year before. The new alliance seemed to establish a balance of forces which would quickly lead to peace, especially since by then Julius II was dead. Even when, against expectations, Julius' successor Leo X continued the war, the Venetians were confident that the French and Venetian military forces would quickly gain the upper hand in northern Italy. But in May 1513, at Novara, the Swiss inflicted a heavy defeat on the French. Padua came under siege; for the rest the entire *terraferma* was lost again to the advancing Germans. The villages along the Brenta were looted. Mestre was burned. After four years of war the situation in the summer of 1513 was as desperate as it had been in the summer of 1509.

To Sanuto, who observed from the bell-tower of St. Mark's the burning and looting of the enemy, the entire area along the Brenta appeared 'red like blood'.[4] His reaction was very much like that of Priuli four years earlier.[5] He ventilated his desperation in bitter criticisms of the Venetian ruling group. He accused them of negligence in taking defensive measures and in arranging for provisions. The patricians were so much wed to their customary soft life that even in the present emergency they convoked the Great Council only to transact routine business. Instead, they ought to call the people together in Piazza San Marco, arm them, send them out against the enemy, and the senators themselves ought to lead them into the battle against the enemy. So advised Sanuto.

Priuli and Sanuto indicated that they spoke not only for themselves but reproduced the opinions which they had heard expressed by their compatriots. Their diaries show that doubts about the political course, which difficulties and defeats inevitably raise, were widened to questions about the efficiency and equity of the Venetian system of government and about the contrast between the reality of the situation and the values from which the Venetian system of government was traditionally believed to draw its strength. The political issues were extended into social and moral areas. Undoubtedly, the war of the League of Cambrai brought about a deep crisis which invited re-examination of Venetian society in all its aspects. How probing was this self-examination? Did it lead to changes in the Venetian political and social system? Did the crisis which the League of Cambrai precipitated represent a turning point in Venetian history? The following does not exactly solve these questions, but perhaps will direct attention to the importance of the problems. [5a]

I

The view that moral corruption was the decisive reason for the decline of Venetian power was expressed not only by private citizens but was an officially held and recognized thesis. In the rare speeches which the doge Loredan (doge 1501–1521) made in the Great Council, he stressed regularly that immorality was the basic reason for the difficulties in which Venice found itself.[6] He argued that the height of power which Venice had reached had made its citizens so proud and overbearing that God was forced to humiliate them, although it was to be hoped that God would not abandon them forever. In the desperate days of October 1513 Loredan discussed Venetian moral failings at greater length than ever before. Venice had been unjust and unfair in its treatment of foreigners. Loredan criticized the pomp with which the Venetian officials on the *terraferma* conducted their lives. But the doge's chief target was the Venetians' indulgence in luxury. He mentioned that the large hall on the ground floor of their palaces which in earlier times had served for the transaction of business and in which weapons had been kept hanging on the wall, was now transformed into a festival dining room. Loredan confessed his own responsibility and guilt for this; he had been among those who had abandoned the traditional custom.[7]

In accordance with the view that the political crisis was the result of divine punishment, measures to regain God's good graces formed a considerable part of Venetian war legislation. At crucial moments of the war or of diplomatic negotiations the patriarch was asked by the doge to arrange that in all churches prayers were said 'so that God would assist this republic against its enemies'.[8] At the occasion of feast days or victories the government ordered the distribution of alms to the indigent or of money to poor monks in order to implore 'the favour and the assistance of all-powerful God'; those who received these gifts were expected to pray to God 'for our state'.[9] The timber of an old galley was ordered to be used for the building of a church and a monastery in honour of St. Joseph 'so that, by means of his merits and his intervention, God might be inclined to pity and mercifulness towards our state'.[10] When success came it was acknowledged to be God's work who, 'without any merits on the part of the Venetians' had shown 'in a miraculous way His power and His mercy'.[11] The day of Santa Marina on which Padua was reconquered was decreed to be a feast day on which it would be strictly forbidden to work or trade and on which the doge would lead the procession to the Church of Santa Marina and then attend a mass at St. Mark's.[12] Certainly, such governmental measures were customary at critical moments in all Renaissance states. Nevertheless, the manner in which the councils gave direct commands to the patriarch and intervened in ecclesiastical affairs reveals an assumption of the existence of a complete integration of all civic activity – political, religious, social and economic.

The view that political salvation depended on calling a halt to moral decline found expression in a legislation regulating the conduct of social life. Of course, this again must be considered as customary, but it is characteristic that just in the critical summer after the battle of Agnadello, on 29th June, 1509, the government decided to give a more stringent form to a law of 1486 directed against immorality in the nunneries.[13] Anyone who had sexual relations with nuns in the monasteries or had lured them away from the nunneries was banned from Venice for life; should such a violator be found on Venetian territory he would be put into prison and anyone denouncing him would receive 500 ducats. Moreover, laywomen were forbidden to use nunneries as their residence and servants had to wear clerical habits; no longer were they allowed to enter the nunnery in secular dress.

Laws regulating morals required a magistracy assuring their observance, and all such legislation, particularly the laws against luxury, were accompanied by attempts to establish such an office.[14] After officials had been elected for this purpose from time to time a special office of three *savi* for enforcing the sumptuary laws was established in 1476, but it was short lived. Closed in 1503, its functions were transferred to other magistrates who were expected to deal with these problems in addition to their regular duties. But the defeat of Agnadello revived the notion of the need for a special magistracy to enforce strict observance of the laws against luxury. In 1510 the Senate decided to elect from the procurators of St. Mark two members who would 'curb, correct and punish' transgressors of the sumptuary laws. However, in these difficult years the procurators found themselves over-burdened with business and unable to give these problems the necessary attention. On 13th March, 1512 the Senate decided that, in the serious situation in which the city found itself, it was urgent to 'placate the anger of Our Lord' and to establish a permanent magistracy consisting of three *provveditori* with the function of preventing 'immoderate and excessive expenditure'.

The *provveditori sopra le pompe* issued a decree covering all aspects of luxury.[15] Some of the articles of the decree repeated previous legislation and others were to become obsolete through subsequent laws, but the decree of 1512 might be regarded as a basic code which allows a survey of Venetian sumptuary law. As such, this code deserves attention because it throws light on the habits of the Venetian upper class.

The decree aimed at restricting luxury in three different categories: dress, housing and festivities. The regulations concerning the manner in which men and women should dress were mainly inspired by regard for morality. The clothes of women ought to be simple and each dress had to be made out of one and the same material. For dressing-gowns transparent materials were forbidden and lace could not be used. Men were forbidden attire which would increase physical attractiveness. Shirts should cover the entire upper part of the body and close neatly around the neck. There were detailed rules about the jewellery which women might wear. The value of golden necklaces or of pearls woven into ladies' hair was not to surpass 100 ducats and the use of golden or silver threads or of golden belts was prohibited. All this points to the fact that status was largely determined by ostentation and that the open display of wealth was customary in the upper class and distinguished it from the rest of Venetian society.

The same basic motives – stricter morals and greater economy – can be seen in the regulations on housing and festivities. A maximum of 150 ducats was placed on expenses for decorating a single room with wood panelling, goldleaf or paintings. In addition, the list of objects which the householder was forbidden to buy was very large: gold boxes, gilded mirrors, cushions of silk decorated with pearls, curtains of brocade or damask, silk hangings, gold or silver vessels; if, after the issue of this decree, anyone acquired any of these objects they would be confiscated and the owner fined.

Under the decree of 1512 marriage celebrations were sharply regulated; what the law still permitted gives us some idea of the immense luxury which was in vogue on such occasions in times when conspicuous waste provoked no criticism. According to the decree, the family of the bride was still expected to give six small parties for not more than twenty people and two big parties for fifty people in the interval between the engagement and the wedding. The bridegroom was permitted to give two parties, one for eighty and the other for fifty people. In decorating the house and the tables expensive novelties should not be introduced and torches or candles for lighting the rooms should be used with economy. Delicacies – pheasants or expensive sweets – should not be served, but the prohibitions did not include marzipan. Responsible for observance of these decrees and susceptible to punishment in case of transgression were not only heads of houses but also cooks.

Modesty of expenditure was one aim of the sumptuary legislation; the other was to discourage lasciviousness. New dances popular with the young were condemned, particularly the 'most shameless dance of the cap and other French dances full of lecherous and sinful gestures'.[16] Balls were to be confined to the palaces of those who gave them; no dancing outside in the streets; masks were forbidden.

These regulations were dictated by a variety of reasons. One was political. If the wealthy patricians in power continued their luxurious manner of life while the majority of the population suffered from the war and had to make sacrifices, dissatisfaction and unrest were unavoidable and the will to resist would be weakened. In a decree of 14th February, 1511, the Senate stated that some 'do not cease to make many superfluous and extraordinary expenses by which they throw away great sums of money. This arouses general dissatisfaction and causes damage. Such people demonstrate that they have no real love for their fatherland; in addition many of these lavish spenders haven't paid their taxes which are raised for no other purpose but for preservation of the state and every person's life'.[17] The last sentence of this decree indicates another cause for the increased attention given to sumptuary laws during the war of the League of Cambrai. Money spent on luxuries could not be taxed and the reason for the restrictions placed on the acquisition of gold or jewels was that the wealthy people invested their capital in such objects to avoid being taxed or forced to give their money to the Venetian state bank, the *Monte*, whose shares were steadily declining the value. There are also indications that these measures were intended to prevent Venetian gold reaching foreign, hostile countries, although the particular emphasis which was given to a ban on foreign fashions and materials may have been simply an outlet of zenophobic emotionalism which always arises in wartime.

Nevertheless, religion was the decisive motive in the legislation against luxury. This is regularly emphasized in the introductions providing justifications for these decrees. Here it is stated that these laws have been made to 'avoid offending the divine majesty',[18] or that, by spending money for the gratification of their desires, people act 'with little reverence for God and show little fear of Him'.[19] To return to God's good graces is the primary reason for reintroducing and reforming the sumptuary laws at the time of the war of Cambrai.

These laws were designed to restore the way of life which had existed in the early times of the Venetian Republic. These measures were necessary because 'we must with all possible zeal and care imitate our ancestors'.[20] For the Venetians, as for all of that time, perfection existed at the beginning; then corruption set in and decline ensued. The true aim was 'to return to the beginnings' and to restore life as it had been then: simple, modest, in accordance with God's law. The simple life had created the strength which had made possible the rise of Venice. To revive this way of life was the precondition for Venice's salvation. It appears that measures towards restoring religious faith and moral discipline required complementation in political and social life.

II

It is easier to appeal for religious and moral renewal than to undertake political reform and institutional change. Did the criticisms which Priuli and Sanuto expressed in their diaries have any political consequences? To what extent did the crisis of the war of the League of Cambrai represent a turning point in Venetian political and institutional history?

A study of the Venetian archives from the years 1509 to 1517 gives the impression that a small group of men was desperately struggling with an endless number of unexpected and diverse tasks.

There was the problem of the refugees from the *terraferma*. In 1509 the peasants from the area around Padua streamed into the city fleeing from the burning and looting of the hostile mercenaries. Homeless, they wandered with their animals through the streets. The government housed them in monasteries – in San Giorgio Maggiore, San Niccolò and Sant'Andrea – which stood empty because the monks were disinclined to share the hardships of the war with the Venetian citizens and had abandoned them 'with scant charity'.[21] The return of the peasants to their homes after improvement of the military situation posed new problems. They needed seed to sow their land and decrees were issued which stated that the landowners must provide seed and how they were to be compensated.[22] But the refugee problem continued to plague the government. In 1510 refugees from Vicenza arrived and were eventually housed in the Fondaco dei Tedeschi.[23] The crowding of the city created serious problems of security and health. Laws against theft, robberies and violence had to be tightened; carrying of arms was prohibited.

The councils were continuously occupied with intervention in economic affairs necessitated by the impact of the war on trade. In general the interruption of shipping, particularly to and from northern Europe, resulted in intensive smuggling against which measures had to be taken.[24] Arrangements had to be made to import wool from Flanders overland.[25] The loss of control over the *terraferma* aroused the fear of famine. Warehouses were built to store grain.[26] Actually the fear of starvation was exaggerated, although at certain times food for the refugees seems to have been minimal or lacking. Because the enemy troops had driven away the cattle there was a serious shortage of meat and measures were taken to bring cattle into Venice by ship.[27] As a result of the war the ordinary course of business was disrupted and emergency situations requiring extraordinary measures arose.[28] At the beginning of the war the government was engaged in winding up the affairs of the Agostini bank which had failed in 1508. In May 1509 there was a run on the Pisani bank; the government intervened and gave assistance in order to avoid a failure which might shake confidence in the financial strength of the Venetian republic. In November 1513 when a run started on the bank of Girolamo Priuli, government officials went to the Priuli office and guaranteed full payment to the creditors; with this act they dispersed the crowd which demanded payment. (The Priuli bank was not saved but an ordinary liquidation had been assured.) Government intervention in business affairs was not unusual but became more pressing and more frequent in wartime.

A wearisome, unending concern of the officials and the councils was the situation on the *terraferma*. Because it was sometimes in Venetian control and sometimes in that of the enemy, administrators left on the approach of the enemy and returned with his retreat. Changes in personnel were common because in the interval of enemy occupation some of the officials were elected to other positions; others became ill or died; and for others the term of office had ended. Careful supervision of the affairs of the *terraferma* was particularly important because the regular administrative functions were now coupled with additional tasks.[29] It was necessary to punish traitors and to reward those who had remained loyal. Compensation had to be determined for those who had suffered losses because of their adherence to the Venetian cause. This was a difficult job because these proceedings offered many opportunities for deception and fraud. Yet, because of the closeness of the enemy, the establishment of a stable situation on the *terraferma* was urgently needed.

In order to be sure of administrators who would handle the affairs on the *terraferma* firmly and effectively the *Collegio* and the Council of Ten made many appointments in disregard of the electoral rights of the Senate and the Great Council. This created friction; indeed, after the emergency was over, the Senate and Great Council annulled the appointments made by the *Collegio* and successfully reclaimed the right to elect.[30]

The war on the *terraferma* also involved the Venetian government in military administration. The government had to take measures to protect the citizens of the towns on the *terraferma* against vandalism and robbery by the soldiery. Among the Venetian troops there was a militia composed of men from the villages and towns of the *terraferma*. If they deserted, the government decreed, their noses and ears were to be cut off.[31] But the inhabitants of villages that had been loyal to Venice were freed from taxes or received special privileges.[32] Jobs had to be provided for individuals who had lost a limb fighting for Venice and could no longer do military service or continue their regular activity; and provision had to be made for the widows.[33] There was no general law covering the various aspects of the ravages of war; each case was determined separately and then presented to the Senate for approval.

The burden of this extraordinary work had to be carried by men whose duties were heavy in peacetime: they were administrators of a city with 100,000 inhabitants and policy makers of a world power. For these responsibilities the number of men in direct authority, as in all states of this time, was small: the *Collegio* with the *savi*, the Council of Ten and the *Quarantia*. The ruling group was well aware of the need to distribute these charges among a greater number. Different methods were used to ease the pressure. Special committees for the execution and supervision of particular tasks were established, although the *savi* set the guidelines for the work of these committees and then selected and defended them in the councils. For the time of the emergency the number of the *savi* was increased – a necessary arrangement because some of the *savi* served as commissioners with the military forces and for long periods were absent from Venice.

Nevertheless, the strain on those who filled the high offices was immense because in addition to the variety of tasks mentioned they were continuously harassed by what was their most important and most arduous task: providing money for the conduct of the war. Campaigns lasted from early spring to October and each year arrangements had to be made with *condottieri* for the army which Venice could field. In 1509, after Padua had been reconquered, expenses for the troops which had to defend it amounted to 50,000 ducats.[34]

Venetian state finances grew precarious during the war because, as with all wars, the usual sources of income declined or dried up altogether. The revenues of the Venetian government consisted, like the finances of the other Italian city-states, of indirect and direct taxes. The indirect taxes comprised a great variety of imposts: tolls, customs on imports, sales taxes on grain and many foodstuffs, on clothes, duties on financial transactions, rents for shops and offices in buildings belonging to the government, particularly on the Rialto, etc. Some of these taxes were raised directly by government officials, others were farmed out. It is obvious that the decline in economic activity, particularly in trade, decreased and in some cases almost extinguished the revenues from these taxes or duties. For instance, the rents on shops had to be lowered continuously and promises of special privileges like exemption from taxes for a number of years were made in order to find occupants. The shrinking of the indirect taxes had its impact on the direct taxes as well, because the revenue from some of the duties was reserved for the payment of interest on the consolidated public debt, the *Monte* from which the government drew money for current expenses.

There were three kinds of direct taxes in Venice. One was a tax on landed property on the *terraferma*; in normal times it produced a good solid revenue but during the war of the League of Cambrai this tax became almost negligible. Secondly there was the *decima*, a property and income tax which was raised from time to time. And thirdly there were the forced loans to which the government took recourse in times of urgent financial needs; for the money which the citizen loaned to the government he received shares in the *Monte* which bore interest. Steadily rising government expenses increased the capital of the *Monte* derived from forced loans and even before the war interest payments were in arrears. The original *Monte*, the *Monte Vecchio*, became complemented by another *Monte*, the *Monte Nuovo* to which other sources of revenue for interest payments were assigned. But when in wartime the indirect taxes failed to produce enough revenue both *Monti* went bankrupt and a new *Monte*, the *Monte Novissimo*, was established in the fall of 1509. But these bankruptcies reduced the citizens' capacity to pay the *decima* and made them much averse to lending money to the government.

The Venetians had to chart their course in a situation of decreasing economic opportunities, of declining revenues, of mounting expenses and of rapid need for ready money. They did what, almost up to the present, governments have always done in such situations: they tried to reduce expenses wherever possible; they tried to discover new sources of revenue, and they raised taxes.

One of the economy measures adopted in previous times was to stop paying the official salaries, and with the exception of some lower offices and of administrators on the reconquered *terraferma*, this policy was maintained throughout the war. Loopholes in the taxation system were filled; an attempt was made to bring up to date estimates of taxable property which frequently had become obsolete.[35] Supervision of accounting methods was tightened.[36] Special committees were appointed to examine possibilities for greater economy in the administration and in the conduct of the war. For instance, in their eagerness to eliminate waste the *savi* investigated the rumour that the painters entrusted with the decoration of the hall of the Great Council had received 750 ducats for two paintings which they had not even begun, whereas other good masters were willing to execute these paintings for 250 ducats. At the end the painters in charge provided a satisfactory explanation and consequently Titian could continue his work.[37]

In the search for additional revenue the obvious method was to eliminate exceptions. In 1509 foreigners were required to pay in taxes fifty per cent of the rent they were paying for houses.[38] And employees in the Fondaco dei Tedeschi were taxed.[39] Goods which the government had confiscated as security for unpaid taxes were sold. And payments which the Jews had to make for being allowed to live in Venice were increased.

Yet all these measures were makeshift. The government had to place its reliance primarily on the *decima* and on forced loans. The *decima* was raised with increasing frequency and the demand for forced loans which was particularly addressed to the wealthy citizens became more immediate and urgent. In speeches to the Senate the doge appealed for loans and then spoke to each member individually.[40] Those who had no cash for taxes or forced loans were asked to deliver household objects made of silver or gold. The government tried to obtain quick and prompt payment of taxes by announcing that those who paid at the earliest set term could use for payment of subsequent taxes part of the assignments on the *Monte Novissimo* which they would receive. Although such promises might have helped to meet a particularly urgent need the final result was to decrease the amount of revenue from further taxes. As the war dragged on the financial situation became increasingly difficult.

Under this pressure the government took a step which was felt to jeopardize a basic tradition of Venetian political life: the government began to sell offices.[41] The process started in 1510 with a category of minor officials employed in the magistracies as scribes, notaries, accountants and assistants; they were allowed to buy the positions which they held either for a limited term or for life and in the latter case they could hand them over to their descendants subject to the payment of a certain percentage of the proceeds from their offices. In the same year nobles who loaned the government a specified sum of money were admitted to the Senate, but without voting privileges. In 1514 young noblemen who were eighteen years old or over but had not yet reached the required age of twenty-five were admitted to the Great Council in recognition of a loan. And nobles could be elected to the *Collegio* as *savi agli ordini* for the sum of 200 ducats even if they were still below the required age. A decree in 1515 made entry to the *Quarantia* possible to men below the age limit in return for 100 ducats. Even admission among the procurators of St. Mark was tied to a financial offering.[42]

The most shocking measure of this kind was adopted late in 1515. It was established that the names of those who made loans to the state together with the amount which they had loaned as well as the names of those who had refused to make loans should be published before the Great Council proceeded to elections. Evidently those who had made loans would be elected and those who had lent the highest amount had the best chance. The functioning of this new decree can be easily studied in Sanuto;[43] for instance, on 30th December, 1515, he reported that Zuan Emo had promised 900 ducats, Niccolò Malipiero 200 ducats, Christofal Canal 800, Sebastian Badoer 1,000, Sebastian Malipiero 300, Andrea Balbi 200 and Girolamo Bragadin 720. The outcome of the election was that both Zuan Emo and Sebastian Badoer–i.e., the two who had given the highest amounts – were elected: the one *governador de l'intrade*, the other to the Council for Cyprus; and Andrea Balbi became judge of petitions. Among the candidates for these offices those whose names Sanuto did not list as having offered a loan received only a small number of votes. It should be noted, however, that some precautions were taken against granting electoral office to the highest bidder; to the four candidates among which the Great Council had to choose, the Senate assumed the right to add a fifth candidate, and the prestige which the candidate supported by the Senate enjoyed could sometimes outweigh purely monetary considerations. There is no doubt that the result of this system of coupling elections with payments resulted in a considerable augmentation of the funds of which the government could dispose. In the following year, in 1516, the list of offices to which this system was applied was extended even to offices such as governors on the *terraferma* or *avogadori di comun*.

By waiving age requirements for membership in councils and by allowing financial considerations to influence elections the Venetian government was driven far off its traditional course. But these arrangements were emergency measures and they were abolished as soon as the crisis was over. In these war years there is no discernible trend towards changing or reforming existing institutions. From time to time appeals were issued for suggestions about new methods for raising taxes; in March 1515, proposals were made for a thorough reorganization of the tax system.[44] This suggestion was justified as a return to the past; as it was said, it is always 'appropriate to follow the steps of our ancestors'. The Venetians of earlier times intended to impose only one tax equal to all, although 'because of the revolution of the times, that changes financial resources', new estimates should henceforward be made every five years. It was suggested that Venice ought to return to the imposition of a uniform tax. But such a fundamental change was rejected as inappropriate for the present. Clearly there was disinclination to make any systematic change.

The war increased the daily business of the ruling group to the limits, and the high-ranking officials were entirely satisfied with taking those measures which helped to get Venice through the extreme crises that rapidly followed one upon the other. The ruling group had neither the time nor the possibility to make institutional or constitutional innovations.

The dangers which threatened the state forced the small group of high officials to take quick action and to assume great responsibility. They worked closely together with the Senate; but with both councils – particularly with the Great Council – there was friction because the councils felt that their functions had been abrogated and their rights slighted. In addition it can be observed that the high officials acted high-handedly and ruled somewhat recklessly over the population, even over the other nobles. Consequently within the Venetian nobility a split developed between those in the highest offices who had a strong base in the Senate and the majority of the nobility sitting in the Great Council. Echoes of this split come to us from the diaries of Priuli and Sanuto with their criticism of the ruling officials, and the existence of this split might be deduced from the complaints about low attendance in the sessions of the councils.[45] Evidently the feeling had spread that it was not worthwhile attending the Great Council because nothing of much importance was done there. It might be added that the advantages – resulting from the financial emergency – which wealthy nobles had in obtaining office widened the distance between the effective ruling group of the nobility and the bulk of the patricians.

Because of the powerful hold over the whole range of Venetian life which this ruling group had, the question with which we are concerned must focus on an examination of the extent to which its attitude and structure was changed by the war.

III

Among the eventful times through which Venice passed in the years of the war of the League of Cambrai, the summer of 1513 was the most dramatic. The high hopes with which the campaign began in spring, and which had been engendered by the conclusion of the French alliance, were dashed to the ground by the French defeat at Novara which, among its consequences, brought the enemy again to the gates of Padua and Treviso.

On 10th July Doge Loredan appeared in the Great Council to speak to the Venetian patricians about what they should do in this critical situation.[46] As in some of his other speeches, he began by attributing the dangers and defeats to the sins and arrogance of the Venetian patricians. He admonished his audience to pay taxes and grant loans because, should defeat be the outcome, gold and silver would profit them nothing. Loredan insisted that those who had failed to pay their tax debts should be dismissed from their offices and excluded from the councils. Then he ended with an appeal – the core of his speech – to the patricians to go themselves out to the field, to the defence of Padua and Treviso.

In connection with this last demand a proposal was made by members of the *Quarantia* that those who did military service could be elected to any office in spite of tax debts, but after their return from the war they could take office only after they paid their taxes. This proposal aroused resentment and was quickly revised: by paying half of one's tax debts one could hold office. Even this revised proposal was not enthusiastically received but nobody dared to oppose it. At this moment Marino Sanuto, who had never before spoken in the Great Council, arose and delivered a speech which he noted in his diary,[47] evidently convinced that this was his finest hour. The gist of the speech was that the poor nobles who scraped together some money to equip themselves for military service and to go to the defence of Padua and Treviso were unfairly treated if, having been honoured for their service by election to an office, they were prevented from enjoying the fruits of this honour, should they be unable to pay their tax debts. Sanuto therefore suggested that payment of tax debts should be suspended for six months after a noble returned from the war. Sanuto's proposal was accepted with an overwhelming majority: 1,019 *vs.* 159.

The interest of this story goes beyond the particular situation which Sanuto described, for it illustrates the attitude of the Venetian ruling group towards participation in politics. This attitude is characterized by contradictory features: patriotism coupled with concern for personal interest and gain.

We cannot doubt that, as Priuli wrote in his diary, the great mass of the people 'loved the republic and were devoted to it'; the people were convinced that 'the freedom of Italy depended on the defence of Venice'.[48] They felt that they had upheld Christianity against the Turks and that, even if their present enemies were Christians, they were again fighting to defend civilization against the barbarians. The only people to whom the Venetians could compare themselves were the Romans.

Gestures in imitation of ancient Roman courage were not lacking. Paolo Nani, who had inherited the magnificent palace of the Doge Agostino Barbarigo outside Padua, ordered the building to be burned so that it could not serve as a stronghold for the enemy. Modelling himself after the Roman example was Andrea Gritti; when he and Giorgio Corner were sent out as commissioners to the army they refused to take any salary.[49] Gritti was almost continuously employed in difficult military enterprises. He spent some time as prisoner in France and when he first returned from there in 1513 he was looked to as the obvious candidate to be placed in charge of the defence of Padua. A decree was proposed which said that a person elected to this position and who refused to take it would be fined 500 ducats. Gritti opposed this law saying that it was intended to make it impossible for him to decline should he be elected. He added that he had suffered much in the service of the state and was exhausted. But when the decree was adopted and, as he had foreseen, he was elected, he went to the *Signoria* 'saying that he had never refused to make efforts for this distinguished state as it was the duty of every good patrician'.[50] All this seems to be in accordance with what Hieronimo Borgia, a contemporary historian who was the secretary of Bartolomco d'Alviano, the chief Venetian general during the war, said: 'Not even the Romans behaved towards Hannibal with greater courage than the Venetians'.[51]

But there is also a different aspect which suggests an unrefrained concern with personal comfort and prosperity even in wartime. The appeal to the Venetian nobles to go as military leaders of small groups of citizens to the defence of Padua and Treviso had a very mixed reception.[52] There were complaints that the sons of some of the influential nobles, among them the sons of the doge, had not volunteered. There seemed to have been many cases in which nobles had declared their willingness to go but did not appear when they were called upon. The long lists of volunteers which Sanuto published[53] deserve more careful study than they have received. The names of members of the upper ruling group are rather few and, not altogether unnaturally, military duties seem to have been undertaken primarily by the younger sons of these families. The possibility of being elected to office, even if in debt for taxes, and the establishment of monthly salaries showed the need to provide some stimuli to take on military duties; apparently the appeal was chiefly aimed at the poorer nobles. Great astonishment was aroused when Bernardo Boldù appeared in Padua with seven men whom he maintained at his own expense and did not ask for any compensation. It is characteristic that when in the summer of 1509 the first appeal to the nobility for military service was made the doge emphasized that 'those nobles and citizens who will go into these cities can be sure that they will be as secure as if they were in Venice'.[54] Their presence would chiefly serve to guarantee and protect the citizens of Padua from molestation by the soldiery.

The financial situation of Venice also throws a rather dubious light on the patriotism of the patricians. Tax morality in Venice – as in most other city-states – was low and the war did not better it. In the urgent need for money the deadlines for payment of tax debts were frequently prolonged because it was deemed more convenient to get cash payments than to confiscate goods or take other measures. A much used procedure for forcing the payment of taxes was to publish in the Great Council the names of those who were delinquent in paying their tax debts and to announce that they would be excluded from the councils and from holding office if they did not pay within a certain time. But there was great hesitation to apply this decree, and when it was finally done it emerged that some of the most prominent and some of the wealthiest members of the ruling group – names that appear in crucial measures during these war years – were on this list:[55] in 1511 we find Gabriele Emo, Paolo Capello, Giro-lamo Quirini and even Andrea Gritti. In 1512 Luca Zen, Antonio Grimani, Giorgio Corner, Antonio Tron and again Paolo Capello, and in the same year Domenico Trevisan, Bernardo Bembo, Piero Badoer, Domenico Malipiero – all men who played a prominent role in Venetian politics in these decades.

Similarly the demand for loans gave occasion to subterfuges. It happened frequently that, when the doge made his appeal in the Senate for forced loans people pledged large sums but did not appear with the money when it was requested. Again it had to be decreed that their names would be published in the Great Council and that they would be excluded from office; it is perfectly clear, however, that such a decree was used primarily as a threat; there was no great willingness to proceed against wealthy and influential patricians.

There are signs that people were aware of the contrast between reality and the façade of public virtue. Priuli, on the occasion of the recalling of Grimani from his exile in 1509, noticed that in its present ruined state Venice no longer maintained the principles of strict and equal justice and had lost its pride in maintaining its own laws and order.[56] Members of the ruling group felt themselves entitled to enjoy special privileges. At the wedding of a niece of the doge and at another wedding of a member of the Grimani family, permission was given to transgress the limits of the laws against luxury;[57] some weddings – for instance, a Contarini wedding – remained within the demands of the laws, but many others evidently did not care to observe the rules. As Sanuto noticed with displeasure in 1513, in spite of the war, amusements and dances were held in great numbers.[58]

Undoubtedly, there were men among the ruling group who were most earnestly concerned with the restoration of what they considered to have been the simple and strict life of earlier times. Some indication of this tension is the contempt shown by older members of the Senate towards those who had bought their entry into the council: some newcomers felt so uncomfortable and excluded that they asked to have their money returned because they wanted to abandon their seats.[59] But attempts to reject those who had paid their way in soon ceased. One cannot suppress the feeling that for many members of the wealthy upper group the main reason for making a show of heroism was to maintain the morale of the Venetian population, of the citizens as well as of the poorer members of the nobility.

It is obvious that this generalizing characterization of the attitude of a group does not do justice to the motives and expectations which influenced or determined single individuals in participating in decisions or in accepting them. There is little reason to doubt that in the days of greatest danger belief in a connection between defeat and sinfulness was widespread, almost general, in Venice and that even if politics played an important part in the official emphasis on renewed piety, in the legislation against luxury and in the establishment of a strict supervision of morality, such measures also corresponded to what many considered a moral duty. Only few, if any, embarked upon such measures for purely pragmatic or opportunistic reasons. We can find in the Venetian life of these years every nuance between worldliness and religiosity. Precisely in these years a group of young patricians withdrew from public life to Murano and the two leaders of this group, Giustiniani and Quirini – both at the beginning of great political careers – became eremites in the mountain wilderness of the Apennines;

T

the cruelties of the war, as they wrote to their Venetian friends whom they tried to persuade to join them, were a sign of the futility of life on this earth.[60] A third member, Gasparo Contarini, although he did not renounce the world, conducted his life in such a manner that when, as a mature man he was appointed cardinal, his election was regarded as a sign that the church was embarking on the path of true reform. Although it seems that for most members of the Venetian ruling group the experiences of the war did not change their outlook on life, for some it did and gradually this had its influence on religious thought in Venice.

Likewise, it might be said that, although the adoption of a Roman heroic attitude was façade rather than reality, it was not without further significance. The government became concerned with rebuilding the School of St. Mark's, the Venetian centre of humanistic studies, as soon as opportunity arose, and it furthered those who found in the Roman past lessons for the Venetian present.[61] It encouraged writings about the war of the League of Cambrai, appointed an official historiographer in 1516, and thereby helped to give a firm form to the Venetian tradition. Again, the years of the war started a development which contributed to giving Venetian society that aspect of awesome discipline for which it became famous in the later sixteenth century.

Nevertheless, I would like to suggest that these developments which started at the time of the war of the League of Cambrai gained importance only because of the impact which the war had on the structure of the Venetian ruling group.

Venice had always been a city with sharply separated strata of population. There were the citizens and above the citizens was the nobility. It seems evident, however, that during the war of the League of Cambrai two groups developed within the nobility: a relatively small upper group drawn from the Senate, among which the high offices circulated, and the rest of the nobles partly from the Senate but chiefly from the Great Council. The weight, the closeness and the exclusiveness of this upper group was strengthened by the war, and the reasons were partly bureaucratic. The tasks of the war required the close co-operation of the officials as well as a certain amount of continuity, which was obtained by creating special committees, or by extending the terms of office, so that even those whose term of office had officially ended continued to play an active role in the conduct of affairs. Another reason for the rigidification of this upper group was financial need (with the accompanying sale of offices) which united the wealthy members of the nobility with them.

Of course the struggle of the young against the old, of the poor nobles against the rich, of the old families against the new has been a constant feature in Venetian history.[62] Nevertheless, it might be suggested that the formation of a firm bloc consisting of the traditional ruling families and of the newer families of great wealth distinctly separate from the rest of the nobility, achieved its completion and perfection in the times of the war of the League of Cambrai. The institutions of Venice were not changed by the war but in these critical years the final step was made in establishing as rulers of Venice a small, closely united group, which kept in its hands all decisions about the life of the inhabitants and the policy of the Republic.

NOTES

1. For the following see Priuli, *Diarii*, iv, 29–45, also 296–7.

2. Priuli, *Diarii*, 44: 'Et il Principe et Padri Veneti volevano stare a chasa loro riposatamente et chomodamente et dormire sopra li sui consueti lecti et avere victoria, et questo he difficile et quasi impossibelle . . . Et veramente, se li Padri Venetti voranno mantenire et conservar statto in Ittallia, sarà necessario che li loro nobelli venetti, et dico deli primi, facino lo exercitio et mestiere dele arme . . .'

3. Sanuto, xiii, 139.

4. Sanuto, xvii, 102: '. . . vidi il sol a hore 23 tutto rosso che pareva sangue per il fumo di tanti incendi . . .'

5. See Sanuto, xvii, 94–323 from Sept. to Nov. 1513.

5a. I am working on a comprehensive study of the importance of the years 1509 to 1516 in the history of Venice.

6. As examples, see the speeches of the doge in Sanuto, ix, 117; xvi, 479, 489; xvii, 119, 245.

7. Sanuto, xiii, 246: '. . . e confessa lui Principe fo di primi che disfè la lanziera a San Canzian in la soa casa per meter la tavola di la soa festa . . .'

8. Sanuto, viii, 119–120.

9. A.S.V., S.T., reg. 16, f. 119v: '. . . acio I priegano ei Signor Dio per el stado nostro'. See also Sanuto, viii, 112.

10. A.S.V., *Maggior Consiglio, Deliberazioni*–25–Deda, 12 June, 1513, f. 102v.

11. S.T., reg. 18, f. 40v.

12. Sanuto, xiv, 420.

13. *Maggior Consiglio, Deliberazioni*–25–Deda.

14. The story of the legislation against luxury has been given, on the basis of the relevant documentary material, by G. Bistort, *Il Magistrato alle Pompe* (*Miscellanea di Storia Veneta*, III, v, 1912), and the following report on the formation of the magistracy against luxury is dependent on Bistort.

15. Sanuto, xiv, 114–117, reproduced the main concepts of the decree, but the official text, which was accepted by the Senate (after a discussion mentioned by Sanuto, xiv, 200) and then published 11 May; 'supra scallis Rivoalti', was more complete; I use the official document in S.T., reg. 18, 8 May, 1512.

16. '. . . un altra vituperosa e damnabile practica e consuetudine e introducta qual summamente offende la divina Maiesta cum dar mal exemplo a le pudiche verzene che stano ale feste driedo le zelosie a veder ballar che la prava zoventu balla certo inhonestissimo ballo de la bereta over del capello et alcuni altri balli francesi pieni di giesti lasciui e dannabili.' For a description of these dances, see Pompeo Molmenti, *Venice, The Golden Age* (London, 1907) vol. ii, chap. xiii: 'Private entertainments, balls and banquets'.

17. A.S.V., S.T., reg. 17, f. 77.

18. See the decree, published in Sanuto, xvi, 151.

19. See the decree, mentioned in n. 17.

20. See Sanuto, xvi, 151.

21. S.T., reg. 16, f. 146.

22. Sanuto, ix, 245.

23. S.T., reg. 17, f. 30v.

24. S.T., reg. 17, f. 61. See also Sanuto, xv, 137–141.

25. S.T., reg. 19, f. 59v.

26. See Gino Luzzatto, *Storia economica di Venezia* (Venice, 1961) 248.

27. Sanuto, xvi, 643.

28. For the following, see Luzzatto, op. cit., 236–262, and, in particular, Frederic C.

Lane, *Venice and history* (Baltimore, 1966), the chapter on 'Venetian bankers, 1496–1533', 69–86.

29. A.S.V., *Consiglio dei Dieci, Miste* 1509–10, f. 214, and many similar instructions.

30. S.T., reg. 17, f. 50v mentions the 'universal murmuratione' against the appointments by the *Signoria* and the *provveditori*; see also S.T., reg. 19, f. 137 for demands for annulment of appointments by the *Collegio*.

31. S.T., reg. 16, ff. 21, 125v.

32. S.T., reg. 16, f. 157, etc.

33. There are many examples of this: see S.T., reg. 16, ff. 26r and v, 81r and v, 82v, 140, 172, 178 for the years 1509 to 1510 alone.

34. Sanuto, x, 37–39.

35. S.T., reg. 16, f. 99.

36. S.T., reg. 16, f. 35v ('Resecar le superflue spese'); reg. 17, f. 52v.

37. S.T., reg. 19, ff. 78v and 79, 30 Dec., 1515, and Sanuto, xxi, 425–426.

38. S.T., reg. 16, f. 120v.

39. S.T., reg. 17, f. 16v.

40. For some of these speeches, see above, n. 6.

41. For details, see the essay by Cozzi in this volume.

42. S.T., reg. 19, f. 100v, and about the doge Loredan's son making use of this decree, see Sanuto, xxii, 258.

43. Sanuto, xxi, 423–424.

44. S.T., reg. 19, f. 18, and Sanuto, xx, 15–19.

45. *Consiglio dei Dieci, Miste*, 1509–1510, f. 210.

46. Sanuto, xvi, 489.

47. Sanuto, xvi, 490–491.

48. Priuli, *Diarii*, 270, 282.

49. S.T., reg. 16, f. 113.

50. Sanuto, xvi, 476–477.

51. Hieronymus Borgia, *Historiae de bellis Italicis ab anno 1494 ad 1541*, B.M.V., Cod. Lat. 3506, f. 82r: 'Neque veri Romani adversus Annibalem fortiores Venetis extitere.'

52. For examples of heroic behaviour, see Sanuto, xii, 378; xvi, 473; xvii, 111, but a certain lack of enthusiasm can be noticed in Sanuto, vii, 254; xii, 570; xvii, 109, 111. The material advantages of this kind of military service are emphasized in Sanuto, xvi, 494. Sharp criticism of the doge and his sons is stated in Sanuto, xvii, 120, 208. An interesting criticism of the doge is to be found in the unpublished diary of Marcantonio Michiel, M.C.V., Cod. Cicogna 2848, f. 89v; Michiel mentioned the speech of the doge in Oct. 1513 and wrote about its effect: 'Ne però alcuno so offerse de andar si perche haveano pocho in gratia el Principe per la mala fortuna sua, si etiam perche tantum li confortava con parole, ne però mandava uno di soi fioli o ne prestava danari.'

53. Sanuto, xvi, 492, 536–538, 568, 576–577, 597, 626, 635; xvii, 160–162, etc.

54. Priuli, *Diarii*, 279.

55. Sanuto, xi, 788; xiv, 639; xv, 329–330.

56. Priuli, *Diarii*, 94.

57. Sanuto, xii, 139, 303; xiii, 423; xvii, 13.

58. Sanuto, xvi, 206–207.

59. Sanuto, xii, 266, 375; xiv, 18.

60. See my article 'Religion and politics in the thought of Gasparo Contarini', *Action and conviction in early modern Europe*, ed. T. K. Rabb and J. E. Seigel (Princeton, 1969).

61. See my article 'Biondo, Sabellico, and the beginnings of Venetian official historiography', *Florilegium Historiale*, ed. J. G. Rowe and W. H. Stockdale (Toronto, 1971).

62. See William J. Bouwsma, *Venice and the defense of republican liberty* (Berkeley, 1968) for a discussion of these issues in the later sixteenth century, although by then the Venice of the Renaissance had developed into the Venice of the Counter Reformation.

XI

GAETANO COZZI

Authority and the Law in Renaissance Venice

For if the government in Cosimo's time had all the weaknesses alleged above, a similar
government today would see them redoubled, for the times have changed from what
they were, and so have the city and its inhabitants.

MACHIAVELLI: *Discursus florentinarum rerum post mortem iunioris Laurentii Medices*

On 4th April, 1456, the *Quarantia criminal* – a constitutional body with chiefly
judicial functions but which also had standing and competence of a political
nature, including the power to initiate legislation – proposed a new statute to
the Great Council. It was observed in the preamble that many men who had
been exiled from Venice after being convicted of crimes were risking a return
to the city and were committing new and worse villainies there. The guardians
of order – 'offitiales' and 'custodes' – were reluctant to pursue them, at least
with the necessary vigour, fearing that should they kill them they could themselves be charged with homicide. The statute therefore established that if anyone,
either outlawed already or to be outlawed in future for crimes which carried a
penalty of death, loss of limb or life imprisonment, tried to resist arrest with
weapons, the 'custodes' could assail him 'per omnem modum'; and it was added
for the sake of full clarity that if it should happen that the outlaw were killed,
'non incurrant propterea custodes in aliquam poenam, sed licite et impune
bannitos praedictos se cum armis defendentes offendere et occidere possint'. The
statute was approved by the Great Council, but against considerable opposition:
645 votes in favour, 105 against, 73 *non sinceri* (or disposed to modify the law).[1]

Another statute which the *Quarantia criminal* brought before the Great Council
on the same day had more success. It, too, was concerned with the disturbing
problem of the spread of crime. In the past, it was said, the laws awarded a cash
bounty to anyone who captured a murderer or a sodomite condemned 'ad
supplitium mortis' of 100 lire *di piccoli* the first time and much more, 500 lire *di
piccoli*, the second time; nothing, however, if it was a matter of theft. This, the
preamble maintained, was unjust both because men who had committed murder

on an angry impulse were treated with far greater severity than those who stole with 'malice aforethought', and because nowadays 'many thefts and numberless larcenies' were perpetrated nightly. To remedy this state of affairs the statute established that whoever – 'offitiales' or 'custodes' or others – arrested a thief would receive a cash reward on a scale running from 200 to 400 lire *di piccoli* – according to whether the culprit was sentenced to death or the loss of two limbs or of one. It was passed almost unanimously: 533 votes in favour, 9 against, 23 *non sinceri*.[2]

On 16th September, 1468, the Council of Ten, the severest and most feared of Venetian constitutional bodies, returned to the question of the arrogant and rebellious behaviour of the 'malefactores et exules' who roamed Venice, impatient of every authority, indifferent to every law. Once, the verbal order of a representative of the government was enough because people hastened to obey: today, they revolted against the guardians of order to the point of snatching those arrested from their very hands. Proposing a remedy, the council ruled that the 'officiales' could kill those who drew weapons against them without risk of penal consequences.[3]

Outlaws were those who, having been summoned by a judge to answer to a crime charged to them, escaped justice by fleeing. Doubly guilty, then: both of the crime for which it was hoped to take proceedings against them and of that of high treason, the refusal to submit to supreme authority; the Barbarian Code, considering their actions to have put them beyond the law and outside its protection, held that they could be killed with impunity.[4] Traces of this conception permeated the statutes of a good many Italian cities, including Venice, which had reached the point of granting the *cinque savi alla pace* a privilege according to which the fine to be paid by anyone who killed a person outlawed by this magistracy was limited to five *soldi di piccoli*, with no further penalty.[5] This was an exceptional case, however; and in 1318 the privilege had been much reduced inasmuch as it had been decreed that if the victim had been guilty of a crime liable to a pecuniary penalty of less than 100 lire *di piccoli*, the murderer would be prosecuted for homicide 'ac si interfectus . . . non fuerit bannitus'.[6] Apart from this case, the Venetian penal code at that time refrained from authorizing or openly favouring the assassination of miscreants and outlaws: the three laws cited above prove this. The Venetians attempted also to limit it in the *dominio* with a law of 1489 which, however, they were compelled to revoke in 1490 because of the reaction of the Vicentini.

Looking at the penal legislation of the third decade of the following century, one becomes aware that in the interval the situation has changed radically. Authorization to assassinate outlaws is normal in Venice and the *dominio*, and whoever does so, apart from receiving a bounty, frequently succeeds in being freed himself from exile caused by some crime of his own. A law of the Council of Ten, of 30th August, 1531, is indicative of this new orientation in the criminal law. After having said that outlaws were able to continue breaking the law because of those who were feeding them and offering them refuge, the law draws rigid consequences: 'let it be decreed', it resolves, 'that whosoever *de caetero* accepts any outlaw into his town house or country house or elsewhere, or, having already accepted him, does not send him away instantly, but keeps company with, follows or accompanies him by day or night, armed or unarmed in places forbidden him by his sentence, even if he be connected to him by the closest ties of blood', that is, father, son or brother, 'immediately incurs, and is understood to have incurred, the same penalty of being outlawed as the real transgressor . . . and, as an outlaw, can be attacked or brought to death with impunity, and for the same reward as that placed on the outlaw's head'. The results were not long in showing themselves. From every side, the Council of Ten was warned that many were taking advantage of the law 'some to obtain rewards and absolution from exile, others to take revenge on their enemies'; any evidence was enough, however vague or uncritically accepted, to allow them to kill and, moreover, to make a profit from it. The same council resolved, on 26th September, 1532, to correct the law: whoever sheltered an outlaw for more than a day would be banished for five years from the territory in which he was living and would have to pay a cash fine. It was an ephemeral remedy, however: the spiral of violence unloosed in these years would not be checked until late in the eighteenth century.[7]

★

The period when the laws we have mentioned were adopted in Venice, represented an epoch of profound upheaval for Europe. National states approached maturity, acquiring the constitutional forms which represented the modern state in embryo. Long and hugely expensive wars were fought, which had their epicentre in Italy but which affected the political and economic life of the entire continent; the religious crisis which had been brewing for some time broke out in a drama which involved the collapse of Christian unity; new lands were discovered across the seas; a new culture was introduced. The world was changing and even penal institutions were affected by structural transformations and by a changing sensibility: witness the bull of Charles V, of 1532, which reformed the penal code of the Empire; the statutes of Henry VIII of 1531, 1533, 1537 and that of Edward VI of 1547; and the 'Ordonnance sur le fait de la Justice', promulgated by Francis I in 1539 at Villers-Cotterets.[8]

The Venetian Republic was to feel the repercussions of these events very powerfully, especially those of a political and economic nature: it emerged, in the fourth decade of the *cinquecento*, deeply scarred, not only, or not so much, in its prestige and wealth (many splendid days were yet to come, as Fernand Braudel says, in the rest of that century and in the following one)[9] but in its spirit and its institutions – and more deeply that it dared allow to be seen.

At the beginning of the second half of the *quattrocento*, it seemed that a long period of peace was about to open. In 1454 Venice concluded, with the Peace of Lodi, the war against the duke of Milan; in the same year Mahomet II, the recent

295

conqueror of Constantinople, confirmed with the Republic the peace drafted in 1452. Instead, it was to be a period of continuous wars. Wars in Italy, with the duke of Ferrara, with Sigismund of Austria. Between 1496 and 1499 Venice supported the Pisans in their struggle against Florence. It remained a spectator in the face of Charles VIII's descent into Italy in 1494, except for making itself the headquarters in 1495 of an anti-French league contracted with the pope, the emperor, the king of Spain, and the duke of Milan. Then it became an ally of Louis XII of France when he launched his attack on the duke of Milan in 1499. And apart from these there were wars with the Turk: one, lasting a good sixteen years, from 1463 to 1479, was fought from Negroponte in the Morea to Albania; another, begun in 1499 and ended in 1502, was darkened by the two serious naval defeats at Zonchio; and this is not to mention the incursions which by the end of the *quattrocento* the Turks were making across the Venetian *terraferma* to the very shores of the lagoon. At the very beginning of the sixteenth century the policy of the last fifty years could seem, from a territorial point of view, not lacking, on balance, in positive elements. In the east, if first Negroponte, then Scutari and then Modone and Corone had been lost, there had been a major acquisition, the island of Cyprus. In Italy the outcome was firmly encouraging. Towards Milan the Venetians possessed Cremona and the Ghiaradadda, towards the Po, Rovigo with the Polesine, and south of the Po, Rimini, Cervia and Ravenna, fertile lands from which a new supply of grain was expected to alleviate, if not actually avert, the danger of recurrent bad harvests; they had even obtained a few ports on the coast of Apulia.

But the price had been very high. 'Now I do not wish to refrain from writing that I have heard', noted Marino Sanuto in his *Diarii* in the February of 1499, 'that Venetian money has vanished especially through the demands necessitated by four wars'.[10] 'The treasuries and the purses of private citizens' are exhausted, confirmed another diarist, Piero Dolfin, in March, 1500.[11] Fernand Braudel and Gino Luzzatto have remarked on the strangeness of the Venetian economic situation at the end of the fifteenth century, when, side by side with clear signs of the recession lamented by contemporaries – especially the successive bankruptcies which occurred between 1495 and 1499 – there was evidence of great wealth:[12] in the city, the construction of splendid palaces, public and private, of churches and monasteries and the pursuit of luxuries ('to build houses and dress sumptuously', said Sanuto), in the *terraferma* purchases of land even in the Romagnol territories which had only just been acquired (Girolamo Priuli, a fierce adversary of the expansionist policy in Italy, suggested that the Venetian government had been driven to it by a 'greedy desire to expand the empire for their own benefit').[13] The richest patrician families, able somehow to take advantage of the times – and of others, too weak to counter them – grew richer. It was symptomatic that in the furore of polemics and resentment, one of the accusations levelled against Antonio Grimani – the immensely wealthy merchant who, having been appointed captain general of the sea, was charged with the responsibility for the serious defeat suffered by the Venetian fleet in the first battle of Zonchio – should have been that he had taken advantage of the war with the Turk, because during the period of slack business he had been able to sell the spices piled up in his warehouses at whatever figure he chose to set on them. On the other hand, the trade recession had taken from the nobles of modest fortune their principal source of income, the posts reserved for them in the 'galie di viazi' which afforded the possibility of carrying a certain amount of goods without paying duty on them. 'Many poor gentlemen ... it used to be their bread and butter', observed Dolfin in December, 1500, deploring the prevailing tendency to concede these posts more as a favour than through the usual electoral route.[14] A nobleman of the Contarini, without public employment for sixteen years, incapable, as he complained, of 'earning a living by any trade' and forced to support a large family on a paltry income, turned to the doge in order to protest against the office charged with the exaction of taxes which, considering him in arrears with his contribution, had sold his house. He received satisfaction: the sale was revoked and the agency was told to make the rich pay and to proceed 'understandingly with the poor who have nothing on which to live'.[15] A patrician who had headed the office, however, discovered to his cost that this was not such a simple task: some of the rich and politically powerful nobles whom he had forced to pay had then taken their revenge. The doge replied to his protests with words of comfort: 'have patience and God will see you compensated'.[16] At the end of 1501, at the height of this crisis, the news reached Venice that the Portuguese caravels, having circumnavigated Africa, had arrived at Lisbon from India; from Levantine emporia like Alexandria came letters saying that spices were nowhere to be found 'owing to the competition of these *signori*, who are the complete ruin of the country'. Similar news would be repeated in the following years, more and more frequent, more and more disturbing. To merchants like Girolamo Priuli, it seemed that this might be the end of the Venetian spice trade, 'the life blood', as he put it, of the Republic's economy.[17]

The crisis which was thwarting one part of the nobility could not but have serious political repercussions on the patriciate as a whole: a unitary body which, through the complex machinery of councils, offices and magistracies, sustained the burden of administration and the government of the state. At the base of this structure was the Great Council: taking part in it by right were all Venetian nobles who were proved to be the legitimate sons of noble Venetians and of mothers of suitable social status and who had reached the age prescribed by law, normally twenty-five years. From the beginning of the century the qualifications for membership of the Venetian aristocracy and, therefore, for admission to the Great Council, were subject to increasingly rigid rules and controls.[18] The Republic exercised its sovereignty over a part of the Po valley which was immensely rich in civic and feudal tradition, inhabited by an ancient nobility which, reluctant from the beginning to accept their new rulers, would have harboured feelings of scorn and antagonism towards an aristocratic body which was not concerned for its own exclusiveness and the purity of its blood. Among the functions of the Great Council apart from voting on laws and granting favours which had been proposed by the relevant constitutional body, there was a distributive one: to elect nobles to the various offices of the Republic. This was particularly delicate in the case of the Senate, the more restricted council which, as Sanuto said, really managed the government of the state. The vast majority of all elections took place in the Great Council and thus the entire body of the nobility had a hand in them. There were marked differences between the various offices. Many, and obviously the most important, were located in Venice; the others, to which government of the empire, by land and sea, was entrusted, were scattered among its cities, towns, and fortresses. There were other differences which arose from the nature and importance of the duties to be performed, from the lustre which they required and gave, from the experience and preparation they presupposed, from the burden they imposed and the profit which could be derived from them. There were offices which were almost exclusively the preserve of the leading noble families; of men who possessed adequate learning and were, moreover, in a position to leave merely economic consideration on one side while they concentrated on going through the *cursus honorum* of appointments in the required order, until they eventually became part of the elite which, in practice, held the reins of government in its hands; and there were offices which attracted only the poorest of nobles, for whom the fundamental problem was simply one of eking out a living, a problem which had become harsher once exclusive notions of the conduct properly becoming a noble forbade recourse to means of making a living which remained open to other men. But for all the disparity among offices and among nobles, there was only one electorate and the rich helped elect the poor, and the poor aided the success of the rich. It was an inevitable result of this that if one group of men was disposed to commit fraud, say to make certain candidates win and to exclude others, everyone suffered the consequences, politically and morally; and so it was if some were disposed to sell their own votes, or if others organized vast networks of common interests. In the Republic, which had never had any illusions about human nature, the electoral system was set up in a way that would offer the greatest possible protection; all the same, anyone who was inclined to cheat could find a way to do so.

Things went well when the numerical ratio between offices and candidates was reasonable. In the fifteenth century it changed; although the number of offices grew it fell out of step with the increased number of candidates. Running through the records of the Great Council one is struck by the difference between the votes with which laws are passed or rejected at the beginning of the century and those that obtained at the end. In the first decades of the century it is difficult to find a piece of legislation voted on by more than 400. By the middle of the century the increase is already considerable; by the end there can easily be 800 votes.[19] In his *Cronachetta* Marino Sanuto wrote of about 1,400 or 1,500 nobles being in the council chamber in 1493 and at times – for instance when prestigious appointments like the procuratorships of St. Mark were being made – 1,800. In 1509, when Antonio Grimani's exoneration from the penalty inflicted on him in 1500 because of the defeat of Zonchio was to be voted on, his sons and grand-sons exerted themselves to their utmost to plead his cause and 1,465 patricians came out in his favour.[20] In 1513, for the decision on a law regarding a magistracy, the *signori di notte al criminal*, to which nobles of low fortune could aspire – an increase in salaries was also under consideration – there were 1,300 voters.[21] Underlying this numerical change there was undoubtedly a demographic increase in the patrician class. Another, though much less important factor arose from the favour extended to young men, who, from 1441 to 1497, after a drawing of lots which selected thirty of them each year, could enter the Great Council at the age of eighteen rather than at twenty as had previously been the rule, and as it would be again.[22] But this throng of patricians in the hall of the Great Council was due to yet another cause: maritime and mercantile sources of income having diminished, and the prospect of taking to the seas having become less enticing owing to the ever greater risks to be encountered there, the poor or moderately-off nobleman had nothing left but to look to the government of the Republic for a livelihood. The pursuit of office was to be the most logical means of resolving the problem: a pursuit by men hungry for the very humblest offices which led to an enhanced demand for the remaining, more important ones. According to certain contemporaries, the frequency of cases of embezzlement in the Venetian administration in this period was due to the fact that many jobs were filled by men forced by their wretchedness to extort profit greater than that offered by the normal salaries.[23] This may have been so, but if this were the only reason, the numerous cases of embezzlement attributed to patricians with substantial fortunes would remain unexplained. What is certain is that towards the end of the fifteenth century the phenomenon of 'broglio' took on disturbing proportions, in other words pre-electoral machinations, bribes, canvassing and attempts to solicit sympathy and favour and requests for votes coupled with the pledge to render a comparable service as opportunity served.[24] This is, of course, an inevit-able phenomenon wherever elections exist. The seriousness of the situation here occurred when it was carried to such excess as to lead to the creation of veritable clans, paralyzing the will of the voters, making them forget for considerations of family or group loyalty that the point of the elections was to entrust offices to the most suitable and deserving. It was worse when impoverished nobles, in extreme need and at the limits of their self-respect – those nobles who, in reference to the mercenaries who figured so largely on the European political scene, came to be called 'Switzers' – actually sold their votes. There will be more to say on this, however, with regard to the years to come rather than to the period I am discussing now. The records of the Great Council abound in regulations which attempted to eliminate these vices in the electoral system. First of all there were rules which imposed rigid conformity within the assembly. Then there were rules aimed at repressing the 'broglio'. Finally the attempt was made to reform the electoral system by imposing a more careful winnowing out of candidates; it was laid down in this period that almost all appointments had to be made from among four candidates rather than two, as in the past.[25] Among the first was one passed in March, 1478, by the Council of Ten according to which the doge and other magistrates (the six ducal councillors, the three *avogadori di comun*, the three *capi* of the Council of Ten) were to be considered 'creti', that is, were to be believed 'on their simple word' should they claim to have seen nobles in the Great Council chamber offending against the law.[26] But the hope expressed by Domenico Morosini, one of the most influential of Venetian noblemen between the end of the *quattrocento* and the beginning of the *cinquecento*, and a man imbued with classical nostalgia like so many of his class, that a special magistracy of 'censors' would be created with a specific assignment to control the 'broglio' and see to discipline within the assembly, was not realized, at least not then.[27]

The situation of the patrician class was pregnant with dangers which were not limited to the battle to secure office for oneself or to foster, through mutual agreements, their acquisition by others. Certain movements of opinion were also much to be feared, certain proposals whose mouthpieces were patricians of the highest rank but of demagogic temperament. In 1492 Gabriele Bon and Francesco Falier, *capi* of the *Quarantia criminal*, let it be known that they had found the way 'to provide poor gentlemen who have no office with 70,000 ducats a year: that is, 100 ducats a year per head to those who are past sixty, and fifty to those who are between twenty-five and sixty, on condition that they pay the *decime*': and they proposed to raise the money from offices, suggesting that those whose term of office was for two years should serve eight months, and whose offices lasted one year, four months "da bando", that is, without payment. This notion was expressed in a measure put before the Great Council, but the nobles who held office in the *terraferma* or who hoped to (as *rettori* of the subject cities) were certainly not attracted by the prospect. The members of the *Collegio* (an even more restricted council of the Senate which was pretty well the leading policy-making body in Venice) and of the Council of Ten declared themselves scornful; they even indulged in classical reminiscences, conjuring up 'the example of the agrarian laws in Rome'; 'it cannot be allowed', they maintained, 'that anyone should try to make himself mighty by handing out public money' and 'that by this means the land be ridden with factions'. It was feared, moreover, that the beneficiaries of the new law would be united in large groups in the Great Council on the day of the election. The *Collegio* therefore asked the doge to summon the law's promoters and urge them to withdraw it 'on pain of the disgrace of the Council of Ten'. This disgrace did in fact fall promptly on the two men, who, after having said they would comply with the doge's request, still appeared determined to present the law. The *Collegio* and the Council of Ten met again: 'without any reservation, nor considering any other matter, to provide that neither these nor others should promote such a thing in the future, and that Falier and Bon should be confined for life at Nicosia, on pain of death'.[28] Ten years later, a similar disgrace fell to the lot of another noble, Zuan Antonio Minio. In the preoccupation with finding money which was tormenting the Republic it was decided to impose a measure, already presented in the Senate and awaiting the sanction of the Great Council, that would halve the stipends of public officials. The demand was still for a 'servir da bando', but not in order to give what was saved to the poor nobles; instead, it was to deprive them of money to the same extent as the rich ones. In the Great Council Minio fervently pleaded the poor nobles' cause, insisting on the injustice of the law and expressing the conviction that the lack of charity of which this was a proof was one of the reasons why God was raining such massive disasters upon the Venetian Republic. This time even Sanuto, who was usually sympathetic – probably because of a certain social affinity with the poor nobles – became indignant; Minio, he noted in his *Diarii*, thought 'to gain great credit in this way by seeking the plaudits of those poor men who lived by their offices'. As for the Council of Ten, it took steps to condemn Minio immediately to perpetual confinement on the island of Arbe.[29] What was taking shape, then, was a movement on the part of the 'grandi' to hold that plethoric and unpredictable organism which the Great Council had become in due subjection. For its own part, or at least on that of those of its members who were most concerned with this issue, there were two possible means of retaliation: to try and get the rules which hampered them revoked, and to frustrate elections to the offices where the 'grandi' had most weight. The latter remedy was to score a success in 1503; for some time it was not possible to elect the Council of Ten because the necessary margin of votes could not be obtained.[30]

Describing the form of government of the Republic in the middle of the *quattrocento*, the nobleman Paolo Morosini put the doge and the Great Council almost on the same level and well above all other councils and magistracies.[31] In 1463 the doge, Cristoforo Moro, asked the Great Council if war should be made on the Turks as the pope was requesting: 'we depend on the goodwill of *la signoria vostra*', he told the assembly.[32] But in the period bridging the *quattrocento* and *cinquecento*, Domenico Morosini (the nobleman mentioned earlier), who was a member of the group of key dignitaries and probably representative of the views of many of them, subjected both the Great Council and the institution of the dogeship to criticism in his *De bene instituita republica*.' It is particularly interesting that his work was not a celebration of the Republic as were those of Paolo Morosini (very restrained), Marino Sanuto and Marc' Antonio Sabellico or as Gasparo Contarini's was to be, but adopted a quite different tone. Domenico Morosini discussed amendments to the Venetian constitution as it stood, it being practically impossible to create a new one – a clear sympton, this, of the dramatic moment in which the Republic was trapped and the crisis which gripped its men and its institutions. The fault of the Venetian nobility, he said, is that it is too numerous: though it managed to set itself apart from the mass of the people it was not exempt from the vices to which every kind of multitude is subject. Taking the state of things as they were, the way to find a remedy would be to distinguish offices suitable for young men from those suited to the old. If today one were suddenly to deprive the young men of the possibility of belonging to any office, they would start a riot. But if one were obliged to create the republic anew – and to 'turn it upside-down', Morosini observes (and one does not know if he is thinking of something actually realizable) would be a formidably difficult undertaking – the magistracies should be entrusted to the older men; this would dissuade youth from ambition, displacing it in the direction of crafts, trade and the liberal professions. If this attack on the swollen body of the nobility expresses the unease that was felt about the Great Council, what Morosini wrote about the institution of the dogeship is in line with the disquiet and hostility it had aroused for some time.[33] In the fourteenth century a doge, Marin Faliero, suspected of conspiring against the state, was sent to his death; in the middle of the fifteenth century another doge was deposed, Sanuto wrote, 'for being incapable of functioning as doge'. Yet again, in the second half of the *quattrocento* there were two cases of doges who had caused public opinion to explode: that of Cristoforo Moro, doge from 1462 to 1471, and of Agostino Barbarigo, who held the office from 1486 to 1501. An assembly as crowded and as pervaded with malcontents and grievances as was the Great Council at the end of the century could be a highly dangerous temptation for ill-intentioned doges to use as an instrument. Especially for a man like Barbarigo. The mere fact that he had managed to succeed his brother Marco as doge, a case unique in Venetian history, reveals both an utterly determined will to have his way against those who saw the risks of a succession within the same family, and the strength of his supporters. He had encouraged men to genuflect before him as a matter of course, newly-married couples to come to touch his hand on the day of their weddings, patricians to come to him in order to pay their respects on the day on which they quitted or were elected to any office or post. As though this were not enough he was also accused of having committed, with the agreement of his intimates and servants, 'horrible, abominable and dreadful peculations and extorsions, and sold justice... without any shame, *tanquam dominus et tyrannus: sic volo, sic jubeo*'.[34]

The 'correzioni alla promissione ducale', or revisions effected immediately after the death of a doge in the complex of rules (the 'promissio') regulating the authority of his office which every doge on election had to swear to respect, reveal in this period the constant care taken to define the constitutional position of the doge within very precise and restricted limits; he was enjoined to represent his role with splendour of exterior demeanour, certainly, but he was also prevented from taking any individual initiative whatsoever, and many were the precautions taken to avoid abuses on the part of his intimates.[35] Domenico Morosini held that even this was not enough. The doge, he wrote, as the guardian of the law and of justice, and as holder of the supreme magistracy, should intervene in decisions in order to safeguard the public interest and prevent private causes from imperilling those of the state. But he himself should be placed under the law as administered by the appropriate magistracies. According to Morosini, then, it was necessary that a review of the doge's behaviour should take place not only *post mortem* but every five years during his life; and whenever he was shown to be incapable or unworthy of filling his office he should be deposed.[36]

These are opinions which might seem to suggest our looking at Venetian policy, especially with regard to its fundamental aspects such as the value of tradition and the relationship between authority and equality of status, from a changed point of view.

'Est preterea supremum et auctoritate perspicuum trium advocatorum tribunal quo nil civitate sanctius, cum communes oppressorum omnium advocati dicuntur; nil scelestis legumque transgressoribus magis formidabile previdentur', Paolo Morosini had written of the *avogadori di comun*; 'est praeterea decemvirorum consilium, in quo princeps sexque consultores assistunt, et si quem in principe, principatumque deliquisse constiterit, indelebili de poena mulctatur. Maxime itaque terrore omnibus extat consilii huius tremenda sententia . . .', he was to say, a little further on, of the Council of Ten.[37] Marino Sanuto is more detailed. As for the *avogadori di comun*, he emphasizes that they must be present at every council on pain of the invalidation of the meeting; that any one of them may 'intrometter quello li par', that is, may suspend all deliberations the legality of which is in question; that they may 'menar' or summon to justice those whom they regard as guilty of a crime 'before what council they choose, either the Great Council, the Senate or the *Quarantia criminal* . . . and within these councils', Sanuto continues, 'they argue as advocates for the commune, whence comes their title "avogadori", and they argue there in support of their suspensions . . . and act as guardians of the law'. He does not omit to mention thereafter, and twice, that the *avogadori* have precedence over the *capi* of the Council of Ten.[38] But it is evident that even in the brief space of time – approximately thirty years – which separates the writings of Morosini and Sanuto the situation had changed. Sanuto, immensely fervid admirer of the *Avogaria* though he is, cannot put it before the Council of Ten itself as his predecessor had done; and he recognizes that – in spite of the longer tradition of the former, in spite of the formal prerogatives which still gave it such an honourable status – the power and repute of the Council of Ten are a good deal greater. Strictly interpreted, its competence was restricted, it was a judicial body and it was responsible for protecting the security of the state. Yet the most dramatic events of the last two centuries were associated with its name: the execution of Doge Marin Faliero and of Count Carmagnola, chief of the Venetian army, the deposition of Doge Francesco Foscari. He emphasized that 'it also determines other matters of great importance', and he concludes by saying that it is an 'extremely awesome magistracy' and a 'highly secret' one.[39]

The two magistracies, despite their different historical and political origins, had duties which were or could become over-lapping and they tended, therefore, to compete with one another. This is confirmed beyond all doubt by the fact that in the space of ten days, from the 18th to the 29th of September, 1468, attempts were made to define the areas of competence of each of them. First it was the turn of the Council of Ten. The proposed statute, after having recorded that the fathers of the Republic had taken care to hold 'in culmine consilium nostrum Decem', be it because of its authority and dignity or the importance of the matters concerning the state entrusted to it, it was deplorable that for some time its members 'excreverunt in tantum occupationes et negotia ipsius Consilii praesertim multiplicibus et diversis rebus impertinentibus indignisque tanti magistratus'. In future, it would be required to concern itself with these matters only: treason, conspiracies and anything else associated with disturbance of the peace of the state, treaties, and 'terrarum et locorum ac aliarum rerum huiusmodi', for which high secrecy was necessary, cases of sodomy, questions relating to the *Scuole grandi* and to the chancery. Its authority to punish the *rettori* and other 'offitiales' of the Republic who refused to obey 'mandatis nostri Dominii' was confirmed, while the *capi* of the Council lost their control over the maintenance of the privileges of subject cities and territories, this trust being given to the *avogadori di comun*. On passing the measure into law the doge's councillors were directed to enforce immediately a penalty of 1,000 ducats for *capi* of the Council who did not comply with its provisions. The preamble to the measure affecting the *Avogaria* was much harsher. It was recalled that it was a good rule that the various magistrates should not arrogate greater authority than that deputed them by law or capitulary passed in the Great Council; in spite of this, the *avogadori* have removed to their own higher court 'omnes casus tam civiles, quam criminales', and even criminal cases which are inappropriate to their office and which belong to others of lesser importance. The *avogadori* were then enjoined to limit themselves to the handling of only those criminal matters which had been allotted them by the Great Council in 1352 and those which might be entrusted to them from time to time by the *Signoria* ('per nostrum Dominum'). The most remarkable section, re-echoing old complaints about the conduct of the *avogadori*, was the final one: 'Item, non possint a se ipsis sine consiliis terrae ordinare, nec jubere Rectoribus de Extra, nec impedire judices vel offitiales de intus super rebus et causis civilibus vel criminalibus per illos Rectores, judices vel offitiales judicandis vel expediendis, salvo quam in executione rerum et causarum ipsis advocatoribus ut supra specialiter commissarum; sed cum consiliis terrae possint et ante et post ordinare et jubere rectoribus, judicibus et offitialibus praedictis sicut sibi iustum videbitur.' And the *avogadori*, too, were threatened with a 1,000 ducat fine in case of any breach of these regulations.[40]

It was the *Avogaria di Comun* which came out worst from these revisions, and not entirely because they reduced the scope of its activity while accentuating the autonomy and importance of another magistracy, the *Auditori Novi*, which was to receive and judge the sentences of the *rettori* 'both of land and sea'.[41] This was inevitable, given that its sphere of jurisdiction was the entire *dominio* and that civil cases superabounded because litigation had been increased by the wars, by changes of sovereignty and by the consequent uncertainty about what law was really relevant (*jus commune* on the *terraferma*, *jus proprium* in the ruling city). It was essential that the Republic guarantee its new subjects a fair, rapid and inexpensive justice. The greatest offence to the *Avogaria* was having been deprived of any possibility of autonomous initiative with regard to the *rettori* of the *terraferma* and the other 'judices vel offitiales' and having its actions made subject to the approval of one of the councils (such as the Senate, the Great Council, or the Council of Ten itself). The *Avogaria* continued to be weakened in subsequent years. A law of 1471, replacing another of 1468, authorized the *capi* of the *Quarantia criminal* to take the initiative in bringing forward any 'intromissioni' which the *avogadori*, for one reason or another, might have omitted or deferred, so as to make sure that all criminal proceedings reached completion.[42] Three years later the *avogadori* were once again under attack. 'A very bad practice has been introduced in this city of ours', said a statute approved by the Great Council on 14th August, 1474, 'that the *avogadori di comun, auctoritate propria sine consiliis*, have begun to nullify certain *intromissioni* of the *auditori novi* or *syndici*, and to have them erased from their books, passing sentence on them themselves . . . making inappellable judgements beyond their constitutional rights and, furthermore, the practice of this city of ours'. However, 'for the honour of the *Signoria*, and also that many of our subjects should not suffer and that errors of this sort shall no longer recur', the *avogadori* were forbidden to quash any 'intromissione' from the *auditori* or the *sindaci*.[43] These were serious charges of arbitrary action, of indifference towards subjects' rights; all the more serious since they were levelled against magistrates whose institutional duty it was to guarantee observance of the law. The *avogadori*, however, were by no means prepared to accept these erosions of their power. In 1505 they brought to Venice under arrest a *provveditore* of the Riviera of Salò who had not complied with their order to suspend the execution of a death sentence he had pronounced. His case was referred to the decision of the Senate; they found the *avogadori's* claims unfounded and the *provveditore* was freed.[44]

The Council of Ten, on the other hand, continued its ascent. On 15th May, 1486, a new statute of the Great Council restored its control over the observance of all the privileges conceded to cities and other components of the empire; only a few years before, as we have seen, this had been assigned to the *avogadori*. The political and military events of the last decade of the century and of the beginning of the following one, the deterioration in the circumstances of many elements within the patriciate, the aggravation of the problem of public order in Venice and its empire all worked to accentuate its power and to enlarge its jurisdiction.[45] Many were alarmed by this. Among them was the chronicler, Domenico Malipiero, who showed irritation in 1497 that the Council was betraying no signs of staying within the limits fixed for it by the law of 1468: 'under cover of doing the most secret things', he wrote, 'it meddles with many matters which are none of its business.'[46] But these protestations died as soon as they were uttered; for the majority the new order of things was inevitable. Even Sanuto, whose attitude was to stiffen when it became clear that the Council of Ten was undermining the power of the Senate, did not raise objections then. On the contrary, when in December, 1501, an inquisitor into the conduct of Doge Agostino Barbarigo pronounced in the Great Council a vehement indictment he noted in his *Diarii*: 'I would not be silent about what most people thought, and in particular . . . that for the honour of the state it would be better to deal with such matters in the Council of Ten and not *coram omnibus*.'[47] A comment worthy of a Domenico Morosini, who was in fact to declare himself an enthusiastic admirer of the Council: 'A quo consilio', he wrote, 'tot et tanta bona profecta sunt ut tranquillitas perpetua nostrae civitatis et diuturnae nostrae libertatis ex magna parte huic consilio possit ascribi.'[48]

When confronting the *avogadori di comun*, Domenico Morosini seems to indicate, in a rather intricate passage of his work, that he is in some perplexity. They are the defenders of the law. It seems to be his view that they are, however, insufficiently strong and autonomous, being too bound to the doge, who is himself traditionally considered an *avogadore*, 'magnus et perpetuus advocator'; he usually lends them his support but by virtue of this succeeds in controlling them and can block them whenever it is a case of their taking effective action on occasions when he disagrees with them. The effectiveness of their action, their ability actually to protect and preserve 'boni mores' and prevent 'mali mores' from establishing themselves depended on the character, good or bad, of the doge. For the *avogadori* to fulfil their function they needed not only the doge's support but power to protect themselves in case he wished to exert pressure on them. For Morosini, as is well known, this would be ensured if the conduct of the doge were made responsible not only to the law but to the close scrutiny of the relevant magistracies.[49] The Council of Ten, on the contrary, was potentially in a position to change the situation, to eliminate the 'mali mores', to impose the good. 'It seems to me very like the dictatorship which the Romans set up at moments of great danger', Trifone Gabriello is made to say in Giannotti's book, adding that 'what they created in dangerous times can also be found in our own Republic.' 'Hic magistratus tenet locum principis tiranni, si non ex toto ex maxima parte', wrote Domenico Morosini in outright terms, praising the services they rendered from a different standpoint and with a different emphasis.[50] To describe the antithesis between the *Avogaria* and the Council of Ten in what can be no more than a tentative formula, one could say that whereas the *avogadori* represented the law as a function of equality the Council of Ten represented it as a function of authority. For the Venetian aristocracy law was not something extrinsic or imposed: it was the expression of themselves, of their own will and nature, the highest and most representative form of self-expression, the most ingrained in their own political and civil experience, the most indispensable for their own existence; it was the fruit of the collective will, accepted and used by all as something peculiarly their own; they subjected themselves to it because they were aware that this was the only guarantee of equality between individuals and liberty within the Republic. The body of the aristocracy was made up of men who were at once sovereigns and subjects, judges and judged. A member of the *Quarantia* or of the Council of Ten could be the judge of a man who, a little while earlier, had judged him or his sons or others of his family; a tax-payer in arrears could share in the promulgation of laws which threatened the most severe penalties for those who, like him, were in debt to the state. It was no easy matter for individuals to distinguish their duty from their interests, to demand from others what, personally, they could not or did not wish to do, to suggest and then later accept the most severe penalties involving sacrifices and heart-searchings which they could entail, for the security of the law was achieved at the cost of these sacrifices and these heart-searchings. This was the price, and it was a high one, of republican government. There was no lack of failings: surrenders to the pressure of friends, to considerations of family solidarity, to the ties of common political or economic interests. 'The wolf does not eat the meat of a wolf', said the Venetians, noble or less than noble, when some collusion of this kind and, as a consequence, the faulty working of justice, was suspected. The patricians, however, were the first to be aware of the existence of these defects and, above all, of the consequences they could have in undermining respect for the law, the cement which guaranteed their own unity and kept the state strong. There was no shortage of suggested remedies. A decree of January, 1471, after having recalled how much had been done in the past to restrain the unlawful pressures which interested parties brought to bear on 'consegli e collegii', decided on measures which were both energetic and, perhaps, a bit ingenuous, to see to it that 'our whole realm is satisfied and that there will be reason for justice to be rendered indifferently to all'. Once a trial was concluded judges were to 'swear solemnly on *Evangelia Sacra Dei*' that they had entertained neither petitions nor other attempts to influence them and that they had not disclosed the nature of their proceedings; otherwise, the sentence issued must be regarded as null and void.[51] Other expedients were adopted in order to ensure that sentences were actually carried out; the most common, and effective, was to lay down rigorous conditions (the so-called 'strettezze') whereby the condemned man might obtain pardon. But the surest protection came from the patrician's own persistent awareness of the necessity to place himself beneath the law; an awareness affirmed by those decisions of scrupulous fairness and impartiality which made him feel the value of the collective obligation which preserved the life of the Republic, and with which he sought to renew a faith which often, and inevitably, tended to falter. Nor was it an easy matter for the offices and the councils to stay within the limits of jurisdiction fixed by the law or to avoid meddling with one another's areas of competence. For all the consideration which the Venetian constitutional system gave to individuals, it depended on a conscientious balancing act between the various office holders and councillors, linking the former group to the latter, more powerful one, by virtue of the presence of members common to either group, and offering each a way of imposing a respect for the law on the others. 'The affairs of Venice are governed with laws', was the proud statement of the Republic, which thus distinguished itself from other forms of government.[52] But the body that represented – in institutional terms – the civic conscience of the governing aristocracy, whose business it was to protect the notion of equality on which everything, in principle, was based, which warned that in all circumstances the law must always be obeyed was the *Avogaria di Comun*.[53]

The increasingly important role played by the Council of Ten in Venetian policy represents a crisis in the conception of equality – that linchpin of the republican regime – which was brought to a head by the political and social factors I have been discussing up to this point. The Council had been set up according to the usual canons of the Venetian constitution; care was taken to avoid its isolation from the other constitutional organs which might have become bases for oligarchical bids for absolute power. Protection against this was supposed to be secured by the presence, apart from the ten members of the Council itself, of six ducal councillors and, although they had no voting rights, of three *avogadori di comun*; 'their office', Rinaldo Fulin noted, referring to the councillors and the *avogadori*, 'had another origin and another purpose than those of the Council of Ten into which they were introduced; the first were to represent, together with the doge himself, the rights of the princely element in the constitution, the others to protect the cause of equality . . .'[54] In reality, the sectors entrusted to the Council of Ten, such as the negotiation of matters requiring maximum secrecy and the safeguarding of the peace and security of the state, were difficult to define precisely and in the difficult times the Republic was going through they necessarily tended to spread. This, added to the fact that in the course of its judiciary activity it could make use of a special procedure – the so-called 'rito' – characterized by its rapidity and secrecy, could not but mean that the Council had a political potential, the possibility of acting in a purely political capacity comparable to the functions of certain other councils and some of the officers of state. More, it was this secrecy which shrouded the activity of the Council, and which depended on the small number of its members and on the absence of the sort of control which could be exercised on the Senate and the *Quarantia*, that separated it most clearly from other elements within the constitution; this is what gave it the upper hand, this was the basis of its authority. And what ensured the effective substance and continuity of the Council's 'authority' was the fact that it was the ambition of the most prominent men in the Republic to become its members. These were the men who were admitted to the *Collegio* and the *Minor Consiglio* and who aspired to be procurators of St. Mark, men who understood how to make use of the means the Council offered of controlling the policy of the Republic and watching over the moods of subjects and patriciate alike. It was, on the other hand, inevitable that those who had assumed or were assuming the responsibilities and powers of the Council should come to over-value their 'authority' and to gain from it to their personal advantage a special and privileged status in comparison with the rest of the patrician class. Thus, for example, in May 1505 a member of the Council, Niccolò Priuli, against whom criminal proceedings had been initiated, tried to evade arrest by claiming that this would damage the Council's prestige; 'We should not act precipitately', he said, 'and disgrace one of the seventeen pillars of this state.'[55] He was not heeded; he was imprisoned and then condemned, to the great relief of one who, like Marino Sanuto, persisted in believing firmly in the equality of republican justice.

The institutional difference between the *Avogaria* and the Council of Ten appears very clearly in the field of criminal law. The *avogadori* could properly initiate proceedings given that it had come to their attention that one of the crimes within their sphere of competence had been committed, or they could take up an objection to or an appeal against the sentence of a subordinate court which had been presented to them; they could also act on the orders of the *Signoria*. In order to arrest criminals – except in urgent cases – they had to have the authorization of the *Quarantia criminale*. The interrogations of the defendants were then conducted by an *avogadore* in the presence of a committee composed of five other persons. The interrogations were minuted. If the defendant were found guilty, he was then remanded for trial. This took place publicly, with a verbal debate between the *avogadore di comun* and the defendant's lawyer, who had meanwhile received the text of the minutes of the earlier phase. It was, then, a mixed proceeding in which there were elements of the old accusatorial process and of the inquisitorial process of medieval origin: a procedure which a Venetian writer at the end of the *seicento* was to say, with evident pride, 'retains some aspects of the ancient Roman decorum'.[56] Indeed, the procedure was admired by foreigners, too, for the liveliness of the debates it produced, and especially for the protection it offered the defendant. As for the Council of Ten, which had been created precisely in the period when the inquisitorial rite was introduced in the early *trecento*, its procedure was quite simply this: secrecy in every phase of the proceedings; rapid settlement inasmuch as the accused was not defended by a lawyer but, apart from what he could do for himself, could hope only for the support which might come from one of the judges. His one protection was, in fact, that in the restricted college composed of four members which conducted these cases, one *avogadore* also took part. But what struck people most – and what constituted the psychological element on which the intimidating power of the Council was founded – was the atmosphere of secrecy, of being alone in the power of the judges. 'And he who falls into the hands of the Council of Ten', wrote Sanuto, 'cannot defend himself with counsel; when they examine him the palace is barred.'[57] It is a procedure which was to be emphasized more and more as time went on, whether in order to enlarge the Council's sphere of influence or to encourage the creation of what can be defined as its satellite magistracies, or by extending to other magistracies, such as the *rettori* of the *terraferma*, the authority to use its procedures for resolving especially serious situations. The collective sensibility, attuned to the realities of social and political change, was to accept this as inevitable.

★

'Who is there who is ignorant', wrote Claude de Seyssel in 1510 in a pamphlet exalting the resounding victory of Louis XII of France over the Republic, 'of how the *Seigneurie* and the very name of the Venetians, through great and continual acquisitions over a period of some eleven hundred years, have arrived at the repute they now enjoy, and how they are feared not only by all Italy, but by Germany, Hungary, Dalmatia, by all Greece and as far as Asia, for all have lost some of their possessions to her? And in time, given the opportunity, they would through fraud and subterfuge have managed to subdue all the rest of Italy and then render others their tributaries just as the Romans did in the past.'[58] Virtually everyone was discussing this theme. Machiavelli and Guicciardini are among the historians who bore witness to it. A good many Venetians, like Girolamo Priuli, talked of it as well, with an anxiousness that grew as the reaction of the pope and of the major European states – France and the Empire were the first – took shape, became confirmed in 1504 by the Treaty of Blois and was then expressed in a more vigorous and polemical way in the League of Cambrai of December 1508. They deplored the unbridled ambition of the leading Venetian policy makers; they feared its consequences, foreseeing a punishment of God which would sweep away, in a single upheaval, the splendour and wealth together with the pride, the ambition and the other innumerable vices of the Venetians. The defeat sustained by the Republic's army at Agnadello on 14th May, 1509, the successive invasions of the entire state of the *terraferma* by bodies of French, Spanish and Imperial troops which immediately followed it; the enemy's thrusts to the very borders of the lagoon: all these events stirred up dark waves of religious perturbation and of intense moral distress among wide sections of the population. Europe had long been oppressed by an atmosphere of foreboding and suspense, infused with the presence of a God meting out punishment for the sins of the world. Venice was to feel it intensely, as something palpable and inexorable, both in these days and over the years to come, as the city groped towards the recovery of its lost ascendancy.

The Republic was to succeed in regaining the *terraferma* – except for the territories it had won most recently – by the beginning of 1517. These were gruelling years. There had been no more pitched battles like Agnadello. But it had been a wearing war; skirmishes, many futile troop movements, crops devastated, villages burned, populations massacred, as in Friuli. Nor was the enemy the only thing to be feared. Just as dangerous were those who fought in the service of the Republic: 'All the soldiers', wrote Sanuto, 'act in their habitual way, dressing up in cloth of gold, and *licet* they are not paid in time by the government, they do so much harm among the villages that they come out very well from it and rejoice, wanting the war to drag on as it does.'[59] Soldiers, commented Girolamo Priuli in his turn, are predators through habit: the real trouble comes when you are dealing with a people like the Venetians, 'poorly trained and inexperienced as soldiers, . . . for in all truth they knew neither how to wage war nor govern troops, they could not make good use of it [the money they raised] but threw it away'. The result was, in fact, that their troops continued to insist on having money, but 'did not use it for any military action, but stood about scratching their bellies'.[60] In certain moments, when other calamities were added to the military reverses, there was a conviction in Venice that the end had come: between 1513 and 1514, after the failure of the attempt to re-conquer

Vicenza, plague broke out and fire destroyed the Rialto, in the very heart of the city. The city, meanwhile, became more crowded than ever. Nobles and *popolari* had taken refuge there from cities occupied by the enemy and found much in its favour; little by little refugee peasants from the devastated country-side sought asylum there, confident that in Venice, the place of fabled wealth and abundance, a roof and subsistence would not be wanting. Even the Jews had preferred to leave Mestre, where they lived near their banks, and to try to settle as best they could in the city; and their co-religionists had followed them from other centres of the *terraferma*.[61] There were too many people amid too much uneasiness and confusion. The religious, and laymen who like Priuli were prompted by a concern for tradition, lamented the pleasure-seeking atmosphere of certain quarters of the city, the modish disregard for civil and religious duties, the adoption of French fashions by men and women, and the spread of blasphemy, of cases of sodomy, of scandal in the monasteries, of gaming and luxury. There was an increase in thefts and homicides and much casual violence. Some measures had been taken to coper with this delinquency; more severe laws against the various crimes; laws against the carrying of arms, which had ended up in the hands of too many people and of which constant use was made. In December of 1514 Sanuto singled out, as something uncommon and worthy of note, that there had been an attempt to commit murder with a gun.[62]

'In this country', the same diarist wrote at the war's end in the October of 1517, 'there is much homicide and petty theft and many scoundrels, and this is because there is no living to be gained, and so the people turn to crime and are not punished.'[63] One could not really count on the action of the 'birri', or 'zaffi': 'poltroons', Priuli called them scornfully, 'who cannot even crush a flea', and he emphasized that through cowardice or corruption they were incapable of pitting themselves against the criminal or the powerful.[64] Things certainly went no better on the *terraferma*. Apart from the damage wreaked by troops in their lodgings or on the march was that done by deserters or by men who, unexpectedly dismissed by their captains, did not hesitate to devote themselves to marauding about the countryside. There was no protection from them and many years went by before it became possible to enforce justice there.[65]

Sanuto and Priuli often had moments of failing confidence in the Venetian ruling class. At such times they would burst into expressions of indignation, accusing all those most responsible for Venetian policy, including the doge, of incapacity, inertia, egoism. The 'grandi' were certainly good at inciting others to action; but then they would do nothing themselves. Even in the most serious circumstances, when it seemed that the situation was crashing about their ears, very few volunteered to serve in the army in the besieged cities of Padua or Treviso; and the few who did were predominantly poor nobles who had been enticed to serve by the prospect that on their return they would gain entrance to the *Quarantia*. The matter of payment of debts to the state was typical. In November of 1512, when, after a vain attempt at collection, it was decided to proclaim the debtors publicly, it was the names of men who through political office and family wealth carried the highest prestige, which came out, such as the four procurators of St. Mark, Luca Zen, Antonio Grimani, Giorgio Corner and Tommaso Mocenigo.[66] In justification, the 'grandi' could adduce the slackness of business due to Portuguese competition in the spice trade, the decline of revenues from estates in the *terraferma*, and so on.[67] But to that it could have been replied that if they did not pay their taxes they nevertheless spent lavishly on luxuries. This was certainly one way of staying cheerful and of not allowing oneself to be depressed in the midst of so much that could lead to anguish; at a time when a monetary crisis was brewing it was probably also a device for investing money in commodities such as gold, silver, jewels, precious stones and dress, which had an intrinsically lasting value and were, in addition, non-taxable. It was no fortuitous coincidence that in August 1512, two months before publication of the names of taxpayers in arrears, an ordinance of the Senate should have complained that the sumptuary laws were being brazenly violated; in charge of executing the new law's provisions was a special magistracy, the *provveditori alle pompe*, which had been set up in the previous April.[68] The 'grandi' made an equally deplorable showing when they refused the responsibility of difficult or burdensome offices, as, for instance, in the January of 1514 and of 1515, when it seemed that no one was disposed to accept the post of *provveditore generale* in the field or to accept an embassy. Not that the minor nobility was blameless. It too was deserting posts which were generally reserved for it, like the *Zudegà di petizion*, a court where law-suits concerning 50 ducats or less were judged, though the justification was more plausible for people of limited resources, the fact being that they could no longer earn enough there. All the same, at Treviso and Padua the poor nobles had not behaved well, and the soldiers, Girolamo Priuli recounts, were 'misled' by them, 'because', he continued, 'there were many poor nobles who did disgraceful things and led shameful lives . . . yet it was necessary to employ them because the rich nobles were not prepared to inconvenience themselves by undertaking works of that kind'.[69] The lesser nobility, already worn down by the events of the preceding period, was really exhausted, and they were now at grips with ever more serious economic difficulties due to the persistence of the trade crisis overseas. In May 1511, on the eve of the departure of a merchant convoy, when the Senate decided to elect two hundred 'nobili da pope' who could sail on it (and the number they fixed on was nearly double the usual one in order to give the opportunity to the greatest number of people), a good four hundred applications were presented.[70] But with the indigence of poor nobles and the ambition of the 'grandi', electoral corruption increased all too easily. We have already referred to the so-called 'svizzeri' in this connection. In May 1515 Sanuto referred to a certain group of poor nobles who, when a gentleman was elected to an office, would call at his house for money in recompense for the advantage their votes had brought him. And he added that they were numerous and well organized, with councillors, a captain and a chancellor and even a vocabulary of secret signs: they would remove their hats if they wanted a candidate elected and touch their beards if they wanted him rejected.[71] Many were urging the Council of Ten to repress this kind of electoral 'mafia', to put it in modern terms. Sanuto, for his part, was sceptical about the actual efficiency of their organization. They were but poor men, he said, going on to play down their significance. Things used to be far simpler. When one of these patricians had been in a position to nominate someone for election to an office he invited contributions from the interested parties without making any bones about it. Nowadays, he lamented, anybody at all who wanted to be proposed as a candidate could get their way through bribery. But whether because it was difficult to single out those really responsible or because it was a question which involved too many people, the Council of Ten decided to do nothing about it.

Sanuto's bitterly conclusive comment referred to the system which the Republic had shortly before decided to adopt in order to deal with the disastrous financial situation and with the continuous, nagging need for money which resulted from it. The war was costly: the army – soldiers and captains and weapons – had to be paid for, so did provisions and lodgings, so did allies wanting to be compensated for services rendered, so did enemies wanting to be abundantly remunerated when they agreed to adhere to a pact, whether secret or official.[72] The normal fiscal sources, direct or indirect taxes, were either exhausted or dormant. Recourse to the public debt was fruitless because of the lack of faith in it that had spread throughout the population. It was absolutely necessary to find other ways of diverting the wealth which still existed – the immense wealth of the richer nobility, the more modest but no less solid wealth of the middle nobility and of some *popolari* – towards the coffers of the state, ways which might well be unjust or downright dishonest: but, said Girolamo Priuli, in such a contingency, when the life or death of the Republic was at stake, one must not have scruples, always providing that one fairly undertook to put things back on their original footing as soon as peace returned.[73]

First, on 10th March, 1510, the Great Council had deliberated selling to those who already possessed them all the 'scrivanie, nodarie, cogitarie, massarie . . . and every other kind of office' (that is, those offices open to citizens, not those reserved for nobles), with the exception of those of the ducal chancery and several others, either for life or for a certain term, allowing the former, if they paid a certain percentage of the proceeds from the office, to leave it after their death to their sons or grandsons, who would hold them in turn for the whole of their lives, or to their brothers, who would, however, be required to pay a percentage of the proceeds.[74] In the same year it was decided to admit to the Senate, but without the right to vote, nobles who lent the Republic a given sum of money.[75] In August of 1511 those responsible for Venetian policy tried to take the big step: to establish that anyone who hoped to be elected to an 'office or magistracy' must lend the Republic a sum of money varying in accordance with the importance of the appointment and the interest that competing nobles showed in it. Despite the seriousness of the moment, the opposition of the majority of the patriciate was very strong, to the point of advising against even putting the text of the proposal to the vote; and it was an opposition made in the name of that equality which should always be the basis of the Venetian aristocratic system. 'In a well-ordered Republic', it was said on behalf of the opposition, 'equality should always be maintained so that all can share in the benefits and advantages it brings; only in this way will nobles who are rich and powerful on account of their money be honoured and appreciated for it, and the poor but clever and prudent who are without wealth be able nonetheless to acquire some honour and standing in the Republic.' To these considerations of principle were added others of a practical nature which arose from the habitual disenchanted realism of Venetian nobles; in the opposition's view those who obtained an appointment by virtue of a loan to the Republic, especially those who had themselves to borrow the money at interest for this purpose, would not want to run the risk of losing money or of allowing the capital paid to the state not to make a profit; and they would therefore be inclined to exploit the offices and magistracies as much as possible for their own gain.[76]

This remedy having failed, others were studied which might not clash with the rights and susceptibilities of the less wealthy members of the patriciate. On 18th September, 1514, the Senate granted that nobles who had not yet reached the age usually required could be elected *savi agli ordini* (a body which was part of the *Collegio*) on making a payment of 200 ducats. At the same time the Great Council opened its doors, as it had done in the second half of the preceding century, to young men of eighteen years who loaned a set sum of money (on the same day, 18th September, Marino Sanuto noted that some sixty-two youths under twenty-five had entered the Council).[77] The Council of Ten made a special concession, authorizing entry to the Great Council to two seventeen-year-olds whose fathers were offering to lend 100 ducats; with another resolution the same Council sold the chancery which handled the affairs of those who had been banished for life for 500 ducats; with yet another, it allowed that a noble, even without having reached the prescribed age, might enter the *Quarantia* by lending 100 ducats.[78] 'And so', Sanuto said bitterly, 'everything is up for sale.'

This was on 2nd August, 1515. In the following days the project which had failed exactly four years before was taken up once again with immense caution and an attempt to give it the most anodyne tone. On 3rd August the Council of Ten with the *Zonta* and the Senate approved laws which guaranteed, with revenue from the *dazi*, the restitution of their money to those who might make loans to the state. On 4th and 5th August the doge and his advisers, together with the entire *Collegio*, proposed first to the Senate, then to the Great Council, where, as we know, the greater part of elections took place, a law which established that the names should be published in the Great Concil of those 'who have made loans, and how much, and also the names of those who wished to meet the amount offered, and in the same way the names of those who have not made loans, so that', it was explained as a clear warning, 'it can be seen where everyone stands'. The doge had driven home the significance and the aims of the law in one of his speeches. Once the law was approved, and the names of lenders published, the elections to vacant appointments were held. The result was as expected. Those patricians who, although rich, had not made loans, were eliminated (although the case would arise, albeit rarely, of men being defeated in spite of having made loans and of others who were successful although they had not done so).[79] This reform was rounded out by the adoption of one particular device, the application of the electoral method known as 'per scrutinio e quattro man di elezioni' to a wide number of appointments. The 'quattro man di elezioni' referred to the way in which the Great Council selected four candidates to run for an appointment: to these was added one other candidate, chosen instead by the Senate according to a procedure called 'scrutinio'.[80] The Senate candidate went forward under favourable conditions: either because he had behind him the endorsement of men of note, experts in the problems of government who were aware of the Republic's requirements, or because during the voting which was held in the Great Council he could count on a block of votes, those of the senators who had proposed him. It was, then, a way of avoiding the risks of candidatures supported by loans, which provided an opening for demagogues capable of making an impression on the emotionalism of a large assembly but otherwise poorly qualified; or, on the contrary, of supporting men who had lent a great deal but who were unpopular. Furthermore, it allowed the 'grandi' to exercise a direct control over access to offices, in other words, to assert their authority. This was the device which most offended the lesser nobility and gave them the feeling that their rights were being prejudiced. But once it had been put into effect and it was seen that the desired advantages were actually obtaining, it was not possible to stop, at least not while the current political and economic difficulties persisted. In the middle of October, 1516, and again on 14th December, it was decided to have a new block of appointments elected 'per scrutinio e quattro man di elezioni'. Among the latter, along with appointments in small centres of the *terraferma*, there were three *avogadori di comun* 'straordinari' who were to enter the ordinary magistracy when those who presently filled it had finished their time in office. 'It was a bad decision', commented Marino Sanuto in this connection, 'to open the field to young men wanting to become *avogadori*', a decision which certainly did not bring prestige to the *Avogaria*, whose reputation, like that of every other magistracy, was based on the quality of the individuals who became its members. Sanuto mentioned another disturbing symptom. In the Great Council many of the benches were empty, the number of those attending having been reduced to 800; this meant that a great many patricians felt themselves excluded and were losing interest.[81] However, with the passing of time, even those in opposition like Sanuto who, man of small fortune that he was, had been barred by these innovations from elections to offices he coveted, were eventually convinced that the remedies adopted had been fruitful: between the beginning of August, 1515 and 15th January, 1517, the day on which the system of electoral loans was repealed, as much as 474,870 ducats found their way into the coffers of the state. And when in the autumn of 1517 the same Sanuto found himself dealing with nobles who were disdainful of those who had succeeded in the elections by means of loans, he commented irritably that 'by this means the state was maintained and Verona recovered, so that without it, *actum erat*'.[82]

This was a valid historical judgement, no longer clouded by the emotionalism and the resentments which naturally took precedence when the crisis was at its height and when deprivation, danger and concern for the future took on an exaggerated intensity. And on re-reading the pages of Sanuto's *Diarii*, and those of the *Diarii* of Girolamo Priuli, one has glimpses through the pervading gloom they record which enable one to understand better the reasons behind the resistance the Republic offered in the face of the tightening circle with which its enemies proposed to throttle its energies. Above all, an examination of the collective consciousness of the time reveals a spirit which not only affected religion, with the result of making Venice one of the cities most responsive to the need for reform, but civic life as well.[82a] The problem of justice – the justice which should have been imposed and had not been and the grievances subjects had endured because of this – took on the dimensions of a moral problem.[83] Thus in 1513, when the position of the right of appeal was faced, the rules governing recourse to it were defined in accordance with the constant aim of legislation in that period: to prevent delays connected with trials. Shortly afterwards, a statute regulated important matters of criminal procedure, such as the number of votes necessary for sentences of not guilty or of condemnation and the rules affecting judicial interrogations.[84] Other penal laws (one, for example, on the problem of preventive imprisonment, another on procedure in cases of contempt) had been approved between 1515 and 1516; at the same time the civil trial was taken into consideration, the preoccupation here too being with making its course more rapid.[85] 'The *Signoria* had held justice closer to its heart than anything else in the world', read a draft statute on 26th January, 1516, which aimed to improve the working of the civil courts 'by bending every care and study towards finding a method and form of bringing litigation to an end and of obviating all impediments and reasons which might hold up their conclusion for long periods.'[86] Not that the trial procedure, civil or criminal, could have been reformed at that time. What is interesting here is the lucid political vision of the Republic, whose members had understood that the war was involving a civilian effort as well as a military one, and that it was necessary to try to adapt its judicial arrangements to the economic and human realities which were being forged in those years.

They were doing the same thing in the more purely administrative field. In 1516 they imposed on the office of the *camerlenghi di comun*, the real treasurers of the Rialto's public offices, precise and detailed instructions concerning the criteria they must apply while keeping their records; in the same year a new office was created, that of the *scansadori alle spese superflue*, in answer to the need which had emerged for a vigilant auditor; two months later another measure regulated the notaries' office.[87] One eye was always kept on commerce, the thorn in the side of the Republic. On 19th February, 1515, a new office came into existence, called the *Cinque Savi alla Mercanzia*, intended to devise measures to remedy the loss of such trade as had adopted other routes.[88] An indubitable sign of political vigour was the resoluteness with which, despite the urgent need in those dangerous times to refrain from a definite breach with the Holy See, the integrity of secular jurisdiction was defended against interference by the patriarch.[89] Another sign of vitality was the attempt of a group of young men, promoted by two *capi* of the *Quarantia criminal*, to secure a provision whereby the Republic saw to it that young Venetian gentlemen were given military instruction in order to avoid in future the calamitous venality which has been responsible, in their view, for the disasters suffered in the war and for the protracted way it had been dragged out. 'It is not possible for any ruler or any republic to defend, let alone extend its rule if it does not possess a strong force infused with military *virtù*,' their proposed statute began, with Machiavellian overtones. They had no luck: not even when, on proposing the law once again, they no longer emphasized the ideal of *virtù* but rather the lustre which would accrue to the aristocracy and the Venetian state from this gesture on the part of its members.[90]

If one takes stock of this period with regard to the two principles, 'authority' and 'equality', which I have mentioned as the linchpins of Venetian policy, we can say that it is unquestionably the first which had the upper hand. It could hardly have been otherwise: the enormous difficulties which had had to be overcome, at home and abroad, had called for government action which was resolute, efficient, and unencumbered by formalistic obstacles or constitutional scruples. A typical example of this had been the electoral legislation of August, 1515, which, introducing a preferential element like the payment of money, had not only damaged equality of opportunity among the patriciate, but had allowed one part of it to acquire an extraordinary weight in relation to the other.

The ascendancy of 'authority' was, as has been said, symbolized by the growth in power of its foremost representative, the Council of Ten. In 1515, while revising his separate little work, the description of the Venetian magistracies which he had placed as an appendix to his *Cronachetta*, Marino Sanuto made additions dealing with the changes which each of them had undergone in the past twenty-two years. In general they were the briefest of notes which were concerned with the differences which had arisen in electoral rules. There are several notes on the Council of Ten, one of them extremely full and eloquent. Its members, he writes, 'nowadays govern the state, for all state affairs are dealt with in this council'. After having said that the Council, composed of seventeen persons – the so-called simple Council – is frequently supplemented by an additional council called the *Zonta*, composed of fifteen persons chosen from the nobles with the greatest prestige, Sanuto observes: 'and these govern nearly everything; they do as they please and have the greatest authority. They used to divide business among various *Zonte*, that is for money, for Cyprus, for rebels, for the state, etc.; now they form one only which attends to everything.'[91] The Council of Ten was not suffered gladly; scorching accusations, obviously exaggerated by the passion which inspired them, were hurled at it unhesitatingly. In March, 1511, following an exchange of prisoners arranged by the Council and judged by public opinion to be iniquitous and harmful to the interests of the Republic (two Venetian nobles who were pledging to lend the state 1,500 ducats each on the security of a captain of the French army), it was said, according to the account of Girolamo Priuli, 'this Council is the ruin of the Venetian Republic. Having so few members it can easily be persuaded and won over, and every bad decision and every bad example follows from that.'[92]

Meanwhile the limits of the council's competence in penal affairs had also been extended. In 1513 it had assumed cases of sacrilege committed in monasteries.[92a] In April 1514 it had taken upon itself the task of prosecuting blasphemers, who, numerous and arrogant as they seemed to have become, were considered, together with sodomites, to be among those most responsible for the unleashing of divine anger against Venice. It should have been the duty of the *avogadori* to bring them to order. They had not succeeded, it was said, probably because of the complexity and the slowness of their procedure. There was no doubt that the Council of Ten would have had more success.[93] Its procedure was more flexible, more capable of being adapted to circumstances, of freeing itself from the constraint of certain formal scruples. The proof of this was an episode which took place in the autumn of 1514. On 15th November, a Paduan rebel, Nicolò Sanguinetto, was brought from Verona to Venice. He was not given a trial, the council having decided to have him strangled without delay in the silence of his cell. 'It is remarkable', commented Sanuto, 'that he was sentenced to death by spoken decision only, without any other form of balloting, a thing that had never happened in the Council of Ten before; still, as a rebel he deserved it.'[94] It is interesting to note this reaction, astonished but at the same time approving, to such a summary proceeding.

The clearest impression of the change which took place in this period, both in the judicial system and in the collective sensibility, in the face of the problems raised by the flood of criminality is furnished by a law against outlaws approved by the Great Council on 28th January, 1515. The hint was given by that very ancient law, or custom, still in force in the office of the *Cinque Savi alla Pace*, which I mentioned at the beginning of this essay; as far as this magistracy was concerned outlaws could be killed with impunity or through a purgation of purely symbolic value, a small sum of money. Recently, this prerogative had been used, and abused. Girolamo Priuli refers in this connection to three somewhat disturbing cases which had had nobles as protagonists. In the first case, which took place in May, 1511, a noble, condemned to death for the murder of a Trevisan horse-dealer, tried to escape the penalty by maintaining that his victim had once been condemned by the *Cinque alla Pace* and could therefore be killed with impunity. To the objection that the name of the dead man did not figure among the records of that tribunal, he answered that the horse-dealer had managed to have his sentence cancelled with the support of one of the tribunal's members (something, Priuli notes, which happened 'almost every day'). The relatives of the murderer, facing the intransigence of the Council of Ten, had requested the *avogadori* and the *Quarantia criminal* to annul the supposed cancellation of the name of the horse-dealer from the records of the *Cinque*. The Council, however, made its authority felt: the noble murderer was beheaded.[95] It went better for two other nobles likewise accused of having murdered *popolari* in the spring of 1512, who did succeed in demonstrating that their victims had been outlawed by the *Cinque alla Pace*. The nobles concerned were extremely rich and it was said around Venice that they had kept the whole thing quiet with their money: 'these people', Priuli relates, 'complain that you cannot get justice against nobles in the city because nobles can do much on account of their money and their relatives, and that justice turns a blind eye to *cittadini* and *popolari*'.[96] In spite of the atmosphere of scandal surrounding the *Cinque alla Pace* and their proceedings, the law of 28th January, 1515, saw fit to maintain that very prerogative. A unique prerogative, it was said. In the past the phenomenon of outlawry had not really been a serious concern, 'assuming and knowing for certain that in those happy times no one could be found, or was found so defiant as to presume to break the terms of his banishment and his obedience to the state'. Now, the situation has become intolerable. Those who are banished from Venice because of the serious crimes they have committed there, dare to remain in the city, indifferent to the sentence which has been passed on them and provoking general scandal, 'with little honour to our state'. Then came the first provision: all outlaws who do not leave Venice within eight days, 'may be attacked without penalty even if they are killed'. Up to this point the law limited itself to extending to all the prerogative which was formerly exclusive to the *Cinque alla Pace*. The true innovation came later: 'and so that this so necessary measure shall produce the desired effect with the most suitable remedy and a severity suited to the offenders', the law continued, 'in imitation of the dictum "vincam inimicos meos de inimicis meis" be it therefore now determined and resolved' that a man outlawed from Venice, who had killed, at Venice, another man also outlawed from the same city, would not have to answer to the crime for which he has been condemned to banishment except in accordance with the extent to which it was graver than the crime committed by the murdered man. Or, in other words: if such a man, outlawed for premeditated homicide, had killed a man also outlawed for premeditated homicide, he would have been acquitted of any charge, having paid off his own crime with the murder of his homologue; whereas if he had murdered a man outlawed for simple homicide, his own crime and punishment would have been mitigated only partially, the other's having been far less grave than his own. The vote was practically unanimous: 1,616 votes in favour, and only 67 against and 1 abstaining. Even Sanuto found the law perfectly satisfactory: 'It is an excellent law', he commented, 'because many outlaws here have no fear of the law, and the *officiali* and *capitani* say nothing to them: now they will go away, fearing lest they be betrayed by another outlaw.'[97]

*

As soon as Verona was recovered the Senate repealed the legislation on electoral loans of the beginning of August, 1515. What deserves special mention is the firmness with which the change of situation was announced: 'Verona being recovered by divine favour, and the fortunes of our state being in the condition well known to this council', the new decree, which bears the date 16th January, 1517, began by saying, 'it is proper to give notice to all, that if certain offerings of money in the form of gifts or loans have been accepted for offices and posts, it was done out of necessity and contrary to our ancient customs and out of the most ardent desire for the restoration of our state'.[98] From now on, the law concluded, no more gifts of money would be accepted for electoral purposes. Just one year later, on 29th January, 1518, a decree of the Great Council completed the work by abolishing the last of the innovations introduced into the electoral systems during the war period – the addition of a candidate chosen by 'scrutinio' in the Senate to the four put up from the Great Council in its elections – and thus restored the full distributive power of the chief assembly.[99]

It was the opening of a season of peace. It was necessary to renew in spirit as well as in the letter the old traditions, overhauling organisms worn out during the past disorders and rediscovering, with the initiative of new days, the pride of belonging to a city which still had an important role to play, with the wisdom of its institutions, the power of an economy which was again thriving and the splendour of its monuments and of its culture. Particular thought had been given to the defence of the *terraferma* against new risks; the advice of Andrea Gritti, the great architect of the reconquest, was welcomed. Gritti had had words for this of a realism which expressed in its very crudity the lucid and vigorous vision of a great political class; he maintained that it was necessary to fortify the cities and to dismiss any illusion about relying on fortunes of the battlefield, because then, if confronted again by the French, nothing could be done. 'Once the French were in the field we would be slaves', he warned; nor was he too perturbed at this thought because, he said, 'it is far better *de coetero* to fight with sword in sheath and with prestige than not to fight at all.'[100] Nor were men prepared to be deaf to the lessons to be learned from people like the Turks; they longed to see the Venetians animated by a more combative spirit, and it was in consequence decided by the Council of Ten and its *Zonta* to have weekly drills, in some remote part of the city, in order to train men to shoot with handgun and arquebus. But the sea had always been closest to the hearts of the Venetians. In June, 1517, they had already spoken of sending galley convoys to Flanders and Syria. Someone who believed particularly in trade with the Levant had thought of opening in the *Merceria* a school where reading and writing in Arabic ('moresco') could be learned. But there were also those who, like Jacopo Tagliapietra, looked with special attention towards India and the route which the Portuguese had opened to it, even asking their king for authorization to go as far as Calcutta with the caravels. Jealous of keeping trade with those lands in his own hands, he had refused. It was not easy to get the Venetian economy moving again; despite attempts to reactivate trade routes, reorganize finances and stabilize the currency, the state remained weak. It was not even successful in collecting what was owed by the taxpayers, to the point, in October of 1517, of not having money to pay workmen in the arsenal. The majority of merchants had not yet recovered. Catching this mood, Marino Sanuto, cheered though he was by the lasting peace, noted in early December, 1518, that 'the crafts do little because trade is slow and the merchant convoys do not sail because of Portugal'. But Luca Tron, the most interesting and genial personality of this period, had faith. The important thing was to realize that 'the world has changed', not to limit oneself always to covering the same old ground, but to seek out a new one in the west: 'so', he concluded, 'following the times we must change our habits and set sail.'[101]

These were also years of fervent intellectual life. In October, 1517, the *studio* of Padua was reopened. This was at the request of the Paduans, but the Venetian government, too, was determined to revive the cultural achievement of earlier days.[102] A chair of philosophy was established in Venice in 1521; it was the discipline which seemed to appeal most to the patriciate although a general flowering of humanistic studies can be seen, an interest in literature and archaeology, a love of the arts.[103] As for the religious life, there were certainly pockets of dismal bigotry, like those which insisted upon the expulsion from Venice of the Jewish community. But the city's tone was given at this time by men who looked forward to a far-reaching renewal of the Church and who opposed the worldly ambition within it, its eagerness for temporal power, the piety which moved between on the one hand an obtuse credulity and on the other a complete scepticism, which was spreading in Rome in the world of the *curia* and casting its reflection everywhere upon monasteries and parish churches. So that when Venice was asked by Brescia to intervene in order to put an end to the widespread phenomenon of witchcraft in the Val Camonica, where many women were convinced of being carried aloft to mount Tonale to frolic with the devil, Luca Tron was to say that it was a matter of mere 'lunacy', and the Council of Ten refused to take action.[104] In Venice, the city where the news of Leo X's death was received with joy and that of the disappearance of Hadrian VI with sorrow, the first reaction to reports of Martin Luther's preachings was one not merely of curiosity but of attentive interest, and his first Venetian follower, Andrea da Ferrara, found an attentive and respectful reception. Sanuto, an assiduous listener to the preachers and even the 'hermits' who were arriving in the city, adopted a similar attitude, an attitude no different from that of Gasparo Contarini as we can gather from a splendid letter of April, 1521. It was, in fact, 1524 before Venice took its first official stand against the German reformer and his teaching.[105]

Venetian religious feeling found its most incisive expression on the occasions of jurisdictional dispute which arose between the Republic and the patriarch or even the Apostolic See. We have seen that in the course of the war there had been a great crisis in the administration of justice due to the near impossibility of administering it in some places or administering it with any regularity in others: a crisis which inevitably carried with it a crisis of faith in the state. In the area of civil law, perhaps the most sensitive to this kind of crisis, the habit had begun to spread of invoking ecclesiastical judges as a way of securing additional time and a wider chance of success, to the point where someone had summoned 'his contestants either to Rome or before other ecclesiastical appeal judges, thus obstructing the sentence of our ordinary civil law judges'. Nor did this practice show any signs of coming to an end when peace had restored territorial unity and full sovereignty to the Republic. A decree published by the Senate on 25th June, 1517, condemned taking legal proceedings before an ecclesiastical judge in cases belonging to the secular courts on pain of perpetual exile and the loss of any redress which might have emerged from the dispute.[106] The Republic, supported with equal vigour by Venetian public opinion, attempted to take action against what had become – probably aggravated in recent times by the increase in criminality – a common abuse. Many defendants were asking to be withdrawn from a secular court and placed under an ecclesiastical one on the grounds that they had taken religious orders. There was also the case of a nobleman condemned for embezzlement of public funds who demanded that since he had taken religious orders his name should not be read out in the Great Council on the first Sunday of March in the list of 'furanti' (it was an old tradition in Venice that those who had committed malversations of public money, the 'furanti', should have as an extra penalty, that of being shown up each year until death to public scorn). He was answered with a refusal: and the patriarch met with a similar response when he came to plead similar cases.[107] When it was Luca Tron's turn to speak on the theme of the defence of the state's sovereignty, the senatorial debate took on a vehement tone. A controversy had arisen between the Republic and certain Benedictine monks with reference to fortification works which it wanted to carry out. The greater part of the members of the *Collegio* would have liked to write a letter to the pope inviting him to advise the monks to take a more submissive attitude towards the Republic. Tron was indignant. 'We are *signori*', he said. 'Do you wish to ask the pope's permission to defend our country?' A nobler retort, one that intimidated his colleagues in the *Collegio* because of the consequences which could have resulted if the pope had been informed of it, was pronounced by Tron on 19th December, 1520. 'When the papal legate came with a certain piece of business, the councillor Luca Tron said a few words about calling the pope's case before a council', wrote Sanuto.[108] It was a topical reference: just one month earlier, on 17th November, Martin Luther had made the second of his appeals from the pope to a general council of the church.[109]

The fact that Luca Tron was, in these same years, the most energetic defender of the *Avogaria di Comun* seems worthy of attention; as it does that it is he who fought, in 1524, to correct the legislation on outlaws in order to give them some protection and guarantee of justice and relieve them from the alternatives of either paying for a pardon or embracing a wandering life in which they were anybody's prey. Tron produced his first defence of the *Avogaria* in the April of 1518, with reference to the competence of this office in matters of crimes of a religious nature. In the October of 1517 the Council of Ten with the *Zonta* had decided to restore blasphemy cases to the *avogadori*: it was a sign, and not the least important, of that desire to return to the old ways which has been mentioned and which was also a return to the equilibrium between the two principles, 'authority' and 'equality'. In the April of 1518 there was an attempt in the Senate to alter the situation radically: it was proposed that a new magistracy be instituted, the *Corectori sopra le Biasteme et i Sacrilegi*, having the authority of the *avogadori*. The *avogadori* saw the move as an outrage and a diminution of their magistracy; the supporters of the proposed law maintained that, on the contrary, it was their intention only to relieve the *avogadori*, swamped as they were by too much work, from some of their burdens. Entering the argument, Luca Tron had, without dodging the point, put his finger on the sore spot – or, rather, sore spots – of Venetian justice. Woe betide taking authority from the *avogadori's* authority: they were being reduced to mere semblances, like the *procuratori alle pompe*, who continuously witnessed violations of their extremely severe sumptuary laws but had no power to take any corrective measures. And wishing to demonstrate that the diminution of authority which the *avogadori* had suffered was harmful, he recalled a recent case: the doge had prevented the *avogadori* from doing their duty in the case of eleven noblemen charged with having had illicit relations with nuns (the so-called 'munegini'). He also directed a blow at the *capi* of the Council of Ten, accusing them of wanting to arrogate authority where they had none, as in the Senate. And he ended with this severe accusation: 'there are three groups among us, great, middling and low, and nothing can be done against the great because of the support they can muster, like the 'munegini', some of them sons of procurators, and others.'[110]

It was the *rettori* of the *terraferma* cities who, as is well known by now, suffered the powers of the *avogadori di comun* in a bad spirit: the quashing of their sentences when reviewed by the Venetian magistrates constituted an obstacle to the exercise of their justice, all the more intolerable as it became more necessary – in everyone's eyes, not only theirs – to exercise justice with inflexible promptness. But when, in the middle of May, 1519, the *podestà* of Padua asked the *Signoria* for authorization to outlaw the murderer of a student of the *Studio* and publish the sentence together with the offer of a reward he certainly had the support of many of the ducal councillors but found Luca Tron hostile; Tron maintained that the trial should be put before the *avogadori*. If the *avogadori* were slow to take action, this resulted from their numbers which were too small in relation to the mass of work they had to despatch; and Tron proposed, that same day, a new law according to which three *avogadori straordinarii* would join the three ordinary *avogadori*.[111]

Their prestige strengthened and their prerogatives assured, the *avogadori* were to succeed in making their voices energetically felt in defence of the law. In January, 1520, two *avogadori* 'suspended' a law passed by the Senate in which a question which had not previously been the subject of judicial process – it related to the failure of the Agostini bank – was referred to the judgement, admitting no appeal, of the *Collegio* of the ten *savi*. A dispute of wide-reaching implications grew out of this action. 'The Senate', one *avogadore* stated, 'cannot remit a ruling to an office or council that can be considered definitive unless it has previously been treated in some court of first instance'; from the other side it was said that there was a distinction to be made between magistracies composed of a small number of judges whose decisions always required the possibility of recourse to appeal, and the councils, from which no appeal could be made. The majority were for this limiting interpretation of the right of appeal.[112] The *avogadori* had better fortune in August of that year. This time they found themselves up against none less than the doge because of a death sentence on three thieves pronounced by the *giudici del proprio* with the intervention (which determined the vote) of the doge. The *avogadori* suspended the sentence *in extremis* just as it was about to be carried out, objecting, with the support of a law of 1346 which seems to have been unearthed just in time, that the doge had the right to intervene in judgements of the office of the *Proprio* only on condition that the judges' opinions were divergent, though not when the point at issue was whether to pass or revoke a death sentence. The case having then been brought to the *Consiglio dei Quaranta* and the individual opinions of the judges of the *Proprio* expounded there, a new sentence was issued under which each of the three thieves was condemned to lose an eye and have a hand amputated.[113] On another occasion the *avogadori* challenged the Council of Ten; Giovanni Emo, who had suffered from an extremely severe sentence of exile and of being designated 'furante' for embezzlement committed during the war years while he had been *governatore alle entrate*, asked, in 1521, to be excused from his penalty against payment of an impressive sum of money. The doge and the Council of Ten would have been inclined to consent, but against the opposition of the *avogadori di comun* there was nothing to be done.[114]

Marino Sanuto always followed the activity of Luca Tron with respectful attention. In the June of 1521 he approved the measure with which Tron intended to modify the system of electing the doge in order that it should be infused with that 'equity and equality' which was indispensable to the institutions of a just Republic.[115] But Sanuto had been sharply at odds with Tron when in May of that year, he had proposed and gained acceptance in the Senate for a measure which affirmed the principle that in order to preserve the 'very great importance, dignity and authority' which the *Avogaria* had had in the past it was necessary that it should be entrusted to 'individuals who are of substance and standing'. The way to attain such an object, the decree maintained, was to have the *avogadori* elected by 'scrutinio' of the Senate as well as by 'quattro mani di elezioni' in the Great Council and to increase their perquisites; it added that 'debitori de la Signoria', that is, tax-payers in arrears, might also be elected. Sanuto always cherished the dream of becoming an *avogadore*: he feared that after this law was passed it would be definitively unrealizable. On the very day that the law was put to the vote in the Great Council (the most important laws had always to be voted on in two different councils), Sanuto launched an extremely spirited attack which was specifically directed towards appealing to the sense of pride in the great assembly of the patriciate. It was a dangerous law; election by 'scrutinio', he told his audience, 'is nothing but the beginning of your loss of liberty; a return to choosing candidates by scrutiny, as happened before, will force your Excellencies to elect one of those chosen in this way, as always happens, and to reject a man chosen after sound and worthy deliberation, so that when an individual is elected who is not one of the country's leaders, he will be held in ill repute'. Next he recounted the various attempts which had been made to have this surreptitious system approved, and repeated that the formulators of the law were aiming at nothing other than the victory of those they had had approved by 'scrutinio' in the Senate, and this in spite of the choices made by the Great Council. Moreover, he pointed out, it had not been said that the 'grandi' on whom electoral favour might fall would then actually be in a position to take upon themselves the extremely onerous duties of the *Avogaria*, which youths but not necessarily older men might be able to endure. Finally it was child's play for him to bring out the contradiction between the intention to give back prestige to the *Avogaria* and to allow those in debt to the state to be admitted there. It escaped him – or he did not want to understand – that in this clause Tron had probably been aiming at making the post available to men who, although capable, were going through a moment of financial difficulty.[116]

The differences among the various magistracies, or rather in the nature of the power which they could effectively exercise, were becoming more and more marked, corresponding with the ever greater distinctions among the several strata of the aristocracy. The smallest magistracies, which in the past century had still had a certain repute, were now reduced, as Gasparo Contarini said, to handling, quite simply 'certain small and ignoble pieces of business which the others scorned'. Things were going no better for the *Quarantia* if the same Contarini, who was highly sensitive to these distinctions, could write that they were accepting nobles who were 'poor, and of little account'.[116a] Indeed, the debasement suffered by this council in the last thirty years was only too evident. In 1525 there was a patrician who tried to deal with the problem on the lines Luca Tron had adopted for the *Avogaria*, devising expedients of the greatest ingenuity to have only men of a certain age – at least forty – and of proven experience accepted in the *Quarantia*. The proposal was dropped after the intervention of Sanuto, who defended the right of young men to hold some offices in order to familiarize themselves with the government of the Republic and begin to make their voices heard.[117] It was a perfectly valid argument. But what was wrong as an approach to the *Quarantia* could be right if applied to the *Avogaria*, if, that is, one wanted it to be a solid and prestigious magistracy, sustained by a vigorous and aware political will, capable of supporting the ideal of constitutional harmony based on the 'law', the law as a guarantee of equality.

Perhaps it was self-deception, given that the standing of the magistracies followed a course determined by so many factors that no single measure could enforce a lasting change; but this was nevertheless the one means one could try.

The problem of the excessive number of the nobility, which we have seen as one of the elements responsible for a loss of equilibrium in the Republic's political and constitutional life, was still far from being resolved. Not long after the end of the war it had been decided to remedy the spreading practice of 'broglio' with a new magistracy, the *Censori* – Domenico Morosini's old idea, it will be remembered – which had the task of anticipating and checking it, in both Senate and the Great Council. At first it seemed to be getting excellent results. But this was a short-lived illusion. In the November of 1519 an anonymous letter informed the Council of Ten of full-scale electoral scandals which were taking place based on the buying and selling of votes. Scandal on every level: on the part of poor nobles, it was in order to have the usual, modest offices with which to cope with the exigencies of every-day life; for the 'grandi', it was to obtain important appointments.[118] There was an attempt to provide for the requirements of the former, on 27th May, 1520, by a decree which enticed the nobles to become 'avvocati alle corti' with the hope of earning a good living. Almost contemporaneously another law emerged from the Senate; after having noted the great increase in the number of gentlemen and having stated that 'it was in the interest of justice and equity to enable everyone to participate in offices and government posts', it established that all offices, in both the city and the *terraferma*, which afforded 'salario et utilità' must also carry a period of quarantine before an individual could occupy the post again, the purpose being to ensure a turn-over of men.[119] Despite these attempts, despite other laws which tended to prevent the formation of factions, the electoral battle continued unbridled. The magistracy of the *Censori* had proved incapable of controlling it: consequently, on 15th October, 1521, it was decided to suppress it and turn over its functions to the *avogadori di comun*.[120]

Not even the *avogadori* succeeded in stemming the practice of 'broglio', which was kept alive by causes which went far beyond a mere bad tradition. Besides, gentlemen who had been conventionally qualified by going through the *cursus honorum* had still been elected. In 1523, even, a gentleman, much celebrated as a lawyer, succeeded in getting himself elected, having been so anxious to achieve that goal as to give up the considerable profits he derived from practising the law. In Sanuto's view, despite all their prestige, despite their power, the *avogadori* were simply standing by, watching but taking no action against the people who were engaged in electoral machinations. And then a ludicrous thing was happening: once the office of *avogador* became thoroughly attractive the flame of the 'broglio' became fanned by the competition for that, too. As a result, on 2nd October, 1524, a day of election for the *Avogaria di Comun*, the *capi* of the Council of Ten decided to take into their own hands the repression of the 'broglio' by sending their men into the Great Council to break up small groups and take note of the names of the offenders. 'A new phenomenon, and a scandal to the *avogadori di comun'*, Marino Sanuto commented, perhaps with just a shade of vexation.[121]

*

The peace had lasted only four years. In 1521 imperial and papal troops entered the duchy of Milan, which had been, after 1515, under the control of the king of France; the Venetians, as his ally, found that they too were involved in the struggle. In the July of 1523 the Republic drew up a peace treaty with Charles V and retired from the military vicissitudes of Lombardy. After the battle of Pavia of February 1525, which saw the utter defeat of the king of France and emperor Charles V now incontestable master of Italy, Venice effected the League of Cognac with England, France, the pope and the other Italian princes, the duke of Milan himself, Francesco Sforza, among them. Its purpose was to try to prevent – and, as Federico Chabod has noted, this was the fundamental task for the Republic – 'the excessive power of any one influence in Italy'. The Venetian army had been involved if only for a short time; the duke of Milan had withdrawn suddenly from the struggle after making peace with the Emperor, and it had not been possible for the Venetians to keep the field alone. Also, the rumour was spreading that huge quantities of soldiers were being concentrated over against Bolzano, *Landsknechts* under the command of the Lutheran George Frundsberg and of the constable Charles of Bourbon who had formerly been on the imperial side. Not long before this the Venetians had been able to follow – through the accounts, which were extremely rich in facts and comment, of their ambassador to the archduke of Austria – the peasant uprisings of southern Germany and Austria, a product of the new religious ideals which the peasants there knew how to turn to good account in mobilizing support. The *Landsknechts*, drawn from their ranks and now making ready to swoop down on Italy, were the incarnation of that myth of fiery and brutal force. These were the very worst years for the Venetian economy. The production of wool was collapsing; exchange rates were rising frighteningly; in 1527 a terrible dearth of grain which was to drag on into the next century affected the countryside as a whole. The descent of the *Landsknechts* from the Alpine valleys, the passage of their starving and predatory troops across the lands of the *dominio* and towards Rome was followed with apprehension; the news of the sack of Rome heard with stupefaction. The Republic had not, however, renounced the temptation to profit from the difficulties of the Apostolic See: it unhesitatingly accepted the offer that Ravenna and Cervia should return to Venetian rule. It was an imprudent move – though its supporters in the government were by no means few – but understandable, considering the urgency of the grain problem and the property which a number of Venetian gentlemen had had to give up there; still more hazardous was their acceptance, in 1528, of ports like Monopoli, Bari, Polignano and Brindisi in Apulia, a region which was subject to the crown of Spain. In the June of 1529, Pope Clement VII and the emperor Charles V put their seals to an agreement: the latter undertook to transfer the Romagnol lands from the Republic to the pope and to come himself to Italy, at the end of the same year, in order to conclude a general peace. Some, including the doge, wanted Venice to oppose this, and to this effect make a new alliance with the king of France; but the French wanted money for coming to Italy, the imposing sum of 20,000 ducats a month, and the majority of Venetians were weary: weary of paying, of being afraid, of continuous uncertainty, of the incubus of the *Landsknechts*, who, it was said, would return to Italy with the emperor. So the Republic accepted, in the winter of 1529–30 at Bologna, the conditions of the peace: to restore the Apulian ports and the lands in the Romagna (except for the right to retain private property), to renounce any expansionistic ambitions that might threaten the duke of Milan or the duke of Ferrara, and to pay a sum of money to the emperor.

The return of peace in 1530, was quite different from that of 1517. There was great joy, now as before; a great desire to overcome as quickly as possible the consequences of past vicissitudes and to eliminate their most typical and important expressions, such as electoral loans, and so forth. But at the same time there was a great sense of fatigue and some doubt as to the possibility of retrieving past glory and continuing to keep step with the states which had come to the fore as the protagonists of political and economic life in the last decades. It was symptomatic that in the October of 1531 two Venetian nobles, Giovan Francesco Giustiniani and Giovanni Contarini, nicknamed 'cazadiavoli', both of them well-known men of the sea, should have left Venice and gone to Constantinople in order to serve the 'Signor Turco'. Giustiniani wanted to embark 'in the fleet which he [the sultan] was proposing to send through the Red Sea against the Indians and the Portuguese'; for Contarini it was enough that he should find 'something new to do'.[122] And it was equally symptomatic that, making his excuses to the advisers of the king of England because the Venetian galley fleet no longer carried spices (the English said that it was useless in that case for them to come to England) the Venetian ambassador to London should have explained that it was not the Venetians' fault 'but that of the changed world'.[123] The very words that Luca Tron had used in 1519, but in another spirit – the spirit of the Renaissance, which the Republic did not now feel or know how to revive.

More than in the institutions, more than in the actions of men in the government – whose capacity, resolute and yet flexible in adapting itself to the new reality, I will speak of later – the fatigue showed itself precisely in the fading of this spirit. After 1524 the official attitude of the Republic to the Lutheran movement (that so many people supported the Reformation, defying the repression of both state and inquisitorial institutions, cannot be dwelt on here) was one of straightforward rejection: it did not want to hear it discussed. Partly this was due to the political and social echoes of the German situation but mainly it was because the Apostolic See, taking advantage of the difficulties in which the Republic continued to flounder and of its need not to aggravate Rome too much, succeeded in obtaining Venice's voluntary submission to a point of view which the pope was reluctant actually to impose on it; a point of view which found in the patriarch Gerolamo Querini its most convinced interpreter in Venice and the man most determined to bring about its implementation. Questions relating to the right of sanctuary and the power of secular authority to judge delinquents who, at the moment of arrest or sentence, claimed to have taken minor orders and therefore wished to be referred to the ecclesiastical authority – frequent, as we have seen, even under the former patriarch, Antonio Contarini – were now becoming acrimonious in the extreme. The Venetian patricians were certainly not inclined to give in easily. In April, 1526, the patriarch Querini, summoned to the *Collegio* to account for a brief of excommunication he had issued against the *signori di notte* for having imprisoned a priest accused of theft, had had an extremely heated encounter with Luca Tron. To these men, Sanuto relates, 'he used haughty and unusual words, as the patriarch did to him. And the doge supported the patriarch'; but as the city was with Ser Luca, the patriarch had to withdraw the briefs of excommunication from the column where he had posted them.[124] In June, 1529, it was the doge's turn to quarrel with the patriarch, because of a citation issued against some parish priests who had registered a complaint with the *Signoria* against certain of his decisions. There was no way, however, of making him revoke them even though the doge exclaimed that he would have him driven from Venice.[125] Querini was a man much valued by Clement VII; his appointment had been one of the consequences, and by no means the smallest, of the Peace of Bologna, and with him he had brought the unbendingness of his religious convictions and his jurisdictional demands.

By now we have reached the point in time which is usually referred to as the 'Counter Reformation'. One no longer sees – at least to judge from Sanuto's diaries – that quaking religiosity, rapt in anguished contemplation of sin and eschatological expectation, of the previous decade, nor the fresh spirit of charitable fervour that marked the period around 1520, when hospitals were being equipped for those ill with the 'mal franzoso', the eager solicitude for the poor which is echoed in the letter of Paolo Giustiniani and (also reported by Sanuto) in the will of Antonio Tron.[126] Not that similar examples, and of the loftiest kind, are not repeated, or that one cannot catch murmurs of a Savonarolan tone, as in 1528 when there was fear of a second invasion by the *Landsknechts*. But, in the main, the atmosphere appears different. The desperate cries of the poor – peasants who had fled from the countryside where they had sunk to eating grass; fishermen or market gardeners from Burano who had deserted their island and flung themselves upon the bridges and under the colonnades of the *piazza* to die of hunger and cold – the cries which resounded in the city for three winters do not seem to have aroused any profound agitation in men's minds as a whole. The state did something through the organizational capacity and the concern for public order it displayed in those years; it put up shelters, in fact, and severely repressed the begging from which the crowd of unfortunates tried to make a living.[127] In contrast with this background was an abundance of wealth and festivities, a jubilant thirst for life. On the evening of one of the worst days of February, 1528, a banquet was given with a ball in the house of Cardinal Grimani. '*Tamen*', observes Sanuto, 'it would have been better to give alms.' And two evenings later the cardinal was at another party, in Murano, where the performance of a pastoral eclogue was followed by a ball.[128] Nor was it only exiles from the *terraferma* or the islands who were numbered among the poor, or the many members of the Venetian plebeian class. The poverty of the nobility persisted, with cases which were often pitiful like that of an old man who, in order to live, asked to be given shelter in the prison where his son already lay, or of others who longed to leave Venice; and the problem of numerical excess persisted too, provoking the usual frenzied chase after remunerative offices, the continual 'brogli', the eternal sale of votes by the 'svizzeri'. At the end of the fifteenth century, two *capi* of the *Quarantia* had thought of charging the maintenance of the poor nobles and their families to those who occupied offices, and it will be remembered that they had aroused such indignation among the prominent men of the Republic that they were sent at once into confinement on an island in the Levant. Some thirty years later, in 1528, the *capi* of the *Quarantia* then in office, supported by four ducal councillors and three other members of the *Collegio*, considered solving the same problem with a proposal which was typical of the new atmosphere. 'With trade and industry falling off every day because of the cessation of the trading voyages and because of the wars and the tribulations of the past years and of the present, the means of support of a good part of these our gentlemen' being lacking, it was necessary, the preamble to the decree stated, to find a solution which would be not merely harmless but, rather, a public benefit, and which would at the same time 'redound to the honour of this Republic.' The solution was this: to obtain from the Holy See authorization to appoint as canons of St. Mark's fifty Venetian gentlemen – five of them chosen by the doge, the other forty-five elected *per scrutinio* by the Senate – endowing them with benefices to a total sum of 10,000 ducats annually, equal to 200 ducats per head. They would receive holy orders for life, and by way of services rendered, they would above all dedicate themselves (probably it would mean staying in Padua) 'to the study of sacred and worthy letters'. The Senate approved the proposal; but then, perhaps due to negative reactions in ecclesiastical circles, it was not presented in the Great Council, so that it was left in abeyance and did not receive the final seal of approval.[129]

In the interest of dignity, of order and good manners, decorum and morality, free and easy habits, boisterous and indecent amusements were repudiated. The theatre had been the great solace of the Venetians even in the hardest years of the two war periods: it remained so after Agnadello. In 1520 a law had indeed been approved which forbade it, but it was not published, and people continued to amuse themselves with performances of Cherea and Ruzante. Something analogous had happened with the lotteries, invented in 1522 and regarded by the Council of Ten with such distrust that they had prohibited them – though later on they not only allowed them to continue but assumed control over them.

Immediately after the conclusion of the Peace of Bologna in February 1530, after the failure of an attempt at a complete prohibition of plays, which was too hard for passionate theatre-lovers like the Venetians to bear, the Council of Ten decided (the carnival was then in progress) that its *capi* could give 'permission to perform plays, as long as they are respectable'.[130] In this framework of hunger and uncertainty about daily life, of wealth and strident social contrasts, of poor people and deserters from the various armies wandering from the countryside to the cities, delinquency was inevitably bound to increase. The phenomenon was not unique to Venice; one has only to read the ordinances issued by Francis I in this same decade to understand what its dimensions must have been.[131] Letters from cities of the *dominio* spoke of outlaws who were terrorizing the countryside, of innumerable murders and acts of violence. 'Here', noted Sanuto, referring to Venice on 25th April, 1524, 'an enormous number of murders are committed . . . in this month there have been twenty-two people killed, and the greatest enormities perpetrated'.[132] And among the murders, as well as those which were committed on a violent impulse or with the purpose of robbery, were those performed under the consenting eye of the police and justices in order to ease their own situation and to help the state in its tremendous effort to enforce public order: that is, murders committed by outlaws on other outlaws, an activity which in these years came to its height.

Turning to a consideration of the internal politics of the Republic in this third decade of the sixteenth century, it seems dominated by the problem of money even more than in the preceding period. It was a need that grew year by year until around 1530 it became obsessive. And to have money was not simply to have a means of making war and calling for peace. For Venice, to have money, to be lavish with it in gifts and loans and financing represented something more: it became the symbol of its own brand of statecraft, its special strength, the substitute for a military power which was lacking and which it was considered neither possible or profitable to have. Squeezed as they were between politically and militarily menacing powers, the Venetians came to think that there was no bargaining counter available to them other than the contrast between the disastrous financial conditions of the great monarchies – Francis I and Charles V and even the Apostolic See would seek support from their banks – and their own great and relatively easily available wealth. The presence, as doge, of a strong personality like Andrea Gritti's, toughened by personal experience of wars on land and sea and aware therefore of the capacities of and the possibilities open to both the Venetians and others, had considerable influence in persuading the Republic to adopt this stance. Evidence of it was the demonstration organized at Venice to celebrate the promulgation of the League of Cognac in July, 1526. The doge was present, 'dressed in gold', Sanuto tells us, 'with a cloak of gold and white over all and his *bareta* of the type that symbolizes peace'. On the 'soleri', or hustings, commenting on the allegories represented there, were inscriptions like these: 'quisquis habet nummos secura naviget aura fortunamque suo temperet arbitrio'; 'Aurum belli materia'; 'Per aurum victoria'; 'Obediunt omnia pecuniae'; 'Divitiae si affluant, noli timere'.[133] Such phrases expressed official opinions. This was confirmed, in the February of 1528, by a decree which discussed the necessity of taking measures to oppose any new passage across the *dominio* and he supported the army of the League engaged in southern Italy. Money, it said, is the chief prerequisite for getting what one wants and the thing on which one must rely: it was necessary, therefore, 'to collect it by all possible means'.[134] But the assumption of the myth of wealth as the emblem of the Republic could not have an impact on its international policy alone. There were, necessarily, reverberations in internal policy, an exaltation of those who possessed this wealth and who were therefore the guarantors of the Republic's political activity, the guardians of its power. Wealth thus had a civic as well as a political value. Not to have it, or to have too little, constituted a lessening of rank and prestige, of the possibility of establishing one's own merits. 'Veh civitas', Sanuto is said to have warned during a discussion held on 4th August, 1526, to protest against the fact that appointments were now being granted only to those with money.[135] Domenico Giannotti, writing in those years, expressed a similar concern through his Venetian gentleman, Trifone Gabriello: the method of raising money prevailing in Venice nowadays – that of electoral loans and donatives – can be justified by the necessity of the moment, the protagonist of the *Repubblica de' viniziani* explains, 'though it is not to be praised, lest it adds repute to wealth by taking it away from virtue'.[136]

Of the remedies applied by the Republic to solving the problem of money, the one which heightened ambition to enter the colleges or to win posts in the government was always the most successful. It had been started in November, 1521, first with the admission to the Senate (as usual without the right to vote) of nobles who paid 400 ducats; then, only a few days later, young men were accepted in the Great Council on making loans of as little as 50 ducats (for 100, which would have been preferred, hardly anyone came forward). Then, in 1522, six procuratorships of St. Mark were put up to be competed for and because of the prestige which still surrounded that honour – but which the increase in the number of men who received it and their recruitment by virtue of sheer cash would eventually tarnish – fetched a very considerable sum of money.[137] Those in opposition spoke up when requests for loans were to be accompanied by the adoption of the electoral system of 'scrutinio' in Senate and the 'quattro mani di elezioni' in the Great Council. Sanuto, who in May 1521 had already expressed his disagreement with the electoral law for the *Avogaria di Comun* proposed by Tron – a law which did not contemplate money loans – protested vigorously when that system was extended to an increasingly large number of appointments.[138] Indeed, it was extended to practically all of them. And once the elections to offices presently vacant were exhausted, another resource was discovered in 1526, that of electing the future successors to offices which were for the time being occupied by the same method. These were the so-called 'expectative' appointments. Sanuto rose to speak in the Great Council against them, too, and received the honour of a reply from the doge himself, who maintained yet again that overriding financial necessity compelled all other considerations to be set aside.[138a]

Also making headway was a tendency to suspend the application of those protective measures, like the 'quarantine' periods and the disqualifications based on personal ties which were aimed at preventing the formation of tight groups of nobles securely ensconced in such important organs of government as the *Collegio*: the excuse was that in times of crisis like the present one could deprive oneself of valuable men by clinging to legal scruple. On 23rd October, 1524, quarantines and disqualifications for the *savi del collegio* were suspended; the next day it was decided to elect three *savi del consiglio di zonta* (that is, 'extraordinary' *savi*) establishing that for them, too, quarantine or disqualification rules need not obtain.[138b] It often happens that an extraordinary solution ends by becoming an ordinary one, and thus on 2nd June, 1525, the election of three *savi del consiglio di zonta* was once again proposed, and accepted. Only for a month, however: but at the beginning of January, 1528, it was decided to elect another three for three months. 'It is the worst of laws', Sanuto commented bitterly this time, 'and the ruin of the state, for it is creating permanent members of the *Collegio*.' Nor was he the only one in the Great Council to think so. In July of the same year and in the April of 1529 proposals to elect the three *savi del consiglio di zonta* were rejected.[139] The protagonist of the *Repubblica de' viniziani*, Trifone Gabriello, shows that he, too, harbours certain suspicions about the existence of a kind of crypto-oligarchy, despite the extreme caution with which Giannotti makes him speak. After explaining that the greater 'magistrates, *savi di mare*, *savi di terra ferma*, *savi grandi*, [ducal] councillors, the [members of the Council of] Ten, the *avvocatori*, *censori*, do not obstruct one another', so that 'as soon as a gentleman has obtained one office he can enter the others as well', Trifone is asked by his interlocutor Giovanni, whether, things being as they are, the result is not that 'all these offices . . . rotate among a small number of gentlemen'. 'You speak to the point', Trifone replies. 'And we', he continues, 'are accustomed to say that whenever one of our gentlemen has attained the office of *savio di terraferma*, he is as likely as not to have achieved a place in some of these magistracies.'[140]

In practice this concentration of power was to centre around the *Collegio* and the Council of Ten with its *Zonta*. The fulcrum was the Council of Ten because of the breadth of its field of action and the unusual range of its judicial activity. One must take care to 'maintain it in the highest possible esteem', it being 'the principal magistracy in our state', the doge once said during a discussion about whether to fill vacant posts with premature elections or to observe the time-limits fixed by the law; and his conclusion was that in order to protect that 'esteem' one could at times come to some compromise with the formal aspects of the law.[141] Foreign and financial policy, the oversight of food supplies, and a good part of the legislation on electoral matters, were to originate in the Council of Ten and its *Zonta* to a far greater extent than had been the case in the past few years, years which had nevertheless seen its emergence as the chief organ of the Republic. It was the Council of Ten and the *Zonta*, for example, which in

September 1528, reformed the statutes affecting the quadrennial re-licensing of the Venetian Jews; they took this upon themselves in order to avoid the outbreaks of anti-Semitism which had occurred in the past on other councils and which had raised doubts about whether the renewal would be effected – a matter which, in the judgement of the most responsible men, would seriously damage the entire Venetian economy.[142] It was the Council of Ten with the *Zonta* which decreed, on the morrow of the Peace of Bologna, the cessation of the practice (electoral or not) which has come to be called the sale of offices.[143] And the Council was to institute new magistracies, like the *Esecutori contro la Bestemmia* and the *Inquisitori di Stato*; it was to keep a strict control over others already in existence, like the *Provveditori sopra i Monasteri*, deciding, in 1528, to elect them itself by the 'scrutinio' method. Again, it was to discuss the old project of Piero Tron, disinterred in 1529, to give military commands to thirty-one nobles; and in the same year it oversaw the three *provveditori* responsible for bringing the greatest possible supplies of grain to Venice.[144] In practice it was to take under its control the body of Venetian nobility as a whole, vigorously imposing respect for it on subject citizens, watching over its behaviour and reserving a good part of the crimes committed by its members for its own judgement (although it was not until 1571 that it was established that nobles were subject to its judgement exclusively). Finally, it was to do a tremendous amount of work, judicial and legislative, on ethical and religious matters (quenching the sparks of Protestant reform) and on problems arising from social *mores*, becoming in this way the most resolute guardian of religion and morality, the pillars which upheld its prime goals, public peace and order.

The Great Council, the Senate and the *avogadori di comun*, on the other hand, paid the price of the political and constitutional upheavals of recent times. As for the Great Council, decline was really incidental, the result of a transitory electoral system; its distributive and ratifying power had not been substantially harmed. For the Senate the story was different; it had in effect been deprived of a good part of its powers, over foreign policy, economic policy, and so on.[145] Once again it was claimed that it was composed of too many people and that any hope that the more delicate decisions of Venetian policy could be kept secret there was absolutely illusory. But to enlarge its numbers with admissions through loans of money was to aggravate this very defect and to make the loss of its control of policy inevitable. Many senators complained about it: 'the Senate is called to weary the senators in reading letters of no importance', said one of them; and another added that 'when the Senate bell rings it is to govern the country, not to do nothing, as is the case at present'.[146] Nor could one predict that peace would allow a return to the methods of the past. By now, unlike 1517, it was observed that the transformation had been too profound; that there had been a radical shift of wealth within the patrician class (so much so that it was held necessary, in 1528, to order a complete revision of the distribution of fiscal burdens 'because of the inequalities involved in the present tax regulations'), and that such shifts inevitably involved shifts in the centres of power; that the nature of the state, in its administrative even more than in its political structures, had become more complex, more exacting, more concerned with precision. In connection with this last point – apart from the need, which had emerged years before, for accurate accounting and well-ordered records – there was a demand for clear biographical data on the individuals, especially nobles, but also all others, who had anything to do with the administration of the law; and it is revealing that in 1530 a decree expressing belief in the utility of studies 'of good letters' to prepare 'for the administration of governorships' instituted public instruction in mathematics as particularly suited to that end.[147] In sum, to control all these concerns and the men who had been placed in charge of them, and at the same time to keep in check subjects who were reluctant to accept what the state proposed and to lend it as much as it requested, required that authority be exercised in a way which was not possible for the Senate. It was to recover somewhat, even so, but the balance had been too disturbed by the Council of Ten for it to return to its former status.

The same was true of the organ I have described as the great antagonist of the Council of Ten, the *Avogaria di Comun*. Luca Tron's attempt to bring it back to life, to being one of the poles of the Republic's political structure, the one bound in duty to protect 'law' and aristocratic equality against the prevalence of scarcely controllable oligarchical inclinations and 'auctorità' could be considered to have failed.[148] Not that there was any lack of *avogadori* capable of firmly imposing respect for the law on even the most powerful patricians: let the case of June, 1526, suffice, when the *avogadori* managed to have a *capo* of the Council of Ten dismissed – he was defended, what is more, by his colleagues sword in hand – for having put off taking up his appointment for a few days.[149] But these cases involved the presence in the magistracy of men of unusual energy. One does not have the feeling that the *Avogaria*, by itself, of its own intrinsic force, constituted an autonomous political influence sufficient to counterweigh, in the Venetian constitutional balance, the energy represented by an organ like the Council of Ten. The most serious blow was inflicted when its prerogative of exercising control over the laws and their application ended by being taken over by the Council of Ten; in July, 1526, for example, the Council, together with the *Zonta*, nullified an edict issued by the ducal councillors because it did not have the number of votes required by law. In 1529, again, a law of the council and the *Zonta* rigorously fixed the principles to which offices which handled money had to adhere. The execution of the law was, indeed, entrusted to the *avogadori di comun*, but it was established that in case of controversy between them and the treasurers of the various offices the *capi* of the Council of Ten would have the last word.[150] Gasparo Contarini, one of the leading actors in the Venetian political life of these years and an extremely close observer of it, summed up the decline of the *Avagaria* in harsh words. After having recalled that the *avogadori* could be likened to the Roman tribunes of the people, with the difference that the latter had been instituted in order to defend freedom and the first to keep potent 'the majesty of the law', Contarini concluded that the authority of this magistracy had been great in the past; 'but now', he continued, 'because the authority of the Ten has spread its roots more widely, the reputation of the *avogadori* has been obscured and diminished by their power'.[151] In substance, the *Avogaria* was above all an organ of criminal justice. This was made clear by a law of 2nd August, 1534, which, in indicating its areas of jurisdiction, stressed above all 'the responsibility for and conduct of criminal affairs, not only in this city but also in all the rest of our state', and then 'the observance' of the laws, but this as though it were a matter for an appendix.[152]

Not even in this connection, however, can one say that the *Avogaria* kept the authority and the full powers and functions it had had in the past, or that it had not suffered from the victorious competition of the Council of Ten. It was inevitable that its decline on the political level should have had repercussions on the judicial one because of the extremely close correlation which existed between them. But the judicial decline of the *Avogaria di Comun* had independent roots as well; it followed from the progressive detachment of judicial methods from the Roman model and thus a widespread intolerance of the formal solemnity of its public proceedings, which fell into several phases, each with its interminable debates between representatives of the prosecution and representatives of the defence, the cavilling that went on in order to suspend the course of the trial, and the endless sequence of appeals. I have already referred to this. In this decade, however, the opposition became even stronger, and lawyers and courts of appeal, symbols of these methods, were the object of continual criticism.[153] And apart from having a name in common, the *avogadori* had come to play a role in the trial which was analogous to that of the lawyers. It was they themselves, moreover, who had confirmed this connection in years when, partly in order to escape procedural burdens, partly to avoid (not being themselves professionals) having to confront, perhaps on technically difficult questions, men who spent their lives in the law courts and understood their every problem and trick, they had had their places taken in criminal trials by ordinary lawyers.[154]As for appeals, they were among the *raisons d'être* of the *avogadori*. It was by virtue of appeals addressed to them that subjects could hope that justice might be done; the quashing of the sentences of inferior judges ordered by the *avogadori* was a restraint on those who might have overridden subjects' rights. But there was no preventing the degeneration of this protection in the hands of able lawyers into a means of protracting trials or of ensuring that the most dangerous offenders might escape the course of justice.[155] These abuses could not happen in the Council of Ten, where lawyers played no part, appeals were not permitted and questions of competence did not arise save in exceptional cases; there the concern was for doing things in a hurry, for penalties that were examples of timeliness and toughness.[156] The Council of Ten had itself intervened in order to try to correct the major procedural vices of the *Avogaria* and of the council through which it habitually worked, the *Quarantia criminale*; on 14th March, 1526, it had limited the number and duration of the interventions and rebuttals both of the *avogadori* and the lawyers.[157] It was not enough, so it continued to take the greater number of trials upon itself, especially those of some importance. The doge had risen one day to protest against the Council of Ten, saying 'energetically that they should not hamper the freedom of the *avogadori*'.[158] But the evidence was before everyone's eyes. In 1529 the Council of Ten in two days condemned a certain man to death for having predicted in conversation with friends – this was 1529 – that Charles V would overrun Italy and sack Venice. It takes months to pursue a case in the *Quarantia* under the present *avogadori*', Sanuto had remarked in 1526.[159] Six years later the *Quarantia criminale* decided to release another man who, after four years in detention, had still not been tried. Under these circumstances the *Quarantia* itself asked the Council of Ten for permission to use its 'authority' in order to take measures (like allowing a prosecutor to free an outlaw) held indispensable for resolving difficult situations connected with trials, and the *avogadori* wanted a case of embezzlement withdrawn from the *Quarantia* and put to the judgement of the Council of Ten. And once again it was the doge who upheld the traditional jurisdictions.[160] Finally, at the end of December, 1530, it was decided thoroughly to reform the competence and the procedure of the *Avogaria*.

'Defiance, homicides and other contumelies both in this our city and in our lands and territories', began the preamble, 'have increased, and are becoming more and more numerous because the delinquents are too certain of being able to rely on impunity'. It was therefore established that 'excepting and reserving the authority of the *avogadori di comun*, and excepting and reserving also that our laws and ordinances concerning lawsuits cannot be suspended or set aside . . . *de coetero* our *avogadori* neither may nor can, by any way or means or under any excuse, impede by calling to see or in any way altering or suspending the course of any case, as within, so without, which by our *rettori* or magistrates is set in train, until the criminals be called to their defence.' If the guilty persons are imprisoned, the *avogadori* may send for the trial documents which concern them, even if they are as yet incomplete, while the *rettori* and the other magistrates may confine themselves to sending, for their greater security, only a copy, and not the originals. At this point the *avogadori* will have a month at their disposal to decide, having heard the opinion of the ducal councillors, whether to distrain on the case or let it go forward; at the end of which term, *rettori* and magistrates will be able to resume the case which has meanwhile been suspended, and bring it to a conclusion. For the setting of a new time limit or any other decision whatsoever to suspend the case the *avogadori* require the permission of the *Quarantia criminale*.[161] The *Avogaria* had come a long way since the law of 1468 had begun to erode its authority.

*

A crisis of law, then, and at the same time a crisis of institutions, involving the nature of the state itself. It was a crisis of institutions in as much as men's relationships with them had changed. Their feelings about life and – both in its material and spiritual aspects – the way they lived, differed from the preceding century. We have pointed out the violence, the long periods of dearth, the economic and financial upheavals, the religious crisis which overran all Europe, the change of manners and morality: all things which could not but have had consequences for the state, for its institutions as well as for the conception of its sovereignty, its way of imposing it and the attitude of its subjects. The state sought to emphasize its authority, to forge it in a way which would make its exercise more rapid and efficient. But it was an authority which, despite this zeal, remained precarious, which found itself forced to accept being conditioned by the power, political and economic, of a part of its subjects, to face and combat the resistance of those who rejected it. It was an authority which showed tears in its fabric, great gaps even, incongruences, things which became all the more evident and dangerous the greater the attempt to overcome or eliminate them with inefficient or inadequate measures: and through these tears and gaps the activity of those who were not disposed to suffer authority filtered and spread. It is interesting that shortly after the Peace of Bologna, and above all between 1532 and 1533, the sense of unease which had been building up within the state found an outlet in Venice itself through angry criticism of the nobles. Judging from the tone of the graffiti which expressed this protest, it came from members of the bourgeoisie, that is, from men who were also in a position to express the state of mind of the unfortunates who were most cruelly affected by the war, dearth and hunger. 'The people will rise and punish you', threatened one of these slogans.[161a] The outlaw problem was another symptom of this dual crisis of men and the state. It assumed particularly grave proportions at this very time, and the government resorted to the wildest and most impracticable ways of containing it.[161b]

As early as 1523, the law of 28th January, 1515 was not only reconfirmed but extended to the whole of the *dominio* – the law which, with its evocation of mythic times gone by when no one aspired 'to break the terms of their outlawry or their obedience to the state' showed, despite its gross exaggeration, an awareness that a new age had dawned. The question of outlawry was still, however, complex and confused. In 1524 Luca Tron had thought of rationalizing it in a single law. In this initiative there was even an aspect which we would call 'liberal', and which was part of the policy Tron sought to promote in these years; that is, while he recognized the acceptability of the murder of those who were 'definitive' outlaws, following their sentence, he maintained that those who were only outlaws *ad inquirendum* or still awaiting judgement should not be the objects of the same treatment; they should have a fixed term for presenting themselves to their judges.[162] The extent of the intellectual and moral confusion of these years, of the alarm in the face of the enormity of the problem of outlawry, of the sense of terror and of atrocity which it raised can be seen in the negative reaction which greeted this proposal even on the part of men like Sanuto, whose lucid and balanced vision of the situation we have come to understand in a different light. 'It is true, *O signori*', he stated in a speech which he reported in his *Diarii*, 'that when the law was made there were attempts to find ways round it and some disadvantages followed, that men killed twice and yet returned, but it is not for this that so good and holy a law should be broken; if it is really needful, change it somewhat, but do not repeal it . . .'[163]

Tron's law remained in force for a few months. In June of the same year, 1524, it was revoked.[164] And yet facts had been uncovered which might well have seemed horrifying. Continuing to exploit the current regulations of the *cinque savi alla pace*, the rascally practice of causing the names of murdered men to figure in the records of the condemned, so that the murderer would be exempt from penalty, had been systematically organized with the support of one of the judges and the clerks. The case assumed massive proportions, so much so that even the responsibility of the grand chancellor was involved and he was forced to resign. But when in May, 1525, the Council of Ten and *Collegio* decided to bring this lamentable turn of events to a close, regulating the functions and jurisdiction of the *cinque savi alla pace* with a new law which branded the office by saying that it would have been more exact to call it the 'stimulus and cause of evil deeds, homicides and unpunished enormities', they restricted the earlier licence to murder by only a little: it was merely forbidden to kill those who, sentenced to fines of less than ten *lire di piccoli*, had not paid them. 'Indeed', the law went on, 'from fifty *lire* up let the custom be retained that they can be attacked and killed without penalty, to bring terror to the evil-living and temerarious.'[165] Once the avenue was open, there was no reluctance to pursue it. There was no lack in these years of cases of outlaws who returned to Venice with the head of another outlaw and displayed it to qualified judges as evidence for having their own sentences remitted. It was mainly a question of patience and information. There was always someone who could help – like a certain priest of Torreglia, in the Euganean hills, who, having realized in confession that he had before him an outlaw from Friuli, hastened to inform another outlaw, also from Friuli, of this in exchange for a suitable recompense, so that the man might make use of it to escape from his own situation.[166]

This was 1532, only a few months after the Council of Ten had authorized, with the statute cited near the beginning of this essay, the killing of anyone, including relatives, who aided an outlaw.

NOTES

1. A.S.V., *Maggior Consiglio, Libro d'oro*, pt. viii, f. 9. Also when there was a preliminary vote in the *Quarantia* the law had met with a certain amount of opposition. Out of 37 voters, 30 had voted 'yes', 6 'no', and 1 '*non sincero*'. In both councils, then, there was the same percentage – 20% in one, 18% in the other – of gentlemen who disagreed with the proposed law.

2. Ibid., f. 10. This law passed unanimously in the *Quarantia criminal*.

3. In *Leggi criminali del Serenissimo Dominio Veneto in un solo volume raccolte e per pubblico decreto ristampate* (Venice, 1751) 14.

4. C. Calisse, *Storia del diritto penale italiano* (Florence, 1895) 105 seq. A. Esmein, *A history of the continental criminal procedure* (New York, 1968) 75.

5. M. Ferro, *Dizionario del diritto comune e veneto* (Venice, 1778) ii, 1778; L. Priori, *Prattica criminale secondo il ritto delle leggi della Serenissima Republica di Venetia* (Venice, 1663) 52 seq., sets out the Venetian legislation on this point in a weighty synthesis. In M. Roberti, *Le magistrature giudiziarie veneziane e i loro capitolari fino al 1300* (i, Padua, 1907; ii and iii, Venice, 1909–11) there are references to outlawry laws; according to a law of 1229 (i, 283) it was accepted that the aggrieved could kill the offending party if he, once outlawed, returned unlawfully to Venice; other laws of 1284 and 1289 (iii, 43 and 84; ii, 54) speak of giving cash rewards to whoever captured an outlaw or arranged the sequestration of the goods of anyone outlawed for homicide.

6. M. Sanuto, *Cronachetta* (Venice, 1880) 200–201. Girolamo Priuli also referred to this custom in his *Diarii* under the date 28 May, 1511 (ms. in B.C.V., *Provenienze diverse*, P.D. 252–c, libro 6°, 206v seq.). In the capitularies of this office, preserved in A.S.V., there is no explicit mention of this: on the other hand, the principle of 2 March, 1318, which is mentioned in the text, is recorded there. On 21 Sept., 1474 a law of the Great Council, designed to put a limit to the excessive number of pardons conceded to the *Cinque alla Pace*, 'la qual cosa', it noted, 'dà materia che senza timor de pena ogni uno ardisce disnudar arme et ferire cum exfusion di sangue', ordered that they could 'far grazia solo del quarto delle condanne pecuniarie' (*Libro d'oro*, pt. viii, f. 187).

7. In *Leggi criminali . . .*, cit., ff. 30v and 31.

8. In J. S. F. Boehmer, *Elementa iurisprudentiae criminalis* (Halle, 1749); the treatise is preceded by the text of the Caroline ordinance; *Recueil général des anciennes lois françaises*, by Isambert, Decrusy and Arnet (Paris, 1828) xii, 600 seq.: cf. on this ordinance A. Esmein, op. cit., 145 seq.; J. F. Stephens, *A history of the criminal law in England* (London, 1893) ii, 204 and 459 seq. For an analogous evolution of the Florentine judicial system in this period, see A. Anzilotti, *La costituzione interna dello stato fiorentino sotto il duca Cosimo de' Medici* (Florence, 1910) 14 and 132, and L. Martines, *Lawyers and statecraft in Renaissance Florence* (Princeton, 1968) 130 and 142.

9. F. Braudel, 'La vita economica di Venezia nel secolo XVI', *La civiltà veneziana del Rinascimento* (Florence, 1958) 101.

10. Sanuto, ii, 390–1.

11. P. Dolfin, 'Annali', *Diarii veneziani del secolo decimosesto*, ed. R. Cessi and P. Sambin (Venice, 1943) i, fasc. i, pt. iv, 5.

12. F. Braudel, op. cit., 85 seq.; G. Luzzatto, *Storia economica di Venezia dall' XI al XVI secolo* (Venice, 1961) 236 seq.

13. G. Priuli, *Diarii*, *R.I.S.* 2, ii, 297.

14. P. Dolfin, op. cit., 219.

15. Domenico Malipiero, *Annali veneti dall' anno 1457 al 1500*, ed. Longo-Sagredo, *A.S.I.*, vii (1843) 535.

16. Sanuto, ii, 616.

17. Ibid., iv, 167–9; G. Priuli, *Diarii*, ii, 187 and passim in the succeeding volumes.

18. Matters were regulated by two laws of the Council of Ten of 6 Sept., 1506. Here and in the rest of this article I will do no more than allude briefly to the various organs of the Venetian constitution by way of introducing, from the point of view of my subject, the particular problems with which I shall try to deal. For a modern view of the constitution, see the two volumes of the classic work by G. Maranini, *La costituzione di Venezia dalle origini alla serrata del Maggior Consiglio* (Venice, 1927) and *La costituzione di Venezia dopo la serrata del Maggior Consiglio* (Venice, 1931) and the perceptive study by G. Cassandro, 'Concetto, caratteri e struttura dello stato veneziano', *Rivista di storia del diritto italiano*, xxxvi (1963) 23 seq. From the point of view of clarity and organization, the course by Paolo Selmi on *La costituzione della Repubblica di Venezia dopo la serrata del Maggior Consiglio* (as yet unpublished) written for the school of history of the University of Warwick, is an admirable introduction to the study of the constitution.

19. *Libro d'oro*, pt. vi. On variations in the numbers of members of the Great Council

(augmented from 1437 to 1510, diminishing thereafter) see G. A. Muazzo, *Del governo antico della Repubblica veneta, delle alterazioni e regolazioni di esso, e delle cause e tempi che sono successe fino a' nostri giorni. Discorso istorico-politico.* Ms. in B.C.V., Cod. Cicogna, 2080, f. 119.

20. *Cronachetta*, cit., 222; Sanuto, viii, 411–2.
21. Sanuto, xvi, 645–6.
22. Maranini, cit., 42–3.
23. See, for example, Sanuto, i, 275, 303, 338; iv, 249–50 and 338.
24. Priuli, *Diarii*, cit., e.g. i, 211 and 245–6.
25. *Libro d'oro*, pts. vii, viii, ix, *passim*.
26. Ibid., pt. viii, f. 232.
27. D. Morosini, *De bene instituta re publica*, ed. C. Finzi (Milan, 1969) 94. See also G. Cozzi, 'Domenico Morosini e il *De bene instituta re publica*', *Studi Veneziani*, xii (1970).
28. D. Malipiero, cit., 691.
29. Sanuto, iv, 201–4, 209. Contrary to the expectation of many gentlemen Minio's sentence was not proclaimed in the Great Council, as would have been the normal course, 'o per più teror, o perché non era da meter cause aperte, ma dubiose da interpretar'.
30. Sanuto, v, 388.
31. P. Morosini, 'De rebus ac forma reipublicae venetae', in G. Valentinelli, *Bibliotheca manuscripta S. Marci Venetiarum* (Venice, 1870) iii, 246.
32. Malipiero, cit., 21.
33. D. Morosini, cit., 113 and 155.
34. Sanuto, iv, 181–182; Priuli, cit., ii, 176.
35. *Libro d'oro*, pt. vii, viii, ix: alterations in the 'promissio' were made on the occasion of a doge's death.
36. D. Morosini, cit., 100, 113–114.
37. P. Morosini, op. cit., 256 and 259. 'Il magistrato degli Avogadori a que' primi tempi fu di grande auttorità et d'incredibile stima: il principale ufficio del quale è la guardia delle leggi, cioè che in parte veruna non si offenda le leggi', wrote Gasparo Contarini, *Della republica et magistrati di Venetia* (Venice, 1630) 91–92.
38. *Cronachetta*, 95 seq.
39. Ibid., 100 seq.
40. *Libro d'oro*, pt. viii, ff. 111 and 112.
41. Sanuto, *Cronachetta*, 170–171.
42. *Libro d'oro*, pt. viii, f. 130.
43. Ibid., f. 184.
44. Sanuto, vi, 137 and 142.
45. Criminal legislation from the fifteenth century on (we have seen an instance in the laws respecting outlaws) bore above all the stamp of the Council of Ten. On the rise in criminality caused by the wars and the misery that accompanied them, see the statute of 22 July, 1475, setting up the institution of 'advocato dei poveri presonieri'. *Libro d'oro*, pt. vii, f. 206.
46. Malipiero, op. cit., 492.
47. Sanuto, iv, 182.
48. Op. cit., 196.
49. Morosini, op. cit., 112–114.
50. D. Giannotti, *Libro della repubblica de' viniziani* in *Opere* (Florence, 1850) ii, 120; Morosini, op. cit., 98.
51. *Libro d'oro*, pt. viii, f. 125.
52. Sanuto, iii, 665.
53. R. Fulin, *Gl'Inquisitori dei Dieci*, in *A.V.*, 1 (1870) 361.
54. Ibid.
55. Sanuto, vi, 133 and 159.

56. G. A. Muazzo, *Storia del governo della Repubblica di Venezia*, ms. in B.M.V., It., VII, 963 (8239); on the procedure of the *avogadori* see D. Giannotti, op cit., 132 seq. and 144–45.

57. M. Sanuto, *Cronachetta*, cit., 100. On the procedure of the Council of Ten, see R. Fulin, op. cit., above all, i (1871) 40 seq. and 361 seq. G. Maranini, op. cit., 455 seq. There is a rapid sketch in G. Contarini, op. cit., 87.

58. Claude de Seyssel, *La victoire du roy contre les Veniciens* (Paris, 1510).

59. Sanuto, xx, 155. A full picture of the situation in the Venetian *dominio* in this period is given in A. Ventura, *Nobiltà e popolo nella società veneta del '400 e' 500* (Bari, 1964).

60. Priuli, *Diarii*, ms. in B.C.V., P.D. 252–c, libro 6° ff. 57, 152v, 383, 400.

61. Ibid., libro 7°, f. 31 (I have taken these details about the situation in Venice from Priuli and Sanuto).

62. 'Schiopeto'. Sanuto, xix, 331.

63. Ibid., xxv, 113 seq.

64. *Diarii*, libro 6°, ff. 64–65.

65. Ibid., f. 462v.

66. Sanuto, xv, 329.

67. Priuli, *Diarii*, libro 6°, f. 344, 9 Aug., 1511.

68. Sanuto, xiv, 109 and 621.

69. Priuli, *Diarii*, libro 6°, f. 466, Aug., 1511. The soldiers were also astonished 'per li modi de li vestimenti chome etiam per la aparentia et presentia loro, et sì per il portar dele arme'.

70. Ibid., f. 226. On the 'nobili da pope' or 'of the galleys', see G. Contarini, op. cit. 130.

71. Sanuto, xxi, 70.

72. In May, 1512, Priuli wrote that the army was costing the Republic 40,000 ducats a month (ibid., libro 8°, f. 74).

73. Priuli, *Diarii*, libro 6°, f. 544v.

74. Sanuto, x, 27. On the sale of offices in Venice – but without reference to the decisions recorded here – see R. Mousnier, 'Le trafic des offices à Venise', now in *La plume, la faucille et le marteau* (Paris, 1970) 387 seq.

75. Sanuto, x, 44.

76. Priuli, *Diarii*, libro 6°, f. 368; Sanuto, xii, 363, refers in detail to the contents of the proposal.

77. Sanuto, xix, 67–70.

78. Ibid., xix, 22 and 83, and xx, 150. On 2 Aug., 1515, there was open talk of the possibility of selling Asolo, xx, 446.

79. Ibid., xx, 451–5.

80. There is an excellent explanation of the electoral procedures used in Venice in Giannotti, op. cit., 114.

81. Sanuto, xxiii, 70 and 317.

82. Ibid., xxix, 530 and 532.

82a. On the religious atmosphere in Venice at this time I limit myself to citing the recent articles of I. Cervelli, 'Storiografia e problemi intorno alla vita religiosa e spirituale a Venezia nella prima metà del '500', and of G. Fragnito, 'Cultura umanistica e riforma religiosa', both in *Studi Veneziani*, viii (1966) and xi (1969).

83. Passim in Priuli's *Diarii*. Sanuto emphasizes this point, though in a less emotional manner than does Priuli. E.g. xvi, 500 seq.

84. Sanuto, xxi, 317, 479, 568.

85. Ibid., xxii, 95–6, 344, 382; xxviii, 516, 554–6.

86. Ibid., xxi, 479.

87. Ibid., xxi, 502; xxii, 84, 223 seq.

88. Ibid., xix, 446.
89. Ibid., xviii, 144 and xx, 40.
90. Ibid., xx, 116, 185–6 and xxi, 147–9.
91. *Cronachetta*, cit., 98–103.
92. Priuli, *Diarii*, libro 6°, f. 128.
92a. A.S.V., *Provveditori sopra monasteri, transunto leggi e capitolari*, B.1, f. 1.
93. Sanuto, xiv, 258 and 473.
94. Sanuto, xix, 141.
95. Priuli, *Diarii*, libro 6°, ff. 206v seq.
96. Ibid., libro 8°, f. 83v and 168.
97. The text of the law referred to here is taken from A.S.V., *Maggior Consiglio, Deliberazioni*, reg. Deda (1503–1521) f. 100r and v.
98. Sanuto, xxiii, 483.
99. Ibid., xxv, 263–4.
100. Ibid., xxiv, 69 seq.
101. Ibid., xxv, 20; xxvi, 243; xxvii, 456–7.
102. Ibid., xxiii, 562 and xxv, 30, 69.
103. Ibid., xxv, 83–4 and xxxi, 60.
104. Ibid., xxiv, 50; xxviii, 250; xxix, 465. It is worth noting certain contradictory features of penal justice which emerge in this period. On the one hand the harshness of penalties; on 3 Aug., 1521, Sanuto recorded (approving the judges' opinion) the first case known to him of a woman condemned to be quartered for premeditated uxoricide and concealment of the body. On the other hand, judgements took insanity into account, though only as an extenuating circumstance: an insane woman, guilty of killing a child who had derided her, was sentenced to life imprisonment after a long debate among the members of the *Quarantia* about the criteria to use in this and similar cases.
105. On the spread of Lutheranism in Venice, see F. Gaeta, *Un nunzio pontificio a Venezia nel cinquecento: Gerolamo Aleandro* (Venice–Rome, 1960) 112 seq. See also Sanuto, xxxiv, 410.
106. An echo of these controversies, and the negative reaction they found among many subjects of the *terraferma* can be caught in one of Luigi da Porto's letters, which reflects the state – and mood – of affairs in that grim period; *Lettere storiche*, ed. B. Bressan (Florence, 1857) 25 seq.
107. For instances of this sort, see e.g. Sanuto, xxix, 45, 192, 206, 256, 282, and xxxiv, 436–7.
108. Ibid., xxix, 297–8 and 468.
109. H. Jedin, *Storia del Concilio di Trento* (Brescia, 1949) i, 151–2.
110. Sanuto, xxv, 356–7; xxix, 45, 192, 256, 282, 316 seq.
111. Ibid., xxviii, 294.
112. Ibid., xxviii, 206.
113. Ibid., xxix, 181–2.
114. Ibid., xxxi, 28–9 and 121–2.
115. Ibid., xxx, 395, 402.
116. Ibid., xxx, 156 seq., 253, 310.
116a. Contarini, op. cit., 102.
117. Sanuto, xxxviii, 377 and xxxix, 24 seq.
118. Ibid., xxxvii, 25 and 216.
119. Ibid., xxviii, 366.
120. Ibid., xxxi, 37.
121. Ibid., xxxvii, 71.
122. Ibid., lv, 37.
123. Ibid., lv, 191.
124. Ibid., xli, 196.

125. Ibid., l, 499.

126. Ibid., xxx, 252, 330 and 299.

127. Ibid., xlvi, 611–2; lxvii, 30.

128. Ibid., xlvi, 611.

129. Ibid., xlvi, 101. For the amount written on the problem of poor nobles by the papal nuncio in Venice, Gerolamo Aleandro, see Gaeta, op. cit., 80. Unfortunately, I was unable to take advantage of B. Pullan, *Rich and poor in Renaissance Venice* (Oxford, Blackwells, 1971).

130. Sanuto, lii, 583.

131. The edicts of Jan., 1521 and Sept., 1523, and Jan. and April, 1534, are in Imbert, *Recueil . . .*, cit., xii.

132. Sanuto, xxxv, 389 and xxxvi, 258.

133. Ibid., xlii, 67.

134. Ibid., xlvi, 641.

135. Ibid., xlii, 317. See also xl, 596.

136. Giannotti, op. cit., 155–6. On the dating of Giannotti's work, *see* R. Starn, *Donato Giannotti and his Epistolae* (Geneva, 1968) 18–19. There are many signs in Giannotti, albeit heavily veiled, of fears about the prevailing influence of money (see 61–2, 84, 88, 126–7). G. Contarini, on the other hand, appears as the spokesman for the new reality of the situation in Venice, e.g. his initial definition of Venice as 'città richissima et abondantissima', and his praise of the Republic for its being ordered for peace and as a place which does not offer nourishment for warlike myths; op. cit., 9, 10–11, 13.

137. Sanuto, xxxii, 96 seq.; xxxiii, 203 seq. And see Giannotti's observations (op. cit., 126) on the decline of the office of *procuratore di San Marco*.

138. Sanuto, xxx, 301.

138a. Ibid., xliii, 235.

138b. Ibid., xxvii, 82.

139. Ibid., xxxvii, 82–3.

140. Giannotti, op. cit., 124–5.

141. Sanuto, xlviii, 300.

142. Ibid., xlviii, 443 and 450.

143. Ibid., lii, 600.

144. *Provveditori sopra monasteri*, cit., B.1, f. 9; Sanuto, li, 147 and l, 495.

145. G. A. Muazzo, in his *Discorso istorico-politico*, cit., f. 191, writes that from about 1470 to 1582 the Senate's authority 'restò in parte offuscata da quella del Consiglio di X con la Zonta'.

146. Sanuto, xli, 664 and l, 368–9.

147. Ibid., liv, 20–1.

148. The most tangible proof of this is that in July 1534 a law of the Great Council made another attempt to attract gentlemen of the highest standing to put themselves forward for election to the *Avogaria*, to this end reducing the tenure of the office, which was indeed an extremely burdensome one, to one year, and guaranteeing that tenure of this office would qualify a man to present himself for the highest honours of the Republic. A.S.V., *Avogaria di comun, capitolari*, reg. 4.

149. Sanuto, xlviii, 88.

150. Evidence of the energy with which many *avogadori* continued to exercise their duties is shown in the protests which papal nuncios continued to bring against them, accusing them of damaging both the secular jurisdiction and ecclesiastical immunities. See the letters of 7 July, 1537, 9 Aug., 1588, 5 Oct., 1540, 9 April, 1541 in *Nunziatura di Venezia*, ed. F. Gaeta (Rome, 1960) ii.

151. Contarini, op. cit., 9.

152. *Avogaria di comun, capitolari*, reg. 4.

153. See Michel de l'Hospital, *Traité de la reformation de la justice* in *Oeuvres inédites*

(Paris, 1825) i, 339 and ii, 274. Francesco Guicciardini, in his *Dialogo e discorsi del reggimento di Firenze* (Bari, 1932) 114 also speaks of the plague of appeals. In England, too, similar protests and similar demands were being raised. In the *Dialogue* between Reginald Pole and Thomas Starkey, written between 1536 and 1538, the English common law is described as 'confused, full of delays which cause suits to be long in decision. Process, therefore, should be made more summary. Similarly, both statutes and the reports of cases are over-many and should be reduced to manageable size by the wisdom of some politic and wise men'. Quo. in S. E. Thorne, 'English law and the Renaissance', in *La storia del diritto nel quadro delle scienze storiche* (Florence, 1966) 437–447.

154. Contarini writes that the authority of the *Auditori*, a magistracy created to control the functioning of civil justice in the *dominio*, is 'molto oscurata e diminuita' because people prefer to trust advocates with the management of their private interests rather than that magistracy. Op. cit., 108–9.

155. Nor was it admitted that a defence could be waived. As has been said, there was an office designed to this end, that of the advocate for impoverished prisoners, but in a case tried in 1530 against the assailant of a noble, the *avogadori* wanted the accused to be defended in the *Quarantia* by one of the most outstanding advocates. Sanuto, liii, 95.

156. In exceptional cases a trial could be reviewed by the Council itself. See the example of Jan. 1531 in ibid., liv, 265.

157. Ibid., xli, 78.

158. Ibid., xlvi, 445.

159. Ibid., l, 417.

160. Ibid., lv, 129, 190. A symptomatic consequence of this state of affairs occurred in 1530 when an *avogadore di comun* had the *Quarantia* arrest a captain of the guard of the Council of Ten; the *capi* of that council hastened to claim that the *avogadori* had no right to intervene because the captain was 'homo sottoposto al Conseio di X'. After discussion, however, the Council disavowed their *capi* so that the *Quarantia* was able to try the captain. Sanuto, liii, 269.

161. *Avogadori di comun, capitolari*, reg. 4.

161a. Sanuto, lv, 18; lvi, 76–8 and 845; lvii, 584 and lviii, 247. Luigi da Porto who, as we have seen, expressed the moods of Venice and the *dominio* in the years before the Peace of Bologna in his *Lettere storiche*, devoted a letter to expounding the conflict between *nobili* and *segretari*. The latter accuse the *nobili* of keeping power exclusively in their own hands and claim that it is only right that they alone should pay the expenses of a war as they alone decide on it and derive 'l'utile e l'onore' from it. The *nobili* reply that the true beneficiaries of the present state of affairs are the *segretari*, for to all intents and purposes they are the owners of their offices, from which they draw a large and secure profit, while the *nobili*, because of the rotation of their offices, live in constant uncertainty – and they add that because of the long tenure of their offices the *segretari* do, in fact, possess the effective power. Op. cit., 128 seq.

161b. For stimulating *aperçus* on the progressive extension of banditry in the Mediterranean area see Fernand Braudel, *La Mediterranée et le monde Mediterranéen à l'epoque de Philippe II* (Paris, 1949) 643 seq.

162. Sanuto, xxxvi, 121.

163. Ibid., xxxvi, 127 seq.

164. Ibid., xxxvi, 408.

165. A.S.V., *Cinque savi alla pace, capitolari*; Sanuto, xxxviii, 339 seq.

166. Ibid., xliii, 502.

XII

UGO TUCCI

The psychology of the Venetian merchant in the sixteenth century

---

The assertion that the great majority of Venetian merchants were of noble birth reflects *trecento* reality[1] and, in a more limited way, that of the following century. The *cinquecento*, on the other hand, saw the progressive detachment of the nobility from trade; though certainly not a new phenomenon, this was the period in which it became most pronounced.

At the beginning of the century Machiavelli could still write that the greatest fortunes of the representatives of the dominant Venetian class were founded on 'trade and movables' rather than on landed property.[2] This was already ceasing to be true. The number of noble merchants had already declined to such an extent that the tendency had not escaped numerous observers. In the eyes of the Florentine secretary, however, there were still too many to cancel out the anomaly of the full civic dignity which the Venetian constitution accorded to commerce in contrast with the political and social customs of all other countries, where the natural order required an aristocracy inseparable from the possession of land, castles, and private jurisdictions. Even later, well into the *cinquecento*, when the Venetian nobility's renunciation of trade had become almost general, it was still thought to be dedicated to its characteristic occupation, so deep was the imprint of the tradition. Involvement in trade was held to be the chief distinguishing mark of the Venetian nobility just as love for the dignity of the papal court was typical of the Roman, luxurious leisure of the Neapolitan, a heartfelt preference for the life of the castle over that of the town of the Piedmontese – and so on, with all the variations on disposition and character which filled the writings on national characteristics which were so widespread in this century. Treatises on the nature of nobility had perforce to accept this divergent behaviour and try to justify it, and the arguments used to allow the practice of trade by the Venetian patriciate were numerous and reasonably consistent. It was made clear, however, that this was simply to come to terms with living reality, the actual commercial ventures of families who by hereditary privilege

346

provided the Republic with its chief magistrates, rather than to express any conviction that the characteristic functions of the merchant could be adapted to fit the ideal portrait of a gentleman which was being impressed on that age.

Thus the Veronese Bartolomeo Cipolla, whose categories were rigidly narrow, had to admit that what was elsewhere an undoubted reason for social inferiority was permitted in Venice for the sake of a 'necessitas loci in quo nulli alii redditus vel fructus nisi ex mercimonio haberi possunt',[3] but he specified – with Cicero – that the exception was valid only where it was a question of 'mercatura magna et copiosa', because were it 'tenuis' it would have to be considered base.[4] Fortunately, there was this famous passage from the *De officiis* (I, 42), to which everyone referred and which lent its authority to justify the anomaly. In fact, if the English nobility were described in Italy as liking to live far from the city while attending nevertheless to the 'basest forms of trade', it was emphasized that the Venetians practised trade, indeed, 'but wholesale'.[5] The difference was by no means unimportant. In big business the manual application which disqualified other forms of work and determined their inferiority, played no part: it required above all organizational energy, broad technical knowledge, a spirit of adventure, 'experience of the things of the world'; moreover, it operated within the bounds of a relatively restricted circle of initiates and obviated the need to mix with people of low estate. A gentleman, Muzio recommended, must not use his own hands but have everything performed by his agents.[6] These were the characteristics which differentiated the merchant from the shopkeeper, and, above all, from the artisan. It was in the name of these principles that in 1527 a noble Venetian[7] – as though in answer to Machiavelli's proposition that precisely because they were dedicated to commerce the gentlemen of Venice 'were more so in name than in fact' – drew attention to the spectacle of the men who ran the Florentine government, who, together with their sons, were engrossed in the manual labours of the wool and silk trades in their shops, and pronounced the disdainful judgement that 'as all the Florentines are employed in these base occupations, they cannot but be craven and base themselves'.

By virtue of another important distinction, which took into account the nature of the goods concerned, the practice of trade in humble things like wood, coal, and ash was designated ignoble, while other business was 'respectable and honourable'. Furthermore, within the framework of the belief that everything in creation is ordained to an end, the activity of the merchants was held to be 'ordained for the conservation of mankind'.[8] In favour of trade was cited the benefit it yielded to the community as a whole, providing it with necessary goods and insuring the livelihoods of many fellow workers and intermediaries.[9] In this way, some saw it as among the concrete demonstrations of altruism and munificence towards which the nobleman must naturally feel inclined. But inevitably this led to an adulterated image of the merchant. He was required to be entirely disinterested, bound to his work not by a desire for profit but for the 'convenience and advantage' of others, and he was not permitted to speculate on time, storing up goods, for example, when they were flooding the market with the aim of reselling them when the price became dear, nor could he make an illicit profit by asking more than a 'just price':[10] if these were the qualities of a nobleman, they could certainly not keep their validity when transplanted into a professional sector instilled with its own, entirely different ethic. The noble merchant of certain authors would have had an extremely hard time of it in the business world, and some of them, in fact, considering the matter from the merchant's standpoint, denied that generosity was as appropriate for business men as it was for *signori*, because 'as it is the function of the *signore* to give, so it is the function of the merchant to collect and organize wealth, this being the purpose of his activity'.[11]

The effort to reconcile nobility and trade did not succeed in finding other equally effective rationalizations, but the debate – which in Venice never reached a conclusion that openly condemned the traditional activity and was never reflected in legislation, which continued to accord full civic dignity to the merchant[12] – went on, gradually wearing itself out and losing its topicality.

The break in mercantile tradition on the part of the patrician order came into sharp focus at the beginning of the *cinquecento* and one of the chief causes of the transformation (the first, in any case, of which men became aware) should probably be ascribed to the years of the war of Cambrai.[13] Of course, it is always tempting to make periods of pronounced socio-economic change coincide with wars and other specific events and thus obtain a ready explanation for them. It is, perhaps, difficult to imagine that a change like this could have evolved except in irregular spurts, accelerations in pace caused by immediate and specific causes; to seek these out is, indeed, an historical task of undoubted importance, though it should not lead to undervaluing the weight of emotional factors, of fashion or of an individual's tendency to adapt his own behaviour to that of the group. Even so, what actually appears as the outstanding feature is a continuous and unpausing progression which, for all its variations in intensity, covers the entire century. Going through the documents, this is the distinct impression one receives, though the absence of sufficient data to define the chronological distribution of the phenomenon in quantitative terms also plays its part.

As we move forward in time the number of merchants belonging to noble families decreases, and what decreases most noticeably is the number of those who work in the Venetian mercantile colonies still scattered throughout the world. At Constantinople in 1594, out of nineteen merchants convened by the *bailo* for a meeting, only four, judging by their surnames, are noble (and it could be fewer if some of them bear the name of a noble family to which they do not belong).[14] At London in 1592 there are no longer any; here, indeed, a single Venetian, originally from Zanthe, is in residence, with the result that many merchants are forced to entrust their affairs to the Florentine Bartolomeo Corsini, an agent of the Capponi, and the Republic has difficulty in choosing a consul.[15] In the past such communities had been largely composed of young noblemen, who served there a useful apprenticeship which was also the preliminary phase of the political *cursus honorum* they were later destined to embark on; at the conclusion of the cycle of studies begun in childhood, when 'the beard begins to sprout' they 'sailed to far-away countries, where they increased their families' wealth with mercantile activity and at the same time became expert in the customs, practices and laws of many peoples'.[16] The diminishing numbers in the mercantile colonies gives the sense of how definitive and radical the desertion must have been; a man who had been kept well away from trade in his youth would hardly be tempted to return to the way of life of his elders, even at times – which were not lacking in the course of the century – when the situation might appear to favour such a return. The effects on the shaping of the new generations were decisive. Those of the first decades of the *cinquecento* grew up in a mood quite different from that of their predecessors, and the changes in experience and educational background left a distinct mark on their nature, accentuating the contrast of feelings, values and aspirations which towards the middle of the century was to lead to an open break within the Venetian patriciate, dividing it between 'vecchi' and giovani', with their different conceptions of the political and economic needs of Venice.[17]

There were many who followed this development with apprehension and feared the consequences which such a narrowing of horizons was bound to produce. The young men, Girolamo Priuli complained in 1509, are brought up 'with no experience of the world';[18] 'with no practice and understanding of the world', repeated in 1584 the procurators of St. Mark who were engaged in an attempt to reinstate Venice, even at an extremely high political price, in the lucrative circuit of the spice trade.[19] And whoever feared the ferment of new ideas that were endangering internal political stability saw them as creeping threateningly among those who were crowding the city instead of taking themselves off in the traditional manner. The spectacle of the inactivity in which youth was growing up aroused their greatest concern; it was to this that they attributed the quarrels and turbulence which – no more seriously, perhaps, than in the good times past – were troubling them. Where trade, with structural characteristics that played so important a part in the framework of society, had been abandoned, it was replaced by the idleness of many sections of the upper class because, in effect, no new activity had been substituted for the old. 'Capti luxuria, facile diverterunt a laboribus ad delitias', wrote Andrea Mocenigo in 1525.[20] The trade crisis had diverted capital funds mainly to the country, accelerating the race for investments in land which formed one of the major themes of the century nearly everywhere in Italy. And if there was no lack of large scale speculation, if agricultural reforms were – especially in the reclamation of land – numerous and sometimes impressive, all of which testified to active participation; if some, again, were able to stimulate considerable governmental intervention and to take advantage of it, all the same the great majority of new proprietors asked nothing more from their possessions on the *terraferma* than the opportunity for recreation and a steady flow of income. The basic cycle of rural economy needed no special encouragement to yield the benefits of its natural fertility. This belief was almost universally held by the men who were now taking over from other owners (who had been equally detached from the actual processes of agriculture) and the belief was strengthened by a faith in the extraordinary fertility of Italian soil which was one of the great myths of this period. The palaces and seignorial villas, made for celebrations, entertainments and the care-free but decorous parties which passed the time with story-telling and discussion, remained for the most part shut off from problems connected with working in the fields. And in fact in the Venetian region this was not a period of technical progress nor of increased agricultural productivity, and the cultivation of cereals, which determines the evolution of agrarian practice so deeply, developed on extensive lines, to the detriment of areas occupied by woods and meadows; any-one who interested himself closely with agricultural matters did so for pleasure, as was befitting a gentleman, limiting himself in any case to the cultivation of trees, because anything that implied the use of hoe or ploughshare must be con-sidered 'rustic and base'.[21]

Although the means by which noblemen were permitted to earn their own living honourably were farming, the army, letters, and trade,[22] even in Venetian society it was in fact farming which, more and more, was gaining favour with the ruling class. In 1288 a Da Canal could be dispensed from a public office in order to deal with business matters which piled up on the eve of the galleys' departure;[23] in 1596 a trial was suspended because one of the judges was out of Venice for the harvest.[24] Clearly the type of occupation which could justifiably excuse a government official from duty had changed completely. It is well known that in the past landed investment had already played a by no means secondary role in the make-up of patrician patrimonies. In the tenth to fourteenth centuries they had represented a form of insurance, a guarantee to set beside commercial and maritime activities;[25] later they came to absorb trading profits which could not be reinvested in new mercantile ventures;[26] finally, they became extensive enough to involve an autonomous need for rounding out and consolidation. Thus, even before the unfolding of the events which according to traditional historiography mark the beginning of the decline of Venice, wealth accumulated through the fortunate operations of many generations was committed to the land. Solidly anchored in a stable tenure, increased indefinitely by the cumulative effects of exorbitantly priced produce, it was real wealth, designed to be the instrument and continual support of family dignity. It became the emblem of the most powerful and illustrious families, and this helped, perhaps to a greater extent than any economic incentive, to encourage and multiply investments in land throughout all the social orders. The nobility of today, observed Tommaso Garzoni, deriding the flood of the new fashion which had taken hold of every-body and was helping to swell the ranks of false titles, 'consists of having a vineyard on four *pertiche* of land, with a cottage in the middle where one sometimes goes for pleasure . . .'[27]

The praises of rural life were sung on every possible occasion, its serenity valued in contrast with the anxieties of trade, as was the sense of security it offered in a changing age which required tremendous efforts of adaptation. Then there was the distinction attached to the exercise of a virtually absolute territorial dominion and the firm support that being overlord of a peasant world gives to the aristocrat's sense of superiority, especially in areas which had preserved a residual feudalism in the relationship between ownership and production. And, in addition, the landed proprietor did not have to involve himself in any initiatives or wearisome negotiations whatsoever in order to realize his profits: without the necessity for quarrels with other men they were bountifully provided for him directly from nature, and by virtue of the incontestable right that accompanied a lawful title of acquisition. By the second half of the century it had become easy to prove that farming was 'more noble by far than warfare',[28] and a treatise published in Venice in 1596 advised the Knights of Malta to stay away from ignoble practices and 'illicit earnings' (i.e., from trade) as they ought to obtain their money from land.[29] It was land which, in effect, constituted what was defined as 'an aspect of nobility and no light ornament'[30] and it was only with reference to land, the only possession that really ennobled, that 'old wealth' could be identified. That old wealth was superior to new was confirmed by the corollary principle that nobility is a quality inherited from antecedents because 'an individual, however virtuous, is not yet noble, but the beginning of nobility: only his descendants, through many generations of virtuous performance, acquire nobility'.[31] The wealth which comes down to us already accumulated by others is more respectable than what we accumulate ourselves because this operation calls for avarice, which is a vice, and a thirst for profit, which entails the practice of base professions; the relationship between a virtuous man and wealth consists in giving it away, not in acquiring it, because a nobleman does not take, he gives.[32] This line of argument took its authority from Aristotle; it was applicable to agriculture and was used to praise it, and at the same time it implicitly constituted a condemnation of trade while not attacking it directly.

While everyone was turning to landed wealth, the merchants, on the contrary, saw themselves as 'despised and vilified by all, and looked on with little respect'; fearful of losing social prestige, many had liquidated their affairs and acquired 'property and suchlike, so as to live from the revenue'.[33] In Bandello's story about the gentlewoman married to a merchant, she hastens on his death to liquidate his commercial business and convert the capital into landed property; thus her son, kept away from trade and given a genteel education, can become refined and magnanimous, open to the pleasures of literature and music as well as accomplished in horsemanship, fencing and 'other similar skills'. The tale is set in Milan, but by now little would have needed changing if it had been set in Venice. At times the rejection of trade seemed to transcend simple economic choice and to realize a craving for purification which was also deeply felt in other social strata. We can see this in the letter of an imaginary merchant, presented in a formula which we can regard as broadly representative because the proposals it contains are addressed to a wide circle of readers: 'I have decided to put aside this infinite greed for lucre and to return to my homeland, where I will pass what remains of my life in valleys, hills and fields . . .'[34]

French and Spanish models, present in so many manifestations of Venetian Renaissance custom, had a by no means negligible influence on this change of outlook: a gentleman of Brescia, albeit mistakenly, attributed the responsibility for the unworthiness of trade being singled out as a reason for exclusion from the *Consiglio Cittadino* to the French occupation of his city.[35] Effective, too, must have been the example of the way of life of the many wealthy families who had fled from the lawlessness of their own tumultuous countries and chosen Venice as a tranquil place of residence where their incomes could be enjoyed in splendid surroundings.[36] It is more difficult to show the extent to which the change is connected with the currents of renewal running through Italian society as a whole. In other urban communities the cultural tendencies of humanism had, taken together, already helped to support a shift in moral attitudes and political and social forms towards aristocratic or noble values, and it is certain that no aspect of the evolution of collective sensibility in the sixteenth century can be isolated from this general background which induced – even when it did not affect it directly – an atmosphere which nourished the sort of ideals that give validity to new types of man and citizen. Research in depth in this direction is certainly called for, research which must aim at a precise estimate of the part played by this withdrawal from business in playing up the spirit of aristocratization and impoverishing that of civic life.

But whatever explanation one might offer for this transformation in the living habits of the Venetian patriciate, two factors lay at the root of it; the demobilization of commercial and maritime efforts prepared during a long period of slack business, and a shrewd awareness of the revolution taking place in the structure of international trade. Girolamo Priuli had no doubts on the subject: 'Venetian merchants, given that voyages are few, without spices and hardly profitable, have retired from trade and have invested their money in property, a little profit being better than nothing or than keeping their capital idle.'[37] Around the beginning of the century and even within the framework of a general crisis, it was still trade which brought wealth; in the winter of 1499 the increased price of spices had yielded a profit on the market of more than 200,000 ducats, and in the February of 1500 the Grimani's share alone had amounted to 40,000. At that time the new *rentiers* drew scarcely enough to keep going on.[38] Later, however, circumstances proved them right. Loss of hegemony in the balance of exchange with the Levant, insecurity on the seas, scanty remuneration from traditional investments, insolvencies, successive bankruptcies: these are the phenomena which historians have clarified in the light of an enormous documentation which leaves little room for divergent interpretations. 'It is less bad to keep capital at home than to put it in circulation with so many risks and without profit': advice like this, addressed in 1555 from Syria to the nobleman Antonio Bragadin,[39] recurs with the frequency of a refrain in business letters in which the graph of overall economic trends can be drawn in terms of proposals to withdraw, regret for the past, reciprocal accusations of operative ineptitude.

And many documents indicate that the crisis was reflected in the economic structure itself. Gasparo Contarini brought one aspect colourfully to life when in 1524 he observed that the five senators with jurisdiction in maritime matters – the *savi agli ordini* – who had had such importance in the past, had now fallen into such low repute that the office was entrusted to 'youths and those barely on the threshold of manhood'.[40]

The modifications which the crisis brought about in its commercial organization deprived Venice of its character as a great collective concern in which the whole city, directly and indirectly, had an interest. Business no longer identified itself with the state, nor did government with its conduct. It follows from this that the technical preparation and the kind of sensibility required of the nobleman entrusted with public office came to have less and less in common with those of a merchant, since they were moving in independent directions. It was a short step from here to seeing themselves in opposition. 'It is one thing to be a merchant, another to govern states and fleets, and one never sees nor hears that a commoner does anything worthwhile unless it is making money', pronounces a nobleman of the new generation. This severe judgement, which is Donado da Lezze's, was delivered against some commanding officers of the merchant galleys which by absconding from the line of battle in the naval encounter with the Turkish fleet in August, 1499, caused St. Mark's fortune to take a turn for the worse;[41] the new awareness of an antithesis between the ideals of those who constituted the patrician class and a profession which, because of the ends it pursues, debases its practitioners, could hardly find a more telling witness. Without the excuse of an equally serious occasion, the argument was taken up later by another Venetian noble, Giovan Maria Memmo. With him, we are in the second half of the *cinquecento*, when it was already possible to observe the end results of the process. He is obliged to admit that in the Venetian Republic 'merchants have always governed and administered public affairs with great and praiseworthy prudence', and this could not but be out of respect for his predecessors who 'have helped the State with trade'; still, he would like them excluded from the government during the entire time that they are attending to business because 'blinded by the desire for their personal gain, they would place their own private interests before the good of the Republic.'[42] Since Memmo makes a clear distinction between craftsmen – absolutely excluded because their profession condemns them forever to an ignoble status – and merchants, for whom he simply sets a period of quarantine, one can see in his position only a veiled condemnation of a too common practice which, even when it did not degenerate into abuse, could lead many patricians astray from the proper performance of duty. Ample illustration of this was not wanting; consider fiscal evasion alone, a phenomenon as widespread in Venice as it was elsewhere and which found ready means in the exploitation of certain administrative offices as well as through a network of relatives, political associates and friends. And despite the ambiguities and the occasional reticences in the dialogue, which plainly reflect the difficulty with which the patrician class was

z

coming to grips with the change in its social criteria, Memmo's conception of the deleterious character of trade, of the incompatibility of its goals with those which anyone who performs a public function must set himself, comes out clearly enough. He addresses himself, moreover, to readers more familiar with the models offered by Castiglione's *Cortegiano* than with those of the perfect merchant, well versed in his duties and alert to the metrological conditions in the four continents. And his approach seems even more valid when applied to the shift towards the more professional and specialized notions of behaviour which were infecting the bureaucratic machine (just as they were the higher spheres of political power) with a new sense of the role of public servants which, in its turn, was coming to 'bureaucratize' their frame of mind and their conduct.[43] The time when 'all merchant nobles of Venice operated as one large regulated company of which the board of directors was the Senate'[44] belongs to the distant past: now the special interest of the merchant no longer coincides with the public good; his activity has ceased to be seen as a civic activity, so that in a well-ordered state the patrician, upon whom the exercise of power is incumbent as a birthright, keeps himself at a distance from trade.

With the progressive disappearance of all those public interventions which made a privileged profession of trade, especially with the end of regular state-organized galley services which for two centuries[45] had been the most concrete aspect of Venetian collective solidarity, the weaker operators felt isolated in their struggle with the course of events. The young patrician lacked many of the opportunities for profit and, therefore, the business incentives which for his ancestors had represented a secure resource. In 1532 a member of the Badoer family, Zuan Alvise, could still travel as a *patronus galearum Flandrie*, a public commission which offered him, with the chance of doing his duty as a citizen, the most favourable conditions for seeking a fortune: from Venice, one of his brothers addressed a letter to him at Southampton in which he urged him to mind his interests 'honourably', to come out on the credit side and think of the future because 'in the world today, and especially in Venice, none but the rich are respected'; he should invest his capital in good kerseys and try to manage things as though he were a small merchant, without showing off; above all, with taxes in mind, on his return home he should make out his customs declaration under a false name.[46] But although we find here a situation and mental attitudes which take us back into the great era of the noble merchant, we are already at its limits. The law had reserved two hundred or more posts for noblemen on board merchant ships and galleys, as much to provide an opening for men from poor families as to encourage new recruits to the marine; by mid-century even these opportunities were not always available.[47] For a man in search of a decorous occupation there remained professions like the law, which, having become the refuge of the disinherited just when the contraction of affairs had brought about a decline in the number of civil actions, offered earnings that were hardly bountiful,[48] or public offices which, fortunately for those seeking an occupation, were by this time increasing in number as the administrative organization of the capital and the *dominio* grew ever vaster and more complex. This last factor is not to be overlooked because with its powerful enticements it played its part in helping to extinguish the spirit of free initiative which is at the basis of mercantile activity. Two examples stressing certain distinctive elements will help to make the contrast sharper. Marco Bollani[49] lost his life in 1497 in the waters of Cherso during the sinking of two galleys laden with eastern merchandise because he was dragged to the bottom while trying to keep afloat with 1,500 ducats (more than 5 kilos of pure gold) which he carried on his back; his is a figure we can think of as typical of the generations which believed in trade. Andrea di Gregorio Barbarigo (d. 1570),[50] on the other hand, is a symbol of how far away from this the new generations had moved. Climbing the ladder of government office as a very young man, he began his career in 1521 by taking part in the Great Council before he was twenty-five, thanks to a donative. Three years later he tried by the same means to get himself elected *savio agli ordini* although he had not reached the prescribed age, and immediately afterwards he was beaten in the ballot for election as consul of Damascus by a competitor who had offered more. After occupying an almost uninterrupted string of offices he was elected in 1554 to the Council of Ten, and in 1561 and 1570 he missed becoming doge by only two votes. It is true that this course earned him a bad reputation, so much so that in 1546 he considered having himself re-elected to the Senate in the ordinary way – after having entered it in 1538 by means of a donation of 500 ducats. This, however, was the unfortunate custom of the time. A law passed under pressure of financial need, but certainly not without disregard for the aspirations of numerous aspirants, had opened the doors of the Great Council to eighteen-year-old noblemen who paid a fixed sum into the coffers of the state; even the office of procurator of St. Mark, which was among the most exalted, had come to be given to young men of twenty-one who were prepared to contribute some tens of thousands of ducats,[51] so that it was not necessary to be a great moralist to regret times when 'only the wisest and those who were judged the best were elected to such a noble and serious rank, and no one attained it by ambition or money.'[52]

For some, to become part of the governmental machine was a solution to the practical problem of insuring the economically secure existence which could no longer be expected from trade; it provided an income, even if not as good a one as land and investment in mortgage loans, which were the signs of a man who had succeeded in making his fortune. For others, however, it served mainly as a way of entering the area of effective power, of preparing the way for sons and grandsons into the round of offices which were a monopoly of the most powerful families. The Venetian ruling class did not really give the appearance of an undifferentiated whole. The economic order flourishing at the end of the great era which had opened with the crusade of Dandolo concentrated wealth in a relatively restricted group of families; the economic standing of many others was incomparably inferior, even to the point of extreme modesty. I do not propose here to investigate the political and social consequences of the division thus created, but to limit myself to observing its effects on traditional forms of investment. The problem for the rich was not so much one of further growth as of the conservation and management of what was already possessed, and trade, with the high margins of profit it could offer in good periods but the grave risks to which it was perennially subject ('Ships are but boards, sailors but men . . .', Shylock justly commented) did not meet their requirements; the function of consolidation was better satisfied, as we have seen, by investment in real estate. This tendency can be seen at work, for example, in a hazardous sector like shipowning. In a list of 22 vessels in 1500, at least 16 belonged to patricians; of 11 requests for state loans for shipbuilding between 1553 and 1559, 7 were made by patricians; out of 40 presented in the period 1558–1603 only 7 requests came from patricians: a fall from 72.73 per cent and 63.63 per cent to 10.72 per cent.[52a] A man who could not avail himself of large capital sums, on the other hand, was only left with the hope of mediocre profits because the productivity of commercial operations was restricted by more and more aggressive competition, quite apart from the risk of incurring large losses without any possibility of salvaging them. One merchant was of the opinion that it was worthwhile to 'leave Venice in order to go among so many dangers' to trade in a foreign market only provided that one had business worth 100,000 ducats,[53] a not inconsiderable sum which few would have at their disposal. This was perhaps an exaggeration, but all the same the time was past when one could rely with good reason on a starting capital of five hundred to a thousand ducats. In addition, the switch from the monopoly on which Venetian commercial ventures had relied in the past to the new conditions of international commerce had been too abrupt for the operators' adaptability. Events which were easily explicable in the light of the current situation stirred up public opinion, even at a high level, to ill-considered reactions and, above all, to a sense of disorientation which was frequently coloured with fatalism. If that was the moment to sharpen their weapons, the Venetian merchants do not really give the impression of having grasped it. Although this was still a period of great prestige for their mercantile institutions, they were satisfied with the pattern established in the *quattrocento* and had taken few pains to bring it up to date. At the moment when in Genoa merchants of the medieval type were transforming themselves into bankers and financiers, in Venice the business world made no move to free itself from the time-honoured forms of its long tradition and remained faithful to the same routine. The principal, if not the exclusive, field of action was still the transfer of goods from a country where they cost less to another where they cost more, the profit being the difference in price; they continued to search for spices, raw silk, and cotton in the Levant in order to exchange them for kerseys acquired in England or with other products of the west or of Italy, even though the loss of certain markets seriously unbalanced the system and warehouses were often out of one commodity or too full of another, according to events whose course was no longer steered from the Rialto. Techniques remained excellent, but obstructing their perfect functioning was an old-fashioned mentality; only rarely do we get the impression that men were in command of the economic situation at hand rather than accepting it passively, almost detachedly; few appear to have widened their vision beyond the mechanics of geographical price variation in which a profit would be made in an elementary way, to the pursuit of bold increases of profit or the nourishing of ideals of accumulated wealth over and above what sufficed for a tranquil old age and the conservation of a family's social position. The treatise of Benedetto Cotrugli – which one would be wrong to restrict to its Ragusan context, as it gives a faithful picture of the vast Mediterranean area dominated by the Venetian mentality – breathes the spirit of the just price, temperance and moderation, and it seethes with rebukes for those who would earn too much, who risk too much, who do not leave room for others: 'who would earn too much loses everything . . .; do not do too much business or on too large a scale, do not hope to catch every bird . . .; if you wish to accumulate infinitely, I regard you as an irrational beast and as an animal, not as a man, because a merchant should practise trade with the aim of satisfying his needs.' Fortunately in Venice there was no inclination to follow his recommendation so far as to adopt a sabbatical year during which no contracts could be made and merchants would have to limit themselves to settling accounts and calling in debts.[54]

In merchants like the Venetians, who had become slaves to routine, whom we see continuing almost by sheer inertia, undauntedly exporting eastern mohairs to Antwerp even when the market was saturated with the local product which was, in any case, thicker and longer, wonderfully coloured, and better value, it would be difficult to trace the distinctive features which mark the protagonists of the new era of commerce in Europe. In 1583 one of these, the Fleming Guglielmo Helman, who, with his brother Carlo, headed one of Venice's most active firms, ordered his agent in Constantinople to sell immediately, and thus at a loss, all the emeralds he had in deposit on his own account so that a competitor who was preparing to embark with a considerable quantity of these goods would find the shops supplied and be forced either to get rid of them below cost or to turn back: those who had sent him in the hope of making a fortune would thus receive a salutary lesson. No noble Venetian could ever endorse such coups, which were foreign in the most absolute way to the old conception of business, even less compete on an equal footing with those who planned them. It was, moreover, these very Helmans who, bringing a new spirit to the Venetian business world, tried to turn one of their agents in Constantinople – who, according to custom enjoyed considerable freedom of action, working partly for the commission on the affairs he handled, partly for friendship's sake – into a mere executor of orders, subordinate in everything and paid a fixed salary. For Niccolò Crotto, on the other hand, who in 1585 went to Ankara to purchase camlets, it was a question of live and let live. God had made the world large so that everyone could benefit from his bounty; 'whoever harms others through his wicked appetite', he pronounced, 'will never prosper in his own affairs.'[55]

A static conception of operative strategy and business ethics was another feature of the nobles' withdrawal from trade. As long as it had been carried on not in a totally absorbing way but as a complement, as it were, to a well-defined phase of life within a political and social context where patriotism and personal interests coincided, business activity had not seemed incompatible with the dignity of the ruling class; indeed, protected by a completely secure barrier of privilege, backed by recourse to force when it was deemed necessary, its aims identified with those of the state: trade on these terms was perfectly suited to the character and values of the patriciate. Now that changes in the patterns of international trade imposed objectives and means which conditioned, in a quite specific and exclusive way, the mental outlook, conduct and way of life of men engaged in trade on more specifically 'bourgeois' lines, the contrast was becoming too apparent. The nobles' insufficient ability to assimilate the new factors which were transforming the nature of mercantile activity revealed them as feeling progressively less like merchants and more like nobles. Those of them who in the *cinquecento* did remain in the breach kept firmly to the old mentality, even though they were trying to keep it alive in a world infused with a radically changed approach. Even in the first half of the century such men seem behind the times, whether they are compared with businessmen of the northern stamp or those who turned to other occupations or simply decided to live as *rentiers*.

If the biography, taken at random, of a noble merchant of this century is transferred to the setting of fifty or a hundred years before, the anachronism, all things considered, is not perhaps so great as to appear improbable. A Pietro Bragadin, for example, appears at home in the preceding century at least as much as in his own. Born in the last part of the *quattrocento*, in his youth we see him employed in the classic pepper trade with Alexandria and implicated (this comes as no surprise) in a dispute with the exchequer over an importation under a false name on behalf of his father, Andrea, also a merchant; he even deals in other goods typical of the exchange between the Levant and the west, and particularly in jewels of which he is an expert connoisseur, and he continues to practice trade even when invested with public office. As *bailo* in Constantinople from 1524, he succeeds in carrying on a flourishing trade with the Black Sea, making a profit on some of his operations of up to 100 per cent; later, entrusted with important public functions, he participates in meetings of the highest assemblies of the Republic, sometimes in the capacity of vice-doge. His son, Zuan Francesco, follows in his footsteps. In 1519 he is in Alexandria, and his letters show that he has profited to the full from an apprenticeship in business training. 'Things are not going very well', he writes, 'because the prices of spices tend to rise in the East while at Venice they are on the decline, but the arrival of the caravan which is expected will bring everything to rights and the galleys will depart well laden . . .' How many times have we read these things in Venetian commercial correspondence of the fifteenth century? It seems that nothing has changed, not even the faith in better times which indicates that the crisis is not seen in terms of a catastrophe. The Bragadin conception of trade is revealed by an exhortation which Pietro addresses in 1525 from Constantinople to his son, who has returned to Venice in order to look after the affairs of the family firm while his father is in the service of the Republic: 'Make two ducats out of one, if you can, so that you may feel the profit and honour of it, and I peace of mind.'[56] Profit and honour: in this context such concepts now seem inadequate because the Venetian aristocracy has long since begun to locate these aims elsewhere among its mental categories.

Nevertheless, we continue to encounter many such figures in the Venetian business world of the *cinquecento*, nobles great and small who behave like Pietro Bragadin. Girolamo Mocenigo, for example, has business connections with Aleppo before becoming *podestà* in Vicenza (1556); Paolo Contarini, while he fills the important post of *provveditore generale in terraferma*, does not neglect his business with Constantinople (1585); there is Zuan Francesco Priuli, an outstanding figure in Venetian financial history because of his plan for the redemption of the public debt, successfully carried out between 1577 and 1594, who, in 1595, sends his agent in Pera wool cloths 'from his *bottega*, the most exquisite stuff' and silk 'bought with great care'; Antonio Priuli, of the Council of Ten, who deals in diamonds for many thousands of ducats (1596).[57] The list could easily be made longer, taking as a starting point the index of eighty-three nobles who 'have dealings in the Levant' compiled in 1610 by the *cinque savi alla mercanzia*, though, to be honest, the list somewhat strains the credulity of an historian.[58]

Still, however many were the nobles who persevered in their traditional activity throughout the *cinquecento*, they were not enough to modify the process which had been set in motion and which reached its climax in the first decades of the following century. It is pointless merely to count them and deduce that their presence testifies to a continuation of the situation of the preceding age or, again, to argue simply from their number that we are in one particular moment or another of Venice's struggle for survival or of its economic decline. What counts is the split which has developed between the patrician and mercantile mentalities, and the growing conviction that their respective moral and behavioural rules are incompatible which has widened it. The conception of the merchant as a better class of citizen, which had been predominant throughout the centuries during which Venice built up its fortune, has had its day: in short, the role of the noble merchant in Venetian history appears to be played out.

Profit and honour. From the moment Venetian noblemen stopped believing that the buying and selling of goods was their special prerogative, the practice of trade was progressively restricted to a group with its own self-sufficient characteristics. Despite defections, this group still appears to be fairly numerous in the *cinquecento* and the forms its activity took show an advanced stage of development based on centuries of experience. The specialization required by the large volume of trade helped to maintain its cohesiveness, as did difficult working conditions in the face of international competition. This concentration of mercantile activity is not a peculiarity of the *cinquecento*; the process had much earlier origins, which can be traced back as far as the second half of the *duecento*, but it tended to be accentuated now because, as always, bad periods tend to eliminate the weaker, the less fortunate, and the non-specialist – a term which must be applied to the patricians, at least in the last phases.

Examining the composition of this restricted merchant class, we come first of all to the order of *cittadini*, half way between nobility and *popolani*, from whom most of its members were recruited. Even in past centuries *cittadini* had co-operated with nobles for the greater glory of Venetian commerce, participating in this sector with equal rights, although the nobles' control of power inevitably ensured much more advantageous conditions for them. They had always worked side by side, and the difference of class, despite the persistence of many of its effects, had never been an obstacle to the establishment of relationships in society or elsewhere or of close personal ties in the pursuit of their common economic occupation. Now, however, if things had not changed on a formal level, in practice social discrimination made itself oppressively felt in the business sector as in every other aspect of civic life: 'Note well, when you have to do with noblemen, how we are treated and how they haggle', complains a *cittadino* merchant in 1553.[59] But in the Venetian business world the nobles who had remained faithful to their ancestors' traditional occupation seemed more and more out of place; when they left the field altogether it was the *cittadini* who took over the most conspicuous part of it. In the second half of the *cinquecento* the Venetian merchant was already beginning to identify himself with the *cittadino*, and in the following century the composition of Venetian society presented observers with no uncertainty: 'The nobleman', wrote Luca di Linda, 'employs his talents in letters or public office, sometimes in the affairs of Mars . . . the *cittadino* of lower standing either takes up the career of government secretary or is employed in trade; the plebeian is entirely occupied with crafts.'[60]

Heterogeneous in structure, although the privileges enjoyed by certain pro-fessional sectors gave it a recognizable identity, the political influence of the *cittadino* class was very modest (in the *cinquecento* as in every other period) but rich in individuals of considerable economic power. Apart from merchants the ranks of *cittadini* – which, numbering 7,209 in 1581 (a thousand more than the nobles) made up 5.3 per cent of the population of Venice[61] – also included those who practised the liberal professions as well as public functionaries and employees. It does not seem that the movement between various types of occupation within this class can be explained in the light of the familiar cycles of accumulation and dispersal of inherited wealth. If some families remained faithful to one specialized profession for several generations and the sons followed in the footsteps of their fathers, still others distributed their members among one or other of the occupational groups which have been mentioned, depending on individual preference and opportunity. In effect the long range changes taking place in the structure of trade had the same problems in store for them as for the nobles, on whom they also, as a rule, modelled their own standards of behaviour. Piero Ventura, cloth and jewel merchant and brother of the perfumier at the sign of

The psychology of the Venetian merchant in the sixteenth century

The Lily, sent one of his sons, Zuan Maria, to do business in Constantinople while in 1592 the younger brother, Agostino, began his university studies in logic at Padua. Michele Legiso, too, wanted to go to Padua to take a degree in law and philosophy, thereby disappointing his father, Antonio, who from Candia took part in the great wine trade with Flanders and England; in 1558 spurred by the problems involved in providing dowries for three daughters, he had placed Michele with the Pisani, in Venice, to serve his mercantile apprenticeship there, but the atmosphere of a patrician house was no longer the place to encourage such a vocation. Tommaso de Freschi – and the examples could go on – embarked as a very young man for Constantinople, in order to work with his uncle, Antonio Paruta, a prominent merchant, but he later had to learn good Turkish so that he could be appointed as an interpreter ('giovane di lingua') by the Republic. It is clear that, without prejudging the careers they would eventually adopt, there was a tendency to send young men abroad for business training so that they had thereby a way of 'making themselves into men'.[62]

The possibilities of choice were strengthened by the desultory and undemanding nature of the basic instruction required at a time when preparation for professional life was entrusted mainly to a good apprenticeship. Again, the reduced range of occupations to which the *cittadino* condition gave access, rigidly barred above by the area reserved by law for nobles and beneath by the zone of manual labour which belonged to the *popolari* (and which could not be entered without serious loss of prestige), tended to level out whatever was peculiar to the various activities of the *cittadini*, apart from their purely technical aspects, and brought about a decided similarity of outlook, and therefore of life styles and their social manifestations. Contacts were especially close between the category of merchant and that of public functionary: the incidence of men employed in both sectors at the same time and equally actively is very frequent. I am not, of course, referring to small or casual trade undertaken in order to round out a meagre stipend, but to an activity involving a certain degree of commitment. Tullio Fabri, to mention one of these men, served the Republic as *rasonato* (accountant); from 1587 to 1590 he had been in Constantinople with the *bailo* Moro, and in 1591 he had accompanied Zaccaria Contarini on his special mission to Rome; when he died – in 1597 – he had been in Constantinople for more than three years, still in the *bailo*'s retinue. Throughout the whole of this period we see him carrying on an intense commercial activity which was so closely bound up with his public office that it would be difficult to establish which of the two was his principal occupation. He went to Rome when offered an opportunity of visiting the city, but he took a good many jewels with him, hoping to dispose of them well, and he intended to go as far as Naples in order to pursue another commercial operation at close quarters. In partnership with his brother, to whom he entrusted the Venetian market, he dealt not only in pearls, rubies, emeralds, but also in cloth of every kind, raw silk and cotton, wax, hides, not disdaining to import grain when the price was high. Tens of thousands of ducats passed through his hands; in 1596 he acquired a ship of 700 *botte* (about 560 tons) and made himself responsible for its cargo on a voyage from Constantinople to Venice, while at the same time he was occupied with explaining an apparent error in his handling of public accounts, following with interest the changes in salary level of some of his colleagues (earning 10 to 12 ducats a month) and presenting the *Signoria* with a proposal for an infallible method of eliminating evasion of the consular taxes. There is no reason to be scandalized by the knowledge that sometimes his merchandise travelled under the seal of St. Mark together with the chests containing the official account books; after all, will not the *bailo* Venier return to his country in 1597 carrying, like so many of his predecessors, jewels, pearls and various other goods destined for various Venetian merchants?[63] Like Fabri, another functionary traded in cloth with Constantinople in direct association with his superior, the noble magistrate Zuan Francesco Priuli, whose own commercial activity we have already mentioned.

This interchangeableness can also be seen in the substitution of one career for another, the official turning merchant and *vice versa*, but it is not easy to bring these tendencies into focus as they often seem contradictory. In 1595 Ottavio Fabri left an important post with the duke of Ferrara, attracted by the prospect of profit offered by business in association with his brother Tullio; Iseppo da Canal, around the same time, leased out his office as *fante* in the *Fondaco dei Tedeschi* and moved to Constantinople to take up trade.[64] This case is the more complex because one might have supposed that the merchant had, rather, acquired the office with the proceeds from business, as the law allowed; it would in any case be risky to generalize from episodes like this. The more common rule would seem to be the abandoning of trade for an occupation that is perhaps comparatively less profitable (in any case incapable of radically transforming a man's economic condition) but dignified, secure and without risks. The attractions and incentives which we have seen as operating powerfully on the noble classes also operated here. On the other hand, one must consider the fact that public administration was able to offer 'native' *cittadini* positions of power and income which were anything but despicable: of *cancellier grande*, for example, who had all the prerogatives of the nobles except their votes in the councils, and funeral ceremonies comparable to those of the doge; residents at certain foreign courts with the functions and rank of ambassadors, secretaries to councils, etc. But even apart from the more elevated ranks, the prospects were often seductive; a post as customs officer *al Purgo*, where the locally produced wool cloths were washed and sealed (and over which a battle flared up in 1597 which even numbered among the protagonists a merchant of considerable standing), meant an hour or two of work a day with an annual stipend of 200 ducats and the certainty of 'helping oneself' to more than 40,000 a year – a figure, this, which in its evident exaggeration well expresses the expectations which rested with jobs of this kind;[65] and to give one more example, the *sopramassaro* at Corfu received, as well as his lodging, an annual salary of 80 ducats, which could be rounded out through commissions, lawful and unlawful, to around 4,000 ducats.[66]

'Native' citizen status, which was bestowed on those born in Venice of three generations of *cittadini* who had not practised 'mechanical crafts', that is manual labour, was the indispensable condition – according to a law of 1569 – for admission to the ducal chancery, but to fill other offices and positions it was sufficient to have citizenship by privilege, which was of two grades: *de intus* and *de intus et extra*. Merchants needed the second more extensive one because it gave the right to trade all over the world as a Venetian, with the benefit of the protection and financial assistance reserved for members of the Venetian community; further, only those who were thus provided could trade with the Levant, whence all foreigners were rigorously excluded. This still left them with a much reduced freedom of manoeuvre because at the Rialto market they were obliged to buy and sell only from Venetians. It was certainly not impossible to avoid such restrictions by referring to fictitious or conveniently sleeping partners, but these expedients must have involved some inconvenience, as non-native merchants incessantly urged a more liberal regime, as did, for example, the English in 1604 through their ambassador Sir Henry Wotton.[67] Citizenship *de intus et extra* was acquired after one had resided and paid direct taxes for twenty-five years in the city, a period which could be reduced in special circumstances. As is well known, it was attained in 1476 by John Cabot, who in a document of some years later was designated *mercator*. In the *cinquecento* the list of concessions is very long and because Venice was still a great centre of attraction includes people of every origin. We find Pasquale Spinola there, a Genoese noble and an oil and grain merchant who had lived in Venice from 1560 to 1583, and two other Genoese, the brothers Francesco and Giovan Ambrosio Marini, who in 1580 obtained the privilege after only fifteen years' residence, as being 'respected merchants and among the principals of the market, who with their very large operations render a great service to the excise duty and toll'.[68] A representative of a new activity in which Venice had acquired the leading role, the typographer Vincenzo Valgrisi, of French origins, asked for full citizenship in 1567 after thirty-six years' residence and a marriage blessed with numerous offspring.[69] Many were the Flemish merchants who made Venice their second country, beginning with Martin de Hane, a native of Brussels, who settled in Venice at the beginning of the century and achieved the prestigious goal of a palace on the Grand Canal. But the greatest influx is recorded in the last decades of the century after the sack of Antwerp in 1576 and the blockade of the Scheldt in 1585;[70] among the most important who obtained citizenship were Guglielmo Helman in 1579, and his brother Carlo, also a 'much respected' merchant, in 1596, and Francesco Urins in 1593.

The largest number of applications for citizenship by privilege came, however, from the inhabitants of the *terraferma*, who converged on the capital as a matter of course. The merchants of Bergamo succeeded in obtaining a more expeditious procedure in 1525; their native soil was so grudging that – as one reads in a story by Bandello where we find a ferocious characterization of those inhabitants – they were forced to 'betake themselves here and there throughout the world, earning what they can with sweat and the greatest pains and saving as much as possible on clothes and food . . .; there exists no place in the world, however distant or remote, where there is not a Bergamasco doing business'.[71] Among them we meet Salomon Rigola, jewel merchant (1584), Zuan Antonio (1590) and Pietro Zois (1595), cloth manufacturers, Bernardino and Agostino Agazzi (1593), merchants, 'with much business and good reputation' who make their way as far as Constantinople and Ankara and at the end of the century become the proprietors of a large ship which they employ on the Levantine routes.[72]

The life of the great city burned up much of this fresh energy. It banished to its borders a large number of immigrants, dashing their hopes of making a fortune and reducing them – as Donato Giannotti bluntly says in his dialogue on Venetian institutions – 'to doing nothing but stay alive'.[73] But it is from this very period of flux that we see the emergence of a few men who are still capable of growing rich quickly. One of them, perhaps the most favoured by luck, was Bartolomeo Bontempelli. A native of the Val Sabbia, in Brescian territory, where to eat meant bitter toil in the iron works, he emigrated to Venice when barely over thirteen, with, one assumes, little or no means. But hardly ten years later, in 1562, he owned in partnership a very advantageously sited shop; in 1578 he came to acquire the full ownership of another, and in 1587, thanks to a shrewdly politic marriage, both of them ended up in his hands. He was granted the privilege of citizenship *de intus et extra* in 1579. He dealt in valuable cloth, cinnabar and mercury; indeed, if the expression were not banal, we might say he sold everything that was saleable.

The complete Venetian, he took shares in the public debt and in mortgage loans (his debtors included noblemen who had got into deep water) and at the same time he ventured along new avenues, such as the lease of a copper mine. His affairs prospered so well that he succeeded in amassing an immense fortune. On his death in 1616 he left his brother heir to palaces and farms, to an enormous sum in cash and goods, without, however, neglecting the good works for which he had distinguished himself during his lifetime, having the church of the *convertite* restored at his expense, erecting altars in the School of S. Rocco and in S. Salvador. To the hospital of S. Lazzaro of the Mendicants alone he left in perpetuity an endowment of 100,000 ducats.[74]

Other groups, apart from *cittadini*, belonged to the mercantile class. There were the foreign merchants, often organized into 'nations', with their representatives officially recognized by the *Signoria*, like the Spanish and the French (the latter from the last quarter of the century) and who had their own consuls in addition to an ambassador. 'In the greatest numbers', wrote Giannotti in 1526, 'they come to Venice from all countries, because, with its easy access to the sea, it is like a common market for the whole world, and they wait for their patrimony to grow and then when it suits them they go away.'[75] Some of these foreigners lived in communities, as did the Germans, but their *Fondaco* at the Rialto, with frescoes by Giorgione and Titian, was a place open for the meeting of people of every origin. Although the foreign merchant tended to band together with his fellow countrymen, especially during brief visits, the frequency of contacts, the substantial solidarity of interests and common working procedures all brought them close to the local merchants, reducing differences and favouring their absorption into a common milieu, which, as a result of this osmosis and of the consequent weakening of national and municipal differences, was bound to have a powerful levelling force. One must not forget that Venice was for many of them primarily a school which they approached in the mood of one who comes to be instructed. A Venetian apprenticeship was an obligatory step for young Germans: Jakob Fugger underwent it at twenty and Marx Christoph Welser was only fifteen when he was sent from Ulm to the city of the *Fondaco* to stay there for five years in 1604.[76] Integration was rapid, especially for the merchants who came from other Italian states, the variety of regional characteristics not constituting a serious obstacle; in 1588 and 1597 the *cinque savi alla mercanzia* had rightly found the pontifical request to open a consulate unjustified (there was already a *nunzio*), considering that its purpose would have been merely to help people with the same language and customs as the Venetians.[77] Tuscan merchants became particularly numerous after the return of the Medici in 1530, and around the same period there was considerable political emigration from Genoa. Families like the Giunti, who had moved from Florence shortly after the middle of the *quattrocento*, became completely integrated in the world of Venice. Luc' Antonio Giunti the younger sent cases of books all over Europe and traded in cloth, sugar, pepper, oil and tin; part of the proceeds of these transactions systematically went towards extending his landed property in the Trevisano, which from 180 *campi* in 1564 grew to more than 400 by 1601.[78]

Only the Jews remained excluded from this great consortium of merchants from every nation; the few Turks who, after the year of Lepanto, grouped together in the Barbaro palace in Cannaregio only to pass on to S. Matteo four years later are not of much importance. There were some thousand Jews around the middle of the century, hardly fewer than 1,700 in 1586,[79] and from 1516 they lived segregated in the *ghetto*, which had become one of the most densely-populated sections of the city. In 1550 the Republic had ordered the banishment of the Spanish and Portuguese Maranos who had become attached to the old Levantine and German community but the enforcement had been mild: one of them, Daniel Rodriguez, a man of great intelligence and a highly fertile imagination, actually succeeded in taking a very important part in the plans to improve the commercial organization of Venice, particularly with a project for new ties with Spalato. Although the Jews were better off in Venice than in other parts of Italy, even here their activity was subject to numerous restrictions: they were not allowed to trade with the Levant but had to make use of a Venetian intermediary, and while Jews on the *terraferma* could practise any kind of business, those who were members of the 'German nation' of Venice, so as not to harm the other inhabitants of the place, had to limit themselves to dealing in second-hand clothes – besides, of course, the practice of usury. But in 1598 they obtained much more liberal terms.[80] Already in 1580 the *cinque savi* had recognized the 'benefit and the great utility to the customs receipts' which ensued from their commerce and they had tried to improve the condition of those who practised trade, separating them from other Jews: crowded together in the over-full ghetto, the rest were left to live in nearly uninhabitable houses and were exposed to violence and threats. Moreover, the tolerance from which they benefited at certain moments never weakened the notion, universally felt, of the difference in function and spirit which characterized the Jewish and the Christian ways of doing business, a constitutional difference which was thought to draw the baser aspects of the profession to the one and to the other modes of behaviour which ennobled it; like Shylock and Antonio in Shakespeare's play, because of the different conception of the activity each pursues, the Jewish merchant and the Venetian, even though they breathed the same air they belonged to two worlds which could never meet.

The aims and requirements of the activity they practised reinforced the solidarity of this mercantile class and helped to consolidate its communal privileges despite the considerable fluidity of its composition. These ties did not bring about a generic spirit of co-operation, but even without attaining a true association, they were frequently expressed in organizational forms, for example through the presentation to government authorities of petitions expressing group requests or through the election of representatives for the solution of questions of general interest. In the mercantile colonies abroad, the most important decisions were taken by a *consiglio* and were binding on everyone. But professional spirit and group consciousness rested mainly on the complex of procedures, techniques, juridical usages and 'moral and political *virtù*' which gave substance to trade as a highly specialized occupation and one of solid civic worth.

Commercial institutions grew up in a particular climate and showed an autonomous evolution which followed criteria that were not always in accordance with those of the common civil law. One must not forget, however, that the title *publicus mercator* was recognized socially rather than legally, and that there was therefore a certain resistance on the part of the legislator to acknowledging special laws and procedures even for matters that were of common and urgent concern like bankruptcy.[81] But the area ruled simply by custom was always very wide and many were the occasions when it ensured justice by filling gaps in the law. One might add that the merchant had an instinctive distrust of professional judges and preferred the arbitration of his peers in the settlement of conflicting interests; they did not drag out the dispute for years and were certainly more likely to interpret the corporative conception which he shared of right and wrong. There is no doubt that even the decisions in these arbitral awards were couched in the vernacular, which was the language the merchant used in the management of his affairs, shunning both at home and in his international dealings the Latin, so rich in ambiguities and snares, of jurists and scholars. The vernacular, moreover, furnished the basic vocabulary of the *lingua franca* which was spoken in the emporia of the Levant and the Barbary coast and was openly receptive, through commercial contacts, to the influence of other idioms (for example, *costuma* from the English 'custom', *carisea* from 'kersey', *celliere* from 'cellar', clearly of Latin origin but actually used only in letters from England, etc.). And by ascribing a broad recognition to private book-keeping and company documentation, the merchants had found their own substitute, as far as was possible, for the agreements – so rigid and irksome in their conservatism – drawn up by public notaries. Even kings and princes could not have aspired to the trust and credit enjoyed by a good merchant.[82] Reciprocal trust and good faith in their dealings were the ethical elements which distinguished the tone of relations between merchants and which were the most important factors in their solidarity. These moral propensities must not be understood as an exact equivalent to honesty – although the Venetian merchant was never deliberately dishonest, even if in the quest for profit he was bound to make the most of circumstances – nor can they necessarily have been applied to every aspect of commercial activity. In the language of the period they came together under the rubric of 'friendship', and, apart from considerations which are obviously applicable to the structural tendencies of any type of group, it was friendship which made the system of reciprocal relationships function within the community, especially where adequate legal competence was lacking; in a sense it ensured the observance of what has been so happily defined as the traditional rules of the game.[83] 'Where many merchants live together', Cotrugli points out *à propos* the selection of the most favourable place for the practice of the profession, 'mercantile customs and practices are observed the better.'[84]

Mercantile honour lay to a large extent in respect for this kind of friendship, as much when displayed in relationships between associates as between *padroni* and *fattori*, or among the people who belonged to the field of power which centred upon Venice. Quite apart from one's place of origin, to be a Venetian merchant, in fact, really meant being on the 'Venetian' side at the moment of the purchase or sale of certain goods according to the division of international commercial labour. This condition involved special collective obligations which were frequently confirmed by pacts between associates or by measures to stem competition.[85] Agreements not to buy or sell except at a prearranged price, for instance, were normally condemned insofar as they were not in accordance with the social function assigned to trade, but the Venetians, who refrained from them in their dealings with one another, practised them regularly and without remorse when faced with anyone who was not part of their own circle, applying the ancient principle that a stranger is one's enemy against whom the use of violence and deceit is legitimate. 'It is legitimate to engage in usury against the enemy of your country, against whom one fights a just war', we read in Cotrugli, who has very clear ideas on the subject; and again: 'cover yourself with conditions against your enemy; with your friend, merely be prudent.'[86] Such an attitude certainly entered into the rejection of cultural patterns different from those with which the Venetians identified themselves, and it was in fact with the Turkish world that conflict, justified by the difference of religion and custom, was particularly inflamed. 'These are the countries of beasts', declared Giacomo Rizzo in no uncertain terms, speaking in 1506 of Syria where he was doing business.[87] But even westerners were not spared, especially when they paid the Venetians back in their own coin; the English were condemued for their habit of 'using every ruse' to raise prices when selling, and then when buying, of making a show of being prepared to pay high prices only to 'try every way and means' of getting them lowered at the moment of contract.[88] England, moreover, was described as a country in which 'there is no justice for foreigners'; all the same, when at Aleppo in 1594 the English were on the side of the Venetians in holding down the buyers' price of raw silk, they were designated, with no reservations, 'merchants'.[89]

When a man incurred the disapproval of his colleagues for a clumsy operation committed in good or bad faith, it was not only their material interests which suffered: it was regarded as a betrayal of values which were measured in a very precise scale of obligations. It was like turning traitor against the very commodities which were the objects of his professional activity and which could almost have been living things, so great was the affection which the merchant felt for them. 'The merchants have disappeared and only cooks are left: few are the good merchants who love these poor bits of merchandise', lamented a merchant in Syria in 1555, blaming a difficult situation on the inadequate professional commitment of his colleagues.[90] A merchant had always to act in accordance with certain moral values, observing set rules. Every judgement, as is natural, changed in relation to its perspective: from abroad his competitors and all those who made use of his services looked for the merchant who was *onesto* – honest, that is, in the sense of being satisfied with a profit which was the just recompense for his labours; inside the mercantile world, however, what was valued most highly was fidelity to traditional practices. Success was valued to the extent that anyone who attained it showed that he possessed the necessary qualities to deserve it and had used them 'with measure and reason', although one was forced to admit the overriding influence of fortune; fortune often revealed itself to be the friend of 'inexpert and almost irrational' merchants, and it could also reward the man who had not earned divine favour by dint of good works, however worthy.[91]

Profit and honour, wealth and honour: the 'glorious merchant', one, that is, who combined all the virtues exalted in the treatises, was not content with achieving easy circumstances but aspired no less to win the respect of his own circle. Honour, which was often coupled with 'glory', was defined as the 'good opinion others have of us as men to be held in esteem'.[92] It was an extremely efficient device within the system of social relationships which centred around the merchant. Often it crystallized in banal forms such as the admonition to keep one's records 'neat and tidy' so that those concerned can find what they want quickly and exactly, or for the sake of people whose capital was at stake to keep one's eyes open so as not to let good opportunities go by,[93] but when we see it described in some documents as 'immortal honour', it is not difficult to see that here is an aspect of the new spirit which was being vigorously asserted in the framework of a general re-evaluation of human action. The merchant shows that he has developed a full awareness of his situation, with its attendant rights and duties, and that he is conscious of the position his profession assigns him in society. He is proud of it, as his very conservatism proves, and it is abundantly justified by the privileges he enjoys. He now feels the prestige of his condition, accepts all its worldly symbols and aspires to attain them. One of the most conspicuous is his house, where he has to strike a balance between functionalism, related to the special activity it has to serve, and the requirements of social prestige.

Writers on the subject discussed at length the most suitable position and the distribution of living space, and they had nothing against rooms being 'magnificent'.[94] In fact the house which Pietro Busello built in 1592 was a beautiful and ornate palace with a large garden,[95] while another merchant, Decher, abandoned his house for a more modest one when he had to compound with his creditors (1597). Antonio Paruta laid plans to bring home (1592) the 'furnishings, most beautiful things' which he had obtained in Constantinople; Ottavio Fabri had his brother's room arranged with leather furnishings and a muslin canopy, and decorated in the Titianesque style of Giovanni Contarini, while he was waiting (1595) for Palma Giovane – cordially mentioned as signor Giacomo – to make up his mind to finish the picture he had been working on for so long. Giacomo Savioni ordered from Constantinople, for his own use, a 'coverlet of green silk, which must be beautiful' (1594).[96] In the house of Francesco Urins stood a clavichord and a spinet (1604), in that of the merchant shipowners, Cabianca, there was a *claviorgano* (1614),[97] and there is nothing here to wonder at; in their childhood future merchants read Donatus and were instructed in letters and arithmetic (that is, 'in the weapons without which they could not have defended or kept track of business and commerce'),[98] nor did they neglect books of lute scores.[99] Antonio and Girolamo Cabianca were no more refined than their colleagues in displaying a silver table service for twenty-four, with knives decorated with damascening, silver cups and salt-cellars (and we can admit that they constituted a good reserve against emergencies) and almost two hundred pewter pieces of various sizes. But what is most striking about the inventories of houses is the number of pictures; unfortunately, as the painters' names are usually omitted, it is not always possible to know their value. In the Urins house, the ground floor of which consisted of spacious warehouses overflowing with goods of various kinds, we find pictures in every room, big and small, sacred and profane, as well as a large planisphere which attests the owner's interest in a knowledge of the world not restricted to the traditional area of his commercial operations, together with numerous family portraits. The portrait had become part of the merchant way of life, and if it is true that in the Renaissance portraiture broke away from the aulic convention which had gripped it for so long, it had certainly lost nothing of its celebratory significance; furthermore, the attention it now paid to settings and objects which drew attention to the pursuits of the person represented faithfully reflects the pride merchants took

2A

in their own social rank. Ottavio Fabri (and I mention him only to stay within the circle of merchants named in this article) invited his brother Tullio (1596) to have his portrait painted on his return from Constantinople by Contarini, a friend of the family but 'not inferior to other painters, past and present'; Pasqualin Leoni, on the other hand, preferred to be painted while at Constantinople by Paolo de Freschi, who made use of the 'scanty evidence' vouchsafed him. De Freschi was not, in fact, new to this kind of undertaking; in the same year he painted (without a model) the portrait of the sultan which the *Signoria* had given to the Turkish *beylerbey* of Greece, [100] but it is clear that what the mercantile world appreciated more than physical resemblance was a style of characterization capable of conveying moral attitudes or qualities inherent in their profession, not to mention the symbolic significance with which the occasion of being painted enriched a man's life, besides its function of prolonging existence by handing down his physical traits to posterity. [101]

In the Cabianca house the walls were adorned with eight 'large Flemish pictures' and with numerous Madonnas, Christ figures, St. Jeromes and Last Suppers. Sacred subjects were much favoured by merchants, whose religious sentiments were undoubtedly sincere despite their concern with carrying out the acts thought necessary in certain circumstances for soliciting the Almighty's aid. Thus we should not conclude that they were religious only to the extent that the uncertain outcome of their occupation constantly called for the aid of a superior power. Without altogether supplanting the purpose of the traditional devotions designed to this end, the diffusion of insurance contracts anticipating the effects of accidents had greatly helped to reduce the margins of risk, especially in the transportation sector most affected by it; it also seemed only too clear that 'to trust in God more than anything' could not, for example, justify sending a ship on a journey without its artillery. [102]

In any case, there still remained plenty of room for elements of chance, especially where the faulty transmission of news was concerned. Cotrugli dedicated an entire book out of the four which make up his treatise to the religion of the merchant, dwelling on matters of conscience, and equally on forms of religious observance in passages which oscillate between stressing the charismatic symbolism of ritual and the ostentatious conformism bound to occur in a society where such behaviour carried much weight. Religious observance was a very important part of the merchant's life, especially in foreign countries where Sunday mass united all the members of the community in a social occasion of high significance. [103] But it was above all matters of conscience which tormented him, despite the fact that in Venice the divergence between a merchant's actions and the teaching of the Church did not seriously disturb businessmen, whether because the boundaries between licit and illicit had been fairly clearly drawn by practices sanctified by centuries of use, or because men preferred to make their money by handling goods rather than cash, which was, as is well known, the chief target of the casuists' and confessors' arrows. Works like *Lume e specchio dei penitenti* by the Reverend Marco Scarsella, published in

Venice in 1587, devoted as much space to the religious problems of merchants as they did to those of other categories of believers: their profession was likely to expose them to dangers acutely detrimental to spiritual health, and sin lay always in ambush. Cases like that of Ippolito Stefani, who, having retired to a convent in the Padovano in 1591 for the usual spiritual exercises, decided to become a friar, leaving his father to answer his letters and liquidate his affairs,[104] were far from rare. But the merchant, as quick to sin as to repent and give liberally to charities, seeking to 'buy paradise' only to fall back into sin in a bizarre succession of events which ends only with his final contrition, was a purely conventional figure, patterned on medieval models and hardly pertinent to the reality of *cinquecento* Venice, even though it may still have been favoured by writers of fiction. Religious feeling developed in a more decorous dimension, and for every one who was tempted towards indifference by a society that had become more concerned with earthly values, there were many whose conduct was informed by a sincere and uncompromising faith. And the building of chapels and the charity to which merchants devoted themselves in such a munificent spirit did not necessarily imply that they were redeeming their guilt; it was a traditional activity and it satisfied a desire to stand out from their colleagues, to emphasize a superiority in their conduct of the common occupation. The tombs also, for which they fought over space in S. Salvadore and other churches near the business centre, vying to win the most eminent position, expressed the same urge together with the anxious hope of somehow surviving in the materiality of the marble. The merchant was resigned to death as to 'a voyage everyone must take' and he was aware of 'not leaving anything but a good name' won through the honourable practice of his profession, and of being unable to carry 'anything but good works' on the eternal voyage.[105]

As we have seen, the Venetian mercantile world of the *cinquecento* lost, among other traditional elements, the one which was certainly the most specifically Venetian, that is to say the large part played in it by the patriciate. At the beginning of the century nobles still constituted its nucleus, if not – as can be conjectured despite the lack of precise information – actually through their numbers or their gross capital, certainly through their overriding influence on social habits and the collective viewpoint. It is, indeed, incontestable that the association of commercial activity with the monopoly of power had had an extremely important effect both in the city's constitution and its economic and social life. When in the course of the century the nucleus of nobles in the commercial world decreased progressively in stability and weight, surviving for a while as an ever more anachronistic appendix that seemed destined to be eliminated altogether, what did such a loss mean to the trading community as a whole?

One could not say that, at least in the short run, great changes in life style followed from it, because it was, in effect, the nobles who changed theirs while the merchant world preserved intact its own ideals and social morality. Again, if between the chief components of that world, nobles and *cittadini*, there had never been any antagonism in the past, neither had there been a perfect fusion, and so the separation developed as though by a natural process without assuming the character of a mutilation. In general the merchant class ended by organizing itself with greater coherence, reinforcing its professional consciousness and better defining its sense of dignity and social rank. Its close identification with the order of *cittadini* gave it a solid base and a stable set of attitudes and characteristics, psychologically definable as middle class, although one must remember that the privileges reserved for it by the Venetian constitution and its economic power brought it closer to the nobility than to the people. The wealthier merchants continued to appropriate the values and forms of behaviour of the nobles even though the gap between them long remained unbridgeable. The pressure the most prominent *cittadino* families exerted to enter the area of the patrician class succeeded only towards the middle of the seventeenth century in overcoming a resistance which had lasted since the admissions of 1381. Of the 127 new families co-opted between 1646 and 1718, three-fifths were merchants and another fifth lawyers and chancery officials.[106] It is probable that many of the latter were originally merchant families who, having attained certain patrimonial objectives, had wanted to attain greater social dignity to the extent that it was realizable within the *cittadino* order; even if we disregard this possibility, however, there is sufficient evidence to show that even after Venice had been cut off from the great trade routes it was still trade which provided wealth; and it would be interesting to know the relationship – in the patrimonial make-up of all these families – between commercial capital and real estate in order to know the extent to which land still operated as a way of conserving wealth accumulated through trade and as a source of social prestige. The large quota reserved for mercantile families in the admission to the patrician class should not, however, make us think that they were accorded preference, as long-standing tradition might suggest; on the contrary, they were treated with the greatest contempt by the old established families, and it was only by virtue of the huge contributions they were obliged to make to the state, burdened as it was with grave financial difficulties, that they were able to win, by buying it, the right to enter the ranks of the nobility. Perhaps this attitude is not worth stressing – it is, after all, a fact that a reception of this kind has, in every time and every place, been in store for the newly-rich man who comes to wear the colours of nobility – but it remains undeniable that as a consequence of the exodus of the nobles the social standing linked with the practice of trade underwent a slow but uninterrupted deterioration. Trade had become a profession like any other and as such, in a society turning economically and spiritually towards income from land and where the ruling class made use of civic power in order to protect its own interests in landed property, it had come to be, if not despised certainly little esteemed: if in 1458 Cotrugli had been able to write that 'the dignity and function of the merchant is grand and sublime', in 1756 a practical manual recommended him to be 'humble and respectful with everyone'.[107]

The psychology of the Venetian merchant in the sixteenth century

But in the *cinquecento*, in a city which still felt keenly aware of commercial and maritime vocation, the merchant class always managed to maintain its prominence even if it had to cope with serious difficulties. Basically, it was this class which constituted the element of continuity in Venetian tradition. With its outlets for exchange with so many countries from the Baltic to the Indian Ocean as one of the characteristics which defined it most sharply within the citizen body, it retained an international stamp, in contrast with the patrician group which as their way of life changed, tended to close in on themselves and, in a sense, to become provincial. The colonies of foreign merchants who were, as we have seen, so quick to absorb the way in which the Venetians thought and acted also had the reverse effect – with the continual infusion of fresh blood into body of *cittadini*, their staying for a while and then being relieved by others, the close ties with their countries of origin – of weaving new threads into the fabric of the Venetian mercantile world. Indeed, Venetian merchants themselves had a comparable effect, exposed as they were to experience abroad, especially in youth when it made the deepest impression. It was they who, 'instead of staying in a country villa, had to attend to navigation, seeing a variety of countries, nations and customs'.[108] Types of organization, technical expedients, and work methods all tended, moreover, to become the common heritage of the more up-to-date centres, thus bringing about a decided similarity of outlook, and Venice contributed largely to its character, although one must admit that its contribution consisted mainly in what it had known how to do in the past, and it was no longer in the vanguard as an instigator of progress or in the development of modern methods; if, because of the more pointedly vocational character of his occupation the merchant appeared as a more autonomous type than his fellow citizens, it became, nevertheless, increasingly difficult to differentiate him from those who practised trade in other countries. By the end of the century to isolate the Venetian merchant from this context is to risk attributing characteristics to him which had by now become common to a vast economic territory comprising the greater part of the western world. But apart from the interchange with other elements within the *cittadino* order and its acceptance of numerous foreigners, the merchant class renewed itself from another source, from below, for it was open to the upsurge of the more enterprising elements of the lowest of the three orders into which Venetian society was divided. Indeed, even under the least favourable conditions the practice of trade did not cease to be an important channel of social mobility, certainly no less significant than the Church. One cannot say that the withdrawal of the nobles left a freer field for new energies which were then able to take advantage of it and replace them. The flight of their capital does not appear to have been balanced by an influx of new money; on the contrary, its negative consequences for the commercial turnover as a whole and the loss of confidence which rapidly infected an atmosphere as emotional as that of Venetian trade certainly did not help to encourage new investments in the business sector. All the same the mercantile world continued to be invigorated by men who had risen from positions of extreme modesty. They did not, perhaps, move at the pace of the Fuggers; their plans developed on predominantly artisan-minded lines without promoting ventures whose size or methods deserve to be classified as capitalistic; but they did succeed in attaining an economic and social standing – sometimes travelling only half-way to this goal while leaving it to their sons to reach it – remarkable enough to repay them for their pains. Despite the great transformation which had taken place, the backbone of Venetian commerce, even in its new form, was still represented by a myriad of small operators. If in certain ways this was at times its weakness, at others it was the strength which allowed it to overcome even the most serious crises, renewing itself and surviving them.

NOTES

1. See G. Luzzatto, *Storia economica di Venezia dall' XI al XVI secolo* (Venice, 1961) 133, for this general point.

2. *Discorsi sopra la prima Deca di Livio*, lib. i, ch. 55.

3. Quo. A. Ventura, *Nobiltà e popolo nella società veneta del '400 e '500* (Bari, 1964) 309.

4. B. Cipolla, *De imperatore militum deligendo* (Lugduni, 1543) f. 120v.

5. T. Garzoni, *La piazza universale di tutte le professioni del mondo* (Venice, 1665) 133–134 (1st ed. 1584). But in another 'discorso' Garzoni not only does not distinguish between the wholesale and retail merchant but maintains that the difference between a merchant and a tradesman is only quantitative, while they have defects in common. Also for Celio Calcagnino, *Disquisitiones in lib. Offic. Ciceronis in Opera* (Basel, 1564) 262–263, 'quaestio non est de rei quantitate sed de qualitate', so he excludes any difference between wholesale and retail business.

6. G. Muzio, *Il gentiluomo* (2nd ed., Venice, 1575) 129. Also G. Lanteri, *Della economica* (Venice, 1560) 94. If, as regards retail trade Jacques Savary was to write in his *Parfait négociant* in 1675, 'il y a quelque chose de servile', as regards wholesale business, 'il n'y a rien que d'honnête et de noble'. The quotation is from H. Hauser, *Les débuts du capitalisme* (Paris, 1931) 282.

7. Mario Foscari, in his *relazione* on his embassy to Florence (1527); *Relazioni degli ambasciatori veneti al Senato*, ed. A. Segarizzi (Bari, 1916) iii, pt. i, 17–18.

8. B. Cotrugli, *Della mercatura e del mercante perfetto* (Brescia, 1602). The first edition was 1573 but the work was written in 1458. Why it was published after such a long delay and with alterations to bring it more into line with the values of the day are problems which remain unresolved in Milorad Zebic, *O trgovini i o savršenom trgovcu* (Titograd, 1963) which does contain, however, much information about the author's life.

9. G. Calcagnino, *De iudiciis . . . in Opera*, cit. 282. For G. M. Memmo, *Dialogo . . .* (Venice, 1564) f. 119. Merchants are useful because they pay duties which cover public expenditures and thus the need to place heavy impositions on other sections of the community is avoided. The doge Leonardo Donà, itemizing the Venetian revenues for 1586, attributed 400,000 ducats to 'dazi delle mercanzie' and 600,000 to those 'dei viveri', but explained that these latter ultimately 'nascono dalle mercanzie' which 'fanno sì che il popolo mangi'. A.S.V., *Codici Papadopoli*, 12, f. 123.

10. G. Muzio, op. cit., 129 seq.

11. B. Cotrugli, op. cit., 148.

12. As distinguished from the Venetian *terraferma* where merchants were excluded from the city councils. A. Ventura, op. cit., 303 seq.

13. On this point, and on changes in Venetian economic activity in general, see S. J.

Woolf, 'Venice and the Terraferma; problems of the change from commercial to landed activities', *B.I.S.*, iv (1962) 415–441, and A. Ventura, 'Considerazioni sull' agricoltura veneta e sull' accumulazione originaria del capitale nei secc. XVI e XVII', *Studi Storici*, ix (1968) 674–722.

14. A.S.V., *Bailo a Costantinopoli*, reg. 381, 4 Jan., 1594.

15. A.S.V., *Cinque savi alla mercanzia*, reg. 138, f. 166v.

16. G. Contarini, *La repubblica e i magistrati di Venezia* (Venice, 1544) f. 63v.

17. On this division see the admirable discussion in G. Cozzi, op. cit. p. 402, n. 2, 2 seq.

18. G. Priuli, *I diarii*, in *R.I.S.* 2, xxiv, pt. iii, iv, 50.

19. *Parere dei clar.mi A. Bragadino e J. Foscarini . . . intorno al trattato fra Venezia e Spagna sul traffico del pepe, ecc.* (Venice, 1870) 17. In the mid-*cinquecento* this cosmopolitan experience was still a distinguishing quality of the Venetian noble. In Venice, wrote the Friulan jurisconsult C. Frangipane, 'there are many nobles who have travelled across different lands in pursuit of commerce or on embassies or simply moved by the desire to see a variety of peoples and customs'. P. Antonini, 'Cornelio Frangipane di Castello, ecc.', *A.S.I.*, ser. iv, ix (1882) 52.

20. Quo. V. Lazzarini, 'Beni carraresi e proprietari veneziani', *Studi in onore di G. Luzzatto* (Milan, 1950) i, 279.

21. I will simply refer to A. Venuti, *De agricoltura opusculum* (3rd ed., Venice, 1546) Proemio.

22. G. Lanteri, op. cit., 60.

23. *Deliberazioni del Maggior Consiglio di Venezia*, ed. R. Cessi (Bologna, 1934) iii, 209.

24. A.S.V., *Misc. Gregolin*, b. 12 ter, Ottavio to Tullio Fabri, 2 July, 1596.

25. G. Luzzatto, *Studi di storia economica veneziana* (Padua, 1954) 141.

26. R. Cessi, *Storia della Repubblica di Venezia* (2nd ed., Milan, 1968) i, 363.

27. T. Garzoni, op. cit., 134.

28. G. Lanteri, op. cit., 67.

29. P. Torelli, *Trattato del debito del cavaliero* (Venice, 1596) f. 120.

30. G. B. Nenna, *Il Nennio, nel quale si ragiona di nobiltà* (Venice, 1542) lib. i.

31. C. Frangipane, *Discorso sopra la nobiltà* in P. Antonini, op. cit., 34.

32. A. Sardo, *Discorso (della bellezza, della nobiltà . . .)* (Venice, 1586). Muzio added that antiquity of wealth proves that it has been virtuously acquired and administered, for ill-gotten gains cannot be enjoyed by an heir and are quickly expended by those who are vicious, woman-lovers, gamblers or gluttons. Op. cit., 44.

33. G. Priuli, op. cit., iv, 121.

34. G. A. Tagliente, *Formulario nuovo che insegna dittar lettere* (Toscolano, 1538). The letter contests the value of the mercantile life of those who 'neither eat, drink nor sleep, but are for ever thinking of how to make and save money . . . they are the most miserable and unhappy men on earth, who cannot enjoy what life has to offer and who are of no use either to themselves or to others'. It is worth noting that the *Formulario* contains only six merchants' letters, four of which speak of retirement from business. The novella about the merchant's widow is in M. Bandello, *Le novelle* (Bari, 1918) i, 254.

35. G. Lanteri, op. cit., 98.

36. Among much evidence to this effect, see the dispatch to the Senate (24 Aug., 1525) of the *bailo* Pietro Bragadin: 'Venice is richer in gold, men and ships than it has ever been because the wars of the world have brought all the rich men to live there.' A.S.V., *Arch. Pr. Costantinopoli*, b. 2.

37. G. Priuli, op. cit., iii, 52.

38. Ibid., ii, 238, 263; iv, 121. He also comments on the scant business that is carried out all over the world. Ibid., ii, 25.

39. U. Tucci, *Lettres d'un marchand vénitien, Andrea Berengo (1553–1556)* (Paris, 1957) 164.

40. G. Contarini, op. cit., f. 36. Also Donato Giannotti in his *Libro della Repubblica de'*

Viniziani observes that 'when the realm of the *terraferma* grew and our citizens began to turn their attention thither, the status of the *savi di mare* declined and passed to the *savi di terraferma*'. *Opere politiche e letterarie* (Florence, 1850) ii, 93.

41. D. da Lezze, *Historia turchesca (1300–1514)* ed. I. Ursu (Bucharest, 1909) 229. Da Lezze (1479–1526) followed a lengthy political career which ended with his being appointed *luogotenente* for Cyprus; his brother Marino was *sopracomito* with the fleet. The contrast between civic and military virtues and the personality of the merchant was also underlined by Fausto da Longiano, for whom Italy had become 'scacciata, battuta qual vile femminuccia' because it was in part dedicated 'all' esercizio vilissimo delle mercanzie' and in part to serving God and scorning any search for glory. *Il gentilhuomo* (Venice, 1544) f. 9. See p. 153.

42. G. M. Memmo, op. cit., 121. A. Ventura notes that Memmo's homage to the past is purely conventional. *Nobiltà . . .* (cit.) 307.

43. On this evolution see R. Romano and A. Tenenti, *Die Grundlegung der modernen Welt* (Frankfurt a. Main, 1967) 301 seq.

44. F. C. Lane, *Andrea Barbarigo, merchant of Venice (1418–1449)* (Baltimore, 1944) 48.

45. On these routes see C. Vivanti and A. Tenenti, 'Le film d'un grand système de navigation: les galères marchandes vénitiennes', *Annales*, xvi (1961) 83–86, and the articles of F. C. Lane collected in *Venice and history* (Baltimore, 1966).

46. *Misc. Gregolin*, b. 12 bis, Zuan Francesco to Zuan Alvise Badoer, 5 Jan., 1532. The notion of a hierarchy of civic values graduated according to wealth – contrasting with the attitude of the Christian Middle Ages – was familiar to the Venetian society of that time; in Venice (26 Dec., 1535) 'life goes quietly, and those with money rule the roost', British Museum, *Cotton* – Nero B VII, f. 118, Bernardin Sandro to Thomas Starkey.

47. G. Contarini, op. cit., f. 64.

48. F. Sansovino, *L'avocato* (Venice, 1554) 9.

49. Sanuto, *Diarii*, 829. Together with Bollani there perished Bernardo Priuli, son of a procurator of St. Mark, 'mercante grossissimo' at Damascus, and other nobles.

50. On Andrea Barbarigo see the entry by A. Ventura in *Dizionario Biografico degli Italiani*.

51. G. Cozzi, op. cit., 7. The twenty-year-old procurator was Polo Nani (1573).

52. M. Bandello, op. cit., i, 171. See pp. 313 seq.

52a. R. Romano, *La marine marchande vénitienne au XVIe siècle* ('Les sources de l'histoire maritime en Europe', Paris, 1962) 42–3.

53. *Misc. Gregolin*, b. 12 ter, Paolo de Freschi to Antonio Paruta, 24 Sept., 1590.

54. B. Cotrugli, op. cit., 57–58, 84, 162.

55. *Misc. Gregolin*, b. 12 ter, B. Zanoli to G. Ferro, 18 Mar., 1559, and G. Helman to T. Fabri, 27 Aug., 1583. N. Crotto to P. Paruta, 30 Nov., 1585.

56. Ibid., b. 12 bis. On Pietro Bragadin see F. Braudel, 'Réalités économiques et prises de conscience: quelques témoignages sur le XVIe siècle', *Annales*, xiv (1959) 732–733.

57. Ample documentation in *Misc. Gregolin*, bb. 12 bis e ter.

58. S.M., *filza* 187, all. 6 of the decision of 6 Aug., 1610, quo. J. C. Davis, *The decline of the Venetian ruling class* (Baltimore, 1962) 39.

59. U. Tucci, op. cit., 322.

60. L. di Linda, *Le relationi et descrittioni universali et particolari del mondo* (Venice, 1672) 536.

61. D. Beltrami, *Storia della popolazione di Venezia* (Padua, 1954) 78.

62. As Marino wrote to Giovan Maria Ventura on 14 Jan., 1595. *Misc. Gregolin*, b. 12 ter.

63. On all the foregoing, see documents, ibid., b. 12 ter.

64. *Bailo a Costantinopoli*, reg. 373, 13 Aug., 1587.

65. *Misc. Gregolin*, b. 12 ter. Pietro to G. M. Ventura and Iseppo da Canal, 20 Apr., 1597.

66. A.S.V., *Relazioni*, b. 55. *Relazione* of Cristoforo da Canal, *provveditore all' armata* (1558). Cf. A. Tenenti, *Cristoforo da Canal. La marine Vénitienne avant Lépante* (Paris, 1962) 106 seq.

67. D. Sella, *Commercio e industrie a Venezia nel sec. XVII* (Venice, 1961) 37.

68. *Cinque savi alla mercanzia*, reg. 137, f. 99; reg. 138, f. 124v.

69. A.S.V., *Suppliche di Collegio, filza* 2.

70. On Flemish immigration, cf. W. Brulez, *Marchands flamands à Venise*, I (Brussels–Rome, 1965).

71. M. Bandello, op. cit., ii, 22.

72. On grants of 'cittadinanza' to merchants there is ample documentation in regs. 137–139 of the *Cinque savi alla mercanzia*.

73. D. Giannotti, op. cit., ii, 35.

74. On this merchant see the entry by U. Tucci in *Dizionario Biografico degli Italiani*.

75. D. Giannotti, op. cit., ii, 35.

76. H. Kellenbenz, 'Le déclin de Venise et les relations économiques de Venise avec les marchés au nord des Alpes', *Decadenza economica veneziana nel sec. XVII* (Venice, 1961) 133.

77. *Cinque savi alla mercanzia*, reg. 138, f. 57; reg. 139, f. 140.

78. A. Tenenti, 'Luc' Antonio Giunti il Giovane, stampatore e mercante', *Studi in onore de Armando Sapori* (Milan, 1957) 1021–1060.

79. D. Beltrami, op. cit., 79.

80. F. Braudel, *La Méditerranée et le monde méditerranéen à l'époque de Philippe II* (2nd ed., Paris, 1966) ii, 152.

81. G. I. Cassandro, *Le rappresaglie e il fallimento a Venezia nei secc. XIII–XVI* (Turin, 1938) 97. The author observes, however, that experience had shown that the greater number of bankrupts had been engaged in commerce.

82. B. Cotrugli, op. cit., 127. For example, in an act of 1605 it is stated that a document written in Venice and signed by the debtor in the presence of two witnesses has as much validity as a notarized instrument. *Arch. Notarile, filza* 3379, f. 297. In a contract of sale for a ship of 7 June, 1567, the contracting parties beg the notary Francesco de Michelis to couch it in the vernacular 'for their greater satisfaction'. Archivio di Stato, Udine, *Arch. Panigai*, b. 87.

83. J. Meuvret, 'Manuels et traités à l'usage des négociants aux premières époques de l'âge moderne', *Études d'histoire moderne et contemporaine*, v (1953) 19.

84. B. Cotrugli, op. cit., 28.

85. E.g., the agreement entered into in Aleppo in 1562 not to sell tin at a price less than that agreed to. A document attached to this agreement gave the penalties that would be incurred were it violated. *Misc. Gregolin*, b. 12 *ter*, Domenico to Zuanne Balbiani, 30 May, 1562. Sometimes action of this sort was promoted by public authority, as in 1581 when the *bailo* in Constantinople notified eighteen members of the Venetian merchant community that they should not purchase barrel staves at a price higher than that already obtaining. *Bailo a Costantinopoli*, reg. 372.

86. B. Cotrugli, op. cit., 44 and 106.

87. *Misc. Gregolin*, b. 11, letter to Zuan Batt. Merlin, 14 Feb., 1507. Among the evidence for this striking dissimilarity we should not forget the common practice whereby Venetian merchants who lived among the Turks took a mistress and reared, without the benefit of matrimony, a family which was left to its own devices when the moment came to return to Venice.

88. A.S.V., *Misc. di atti non appartenenti ad alcun archivio*, b. 24, B. Corsini to S. Patti, 16 Nov., 1588 and 4 Jan., 1589.

89. Ibid., B. Prandini to S. Patti, 1 Apr., 1592; *Misc. Gregolin*, b. 12 *ter*, Carlo to G. M. Savioni, 15 Jan., 1594: 'There will be English merchants coming but they will do no harm to business because as merchants they will always keep profit in mind.'

90. U. Tucci, op. cit., 30.

91. B. Cotrugli, op. cit., 139. But the real feeling of the writer seems nearer the surface when he writes that fortune, 'commonly supports those who conduct themselves with prudence and according to rule . . . and if it sometimes happens that those who order their affairs badly nevertheless do well, this happens exceptionally and by chance'. Ibid., 23–24. The support of God and of fortune were seen as two distinct elements; e.g. a letter from P. de Freschi to A. Paruta of 24 Apr., 1592, contains the advice to be content with what God and fortune will bring because if one desires more than is in His will, fortune will scorn one and turn her face away. *Misc. Gregolin*, b. 12 *ter*.

92. G. Zuccolo, *Discorso intorno all' onore* (Venice, 1575), 76. 'Onore e gloria' in a letter from Agostino to his brother G. M. Ventura, *Misc. Gregolin*, b. 12 *ter*, 12 Oct., 1592.

93. Ibid., Pietro Ventura to his son Giovan Maria, 20 Apr., 1597, and Tomà Mocenigo to Benetto de Daniel, 9 May, 1580.

94. G. Lanteri, op. cit., 30.

95. The merchant – perhaps imaginary – who was the dedicatee of the 1592 edition of Marco Bussato's *Giardino di agricoltura*.

96. For this see *Misc. Gregolin*, b. 12 *ter*.

97. The inventory of Francesco Urins, who we know became a Venetian citizen in 1593, has been published by W. Brulez, op. cit., 630–643; for those of Antonio and of Ieronimo Cabianca, see *Giudice di petizion, filza* 345/10/63.

98. The expression is G. M. Memmo's, op. cit., 123.

99. *Misc. Gregolin*, b. 12 *ter*, P. de Freschi to A. Paruta, 26 July, 1589.

100. On Fabri, de Freschi and Leoni see, again, ibid.

101. On this function of the portrait see R. Romano and A. Tenenti, op. cit., esp. 126, but the whole chapter is fundamental to an understanding of these aspects of the evolution of sensibility.

102. *Misc. Gregolin*, b. 12 *ter*, Ottavio to Tullio Fabri, 2 July, 1596.

103. At Aleppo in 1555, for example; mass and a lengthy meeting of merchants after the service. U. Tucci, op. cit., 22.

104. *Misc. Gregolin*, b. 12 *ter*, Zuanne Stefani to T. Fabri, 31 May, 1591.

105. Ibid., Ottavio to T. Fabri, 2 July 1596 and G. Cucina to A. Paruta, 31 Jan. 1593. But Bernardo della Croce, who made his will in Constantinople in 1587, wished to be buried in the open, three *passi* underground and not in a church, 'to avoid expense'. *Bailo a Costantinopoli*, reg. 373, 2 Sept., 1587. On the problems of attitudes to death in collective psychology see, again, R. Romano and A. Tenenti, op. cit., esp. 116 seq.

106. J. C. Davis, op. cit., 109 seq. The other fifth were nobles of the *terraferma*.

107. B. Cotrugli, op. cit., 124; A. M. Triulzi, *Bilancio dei pesi e misure di tutte le piazze mercantili dell' Europa* (Venice, 1756) 186.

108. G. M. Memmo, op. cit., 124.

XIII

BRIAN PULLAN

The occupations and investments of the Venetian nobility in the middle and late sixteenth century

---

The legend of Venice is well known – the myth of the enduring Republic with the caste-like patriciate, combining the maximum of stable conservatism with the minimum of social mobility.[1] This essay is an attempt to inquire into those activities and investments of the ruling class which, during the middle and later sixteenth century, brought it wealth and maintenance. For the character of any élite is extensively described, if not defined, by the economic and other habits deemed compatible with belonging to it, and by the duties which society and the state impose upon its members. In legend, the Venetian aristocracy was distinguished by its devotion to commerce and its loyal dedication to the service of the state, by the subordination of the individual nobleman to the interests of his class. The facelessness of the Venetian nobility has made it hard to lift the veil of anonymity which clouds its history, and to distinguish different socio-economic groups within the heterogeneous mass of some 2,000 adult male noblemen – though a few outstanding figures have found able and devoted modern biographers to chart their political careers and analyse their opinions.[2]

The remarks which follow are based extensively on the personal stories of about 140 Venetian noblemen or noble households, few of them distinguished or peculiar, told in the stereotyped phrases of their own petitions to the Senate between the middle 1530s and the end of the sixteenth century.[3] Such sources have obvious pitfalls. Many of the petitions are requests for favours, or demands for the readjustment of taxation, and contain some element of the hard-luck story. Nonetheless, they betray many significant assumptions, and most of the facts they recite could presumably have been verified by the Senate, which was not a gullible body. Indeed, there is ample evidence that in the late sixteenth century they were so verified by the government's fiscal magistracies, whose incumbents commonly insisted on seeing written confirmation from some official source (such as a notarial document or a certificate supplied by a parish priest) of the petitioners' assertions about their economic affairs. These statements did, at least, need to be plausible. A more serious disadvantage is that this form of testimony cannot easily be quantified – it tends to suggest that certain things were being quite commonly done by Venetian patricians, but cannot accurately establish the extent to which they were being done. But even a rough indication of the possibilities, however tentative, may serve as a point of departure for future inquiries, and establish a useful *prima facie* case. In this hope, the following suggestions are put forward.

Most of the forms of economic activity associated by modern historians with the medieval Venetian aristocracy[4] continued to appeal in some degree to their successors in the sixteenth century. But their relative importance had certainly changed by 1600. Investment in mainland properties, in their improvement or reclamation, and in the erection of country houses, absorbed a larger proportion of Venetian capital. Banking, combined with commercial enterprise by patricians, suffered very severe blows, whilst there was certainly a fall in the number of nobles building and fitting out ships, and probably a contraction both in passive investment in maritime commerce and in the number of noblemen personally engaged in trade. Despite the spectacular development of the woollen industry during the sixteenth century, it seems unlikely that many patricians were deeply interested in the actual manufacture of textiles (as distinct from the importing of wools or dyestuffs and the export of cloth) – or, indeed, in other industries.[5] The popularity of government bonds probably waned, to be partially replaced, at least in the second half of the sixteenth century, by an extensive network of personal loans, especially in the form of *livelli* (loans disguised as leases of real property). Before that time, many noblemen were clearly speculating, some unwisely, on the yield of indirect taxes or *dazi*. No account of the wealth of the Venetian patriciate – as distinct from its economic actions and interests – would be complete without some discussion of the profits and burdens of office in the Republic, or without a mention of the episcopal revenues which enriched great families, and of the benefices (eagerly sought from Rome) which offered penurious or embarrassed households some chance to recoup their fortunes.

The question of the balance between commercial and landed investments on the part of Venetian patricians exercised commentators in the sixteenth and seventeenth centuries as much as it now occupies economic historians. In medieval Venice there had not been the same intimate relationship between town-based capitalism and the purchase of land as in most inland communes – although Venetian noblemen had owned fiefs in the Ferrarese and estates in the regions of Padua and Treviso.[6] This situation had arisen partially from Venice's slowness to bring the east Lombard hinterland under her direct dominion, although she had had zones of influence there where Venetians held the office of *podestà*. Grave risks had always been attached to investment in lands subject to alien and potentially hostile jurisdiction. Hence, large-scale movements towards sinking capital in the territory of the neighbouring provinces of the Padovano and

Trevigiano were not simply taken for granted. They were liable, in the sixteenth century, to be stigmatized by critics as a betrayal of Venice's ancient maritime tradition: as an unworthy attempt to exchange the austerities and risks of commerce for the pleasures and security of life in the countryside.[7] Parties anxious to perpetuate the maritime tradition of Venice, and others eager for closer links with the mainland, had probably existed since the thirteenth century, and hence landed and commercial investment were frequently seen as urging rival claims on a limited reserve of wealth: any advance by one must needs be at the expense of the other. Few writers argued, as did Paolo Paruta, that the two might be complementary – he was prepared to point out that the territorial acquisitions of the Republic enabled it, in the late sixteenth century, to put into operation a much larger fleet even than in the death-struggle with the Genoese two hundred years before.[8] Contemporary comment, distorted by this debate, is still more plentiful than adequate statistical evidence of the withdrawal of Venetian nobles from commerce and of a stronger tendency to invest in land.[9]

Nonetheless, it seems likely that a significant tip in the balance of investment did occur during the second half of the sixteenth century. For the first time, the Venetians were confronted simultaneously with fertile and accessible mainland territories under their own dominion; with the challenge of a growing population and the public problem of maintaining social stability by supplying victuals to an expanding capital city periodically afflicted by famine, at a time when imported food was increasingly difficult to obtain; and with the opportunities for private profit afforded by high grain prices. Some distinction must be made between the periods before and after 1570. Between about 1540 and 1570, local population pressure was acute, the Venetian economy was expanding (as witness the statistics for the woollen industry and for the growing arsenal labour force), and extensive land reclamation in the Basso Padovano and Basso Polesine was in progress.[10] But during the 1570s, the weight of population was reduced by savage epidemics of bubonic plague and typhus in Venice and elsewhere, by naval recruiting, and by emigration to avoid conscription for onerous service in the galleys which fought the Turk. Land reclamation appears to have ceased, but investment in land by Venetian noblemen persisted,[11] partly, no doubt, because of the buoyancy which grain prices retained up to the close of the century. Local population pressure had been relieved, but other Mediterranean regions from which Venice could still be compelled to import in seasons of foul weather were suffering variously from overpopulation or from desertion of the countryside, and were becoming increasingly reluctant to supply Venice with victuals. In 1589–98, wheat prices in Venice stood nearly twice as high as in 1567–76.[12] It may be that the attractions of landed investment and the discouragements to commercial enterprise on the part of the Venetians themselves both struck their highest pitch in the decades 1570–1600; a period opened by the outbreak of war with Ottoman Turkey in 1570 and by the loss of Cyprus a year later.

The Turkish war, which consumed much Venetian wealth, underlined the hazards of engaging in commerce in the Levant, Venice's traditional sphere of action, on the territory of a potential enemy. The goods of Venetians were seized in Constantinople and Alexandria, and the experience of one patrician merchant, Giuseppe di Benedetto Dolfin, who petitioned the Senate for tax-relief in 1577, serves to illustrate the heavy losses sustained by certain individuals. Before the war he had specialized in the sale of coral, in which he had invested some 200,000 ducats between 1563 and 1568. He had also run a timberyard, and had attained a level of prosperity which equipped him to provide suitable dowries for five daughters. But on the outbreak of hostilities, two of his sons had been arrested in Alexandria, and the family had sustained losses sufficient to prevent them from continuing any form of mercantile activity and to compel them to sell the timberyard and some of their land. Investigating Dolfin's story, the *dieci savi sopra le Decime* (magistrates responsible for the assessment of direct taxation) obtained from Giorgio Emo, sometime vice-consul in Alexandria, a certificate confirming that much of Dolfin's merchandise had in fact been sequestrated and that he had been forced to pay 13,000 ducats – a sum representing 46 per cent of their value – to get his goods released.[13] On another occasion, the same magistrates, scanning the account books of the late Lorenzo Giustinian of San Moisè, established that he had lost over 5,000 ducats on the voyage to Alexandria between 1566 and 1572 – though the family's losses through the Turkish conquest of Cyprus were far more serious.[14] Moreover, the procurator Alessandro Bon testified in 1574 that in the course of the war his entire fortune, of some 33,000 ducats, had sunk with a new roundship of 1,300 *botte* capacity, converted to government service and wrecked on its maiden voyage.[15]

Still greater, however, were the misfortunes suffered by Venetian families which had held estates and merchandise in Cyprus, a fertile source of salt, sugar, cotton and grain, and an important, if not indispensable base for navigation to Syria. Some patricians experienced not only grave financial losses, but also the indignities of enslavement after capture by the Turks, and were forced to cut into their surviving resources by ransoming themselves and their relatives. Some described graphically to the Senate their plunges from wealth to poverty. Andriana, widow of Federico di Gabriele Cornaro, testified in 1584 that on the capture of Cyprus she had forfeited an income of 10,000 ducats per annum, and had, with her son Ambrogio, served for a spell as a Turkish slave. She was now sixty-five, with no means of support, and had to be granted a state pension.[16] A few years later, Marc' Antonio di Pietro Cornaro, coming from another branch of the same clan, declared that he had lost an annual income of 5,000 ducats through the conquest of Cyprus, as well as having had to contribute generously to the cost of defending the island. Left with only 400 ducats a year on which to provide for five male and five female children, he now hoped to restore the family fortunes by obtaining ecclesiastical benefices for his eldest son, Pietro.[17] Even he proved a shade better off than Geronimo di Pietro Giustinian, whose assets had been held entirely in Cyprus and Alexandria. Having lost revenues from Cypriot estates to the value of 1,600 ducats a year, he found himself with no economic activity and a large family of seven children to support.[18] Leonardo di Lorenzo Giustinian had unfortunately shifted capital into Cyprus shortly before the war. He had sold valuable property in or near Venice to raise 23–24,000 ducats in 1566, in order to repurchase the Cypriot estate of Lefronico, which had probably formed part of his mother's dowry, and would otherwise have left the family on her death. That year, the property had yielded about 7,000 local measures or *moggia* of wheat, with over 10,000 of barley, and smaller quantities of beans and lentils – produce valued at over 4,000 ducats. The Giustinian brothers claimed that the seizure of the island and expropriation from this estate had cut their income by more than 70 per cent – this had now dropped to 1,480 ducats per annum (two-thirds from house property, the rest from government bonds). They declared in 1577 that they had engaged in no mercantile or industrial activity over the past five years.[19]

Dramatic stories of enslavement and ransom were told by Bartolomeo da Ca da Pesaro, whose family, probably resident in Cyprus, had inter-married with the local gentry – with the counts of Rocca and the Podacattaro. His father, a prosperous trader with merchandise, cash and credits in the island, was killed in the siege of Nicosia, whilst Bartolomeo himself became the slave of Mustapha Pasha for four and a half years, and was lamed in one leg by the savage beatings he received. He succeeded, however, in negotiating the sale of a house in Venice for 1,000 ducats through the intervention of the Cavalier Antonio Tiepolo, the Venetian *bailo* or ambassador-consul in Constantinople, and in ransoming himself with this and with a further sum of 400 ducats advanced to him by the kindness of the *bailo*. His mother had drowned in the wreck of a ship laden with gentlewomen being sent as a present to the sultan. But he still had an aunt and sister to redeem, and was forced to sell more houses and land in order to rescue them and to clear his father's debts.[20]

The experiences and financial losses of these noble families clearly indicated the dangers latent in trade with the Levant and residence in the surviving colonies of the eastern Mediterranean. The level of naval preparedness which the Venetians felt obliged to maintain from 1577 onwards bore witness to official fears of another outbreak of war with Ottoman Turkey. None came for seventy years, but this could not have been predicted.[21] Moreover, the misfortunes of merchants in the east helped to disrupt the system of credit in Venice itself by provoking runs on Venetian banks known to have backed them, or to have engaged, with the aid of their clients' money, in eastern commerce on their own account. Two of the three private patrician banks officially recognized by the Venetian government in 1570[22] failed during that year. In August, partners in the Dolfin bank described the withdrawal of over 200,000 ducats in the panic of the past few days: a run caused, or so they said, by 'bankruptcies in Venice and the west, by the capture and wreck of ships in east and west, by the outbreak of the present war, and above all by the opportunity of depositing capital in the Mint, which has been responsible for most of the withdrawals'. In other words, the government's demands for loans – and it eventually borrowed at least 5.7

million ducats in the course of the war – had thrown a heavy strain on the bank, which its liquid reserves did not equip it to withstand.[23] The Dolfin might claim that their liabilities amounted only to 350,000 ducats, and their own and the bank's assets (with some assistance from a relative, the bishop of Torcello) to 441,000. But many of these probably consisted of bad debts and of securities not easily realized – including, for example, nearly 90,000 ducats tied up in estates and houses. Many depositors in the Dolfin bank may have lost a proportion of their capital outright. At all events, it was thought in June 1572 that they would still have to wait another four and a half years for payment in full, and the bank's affairs were apparently still not entirely settled by 1577–78.[24]

The bank of Angelo di Francesco Sanuto had failed early in February 1570[25] – certainly before the Turks' demands were officially presented to the Senate, and before unambiguous news of their designs on Cyprus reached Venice, but some weeks after the first seizures of Venetian merchandise by the Turks.[26] The bank was strongly committed to enterprises in Constantinople and Cyprus. Listing his assets, Angelo Sanuto referred to clocks, jewellery, woollens, velvets, damasks and silks in the hands of his brother Marco in Constantinople; to various oriental goods, such as pepper, rhubarb and dyestuffs, laden on the merchantman *Balba*; and to the bank having entered into two partnerships with Venetian merchants, Lazzaro Mocenigo and Giovanni Contarini, for the purpose of trading with Cyprus.[27] It seems probable that with the growing threat of war and confiscation of goods in the Levant, the knowledge that a bank was trading heavily with the East sufficed to provoke a crisis of confidence acute enough to bring it down.

The war of Cyprus contributed significantly, but not conclusively, to undermining the system of credit in Venice by destroying trust in the private banks which were, in the third quarter of the century, extensively subsidizing commerce. The bankruptcies of the Sanuto and Dolfin concerns were neither the first nor the last great failures of this period.[28] Most disastrous of all was the Pisani–Tiepolo crash in 1584, in which the sum involved was certainly over a million ducats. Its immediate cause was the default of a Tuscan man of business Andrea dell' Oste, with whom the bank was known to have extensive dealings. His debts to the Pisani and Tiepolo were not really as large as rumour drew them, but false reports had as much power as the truth to start a run. Hence, in the words of a patrician chronicler, Francesco da Molin, 'the bank failed, causing grave losses to innumerable persons and incredible damage to this city – which was left for four years without a bank, so that business contracted to an unbelievable extent'.[29] The balance sheet compiled by Giovanni Pisani and Giovanni Tiepolo under the supervision of the government commissioners, the *provveditori sopra banchi*, revealed that the bank's total liabilities stood at 1,045,568 ducats. These included certain deposits, to the extent of over 200,000 ducats, classified as *partite conditionate*, which had evidently not been used for commercial speculation, and were, as Professor Lane has described them in a study of Venetian banking in an earlier period, 'deposits earmarked for specified future payments under certain conditions', including those intended for dowries.[30] Since these had not been touched, there would be no difficulty in paying them. Pisani and Tiepolo maintained that their own estate, liable to seizure to satisfy the bank's debts, was valued at 460,000 ducats, leaving the bank owing about 360,000. They were forced to admit that Andrea dell' Oste's debt of 150,000 ducats was a bad one, but still maintained that 'good debtors to the bank' would meet the remaining liabilities – to the tune of some 210,000 ducats. The failure of Andrea dell' Oste was the effective cause of the disaster, but the Pisani and Tiepolo had also suffered heavily through the earlier bankruptcy of the Piperari of Mantua (probably about 1562),[31] with which they were also associated. This had initially caused a hiatus in their business operations by withholding from them the sum of 140,000 ducats and so forcing them to borrow at high rates of interest to satisfy their own creditors. After twelve years, they had sustained an eventual outright loss of 35,000 ducats. The war of Cyprus and the plague of 1575–77 had also contributed to their downfall – these represented a total of five years in which trade had virtually ceased, but they had still been forced to bear the expenses of keeping the bank open.[32]

THE PISANI–TIEPOLO BANK IN 1584:
ASSETS OF THE BANK AND ITS PARTNERS

Partite conditionate	221,659 ducats, 8 grossi
Personal estate of Pisani and Tiepolo	462,216 ducats, 11 grossi
'Bad' debts of Andrea dell' Oste	153,415 ducats, 21 grossi
'Good' debts	208,276 ducats, 14 grossi
	1,045,568 ducats, 6 grossi

Even when the vacuum created by the Pisani–Tiepolo failure was partly filled by the foundation of the *Banco della Piazza di Rialto* in 1587, this new public bank discharged only limited functions, since it was designed chiefly to keep money safe without employing it in commercial speculations, and to enable businessmen and others to make payments by simple transfers on the books without the exchange of cash.[33] Despite the existence of such a bank, the Venetian economy may, especially in the late sixteenth century, have suffered seriously from the failure to maintain a system of banks prepared to advance credit to entrepreneurs or to engage in commerce themselves. The fall of the Dolfin, for example, had deprived Venice of a bank which maintained connections with Milan, Florence, Naples, Lyons, Flanders and Alexandria.[34] Moreover, at a time when there were strong discouragements to commercial investment, the instability of private banks, coupled with the price-rise, may have created a strong incentive to take money out of them and put it into goods. This may, again, partially explain the continued popularity of land purchases.

The willingness, in the last quarter of the century, of the Venetian government to tolerate, and indeed to encourage, the formation of foreign merchant communities in the city may well be a symptom of increasing tendencies on the part of patricians themselves to withdraw from commerce, whilst at the same time they tried – with a fair measure of success – to keep up the level of activity in the port of Venice.[35] They did so even to the point of permitting another Jewish community, ultimately of Spanish or Portuguese origins, to settle in Venice beside the old resident corporation of 'German' Jews, and to engage in trade with the Levant:[36] an activity otherwise still strictly reserved for Venetian nobles and citizens of long residence. The government's permissive attitude to foreign traders in the late sixteenth century contrasts markedly with the determination it displayed in the early seventeenth to halt their advance and to discriminate against foreign shipping – at the cost of inflicting severe blows on the prosperity of Venice.[37]

Certainly, in the late sixteenth century, Venetian noblemen appear to have been withdrawing from one of their most important traditional activities, ship-owning and shipbuilding. Between 1553 and 1559, seven out of eleven demands for government subsidies to build ships had been presented by Venetian noblemen. But between 1588 and 1603, only seven out of forty requests for such loans came from Venetian nobles.[38] Two of the remaining patrician shipowners, Vincenzo Barozzi and Francesco Morosini, bore grim witness to the misfortunes they had encountered. Barozzi had built five ships between 1582 and 1599, and they had plied on the voyages to Alexandria and Constantinople and to Cyprus and Syria. But three of these had been wrecked in 1592 and a fourth in 1599, when the last vessel also sustained great damage.[39] Francesco Morosini declared in 1606 that in the past ten years he had lost 'four good ships and a galleon, some being wrecked and others seized by pirates'. He had, thereby, lost 48,000 ducats, with a further 14,000 forfeited when one of his roundships, with a capacity of 1,200 butts, was burnt in Cyprus.[40] Barozzi and Morosini are unlikely to have been isolated victims of exceptional misfortune – for at this time piracy was rife, standards of seamanship were falling, and the Venetian navy (for all the vast sums spent on its upkeep) was failing to guarantee adequate protection to merchantmen.[41]

Circumstantial evidence is strong enough to support the hypothesis that, while the first third of the seventeenth century marked the decisive decline of Venice as a port and industrial centre,[42] the last third of the sixteenth may well have seen a decisive, though by no means total, withdrawal of the Venetian nobility from commerce, shipping and banking. This withdrawal was provoked by heavy capital losses through war and Turkish conquest, and by the coincidence of strong discouragements to Levantine trade, of the collapse of stable credit facilities for the support of commerce, and of the persistence of countervailing incentives to invest in land and food production even after the epidemics of 1575–77. However, in view of the serious risk of flood damage to low-lying properties on the mainland, investment in estates in the Veneto can hardly be described as a coward's alternative to commercial speculation.

Although such authors as Traiano Boccalini continued, even in the early seventeenth century, to refurbish the image of the Venetian patriciate as a rational and calculating commercial aristocracy,[43] several of its members, by their own accounts, somewhat resembled the Zeno of San Pantalon and lived in a similar condition of genteel poverty. Distress, no doubt, had made the Zeno huddle together in a large family unit under one roof – the household numbered twenty-four persons, and included the five brothers, two of whom had wives, a widowed mother and aunt, a sister of marriageable age, the brothers' children, and a few servants. They told the Senate, in 1594, that their house had never within living memory embarked on any commercial ventures, and swore that their present assets consisted almost entirely of old and dilapidated houses – very costly to repair – in the city of Venice. With undertones of bitterness, they added that if they ever had engaged in commerce they would not have been forced, on the outbreak of the war of Cyprus, to terminate the personal loans or *livelli* from which they had previously derived an income. They had cashed these assets to meet their obligation to arm two galleys and a *fusta* for the battle against the Turk. They also owned property on the mainland at Castelbaldo in the Padovano, but this had been damaged by floods. They had incurred heavy but vain expenses in making dikes and ditches to protect their country estates, and had run into debt with two government magistracies, the *Ufficio dei Beni Inculti* and the *Ufficio delle Acque*, who had foreclosed on their loans and seized some of the land. The Zeno, who claimed to have an income of only 1,000 ducats between them, did not, as it happened, get any tax reduction for the losses they had suffered on the mainland, because the *dieci savi sopra le decime* believed that there had been compensations for these elsewhere: but the main facts in the petition were not disputed.[44]

In all probability a large fraction of the patriciate consisted, not of merchants, but of *rentiers* and property owners intermittently seeking and holding magisterial office. It is well known that in the late Middle Ages Venetian noblemen frequently invested a thick slice of their capital in the *Monti*, or government consolidated loan funds, originally based on interest-bearing forced loans. Probably, in the course of the sixteenth century and in periods of peace, the Venetian patriciate showed a tendency to invest proportionately more of its capital in personal loans like the *livelli* terminated by the Zeno, and somewhat less in government stock. Between about 1250 and the late 1370s, government bonds had offered an excellent security for those who could afford to retain them and accumulate large holdings. But during and after the last war with Genoa, in 1379–81, there had been periods in which their market value tumbled: especially in years of naval or military crisis.[45] The price of government bonds would then fall steeply, partly because a moratorium on interest payments would almost certainly be declared, and because such events as the invasion of the Veneto in 1509 threatened to cut off permanently the revenues on which interest was secured, if not to annihilate the entire Venetian Republic. Bondholders on whom the state was making heavy demands would be forced to sell their securities at very low prices. Hence, in the summer of 1509, the diarist Girolamo Priuli reported that holdings in the *Monte Nuovo* – a recently floated loan fund –

had dropped from 102½ points to 40, and those in the longstanding *Monte Vecchio* from 25 points to 15. He described the general opinion that, despite the invasion of the mainland, investment in estates would have been more sensible – the enemy could not take these away, and there was every chance that they would eventually be recovered, whereas 'these *Monti Vecchi* and *Nuovi* are up in the clouds, and are nothing but books, made of paper and ink . . .'.[46] During the Italian wars of the first third of the sixteenth century, the government often failed to pay interest – as witness the frequency with which noblemen sought and obtained permission, in the 1530s, 1540s and 1550s, to clear debts to the state by renouncing arrears of interest due on account of bonds held by themselves or their ancestors during these wars.[47] The policy of retaining government bonds for several generations could, admittedly, prove rewarding. In 1542–76, Antonio Barbarigo succeeded in collecting interest payments for the years 1487–1503, which had been missed by his grandfather.[48] But there must have been many whose pressing financial obligations did not permit them to hold their stock for such long periods. Thus, in 1534, Vitale di Alvise Miani declared that he had been forced to sell all his government securities since 1521 in order to pay his taxes during the recent wars.[49]

In the course of the sixteenth century, the Venetian government introduced new methods of rapidly floating loans – as in 1538, during the war of 1537–40 against the Turks, when interest at the high annual rate of 14 per cent was offered to all who would lend sums of at least 100 ducats to the government within a specified period, on the understanding that after his death the bondholder's heirs would have no claims on the state – either to the payment of interest or to the restitution of the capital.[50] These life-loans or annuities obviously had a wide appeal, which embraced both patricians and professional beggars,[51] and in 1554 the impoverished children of Piero Malipiero complained that a large part of the family income had stemmed from the 14 per cent loan funds, and had been extinguished on the death of their mother.[52] However, in the last quarter of the century, the government showed determination and ingenuity in amortizing a large part of the state debt – first, in 1577–84, by repaying loans to the total value of 5.7 million ducats incurred during the war of Cyprus,[53] and secondly, from 1596 onwards, by the liquidation of the older consolidated loan funds, the *Monte Vecchio, Monte Nuovissimo* and *Sussidio.*[54]

Such measures undoubtedly reduced the opportunities for living as a *rentier* and using the state as a source of profit. But there are signs that, even before this time, the popularity of loans to private individuals, particularly in the form of *livelli*, was increasing. The *livello* was in effect a personal loan disguised as a lease of real property for the purpose of circumventing the laws against usury.[55] To take an imaginary example: the borrower, A, wishing to raise a loan of 5,000 ducats from the lender, B, would fictitiously sell certain property to B, and receive the 5,000 ducats in exchange. B would then fictitiously lease him the property he had sold, in return for an annual rent corresponding to a certain percentage of the 5,000 ducats. B would technically be charging for the use of the 'fruitful' property, which was legitimate in the eyes of the canon law, and not for the use of the 'sterile' money, which would have been usurious. In the late sixteenth century, the official rate of interest on such loans seems to have been 6 per cent, though the return on life-loans *a livello* (where the lender would have no claims on the borrower's estate or on his heirs after the borrower's death) was naturally much higher, and could exceed 12 per cent. Almost certainly, the rate varied according to the age and expectancy of life of the borrower. The rates of interest on ordinary *livelli* were somewhat lower than those yielded by the short-term government loans of the 1570s – for the government, up to 1577, was paying interest of half a million ducats on debts of 5.7 million, at rates varying between $7\frac{1}{2}$ per cent and 14 per cent. But the *livello*, giving the lender claims on the entire estate of the borrower, and not only on the properties on which the transaction was theoretically based, may have seemed a more reliable security than government stock. A private person could, after all, be called to account more effectively than could a government, against which no sanctions could be applied by an individual creditor. It was also possible to secure interest payments in the form of agricultural produce, thus mitigating some of the effects of inflation.

Venetian patricians entered into these contracts, not only among themselves, but also with nobles and other inhabitants of subject territories on the Venetian *terraferma*. Matteo di Marco Cornaro, for example, declared that in 1565 he had had 2,000 ducats invested in a *livello* at 6 per cent with Count Ottaviano da Thiene of Vicenza, and a further 1,000 ducats, also at 6 per cent, with Giovanni Nicolò Villibruna of Feltre. He had (like the Zeno of San Pantalon) been forced to terminate these agreements during the war with the Turk, when he was made responsible for fitting out and manning a galley.[56] Probably, many of these *livelli* were not designed to further any kind of economic enterprise, but were simply destined to enable persons of social rank to keep up their style of life and meet the obligations appropriate to their position. An onerous duty, and a recurrent cause of indebtedness or embarrassment which could be palliated through *livelli*, was the obligation to provide suitable marriage portions for daughters or sisters, or else to settle them (at smaller but still considerable expense) in convents – for which dowries were also required. Despite all the attempts of the Senate to restrain it by laws, inflation on the marriage market proceeded inexorably throughout the sixteenth century and outstripped the general price rise. The legal limit on the size of a dowry rose from 3,000 ducats in 1505 to 4,000 in 1535, 5,000 in 1551, and 6,000 in 1575. But these official limits bore no relation to the reality. In 1560–61, a senatorial preamble admitted that certain dowries were reaching the level of 20–25,000 ducats, and between 1560–62 and 1564–75 all legal restraints were removed as being unenforceable. When the Senate restored them in 1575–76, it probably did not seriously expect them to be observed, and may have acted merely from a desire to register official disapproval rather than actively encourage further inflation by the removal of all hindrances to it.[57] The dowry, though not permanently alienated from the family which provided it, frequently created the need to borrow large sums. Its phenomenal inflation was almost certainly caused by the widespread desire to purchase sons-in-law of slightly higher standing and influence than oneself.

In 1590, for example, the brothers Marc' Antonio and Piero Grimani testified that they had incurred debts to the tune of 19,510 ducats, mostly through loans *a livello*, and were paying interest on this sum at an average rate of about 7 per cent – to a total of 1,438 ducats per annum. They had raised a life-loan of 5,000 ducats at approximately 12 per cent, other *livelli* at 6 per cent to a total of 9,400 ducats, and a loan of 3,100 ducats, in return for which they were obliged to produce 122 Venetian bushels or *staia* of corn – valued that year at 244 ducats, corresponding to approximately 8 per cent of the principal. The indebtedness of the Grimani brothers originated in two familiar causes – the demands of state service, and the obligation to provide appropriate dowries for two sisters, which ought for reasons of prestige to match those brought temporarily into the family by Marc' Antonio's brides, Betta di Andrea da Lezze and Paolina di Giovanni Mocenigo. Their father, Ottaviano Grimani, had bought the highly prestigious office of procurator after the outbreak of war with the Turks for the sum of 20,000 ducats and had then donated a further 2,000 ducats outright to the government. Marc' Antonio Grimani himself had the misfortune to be serving as *podestà* of Chioggia when the grand duchess of Tuscany paid the town a state visit, and incurred (or so he said) heavy expenses from his own pocket in ensuring that she was received with due pomp and ceremony. One sister, Lucrezia Grimani, had borne with her a dowry of 23,000 ducats to Giovanni Marcello, and another a portion of 18,000 ducats to her marriage with Giacomo Giustinian. To equip the second sister for her marriage, the brothers borrowed 6000 ducats *a livello* from a creditor bearing the patrician name of Giovanni Vitturi.[58]

The Morosini dalla Sbarra provide another instance of the use of *livelli* for purposes unconnected with economic enterprise. Giovanni di Vincenzo Morosini died, heavily indebted, in 1588, and his wife, 'fearing that his debts would swallow up what little we had left in the world, saw fit to have her dowry repaid'. The inviolability of the mother's dowry could be a decided advantage: unlike the estate inherited by sons, it was immune from seizure to meet the father's debts. The widow then raised money by taking out *livelli*, and from this borrowed capital made further loans to her sons Vincenzo and Vittore to permit them to preserve their house in San Polo and small estate on the mainland at Pieve di Sacco. Paying interest of 126 ducats a year, the brothers then removed to Padua, partly to study, partly to let their house in San Polo, and partly to lodge their sister in a Paduan convent, because they could afford neither to marry her off nor to make her a nun at the high rates prevailing in Venice.[59]

Hints at the importance of *livelli* to the investors of Venice are conveyed by the statement of the banker Andrea di Giovanni Dolfin, listing his assets in 1570. He described them as follows, declaring the annual revenue derived from each form of security:[60]

	Capital	Income	Return
Livelli	34,000 ducats	2,171 ducats	6.4 per cent
Government stock	9,200 ducats	625 ducats	6.8 per cent
House property	33,590 ducats	1,050 ducats	3.1 per cent
Other real estate	55,800 ducats	2,229 ducats	4.0 per cent
Jewellery	21,500 ducats		
	154,090 ducats	6,075 ducats	

The statement suggests that the banker had placed over 20 per cent of his capital in *livelli*, and as little as 6 per cent in government stock, even though the return on government bonds was marginally higher. The yield of house property and other real estate seems markedly low by comparison, though Dolfin may have been content with an initially low return from property he was reclaiming, improving or repairing. There must have been some incentive to sink 60 per cent of his capital in real estate, even when the proportional yield from loans was considerably greater.

Institutional mechanisms for advancing consumption loans to people of social standing were highly developed on the mainland territories of the Republic in the second half of the sixteenth century, through the further extension of credit facilities offered by *Monti di Pietà*. These organs had started in the fifteenth century as Christian pawnshops supported mainly by charitable gifts or bequests, extending small loans on pledges at low rates of interest to poor persons. However, by the middle of the sixteenth century, certain *Monti di Pietà* – undoubtedly including those of Verona and Vicenza – had begun to accept interest-bearing deposits and to extend larger loans to persons who were not in the normal sense poor. The development of a network of *livelli*, loans made by private individuals, complemented the facilities offered by *Monti di Pietà*. *Livellatori* lent on the security of real property, whilst *Monti di Pietà* were supposed to lend only on the security of chattels or movable goods, such as rings and other jewellery, though in practice they often put their funds at risk by illegally accepting unsalable promissory notes as collateral. The importance of *livelli* to Venetian noblemen may have been enhanced by the absence of any *Monte di Pietà* from Venice itself. With remarkable conservatism, the Venetians had resisted the introduction of a *Monte di Pietà* (seriously proposed in 1524) into their own city, and had preferred to retain the moneylending services of the community of 'German' Jews which had moved into Venice during the disturbances of 1509, when the Veneto was invaded. Having narrowly escaped expulsion as a thanksgiving gesture for the Christian victory of Lepanto, the Jews were (after 1573) compelled to run a bank which performed some of the functions of a *Monte di Pietà*, by making small loans at 5 per cent for the benefit of devotees of the alien Christian faith. They themselves complained that their services were frequently misused by persons of high social rank who borrowed large sums by taking out numerous pawn-tickets. But in Venice there was no proper, formalized provision for a public pawnshop to advance relatively big loans to persons of 'civil' or 'noble' condition. The need for credit through *livelli* may, therefore, have been all the greater.[61]

Up to the early 1560s, if no longer, speculation on the yield of indirect taxes was also a reasonably popular form of investment with noblemen. The government itself shouldered responsibility for the collection of direct income taxes or *gravezze*, but would normally commit the exaction of *dazi*, indirect taxation, to private individuals – who were, however, accountable to the fiscal office of the *Rason Nuove*. These *dazi*, which provided the bulk of the state's ordinary revenues, included excises on wine, foodstuffs and industrial raw materials, together with customs duties, transit dues, sales and brokerage taxes. A given *dazio* would normally be 'let' to the person or persons ready to guarantee the largest sum of money to the state. These taxfarmers would make their own arrangements for the collection of the revenue, pocketing any surplus over and above the sum guaranteed, and bearing any losses, should the *dazio* fail that year to meet their expectations.[62] There were several degrees of involvement, both active and passive, in the administration of *dazi*. One or more *conduttori* would administer the *dazio* and keep the accounts; he, or they, would raise the capital from a number of shareholders, among whom the profits or losses would later be distributed; and the shareholders would be required to provide guarantors against failure on their part to make good any losses sustained. For example, in 1562, the principal wine excise was divided into twenty-four shares or *carati*, and sold or 'let' for the year for 138,601 ducats, each of the two *conduttori*, Eustachio Zorzi and Antonio Bambarara, undertaking to find persons to take up twelve shares. Zorzi, a nobleman, asserted years later that he had been persuaded to embark on the enterprise by a certain Orazio dei Cancelieri, who undertook to provide ten and a half shares himself and to leave Zorzi to find only the other one and a half, which Zorzi was unwillingly compelled to take up himself.[63]

The one-time popularity of taking shares in *dazi* is well attested by a number of noblemen – of whom Eustachio Zorzi seems to have been one of the last – who complained to the Senate of losses incurred through their own innocence, and begged for special terms on which to pay their debts to the state. Hence the losses, ranging from several hundred to several thousand ducats, sustained by some shareholders are well documented, though nothing is known about the profits which could be realized from such investments. Fraud or incompetence on the part of a taxfarmer was frequently blamed for these losses. The alleged misconduct of Matteo di Moretto, who administered the taxes on iron and dairy produce in the late 1520s,[64] and of Andrea Bon, a *conduttore* of grain taxes in mid-century, caused great distress and indignation among noblemen involved in the débâcle. So, in 1553, Giovanni Maria di Alvise Muazzo complained of having been beguiled by his supposed friend Bon into guaranteeing two shares in the *dazio della macina* (a tax on corn-grinding) and half of one share in the *dazio della grassa* (on dairy-produce), managed by Nicolò Ciuran, for the years

1549 and 1550. Bon's peccadilloes had cost Muazzo 400 ducats, and he declared, resentment bursting through the stilted phraseology of his petition, that 'I can promise you this, most Serene Prince, that if it lasts for a thousand years nobody else in my family will ever have anything to do with the *dazi* of this Most Illustrious Dominion . . .'[65]

Apart from these hazards, however, other unpredictable fluctuations could occur in the yield of the taxes. Thus, in 1528, several nobles took shares in a tax imposed on merchandise arriving in Venice by sea, the *dazio delle tre per cento da mar*, whose grave losses resulted in part from the unexpectedly late return of the galleys. According to the conditions of their auction by the state, the galleys destined for Beirut and Alexandria were due to leave in July, but in fact departed in October, and failed to return within the period (from March 1528 to February 1529) for which the *conduttore*, Antonio Botazzo, and his associates had undertaken to collect the tax. Again, many vessels, normally used for the transport of merchandise subject to this particular duty, were converted into food ships, and used to relieve the terrible famines which struck Venice in 1528. This naturally affected the yield of the *dazio*, which lost as much as 12,000 ducats.[66]

Several petitions indicate that minors, aged fifteen, seventeen or eighteen, were allowed to take shares in *dazi*.[67] Their authors naturally stressed their tender age with maximum pathos, and doubtless overemphasized their own naïveté. But at least their remarks provide useful evidence that this form of passive speculation was considered suitable for the young and undiscriminating.

For some reason the records in the series *Senato, Terra*, contain no references to noblemen being involved in tax farming after 1562, although the practice of farming taxes certainly continued after that date.[68] This disappearance may point to the withdrawal of nobles from that form of activity, or may, on the other hand, simply have resulted from procedural changes or in methods of keeping the records.

Beyond these forms of private economic action, much of the time and energy of Venetian noblemen was devoted to the service of the state, and to some extent the poorer members of the nobility were able to scrape a living, if not repair their fortunes, by seeking and holding magisterial office. For Venetian men, nobility was ultimately equated with the hereditary right to full citizenship through access (on reaching the age of twenty-five) to the Great Council, which in theory created and elected to all magistracies, as well as to smaller legislative councils. One theory to justify the Venetian system of distributing office was advanced by the Savoyard commentator, Giovanni Botero. He suggested that the Venetians succeeded in smoothing away the most serious inequalities of wealth within the patriciate by assigning offices of great honour to the rich (who had to draw on their private fortunes in order to keep up the pomp and ostentation expected of the Republic's representatives), and by reserving offices of profit to the poorer members of the nobility.[69] The poor clearly showed interest in naval or military commands, in legal, judicial and fiscal posts, and in the obscurer governorships of the Republic's mainland, Dalmatian or other overseas possessions. All of these carried modest salaries and did not demand heavy expenditure, whilst some may – though this is impossible to document – have opened opportunities for illicit profit.[70]

Distinguished military and naval officers recruited from the poor nobility included Andrea Ciuran, captain of the Stradiots or Albanian cavalry during the Italian wars, who died in Apulia in 1529 after twenty years' service 'in Friuli, throughout Italy, and in Dalmatia'.[71] Gasparo Contarini described the abandonment in his own time – which was also Ciuran's – of the ancient convention whereby no command of more than twenty-five soldiers was ever entrusted to a Venetian noble.[72] Cristoforo Da Canal, the naval officer who in the mid-sixteenth century campaigned in favour of the massive employment of convict labour in the regular fleet, also came of a family in very straitened circumstances. On his death, in 1562, it was assumed that his son, Girolamo, would follow the same employment, and the Senate voted him a bounty of 2,000 ducats on the occasion of his becoming a *sopracomito*, or galley commander.[73]

Certain remarks of Francesco di Geronimo Zeno in 1575 illustrate the importance which office could assume for a poor noble. He asserted that in 1568 he had enjoyed a regular income of only 63 ducats per annum, entirely derived from letting urban property. He had nothing in the state loan funds and joined in no form of business enterprise; five children and an unmarried sister (a tertiary in feeble health) looked to him for support. 'I reveal my needs to no one', he wrote, 'but seek to manage my household as best I can without troubling anybody, and to support myself with some form of office, which has sometimes been granted me by their Most Illustrious Lordships, because I certainly could not do without such assistance. Being unable, like the others, to await the opportunity to enter the *Quarantia*, I lately went at the age of forty-four to serve as *podestà* at Castelfranco, although, on account of various misfortunes, I was forced to renounce this governorship before the end of my term.'[74] The *Quarantie* to which he referred were, for normal purposes, the supreme civil and criminal courts of the Republic, and the three organs of the *Quarantia al criminal*, the *Quarantia civil vecchio* and the *Quarantia civil nuovo* provided between them 120 places. Stipends of perhaps 130–160 ducats a year were attached to these posts during the 1580s. In Venice, there was no separation between the legislative and judiciary, and members of the *Quarantia al criminal* were entitled to sit in the Senate. Their three heads, or *capi*, chosen afresh every two months, were the natural tribunes of the poor nobility, whilst at intervals the *Quarantie* became foci of radicalism, attacking and criticizing the established *savi* and senators.[75]

Besides judicial offices, whose sum total, including courts other than the *Quarantie*, was about 220, some noblemen could procure election to the post of advocate in the civil courts at the Ducal Palace and at the Rialto. No formal legal education was required for this purpose, and these jobs – twenty-four were available in the 1520s – could easily become sinecures. Litigants were obliged formally to retain the services of one of these advocates chosen by the Great

Council, though they could employ expert pleaders of their own in addition, and the official advocates could make no further effort and merely draw their fees. According to the Florentine Giannotti, these offices were, in the 1520s, becoming much less sought-after by noblemen, and were no longer a monopoly of the patriciate, for persons merely of 'citizen' rank were now admitted to them.[76] However, certain noblemen did continue either to avail themselves of this provision, or to practise privately as advocates. Giovanni Battista di Pietro Maria Contarini, who subsequently followed a distinguished career, and whose family produced an historian, philosophers and an archbishop of Crete, served as an advocate up to the year 1555.[77] Later, in 1598, Piero di Paolo Rimondo said that for some time he had drawn support from the office of advocate in the Ducal Palace, but had forfeited this income on his election to the office of *avogador di comun*.[78]

Places in the *Quarantie* and provincial governorships were held for spells of not more than two years at a time, it being a cardinal principle of Venetian statecraft that magisterial offices must be continuously rotated within the patriciate, so as to extend the hope of employment to the greatest number of persons, rather than guarantee security to a few. Venetian noblemen had, therefore, to face periods out of office. They could also be excluded indefinitely from such benefits if they fell into debt to the state – for arrears of taxation, from ill-fated speculations on *dazi*, or from any other cause. This was a questionable provision, since it threatened to frustrate the victim's attempts to recoup himself through holding office and so clear his debts. In 1535, Vittore di Giorgio Duodo and Marino di Antonio Pisani wrote of their failure to obtain office. Duodo had held none in the past twelve years, whilst Pisani had reached the age of fifty and never held a single government post. Debts to the state for unsuccessful *dazi* partly explain their exclusion.[79] Sebastiano di Nicolò Foscarini complained in 1536 that, twenty-three years earlier, he had incurred trivial debts, amounting to only 154 lire or about 25 ducats, for his part in two *dazi*. All his property was bound by legal ties – it was entailed, his wife's dowry was 'secured' upon it, and he was therefore prevented from selling any part of the estate for cash. Hence, 'so long as this debt remains, your petitioner is, as it were, deprived of noble rank' – a disaster for one with five children and no employment.[80] Indebtedness to the fisc seems, in practice, to have been the most important form of derogation from noble rank liable to occur among the Venetian patriciate. In 1550, Francesco di Carlo Contarini called himself a 'gientilhomo conditionato', or 'suspended nobleman', because his poverty – and the income tax he consequently owed – had 'deprived me of nobility'.[81] However, the authorities were not totally inflexible. When Leonardo di Alvise Rimondo told the Senate in 1539 that his debts to the state prevented him from 'partaking of the usual benefits and salaries enjoyed by our other noblemen', they agreed to 'suspend' his debts for a period of three years, 'so that in this time, enjoying the rewards bestowed by our commonwealth, he may earn a living and clear these and other debts'.[82]

Whilst poor noblemen competed for offices of magisterial rank which were filled by election and rotated among them, the state was sometimes ready to grant the reversion of lesser offices of profit, which could be held permanently or for much longer periods, to the families of men who had served with distinction in its armed forces. These ranged from military charges in Corfu and Crete to posts in the government warehouses in Venice itself – jobs which, given their menial nature, would presumably be actually done by hired substitutes. Pensions, in cash or flour, were frequently drawn on the treasuries of provincial towns.[83]

At the other extreme, the most honourable offices – especially those which entailed representing the Republic abroad – threw a heavy burden on the finances of those who undertook them. Expenses far outstripped inadequate official salaries. Private 'magnificence' and personal display in Venice itself were discouraged, and, at least in the opinion of travellers and foreign visitors, successfully restrained.[84] But great importance was attached to ostentation in the name of the commonwealth. Notoriously costly were embassies and the governorships of the major provincial towns on the Italian mainland – Padua, Verona, Brescia and so on. Admittedly, the salaries of provincial governors were raised in 1549 and 1565,[85] and in 1549 and 1559 the Senate issued sumptuary laws designed to curb certain forms of extravagance on their part.[86] The preamble to the law of 1559 declared that the *rettori* had 'so increased their expenditure that they are consuming 5,000 or 6,000 ducats or even more, and this causes them grave losses and is of little advantage to our cities and loyal subjects'. This expenditure was five or six times the amount of the official allowance on the most highly paid governorship, the podestariate of Padua.[87] The laws themselves are more valuable as indices to the kind of excesses habitually committed than as evidence that they were successfully restrained. The Senate was clearly, at this time, concerned about evasions of office on the part of noblemen elected to governorships, unwilling to incur the expense they entailed. To refuse office directly meant a heavy fine – but some took advantage of the law that persons indebted to the state were not entitled to hold office and deliberately disqualified themselves by this means. Hence, in 1550, the Senate provided that such indebtedness should not act as a bar to taking up the post of governor.[88]

The charge on the private resources of patricians chosen as ambassadors certainly grew very substantially in the second half of the sixteenth century. Official salaries and allowances failed to increase over the years 1561–1615,[89] thus stagnating throughout a period of acute inflation in the European countries to which ambassadors were sent. The Senate, in 1561, optimistically tried to 'give our ambassadors some means of upholding the dignity of our state without consuming their own fortunes', and provided for an additional allowance of 1,000 gold ducats payable to 'ordinary' ambassadors headed for the imperial or papal courts or for those of France or Spain. A further 1,000 gold ducats would henceforth be paid to any ambassador compelled to remain more than two years at his post.[90] The same year, ambassadors serving abroad, or their relatives, bore witness to heavy expenditure unavoidably incurred – especially in Spain, where 'all prices are two or three times as high as anywhere else'. The ambassador Paolo di Stefano Tiepolo had served as much as four years in Spain, and was facing a fifth year at that Habsburg court because no successor had yet been found. He was said to have spent all the money earmarked for the dowries of two nubile daughters, and his brothers felt unable to give him further financial assistance. Court weddings, funerals, and spells of mourning had taken a heavy toll of Tiepolo's resources, and he himself wrote, a few months later, of 'the incredible costliness of this court, which is saturated with luxuries, and of this country, which is void of all economic activity'; droughts, crop failures, and high animal mortality in 1561 had forced the cost of living in Spain to still higher levels.[91] Thirty years later, distress as sharp as Tiepolo's was experienced by the Cavalier Tommaso di Marc' Antonio Contarini, who wrote in 1594 from the Imperial Diet at Ratisbon that 'the salary which has been given me barely suffices for food for the stables and for bread and wine, and since I cannot with dignity reduce my expenditure I will go on consuming my substance, rather than fail to keep up what I have begun'.[92]

Naturally, the opposing effects of the heavy costs of embassies and governorships, and of the profits to be made from humbler offices, did not really produce a parity of wealth among Venetian noblemen. But the high cost of office, particularly in the field of diplomacy, did serve as a form of supertax which partially curbed the tendency towards the formation of rigid and contrasting groups of over-rich and abjectly poor persons. On the other hand, it may have diverted a significant amount of capital from economic enterprise, especially in the period of rising prices, and over the years 1570–1600.

For certain families, the enjoyment of ecclesiastical benefices offered a partial alternative to the pursuit of magisterial office within the state. Careers in church and state could not be pursued simultaneously, though they might be successive. The laws of the Republic excluded clerics from magisterial office and from seats in legislative councils. Men with an income from ecclesiastical sources were not to invade offices of profit designed for persons with no other means of support,[93] and in any case clerics, who might have gained preferment by currying favour at Rome, were liable to serve two masters. To the Venetians, the pope stood not merely for a distant foreign jurisdiction, but for a neighbouring principality whose territorial ambitions might easily clash with those of the Republic. Hence the advent within the Venetian governing class of antagonistic groups of *papalisti*, families which had formed connections with the Roman curia, and of patriotic anti-clericals, to some extent identified with the party of the *giovani* – who often treated the quest for preferment as tantamount to courting the favours of a foreign prince.[94] For such reasons, no clerk could be a magistrate – but men who had distinguished themselves in the service of the state (especially diplomats) frequently took orders and became bishops at a late stage in their lives. As the Senate officially declared in July 1600, concerning the appointment of the Cavalier Matteo Zane to the patriarchate of Venice, 'we have seen clearly from the past that those who have held secular appointments and offices, and have experience of wordly affairs, have proved to be better prelates than those recruited from libraries and bare monastic cells . . .'[95] The Venetian government may even have tacitly undertaken to back for ecclesiastical preferment persons who had spent large sums on its behalf, and who could then partially recoup their losses.[96] Moreover, the state had an obvious interest in ensuring that its bishops were persons already proven in its service.

The Venetian government had, in theory, lost control over appointments to most bishoprics since the concessions made to appease Pope Julius II in 1510, although it continued after that time to appoint to the patriarchate of Venice and could present the pope with a band of four candidates for the archbishopric of Crete – of whom he would choose one. Nevertheless, episcopal office on the mainland territories was in practice almost completely monopolized by Venetians, and most bishops occupying the major sees were noblemen. Certain family connections in the first half of the sixteenth century, especially the Grimani–Barbaro and Cornaro–Pisani, succeeded in engrossing an excessive amount of ecclesiastical patronage, occasionally provoking jealous reactions on the part of the less fortunate.[97] The famous anti-clericalism of the Venetian Republic stemmed chiefly from families of modest fortune which had established no connections with Rome. For several years, in and after 1528, a majority in the Senate obstructed Clement VII's endeavours to confer the bishopric of Treviso on the pluralistic Cardinal Francesco Pisani, who already held the bishopric of Padua and the archbishopric of Narbonne. Opponents succeeded in delaying his entry to Treviso for about 10 years.[98] The distribution of patronage may have evened out in the second half of the sixteenth century,[99] but the type of the family over-enriched through the accumulation of benefices survived into the seventeenth, in the Cornaro of San Polo. According to an observer in mid-century, 'the house of Cornaro of San Polo, on which has descended the wealth of the doge, of Cardinal Cornaro, and of the bishopric of Padua (now under Federico Cornaro), reckons over 35,000 ducats of annual revenue'.[100] During the 1620s, Doge Giovanni Cornaro and his family had presented a wide target to Renier Zeno, the demagogic leader of the poor nobility, whose bolder proposals included the suggestion that the most lucrative sees, such as Padua, should be left vacant and their revenues be employed to furnish pensions for poor noblemen.[101] Another career priest unpopular with the anti-clericals was Giovanni, second son of Benedetto di Giuseppe Dolfin, a merchant who had suffered heavily during the war of Cyprus.[102] Giovanni Dolfin became ambassador to Rome at the close of the sixteenth century, and rose high in the esteem of Clement VIII: hence his promotion to the bishopric of Vicenza in 1603, and to the College of Cardinals the following year. Certain clans, such as the Cornaro and Dolfin, succeeded in keeping bishoprics in their families for several generations by such devices as resigning to relatives, or appointing them coadjutors with the right of future succession. On the other hand, a prelate of less eminent family, enjoying neither the sympathy of Rome nor the support of the Republic, Alvise da Molin, bishop of Treviso from 1595 to 1604, proved unable even to guarantee benefices within his diocese to members of his own family and the children of his brother-in-law.[103]

It was also possible, with the official support of the state, to seek more modest benefices, to the value of a few hundred ducats a year, for the purpose of repairing the family's fortunes. Indeed, the diarist Priuli recorded in the summer of 1509 that the proliferating Venetian nobility, finding that the Portuguese discovery of oceanic sea-routes to the far East had reduced opportunities for commercial investment, had begun to seek alternative support through the revenues of the church. They had been importuning the Senate to intercede with Rome on their behalf, though the recent misunderstanding with Julius II had discouraged such proceedings. It was still true, however, that 'when a nobleman had many sons, he would make one of them a priest, and all would live under his wing until they reached an age at which they could be provided with other sources of income'.[104]

There is no statistical evidence of the fluctuations in the number of beneficed patrician clergy during the sixteenth century – though they undoubtedly became more numerous in the subsequent era. The proportion of noble clerics to the total number of noblemen aged over twenty-five rose from about 4 per cent in 1615–20 to approximately 12 per cent in 1760.[105] However, there is later evidence to corroborate Priuli's other statements. At intervals, the government would indeed agree to send instructions to the ambassador in Rome to ask the pope for reservations of benefices to a specified annual value for the support of deserving patricians and their families. Such representations were not to be made lightly. A decree of 1491 – re-issued in 1569 – laid down stringent rules of procedure, and stated the principle as follows: 'To discriminate between persons by writing in support of one and passing over another is unworthy of the traditions of our Republic, and gives cause for complaint to many. It also quite frequently happens that the Supreme Pontiff, having acceded to such requests made on our part on behalf of private individuals, raises difficulties over matters of greater delicacy and importance which involve the safety of our state . . .' The law therefore ordained that any proposed letters of commendation must win the support of all members of the *Collegio* and of a five-sixths majority in the Senate before they could be sent to Rome.[106] These stiff requirements were by no means always met.[107]

Patricians of numerous family, state servants of exceptional distinction and victims of the war of Cyprus were among the successful candidates for support. The Senate agreed to assist by this means the children of Marc' Antonio Barbaro, the ambassador-consul arrested in Constantinople at the outbreak of war;[108] those of Angelo Barozzi, imprisoned by the Turks when serving as consul in Alexandria;[109] and those of Lorenzo Tiepolo, killed at the siege of Famagusta.[110] Swarms of dependent children constituted a valid reason for approaching the state, and for the state approaching the pope. So, in 1551, Nicolò Contarini, an advocate-fiscal responsible for defending the interests of the state in litigation with private persons, announced that he already had five boys and three girls, and was certain to sire other children. His preoccupation with government business left no time to make them money through other pursuits, and he therefore wished to make one son a priest and to have him recommended for reservations of benefices to the annual value of 500–600 ducats.[111] At it happened, the pope subsequently announced that he had cancelled all existing reservations, but was prepared to assign benefices to the annual value of 2,500 gold ducats to his nuncio in Venice, to be conferred on candidates nominated by the government.[112]

As Priuli had implied, benefices were often openly sought and obtained in order to provide for the whole family, and not merely for the support of the priest himself. With apparent disinterestedness, Nicolò di Marco Priuli, in 1566, wanted 500 ducats a year for his eldest son, Marco, 'so that he can support himself and perform the duties required of a good servant of the Lord God, and at the same time become equipped to serve Holy Church'.[113] But, in the same year, Giovanni Francesco Salamon lamented that he had pinned all his hopes on his son Nicolò, who, being destined for the priesthood, had died at the age of twenty. A relative, the late Monsignor Andrea Salamon, had renounced in favour of Nicolò a canonry of Treviso, worth over 600 ducats a year, and from this Giovanni Francesco 'had hoped to be able to draw enough income to place in a nunnery some of the seven girls I have at present, and also to support three boys in the best style possible'. But Nicolò's death had extinguished his hopes and the father could only request that benefices to the value of 400–500 ducats per annum might be conferred on one of his other sons.[114] The convenience of the family, rather than the spiritual fitness of the youth concerned, may have been uppermost in the distressed father's mind. In 1615–20, eighty-three out of some 2,000 adult noblemen were in holy orders[115] and were probably spreading the benefits of their preferment to a much larger circle of patricians – to brothers, nephews, fathers, and so on.

In general, the 2,000 members of the Venetian patriciate in the early seventeenth century formed a large, heterogeneous body, identified and separated from the bulk of the *cittadini* by legal and historical distinctions and by the privileges of full citizenship,[116] rather than by conspicuous differences in the extent of their wealth or in the sources from which it derived. They could still, in the eyes of such commentators as Traiano Boccalini, appear as a united and secretive élite, maintaining an ethic of honourable gain through commerce which contrasted with the vain and irrational pursuit of plunder and glory to which the militaristic monarchs and aristocrats of France and Spain were dedicated. Other writers, sympathetic to the Habsburgs, and propagating the 'anti-myth' which stressed the grave internal weaknesses of Venice, saw only the divisions within the patriciate, the oppressions of the government, the development of extremes of wealth and poverty within the ruling class.[117] In fact, the ideal portrait of the Venetian patriciate, as an aristocracy devoted to the selfless service of the state and to the pursuit of gain at sea, had still further parted from reality with the acquisition of a mainland empire and with the erosion by Turkish conquest of the old colonial stepping-stones to the Levant. The ranks of the patriciate comprised many property owners and *rentiers*; consumption loans to private persons were clearly competing with government bonds and commercial investment; and passive speculation on the yield of *dazi* had for a time proved a popular outlet for patrician capital. For many noble Venetian families the pursuit of ecclesiastical preferment offered a welcome supplement to the modest gains made in offices of profit bestowed by the Great Council, and provided an alternative to stare service – though the wealth of the church could sometimes be employed, deliberately or incidentally, as compensation for the heavy charges laid by 'honourable' offices on the purses of those who filled them.

Certain analysts of the sixteenth-century Venetian state, such as Gasparo Contarini, loyal to Aristotelean theory, depicted Venice as a mixed polity which contained monarchic, aristocratic and 'popular' elements.[118] Within this, however, only a restricted group of full citizens, corresponding to the patriciate, came within the pale of the constitution at all or became in any sense political beings. Bodin rejected the concept, and saw Venice as a pure aristocracy.[119] But, granted the assumption that citizenship ought to be the prerogative of a narrow élite perpetuated by hereditary privilege and freed of 'filthy artes, and illiberal occupations',[120] Contarini's views have a certain cogency. Huge differences of wealth separated the large propertied families and successful benefice-hunters from the ranks of the poor nobility, the so-called 'Cypriots, Cretans and Dalmatians', who followed their demagogic leader, Renier Zeno, in 1627–28.[121] During the sixteenth century, a certain number of noblemen was undoubtedly receiving charity in the simplest sense of the term – in the form of alms dispensed by the *Scuola Grande* of San Rocco under the provisions of a charitable trust. Between 1545 and 1589, on average, some twenty-five poor noblemen and women presented themselves, every two years, to receive alms from the *Scuola*. The families of Zorzi, Zane, Da Canal, Pasqualigo, Balbi, Diedo and Bollani were strongly represented, whilst rather less than half the noble clans of Venice produced some paupers, who were compelled to resort to this charity.[122] Within the sphere of the patriciate, the relationship between the established rich and the poor nobility was not unlike the relationship between a narrow aristocracy (or oligarchy) and a plebs which could occasionally, by sheer weight of numbers and votes, make its influence felt – but was not equipped, by wealth or education, to exercise continuous responsibility.

The problem of 'poverty and broken estate in the better sort', as Francis Bacon called it, was certainly not peculiar to the sixteenth and early seventeenth century. But some of the phenomena described in this essay may have accentuated the tendency for rigid and mutually alienated groups of rich and poor to form within the patriciate. The movement towards less hazardous forms of enterprise may have curtailed opportunities for the small investor, who had been well situated when commerce was flourishing, and may also have diminished the chances of rich families losing their wealth rapidly through disasters at sea, or of

2C

poor ones redeeming their fortunes through the high gains of international commerce.[123] The costliness of certain 'honourable' offices may have pared down the wealth of the rich, but may also have created a schism – since it effectively ousted the poor from many influential forms of decision-making. The disproportionate inflation of dowries, itself a result of social climbing, almost certainly caused wealth to be pumped up towards the top of the social scale rather than percolate evenly through it.[124] The practice of denying office to persons indebted to the state, no doubt intended as a stimulus as well as a punishment, could have a paralytic effect on the poor and frustrate the recovery of their fortunes. The development of extremes of wealth and poverty ought, in theory, to have shaken the legendary stability of the Republic – but in fact it survived, free of deep-seated endogenous disturbance, until the surrender to Napoleon in 1797. Even in the late eighteenth century, such leaders of the poor nobility as Carlo Contarini or Giorgio Pisani showed no desire to undermine the aristocratic foundations of the Republic – but clung, instead, to the status which differentiated them from the people.[125]

NOTES

1. On the 'myth of Venice' in general, see Franco Gaeta, 'Alcune considerazioni sul mito di Venezia', *Bibliothèque d'Humanisme et Renaissance*, xxiii (1961). Its influence on Florence is discussed in Renzo Pecchioli, 'Il "mito" di Venezia e la crisi fiorentina intorno al 1500', *Studi Storici*, iii (1962), and in Felix Gilbert, 'The Venetian constitution in Florentine political thought', in *Florentine studies: politics and society in Renaissance Florence*, ed. Nicolai Rubinstein (London, 1968). On its influence in England, see Z. S. Fink, *The classical republicans: an essay in the recovery of a pattern of thought in seventeenth-century England* (Evanston, Illinois, 1945). On the caste-like character of the Venetian nobility, see J. C. Davis, *The decline of the Venetian nobility as a ruling class* (Baltimore, 1962).

2. For example: Charles Yriarte, *La vie d'un patricien de Venise: Marcantonio Barbaro* (Paris, 1874); Giorgio Candeloro, 'Paolo Paruta', *R.S.I.*, ser. V, vol. i (1936); Gaetano Cozzi, *Il Doge Nicolò Contarini: ricerche sul patriziato veneziano agli inizi del Seicento* (Venice–Rome, 1958); Federico Seneca, *Il Doge Leonardo Donà: la sua vita e la sua preparazione politica prima del Dogado* (Padua, 1959); Gaetano Cozzi, 'Federico Contarini: un antiquario veneziano tra Rinascimento e Controriforma', *B.I.S.*, iii (1961).

3. Similar statements, presented by noblemen to the Venetian Senate between about 1590 and 1620, are discussed in my article, 'Service to the Venetian state: aspects of myth and reality in the early seventeenth century', *Studi Secenteschi*, v (1964).

4. Cf. Gino Luzzatto, 'Les activités économiques du patriciat vénitien (Xe–XIVe siècles)'; and 'L'attività commerciale di un patrizio veneziano del Quattrocento', both reprinted in his *Studi di storia economica veneziana* (Padua, 1954); F. C. Lane, *Andrea Barbarigo, merchant of Venice, 1418–1449* (Baltimore, 1944).

5. Cf. Davis, *Decline of the Venetian nobility*, 41–42. Exceptions included the Vendramin, who manufactured soap – see A.S.V., S.T., *filza* 53, 29 June, 1569.

6. Cf. Luzzatto, 'Les activités économiques du patriciat', 139–141; Vittorio Lazzarini, 'Possessi e feudi veneziani nel Ferrarese', in *Miscellanea in onore di Roberto Cessi*, i (Rome, 1958); Giorgio Cracco, *Società e stato nel medioevo veneziano (secoli XII–XIV)* (Florence, 1967) 123 seq.

7. Cf. Girolamo Priuli, *Diarii*, iv, ed. Roberto Cessi (Bologna, 1938), 48 seq. It is

worth comparing Priuli's remarks with the somewhat similar observations made in the early seventeenth century, (a) by a senator of the Donà family in 1610 (speech reproduced in Romanin, vii, 530–535); (b) by the Venetian ambassador in England in 1611, reporting on London opinion of the Venetians (*Calendar of State Papers, Venetian*, xii, doc. no. 383); (c) by the English ambassador in Venice about 1612 (quoted in Cozzi, *Nicolò Contarini*, 15).

8. Paolo Paruta, *Discorsi politici* (Genoa, 1600) 390–391.

9. Cf. Daniele Beltrami, *La penetrazione economica dei veneziani in terraferma. Forze di lavoro e proprietà fondiaria nelle campagne venete dei secoli XVII e XVIII* (Venice–Rome, 1961), and the critical essay by S. J. Woolf, 'Venice and the Terraferma: problems of the change from commercial to landed activities', reprinted in Brian Pullan, ed., *Crisis and change in the Venetian economy in the sixteenth and seventeenth centuries* (London, 1968).

10. For the increase of population in Venice and on the mainland, see Daniele Beltrami, *Storia della popolazione di Venezia dalla fine del secolo XVI alla caduta della Repubblica* (Padua, 1954) 59; Beltrami, *Veneziani in Terraferma*, Appendice al Capitolo I. On the labour force at the arsenal, see Ruggiero Romano, 'Economic aspects of the construction of warships in Venice in the sixteenth century', in Pullan, *Crisis and change*, 70–76; on the woollen industry, Domenico Sella, 'The rise and fall of the Venetian woollen industry', ibid., 109. For evidence of land reclamation, see especially Aldo Stella, 'La crisi economica veneziana della seconda metà del secolo XVI', *A.V.*, lviii (1956), 21 seq.

11. Cf. Woolf, 'Venice and the Terraferma', 194–199.

12. See Maurice Aymard, *Venise, Raguse et le commerce du blé pendant la seconde moitié du XVIe siècle* (Paris, 1966) 109. For evidence of comparable price movements in Bassano over the same period, see Gabriele Lombardini, *Pane e denaro a Bassano: prezzi del grano e politica dell' approvigionamento dei cereali tra il 1501 e il 1799* (Venice, 1963) 58–60. For the general situation described above, see the evidence presented in Brian Pullan, *Rich and Poor in Renaissance Venice: the social institutions of a Catholic state, to 1620* (Oxford, Blackwell–Cambridge, Mass., 1971) pt. ii.

13. S.T., *filza* 72, 31 Dec., 1577.

14. S.T., *filza* 71, 21 May, 1577.

15. S.T., *filza* 64, 16 Sept., 1574.

16. S.T., *filza* 91, 15 June, 1584.

17. S.T., *filza* 105, 11 Feb., 1588. Information given by the genealogist who traced the family tree of the Cornaro dalla Tresca suggests that Pietro did in fact become a canon of Padua, whilst three of the four younger sons pursued the type of career, in the *Quarantie* and in minor legal and fiscal magistracies, normally associated with poor noblemen (A.S.V., Marco Barbaro, *Arbori de' patritii veneti*, iii, 88).

18. S.T., *filza* 57, 18 Aug., 1571.

19. S.T., *filza* 71, 21 May, 1577. For the separate genealogies of Geronimo and Leonardo Giustinian, who came of different branches of the clan, see A.S.V., *Arbori*, vii, pp. 454, 459.

20. S.T., *filza* 82, 21 Mar., 1581; *Arbori*, vi, p. 81.

21. Cf. Romano, 'Construction of warships', 82–83.

22. In the winter of 1568–69, there had been four officially recognized private banks in Venice, those of the Dolfin, of the Pisani and Tiepolo, of the Correr, and of Angelo Sanuto. Of these, the Correr bank had dissolved, paying its creditors in full, by 1570 – see S.T., *filza* 52, 2 Dec., 1568, 24 Jan., 1569; *Cronaca Agostini*, ii (M.C.V., Cicogna Mss. 2853), f. 168v.

23. For the affairs of the Dolfin bank, see S.T., *filza* 55, 9 Aug., 1570.

24. S.T., *filza* 59, 3 June, 1572; *filza* 72, 3 Dec., 1577; *filza* 74, 19 June, 1578.

25. S.T., *filza* 54, 8 Feb., 1570.

26. Fernand Braudel, *La Méditerranée et le monde méditerranéen à l'époque de Philippe II* (new ed., 2 vols., Paris, 1966) ii, 374.

27. See Arturo Magnacavallo, 'Proposta di riforma bancaria del banchiere veneziano Angelo Sanuto (secolo XVI)', *Atti del Congresso Internazionale di Scienze Storiche*, ix (Rome, 1904) 413–417.

28. For the failure of the bank of the procurator Antonio Priuli in 1551, see S.T., *filza* 14, 26 Sept., 1551; reg. 1551/52, ff. 12v–13, 16v–17v, 18v, 81v–82, 101v–111v.

29. Francesco da Molin, *Compendio . . . delle cose che reputerò degne di venerne particolar memoria*, B.M.V., mss. Italiani, Cl. VII, dliii (8812) 123–124: for the affairs of the bank, S.T., *filza* 90, 17 May, 1584; *filza* 91, 2 June, 1584.

30. F. C. Lane, 'Venetian bankers, 1496–1533', reprinted in *Venice and history: the collected papers of Frederic C. Lane* (Baltimore, 1966) 72–73.

31. According to Pisani and Tiepolo, their bank had in 1584 been in existence for about 25 years, and the failure of the Piperari of Mantua had occurred in the third year of its life. Vittore Pisani and Giovanni di Geronimo Tiepolo also refer to the Piperari failure in a petition considered by the Senate early in 1572: S.T., *filza* 58, 5 Jan., 1571.

32. See Sella, 'Venetian woollen industry', cit., 109, for statistical evidence of the recessions in textile production in 1570–1573 and 1576–1577.

33. C. F. Dunbar, 'The Bank of Venice', *Quarterly Journal of Economics*, vi (1892); Gino Luzzatto, 'Les banques publiques de Venise – siècles XVIe–XVIIIe', in *History of the principal public banks*, ed. J. G. Van Dillen (The Hague, 1934).

34. S.T., *filza* 60, 6 Dec., 1572.

35. For the circumstances favourable to the Venetian economy in the late sixteenth century, see Pullan, *Crisis and change*, cit., 8–9, with references.

36. On the Jewish community, cf. Cecil Roth, 'Les Marranes à Venise', *Revue des études juives*, lxxxix (1930) 205–206; Bernard Blumenkranz, 'Les juifs dans le commerce maritime de Venise (1592–1609)', ibid., ser. III, vol. ii (1961). On the growth of a new Flemish community, see Wilfrid Brulez, *Marchands flamands à Venise*, i (1568–1605) (Brussels–Paris, 1965) xii seq.

37. Domenico Sella, 'Crisis and transformation in Venetian trade', in Pullan, *Crisis and change*, 92 seq.

38. Ruggiero Romano, 'La marine marchande vénitienne au XVIe siècle', in *Les sources de l'histoire maritime en Europe, du Moyen Âge au XVIIIe siècle: actes du quatrième colloque international d'histoire maritime*, ed. Michel Mollat (Paris, 1962) 42–43.

39. S.T., *filza* 154, 20 Apr., 1600.

40. S.T., *filza* 179, 26 Aug., 1606. On the activities of Francesco Morosini, cf. the numerous references in Alberto Tenenti, *Piracy and the decline of Venice, 1580–1615* (London, 1967), esp. at 26, 177–178; also Pullan, 'Service to the Venetian state', 114–115.

41. For the general theme, see Tenenti, *Piracy*, passim, and the Introduction to his *Naufrages, corsaires et assurances maritimes à Venise, 1592–1609* (Paris, 1959); for expenditure on the arsenal, Romano, 'Construction of warships', 79 seq. Braudel, *La Méditerranée*, i, 267–268, argues against this thesis by drawing attention to the low rates of insurance on Venetian shipping at the close of the sixteenth century: but the evidence he actually cites suggests that the rate of insurance on ships destined for Syria rose from 5 per cent in 1593–94 to 8–10 per cent in 1607.

42. Braudel, in the same place, points out that the volume of trade handled by the port of Venice in 1725 was in fact somewhat higher than in 1607–10, but the period 1607–10 was one of depression (see Sella, 'Crisis and transformation', 94 seq.) and cannot fairly be used as a standard of measurement in this context. Customs receipts in 1609 were over 30 per cent lower than in the late 1590s. In any case, Braudel is discussing only the question of the absolute decline of the port of Venice, and not that of its relative decline.

43. Cf. *Ragguagli di Parnaso, con la pietra del paragone politico*, ed. Giuseppe Rua and Luigi Firpo (3 vols., Bari, 1910, 1912, 1948) ii, 161–163; Pullan, 'Service to the Venetian state', 100 seq.

44. The *Ufficio dei beni inculti* was a commission of the Senate established in 1556 for the purpose of planning land reclamation and irrigation schemes in the regions of Padua, Vicenza, Verona, Asolo, the Polesine di Rovigo, and Istria (S.T., reg. 1555–56, ff. 136 r–v, 10 Oct., 1556). A *fusta* was a small galley. For the information about the Zeno, see S.T., *filza* 134, 30 Dec., 1594; for their family tree, *Arbori*, vii, 374. Other nobles prepared to swear that they had little or nothing to support them besides house property (often decaying) or land (frequently flooded) were: Vitale di Alvise Miani (S.T., reg. 1534–35, f. 9v, 31 Mar., 1534); Alvise di Luca Vendramin (ibid., f. 187v, 16 Oct., 1535); Giovanni di Paolo da Molin (*filza* 17, 9 May, 1553); Camilla Zane, widow of Pietro di Alessandro Donà (*filza* 34, 20 Sept., 1561); Giovanni Francesco di Alessandro Bondumier (*filza* 74, 7 June, 1578); Marino di Andrea Zorzi (*filza* 132, 14 June, 1594).

45. See Gino Luzzatto, *I prestiti della Repubblica di Venezia (secoli xiii–xv)* (Padua, 1929) Introduzione; Gino Luzzatto, *Storia economica di Venezia dall' XI al XVI secolo* (Venice, 1961) 73–74, 111–116, 140–145; Lane, *Andrea Barbarigo*, 34, 37–38; F. C. Lane, 'The funded debt of the Venetian Republic, 1262–1482', in his *Venice and history*.

46. Priuli, *Diarii*, iv, 15–17. According to his fellow-diarist, Marino Sanuto, *Monte Nuovo* bonds stood at 90 in February, 1509 – see Sanuto, viii, 11, 6 Mar., 1509. The *Monte Nuovo* had been established in 1482, during the war of Ferrara.

47. Cf., for example, the cases of Andrea di Alvise Loredan, 20 Sept., 1535, Vittore di Giorgio Duodo, 25 Sept., 1535, Antonio di Giovanni Venier, 11 Oct., 1535, Marino di Antonio Pisani, 16 Oct., 1535, Alvise di Luca Vendramin, 16 Oct., 1535; all in S.T., reg. 1534–1535, ff. 172v, 175v–176, 182r–v, 186, 187v. There are many other instances.

48. See Lane, *Andrea Barbarigo*, 42.

49. S.T., reg. 1534–1535, f. 9v, 31 Mar., 1534.

50. See Fabio Besta, *Bilanci generali della Repubblica di Venezia* (Venice, 1912) 216–218, doc. 162.

51. 'Antonio of Verona, called Vittore', a blind beggar, was found in 1545 to have savings of 325 ducats, which he had invested in the name of a man of straw, Antonio, a soapmaker at the *Fondaco dei Tedeschi*, in the 14 per cent loan funds in January, 1540: A.S.V., *Provveditori alla Sanità, Notatorio V*, vol. 729, ff. 65v–66, 71v.

52. S.T., *filza* 20, 29 Sept., 1554.

53. Besta, *Bilanci generali*, 250–253; Ugo Corti, 'La francazione del debito pubblico della Repubblica di Venezia proposta da Gian Francesco Priuli', *N.A.V.*, vii (1894); Daniele Beltrami, 'Un ricordo del Priuli intorno al problema dell' ammortamento dei depositi in Zecca, del 1574', *Studi in onore di Armando Sapori*, ii (Milan, 1957); published extracts from the *Historie Venetiane* of Nicolò Contarini in Cozzi, *Nicolò Contarini*, 313–315.

54. Ibid., 316–317; Corti, 'La francazione', 338.

55. Cf. Marco Ferro, *Dizionario del diritto comune e veneto* (10 vols., Venice, 1778–1781) vii, 40–41.

56. S.T., *filza* 69, 15 Mar., 1576.

57. See Pullan, 'Service to the Venetian state', 135–143. For instances of dowries in the late sixteenth century, cf. the cases of Marietta Capello, who married Alvise di Marc' Antonio Michiel in 1583 with a dowry of 10,000 ducats (S.T., *filza* 129, 25 Nov., 1593); of the widow of Silvano Capello, who recovered a dowry of 10,000 ducats on her husband's death, about 1592 (*filza* 129, 26 Nov., 1593, *filza* 163, 24 Aug., 1602, *Arbori*, ii, p. 256); of Elena Vitturi, who married Zaccaria Gabriele, some time between 1585 and 1594, with a dowry of 11,000 ducats (S.T., *filza* 132, 20 Aug., 1594); of Agnese Foscarini, who proposed to recover a dowry of 12,000 ducats on the death of her husband, Leonardo di Francesco da Molin (*filza* 134, 17 Dec., 1594); of the daughter of Michele da Lezze and Lucrezia Contarini who married Marco Barbaro about 1595 with a dowry of 9,000 ducats (S.T., *filza* 148, 29 Sept., 1598). These dowries, evidently given in families of moderate wealth, were all far above the official limit imposed by

the Senate in 1575–76, and the petitioners saw no reason to apologize to the Senate for this fact. I have encountered only one reference to a prosecution for breach of the laws governing dowries – that of the Cavalier Lorenzo Priuli, who was fined in 1555 by the Senate for giving a dowry of 8,500 ducats to his daughter Paola for her marriage to Antonio di Piero Morosini. The legal limit was then 5,000 ducats (S.T., reg. 1555–56, f. 52v, 12 Sept., 1555).

58. S.T., *filza* 116, 25 Sept., 1590. They belonged to the family of Grimani of San Boldo – *Arbori*, i, 141.

59. S.T., *filza* 132, 12 June, 1594; *Arbori*, v, 345. For some other references to *livelli*, see the petitions of Chiara Foscarini, widow of Paolo di Piero Capello (S.T., *filza* 128, 7 Sept., 1593); of Cornelia, Elena and Cecilia, daughters of Alvise di Marc' Antonio Michiel (*filza* 129, 25 Nov., 1593); of the five sons of Silvano Capello (*filza* 129, 26 Nov., 1593); of Piero di Paolo Rimondo (*filza* 148, 29 Sept., 1598); of Antonio, Nicolò and Angelo, sons of Vito Morosini (*filza* 150, 20 Mar., 1599); of Bernardo Zane and his brother the Cavalier Matteo, sons of the Cavalier Procurator Geronimo Zane (*filza* 153, 30 Dec., 1599).

60. S.T., *filza* 55, 9 Aug., 1570. On the one hand, since his own estate was liable for the bank's debts, Dolfin had some incentives to conceal his resources; on the other, he was trying to prove that the bank would have no difficulty in meeting its commitments. These conflicting motives may have cancelled each other out.

61. See Pullan, *Rich and Poor*, cit., pt. iii.

62. Besta, *Bilanci generali*, Introduction, xxxviii seq.

63. S.T., *filza* 47, 23 Sept., 1566; *filza* 67, 29 Sept., 1575.

64. Among those involved in the Moretto affair were Domenico di Giovanni Michiel (S.T., reg. 1534–1535, f. 71, 24 Oct., 1534); Vittore di Giorgio Duodo (ibid., ff. 175v–176, 28 Sept., 1535); Almorò di Giovanni Venier (ibid., ff. 182v–183, 11 Oct., 1535); Marino di Antonio Pisani (ibid., f. 186, 16 Oct., 1535).

65. S.T., *filza* 18, 21 Dec., 1553. Also affected by Bon's misconduct were Francesco di Paolo Malipiero (ibid., *filza* 21, 12 Aug., 1555) and Piero di Alessandro Donà and his widow Camilla Zane (ibid., *filza* 34, 20 Sept., 1561).

66. A.S.V., S.T., reg. 1534–35, f. 175, 23 Sept., 1535. Another noble, Tommaso Donà, said that he had lost heavily on the *dazio dell' insida*, in which he had taken two shares in 1508, as a result of wartime restrictions imposed on the movement of metals and minerals, such as sulphur, tin and lead: ibid., reg, 1536–37, f. 18v, 26 Apr., 1536.

67. E.g. the cases of Andrea di Alvise Loredan (S.T., reg. 1534–35, f. 172v, 20 Sept., 1535); of Fantino di Bernardino Dandolo (ibid., reg. 1536–37, f. 72, 24 Nov., 1536); and of Piero di Marco Marcello (ibid., *filza* 17, 17 Aug., 1553).

68. See, for example, the information on the farming of the anchorage tax in F. C. Lane, 'The merchant marine of the Venetian Republic', *Venice and history*, 154.

69. Giovanni Botero, *Relatione della Republica Venetiana* (Venice, 1605) f. 88.

70. See Pullan, 'Service to the Venetian state', 120 seq.

71. Cf. Sanuto, l, 80, 23 Mar., 1529; S.T., reg. 1550–51, f. 54, 27 Sept., 1550; *filza* 14, 31 Dec., 1551.

72. Gasparo Contarini, *De magistratibus et republica Venetorum libri quinque* (Basel, 1547) 179–182.

73. See Alberto Tenenti, *Cristoforo Da Canal: la marine vénitienne avant Lépante* (Paris, 1962) 182–183; S.T., *filza* 75, 25 Sept., 22 Nov., 1578.

74. S.T., *filza* 67, 29 Sept., 1575.

75. Cf. Contarini, *De magistratibus*, 134–136; Brian Pullan, 'Poverty, charity and the reason of state: some Venetian examples', *B.I.S.*, ii (1960) 30–32, 48–49; Pullan, 'Service to the Venetian state', 121–122.

76. Donato Giannotti, *Libro de la Republica de Vinitiani* (Rome, 1542) ff. 79v–80. For

the use made of such office by a nobleman in the early fifteenth century, see Lane, *Andrea Barbarigo*, 18–19.

77. S.T., *filza* 52, 9 Oct., 1568; *Arbori*, ii, 457, 459 (family of Contarini da San Paternian).

78. S.T., *filza* 148, 29 Sept., 1598.

79. S.T., reg. 1534–35, ff. 175v–176, 186, 25 Sept., 16 Oct., 1535.

80. S.T., reg. 1536–37, f. 63v, 28 Oct., 1536.

81. S.T., *filza* 11, 10 July, 1550.

82. S.T., reg. 1538–39, f. 142, 5 Dec., 1539. Cf. also *filza* 69, 15 Mar., 1576, for the case of Matteo di Marco Cornaro, who asked for his tax assessment to be re-adjusted 'because if I became indebted on account of some unjust tax I would thereby lose the vote, much to my shame and discomfort'.

83. For examples, see S.T., reg. 1540–41, f. 15v, 22 Mar., 1540 (Alvise and Cristoforo Ciuran); reg. 1542–43, f. 36, 2 June, 1542 (Giacomo Morosini); reg. 1543–44, ff. 138v, 174v, 8 Nov., 9 Jan., 1545 (children of Tommaso di Nicolò Permarin); *filza* 11, 31 July, 1550 (Giovanni di Andrea Zane and brothers); reg. 1550–51, f. 54, 27 Sept., 1550, *filza* 14, 31 Dec., 1551 (family of Andrea Ciuran); *filza* 16, 31 Dec., 1552 (family of Alvise di Silvestro Contarini); *filza* 20, 29 Sept., 1554 (children of Piero Malipiero); reg. 1557–58, ff. 171r–v, 26 Nov., 1558 (children of Antonio Bollani); *filza* 75, 25 Sept., 1578 (Hieronimo di Cristoforo Da Canal); *filza* 91, 15 June, 1584 (Andriana, widow of Federico di Gabriele Cornaro).

84. For example: Giuseppe Soranzo, 'Rapporti di San Carlo Borromeo con la Repubblica Veneta', *A.V.*, xxvii (1940) 36–37; Montaigne, *Journal de voyage*, ed. Louis Lautrey (Paris, 1906) 169; Thomas Coryat, *Coryat's Crudities* (2 vols., Glasgow, 1905) i, 415.

85. S.T., reg. 1548–49, ff. 160v–163v, 6, 25 Nov., 1549; reg. 1564–65, ff. 179–180, 13 Nov., 1565.

86. S.T., reg. 1548–49, ff. 170v–171v, 21, 25 Nov., 1549; reg. 1559–60, ff. 62v–63, 29 Sept., 1559.

87. The salary of the *podestà* of Padua was fixed in 1549 at 50 ducats per month, plus further payments classified as *utili*, to the extent of 12 ducats per month. Over a period of eighteen months (the average length of a *reggimento*), the *podestà* might therefore receive just over 1,200 ducats from official sources.

88. S.T., reg. 1550–51, ff. 33v–34, 5 July, 1550.

89. S.T., *filza* 214, 29 June, 1615. The preamble to this decree specifically declares that between 1500 and 1561 the allowances to ambassadors had more than once been increased, 'but in the last 54 years there has been no increase at all'.

90. S.T., reg. 1560–61, f. 78v, 2 June, 1561.

91. S.T., *filza* 34, 29 Sept., 1561; *filza* 36, 7 Mar., 1562. Cf. also similar petitions from Geronimo Soranzo, ambassador in Rome, *filza* 33, 28 June, 1561, *filza* 37, 10 Sept., 1562.

92. S.T., *filza* 132, 18 Aug., 1594; Pullan, 'Service to the Venetian state', 119–120.

93. Bartolomeo Cecchetti, *La Repubblica di Venezia e la Corte di Roma nei rapporti della religione* (2 vols., Venice, 1874) i, 133.

94. Cf. the general theme of Cozzi, *Nicolò Contarini*, cit.

95. Quoted in Gino Benzoni, 'Una controversia tra Roma e Venezia all' inizio del '600: la conferma del Patriarca', *B.I.S.*, iii (1961) 127.

96. Cf. Pullan, 'Service to the Venetian state', 128–129.

97. For a most valuable survey of ecclesiastical patronage in the Venetian Republic, see O. M. T. Logan, *Studies in the religious life of Venice in the sixteenth and early seventeenth centuries: the Venetian clergy and religious orders, 1520–1630*, Ph.D. thesis (Cambridge University, 1967) 178 seq.

98. See Rodolfo Gallo, 'Una famiglia patrizia: i Pisani ed i palazzi di S. Stefano e di Strà', *A.V.*, xxxiv–xxxv (1944) 83–85.

99. Logan, *Religious life*, 178.

100. From an anonymous description of Venice, dated between 1659 and 1665, written either by a Venetian noble or by a representative of a foreign state: printed in P. G. Molmenti, *Curiosità di storia veneziana* (Bologna, 1919) 416–417.

101. See Agostino Zanelli, 'L'elezione del Doge Cornaro, 4 gennaio, 1625', *A.V.*, viii (1930) 4–5; Cozzi, *Nicolò Contarini*, 294.

102. See above, n.13.

103. See Pullan, 'Service to the Venetian state', 129–133.

104. Priuli, *Diarii*, iv, 37–38.

105. I.e. from 83 out of 2,000 in 1615–20 to 166 clergymen in 1760, where the total number of noblemen over 25 was 1,300 in 1775: see Davis, *Decline of the Venetian nobility*, 58, 67.

106. S.T., *filza* 54, 15 Oct., 1569, with a copy of the decree of 1491.

107. See, for example, the cases of Vittore Trevisan, S.T., reg. 1538–39, ff. 129r–v, 29 Sept., 1539, and of Vincenzo di Francesco da Molin, nephew of the dying bishop of Treviso, ibid., *filza* 172, 11 Sept., 1604.

108. S.T., *filza* 55, 13 Apr., 1570.

109. S.T., *filza* 57, 4 Aug., 1571.

110. S.T., *filza* 60, 27 Dec., 1572.

111. S.T., *filza* 14; cf. also the similar case of Francesco di Silvestro Pisani, ibid., *filza* 16, 15 Dec., 1552.

112. S.T., reg. 1553–54, ff. 159r–v, 15 Sept., 1554.

113. S.T., *filza* 47, 29 Sept., 1566.

114. S.T., *filza* 46, 18 May, 1566.

115. Davis, *Decline of the Venetian nobility*, 67.

116. In Venetian terminology, the status of *cittadino* conferred economic privileges and, in certain circumstances, the right to form part of the permanent bureaucracy. It did not bestow the right to hold offices of magisterial rank, which were formally concerned with the making of policy – see for example, Pullan, *Rich and Poor*, pt. i.

117. Cf. Pullan, 'Service to the Venetian state', 95–108.

118. Contarini, *De magistratibus*, 27–28, 32–33; Gaeta, 'Mito di Venezia'. Below, pp. 431 seq.

119. See Elio Gianturco, 'Bodin's conception of the Venetian constitution and his critical rift with Fabio Albergati', *Revue de littérature comparée*, xviii (1938).

120. The phrase is Contarini's (ed. cit., 30–31). I quote from the English translation, *The commonwealth and government of Venice*, by Lewes Lewkenor (London, 1599) 17.

121. Cozzi, *Nicolò Contarini*, 247, n. 1. The term 'Cypriots' doubtless refers to families impoverished through the loss of Cyprus. 'Dalmatians' were almost certainly those who habitually sought governorships and castellanships in the remoter and poorer of the Republic's possessions, on the Dalmatian coastline. 'Cretans' may either have been those who sought office in Crete, or the descendants of noble families who had emigrated to Crete since the early thirteenth century and retained the right to membership of the Great Council in Venice.

122. Pullan, 'Poverty, charity and the reason of state', 37–40. This evidence is drawn from the records of the trust founded in the late 1520s by Maffeo di Bernardo Donà, of the parish of Santa Maria Zobenigo.

123. Cf. Davis, *Decline of the Venetian nobility*, 36 seq.; Lane, *Andrea Barbarigo*.

124. Cf. Pullan, 'Service to the Venetian state', 138.

125. Cf. Romanin, viii, 244 seq.; Roberto Cessi, *Storia della Repubblica di Venezia*, ii (Milan–Messina, 1946), 234 seq.; Carlo Grimaldo, 'Giorgio Pisani perseguitato ed incompreso', *A.V.*, lii (1953).

XIV

PAOLO PRODI

The structure and organization of the church in Renaissance Venice: suggestions for research

---

The religious institutions and the ecclesiastical organization of Venice have hardly begun to be the subject of research in depth: and this is true of the basic, preliminary aspects of the subject. The archives have hardly been touched and even the most recent literature – apart from a few notable exceptions – simply follows the lead given by the burst of scholarly erudition in the *settecento*. If anything, our understanding of Venetian ecclesiastical institutions in their historical setting has taken a step backwards. The responsibility lies with the division – and while especially true of Venice this is typical of the post-Risorgimento mood of Italy as a whole – between a clerical, confessional historiography, increasingly local in scope, and a secular historiography which feels ill at ease in tackling problems arising within the church itself or simply neglects them – while nonetheless claiming to furnish an overall view of Venetian society in the Renaissance. In the absence of the requisite frame of mind no adequate synthesis can at present be presented; all that can be done is to point to the chief problems and cautiously suggest some working hypotheses.

It should also be recognized that the copious research that has been carried out into relations between Rome and Venice, especially for the period of the Interdict, have suffered greatly from the lack of knowledge about Venice's ecclesiastical traditions. On the one hand historians still speak of a lay and thoroughly politicized Venice, of a 'cesarismo veneziano',[1] dedicated to protecting the overriding interests of the state against monastic and ecclesiastical interests; on the other the best known and most solid historical writing has demonstrated the confessional nature of the Venetian state beyond any shadow of doubt, locating the origins of its jurisdictional practice in the theological and spiritual currents of medieval Christianity. But this line of inquiry has not been developed in such a way as to show how far these origins are to be seen as common to Italy or medieval Europe as a whole, or to what extent they should be seen as peculiar to the religious traditions of Venice.[2]

Indeed, we know very little about the religious history of Venice between the Middle Ages and modern times. One important element (though isolated from its social and institutional context) has emerged through a study of the contribution made by a number of outstanding Venetian personalities to Catholic Reform;[3] with masterly insight Giuseppe De Luca has opened up the possibility that the problem of 'piety' might provide a fresh approach to understanding what was happening in Venice, but his imaginative lead has not been followed up with studies based on adequate research.[4] In many of his works Gaetano Cozzi has perceptively called attention to the nature of religious feeling in Venice, but by their nature they do not look to deeper understanding on the ecclesiological or institutional levels.[5] Again, the most recent studies of Sarpi have been more concerned to show the nature of his relationship to northern attitudes (Gallican, Anglican, Reformed) than his links with Venetian tradition.[6]

Leaving the large and complex question of religious feeling on one side and limiting the theme to the internal structure of the church in Venice, the first question we have to face is that of the influence exerted on it by the confessional and sacral tradition of the state. This is important not only as a means of increasing our understanding of the tense relations with Rome and the background of the Interdict, but also to help towards a deeper interpretation of the religious background to modern jurisdictional thought.[7] What, then, is the sacral significance of the state in Venice?

It was Sarpi himself who repeatedly and explicitly referred to the specifically Venetian relationship between lay and religious society, and he put himself forward as the defender of a thousand year old tradition now threatened by the enhanced pretensions of the Counter Reformation papacy. The real innovator in recent times, he wrote to Jacques Leschassier, had been the papacy, which in order to impose its own power had taken advantage of the weakness of the governing class in Venice to pervert its liturgy, its worship and its devotion: 'Imo cum pontificibus haec nobis contentio, quod illi ritus et leges religionis quotidie, mutare volunt, quas nos manere cupimus, ne status reipublicae mutatio consequatur. Nescio an apud vos id tentatum, vel obtentum fuerit, sed apud nos, cum olim dormiremus vel dormitaremus, sacramentorum et sacrae missae ceremonias omnes immutarunt, missales libros veteribus abrogatis novos substituerunt, alios sacros correctionis nomine alterarunt, omnem spem christianorum in aereis imagunculis quibusdam ponendam docuere, doctrinam de peccatis totam novam constituerunt, omniaque ad fulciendam dominationem propriam attemptarunt.'[8]

The exercise of jurisdiction over ecclesiastics did not derive, in Sarpi's eyes, from an abstract principle of political sovereignty, but from a living tradition which was at once political and religious: 'The ground whereby the Republic judges ecclesiastics lies in the fact that it received this power from God at its birth, and that it has exercised it continuously and without interruption whenever it seemed to be to the advantage of the common good, and in the records that survive we see that at all times all kinds of ecclesiastics have been subject to the magistrates on account of any crimes it seemed proper to charge them with. And if popes have passed laws subsequently, the city has not renounced the power given it by God . . .'[9]

It could be shown through countless quotations that Sarpi was profoundly convinced of being not an advocate urging the power of the state but the defender of a tradition that had only been kept alive in Venice, albeit in the face of many difficulties. Venetian diplomacy appeared, in effect, to take the directly contrary line. To rebut the accusations of the curialists and to secure the support of other rulers during the conflict with Rome, it tried to make the situation of the Venetian government and the positions it took up against the Church of Rome appear precisely analogous to those maintained by the other European powers, and to leave one side anything that might make Venice seem to be a special case. It was papal diplomacy that tried to convince the other sovereigns that the case of Venice was altogether individual and anomalous and had nothing in common with other jurisdictional issues: '. . . for the crux is that the Venetians lay hands on ecclesiastical matters and persons as if they were bishops and had the whole spiritual jurisdiction in their hands.'[10]

Thus the rival arguments of Sarpi and papal diplomacy had one thing in common: the assertion that Venice had remained at least to some extent apart from the great historical process which had transformed church–state relations throughout western Europe through the Gregorian reforms of the eleventh century and the Investiture contest. Traditional ecclesiastical historiography had itself accepted this interpretation, underlining 'how different was the Venetians' ecclesiastical discipline from that of all the rest of the Catholic church'.[11] Again, the collections concerned with Venetian ecclesiastical legislation confirmed its unusual nature as well as its long tradition all the more for examining individual decrees in isolation from the dynamic process of development in ecclesiastical and lay society in Venice during the last centuries of the Middle Ages.[12]

It was in fact the sacral character of the state that was most discussed and most sharply challenged in these centuries. Leaving aside the whole important question of the formation of Venetian ecclesiastical institutions and their symbiosis with society and the state through the symbol of St. Mark,[13] it is clear that a lengthy historical process had led to church and state finding themselves drifting apart, laymen and ecclesiastics tending to become distinct and distrustful groups, and the conduct of the internal and foreign policies of the Republic reflecting a changed balance of forces.[14]

Given the present state of our knowledge it is, I think, impossible to chart the stages in this process of disassociation chronologically. It can be said, however, that it accelerated rapidly from the first half of the fifteenth century under the pressure of changing political and ecclesiastical circumstances and that it introduced an irremediable rift in the social fabric of Venice. And it was the presence of that rift that was to render unhistorical the appeal to the ancient and long-cherished traditions of the holy Republic made by Sarpi at the beginning of the seventeenth century.

For ecclesiastical institutions, as in the political field, the key to the changes in the fifteenth and sixteenth centuries has to be looked for in the Venetian conquest of the *terraferma*. The government's need to put trusted men in charge of dioceses and the other chief ecclesiastical offices on the mainland, and the eagerness of the chief patrician families to take advantage of the fat and secure ecclesiastical revenues there, radically changed the Venetian ecclesiastical structure and also Venice's relations with the papacy. As far as relations with Rome were concerned, Venice's entry into the territorial system of Italy and Europe involved the absolute precedence of political themes – liberty and balance of power within Italy, the Turkish menace, freedom of navigation in the Adriatic, frontier and other minor territorial issues – over ecclesiastical ones. At the turn of the sixteenth century nuncios' correspondence was filled almost exclusively with political matters, and these in turn dictated the way in which questions relating to benefices and to jurisdiction were to be settled.[15] Rather than recalling the events and the conflicts which characterized relations between Venice and Rome during the pontificates of Innocent VIII and Alexander VI, it is enough to refer to one well-known episode: the forced acceptance by the Republic of the capitulation imposed by Julius II in February, 1510, after Agnadello. Quite apart from the political clauses, the *Serenissima* had to accept the whole of the papal demands *in spiritualibus*: the renunciation of an appeal to a council, no more taxation of clerics, recognition of the pope's right to collate unchallenged to benefices in Venetian territories.[16]

In the world of ecclesiastical affairs in these two centuries there were, moreover, radical innovations within Catholicism which could not but complicate matters for the church in Venice, though their epicentre lay elsewhere. The strengthened authority of the Renaissance papacy, the dwindling of any possibility of regional differentiation in matters of faith and organization due to the existence of opposed religious blocs after the Reformation, the Counter Reformation drive towards uniformity and centralization: all these were factors which modified and almost completely transformed the Church's local organization which at the end of the Middle Ages was far more complex and diverse than is usually recognized. In the dioceses and ecclesiastical provinces which did form the epicentres of Catholic Reform, like Milan, the renewal imperilled the whole diocesan structure and even its relationship to the papacy.[17] The disciplinary reform advocated by the Council of Trent tended to fracture the links between and the shared values of lay and ecclesiastical society through its desire to rid the former of any worldly interests and to help it concentrate on nothing outside the cure of souls. So this, too, represented a real and deliberate threat to the structure of the medieval church, in which this link, for all the complications and tensions it involved, was by no means something accidental but a valuable part of its overall character.

There can be no doubt that Venetian ecclesiastical institutions saw the inheritance of traditions on which their life in the Middle Ages had been based challenged by this double pressure, political and religious. The result was a serious crisis, made up of many attempts in various sectors of the church to reach a new sense of equilibrium, each of which had its own individual characteristics. It would certainly be interesting to follow each institution as it tried to come to terms with the problems arising from the relationship between lay and ecclesiastical society, from the mid-*quattrocento* to Paul V's interdict. But as we have seen, the preliminary research necessary to forming an opinion is simply lacking; all that can be done here is to try to indicate the fields in which it can be hoped that new research, together with the re-examination of familiar sources, will contribute most to revitalizing the historiographical approaches of today.

I. THE SACRAL ROLE OF THE PRINCE

Sarpi's frequent references to the model of the imperial church of Constantine, Theodosius and Justinian are well known.[18] Are these merely historical allusions or do they correspond to an actual state of feeling in Venice? According to the evidence of the chronicle of Doge Dandolo in the mid-*trecento*, Venice still regarded itself as the true heir to the imperial Church: the doge, *princeps in republica* and *princeps in ecclesia*, a latter-day Constantine, is responsible for the unity and prosperity of both church and state in an equilibrium elsewhere lost in both east and west.[19] A similar attitude appears to have persisted into the second half of the *quattrocento* in patrician consciousness. Exalting the grandeur of Venice's role in the history of religion, Bernardo Giustiniani emphasizes the sacral nature of ducal power, visible in both costume and function; but his pages already bear witness to the hampering presence of papal Rome, a presence which makes Rome and Venice seem to be rivals on the religious rather than the political level.[20] In Gasparo Contarini, in the first decades of the *cinquecento*, the religious concept of the state remains a matter of profound conviction as far as the individual's duty, part political part religious, is concerned,[21] but a grave crisis is foreseen both in theory and practice; only a very thin thread seems to connect his youthful *De officio episcopi* and his *De magistratibus et republica Venetorum*, while from the shadows emerges the spectre of heresy: 'Nulla enim capitalior pestis . . . quam haeresis est, quae fundamenta fidei cum tollat, etiam omnem reipublicae statum subito evertit.'[22] For Paolo Paruta, at the end of the century, the defence of the moral purpose of political life seems an attempt to cover up a division which in reality dominates Venetian society and has put an end to the sacral concept of power.

An understanding of the development of this theme in Venetian consciousness between the *quattro*- and *cinquecento* could be deepened through another approach: through narrative and documentary sources, by looking afresh at the now classic distinction between 'vecchi' and 'giovani' based on generational differences. Even politically sophisticated papal diplomats seem thoroughly surprised, at the outset of their missions to Venice, to find that the supremacy of state over ecclesiastical jurisdiction is not based on 'raison d'état' but on an ecclesiastical and spiritual tradition. Thus Gerolamo Verallo writes in 1536: 'There are arguments every day about ecclesiastical liberties, for they take priests and friars and want to decide between spiritual, civil and criminal procedure, and there is no use in protesting and urging other remedies, for *certe volunt esse domini utriusque gladii* . . . so that if the holy Council or N.S. does not provide, things will not go well, for I am told that it has always been like this.'[23] And here is G. Antonio Facchinetti in 1566: 'I perceive a good intention in the prince and the older men, but they are deceived by a bad tradition and by believing that they can do what in fact they cannot, so it is uphill work to disabuse them skilfully, and a little at a time, as I shall not fail to do.'[24] And there is considerable fascination in watching the 'uphill work' of the nuncio when, as a good canonist, he explained the principle of the separation of powers to the *Collegio* on several occasions.[25] This, too, represents a step in Venice's move towards the secular state. While neither capable of arriving at any definite conclusion nor, at present, wishing to, one can say, I think, that it would be worth while to re-examine the dualism between personal religious feeling and political commitment as exemplified in recent work on the leading protagonists of the Interdict crisis, notably Doge Leonardo Donà.[26] Even if the doge's sacral role has by now run its course, his religion has not yet become a purely personal affair; it is not without significance that Doge Pasquale Cicogna, who died in 1595, was associated with a classic type of miracle: the consecrated host, it was said, was blown into his hands by a gust of wind.[27]

It would also be of considerable interest to examine the evolution in this period of changes in ducal liturgy and ceremony. The problem has been posed for the Middle Ages, from its complex origin to the *trecento*, by Gina Fasoli. From an examination of elections and investitures, from ducal eulogies and insignia and from public ceremonial, she draws the conclusion that while the doge was not considered sacred in any strict sense, neither was he simply seen as a civil magistrate – as witness the ducal *cultus* centred on the church of St. Mark.[28] The history of these ceremonies and this *cultus* is completely unexplored for the fifteenth and sixteenth centuries. It could be significant that the first ducal ceremonies, at least the first that have been preserved, come from the second half of the *cinquecento* and are clearly of Byzantine inspiration.[29] A 'renewal of Byzantinism' has been spoken of, and it can tentatively be suggested that what we see is an attempt to bolster the sacral aspect of ducal authority in the face of the Counter Reformation emphasis on the separation of powers. As for the church of St. Mark ('cappella nostra et libera a servitute Sancte Matris Ecclesie'), the doges as its spiritual heads continued for centuries to control it directly through the *primicerii* they nominated and had powers far greater than those involved in any other form of patronage. It would be interesting to examine the resistance opposed to any attempted interference on the part of the ecclesiastical authorities.[30]

Parallel to studies relating to the doges themselves, it would also be worth investigating the 'de-sacralizing' of the lesser magistracies, from those whose sacral character was emphasized by the circumstances of their origin, like the procurators of St. Mark, to the others. To my mind insufficient attention has been paid to the parallel advanced some decades ago by Kretschmayr between the complete abolition of the *Arengo*'s political significance in 1423 and the exclusion by the Senate in 1494 of any ecclesiastical intervention on the part of the 'spiritual *Arengo*' – the *Arengo* 'der Geistlichkeit' in Kretschmayr's formulation[31] – when matters as important as episcopal elections were debated.

II. THE PATRIARCHATE

The establishment of the patriarchate of Venice in the mid-*quattrocento* is not only important as a chronological landmark but for the light it throws on the transformation of Venetian ecclesiastical institutions as a whole; Nicholas II's bull suppressing the 'realtina' diocese of Castello and the patriarchate of Grado and combining them in the new patriarchate of Venice dates from 8th October, 1451. If we cannot accept the thesis that this represented the first stage in the transformation of St. Mark's from ducal chapel to cathedral church[32] (after all, S. Pietro di Castello remained the cathedral for centuries, the transference only taking place in the Napoleonic period), it is nevertheless clear enough that S. Lorenzo Giustiniani, who passed from the bishopric of Grado to become the first patriarch of Venice, had sufficient force of character to overcome the *Signoria*'s distrust of any increase of power on the part of the patriarchate.[33] Or perhaps it was simply that in changed political and ecclesiastical circumstances the time was ripe for this development; in any case, the transference of the seat of the patriarchate to within the city allowed closer relations with and a more ready surveillance of it. It is an event which deserves investigation in all its aspects.

The relationship between the new patriarchate of Venice and the Venetian political class is still on open subject, even though its general outlines, together with the careers of a few individuals, have been looked at.[34] Its development cannot be treated in straightforward linear terms, but certain strands can be brought together. The method of elections did not change, remaining in the hands of the Senate. Though naturally all the patriarchs came from the patrician class there were no great struggles or rivalries between the leading families; the revenues from the patriarchal treasury were too small. As a result, it should be all the easier to determine the religious criteria which underlay the choice of candidates. During the second half of the *quattrocento* and in the early *cinquecento* the choice typically lay among members of the long established monastic orders associated with Venice itself. The break came in this apparently tranquil tradition with the patriarch Girolamo Querini (1524–1554), a Dominican. How far this was due to the difficult nature of his own character, to his upbringing as a mendicant friar or to his close connection with certain aspects of Catholic

Reform, especially through Pietro Carafa, cannot be determined with any confidence at present. Certainly the breach affected all fronts: relations between the patriarch and lesser clergy (especially, as we shall see, through the laws affecting the election of parish priests), and between patriarch and government; also relations between patriarchs and the Holy See became increasingly complex, particularly through their sense of rivalry with papal nuncios.[35] In reaction to Querini's term of office, subsequent elections up to 1619 resulted in the promotion to the patriarchate of candidates all of whom were laymen – with one conspicuous exception in the person of the Benedictine Giovanni Trevisan (1559–1590). But what does this mean? It certainly cannot be reduced to such simple terms as the subordination of the church to the state or to a growing sense of worldliness among the higher prelacy such as can be observed in other countries. It was a political response to the danger presented by the centralizing tendency of the Counter Reformation, but it also amounted to a choice made on religious grounds. This was explained in a speech by Leonardo Donà, who defended it 'by pointing out that he had read in St. John Chrysostom that it was often more useful to the Church to have a bishop chosen from among the advisers of a state than from monasteries or seminaries'.[36]

The *Signoria* clearly had a better chance of reaching an understanding with patriarchs chosen from the magistracies of state, even if the patriarch most soundly abused for collaboration with the government was in fact the Benedictine Trevisan, who was criticized very severely by Borromeo when he paid a visit to Venice in 1580[37] and who appears in the apostolic visitation of the following year almost in the guise of an accused offender.[38] The situation seemed intolerable to Rome and the attack was fully pressed home in the first years of the *seicento* when Clement VIII and Paul V made an examination in canon law and theology before a congregation of cardinals in Rome a condition of the elections of the patriarchs Matteo Zane (1600–1605) and Francesco Vendramin (1605–1619) being ratified.[39] Venice saved diplomatic face by avoiding the formal procedure of the examination but was the net loser nevertheless. To see how far matters had gone since the middle of the *quattrocento* it is only necessary to look again at the words with which Pius II invited the patriarch-elect Andrea Bondumier, who was reluctant to accept the heavy responsibility, to Rome in 1460: 'quia tum dignitas haec patriarchalis est magna, et qui eam accipit recognoscere Sedem Apostolicam debet, et ab illa cognosci: contentamur et in virtute sanctae oboendientiae tibi mandamus ut sine mora ad nos venias . . .'[40]

The turning point in this move to restore papal rights can be seen as the bull in which Pius IV, on 15th September, 1561, renewed the traditional right of the Republic to propose a candidate for the patriarchate: the bull put this in the form of a concession of patronage rights but proclaimed the Holy See's exclusive right to nomination. The exhumation of this bull in the context of post-Risorgimento Italy has led to the problem of the *Signoria*'s role as patron of the patriarchate being seen in a false light.[41] Sarpi was right to have strongly advised the government not to base the defence of their patronage rights on the papal concession of Pius IV.[42]

III. The End of the Patriarchal Rite and Changes in Worship

This aspect of our subject is shrouded in darkness. Nothing is known for sure about its origins, its special character, the close connection which must have existed between the rites of the patriarchates of Grado and Aquileia, or the possibility of Byzantine influence. What little material has been collected was put together by the antiquarian scholars of a past age.[43] But we have a point of entrance to this topic in the brief by which on 12th December, 1456 (a date interesting, too, in the wider context of the other subjects whose development we have looked at) Calixtus III granted the patriarch of Venice permission to celebrate in the cathedral according to Roman practice instead of the ancient patriarchal rite, 'non ostante quod secundum consuetudinem olim patriarchalis ecclesiae Gradensis hec omnia facere consueveritis quibuscumque'.[44]

The crisis confronting the rite seems already to have begun in the late *trecento*; at any rate, after Callixtus III's decree the decline was rapid, thanks to the uniformity with which other churches were following the usage of the cathedral. Thus the move set afoot by Pius V to secure uniformity among liturgical books encountered no resistance in Venice – at least so far as is known – notwithstanding the survival of a few idiosyncratic ceremonies and the persistence of the old rite in the ducal basilica of St. Mark's.[45]

Relatively more is known about the cult of the saints, which in medieval Venice presented a number of unusual features: one has only to think of the number of churches dedicated to Old Testament saints, to prophets and to saints of Byzantine origin.[46] Completely unexplored, in contrast, is the whole question of the emergence in the fifteenth and sixteenth centuries of new dedications and new forms of worship, especially their connection with the spread of the religious orders and confraternities, and with the influence of Counter Reformation ideas.

IV. Bishoprics and the Chief Benefices in the *Dominio*

We have already noted that the conquest of the *terraferma* in the first decades of the *quattrocento* brought about an immediate and radical transformation in the whole Venetian ecclesiastical structure because of the political need to entrust keys posts to trustworthy subjects of the Republic, and because of the way in which the leading patrician families of Venice sought after the chief benefices on the mainland. The replacement of Jacopo Rossi with Angelo Barbarigo on the bishop's throne in Verona in 1405 is an example of a process that recurred over and over again without any hesitating or breach in its continuity.[47] The method of nominating to bishoprics which had already been in force in Venice from the *trecento* – that is, by presenting to Rome the candidate who had received the greatest number of votes during the senatorial *proba* – was gradually extended to the dioceses that were absorbed into the *Dominio*.[48] In spite of every legislative precaution, however, prohibiting personal intervention in negotiations with Rome, forbidding members of the leading magistracies to accept benefices, excluding ecclesiastical office holders from councils and offices (through decrees that were repeated in a crescendo throughout the *quattrocento*)[49] – nothing could prevent the Venetian situation with regard to benefices from coming to resemble that already widespread throughout the west. Ecclesiastical benefices, that is, were treated as part of a family's patrimony; they were transferred from one member of a patrician family to another through the technique of anticipatory resignations and by means of deals ('composizioni') made with the Roman *curia*.

Another interesting inquiry would be to examine in connection with the choice of bishops and prelates the restrictions Venice had to accept in the agreement with Julius II after Agnadello: renouncing the election of bishops by the Senate and recognizing free papal collation to major benefices. This clearly represented another stage in the decline of Venetian tradition. Venice, like other Catholic powers, succeeded during the next decades in sustaining its own political requirements;[50] throughout the *cinquecento* almost all bishops and prelates in the *Dominio* were Venetian nobles[51] and the few exceptions – the best known being Giberti in Verona[52] and Ormaneto in Padua[53] because of their outstanding personalities and the unusual political circumstances in which they were nominated – only proved the rule. But if the impression we are left with on the political and economic planes is one of an underlying continuity before and after the agreement with Julius, on the more purely religious plane the sacrifice of public discussion and senatorial voting must have involved a real break with tradition.

In the following decades, and especially when the papacy was on the defensive, the repeated efforts to restore the original method of nomination reveal a nostalgia which must have been deeply rooted in public consciousness. Evidence of this can be seen in the decision taken by the Senate on 17th August, 1527, with reference to the bishopric of Treviso: 'Anciently it was the custom of our most wise ancestors to nominate the bishops of our cities and territories in our Senate and then to seek conformation for this nomination from the pope; a thing certainly done with great consideration as we can see from the fact that the worthy quality of the pastors nominated produced excellent and exemplary behaviour among both clerics and laity, with not only the conservation of ecclesiastical properties but also their increase. And this praiseworthy custom endured until the time of Pope Julius . . .'[54]

This was the feeling so strongly expressed in the speeches in which the senator Alvise Mocenigo denounced the collusion with Rome of the influential Pisani family, who had nothing but the accumulation of benefices in their minds: 'vol privar questo Stado non fazi mai nomination di alcun, che quando i se feva erano santi.'[55] But this referred to a point of view which belonged to the past. It was entirely peripheral to the current attack centred on abuses and disciplinary reform that Catholic Reform was then getting under way.

V. The Clergy of the City

As we have seen, the formation of a clerical world that constituted a class existing outside the ordinary social and political scene took place in Venice in the last centuries of the Middle Ages, that is, with a certain lag behind other western nations and with characteristics of its own. This happened under the impact of two contrary pressures: the clergy tried to gain the privileged status that obtained elsewhere and the state intervened with continuous and intricate legislation designed to moderate their political and economic role. We have also noted the need to study the acceleration of this tendency after Venice's entry into the political and territorial play of forces in Italy and the ecclesiastical organization of the *terraferma*. It would also be worth looking carefully into the support which the papacy, for political reasons, extended from time to time to the Venetian government to help them keep a tight rein on their clergy.[56] But leaving aside the themes relating to clerical immunity and ecclesiastical property[57] to which most attention has been paid – because the Interdict crisis arose from them – I will confine myself to suggesting the outstanding problems which arose from the internal organization of the clergy in Venice.

In the fifteenth and sixteenth centuries the relationship between the four mother churches ('matrici') and the others had disappeared, or had at least dwindled into a purely honorific recognition of their primacy. The core of religious life consisted in about seventy parishes administered by parish priests elected by their own parishioners, almost all of whom were assisted by a large number of clerics called 'titolari' (because they were bound to a church through a *titolo* or title) organized in chapters or collegiate churches.[58] Towards the end of the *seicento* Stefano Cosmi noted in Venice two 'ecclesiastical prerogatives which do not obtain anywhere else in the Catholic world'; the first was the institution of the patriarchate, 'the other special excellence in our theme is that in this glorious city ecclesiastical benefices are not conferred by the Roman datary or by the will of the patriarchs but by the freely expressed wish of parishioners, that is, the parish district, the local chapters and the *titolari* of the churches. These, Most Serene Prince, are the incomparable ornaments, the most exceptional privileges of this our wonderful principate . . .'[59]

Ignoring the hyperbole – natural enough, in any case, in the work's dedication to the doge – the Venetian tradition does clearly emerge as something dissimilar from the patronal role of other ecclesiastical communities in the medieval west and nearer to the custom of the first centuries of Christianity, when not only the clergy but the whole community was responsible for appointment to and the supervision of ecclesiastical offices.[60] The organized participation of laymen in the administration of church property was by no means over by the late thirteenth century, the local inhabitants having to approve the priest's desire to sell any ecclesiastical land.[61] But the history of the structure of the Venetian church at this local level is still unwritten; what I have said is enough to suggest that Venetian state legislation concerning ecclesiastics and their property should not be judged without first grasping the factors that gave the relationships between church and society their individual character.

This system came under discussion in the first decades of the *cinquecento* thanks to the patriarch Antonio Contarini and, far more, to Gerolamo Querini, whose attempts to secure the nomination of parish priests himself, and to abolish the electoral rights of parishioners, became the chief battleground of his episcopate.[62] Despite abuses and the muddle into which voting procedures had got, the tradition was too strong to be eradicated. The Venetian government vigorously upheld the opposition raised by the parishioners and obtained the support of Leo X and Clement XII. The latter issued a bull which became famous as the 'bolla Clementina': 'Ad b. Petri sedem' of 7th February, 1526 – though it was not published until 1530. This recognized and regularized the electoral system based on parishioners and placed it under the supervision of an office created for this purpose, that of the 'conservatore della bolla Clementina' which was to ensure that elections were carried out legally and keep an eye on such consequential features as investigating the qualifications of candidates and their confirmation by the ordinary or the authorities in Rome.[63]

This was not the only question over which the overhaul of clerical discipline promoted by Catholic Reform had to come to terms with Venetian tradition. I will draw attention to but one more example. We have seen that parish churches were for the most part collegiate. In these the clergy who were appointed to serve a church under the old patriarchal regulations advanced from lesser to greater 'titoli' not according to nominations imposed from outside but to decisions taken by the chapter on the score of seniority. In spite of the disquiet this aroused in the nuncios[64] this practice not only survived but gained strength through the concession granted Venice by Sixtus V to ordain clergy simply on the grounds of the service they had rendered their church, a concession which departed from one of the most rigid Tridentine disciplinary norms – set by canon 2 of session xxi – which forbade the ordination of clergy who were not already in possession of a benefice or adequate personal means.[65]

Another vital but unexamined problem (and which can therefore only be barely mentioned here) concerns the evolution of the clerical 'congregazioni' in the fifteenth and sixteenth centuries which looked after the most purely corporative interests of the Venetian clergy. In 1434 the nine congregations were powerful enough to elect representatives of the Venetian clergy to attend the Council of Basel.[66] After that we only know something about the arbitral functions assumed by the patriarchs in their dealings with them and the attempt made by the patriarchs at the end of the *cinquecento* to regulate and control them: an attempt foiled after an appeal to the Roman congregation of the Council.[67]

Lastly, we come to the professional and cultural training of the clergy. Traditionally this was based on parochial schools supplemented early in the *cinquecento* by the better organized schools of the *sestieri*. All these schools remained very much alive until the end of the century, in marked contrast to their fortunes in other dioceses, where the standing of the original schools attached to cathedrals collapsed under the challenge of the seminaries which the Tridentine reforms brought into being; in Venice these new institutions developed slowly and painfully.[68] This too is a comparative study which would help to indicate what was specifically Venetian in the professional and cultural preparation of the clergy – relative, that is, to the progressive detachment of the clergy from society at large which the establishment of seminaries did much to foster. More than this: Venice also poses a specific problem through the foundation of two seminaries, a ducal one, attached to St. Mark's, founded before a patriarchal seminary was established, but which nevertheless found it difficult to make headway against the greater attraction of the religious orders. But this, too, is an as yet unwritten story.[69]

VI. THE REGULAR CLERGY

For centuries Venice had nurtured monasteries of its own; what the spread of the mendicant orders from the late thirteenth century meant to its religious structure and to Venetian society as a whole, is still unclear.[70] Signs of conflict – in contrast, that is, to the mood of the previous regime, which though open to spiritual influences from various sources was based on the city and its local churches – were only too open in the fifteenth and sixteenth centuries and became, as is well known, one of the chief elements in church-state tension. It was not simply a question of a quantitative, numerical increase in the power and wealth of the religious orders which forced the state to intervene constantly and firmly in order to protect the purely local structure: a more important issue was the centralizing pressure which forced the old orders to respond to demands for tautened discipline and which, urged still further by the new orders of the Tridentine era, led to the creation of a large body which kept apart from the native ecclesiastical structure and from Venetian society. It was these two centuries which saw the creation of the 'machine' whose destruction only began with the suppression decrees of 1769: '. . . the huge machine of monasticism in the Venetian possessions, a formidable moral bloc which – though its components were often at loggerheads – always constituted a solid and united opposition to the secular power.'[72]

Though the struggle had not yet come into the open in the period with which we are dealing, the state was alert to the danger inherent in this extraneous body and tried to neutralize it. On the one hand it continued its attempt to dominate it, to keep it within the traditional pattern by supporting the autonomy of the Venetian monasteries and insisting that all the most influential positions should be held by loyal subjects of the Republic;[73] on the other, the state itself took disciplinary reform in hand with the creation of a 'Magistrato sopra i monasteri' for this purpose. This emerged as a temporary organ in 1521 and then, after painful negotiations with the patriarchate and Rome, became permanent and steadily more powerful in its oversight of the economic life of monasteries and convents.[74]

There was also the question of the corruption and the reform of convents.[75] Here it is enough to suggest that this too should be seen in the same perspective. The conflict did not arise simply from the desire of the aristocracy to solve the problem posed by unmarried women; that was part of the question, but it merged into the wider aim of abolishing all compromise situations, whether 'social' convents or near-hostels – situations particularly encouraged by the largely undifferentiated socio–ecclesiastical structure of medieval Venice. The campaign of Pius V to impose strictly enclosed convents represented for Venice, then, an important step on the road towards a breach between secular and religious life, even if it did no more than take advantage of the Venetian church's own inability to resolve the problems raised by the issue of Reform.

VII. Confraternities, Pious Foundations and Welfare Institutions

This is a complex issue, and before investigating the widely differing significance of Venetian confraternities or *scuole* they must be differentiated and listed (a task that has so far been hardly begun)[76] bearing in mind the frame of reference suggested by Giuseppe Alberigo in his inquiry into the gradual decline in local support to the confraternities in the Tridentine period,[77] and relating this information to a social context characterized by the progressive hardening and self-assertion of the aristocracy as the dominant class.

As for the symbiosis of civic and religious ideals and practice in the organization of pious foundations and welfare institutions, we are fortunate in that the problem was lucidly outlined a few years ago by Brian Pullan and that he has recently published an analysis in depth.[78]

VIII. Repression and Tolerance. The Greek Orthodox Minority

The *Signoria*'s attack on heresy and especially on the creeping infection of Lutheranism is not an essential part of the study of ecclesiastical institutions even if, as we have seen, it obviously had an important indirect effect; thus the persistent attempt of the Venetian government to control, if not actually to take over the inquisitorial machine – whether the motives were religious or political – has been taken note of. Heresy threatened the spiritual and moral roots of civic life.[79] Less notice, if any, has been taken of the background to the confrontation with heresy itself: the unexplored territory of day to day repression and control over devotion and public morality. Gaetano Cozzi has shown how profitably work in this area can add new dimensions to our understanding, especially through his research into the 'Esecutori contro la Bestemmia', a magistracy set up in 1537 whose functions slowly broadened during the following decades, covering gambling, improper behaviour in religious institutions, violations of the censorship laws, and so forth.[80]

Directly concerning religious institutions were the motives behind and the consequences that followed from the Republic's attitude towards the Greek

Orthodox population of the Levant and the large Greek colony in Venice itself. The most up to date research agrees that in the late Middle Ages the Republic, for political reasons, took a tolerant stance in its dealings with the Orthodox Church in the conquered parts of 'Romania'. If it introduced a Latin hierarchy and tried to break the authority of the Greek episcopate, it nevertheless allowed a remarkable degree of autonomy to the Orthodox clergy, even resisting pressures from Rome and the mendicant orders.[81] The situation became much more complicated after the middle of the *quattrocento* and the Council of Florence, with the papacy moving towards the creation of a Uniate, Greek Catholic hierarchy in open conflict with the Orthodox hierarchy which rejected the decree of union. Venice adopted a cautious and guarded attitude with respect to the Uniate movement, though forced to support it because of the political consequences of Ottoman expansion.[82] We know little about the religious situation in the Levant in the sixteenth century, but Venice's position does not seem to have changed; even after the Council of Trent had concluded its meetings papal diplomacy laboured in vain to detach the Republic from its attitude of toleration.[83]

More can be learned from the history of the Greek colony in Venice itself, and its influence on the city's life in the second half of the *quattrocento* and during the *cinquecento* has been studied in depth. The community developed a liturgical autonomy as a result of the ambiguities left unresolved by the Council of Florence and even obtained papal protection for the construction of its own church. Thereafter, the *Signoria* not only protected the liturgical but also the ecclesiastical autonomy of the Greek community, assuring contacts with the patriarchate of Constantinople in spite of pressure from the popes of the Counter Reformation.[84]

'Hi christiani vere sunt, nos vero semipagani', the Venetian Camaldolensian monks Querini and Giustiniani had written in 1513 in their well known *Libellus ad Leonem X*. This comparison between the religious zeal of catholics and orthodox[85] was no mere rhetoric. It was based on the co-existence which Venice permitted during the Renaissance in the capital and in the Levant, a co-existence which was not only operative in the political and economic fields but continued to characterize Venetian religious life[86] even in the midst of the crisis of the sixteenth century.

These, then, are the outlines (others could, of course, be added) of the chief areas where further investigation is required. No conclusion can be reached; all we can do after this inquiry is to look again at the problems posed at the beginning of this survey. The state of affairs in Venice shows how various and distinctive the local churches of Europe were at the beginning of the modern period. Certainly Venetian ecclesiastical institutions had a clearly defined character of their own whose roots lay in a venerable tradition; it is a matter of habits inherent in the nature of an aristocratic Republic whose structure tended naturally to conserve institutional features which came to drop away from other contemporary polities – or did this personality correspond to a specific feeling about the management of ecclesiastical affairs which sprang from Venice's unique position as a bridge between East and West? It is still an open question. What is certain is that this tradition lost some of its hold in the period with which we are concerned under the pressure of two opposed tendencies: the political victory of Counter Reformation ideas and the progressive laicization of the modern state.

The resulting crisis is seen most starkly not in the conflict over the Interdict – that is more in the nature of a solemn epilogue – but in the imposition of the Tridentine disciplinary reforms which culminated in the apostolic visitation of 1581.[87] The opposition made to the entrance of the visitors and to their activities did not simply arise from political or social considerations of the moment, but was based on the fact that this constituted an innovation the like of which had never been encountered, an innovation which threatened the autonomy of the Venetian church. There is no need for such a visitation, said the patriarch Giovanni Trevisan, because the patriarch himself lives in daily touch with the communities under his care, 'and the ordinaries function well if they are left alone to carry out their duties'.[88] No matter that a diplomatic compromise was reached or that the visitor was in fact Agostino Valier, bishop of Verona and a loyal subject of the Republic; the fusion between the ecclesiastical body and Venetian society as a whole was not merely imperilled in a particular aspect here and another there as had been the case in the past, but totally. It was a situation in which a deterioration in the international political scene or a hardening of the attitudes of the two parties concerned would suffice to change the position from one of mutual sparring to one of open conflict.

The continual recourse we find Sarpi having to the self-sufficiency of local churches as the only possible meeting point between the eschatological and spiritual reality of the church and its human and social incarnation,[89] certainly arose in his case from his practical experience of the Venetian tradition, though by then it sounded like the evocation of a vanished past. After the breach caused by the Interdict Tridentine reform was to take up its mission of spiritual and disciplinary renewal in Venice through the work of zealous pastors, but, as the historian Sandi wrote in the middle of the eighteenth century, 'this period is apparently empty of facts or episodes relating to ecclesiastical life which had any relation to the secular policies of the Republic'.[90]

NOTES

1. See G. Benzoni's cogent remarks in *Studi Veneziani*, viii (1966) 560–578, arising from his review of A. Stella, *Chiesa e stato nelle relazioni dei nunzi pontifici a Venezia. Ricerche sul giurisdizionalismo veneziano dal XVI al XVIII secolo* (Città del Vaticano, 1964). On the idea and scope of 'cesarismo', which is still discussed in relatively uncritical terms see e.g. A. Niero, *I patriarchi di Venezia. Da Lorenzo Giustiniani ai nostri giorni* (Venice, 1961) 235 – it is well worth looking at the revisionist interpretation offered by D. J. Geanakoplos in *Byzantine East and Latin West: two worlds of Christendom in Middle Ages and Renaissance* (Oxford, 1966) 55–83.

2. Among many works I restrict myself to citing L. Salvatorelli, 'Venezia, Paolo V e fra Paolo Sarpi' in *La civiltà veneziana nell' età barocca* (Florence, 1959) 67–95; W. J. Bouwsma, *Venice and the defense of republican liberty* (Berkeley–Los Angeles, 1968) esp. 71–83.

3. Among the numerous contributions by H. Jedin, see 'Gasparo Contarini e il contributo veneziano alla riforma cattolica' in *La civiltà veneziana del Rinascimento* (Florence, 1958) 103–124. Interesting, too, is C. Dionisotti's reference to the link between the religious feeling of G. Contarini and the Venetian tradition, *Geografia e storia della letteratura italiana* (Turin, 1967) 172. J. B. Ross, 'The emergence of Gasparo Contarini. A bibliographical essay', *Church History*, XIL (1972) 22–45.

4. G. De Luca, *Letteratura di pietà a Venezia dal '300 al '600* (Florence, 1963). And see the lengthy review of I. Cervelli, 'Storiografia e problemi intorno alla vita religiosa e spirituale a Venezia nella prima metà del '500', in *Studi Veneziani*, viii (1966) 447–476.

5. In particular, G. Cozzi, *Il doge Nicolò Contarini. Ricerche sul patriziato veneziano agli inizi del seicento* (Venice–Rome, 1958) 28–41; Idem, 'Cultura, politica e religione nella "pubblica storiografia" veneziana del '500' in *B.I.S.* (1963–64) 215–294.

6. A model, however, of this approach is B. Ulianich's long introduction to the *Lettere ai gallicani* (Wiesbaden, 1961).

7. The problem has been raised in C. A. Jemolo, *Stato e Chiesa negli scrittori italiani del Seicento e del Settecento* (Turin 1914) introduction. On the ideology of the sacral character of the Venetian state, even during the most critical period of the religious conflict, see S. Caponetto,' B. Spadafora e la riforma protestante in Sicilia nel sec. XVI', *Rinascimento*, VII (1956) 304–5.

8. Dated 12 May, 1609, in Ulianich, op. cit., 42, n. 21.

9. *Istoria dell' interdetto e altri scritti editi ed inediti*, ed. M. D. Busnelli and G. Gambarin, II (Bari, 1940) 132.

10. Cardinal Borghese to the *nunzio* in Savoy, 16 Dec., 1605, in *Carlo Emanuele I e la contesa fra la repubblica veneta e Paolo V (1605–1607)*, ed. C. de Magistris (Venice, 1906) 7.

11. G. Cappelletti, *Le chiese d'Italia dalla loro origine sino ai nostri giorni* (Venice, 1855) 89.

12. The fullest survey of Venetian ecclesiastical legislation is still to be found in E. Friedberg, *Die Grenzen zwischen Staat und Kirche und die Garantien gegen deren Verletzung* (Tübingen, 1872) 688–704 and E. Friedberg and F. Ruffini, *Trattato di diritto ecclesiastico cattolico ed evangelico* (Turin, 1893) 99–103. The collection of references and documents in B. Cecchetti, *La repubblica di Venezia e la corte di Roma nei rapporti della religione*, 2 vols. (Venice, 1874), is still valuable and could be made the basis of a re-examination of the juridical position on strictly historical lines.

13. P. Kehr, 'Rom und Venedig bis zur XI Jahrhundert' in *Quellen und Forschungen aus italienischen Archiven und Bibliotheken*, xix (1927) 1–180. H. C. Peyer, *Stadt und Stadtpatron im mittelalterlichen Italien* (Zurich, 1955) 8–24 and 63–68. G. Fasoli, 'Nascita di un mito' in *Studi storici in onore di G. Volpe* (Florence, 1958) i, 444–479. The information given in O. Aureggi Ariatta, 'Influssi delle relazioni col Levante sul diritto ecclesiastico della repubblica veneta', in *Archivio Storico Lombardo*, ser. IX, vii (1968) 214–223 would be well worth following up and elaborating.

14. G. Cracco, *Società e stato nel medioevo veneziano* (Florence, 1967) 164–167.

15. F. Gaeta, 'Origine e sviluppo della rappresentanza stabile pontificia in Venezia (1485–1533)', *Annuario dell' Istituto storico italiano per l'età moderna e contemporanea*, ix–x (1957–58) 3–282.

16. F. Seneca, *Venezia e papa Giulio II* (Padua, 1962) 146.

17. P. Prodi, 'Charles Borromée, archevêque de Milan, et la papauté', *Revue d'histoire ecclésiastique*, lxii (1967) 379–411; by the same author 'The application of the Tridentine decrees: the organization of the diocese of Bologna during the episcopate of Cardinal Gabriele Paleotti' in *The late Italian Renaissance, 1525–1630*, ed. E. Cochrane (London, 1970) 226–243.

18. Ulianich, op. cit., p. cxli.

19. Cracco, op. cit., 399–435.

20. Cf. H. P. Labalme, *Bernardo Giustiniani. A Venetian of the Quattrocento* (Rome, 1969) 296. It may have been Giustiniani whom F. Sansovino had in mind a century later when emphasizing the similarity between the ducal *corno* and the episcopal mitre: '. . . in segno, cred'io, ch'egli fosse quasi un Principe che partecipasse a un certo modo del Sacro', *Venetia città nobilissima et singolare* (Venice, 1604) 471.

21. F. Gilbert, 'Religion and politics in the thought of Gasparo Contarini', in *Action and conviction in early modern Europe*, ed. T. K. Rabb and J. E. Seigel (Princeton, 1969) 90–116.

22. G. Contarini, *Opera* (Paris, 1571, repr. Farnborough, 1968) 425. These hasty and general remarks should be read against the searching analysis of G. Fragnito, 'Cultura umanistica e riforma religiosa: il "De officio viri boni ac probi episcopi" di Gasparo Contarini', *Studi Veneziani*, ii (1969) 75–189.

23. *Nunziature di Venezia*, ed. F. Gaeta, ii (Rome, 1960) 68, to Ambrogio Recalcati, 13–14 July, 1536; Verallo writes to him again some months later, on 8 Dec., 1536 (ibid., 96): '. . . ma V. S. ha da sapere, si come più volte ancora ho scritto, che questa Signoria vole essere alle volte et papa et principe, né però temeno scomuniche né minacce quando non li va de fantasia.'

24. *Nunziature di Venezia*, ed. A. Stella, viii (Rome, 1963) 48, to Michele Bonelli, 21 May, 1566.

25. Besides the letter quoted in the previous note, see ibid., 511, the same to the same, 16 Mar., 1569: '. . . onde tutti si guardorno l'un l'altro, et qui soggiunsi che le potestà temporali et spirituali erano distinte et che non toccava a S. Ser. tà a intromettersi in simili materie . . .'

26. F. Seneca, *Il doge Leonardo Donà. La sua vita e la sua preparazione politica prima del dogato* (Padua, 1969) e.g. 166, 194.

27. De Luca, 69.

28. G. Fasoli, 'Liturgia e cerimoniale ducale' in *Venezia e il Levante fino al secolo xv* (Venice, 1971).

29. A. Pertusi, 'Quedam regalia insignia', *Studi Veneziani*, vii (1965) 77; Fasoli, op. cit.

30. F. Corner, *Ecclesiae Venetae antiquis monumentis . . . illustratae* (Venice, 1749) x, 178, 189, 197, 295; A. Galante, 'Per la storia giuridica della basilica di S. Marco', *Zeitschrift der Savigny Stiftung für Rechtsgeschichte*, xxxiii, pt. ii (1912) 283–298. For an example of the jealous control exercised by the doge over St. Mark's in the sixteenth century, see the opposition made by the doge to a patriarchal intervention in 1501; Sanuto, iv, 245: 'Non li par meti a S. Marco, ma ben in altre chiesie.'

31. H. Kretschmayr, *Geschichte von Venedig* (Stuttgart, 1934) iii, 108. For the earlier custom of popular participation see P. Molmenti, *La storia di Venezia nella vita privata* (Bergamo, 1928) i, 136–137.

32. De Luca, 36.

33. L. Thomassin, *Ancienne et nouvelle discipline de l'église* (Bar-Le-Duc, 1864) i, 121. On the earlier history of the patriarchate of Grado see H. Fuhrmann, 'Studien zur Geschichte mittelalterlicher Patriarchate', *Zeitschrift der Savigny Stiftung für Rechtsgeschichte*, Kanonistische Abteilung 40 (1954) 43–61; V. Piva, *Il patriarcato di Venezia e le sue origini*, 2 vols. (Venice, 1938 and 1960).

34. Niero, *I patriarchi di Venezia*, cit.

35. F. Gaeta, *Un nunzio pontificio a Venezia nel Cinquecento (Girolamo Aleandro)*, (Rome, 1960) 16–17. Relations between nuncios and patriarchs involved larger and continuing issues of jurisdiction and ecclesiastical practice; a few years later the nuncio G. A. Facchinetti, writing to Michele Bonelli on 15 Nov., 1567, on the open conflict over precedence with the patriarch on the occasion of the doge's funeral, noted that '. . . La premura del patriarcha a me non dà fastidio, ma è cosa se venesse aiutata da questi

signori che meriterebbe d'essere ripressa, perché non solo i patriarchi, ma anco gli arcivescovi in Italia favoriti da prencipi sono passati a poco a poco a tanta insolenza c'hanno voluto competere insin coi Papi.' *Nunziature di Venezia*, viii, 303.

36. Cozzi, *Il doge Nicolò Contarini*, 222.

37. G. Soranzo, *Rapporti di S. Carlo Borromeo con la repubblica veneta* in *A.V.*, ser. V, xxvii (1940) 24–5.

38. S. Tramontin, 'La figura del vescovo secondo il Concilio di Trento ed i suoi riflessi nell' interrogatorio del patriarca Trevisan', *Studi Veneziani*, x (1968) 423–456. It seems to me, though, that the author treats his material in a quite inappropriate way; that is, he applies the general principles of Catholic Reform to the document (which has its own special significance) and ignores everything that is individual or peculiar to it: the fact that there was no similar examination in other apostolic visitations is of some importance.

39. G. Benzoni, *Una controversia tra Roma e Venezia all' inizio del '600: la conferma del Patriarca* in *B.I.S.* (1961) 121–138. Of interest is the public declaration of Leonardo Donà to the effect that to accept Rome's conditions would be to have 'un frate per metropolita col quale s'abbia a contendere ogni giorno del governo de monasteri, del clero e de antichi instituti della città' (ibid., 124); and again 'La Republica non ha altro che un patriarca, che è patriarca della sua propria città, capo di tutto il Stato: il voler trattar di levarli questo o d'interromperli la giurisditione et privilegio di ellegerselo a modo suo è cosa acerbissima . . .' Seneca, *Il doge L. Donà*, 250, n. 2.

40. Corner, *Ecclesiae Venetae*, xiii, 146–147.

41. A. Rinaldi, *Il regio patronato sulla chiesa patriarcale di Venezia* (Rome, 1893) 191–196.

42. Sarpi, *Istoria dell' Interdetto e altri scritti*, iii, 260.

43. G. B. Gallicciolli, *Delle memorie venete antiche, profane ed ecclesiastiche* (Venice, 1795) iii, c. iv; G. Cappelletti, *Storia della Chiesa di Venezia dalla sua fondazione sino ai nostri giorni*, vol. ii (Venice, 1851) 727–728; G. Moroni, *Dizionario di erudizione storico-ecclesiastica*, xc (Venice, 1858) 308–310.

44. Corner, *Ecclesiae Venetae*, xiii, 271.

45. *La basilica di S. Marco in Venezia illustrata nella storia e nell' arte da scrittori veneziani*, ed. C. Boito (Venice, 1888); G. Fiocco, 'Tradizioni orientali nella pietà veneziana' in *Venezia e l'Oriente fra tardo Medio Evo e Rinascimento* (Florence, 1966) 117–124.

46. See the miscellanies *Culto dei santi a Venezia* and *Culto dei santi nella terraferma veneziana* (Venice, 1965 and 1967).

47. P. Brugnoli, 'Il primo vescovo veneziano sulla cattedra di S. Zeno (Angelo Barbarigo)', *Atti e mem. della Accademia di Verona*, ser. VI, xx (1968–69) 25.

48. C. Cenci, 'Senato Veneto: 'probae' ai benefizi ecclesiastici' in C. Piana and C. Cenci, *Promozioni agli ordini sacri a Bologna e alle dignità ecclesiastiche nel Veneto nei secoli XIV–XV* (Florence, 1968). In 1488 the Senate claimed that all the benefices in the *terraferma*, both great and small, were in the hands of Venetian nobles (ibid., 325).

49. V. Sandi, *Principi di storia civile della repubblica di Venezia*, pt. ii, vol. ii (Venice, 1756) 661–673; A. Sagredo, 'Leggi venete intorno agli ecclesiastici sino al secolo XVIII', *A.S.I.*, ser. III, ii (1865) 92–132. We may recall Sarpi's furious reaction to papal usurpations in matters concerning benefices, as in a letter to Leschassier of 14 Oct., 1609. 'Beneficiorum collatio forte ea est potio, qua dementes reddidit plures populos . . . Ego fateor, nihil magis e republica veneta esse, quam si electiones collegiis, et collationes ordinariis restituerentur' (Ulianich, *Lettere ai Gallicani*, 57–58).

50. Gaeta, *Un nunzio*, 59–60.

51. G. Alberigo, *I vescovi italiani al concilio di Trento, 1545–1547* (Florence, 1959) 47–89. The inquiry needs extending by exploiting the methodology applied by Alberigo to the sample of 15 secular Venetian bishops who took part in the first stages of the Council of Trent.

52. A. Prosperi, *Tra evangelismo e controriforma. G. M. Giberti, 1495-1543* (Rome, 1969) 130-133.

53. P. Preto, 'Un aspetto della riforma cattolica nel veneto: l'episcopato di Niccolò Ormaneto', *Studi Veneziani*, xi (1969) 325-363.

54. Sanuto, xvl, 623-624.

55. Sanuto, lii, 82.

56. Gallicciolli, v, 291-314.

57. On this last point see A. Stella, 'La proprietà ecclesiastica nella repubblica di Venezia dal secolo XV al secolo XVII', *Nuova Rivista Storica*, xl (1958) 50-77. An investigation into taxes and tithes with particular reference to relations with Rome and the exemptions granted to the major prelates would be desirable.

58. Described most recently in Piva, ii, 139-162.

59. *B.M.V.*, Cod. Ital. cl. VII, 326 (8953), 'Instrutione per la bolla Clementina composta da mons. Stefano Cosmi arcivescovo di Spalato già conservator della medema bolla' in the work's dedication to the doge. Cf. F. Gaeta, *Un nunzio . . .*, 52, where the work is dated 1768, however, instead of 1678 (the Council of Ten's authorization, placed before the list of contents, is dated 30 Jan., 1679).

60. D. Kurze, *Pfarrerwahlen im Mittelalter. Ein Beitrag zur Geschichte der Gemeinde und des Niederkirchenwesen* (Köln–Graz, 1966) 65-73.

61. H. F. Schmid, 'Das Weiterleben und die Wiederbelebung antiker Institutionen im mittelalterlichen Städtewesen', *Annali di Storia del Diritto*, i (1957) 104-105.

62. Besides the historical documentation contained in Cosmi's 'Instrutione' (see n. 59): Sandi, pt. iii, col. i, 469-488; Gallicciolli, iv, c. xi; Cappelletti, *Storia della Chiesa di Venezia*,ii, 261-288.

63. Stefano Cosmi was, in fact 'conservatore della bolla'. In the eighteenth century the institution had reached a point of crisis for one chief cause: the right to vote was formerly dependent not only on possessing property in the parish but also on living and taking the sacrament there; now property only was required. A. Lamberti, *Ceti e classi nel '700 a Venezia*, ed. M. Dazzi (Bologna, 1959) 45.

64. Gaeta, *Origine*, 222.

65. Gallicciolli, v, 263-270. The provision was also made on the grounds of the lamentable shortage of Venetian clergy and encouraged the entry into the clergy of men of the lowest social class 'per desio d'innalzarsi alla sacerdotale dignità ed astenersi da meccanici esercizi'. Lamberti, 46.

66. A. Niero, *L'azione veneziana al concilio di Basilea (1431-1436)* in *Venezia e i concili* (Venice, 1962) 26.

67. *Cleri et collegii novem congregationum Venetiarum documenta et privilegia* (studio Flaminii Cornelii, Venice, 1754); Moroni, xc, 313-320. And now: *Indice inventario sommario dell' archivio storico delle nove congregazioni del clero di Venezia*, ed. G. Bortolan, O. Marchi and S. Tramontin in the supplemt. to the *Rivista Diocesana* of the patriarchate of Venice, v (1964) 41-85.

68. S. Tramontin, 'Gli inizi dei due seminari di Venezia', *Studi Veneziani*, vii (1965) 363-377.

69. Cf. G. Cozzi, 'Federico Contarini: un antiquario veneziano tra Rinascimento e Controriforma', *B.I.S.*, iii (1961) 190-220.

70. For a general survey up to the fifteenth century see Piva, ii, 181-191.

71. From a Senate decision of 1515: '. . . s'el non vien provisto opportunamente, questa città serà occupata ne la parte più frequente de inclaustri, monasterii et campi sancti . . .', Sanuto, xx, 5.

72. Lamberti, 61.

73. Among innumerable examples, see the case of the Servite monastery of S. Giacomo della Giudecca on whose behalf the procurators *de ultra* wrote to Cardinal Cervini on 12 Mar., 1552, appealing to the laws and customs so that he '. . . dia tale ordine che in

executione delle preditte leggi et ordini nostri, sia eletto priore in questo loco persona da bene et venetiano, a ciò habbiamo causa di accettarlo et tenerlo a questo governo'. *Nunziature di Venezia*, ed. F. Gaeta, vi, 101.

74. I. Giuliani, 'Genesi e primo secolo di vita del Magistrato sopra Monasteri. Venezia 1519–1620', *Le Venezie Francescane*, xxviii (1961) 42–68, 106–169.

75. P. Paschini, 'I monasteri femminili in Italia nel '500' in *Problemi di vita religiosa in Italia nel Cinquecento* (Padua, 1960) 31–60; R. Creytens, 'La riforma dei monasteri femminili dopo i decreti tridentini' in *Il concilio di Trento e la riforma tridentina* (Rome, 1965) 45–84.

76. L. Sbriziolo, *Le confraternite veneziane di devozione* (Rome, 1968); idem., 'Per la storia delle confraternite veneziane: dalle deliberazioni miste (1310–1476) del Consiglio dei Dieci. Le scuole dei battuti', *Miscellanea G. G. Meersseman* (Padua, 1970) 715–64; idem., 'Per la storia . . . Scolae comunes, artigiane e nazionali' in *Atti dell' Istituto Veneto di Scienze, Lettere ed Arti*, Classe di scienze morali, cxxvi (1967–68) 404–442.

77. G. Alberigo, 'Contributi alla storia delle confraternite dei disciplinati e della spiritualità laicale nei secc. XV e XVI' in *Il movimento dei disciplinati nel VII centenario dal suo inizio* (Perugia, 1961) 156–252.

78. B. Pullan, 'Poverty, charity and the Reason of State: some Venetian examples', *B.I.S.*, ii (1960) 17–60; and, by the same author, *Rich and poor in Renaissance Venice* (Oxford, 1971).

79. E. Pommier, 'La société vénitienne et la Réforme protestante au XVIe siècle', *B.I.S.*, i (1959) 3–26; P. Paschini, *Venezia e l'inquisizione romana da Giulio III a Pio IV* (Padua, 1959).

80. G. Cozzi, *Religione, moralità e giustizia a Venezia: vicende della magistratura degli Esecutori contro la bestemmia (secc. XVI–XVII)*, (typescript Padua, 1969). After this preliminary assessment historians will no longer be able to ignore the change that took place around 1580 from primarily religious preoccupations to chiefly social ones.

81. F. Thiriet, *La Romanie vénitienne au Moyen Âge. Le développement et l'exploitation du domaine colonial vénitien XIIe–XVe siècles* (Paris, 1959) 283–291; F. Thiriet and P. Wirth, 'La politique religieuse de Venise à Négropont à la fin du XIVe siècle', *Byzantinische Zeitschrift*, lvi (1963) 297–303; D. J. Geanakoplos, *Greek scholars in Venice* (Cambridge, Mass., 1962) 43–44.

82. Thiriet, *La Romanie*, 429–433.

83. See G. Fedalto, *Ricerche storiche sulla posizione giuridica ed ecclesiastica dei Greci a Venezia nei secoli XV e XVI* (Florence, 1967) 91–96; idem., *Massimo Margunio e il suo commento al 'de Trinitate' di S. Agostino (1588)* 18, 68–69. For the secret negotiations between Venice and the patriarch of Constantinople to secure the support of the Orthodox hierarchy on the eve of Lepanto, see V. Lamansky, *Secrets d'État de Venise . . .* (St. Petersburg, 1884) ii, 077–078, 083.

84. Besides Fedalto (n. 83), see D. J. Geanakoplos, *Byzantine East . . .*, 112–135, and now M. I. Manousakas, *'Ανέκδοτα πατριαρχικὰ γράμματα (1547–1806)* (Venice, 1968), facsimile edition of 44 letters from the patriarchs of Constantinople and Alexandria to the metropolitans of Philadelphia and the Greek community in Venice. The continuity of the link between the Greek community in Venice and the patriarchate of Constantinople has recently been emphasized by V. Peri in 'La congregazione dei Greci (1573) e i suoi primi documenti', *Studia Gratiana*, xiii (Bologna, 1967) 175. The same author has recently developed this theme in a forthcoming study, *Chiesa latina e chiesa greca nell' Italia post-tridentina (1564–1596)*. The connection was still a matter of concern to the Roman *curia* in the last decades of the seventeenth century; S. Tramontin, 'L'attività diplomatica di S. Gregorio Barbarigo a Roma nel 1679', *Studi Veneziani*, ii (1969) 473–476.

85. Cf. S. Tramontin, 'Il problema delle Chiese separate nel Libellus ad Leonem X dei veneziani Paolo Giustiniani e Pietro Querini (1513)', *Studia Patavina*, ii (1964) 275–282.

86. The statements attributed to certain senators and to the doge Niccolò da Ponte himself during the conflict with Rome over the apostolic visit, that they wished to receive the sacraments from 'preti greci' if not actually to embrace Orthodoxy (Stella, *Chiesa e stato*, 38 and 52), together with the intention attributed to Niccolò Contarini of having his position confirmed by the patriarch of Constantinople were he elected patriarch in 1609 (Cozzi, *N. Contarini*, 119), seem to be worth considering – despite the uncertain nature of the evidence – as representing a state of mind that was deeply rooted in Venetian society.

87. S. Tramontin, 'La visita apostolica del 1581 a Venezia', *Studi Veneziani*, ix (1967) 453–533; Stella, *Chiesa e stato*, 30–43. To understand the full effect of the application of the Tridentine decrees to Venice it would be necessary to compare them to the old statutes of diocesan synods and patriarchal councils which – and this cannot be without significance – were gathered together and published by the patriarch Giovanni Trevisan: *Constitutiones et privilegia patriarchatus et cleri Venetiarum . . .* (Venice, 1587). On a specific issue see A. Niero, 'L' "honestas vitae clericorum" nei sinodi di Giovanni Trevisan patriarca di Venezia' in *Il concilio di Trento e la riforma Tridentina*, ii, 745–48.

88. Tramontin, *La visita*, 458.

89. V. M. Buffon, *Chiesa di Cristo e Chiesa romana nelle opere e nelle lettere di fra Paolo Sarpi* (Louvain–Venice, 1941) 40–69 and passim; B. Ulianich, 'Considerazioni e documenti per una ecclesiologia di Paolo Sarpi', in *Festgabe J. Lortz* (Baden-Baden, 1958) ii, 363–444.

90. Sandi, *Principi di storia civile*, pt. iii, vol. ii, 1015.

XV

MYRON GILMORE

Myth and reality in Venetian political theory

I. THEORISTS OF THE CONSTITUTION

The two most famous books on the Venetian constitution and administration were written in the second and third decades of the sixteenth century, one by a Venetian patrician and the other by a Florentine exile. Gasparo Contarini's *De magistratibus et republica Venetorum libri quinque* was probably composed in two stages, the first four books in 1523–24 and the last in 1531.[1] It was posthumously published in 1543. Donato Giannotti's *Libro della repubblica de' viniziani* appears to have been written in 1526–27, subjected to minor revisions in the thirties, and finally published in 1540 in Rome.[2] Both these works contain technical and detailed descriptions of the Venetian constitution and the working of the government and administration. They also contain general propositions about politics and, although the two authors are very close in their accounts of Venetian institutions, their more abstract theoretical views on what constitutes the best regime do not coincide.

Very early in his exposition and throughout the treatise Contarini emphasizes the responsibility of the patrician class who alone had Venetian citizenship. In discussing the possible forms of regime he recalls the long tradition which maintained that the government of one was absolutely the best but, given the fact that there is no monarchy which has not eventually lapsed into tyranny, concludes that a republic is better than a monarchy. Such a republic however must not be a government of all the people because the multitude itself is not fit to govern. No mere agglomeration has ever existed in which there is not 'viltà', and any city or regime will be ruined without a principle of unity and organization.[3]

The 'ordine' or unity which Contarini set himself to describe he explains in terms of the traditional organic metaphor. Just as an animal has many parts that do not have a soul so the city has many men who are not citizens. Every society must have artisans and mercenaries and private servants but these cannot be citizens because they serve or are in reality the slaves of private or public interests, whereas the citizen must be a free man. The wise ancestors of the Venetians put in charge of the Republic those who were noble by blood, virtuous by character and those who had deserved well of the Republic because of some service to the state. Here again Contarini draws on traditional arguments about the best constitution of society which go back at least to Plato and bear a striking resemblance to the ideas of the Florentine Leon Battista Alberti in his *Della famiglia* and *De re aedificatoria*.[4]

The republican regime, however, should not be a simple aristocracy but mixed. In Venice the doge supplies the monarchical element, the Senate, Ten, and councillors the aristocratic, and the Great Council the popular. Famous philosophers, declares Contarini, have maintained that a republic ought to be tempered or a mixture of the noble and popular elements in order to avoid the disadvantages and realize the benefits of both. The republic of Sparta has been widely admired in which the authority of king and ephors was so mingled that it is difficult to know under what category of government it ought to be placed.[5]

Although Sparta and Rome have both been praised for having a mixed constitution, they both show the danger of being too much oriented toward war and too little concerned with dispositions necessary in time of peace or *ozio*. Consequently when Sparta ceased to be at war, the republic began to decline and the same thing happened at Rome for the same reason. This is why Nasica judged that Carthage should not be totally destroyed, so that the Romans should always have an enemy with whom to take up arms, instead of being tempted to turn their arms against themselves. The outcome in Rome showed Nasica's judgment to be correct. As soon as Carthage was ruined, the civil wars broke out through which ultimately the greatest, most flourishing and richest republic that ever existed – the city that was lord of the world – became the prey of the barbarians.[6]

Nothing is more to be feared than intestine disturbances. Every republic must be on guard against the revolt of one who, like Caesar, may rise to destroy the constitution. Contarini recalls that most of the cities of Italy which had a popular regime have in his time fallen under the tyranny of one or more of their former citizens. This can be avoided by creating collegiate magistracies such as the Ten in Venice and limiting their term to one year.[7]

In the governance of the Venetian *terraferma* the danger of one citizen becoming too powerful by controlling the army is arrested by the practice of depending on mercenary officers. Contarini feels that the natives of the subject territories should be encouraged to serve in the army, which can provide incentives to encourage loyalty to the Republic. His great example is Bartolomeo Colleoni of Bergamo, who rose to high rank and recognized what he owed to a grateful government. On the other hand, in Contarini's opinion for the control of the overseas empire and the command of the navy it is better to have officers drawn from the Venetian patrician families.[8]

In the judicial colleges Contarini finds another example of the participation of the non-citizen in the tasks of administration. The secretaries of the judicial colleges are drawn from the plebeian group who are not citizens rather than from the members of the Great Council.

The general propositions which these examples illustrate can hardly be said to form a political theory which is consistent, profound, or original. At the beginning Contarini gives the credit for the creation of the Venetian constitution to those wise ancestors who perceived that they had but to follow nature in order to design a perfect polity. At the end however he proclaims that divine miracle has created the government of Venice. Although the fact of being 'secundum naturam' is adduced as an explanation of how the Venetian constitution has maintained itself unchanged through the centuries, we are told on one of the last pages that 'every human thing tends to decay and as it approaches its end has to be restored just as a body which has been subject to fasting needs to be regenerated with food'.[9]

The major theme which runs through the whole of Contarini's discussion is that of the importance of stability or order. Civil dissensions and factional disputes must always be avoided and this can be done by an elaborate system of checks and balances which allows some degree of participation to each element in the body politic. In the macrocosm of the Venetian state this is to be seen in the ideal of the mixed constitution with the doge representing monarchy, the Senate aristocracy and the Great Council democracy. But there is also a balance between war and peace, between citizens and mercenaries, and between citizens and artisans. Even within the magistracies the restrictions governing the complicated electoral procedures by which not more than two members of the same family were allowed to serve on the same electoral committee are part of the same pattern. Every committee and collegiate body in the whole complicated machinery of government is in a way 'mixed' and so the microcosm reflects the general principle of organization.

It is well known that Contarini's great contemporary, Niccolò Machiavelli, did not have a high opinion of the Venetian constitution. He conceded that republics like Sparta and Venice where the protection of liberty was entrusted to the nobility were well adapted to maintaining stability and order so long as they were content not to expand their territory. In both these cases, however, expansion was followed by disaster and Machiavelli notes that Venice, whose empire on the Italian mainland he contemptuously describes as acquired 'not by dint of arms but of money and astute diplomacy', lost everything in a single battle.[10] Machiavelli's real admiration was reserved for the Roman republican constitution with its emphasis on the military virtues and its capacity for combining a degree of order with the possibility of expansion.

It is interesting to speculate on whether Contarini had any acquaintance with the ideas of Machiavelli at the time of writing the *De magistratibus*. He could have seen the *Arte della guerra* published in 1521 and he could well have had an account of Machiavelli's other writings from Giannotti and other Florentine friends, but there is no evidence that he did so. Certainly later in life in his association with

Cardinal Pole he must have been familiar with Machiavelli's political princi-ples.[11]

In any event there are some interesting points of agreement and disagreement in their conclusions on the lessons of history and their prescriptions for the best way of preserving order with liberty. Contarini's remarks on the decline of Rome after the destruction of Carthage would certainly have been approved by Machiavelli who in several passages of the *Discorsi* comments on the evil effects of *ozio*. 'It appears that the world has become effeminate because the weakness of men has interpreted our religion in terms of "ozio" not "virtù".'[12] The gentlemen whom he condemns and whose existence makes a republic impossible are those who live as 'oziosi' on their incomes.[13] The decadence of the present time is described as due in part to 'uno ambizioso ozio'.[14] Most particularly and exactly anticipating Contarini, Machiavelli states that 'when Heaven is so favour-able to a commonwealth that it has no need to go to war, it will then happen that "ozio" will make it effeminate or give rise to factions'.[15] And again the cause of disunion in republics is most often 'ozio e pace'.[16]

In addition to the relationship between idleness and faction Contarini seems to share with Machiavelli especially in the remarks in the last book that belief so common in many areas of Renaissance speculation that all human institutions tend to decay and have to be periodically restored.[17]

On the other hand, there are of course many points where there is no con-vergence of views between Contarini and Machiavelli. The former praises the Roman institution of the *Decemviri* with a view to defending the collegiate principle and the year's tenure of the Venetian magistracy of the same name,[18] while Machiavelli asserts that the appointment of the *Decemviri* was harmful to the Republic.[19] Contarini's argument for the use of mercenaries for the defence of the *terraferma* and his reliance on the example of Colleoni is entirely contrary to Machiavelli's well-known views on the importance of a citizen army.

Regardless, however, of agreement or disagreement on specific points, any comparison serves to bring out once more the originality and penetration of Machiavelli. Both authors built on the heritage of Graeco–Roman political thought and historical example. Both were interested in the problems of wise founders of regimes, the avoidance of civil strife, the preservation of the independence of the state and the liberty and welfare of the citizen. Yet Machia-velli transcends his Florentine background, whereas Contarini reflects perfectly the views of the Venetian patrician class especially in the period after the successful recovery from the period of the attacks of the League of Cambrai and the battle of Agnadello. He provided in its most developed version the idealized Venetian constitution, the elements of which were the exaggerated claims of the longevity, stability and independence of Venice, the theory of the mixed constitution and the conviction that not only the citizens who composed the Great Council but all the inhabitants participated in the good life which the Republic offered. He is above all the expositor of the myth of the Venetian constitution.[20]

Donato Giannotti who was a close friend and admirer of Machiavelli wrote his dialogue on Venice partly or perhaps mainly as a contribution to the continuing debate on the Florentine constitution. The setting is Pietro Bembo's villa near Padua and the interlocutors are Trifone Gabriele, a Venetian aristocrat now retired from public life, and Giovanni Borgherini, a Florentine on a visit to Padua and Venice and eager to improve his understanding of the Venetian constitution and administration which he greatly admires. The dialogue – so favoured a form of Renaissance exposition whether of philosophy, politics, literature or art – in this case cannot be described as a literary masterpiece. Gabriele appears in the role of a complacent and pompous preceptor and Borgherini's interventions are only too obviously naïve and contrived. There does however emerge a clear, detailed and well-organized picture of the Venetian government. Perhaps because of Giannotti's familiarity with Machiavelli's *Istorie fiorentine*, he gives a much more historical view than does Contarini of the development of Venetian institutions, especially the dogeship and the Great Council.

At the very beginning Gabriele is made to reply to a question of his friend about the periodization of history and the problem of historical recurrences. Gabriele declares as Contarini had done that the decline of Rome began with the overthrow of the republic by Caesar's armies. The fall of the empire and the barbarian invasions brought on a second critical period from which have stemmed the troubled times that Italy has suffered down to the present. The invasions of Italy by the northern monarchs, beginning with Charles VIII in 1494 make this present worse than the previous crises.[21] Gabriele criticizes the historian Sabellicus for comparing wars fought by Venice with those fought by Rome and then undertakes the exposition of the Venetian constitution requested of him by Borgherini. In his view a citizen should know a city's wealth, military capacity, geographical situation, exports and imports, and government. A foreigner, on the other hand, must know the form of the administration and the relationship of the various parts with each other.[22]

After a description of the geographical situation of Venice and a brief historical survey, Gabriele comes to the division of the social classes, the large group of *popolari* or plebs, the small number of citizens and the still smaller number of patricians. He gives a brief account of the foundation of the city by the refugees fleeing from the Huns and the formation of the first popular government and then suggests that the history of the city is to be divided into three periods, the first from the beginning to the creation of the Great Council, a period in which the city was governed first by tribunes and then by doges, and which was characterized by the struggle for survival. The second period, which saw the beginning of Venetian greatness extends from the creation of the Great Council to the closing of its membership in 1298. And the third period, which has brought Venice to the pinnacle of glory above other cities of Italy, comes down to the present. Gabriele emphasizes that it is only in this last stage when the administration of the Republic has been 'tutta in potestà de' gentiluomini' that this splendid position has been attained.[23]

The principal organs of the administration are according to Gabriele the Great Council, the Senate, the College and the doge. When Borgherini objects that he has often heard mentioned also as important the Ten, the procurators of St. Mark and the *avogadori*, Gabriele agrees that they are indeed important but are not strictly part of the 'corpo' of the Republic and therefore will be dealt with later. Everything must be taken up in its place.[24] The 'corpo', he explains, has the form of a pyramid with the Great Council as the base, the Senate more restricted in number as the next stage, then the still more exclusive College and finally the doge at the top.[25]

There follows a detailed description of the electoral procedures and competence of each of these bodies. In the case of the description of the election of the doge the poor interlocutor is forced to confess: 'This is a very laborious business and I don't think it would be really profitable.'[26] Eventually Gabriele in his pedantic way reaches the other magistrates, the Ten, the *avogadori*, and the treatise concludes with an exposition of the judicial system and the financial administration.

The entire dialogue contains very little of what may be properly called political theory. Throughout there is an emphasis, as there is in Contarini, on the superior class of citizens who are contrasted with their 'servitors' the greater part of the population. Gabriele explains that the 'nerves' of a republic – again the organic analogy – are to be found in the principal powers of government, which are the authority to create magistrates, to declare war or peace, to introduce legislation and to inflict punishment and hear appeals.[27] He shows in what organs of the 'body' each of these powers is vested in Venice, but, in spite of the fact that this division of powers would support the conception of a mixed constitution, he nowhere mentions the term. At the very end in connection with explaining the process of legislation, Gabriele tells his friend that if he wishes to know whether the republic is simple or compound, and if simple of what species, and if compound whether closer to one type or another, he should first reflect carefully on all the facts that have been put before him. If he wants a further opinion he should apply to Niccolò Leonico Tomeo, the Epirote Greek who held the chair of philosophy at the University of Padua and who was in the opinion of Gabriele most skilled in discussing such subjects.[28] Giannotti thus avoided the theory of the mixed constitution which had been so much emphasized by Contarini. His description of the powers of government, like the right to make war, coin money, appoint ambassadors, etc., was traditional and borrowed from the legists, but both method and conclusion on their location in the structure of the Venetian government were borrowed by many writers on political thought down to the eighteenth century. No doubt Giannotti's primary purpose may have been to offer a prescription for the conditions of stability which might be applied to the situation in Florence.[29] However, the arguments which he puts into the mouth of Gabriele do reflect, although less explicitly than in the treatise of Contarini, the convictions of the Venetian governing class on the merits of their constitution.

II. AMBASSADORS

The institution of resident ambassadors was an Italian invention, and Venice was among the earliest of the Italian states to establish a system of more or less regular missions to the other states of the peninsula, to the northern monarchies and to the Ottoman empire.[30] The Venetian ambassadors were drawn from the class of patrician citizens who composed the Great Council and who were trained from the earliest age in the ideal of service to the state. Since these ambassadors belonged to the same class as Contarini, who had himself served on such a mission, and since they constituted so closed a group, it is relevant to enquire how far assumptions based on their political experience in Venice and derived from their judgments on its constitution enter into their accounts of the various governments to which they were accredited. In other words, how far do the despatches and *relazioni* contribute to our knowledge of the political thought of the governing class in Venice in the fifteenth and sixteenth centuries?

It must be said at the outset that these ambassadors were on the whole very empirically minded men more often occupied with particular negotiations and estimates of revenues and military strength than they were in making generalizations of a theoretical kind. This is particularly true of the dispatches, which are almost always brief reports of a conversation with a ruler or minister and the conclusion of an agreement on a specific subject. Even the great series of *relazioni* to the doge and Senate on the northern monarchies in the sixteenth century present descriptions of political conditions rather than judgements on them. Contarini himself served as ambassador to Charles V from 1521–25 and gave his *relazione* to the Senate on 16th November of the latter year, that is, in the same period when he was presumably writing the first part of his treatise on the Magistrates of Venice.[31] At the beginning he says that, omitting all superfluities, he will speak principally of three things, the kingdoms and provinces subject to Caesar, the councillors, and finally the characters of the emperor and his relatives. In his brief description of the Empire he barely alludes to the fact that the Germans show little obedience to the emperor and briefly reports that Charles and his brother Ferdinand are hated because of their Spanish customs. In contrast the people in the Low Countries are said to hold the emperor in great affection, while Aragon, Catalonia and Valencia are ill-disposed to him and disaffection is reported also in Naples, Castile and other subordinate territories. These rather vague generalizations are based on impressions of the psychological reactions of the various peoples in the Empire rather than on any analysis of the institutional position of the emperor. The remainder of this *relazione* is devoted to presenting the grand lines of imperial policy and the conflicts among the emperor's advisers with particular attention to the position of the chancellor Gattinara whose counsel in the opinion of Contarini generally prevails.[32]

A similar preoccupation with the role of personalities appears in most of the *relazioni* to the northern courts in the sixteenth century. Examples are Niccolò Tiepolo's account of his embassy to the meeting at Nice in 1538 of Paul III,

Charles V, and Francis I, Marino Giustiniani's mission to Ferdinand of Hungary in 1541, and many of the reports on Tudor England.

In the same Tiepolo's *relazione* of his embassy to Charles V in 1532 there is, however, an interesting comment on the social scene in Germany. The Venetian patrician reports that in almost all the imperial lands the people, 'la plebe' have acquired authority and have so established themselves that the nobles have no share in it. In some towns and provinces the 'citizens' have no more power than the meanest artisans and in others the lower classes have achieved such a mastery that they govern alone. The Swiss cantons and some of the free cities of the empire are cited as examples.[33]

At the other extreme from these democratic regimes was the despotism represented by the Ottoman empire. A series of Venetian ambassadors to the *Porte* condemned the arbitrary power of the sultan in an empire which was largely dependent on the fanatical devotion of converted Christian slaves. The Senate was informed that in spite of the apparent strength and security of the Turkish state, the possibility of revolution was inherent in the system itself. If the sultan died leaving minor children there could be a quarrel over the succession, and the rivalries between pashas opened the possibility of creating independent principalities.[34] Thus the Ottoman empire was presented to the Senate as an example of the dangers inherent in the concentration of power in the hands of one man while the free cities and the Swiss cantons showed the fatal results of sharing political authority with the lower classes. These examples must have strengthened the conviction of the Venetian patricians that theirs was the ideal solution as Contarini had proclaimed.

In general the ambassadors to Germany, England, France, Spain and the Low Countries, coming to their missions with a firm belief in the Venetian myth, show a sensitivity to the responsibility of the governing class and a preoccupation with the maintenance of stability, whether threatened by the disloyalty of feudal nobles or the agitation of heretical sects. However, while their *relazioni* often reflect the experience of their class in Venice, they do not contain abstract speculation on political theory any more than they do discussions of theological questions when describing the progress of the Reformation in Germany.

In the case of the embassies to the other Italian states, however, there was more occasion for comment and judgement on changes of regime. Although Venice was unique in having an overseas empire, she was with her territory on the mainland a city state among other city states and this situation invited comparisons with rival powers which would have been meaningless with the German empire or the kingdom of France. Hence the reports resulting from missions in the Italian peninsula are more articulate on fundamental problems of political theory. This is particularly true of the embassies to Florence.

Marco Foscari was the Venetian envoy to the Florentine republic in the critical first six months of the year 1527. His *relazione* given on his return quotes Aristotle on the conditions necessary for stability in government and finds that they do not exist in Florence. The Florentines, he maintains, have put faction and self-interest above the common good; they all follow base trades, and their governors come from the wool and silk shops. They are poor in defence because their rich men are afraid of losing their villas and palaces built outside the city walls. The ambassador is forced to conclude that some great sin on the part of the city must be the cause that the Florentines 'nunquam in eodem statu permanserunt', nor have they ever been content with their government. They have never had a regime which has lasted in the same form for more than forty years. He ends his report with a contemptuous description of the institutions of the *parlamento* giving authority to a *balìa* to change the government of the city.[35]

Similar judgements are made by his successors in the following years. Antonio Suriano reported to the Senate that the Florentines had recovered their liberty of which they had been deprived since 1434 with the exception of the years during which the Medici had been banished from 1494–1512. He presented the house of the Medici as having established a tyranny over all the other families of the city, so that it had suffered ninety years of servitude with the brief interval of the sixteen-year republican revival. Now, however, he reports that 'la plebe' who are given entirely to the mechanical arts have taken over power and since they cannot know the true art of governing, it is unlikely that the popular republic will last, without external assistance.[36]

Later in the century when the duchy had been established, another ambassador, Vincenzo Fideli, laments that the inhabitants of the province of Tuscany, although formerly free, had destroyed themselves by faction and in consequence have now come into servitude, with no possibility of an uprising to recover their former condition. He declares that he is sad to see the tyranny of a single individual imposed on a free people.[37]

With similar sentiments the Venetian envoys at various periods during the century expressed admiration for the republican institutions of Lucca, Genoa and Siena, while expressing some reservations on the ducal governments of Urbino, Milan and Ferrara.

Judgements such as these permit us to see how deeply held by the Venetian upper class were the convictions which Contarini had articulated into a political theory. The city's long-continued independence, the stability of its institutions, the existence of an aristocratic governing class distinguished from the large mass of labourers and artisans, the 'mixed' quality of the régime, which prevented the domination of a single individual or faction, these were the elements from which the Venetian myth was constructed. These ideas existed in a somewhat unformulated way in the consciousness of the Venetian patricians and they found occasional expression in the ambassadors' reports. Systematized by Contarini, the myth continued with some modifications to command the allegiance of the Venetians as an argument for republicanism throughout the period of Paruta and Sarpi but enjoyed its greatest fortune abroad in the political debates of the sixteenth and seventeenth centuries in Florence, France, England and Holland.

III. Jean Bodin and the Myth of Venice

Jean Bodin, certainly the most learned and probably the most profound political theorist of the sixteenth century, made his first attack on Contarini's theory of the Venetian constitution in the *Methodus ad facilem historiarum cognitionem* published in 1566.[38] This work was conceived as the systematic organization of historical materials with the purpose of making them available for the comparative study of government. The understanding of changes in political structures constituted for Bodin the essence of history from which, like Machiavelli, he hoped to draw lessons of universal validity.

Bodin devotes a good deal of attention in this treatise to the Venetian constitution as described by Contarini and Giannotti. He is already working towards a theory of sovereignty or *imperium* in the conviction that if the universal characteristics of supreme power in a political society could be defined, then the different types of regime could be classified according to who held the sovereign power. In the *Methodus* Bodin's description of this power is in substantial agreement with what Giannotti had called the 'nerves' of a republic, that is, the power to create magistrates, make or abrogate law, declare war and make peace, inflict capital punishment and preside over the highest court of appeal.[39]

Bodin considered that this group of powers must be held by the ruler in any state and, according to whether the ruler was one, few or many, the state was a monarchy, aristocracy, or democracy. Unlike Aristotle he did not allow the degenerate forms, holding that the moral quality of a regime was irrelevant to the type of government.

For his knowledge of Venice Bodin depended not only on the works of Contarini and Giannotti but also on conversations he had had with Michele Suriano when the latter served as Venetian ambassador to France. In the *Methodus* Bodin recalls with gratitude their exchanges of information on the constitutions of France and Venice and their agreement that it was better to discuss relative merits than to attempt judgements of absolute superiority.[40]

In spite of this disclaimer, however, Bodin proceeds to attack the Venetian polity. If his analysis is to be applied to Venice, he says, it necessarily follows that the government of that republic must be in the hands of a single individual or of a small number of notables or of the whole body of citizens or a majority thereof. Following Giannotti he recognizes that Venice began as a popular government and subsequently came under the domination of the nobles. The doge has never had anything but the appurtenances of royalty without the reality.[41] Venice is therefore a republic popular in form in that she is ruled by the citizens but, since the latter are a very small number (some 3,000) in comparison with the total number of inhabitants, she is really an aristocracy. Since Bodin is a defender of monarchy as not only the best possible government but also that which is most according to nature,[42] he is concerned to point out that the boasted stability of the Venetians under what Contarini had called the mixed constitution is an illusion. Venice, he declares contemptuously, has always been the laughing stock of its enemies, and has been able to maintain social peace only by condemn-ing eighteen doges to punishment or exile and undergoing civil wars, con-spiracies, attacks on the senate – in short like a ship without a captain, comparable to devastated Germany during its feudal period.[43]

By the time when the *Six livres de la république* were published in 1576, Bodin had refined and developed the conception of sovereignty which is his most famous contribution to political theory. He now proclaimed the unity and inalienability of the sovereign power which consisted principally in the power to make law. In formulating this definition Bodin broke with the medieval tradition of regarding law as something pre-existent which it was the business of the ruler to declare, and he set up the theoretical framework for the modern dynamic national state with its exaltation of the law-making or legislative power. Reviewing the examples of the Spartan, Roman and Venetian constitutions he now more emphatically repudiates the theory of the mixed regime. Venice is a true aristocracy or oligarchy. Out of all the inhabitants only a small minority of some 3,000 share the rights of citizenship and participate in the exercise of public power. Although Giannotti had rather vaguely divided the power to introduce new laws between the Great Council, the Senate and the Ten,[44] Contarini gives such power to the Great Council that Bodin is convinced that this is the organ of sovereign power in Venice, and he accuses Contarini of inconsistency in trying to maintain the myth of the 'mixed' constitution while at the same time exalting the authority of the Great Council.[45] He further condemns Contarini's attempt to make the doge represent the monarchical element in the constitution, which is as unfounded as the claim that the Great Council is 'democratic'. In Bodin's eyes the doge is a purely ornamental figure deprived of any reality of power.

Venice is therefore a type of aristocratic regime, and in comparing this type with monarchy, which Bodin considers ideal, he points out that aristocracies are less stable since they are always subjected to pressure from below for greater participation in power. Nevertheless Venice has succeeded in maintaining more stability than most such régimes because she has wisely controlled this pressure by allowing to the people minor offices in the administration and occasionally conferring citizenship on one who has done some service to the state (the case of Colleoni), and by maintaining freedom for all inhabitants to engage in industry and commerce so that the non-citizens have little occasion to attempt a revolution and even less power to do so. Even here, however, Bodin recalls that the Venetians have had more seditious attempts against their government than their publicists recognize.[46]

In the last of the six books on the republic, devoted to administration including both taxes and justice, Bodin presents a much more positive view of the Venetian constitution. He reiterates his judgement that monarchy is the best of all regimes using elaborate analogies from macrocosm to microcosm. Among types of monarchy that which is superior to all others he describes as royal, in which the monarch respects not only the laws of God and of nature but also the fundamental laws of the realm. Here Bodin introduces the distinction between state and government or administration. The administration of justice for example may be of three types which he calls distributive, commutative and harmonic, and these correspond to geometric, arithmetic and harmonic proportions. In the first case rewards and punishments may be distributed on the basis of rank, that is, unequally, in the second they will be awarded with absolute equality, the same treatment for senator and shopkeeper, but in the third there will be an appropriate mixture of the two. As an example of such a mixture Bodin offers the division of property according to the Biblical law. The male children inherit the landed property and the female children the moveables, but among the males the eldest has two portions compared to the one of the younger brothers. This Bodin calls an harmonic mixture because giving all the inheritance to the eldest world be in his terms 'geometric', whilst an equal division among all the children would be 'arithmetic'.[47]

Applying this rather complicated analogy to political institutions Bodin points out that, although there are in his opinion only three types of state, each type may be administered or governed in three different ways: that is, monarchy, aristocracy or democracy may each have an administration distributive, commutative or harmonic. The location of sovereignty determines the form of the state but not the nature of the government. The example of Venice is again invoked by Bodin to illustrate this principle and now in terms far more flattering to the Republic than he had previously used. Although an aristocracy, Venice has maintained an harmonic administration. Non-citizens have been able to aspire to some important offices such as the chancellorship. The judicial system permits a wrong done to the meanest citizen to be redressed immediately. Perhaps forgetting what he had earlier alleged about conspiracies, disorders and exiled doges, Bodin's final opinion is that the long continued stability of Venice is due less to her aristocratic constitution than to the administration, which with its genuinely mixed forms perpetuates a style of popular liberty rather than one of oligarchic oppression.

The great fame of Jean Bodin as a political theorist rests on his definition of the concept of sovereignty. By applying the powerful logic of the necessary existence of a unitary, inalienable, law-making power the location of which must determine the form of any political society, Bodin attacked the myth of the mixed constitution as exemplified by Venice. In the end, however, he recognized the reality and importance of a mixture of democratic and aristocratic elements in administration, and used the Venetian experience as a convincing example. We are today in a position to recognize that Bodin's theory of sovereignty is as much a 'myth' as Contarini's mixed constitution, although it is one by which the modern world has unhappily lived for more than three centuries. If the Venetian myth proved in the long run to be not very acceptable political theory, it at least perpetuated the description of a political reality which not only kept alive a tradition of republicanism but also served as a model for a tempered administration to republicans and monarchists alike.

NOTES

1. See F. Gilbert, 'The date and composition of Contarini's and Giannotti's books on Venice', *Studies in the Renaissance*, xiv (1967) 174–176. Also W. J. Bouwsma, *Venice and the defense of republican liberty: Renaissance values in the age of the Counter Reformation* (Berkeley, 1968) 144–161.
2. Gilbert, 'The date and composition', 174–182.
3. G. Contarini, *Della republica e magistrati di Venezia libri V di M. Gasparo Contarini . . .* (Venice, 1630) book i, passim.
4. Leon Battista Alberti, *De re aedificatoria* (first ed., Florence, 1485) bk. iv.
5. Contarini, *Della republica*, 18.
6. Ibid., 19–21.
7. Ibid., 85. Cf. also 99.
8. Ibid., 137.
9. Ibid., 132.
10. Machiavelli, *Discorsi sopra la prima deca di Tito Livio*, ed. Sergio Bertelli (Milan, 1960) bk. i, chs. 5 and 6. Cf. also F. Gilbert, 'Machiavelli e Venezia', *Lettere Italiane*, xxi (1969) no. 4.
11. Giannotti, who was familiar with Machiavelli's works in ms., had been in Padua and Venice in 1525. In 1533 he wrote that he had shown to Marco Foscari, at the time of that visit eight years before, the ms. of Machiavelli's *Historie di Firenze* (see D. Giannotti, 'Lettere inedite', ed. L. A. Ferrai, *Atti del R. Istituto Veneto di Scienze, Lettere ed Arti*, ser. IV, vol. iii (1884–85) 157 seq. The manuscript of *Il Principe* offered at Sotheby's in the sale of 25 June, 1968, appears to have been copied in Venice where it was perhaps being prepared for publication by the Venetian printer Joannes Tacuinus (see Sotheby's Sale Catalogue 'Biblioteca Philippica', New Ser., pt. iv, 47–48). If as Gilbert has maintained, Contarini was writing the last book of his treatise in the thirties, it is possible that he could have seen in print *Il Principe* and the *Discorsi* in the edition of Blado, Rome, 1532. Contarini also had an extensive correspondence with a Florentine friend, Pier Francesco da Gagliano, son of a former partner in the Medici Bank, beginning at least as early as 1515 and this individual may have supplied him with information on Machiavelli's writings (see F. Gilbert, 'Contarini on Savonarola: an unknown document of 1516', *Archiv für Reformationsgeschichte*, lix [1968] 145–146).
12. Machiavelli, *Discorsi*, bk. ii, ch. 2.
13. Ibid., bk. i, ch. 55.
14. Ibid., *proemio*.
15. Ibid., bk. i, ch. 6.
16. Ibid., bk. ii, ch. 25.
17. Machiavelli, *Arte della guerra*, ed. Sergio Bertelli (Milan, 1961), speech of Fabrizio Colonna, 499–520.
18. Contarini, *Della republica*, 85.
19. Machiavelli, *Discorsi*, bk. i, ch. 35.
20. See, W. J. Bouwsma, *Venice and the defense of republican liberty*, 144–154. Also F. Gilbert, 'The Venetian constitution in Florentine political thought', *Florentine studies: politics and society in Renaissance Florence*, ed. Nicolai Rubinstein (London, 1968) 463–501.
21. D. Giannotti, *Libro della republica de' Veneziani*, in *Opere* (Florence, 1850) ii, 12–13. See also Bouwsma, *Venice*, 158–159.
22. Giannotti, *Libro* etc., 19.
23. Ibid., 34–35.
24. Ibid., 37.
25. Ibid., 38.

26. Ibid., 105.

27. Ibid., 39.

28. Ibid., 172. On Niccolò Leonico Tomeo see *Opus Epistolarum Des. Erasmi Rotero-dami*, ed. P. S. Allen (Oxford, 1924) v, 520–521. Also Mario Cosenza, *Dictionary of Italian Humanists* (Boston, 1962), sub verb. Tomeo died in 1531. He held the chair at Padua for many years and left a large body of writing on ancient mythology, history and geography, as well as editions of Aristotle and other ancient texts, and a volume of dialogues. I cannot find that he ever wrote on the Venetian constitution.

29. F. Gilbert, 'The Venetian constitution in Florentine political thought', 492–498.

30. See Garrett Mattingly, *Renaissance Diplomacy* (London, 1955), esp. chs. v–vii.

31. Albèri, ser. I, vol. ii, 11–115.

32. Ibid.

33. Ibid., ser. I, i, 25–74.

34. Ibid., ser. III, i, esp. 325–327.

35. Ibid., ser. II, i, 324.

36. Ibid., ser. II, ii, 429–453.

37. Ibid., ser. II, ii, 455–463.

38. On Bodin see Kenneth McRae, 'Introduction to John Bodin', *The six bookes of a commonweale, a facsimile reproduction of the translation of 1606* (Harvard, 1962) 3–67.

39. J. Bodin, *Methodus*, text and translation by Pierre Mesnard (Paris, 1951) 174b–175a.

40. Ibid., 415a.

41. Ibid., 367b–368a.

42. Ibid., 414a.

43. Ibid., 418a.

44. J. Bodin, *Six livres de la république* (4th ed., Paris, 1579) 260–272.

45. Ibid., 953.

46. Ibid., 1046–1047.

47. Ibid., 952.

XVI

WILLIAM BOUWSMA

Venice and the political education of Europe

Renaissance Florence has long been considered the origin in European history of a concern with politics as an autonomous study. Faced with the problems of governing a turbulent but independent republic, anxious to insure her survival in a precarious world that seemed to be ruled only by power, and nourished by the rediscovered political culture of antiquity, thoughtful Florentines, in a process that reached a climax with Machiavelli and Guicciardini, began to articulate realistic principles of political effectiveness and to define its limits. In this sense Florence contributed to the education of modern Europe as a congeries of particular powers, like Florence the products of their separate histories, whose policies would be determined by some calculation of political interest.

The role of Venice in transmitting the attitudes and the lessons of Renaissance politics to the larger European world has been less clearly recognized, partly because of the preoccupation of recent historians with Florence, partly because the Venetian contribution to political discourse was relatively late.[1] The government of Venice impressed other Europeans primarily when Italy as a whole was no longer an inspiring spectacle; for this, as well as for other reasons, Venice presented herself as a unique example of political wisdom. Furthermore her own major spokesmen, Gasparo Contarini, Paolo Paruta, Enrico Davila and perhaps above all Paolo Sarpi, were men not of the fifteenth but of the sixteenth and early seventeenth centuries. This chronology, however, should not obscure the fact that Venice represented in the modern world the central political values of Renaissance republicanism, which she made available to the rest of Europe in a singularly attractive and provocative form.

The European perception of Venice was not entirely, or perhaps even primarily, the consequence of reading Venetian writers, although their works were widely studied and deeply admired. Furthermore, men saw in Venice what they wanted to see. Venice possessed, nevertheless, a definable political culture;[2] and what

445

the Venetians had to say will therefore be helpful in understanding the general interest of Europeans elsewhere in the Venetian achievement.

The most general element in the political ideal to which Venetian writers exposed their audience was an ubiquitous secularism. They were not hostile to religion; indeed, like most of their compatriots, they were demonstrably men of faith, albeit of a kind uncongenial to the developing orthodoxy of the Counter Reformation; and this fact doubtless contributed to the esteem for Venice among pious Gallicans and Protestants. Their secularism was expressed rather in an antipathy to speculative systems that impose an artificial coherence on all values and experience and thereby claim a right to supervise, among other matters, the political order. They were the enemies not of religion but of metaphysics, and of the notion that the conduct of human affairs should be determined by some comprehensive vision of the nature of things. Their secularism was thus the necessary condition of an autonomous politics, an autonomous culture, and the full appreciation of human freedom.

This characteristic of the Venetian mind found especially vigorous expression in the hostility to scholasticism and to the dogmatic temperament in general that permeated Sarpi's treatment of the Council of Trent and makes him seem so clearly a predecessor of Gibbon. Sarpi displayed much the same zest as some leading figures of the seventeenth and eighteenth centuries in showing up the presumption in all intellectual system-building, its tendency to close men off from the actualities of human experience, and its exploitation to disguise and advance a crude *libido dominandi*. The Venetian approach to human affairs – though Contarini was a partial exception – was earth-bound and empirical. Its refusal to force the data of human experience into large systems was notably exhibited in the preference of Venetian writers for exposition through dialogues in which various points of view may find expression without explicit resolution. This familiar Renaissance form was employed by Paruta. It was also, slightly disguised, a favourite device in Sarpi's great work.

Their rejection of system was fundamental, for the Venetians, to the appreciation of a wide range of human concerns. If there was no universal pattern which bound all things into a single scheme, the subordination of one set of values to another, of one area of experience to another, and indeed of one class of men to another was no longer defensible, except perhaps on the most practical grounds. The implications for political life were here especially clear. Reason of state could no longer find its justification in eternal reason, and there was thus no alternative to a secular politics. The consequence was full recognition of the dignity of the lay estate and of political activity; and this tendency in Venetian discourse was, I suspect, a substantial element in its attractions for European readers. It provided another of Sarpi's major themes, but it emerged with particular clarity in Paruta's defence of civic life.[3] We may also take Paruta as an example of Venetian appreciation of the autonomy of other dimensions of human culture.

Paruta artfully set his dialogue on this subject at the final session of the Council of Trent. This setting enabled him to divide its participants into two groups: on one side, representing the systematic approach to politics, a number of learned bishops; on the other, several Venetian ambassadors. The issue was joined by one of the bishops who, having listened impatiently as the laymen discussed their embassies, their travels, and their experiences throughout Europe, belligerently denounced their worldly activities and contrasted the tedium of service to society with his own leisurely contemplation of higher things. He argued that active commitment to the service of an earthly community is inferior, both relatively in the degree of happiness it provides, and absolutely in the values it represents, to a life devoted to the eternal verities. The active life is a weariness to the flesh and filled with sinful temptations. Above all it tempts men to prefer an earthly city to the City of God, and of course it is obvious to what city he refers. The wise man, he argued, perceives 'that all men ought to be regarded as citizens of this great city of the universe, just as we have all been given one identical eternal law for our governance, one same heavenly father . . . one same head and ruler to govern us and give us everything that is good among us, God, best and greatest. No other homeland have we than nature, no other law, no other family, no other prince'.[4] And Paruta's Venetians understood immediately that what was here proposed was a comprehensive ideal at every point antagonistic to their own: a life without particular foci of experience or particular attachments to persons or places; a life that finds no value in the daily emotional and sensory encounters of human existence; a life in which the entire moral experience provided by society has only a negative value. Their defence of civic life was mounted on many fronts, but precisely because only life in society can provide for the whole, complex range of human capabilities, which cannot legitimately be prejudged, subsumed under any single principle, and organized in hierarchies. They insisted on the claims to human affection not only of particular states, which supply the context for all other values, but of family and friends, of the arts, and even of wealth. Political life was *perfect* for Paruta, because of its range and its refusal to discriminate: i.e., because of its secularity. The relation of these attitudes to some belief in the dignity and value of human freedom is also close. Hostility to the authoritarianism of the Counter Reformation in matters of belief permeated the writings of Sarpi, who condoned coercion only where the social order was at stake; and the personal liberty afforded by Venice was a perennial element in the European image of the Republic. In various ways, therefore, the Venetians supplied an idealistic justification for modern patriotism.

As the reflections of Paruta have already suggested, the rejection of universal intellectual systems had a counterpart in the rejection of political universalism, and this bias in the political culture of Venice doubtless also contributed to its wider acceptability. The values attributed to Venice and the patriotism they called forth were equally applicable to other particular states, but not to a universal empire. Paruta himself devoted many pages to a criticism of ancient Roman universalism, which he judged both politically ineffectual and, in comparison with the small states of ancient Greece, artistically and intellectually sterile.[5] The same arguments were equally effective, as the Venetians were aware, against the universalism promoted by the Counter Reformation papacy.

Venetian politics were based, therefore, on the need to defend the integrity of particular states. The Venetian interdict of 1606–1607, so widely publicized throughout Europe, was, among other things, the first of the great seventeenth century conflicts over sovereignty; and Sarpi had argued the cause of Venice in terms well calculated to have a broad appeal. 'I cannot refrain from saying', he advised his government, 'that no injury penetrates more deeply into a principate than when its majesty, that is to say sovereignty, is limited and subjected to the laws of another. A prince who possesses a small part of the world is equal in this respect to one who possesses much, nor was Romulus less a prince than Trajan, nor is your Serenity now greater than your forebears when their empire had not extended beyond the lagoons. He who takes away a part of his state from a prince makes him a lesser prince but leaves him a prince; he who imposes laws and obligations on him deprives him of the essence of a prince, even if he possesses the whole of Asia.'[6] And the case for the local settlement of local issues was still another important theme in his history of the Council. As he made a Gallican prelate at the Council remark, 'It would be a great absurdity to watch Paris burn when the Seine and Marne are full of water, in the belief that it was necessary to wait to put out the fire for water from the Tiber'.[7] Venetian political culture corresponded, then, to what was more and more clearly destined to be the shape of the European community of nations.

The rejection of systems and of the notion of hierarchy posed a serious danger to political existence, however, because it deprived society, both domestic and international, of its traditional principle of order. The Florentines had discovered the solution to this problem in the idea of balance, which was destined to supplant the hierarchical principle of order at almost the same time in both science and politics. Venice largely owed her survival, in a world dominated by great powers, to a calculated exploitation of the balance of power, and her writers tended to take this for granted. The case was quite different, however, for the internal structure of states; and Venetian publicists were long concerned to account for the order and effectiveness of the Republic by describing its balanced constitution. Contarini's classic work on this subject at times justified Venetian arrangements by appealing rather mechanically to the eternal order of nature, an argument which doubtless did not weaken his case with some of his later readers.[8]

But Contarini was too much of a Venetian to remain long with metaphysics; the order with which he was really concerned was that provided by effective government. 'In our city', he boasted, 'no popular tumult or sedition has ever occurred';[9] and his explanation of this remarkable fact was understandably of peculiar interest for Europeans whose own societies had been demonstrably less fortunate. The secret of Venetian success, Contarini revealed, was her constitution, which held the potentially antagonistic forces of the political arena in a complementary equilibrium. 'Such moderation and proportion characterize this Republic', he declared, 'and such a mixture of all suitable estates, that this city by itself incorporates at once a princely sovereignty, a governance of the nobility, and a rule of citizens, so that the whole appears as balanced as equal weights.'[10] And since this happy arrangement of checks and balances was severely impersonal, it pointed also to a government of laws rather than of men. But its ultimate test was utilitarian. 'The whole purpose of civil life consists in this', Contarini insisted: 'that, by the easiest way possible, the citizens may share in a happy life.'[11] Venice supplied, therefore, both a secular ideal and the means for its fulfilment.

Venetian constitutionalism received even wider, if less explicit, dissemination through the great work of Sarpi, which submits the papacy, as a species of governance, to searching scrutiny and finds it wanting largely because of its failure to realize the admirable principles exhibited by the Venetian government Sarpi argued that the church had originated as a free, spiritual and democratic body; and he showed how it had degenerated, step by step, through the classic sequence of forms described by Machiavelli, until it had at last emerged as the naked tyranny of the contemporary papacy, a particularly odious example of government by men rather than by laws. Here too the popularity of Sarpi's masterpiece had far more than a religious meaning.

Sarpi's vision of the development of ecclesiastical government over the centuries brings us to a final major contribution of Venetian political culture to the rest of Europe: its increasingly sophisticated historicism, which brought into a single focus the secularism, the particularism, and the constitutionalism of the Venetian tradition. These impulses were combined with a grasp of history as a process largely transcending individual acts which, it seems to me, went substantially beyond the hints at this conception in Florentine historiography. Even Contarini's *De republica Venetorum*, which otherwise displayed little historical sense, had suggested the idea of temporal process in applying the familiar platitude that Venice, following the course of biological nature, might decay;[12] and Paruta, an admirer of both Thucydides and Guicciardini, coolly analysed the evolution of curial institutions,[13] described the broad changes in Venetian policy over the centuries,[14] and dealt with Roman history as a long decline through such natural causes as her limited economic base, her defective constitution, her militarism and her excessive greatness.[15] He also expounded the idea of the progress of civilization to account for the contemporary splendours of Venice.[16] Davila was deeply interested in the remote causes for the recent tribulations of France, finding them in her constitution.[17] And Sarpi blamed the papal tyranny not primarily on the wickedness of worldly and ambitious popes but on the general decay of political authority in the early Middle Ages. To those who attributed the Protestant revolt to the actions of a single, nefarious man, he replied that Luther 'was only one of the means, and the causes were more potent and recondite'.[18]

Notable among the Venetian writers was a strong sense of the autonomy of

2F

history, of the obligation to confront the data exposed by historical research directly, without dogmatic preconceptions, and so to get at truth. During the interdict an anonymous Venetian pamphleteer had been bold enough to express a doubt that Charlemagne had truly received the Empire as a gift from the pope, and Bellarmine had angrily accused him of 'heresy in history'. The Venetian had not hesitated to set the matter straight; he retorted, 'There cannot be heresy in history which is profane and not contained in Holy Scripture'.[19] Sarpi insisted more than once that historical truth was a matter not of authority but of fact; and authority, he noted, 'cannot alter things already done'.[20] The famous history of his Venetian contemporary Enrico Davila also owed much of its conviction to its cool objectivity and its apparent freedom from confessional prejudice, and Davila was explicitly sensitive to the problem of bias.[21] Sarpi's bias is, of course, strongly evident, but his professedly empirical method was well calculated to make it appear the product, rather than the motive and organizing principle, of his research. He once compared the Council to a great lake fed by numerous tiny rivulets and gradually spreading out over Europe; the task of the historian, in this light, was to follow each of these brooklets to its source.[22] At the same time Sarpi was not naïf; he recognized the problem of selection, comparing himself to a harvester who found some fields more productive than others.[23]

But there was nothing detached about the Venetian pursuit of historical truth; and if Sarpi devoted himself to ferreting it out, he did so because he thought it useful. When a Gallican correspondent requested his opinion on the delicate question of Pope Joan, Sarpi replied that he found no solid evidence for her existence and personally doubted it; but, he went on to say, 'I should not care to trouble myself to prove something that, once proved, would be of no further use to me'.[24] History, for Sarpi, was not a matter for idle contemplation but an instrument of the active life celebrated by Paruta; the truth was useful, he profoundly believed, because the truth would set men free. Historical study, as the pursuit of truth, was for him the natural solvent and enemy of dogma, which sought, in the interest of an illegitimate empire over mankind, to obscure the truth. History thus became, in Sarpi's hands, the great unmasker, and therefore the one sure means of approach to a better world. By revealing the lost perfection of the past and the causes of its decay, it could display both the goal towards which contemporary reformers must struggle and the problems with which they must contend. Sarpi thus transmitted the secularism, the empiricism and the reformist impulse of the Renaissance to the militant reformers of a later age.[25]

The popularity of the major Venetian political writers and the esteem in which they were held is one symptom of the congeniality of these conceptions in early modern Europe. Their works were widely printed outside Italy, both in their original Latin or Italian texts and in translation; these were in addition to Venetian editions exported abroad. Contarini's *De magistratibus et republica Venetorum* was printed many times in Latin, and was translated into both French and English;[26] Naudé thought this 'admirable work' essential for the understanding of a republic.[27] Paruta's eloquent *Della perfezione della vita politica* was turned into French, his more mature *Discorsi politici* into English and German, and his Venetian history into English;[28] Naudé described him as an 'ornament of erudition',[29] and he was widely admired as one of the great political thinkers of his time.[30] Davila's *Istoria delle guerre civili di Francia* was twice translated into English,[31] appeared many times in French and Spanish versions, and was also put into Latin.[32] Bolingbroke praised Davila as the equal of Livy;[33] and while he sat as vice-president under Washington, John Adams composed a set of *Discourses on Davila*.[34] Even better known was, of course, Paolo Sarpi. His lesser writings were widely read outside of Italy, and editions of his *Istoria del Concilio Tridentino* multiplied rapidly. After its first appearance in an Italian version in London in 1619, it was quickly translated into Latin, French, German and English;[35] the English edition was among the few books carried to the New World by William Brewster, spiritual leader of the Plymouth colony.[36] It might have had a second English translation if Dr. Samuel Johnson had managed to carry out all the projects he devised for himself,[37] and it was twice more translated into French.[38] And Sarpi's distinction as a political sage was soon recognized. His enemies suggested this by associating him with Guicciardini;[39] among his admirers, Naudé ranked him with such ideal counsellors of government as Epictetus, Socrates, Seneca and Cato.[40] His French translator of the later seventeenth century, Amelot de la Houssaye (no blind admirer of Venice) praised him as a '*bon Politique*' and recommended his great history because of its excellent lessons for princes.[41] By the eighteenth century Sarpi's reputation for political cunning had so grown that spurious collections of political maxims circulated over his name, for example, in the Berlin of Frederick the Great, a book of worldly counsel under the title, *Le Prince de F. Paolo*.[42] To these works, which directly transmitted the political culture of Venice to the rest of Europe, should be added various writings of Giovanni Botero, and especially of Traiano Boccalini, both widely read abroad and inclined to dwell on the virtues of Venice. Boccalini, in the first century of his *Ragguagli di Parnaso*, included an eloquent and diverting summary of all that had seemed most admirable in the Republic.[43]

But these books did not by themselves create an interest in Venice; they are significant because they nourished, and can therefore help us to understand more clearly, a taste that had deeper sources. The Venetian achievement and the attitudes surrounding it corresponded to the emerging needs of the European nations. And Venice had particular advantages for bringing into focus the political conceptions of modern Europeans. For the Venetian state was not a utopia reflecting merely theoretical values but a living reality, a palpable part of their own world, superior in this respect even to the Florentine republic. She could be wondered at and admired, and the perennial admiration of travellers attracted other sorts of attention to her; her government and the kind of society that accompanied it could be studied empirically and in detail; and the degree to which it actually worked could apparently be evaluated. Venice therefore corresponded naturally to the growing taste for concreteness in political discussion that had emerged with the great Florentines.

She had also figured prominently in events of European resonance that demonstrated conclusively, before an international audience, her effectiveness in meeting crises of enormous danger and her capacity for survival. Her ability to resist the dreaded Turk was generally recognized, but she had also participated actively in the international conflicts of the West. In the war of the League of Cambrai she had withstood the onslaught of all Europe; and, though brought to the brink of destruction, she had nevertheless emerged as powerful as before. This miracle, indeed, had stimulated the work of Contarini, which so effectively conveyed an appreciation of the Venetian government to the rest of Europe.[44] It also transferred an impression previously confined largely to Italy, where it had already attracted the notice of Florence, to a larger world.[45]

Even more stimulating to the European imagination was the Venetian triumph over the pope in the great interdict of 1606-1607. This episode, which was followed with keen attention abroad, was the occasion for a flood of writings, for and against Venice, that circulated everywhere and in various ways called attention to the political values she claimed to incorporate; indirectly the Interdict also produced Sarpi's great work on the Council of Trent. Various Interdict writings were translated into French, German and English; they were sold at the Frankfurt fair; Pierre de l'Estoile acquired them in duplicate so that he could circulate them among his friends;[46] the Interdict was carefully reported and documents relating to it were extensively reproduced in the *Mercure François*.[47] Later writers on Venice would give special attention to the event. For Pierre d'Avity it showed Venice as 'an immovable rock in the defence of the state'.[48] To the Duc de Rohan the Venetians in this affair 'had transcended themselves' and given 'an example of perfect conduct to posterity'.[49] James Howell devoted a special section to this 'high Contestation', of which 'ev'ry Corner of Christendome did ring aloud, and sounds yet to this day'.[50] Even Amelot de la Houssaye devoted the whole of his second volume to the 'good cause' of Venice against the pope.[51]

The capacity for survival that Venice had revealed in the course of such trials demonstrated, in short, that she had access to a general political wisdom, universal, eternal, and utterly dependable, that might be made available to others in an age of peculiar turmoil and political discontent, and therefore an age with a special need for stable principles.[52] Thus Howell opened his *Survay*: 'Were it within the reach of humane brain to prescribe Rules for fixing a Society and Succession of people under the same Species of Government as long as the World lasts, the Republic of *Venice* were the fittest pattern on Earth both for direction and imitation.' And, he declared, 'If ever any hath brought humane government and policy to a *science* which consists of certitudes, the Venetian Republic is She, who is as dextrous in *ruling* men as in *rowing* of a gallie or gondola'.[53] The Duc de Rohan was attracted to Venice because he perceived in her the triumph of rational calculation over passion: science, perhaps, in a more modern sense.[54] Other writers, including even Bodin, made the point more obliquely by noting the gravity of Venetian political deliberation,[55] or more simply (following Contarini) by attributing the form of the Venetian government to philosophers.[56]

Venice, then, was the embodiment of political reason, a virtue that had previously been manifested chiefly by the ancients. And because of certain peculiarities claimed for her history, she could be seen as the means by which ancient political wisdom had been transmitted to the modern world.[57] For she had, as her admirers insisted, come out of the ancient world but had avoided its general collapse. She was living proof, therefore, of what men longed to believe: that ancient political virtue could find effective expression in the modern world. Thus, in a poem attributed to Marvell, Brittania, after expressing disgust with conditions at home, declares:

> To the serene Venetian state *I*'*le goe*
> From her sage mouth fam'd Principles to know,
> With her the Prudence of the Antients read,
> To teach my People in their steps to tread.
> By those great Patterns such a state *I*'*le frame*
> Shall darken story, Ingross loudmouthd fame.[58]

The comparisons between Venice and the admirable polities of antiquity – occasionally those of Greece but primarily that of Rome – that fill seventeenth and eighteenth-century discussions of Venice were therefore more than routine embellishment; they made a reassuring point. Venetian historians had themselves sometimes seen a parallel, and such writers as Fougasse and Gregorio Leti were inclined to press it.[59] Fougasse's English translator, W. Shute, pushed from similarity to continuity. 'It seemes in the dissolution of the last Monarchie, the *Genius* of it made transmigration to *Venice*. In her the Wisdome, Fortitude, Iustice, and Magnanimitie of old *Rome* doe yet move and stirre . . . All but her Ruines, and the Cause of them, (her Vice) is removed to *Venice*.'[60] But other writers did not hesitate to find Venice far superior to Rome, above all in meeting those ultimate criteria for governments, domestic stability and length of life. Boccalini, in describing Venice, recalled with scorn 'those reformations of government, those restorations of state that, with infinite disturbance' beset the Roman Republic;[61] and Howell observed that all ancient commonwealths, including the Roman, 'may be sayed to have bin but Mushrumps in point of *duration* if compared to the Signorie of Venice.'[62] Such comparisons also reveal another dimension of the Venetian role in later political discussion. Venice helped to strengthen the cause of the Moderns against the Ancients, and thus she played a part in the gathering self-confidence of modern Europe. It is significant that Sarpi and Davila were among the modern historians whom Perrault found equal to the best historians of antiquity, Thucydides and Livy.[63] Even William Temple, if a trifle grudgingly, acknowledged Sarpi (with Boccaccio and Machiavelli) as one of 'the great Wits among the moderns'.[64]

The notion of Venice as the supreme European representative of a generalized political wisdom meant that she could function as the standard by which all particular arrangements might be judged. For an anonymous pamphleteer during the early stages of the Puritan Revolution, a Venetian observer seemed the appropriate mouthpiece for a sensible perspective on the disturbing English scene.[65] A French writer on Venice, finding her utterly different from every other European state, compared her in this respect to China, which had by now seen long service in showing up the defects of Europe.[66]

The general character of the political wisdom attributed to Venice also meant that Europeans from various traditions, concerned with quite different problems and with conflicting aspirations, could (with the partial exception of those Frenchmen, beginning with Seyssel and Bodin, who were committed to proving the superiority of monarchy over all other forms of government) all find inspiration in the Venetian model. They could discern in her whatever they happened to yearn for: both frugality and luxury, valour and love of peace, aristocratic responsibility and broad political participation, order and personal freedom. But whatever they chose to emphasize, they were in general agreement that Venice met certain fundamental criteria of effective government.

The first of these, as I have already suggested, was the capacity for long survival, and the durability of Venice inevitably implied other virtues. Avity declared that she had lasted 'longer than any other [state] that has come to our knowledge';[67] Howell thought her closer to immortality than any other government;[68] Amelot de la Houssaye paid tribute to her long existence;[69] Harrington saw her 'at this day with one thousand years upon her back . . . as young, as fresh, and free from decay, or any apperance of it, as shee was born.'[70] And as Howell observed, 'Length of Age argues strength of Constitution; and as in Naturall bodies, so this Rule holds good likewise in Politicall: Whence it may be inferred, that the Signorie of Venice from Her Infancy was of a strong Symmetry, well nursd, and swadled with wholsom Lawes'.[71] The durability of Venice was a result of, and therefore implied, an effective government capable of maintaining domestic peace. Even Seyssel, though he felt compelled to minimize this troublesome fact, had described Venice as 'the most perfect and best administered empire and state of community that one has seen or read of up to now';[72] and though Bodin emphasized (against those who admired her immutability) that Venice had altered over the years, he too was compelled to acknowledge the gradual and peaceful character of the changes she had endured.[73] Boccalini celebrated the good order of Venice; she had avoided the conflicts between rich and poor so disastrous for other societies, her nobles willingly forgave each others' injuries instead of seeking revenge, she had consistently managed to control her military leaders.[74] Howell observed that Venetians were not 'of so volatil an humor, and so greedy of change as other Italians', and that Venice was therefore free 'from all intestin commotions and tumults'; he also appreciated the cleanliness of her streets, an outward and visible sign of her inner devotion to order.[75] Harrington echoed these sentiments.[76] And this impression of Venice was destined for a particularly long life. The *Encyclopédie*, though aware of her decline in other respects, applauded in Venice 'an internal tranquillity that has never altered'.[77]

It was usual to attribute the internal stability of Venice to the excellence of her laws, their strict enforcement and their impartial application to all classes. In Venice alone among republics, Boccalini suggested, the ruling group had abstained from oppressive legislation in its own interest;[78] and her reputation in this respect was celebrated by Spencer in a sonnet which praised Venice above Rome because she 'farre exceedes in policie of right'.[79] Boccalini praised the vigorous administration of her laws, attributing to this her perpetual youth and beauty;[80] and Bodin admitted that 'an injury done by a Venetian gentleman unto the least inhabitant of the city is right severely corrected and punished'.[81] Behind each of these observations, we may assume, lurks some experience with situations in which so happy a condition did not prevail.

Corresponding to the internal peace Venice seemed to represent was a peacefulness abroad that was equally attractive to many other Europeans. The interest of French observers in this quality, to be sure, sometimes was ambivalent. Bodin remarked that the Venetians were 'better citizens than warriors', though he also saw their pacifism as a cause of happiness;[82] and if Amelot de la Houssaye emphasized Venetian neutralism and aversion to war, he also noted their occasional disadvantages.[83] But the Englishman Howell had no doubts about the benefits of Venetian pacifism: 'Another cause of the *longevity* of this Republic may be alleged to be, that She hath allwayes bin more inclined to *peace* than *war*, and chosen rather to be a Spectatrix or Umpresse, than a Gamestresse.' She had been, indeed, the great peace-maker of Europe: 'All Christendom is beholden unto this wise Republic, in regard She hath interceded from time to time, and labourd more for the generall peace and tranquility of Christendom, and by her moderation and prudent comportment hath don better Offices in this kind then any other whatsoever.'[84]

In addition to all this, Venetians were regularly seen as exemplars of all the old-fashioned political virtues; these both proved the general excellence of the Venetian system and helped to explain its strength. As Howell declared, 'Ther are few Cities which have brought forth men more celebrous for all the Cardinall Virtues than *Venice*'; he also noted, as though it were a further proof of the vitality of Venetian society, her numerous 'scientificall contemplative men, and greater Artists'.[85] Fougasse treated Venetian history as a rich body of patriotic examples, presumably for imitation;[86] and Gregorio Leti also discovered in Venice instructive models of 'service to country and the effects produced by love accompanied by zeal'.[87] Both Amelot de la Houssaye[88] and Louis Dumay[89] defended, in addition, the piety of Venice.

Two characteristics of the Venetian ruling group, however, especially impressed other Europeans. The first was the absence of personal ambition on the part of even its most talented members, as shown by their readiness to descend from positions of power to the anonymity of private life. As Amelot de la

Houssaye remarked, the citizens of Venice 'know how to obey'.[90] A reflection of this virtue was the modesty of life that prevailed even among the wealthiest Venetians, a quality that made them so different from powerful men elsewhere.[91] The second remarkable trait of this group was its acceptance of the obligation to support the state by paying taxes. Boccalini had emphasized the point, in which he would be echoed by others: 'The great marvel of Venetian Liberty, which filled the whole world with wonder, was that the same nobility who governed not only patiently paid existing taxes into the public treasury, but also, with incredible quickness and facility, often decreed new ones against themselves which were then rigorously exacted by the public collectors.'[92] Of what other society in Europe, although most governments were perennially close to bankruptcy, could this have been said?

But the peculiar virtues of Venetians themselves required explanation, as Howell recognized: 'Now, ther are few or none who are greater *Patriotts* than the Venetian Gentlemen, their prime *study* is the public good and glory of their Countrey, and *civil prudence* is their principall *trade* whereunto they arrive in a high mesure; Yet as it may be easily observd, though these Gentlemen are extraordinary wise when they are *conjunct*, take them *single* they are but as other Men.'[93] Even here, therefore, we have been primarily concerned with the evidence that Venice was admirable, and that she was therefore a potential source of instruction for ailing polities elsewhere. With Howell's implicit question about the causes of virtue, we may now turn to the identification by other Europeans of those more specific elements in the Venetian system that seemed to explain its peculiar capacity for survival, the maintenance of order and the encouragement of the civic virtues. The question was of the highest importance. If these could be imitated elsewhere, they might be expected to produce similar results.

We may note first the general European approval of the secular character of the Venetian state. The point is largely left implicit, or it emerges superficially as applause for the exclusion from political responsibility in Venice of the clergy or members of clerically-oriented families.[94] But Howell, who had been imprisoned as a royalist and wrote of Venice during the Puritan domination of England, expressed fuller appreciation for the Venetian effort to separate politics from religion: 'She hath a speciall care of the Pulpit (and Presse) that no Churchman from the meanest *Priest* to the *Patriarch* dare tamper in their Sermons with temporall and State-affairs, or the transactions and designes of the Senat; It being too well known that Churchmen are the most perilous and pernicious Instruments in a *State*, if they misapply their talent, and employ it to poyson the hearts of the peeple, to intoxicate their brains, and suscitat them to sedition, and a mislike of the Government . . . Yet they bear a very high respect unto the Church.'[95] And Amelot de la Houssaye charged that much of the criticism of Sarpi came from a failure to distinguish politics and religion.[96] Venice was a lesson, therefore, for a Europe in which political order was still regularly disrupted by the imperious demands of religion: Venice revealed that the first condition of effective statecraft was that it must be secular and therefore autonomous.

Hand in hand with the separation of realms went the separateness of states; Venice was also admirable because she had insisted so strenuously on her particularity and her sovereignty. This, indeed, was the primary meaning of that Venetian freedom which was the most widely celebrated element in the myth of Venice; its attractiveness signified resistance to the idea of a universal empire and devotion to one's own fatherland. Bodin noted this aspect of Venice;[97] Fougasse thought nothing more certain than that, in this sense, Venice had been always free;[98] Voltaire was still to celebrate the perpetual independence of Venice as though it represented for him some great human value.[99]

In England the unconquerability of Venice was associated with virginity, a virtue recently given prominence by a beloved queen; and erotic language was used to embroider an interesting image. Coryat noted with satisfaction, in writing of Venice, the frustration of all those who, 'being allured with her glorious beauty, have attempted to defloure her';[100] and Howell, who noted more soberly that 'this *Maiden* city . . . had the Prerogative to be born a *Christian*, and *Independent*, whereof She Glorieth, and that not undeservedly, above all other States or Kingdomes', composed verses exploiting an obvious pun:

> *Venice Great Neptunes Minion, still a Mayd,*
> *Though by the warrlikst Potentats assayd . . .*
> *Though, Syren-like on Shore and Sea, Her Face*
> *Enchants all those whom once She doth embrace . . .*
> *These following Leaves display, if well observd,*
> *How She so long Her Maydenhead preserved . . .*
> *Venus and Venice are Great Queens in their degree,*
> *Venus is Queen of Love, Venice of Policie.*[101]

In what may also have some interest for the development of a poetic metaphor, these crudities were eventually refined by Wordsworth into a famous sonnet after the extinction of the Venetian Republic by Napoleon:

> *. . . Venice, the eldest Child of Liberty*
> *She was a maiden City, bright and free;*
> *No guile seduced, no force could violate . . .*

The independence of Venice was the basis for what was widely regarded as her admirably successful foreign policy. Because she was free, she could balance among the various powers of Europe, and so protect both her liberty and her peace. Howell, again, noted this with particular clarity: 'Now, one of the wayes wherby the Republic of *Venice* hath endeavourd to preserve her Maydenhead and freedom so long, hath bin to keep the power of the potentat Princes in a counterpoise; wherby She hath often adapted her designes, and accommodated Her-self to the conditions of the times, and frequently changd thoughts, will, frends, and enemies. She hath bin allwayes usd to suspect any great power, to fear much, and confide little, to be perpetually vigilant of the operations of others, and accordingly to regulat her own consultations and proceedings; wherby She hath bin often accusd of exces in circumspection.'[102] Amelot de la Houssaye also remarked on this tendency in Venetian policy, though with less approval; he would have preferred a Venice more consistently allied with France.[103]

As Howell will have suggested, the Venetian talent for balancing among changing political forces abroad pointed more profoundly to a general adaptability to shifting circumstance that was seen as the necessary condition both of her survival and of her apparent invulnerability to change. She could remain 'forever young' because she had learned how to master the successive challenges of political life and in this sense to triumph over time. Nothing was more attractive to anxious European observers than this aspect of the Venetian achievement. This was the major impulse behind their admiration of her constitution and of those qualities of flexibility and finesse in her policy that less friendly and less secular minds perceived as unscrupulous, opportunistic, in short Machiavellian.

There was a good deal of discussion about the nature of the Venetian constitution, and the earlier view that it was a mixture of monarchic, aristocratic and democratic elements maintained (somewhat like the equilibrium in Venetian relations abroad) in a perfect balance tended to give way by the later sixteenth century to the recognition that Venice was a pure aristocracy.[104] Although some observers were critical of the limitations on the doge as a reflection on the competence of kings and therefore a threat to good political order,[105] the elimination of a democratic taint from the image of the Republic doubtless increased the attractiveness of the Venetian model for the seventeenth and eighteenth centuries. As an aristocratic republic of the most responsible and effective type, Venice acquired a new kind of interest.[106] Much was therefore made of the general competence of her nobility, of the systematic way in which younger nobles were advanced through positions of steadily increasing responsibility, and of the contentment of the lower classes under this régime.[107]

But however it was regarded otherwise, the main point about the Venetian constitution as it was perceived abroad was that it was a regular structure ('a great and ingenious machine' in the suggestive words of Saint-Didier[108]), and that it worked. As early as Thomas Starkey, Englishmen had recognized its effectiveness in preventing tyranny;[109] Howell identified this as a factor in the survival of Venice and a safeguard against 'trenching upon the Common Liberty, and doing injustice';[110] and Venice figured prominetly in the constitutional discussions carried on in the England of Cromwell and the Holland of De Witt.[111] Even in the France of Louis XIV Saint-Didier was bold enough to describe at length the limits on the power of the doge, in a work that generally represented the Venetian government as perfect.[112] Other writers emphasized the virtues in the Venetian system of broad participation by citizens in the affairs of the government. Even Bodin may have hinted at this in recognizing that although

Venice was 'pure and simply Aristocratic', she was 'yet somewhat governed by Proportion Harmonicall', language that suggests multiple participation.[113] The point was evidently important to Voltaire in his contrast between Rome and Venice: 'Rome lost, by Caesar, at the end of five hundred years, its liberty acquired by Brutus. Venice has preserved hers for eleven centuries, and I hope she will always do so.'[114] In the same interest some writers persisted in the old view that the Venetian constitution retained a democratic element, among them Howell,[115] Harrington,[116] Saint-Didier, [117] and perhaps even Rousseau, who declared: 'It is a mistake to regard the government of Venice as a genuine aristocracy. For while the Venetian people has no part in the government, the Venetian nobility is itself a people.'[118]

By permitting the representation of diverse and changing interests, the Venetian constitution kept the Republic in touch with changing conditions and needs; and in the flexibility and shrewdness of Venetian policy European writers found additional grounds for admiration and emulation. This was the general lesson to which numerous particular examples pointed; Venice could be seen to incorporate not only eternal reason but also (however inconsistently in particular cases) practical reason, reason of state. Venice, Howell declared, had 'allwayes bin one of the most politic and pragmaticall'st Republics on Earth';[119] Louis Dumay expressed somewhat the same thought in saying that she had been preserved 'rather by prudence than by valour'.[120] The Duc de Rohan put it more baldly in celebrating the degree to which the Venetians followed 'all the maxims of their true interest',[121] and Naudé most sharply of all in describing them as 'steeped in a continual Machiavelism': in Naudé's eyes a point in their favour.[122]

Some manifestations of the political astuteness attributed to Venice seem innocent enough: for example insistence on the equality of all nobles as a means of maintaining their unity, or the requirement of a *relazione* from ambassadors.[123] Others, though usually mentioned with admiration, are more ambiguous: the capacity of 'the sagacious Senate' for double-talk,[124] the secrecy with which official deliberations could be carried on even in large assemblies,[125] the wisdom of keeping arms out of the hands of subjects,[126] the use of ambassadors as spies, the astuteness with which residents of the city were kept divided.[127] Still others are presented as useful, but with some sense of distaste and occasionally with an argument for their necessity: skill in the exploitation of political symbolism;[128] the oppression of subject peoples on the mainland;[129] the secret denunciations, internal spying, and terrorization of the people increasingly attached to the image of Venice.[130] Of particular interest from this standpoint was the political explanation some French writers advanced for the moral permissiveness regularly attributed, with peculiar fascination, to Venice. Bodin saw it as a device on the part of the rulers of Venice to manage the populace: 'to make them more mild and pliable, they give them full scope and liberty to all sorts of pleasures.'[131] A century later Amelot de la Houssaye gave a similar account of the notorious indiscipline of the Venetian clergy; it served both to discredit them with the people and to keep them content and loyal to the state, in spite of their exclusion from positions of influence.[132]

In another sense, too, Venetian flexibility appealed to other Europeans; as a political model she displayed a remarkable responsiveness to what were, for them, material realities that required just such recognition as they received in Venice. French writers observed in her, with some approval, a degree of social mobility. Bodin noted that, as in England, the nobles participated in trade, and that 'a Venetian gentleman may marry a base woman, or a common citizen's daughter',[133] and Amelot de la Houssaye thought the sale of titles of nobility in Venice a good custom since it renewed the ruling class, eased the tax burden and increased attachment to the state.[134] The English were impressed with the commercial and financial foundations of her greatness. Howell praised her for opening up trade with the Levant, Africa, and the Indies, and for 'her Bank of money', which, he asserted, 'as it hath bin the Ground and Rule of all other banks, so is it the most usefull for Marchants or Gentlemen to any part of the world, nor do I see how Christendom can subsist conveniently without it'.[135] John Dury lauded Venice for encouraging invention.[136] Nor did the Venetian system of poor relief, the government's sponsorship of public works, its responsibility for the provision of food to the populace and its regulations for the control of epidemics go unnoticed.[137]

Although its importance was yet scarcely recognized, it may be worth pointing out also that the historical aspect of Venetian political culture had some relation to its pragmatism. Like the statesmen of Venice, her historians too were concerned not with eternal principles but with particular and changing circumstances, about which they sought the same kind of clear and certain knowledge of the actual world as that on which Venetian statesmen were supposed to base their decisions. History too was in this sense amoral, and Venetian historiography was admired because of its capacity to get at and effectively to reveal the truth.

Most of the admiration focused on Sarpi, whose *Concilio Tridentino* in many ways brought the Renaissance tradition of historical writing to a climax. He appeared to have solved supremely well both the scientific and the rhetorical problems of a modern historian. Amelot de la Houssaye, who thought him the equal of Thucydides, Xenophon and Tacitus, praised his truthfulness, his responsibility to the realities of the human world, his exactness. 'Everything', he declared, 'is *ad rem*, everything is instructive, natural, without art, without disguise. He proceeds always bridle in hand, and always arrives where he is going.'[138] Le Courayer praised his impartiality: 'Has he not entirely filled the character of a perfect historian, who must not show either his religion or his country, but consider himself a citizen of the entire world, and make as a law for himself the simple exposition of facts, whether favourable or prejudicial to anyone whomsoever?'[139] The *Encyclopédie* admired the naturalness and energy of Sarpi's style and the 'judicious reflections' with which he sowed his work;[140] and Samuel Johnson praised the moral qualities of his work, quoting Wotton with approval to the effect that in it 'the Reader finds Liberty without Licentiousness, Piety without Hypocrisy, Freedom of Speech without Neglect of Decency, Severity without Rigour, and extensive Learning without Ostentation'.[141] Both Hume[142] and Gibbon[143] acknowledged Sarpi and Davila among their own masters and models. Thus Venetian historiography, so closely related in the Renaissance republics to the needs of political life, continued to affect the ways in which later Europeans viewed the past; this, indeed, may have been the most persistent among the legacies of Venice.

Much of what, in Venice, interested European observers might also have been discerned in Florence, though perhaps less readily and, because the Florentine Republic had perished, less persuasively. But one final attribute of Venice that vividly impressed the European imagination was regarded as clearly unique: the remarkable personal liberty enjoyed by all Venetians. Because it was general and took many forms, and because of the peculiar capacity of personal freedom to induce anxiety, it produced a variety of reactions, often ambivalent. Thus Saint-Didier: 'The liberty of Venice permits everything, for whatever life one leads, whatever religion one professes; if one does not talk, and undertakes nothing against the state or the nobility, one can live in full security, and no one will undertake to censure one's conduct nor oppose one's personal disorder.'[144] In its religious dimension the freedom of Venice won the approval of Salmasius,[145] and Milton was grateful to Sarpi for his contribution, as a historian, to liberty of conscience.[146] But although Saint-Didier was impressed by the religious latitude allowed in Venice, he was dubious about it: 'The tolerance there is so great that they close their eyes' to all sorts of deviations.[147] Leti doubted whether liberty in Venice was good for civil life.[148]

These ambiguous reactions to the personal freedoms of Venice were all based on a failure, perhaps even a refusal, to distinguish between liberty and licence. It is apparent from them that no real separation between the two yet seemed possible; personal liberty was generally supposed to merge inevitably into licence; and, however fascinating either of these conditions might be, liberty was therefore always dangerous. The almost obsessive preoccupation of foreigners with the licentiousness of Venice,[149] which was given increasing substance as she became a purveyor of pleasures to the upper classes of Europe, the gaudiest stop on the Grand Tour, should thus be seen as a kind of negative tribute to the more general freedom of Venetian society. The sexual temptation that Venice represented and its very confusion with more obviously political aspects of personal liberty pointed, indeed, to the possibility that orderly and effective government might after all be consistent with permissiveness in the more private dimensions of life, though the lesson was slow to emerge. Venice, in any case, could be seen increasingly to possess all kinds of freedom, and by the second half of the eighteenth century the appropriate distinction could at last be made. Thus the *Encyclopédie*, delicately distinguishing among the satisfactions of life, observed that in Venice one tasted both *'la liberté et les plaisirs'*.[150]

By this time, of course, the importance of Venice for the political education of Europe was nearing its end. Venice herself was in decline, and the discrepancy between the tawdry realities of the age of Casanova and the ideal Venice imagined by generations of admirers was increasingly difficult to ignore. Further-more, a new source of political wisdom, a new political model, was now emerging; the *philosophes* were discovering in England an inspiration Venice could no longer supply. Yet the virtues Voltaire and Montesquieu discovered across the Channel were still suspiciously like those previously associated with Venice. England too was admired as a free nation, with a secular and constitu-tional government in which tyranny was prevented by dividing and balancing powers; and, like Venice, England seemed to be ruled by laws rather than men, gave merchants their due, based her policies on a realistic perception of the needs of her people, and afforded them a remarkable degree of personal liberty. Even the distortions in this vision of England had their origins in the Venetian model.

I do not mean to suggest that Europeans learned their politics from Venice, as a student learns, for example, his chemistry. Her pedagogy, to borrow a piquant phrase from Sarpi, was 'obstetrical'.[151] She kept alive, for whoever found them useful, the political attitudes and values of the Renaissance, through her own political writings and above all through her survival as living proof of their validity; and from time to time, when conditions were favourable. Europeans could recognize that these attitudes and values were also their own, In this way Venice helped to transmit the political tradition of the Renaissance to the Enlightenment, and thus she prepared the way for the fruitful recognition of the political achievement of England.

NOTES

1. But see J. R. Hale, *England and the Italian Renaissance: the growth of interest in its history and art* (London, 1954), which does recognize that before the eighteenth century Venice was the primary source of European impressions of the Italian Renaissance. See also Zera S. Fink, *The Classical Republicans: an essay in the recovery of a pattern of thought in seventeenth century England* (2nd ed., Evanston, 1962).

2. For fuller treatment of the Venetian political tradition, see my *Venice and the defense of republican liberty: Renaissance values in the age of the Counter Reformation* (Berkeley, 1968).

3. *Della perfezione della vita politica*, in his *Opere politiche*, ed. C. Monzani (Florence, 1852) i, 33–405.

4. Ibid., 41–57, 214–216.

5. In his *Discorsi politici*, in *Opere politiche*, ii, 1–371.

6. *Sopra la forza e validità della scommunica*, in *Istoria dell' Interdetto e altri scritti*, ed. Giovanni Gambarin (Bari, 1940) ii, 40.

7. *Istoria del Concilio Tridentino*, ed. Giovanni Gambarin (Bari, 1935) ii, 250.

8. *De magistratibus et republica venetorum* (Venice, 1543).

9. I cite from the edition of J. G. Graevius, *Thesaurus antiquitatum et historiarum Italiae* (Leyden, 1722) v, col. 58.

10. Ibid., cols. 7–8.

11. Ibid., col. 4.

12. Ibid., cols. 56–57.

13. In his *relazione* of 1595 after his Roman embassy, Albèri, II, iv, 355–448.

14. In his *Historia vinetiana* (Venice, 1605).

15. In his *Discorsi*, cited above.

16. *Vita politica*, 254–256.

17. *Istoria delle guerre civili di Francia* (Milan, 1807) i, 7–13.

18. *Concilio Tridentino*, i, 236.

19. Bellarmine's charge appeared in his *Risposta a un libretto intitolato Risposta di un dottore di Theologia* (Rome, 1606). It was directed against Giovanni Marsilio, who replied in his *Difesa a favore della risposta dell' otto propositioni* (Venice, 1606). Both works are included in *Raccolta degli scritti usciti . . . nella causa del P. Paolo V. co' signori venetiani* (Chur, 1607) i, 166–167 and 243 for these passages.

20. *Concilio Tridentino*, ii, 437.

21. *Guerre civili di Francia*, i, 3–5.

22. *Concilio Tridentino*, i, 187.

23. Ibid., i, 4–5.

24. Letter to Jcrôme Groslot de l'Isle, 28 Feb., 1612, in his *Lettere ai Protestanti*, ed. Manlio D. Busnelli (Bari, 1931) i, 219.

25. For a vision of Sarpi as reformer, see Pierre F. Le Courayer, *Défense de la nouvelle traduction de l'histoire du Concile de Trente* (Amsterdam, 1742) 38.

26. The French translation was by Jehan Charrier (Paris, 1544), the English by Sir Lewes Lewkenor (London, 1599).

27. Gabriel Naudé, *Bibliographia politica* (Frankfurt, 1673) 111.

28. For these translations see Carlo Curcio, *Dal Rinascimento alla Controriforma* (Rome, 1934) 211, n. The translation of the history (London, 1658) was the work of Henry, Earl of Monmouth.

29. *Bibliographia politica*, 33.

30. Curcio, 211.

31. By Charles Cotterell and William Aylesbury (1647) and Ellis Farnesworth (1758).

32. The French translation (1644) was by I. Baudoin, the Spanish (1675) by P. Basilio Varen de Soto, and the Latin (1735) by François Cornazanus.

33. Henry St. John, Lord Viscount Bolingbroke, *Letters on the study and use of history* (London [1st ed., 1752] 1770) 136–137. For English interest in Davila, see also Christopher Hill, *Intellectual origins of the English Revolution* (Oxford, 1965) 2, 278–279.

34. It was first published in Boston, 1805. It must be admitted that the work is very little concerned with Davila.

35. See Hubert Jedin, *Das Konzil von Trient, ein Uberblick über die Erforschung seiner Geschichte* (Rome, 1948) 93.

36. Giorgio Spini, 'Riforma italiana e mediazioni ginevrine nella Nuova Inghilterra', in *Ginevra e l'Italia* (Florence, 1959) 454–455.

37. For Johnson's interest in Sarpi, see, most recently, John Lawrence Abbott, 'Dr. Johnson and the making of "The Life of Father Paul Sarpi"', *Bulletin of the John Rylands Library*, xxxxviii (1966) 255–267. The first translation was by Nicholas Brent (1620).

38. The first was by the Calvinist Giovanni Diodati (Geneva, 1621); the later translations were by Abraham Nicolas Amelot de la Houssaye (Amsterdam, 1683) and Pierre F. Le Courayer (London, 1736).

39. For example, Cardinal Pallavicino, in his own *Historia del Concilio Tridentino*; on this point see V. Luciani, *Francesco Guicciardini and his European reputation* (New York, 1936) 208.

40. *Science des princes, ou considérations politiques sur les coups d'état* (Paris, 1757) iii, 238

41. In the preface of his *Histoire da Concile de Trente* (2nd rev. ed., Amsterdam, 1686).

42. See Francesco Griselini, *Memorie anedote spettanti alla vita ed agli studi del sommo filosofo e giureconsulto F. Paolo Servita* (Lausanne, 1760) 260.

43. For the numerous translations of this work, see Luigi Firpo, *Traduzioni dei 'Ragguagli' di Traiano Boccalini* (Florence, 1965).

44. Cf. Franco Gaeta, 'Alcune considerazioni sul mito di Venezia', *Bibliothèque d'Humanisme et Renaissance*, XXIII (1961) 63. Among Europeans particularly impressed by this was Claude de Seyssel, *La monarchie de France* (1519) ed. Jacques Poujol (Paris, 1961) 107.

45. For earlier impressions of Venice, see Gina Fasoli, 'Nascita di un mito', *Studi storici in onore di Gioacchino Volpe* (Florence, 1958) i, 445–479. For Florentine interest in Venice see also Rudolph von Albertini, *Das florentinische Staatsbewusstsein im Ubergang von der Republik zum Principat* (Berne, 1955); Renzo Pecchioli, 'Il "mito" di Venezia e la crisi fiorentina intorno al 1500', *Studi Storici*, iii (1962) 451–492; and Felix Gilbert, *Machiavelli and Guicciardini: politics and history in sixteenth century Florence* (Princeton, 1965).

46. *Mémoires-Journaux*, ed. G. Brunet, (Paris, 1875–1896) viii, 198–310.

47. I (1614) leaves 48–70, 89–104, 120–128.

48. *Les estats empires royaumes et principautés du monde* (Paris, 1635) 497.

49. *De l'interest des princes, et des estats de la Chrestienté* (Paris, 1692) 122–123.

50. *S.P.Q.V. A survay of the signorie of Venice* (London, 1651) 142.

51. *Histoire du gouvernement de Venise et l'examen de sa liberté* (Paris, 1677).

52. On the general point see, for example, the recent works of E. Thuau, *Raison d'état et pensée politique à l'époque de Richelieu* (Paris, 1966), and Leonard Marsak, 'The Idea of Reason in Seventeenth Century France', *Cahiers d'Histoire Mondiale*, xi (1969) 407–416.

53. Pp. 1, 10.

54. See, for example, his *Interest des princes*, 102.

55. Jean Bodin, *The six bookes of a commonweale*, Richard Knolles, trans. (London, 1606), in the facsimile edition of Kenneth D. McRae (Cambridge, Mass., 1962) 563. The Knolles translation made use of both the slightly differing French and Latin editions.

56. Avity, 477, for example.

57. The point has been made by Fink, 34–35.

58. 'Brittania and Rawleigh', in Andrew Marvell, *Poems and Letters*, ed. H. M. Margoliouth (Oxford, 1952) i, 188. Margoliouth thinks the poem is not Marvell's.

59. Thomas de Fougasse, *The generall historie of the magnificent state of Venice*, W. Shute trans. (London, 1612) i, 25, 162, from the French edition of 1608; Gregorio Leti, *Ragguagli historici e politici delle virtu, e massime necessarie alla conservazione degli stati* (Amsterdam, 1699) i, 103–105. In this work Leti attempts to substitute Holland for Venice as a new model of political perfection, but he does so by magnifying in the Dutch the virtues elsewhere attributed to Venice.

60. In his epistle to the reader.

61. Traiano Boccalini, *Ragguagli di Parnaso*, ed. Luigi Firpo (Bari, 1948) i, 21–22.

62. P. 203. See also 204–207.

63. Charles Perrault, *Parallèle des Anciens et des Modernes* (Paris, 1688), in the facsimile edition of H. R. Jauss (Munich, 1964) ii, 100.

64. *An Essay upon the ancient and modern learning*, ed. J. E. Spingarn (Oxford, 1909) 36.

65. *A Venice looking-glasse: or, a letter written very lately from London to Rome, by a Venetian clarissimo* (London, 1648). This has been attributed to Howell.

66. Alexandre Toussaint de Limojon, sieur de Saint-Didier, *La ville et la republique de Venise* (Paris, 1680) 4.

67. P. 476.

68. P. 1.

69. P. 12.

70. James Harrington, *Oceana*, ed. S. B. Liljegren (Heidelberg, 1924) 185.

71. Opening words of the epistle to Parliament.

72. Pp. 107–108.
73. P. 433.
74. Pp. 22, 28–29.
75. Pp. 5, 8, 35.
76. Pp. 32, 137.
77. Article 'Venise', *Encyclopédie, ou dictionnaire raisonné des sciences, des arts et des métiers* (Paris, 1751–1765) xvii, 12.
78. P. 24.
79. This prefaced Lewkenor's English translation of Contarini.
80. Pp. 21–22.
81. P. 785.
82. Pp. 428, 606.
83. Pp. 108, 114.
84. Pp. 4, 208. See also Boccalini, 26.
85. Pp. 200–204.
86. For example, i, 114.
87. II, 344.
88. P. 549.
89. Against Naudé, in his notes to the *Science des Princes*. Dumay was a Counsellor-Secretary to the Elector of Mainz.
90. P. 547. See also Boccalini, 25–26.
91. Boccalini, 24.
92. P. 23. See also Amelot de la Houssaye, 48–49; Howell, 5; and the Sieur de la Haye, *La politique civile et militaire des Venitiens* (Paris, 1668) 65–67.
93. P. 23.
94. Amelot de la Houssaye, 37; Howell, 183; Harrington, 173.
95. P. 7.
96. In the preface to his translation of Sarpi's *Concilio Tridentino*.
97. P. 128.
98. I, 23.
99. 'Venise, et, par occasion, de la liberté', *Oeuvres complètes*, ed. Louis Moland (Paris, 1877–1885) xx, 552–554, often included in the *Dictionnaire philosophique*.
100. Thomas Coryat, *Crudities* (Glasgow, 1905) i, 415–416.
101. P. 1 and prefatory verses.
102. P. 180.
103. P. 160.
104. Gaeta, 69–72.
105. And not only in France; see G. P. Gooch, *English democratic ideas in the seventeenth century* (Cambridge, 1954) 243.
106. Cf. Fougasse, i, 208; and Fink, 46.
107. Boccalini, 23, 26–27; Amelot de la Houssaye, 37 seq., 49–50, 61.
108. P. 151.
109. *Dialogue between Pole and Lupset*, ed. K. M. Burton (London, 1948) 167.
110. P. 12; see also 6.
111. Gaeta, 71–72.
112. P. 178.
113. P. 112.
114. P. 554.
115. Pp. 10–11.
116. P. 19.
117. Pp. 152–153.
118. *Contrat social*, bk. iv, ch. 3.
119. P. 55. See also 4, with special reference to Venetian foreign policy.

120. II, 457–458 in Naudé, *Science des Princes*.

121. P. 128. See also 92, 122.

122. *Science des Princes*, i, 146; cf. 144.

123. Amelot de la Houssaye, 99–101, 54–55.

124. Howell, 92.

125. Boccalini, 30–31; Amelot de la Houssaye, 76–77; Saint-Didier, 227–228.

126. Amelot de la Houssaye, 102.

127. Dumay, in Naudé, *Science des Princes*, i, 163; iii, 115.

128. Rousseau, *Émile*, in *Oeuvres complètes* (Paris, 1969) iv, 646 n.

129. Leti, i, 74–76, on the ground that it is the way of nature for the great to oppress the weak.

130. Saint-Didier, 274 seq., where these practices are seen as both debasing and useful; cf. Amelot de la Houssaye, 309 seq., where distaste and fascination seem equally mixed.

131. P. 711.

132. Pp. 99, 135–142, 383.

133. Pp. 235, 398.

134. Pp. 133–134.

135. P. 208.

136. *A seasonable discourse* (London, 1649), cited by Hill, 278.

137. Fougasse, i, 112–113; Howell, 18, 185; Dumay, in Naudé, *Science des princes*, cit., i, 204.

138. Preface to his translation of Sarpi, *Concilio Tridentino*.

139. *Defense de la traduction*, 72, 94.

140. Article 'Venise', 8.

141. 'Father Paul Sarpi', *Works* (London, 1820) xii, 6–7.

142. Letter to Walpole, 2 Aug., 1758, in *Letters*, ed. J. Y. T. Greig (Oxford, 1932) i, 152.

143. *Decline and fall of the Roman Empire*, ed. H. H. Milman (Philadelphia, n. d.) v, 537 n. 89.

144. P. 353.

145. René Pintard, *Le libertinage érudit dans la première moitié du XVIIe siècle* (Paris, 1943) i, 104.

146. *Areopagitica and other prose works* (Everyman ed., 1927) 8.

147. P. 171.

148. I, 260.

149. As in Coryat, i, 401–409; Amelot de la Houssaye, 88, 142 seq., 331–332; and even Howell, 8: 'She melts in softness and sensualitie as much as any other [place] whatsoever; for, 'tis too well known, ther is no place where ther is lesse Religion from the girdle downwards . . .'

150. Article 'Venise', 12.

151. Fulgenzio Micanzio, *Vita del Padre Paolo* (n.p., 1658) 79.

Index

Index

Index

Index